WOMEN'S WRITING IN ITALY, 1400–1650

❀ ❀ ❀ ❀

# Women's Writing
# in Italy
## 1400–1650

❀

*Virginia Cox*

THE JOHNS HOPKINS UNIVERSITY PRESS
Baltimore

This book was brought to publication with the generous assistance
of the Gladys Krieble Delmas Foundation.

© 2008 The Johns Hopkins University Press
All rights reserved. Published 2008
Printed in the United States of America on acid-free paper
2 4 6 8 9 7 5 3 1

The Johns Hopkins University Press
2715 North Charles Street
Baltimore, Maryland 21218-4363
www.press.jhu.edu

Library of Congress Cataloging-in-Publication Data
Cox, Virginia.
Women's writing in Italy, 1400–1650 / Virginia Cox.
p.   cm.
Includes bibliographical references and index.
ISBN-13: 978-0-8018-8819-9 (hardcover : alk. paper)
ISBN-10: 0-8018-8819-0 (hardcover : alk. paper)
1. Italian literature—Women authors—History and criticism.
2. Italian literature—History and criticism.  3. Women and literature—
Italy—History.  I. Title.
PQ4063.C69 2008
850.9'9287—dc22        2007036098

A catalog record for this book is available from the British Library.

*Special discounts are available for bulk purchases of this book. For more information,*
*please contact Special Sales at 410-516-6936 or specialsales@press.jhu.edu.*

The Johns Hopkins University Press uses environmentally friendly book materials, including recycled text paper that is composed of at least 30 percent
post-consumer waste, whenever possible. All of our book papers are acid-free,
and our jackets and covers are printed on paper with recycled content.

For Paul

# CONTENTS

# ACKNOWLEDGMENTS

This book pulls together the findings and musings of almost twenty years of teaching and researching the literary history of women's writing in Italy. My intellectual debts are correspondingly vast, and I cannot hope to summarize them adequately here. The field has expanded and developed beyond measure since I first started to interest myself in it in the late 1980s. It has been an immensely gratifying experience, in all kinds of ways, to participate in this exploratory and still pioneering phase in the critical tradition, but not least of the gratifications it has offered has been the opportunities for dialogue and collaborative work.

I feel a particular debt to my earliest interlocutors on the subject, back in the late 1980s and early 1990s, Letizia Panizza, Pam Benson, and Adriana Chemello; also to Letizia Panizza, again, and to Pam Benson (in collaboration with Vicky Kirkham) for organizing two superb conferences in this area, respectively at Royal Holloway and Bedford New College, London, in 1994, and at the University of Pennsylvania in 2000, which did much to shape my understanding of the field.[1]

Another particular debt I should like to mention is to Al Rabil, who has proved himself an extraordinary promoter of work in this area. Two National Endowment for the Humanities institutes Al organized in North Carolina in 2001 and 2003 on *Women's Writing in Venice, Paris, and London, 1550–1700* contributed immensely to my scholarly development in this field, by offering me the opportunity to work together with Anne Schutte as a coordinator of the Venice segment and to meet and learn from a series of younger emerging scholars in the field such as—to mention only those active in the area of Italian studies—Babette Bohn, Julie Campbell, Maria Galli Stampino, Julia Hairston, Liz Horodowich, Julia Kisacky, Suzanne Maganini, Marjorie Och, and Lori Ultsch.

I had the great good fortune to have as my earliest PhD students at Cambridge in the 1990s Abigail Brundin and Lisa Sampson and have greatly profited from my conversation and collaborations with them over the years. It is my equal good fortune now to have Jane Tylus as a colleague and interlocutor in the Department of Italian at NYU.

Other scholars and graduate students working in the field from whom I have had the opportunity to learn in person as well as through their published work, or who have shared their work with me or helped me with my researches in other ways, include Dick Andrews, Laura Benedetti, Amy Brosius, Judith Bryce, Barbara Burgess-Van Aken, Stephen Campbell, Eleonora Carinci, Alex Coller, Suzanne Cusick, Corinna da Fonseca Wollheim, Massimo Danzi, Valeria Finucci, Margaret Franklin, Susan Haskins, Ann Rosalind Jones, Vicky Kirkham, Stephen Kolsky, Kate Lowe, Molly Martin, Francesca Medioli, Giovanna Rabitti, Diana Robin, Tristana Rorandelli, Deanna Shemek, Gabrielle Sims, Janet Smarr, Alison Smith, Evelyn Welch, Emily Wilbourne, and Niccolò Zorzi.

Where the preparation and editing of the book are concerned, I should like to thank my editors at the Johns Hopkins University Press, Henry Tom and Claire McCabe Tamberino, MJ Devaney for her copy editing, and Anne Schutte for reading and commenting on the introduction. My greatest institutional debt is to NYU, though I would also like to thank the National Endowment for the Humanities, Harvard University Center for Renaissance Studies (Villa I Tatti) and the Gladys Krieble Delmas Foundation for support received across the broader time range of research for this book. I would also like to record my gratitude to the staff of the Rare Book and Manuscript Library of the University of Pennsylvania Library, the Houghton Library, Harvard, and the Biblioteca Aprosiana of Ventimiglia for help in obtaining copies of rare early printed books.

# INTRODUCTION

Did women have a renaissance? In the three decades since Joan Kelly posed this question in her now classic essay of that title, an immense volume of work has been devoted to examining the position of women in the cultural era to which the slippery but convenient chronological label of "Renaissance" still clings.[1] This recent work has added vastly to our knowledge of the lives women lived in this period and the social, cultural, and economic factors that constrained and occasionally empowered them. Noblewomen, queens, working women, courtesans, nuns, and saints have all, to varying extents, been the object of meticulous scrutiny, as have the differing possibilities for female agency offered by different geopolitical and social environments, from the courts, cities, and convents of Catholic Italy to the country houses and market towns of Protestant England and Germany.[2] Much work has focused on women's status in the family, their legal position, and their educational opportunities; much, too, on their role as patrons and consumers and producers of culture. At the same time, attitudes to women—and, more broadly, to sex and gender—have been the subject of an intense and increasingly sophisticated analysis that has revealed ever more clearly the complexity of the role gender plays in the construction of identities, from the individual to the civic to the national.[3] Although the very copiousness of recent work on women can be daunting, we are undoubtedly now, as a result of the endeavors of the past few decades, in a better position to answer Kelly's question than she was at the time she asked it. While it would be unfair to claim that attention to women's history is an exclusively modern phenomenon, as that would neglect the considerable achievements of earlier scholars in this area, it is unquestionably true that our level of expertise in this field has been quantitatively and qualitatively immeasurably enhanced.[4]

So, *did* women have a renaissance? The question is a complex one, and any answer must be correspondingly nuanced: perhaps more so than that of Kelly herself, who replies to her own query with an emphatic negative. Kelly's central point, trenchantly argued, is that the period from around the fourteenth to sixteenth centuries in Europe saw a significant reduction of opportunities for women. Specifically, within the upper strata of society, on which Kelly focuses, changes in inheritance patterns and configurations of political power are presented as having conspired to restrict elite women's economic, social, and cultural agency. Kelly takes as paradigmatic here the contrasted figures of the medieval feudal chatelaine and the Renaissance court lady, arguing that, where the former had often wielded considerable power, whether ruling in her own right or in proxy for a husband who might be absent for periods of years, the latter, sidelined by patrilineal inheritance practices and blessed or cursed by a typically more sedentary spouse, found herself increasingly corralled into the subordinate and largely decorative role of dynastic consort. More generally, both within these exalted circles and beyond them—for example, in the bourgeois elite of mercantile cities like Florence—Kelly sees the division of gender roles becoming more marked in this period, with the public sphere being increasingly demarcated as male, the domestic as female. This was culturally reflected in a prescriptive literature that delineated increasingly sharply dichotomized ideals of male and female behavior, the male defined by the active virtues of leadership and intellectual vigor, the female by docility and obedience. Kelly concludes that the very social and political forces that are often seen as heralds of modernity in this period—the decline of feudalism, the development of mercantile protocapitalist economies, the emergence of the nation-state in much of Europe—may be seen as having worked in many ways to the detriment of women. Thus, seen from the perspective of women's history, the teleological narrative underlying the notion of the Renaissance is inverted in that a greater enlightenment is apparent the more nearly the "dark ages" are approached.

To what extent has Kelly's pessimistic vision of women's history in the transition from medieval to early modern Europe been borne out by subsequent research? The results are, perhaps inevitably, mixed.[5] While Kelly focuses near exclusively on secular women of the nobility and relies—to a contentious extent—on literary evidence to prove her thesis, her analysis ultimately takes as its starting point a broader tradition within the Marxist-inflected feminist history by which she was influenced that saw early capitalism as a turning point in women's relationship with the world of work. In the later middle ages, this tradition argued, women's possibilities for engaging in paid work outside the home were progressively curtailed by guild protectionism and changing working practices, in a way that plausibly diminished their status within the family and enhanced the distinctness of sex roles.[6] This reading of history has been widely contested, and a more nuanced and less dramatic pattern now tends to be preferred, stressing continuity over change and emphasizing the distinctiveness of particular local contexts and trades.[7]

Concomitantly and relatedly, something of the same shift has also been seen on the home terrain of Kelly's thesis: the situation of those women of the upper strata of society, especially within the privileged domain of the princely courts. Much recent work in this area has tended to react against what is perceived as the overdeterministic and overgeneralized character of earlier studies by stressing the possibilities for individual agency that existed even within the most seemingly unpromising environments.[8] Similarly, it has been argued that general social factors that appeared to work to the detriment of elite women, such as the dowry system that made them pawns in families' social and economic strategies, could in some circumstances contribute to their financial empowerment and hence, arguably, enhance their status within the family.[9] Despite these revisionist trends, however, the notion that women did not experience any kind of true "renaissance"—however we might like to define that—remains widely shared. If the period between the fourteenth and sixteenth centuries did not see the kind of dramatic deterioration in women's position that Kelly posits, it would be difficult to argue conversely that this was a time that saw a general improvement in women's social or economic position, either universally or within given environments or social groups. Where their legal status was concerned, certainly, women remained firmly subordinate to men, and their position within the family was generally one of subservience. Women had fewer choices than men in most areas of their life, and those choices did not substantially increase in this period. The professions remained closed to them, as did most lucrative fields of work; with a few notable exceptions, they were excluded from political life, and their educational opportunities were—again, with some exceptions—far inferior to those of their brothers. Further, the Aristotelian notions of gender difference dominant within law, medicine, theology, and natural philosophy served to reinforce and perpetuate this social inferiority, justifying women's subordinate status as the reflection of a hierarchy hardwired into the divine order of creation.[10]

Looking at women's concrete opportunities in this period, then, and their position within dominant ideological constructions of gender, the general picture would appear to be one of stasis, if not of deterioration. Intriguingly, however, within some circumscribed areas, this is eminently not the case; on the contrary, within these areas, the evidence for a renaissance—or perhaps a "naissance" tout court—seems clear. The most striking instance of this is the emergence of secular women in this period as cultural protagonists in a quantity and with a prominence unprecedented in the ancient or medieval world. This is most apparent from the sixteenth century, and particularly from the 1530s and 1540s, when the first literary works by living secular women began to be published in any numbers. While the development was to an extent pan-European, its center of gravity was undoubtedly Italy: a recent comparative study of published women writers in the sixteenth century across Europe lists just over two hundred Italian writers for the period, where France, Italy's closest competitor in this field, can supply only around thirty.[11] Italian women also began to emerge strongly as artists, particularly painters, especially in the later sixteenth century, while the last decades of the century saw some achieve extraordinary success as actresses, composers and singers. The remarkable extent of women's creative activity in this period has only very recently begun to become apparent, as literary historians, art historians, musicologists, and historians of theater have worked to uncover this underexplored area. A further striking fact that has emerged in this process is the level of acceptance and appreciation many of these women artists enjoyed in their lifetime. We are not confronted here—or not inevitably—with the marginalized and stifled voices that so often greet us in later women's history; on the contrary, in many cases in the Italian sixteenth century we encounter figures later sidelined by history who were the object of much acclaim in their day. The painter Sofonisba Anguissola (1532–1625)—little known within art history until her recent rediscovery—was the recipient of a court appointment for which many male painters of her day would have happily sold their soul to the devil.[12] Similarly, the top performers in late sixteenth-century female vocal consorts were paid at a rate their male peers could only envy.[13] Women writers, too, received much appreciation, though of a type generally less susceptible to quantitative analysis: leaving aside durably canonical figures such as Vittoria Colonna and Veronica Gambara, it is not difficult to cite cases of women writers, now forgotten, who received signal tokens of respect in their lifetime from their male peers, ranging from election to literary academies, to inclusion in anthologies, to selection as public speakers on civic occasions.[14] Although their place within Italian literary culture remained undoubtedly marginal, we are not talking of a silence broken by a few exceptional voices but of something more like an established minority presence, increasingly accepted over time as a matter of course.

If this flowering of female creative talent may give pause for thought to those who would dismiss the notion of a Renaissance *al femminile,* so too might the emergence in this same period in certain circles of powerfully affirmative new attitudes to women. The sympathy and acclaim that often characterized the reception of women's creative endeavors was rooted in a more general appreciation among the Italian elites of women's moral and intellectual virtues and their contribution to society—their "dignity" or their "nobility and excellence," to cite the most frequent formulae of the day. If one considers both general theoretical or exemplificatory treatises on female virtues and celebrations of individuals or of groups of contemporary women, the quantity of literature in praise of women in this period is immense.[15] Nor is this praise literature entirely limited, as might be expected, to lauding the qualities conventionally considered as comprising female virtue: while modesty, chastity, and beauty can hardly be said to be underrated, less obviously "feminine" qualities such as fortitude, erudition, and articulacy also receive their due share of attention. Most strikingly, a notion sufficiently voiced in this period to rate as a commonplace is that women were created men's equals and that their subordination to men derives from social custom and inadequate opportunities rather than any inherent inferiority.[16] These arguments for female equality, generally deriving from courtly and humanistic environments, stand as a counterweight to the powerful discourse of female inferiority that continued to prevail in scholastic contexts. As was noted above, within law, theology and the natural sciences, the dominant position on gender was that most authoritatively articulated by Aristotle, in which women's subordination to men was regarded as justified by their natural "imbecility." By the sixteenth century, however, this dichotomizing and hierarchical scheme was far from being the only available means of conceptualizing gender difference. On the contrary, it is not the least of the intellectual achievements of Renaissance humanism to have formed a cogent set of arguments to counter this position, based both on an internal critique of the logical defects of Aristotelian arguments for women's inferiority and a massive barrage of empirical evidence of women's capacity for "masculine" virtues, drawn initially, as one might expect, from the ancient world, but increasingly, as time went on, also from the modern.[17]

Returning, then, to the question of whether women had a renaissance, we are confronted with a paradox. On the one hand, where women's legal, socioeconomic, and political position is concerned, we find substantially no change in this period. However we choose to assess male "progress" in this period—and, as the shadow of Burckhardt fades, it becomes ever more tendentious to claim that *men* had a renaissance in this kind of concrete sense—it cannot be claimed that women entered the seventeenth century more men's "equals" than they had been in the thirteenth or fourteenth. On the other hand, however, if we turn to the cultural sphere, it is evident that something has changed in women's position. In what has been called a cultural "Copernican revolution in miniature," women had passed from a status as consumers of culture to producers, and by the end of the sixteenth century could cite an impressive, two centuries-long record of attainment as writers, as well as shorter, but still striking, histories of creative achievement in music and the visual arts.[18] Moreover, this record of female creative activity was not limited to private, family circulation; on the contrary, the names and works of female writers, artists, and musicians circulated widely and were touted routinely as a source of pride and cultural capital by families, acquaintances, and hometowns. At the same time, within polite literary culture, at least, the view that saw women's energies as properly directed only toward silence and obedience had been marginalized, and women were routinely lauded for "exceeding their sex" in their "noble" aspirations to creative immortality and for "abandoning the needle and spindle" for the higher pursuit of letters.[19] Of course there was much that was patronizing and trite about these wearily circulating commonplaces: as has often been noted, female writers continued to be eulogized hyperbolically rather than seriously critically assessed and to be considered apart, as a separate canon of "miracles of nature," rather than being genuinely integrated into the ranks of their male peers.[20] Nonetheless, our justified skepticism regarding the seriousness with which female artists were taken should not eclipse the remarkable fact of their ascendancy in this period; that this was a period in which female artistic creativity and eloquence were publicly celebrated and in which female aspirations to fame and glory were regarded as laudable and proper marks it out as a remarkably rare moment in the premodern history of the West. It is all the more remarkable, and the more demanding of close analysis, precisely *because* this was not a period of significant advances in women's social, economic, and legal status. Cultural ascendancy seems here, very oddly to the post-Marxist eye, detached from any material base.

What should we conclude from all this? How can we square the fact of women's continuing social inequality in this period with their unprecedented self-assertion in the field of elite culture? How can we account for the encouragement women seeking a public voice seem often to have received from the men in their circle, within a culture that, in other respects, appeared so intent on restricting their actions to their "proper," domestic sphere? And how should we read the many texts from the period proclaiming women's aptness for "masculine" endeavors and condemning their subordination as a social injustice when these same texts seem so assiduously to stop short of pursuing their argument to its logical conclusion and calling for reform in this area?[21] One response to these conundrums—a frequent one in feminist scholarship—is to regard the seemingly "progressive" or protofeminist trends apparent within Renaissance culture as little more than a distracting froth of gallantry playing across the surface of an unchanging patriarchal society. Thus, discourses on women seemingly affirmative of their equality with men, such as we encounter in texts like Castiglione's *Cortegiano* or Ariosto's *Orlando furioso,* are found, on closer examination, to reinforce the masculinist gender attitudes they ostensibly seek to challenge or critique.[22] Male attitudes to women writers and artists are susceptible to the same skeptical scrutiny: as was just noted, the hyperbolically inflated praises routinely addressed to creative women can easily be dismissed as vacuous rhetorical window-dressing. Within this perspective, "real" attitudes to gender are perceived as those revealed in the concrete ordering of society. Cultural attitudes that seem inconsistent with these are, by contrast, dismissed as inauthentic.

Obviously, there is much that is justified in this approach. A naive reading of the textual evidence of Renaissance "feminism" would today be rightly regarded as untenable: no one would wish for a return to the days in which Burckhardt could blithely state, on the basis of the type of cultural evidence alluded to above, that women in Renaissance Italy, "stood on a footing of perfect equality with men"—or, indeed, the more recent ones where a study of the figure of the warrior heroine in Renaissance epic could be subtitled "an index of emancipation."[23] Women in the Renaissance were not "emancipated" in any modern sense of the word, and Renaissance texts that appear to evoke the specter of female emancipation deserve to be the object of skeptical and historicizing analysis. This said, however, there are problems implicit in a mode of proceeding that operates, essentially, by measuring Renaissance texts against modern parameters and finding them lacking. Faced by a phenomenon as wide-ranging and culturally salient as the emergence of "protofeminist" or "profeminist" or "prowoman" discourses within elite society in Renaissance Italy, it seems unsatisfactory to concentrate our analytic energies entirely on the fact of its failure to translate into a coherent and radically transformative critique of social values such as might merit it the epithet of "feminist" tout court. More productive would be simply to accept this limitation as a historical fact and to attempt to interrogate this phenomenon on its own terms. Indeed, if we accept as our starting point that, despite some thematic similarities and consonances of argumentational strategy, Renaissance "'feminism" does not overlap with modern feminism, the questions that we can ask of it, and, potentially, the answers it can provide, become in some sense more interesting. If Renaissance men had no interest in "emancipating" women, what were their agendas in proclaiming women's *potential* for emancipation? If they found it difficult genuinely to conceive of women equaling men's achievements as writers or artists, what investment did they have in encouraging women's creative activity and in praising—often hyperbolically—its results? Even if we dismiss these "profeminist" gestures as attempts to please female patrons, or influential female contacts, or a female reading public in general, the question remains of why such female addressees should have attained a position of sufficient power, real or symbolic, in this period as to influence literary output in such a significant way. A further question is why these *particular* forms of discourse should have evolved in response to female patrons' and readers' perceived tastes and interests—as opposed to, say, simple encomia of female beauty, or female sanctity, or devotion to the hearth.

These questions become the more pressing, and the more interesting, when we observe that, where Italy is concerned, at least, the closely-linked phenomena of female literary and artistic creativity and the "profeminist" discourses that enabled and promoted it, are, though durable, quite clearly historically circumscribed trends. This fact tends to be obscured when these phenomena as they occur in Italy in the Renaissance are studied as part of a more widespread and chronologically extended story, such as the history of the so-called *querelle des femmes* in medieval and early modern Europe. Several factors here collude to blur the distinctness of the Italian phase in this tradition. One is that a sharp enough distinction is not always drawn between debate in general on the merits and demerits of women, as it may be traced from classical antiquity through patristic, medieval, and early modern culture down to the present day and the specific humanistic discourse on sex and gender difference that we see emerging in Europe— and particularly in France and Italy—in the fourteenth and fifteenth centuries. While the Renaissance "defense of women" is continuous in certain respects with previous traditions of prowoman argument, it is also quite distinct in its methods and emphases, not least because its prime theoretical arguments evolved as a response to a particular, scholastic position, in itself the product of a defined historical moment, though admittedly durable in its influence.[24] It is only if we recognize the historical distinctiveness of this discourse that we can properly identify its originating contexts, which is in turn essential if we are to understand the dynamic through which secular women's writing emerged.

If Renaissance "feminism," in the sense just defined, had a beginning, it also had an end, at least if we keep our focus on Italian contexts. Between the end of the sixteenth century and the beginning of the seventeenth, a distinct shift is apparent in the prevalent gender attitudes within elite literary culture in Italy. While discourses supportive of women do not vanish from the scene, they certainly lose something of their cultural centrality in this period, while misogynistic discourses of a type that had enjoyed only a relatively marginal status throughout most of the sixteenth century began to feature more prominently within elite literary culture, initially exciting quite sharp polemics, but later, in the course of time, seemingly gaining an increasing acceptance.[25] At the same time, and relatedly, the sympathetic reception that had greeted women's creative activity to a great extent in the sixteenth century gave way in numerous instances to something more rancorous and negative: one finds women writers, in particular, increasingly subjected to damaging imputations of unchastity or jeered at for the indecorousness of their ambitions or the poverty of their output. As a consequence, in this period—especially, again, where literature is concerned—one finds a sharp drop in women's creative output, persisting at least to the 1690s when the Arcadian movement emerged.

This chronological narrative is distinctive to Italy, and tends, again, to be obscured within treatments of early modern women's writing that examine this phenomenon on a pan-European scale. Within this geographically more expansive perspective, it is possible to reconstruct some kind of satisfyingly teleological narrative, in which the pioneering women writers of sixteenth-century Italy pass on the baton of female creativity to their successors in the salons of seventeenth-century and eighteenth-century France and England, in a manner that takes us to the threshold of modernity with a figure like Mary Wollstonecraft. A similar trajectory, involving many of the same protagonists, may be traced for the history of protofeminist discourse.[26] It is perhaps this perspective—a local variant, of course, of the more general habits of teleological vision implicit in the notion of "Renaissance"—that leads us to scrutinize the fragile tissue of Italian Renaissance feminism through the distorting lens of anachronistic expectations. Refocused in a more geographically localized manner, the oddly circumscribed historical character of Italian Renaissance "feminism" becomes apparent. Rather than regarding it typologically, as the first glimmerings of a revelation destined to be realized with increasing clarity with the progression of "reason," we may be in a better position to see this phenomenon for what it was: a defined historical development, reflecting a particular set of cultural circumstances obtaining within a society very different from our own.

All this is important for the project of this book because it is one of its central contentions that the history of women's writing in this period cannot be studied in isolation from that of the cultural discourses that enabled it. The chronological trajectory just sketched for the emergence and decline of the specifically Italian Renaissance discourse on "women's dignity" coincides more or less exactly with that of the parallel narrative of women's emergence as writers. As we will see in chapter 1, the first humanistic formulations of a rhetoric affirmative of women's capacity for "masculine" attainment may be dated to the later fourteenth century, with Boccaccio and Petrarch, while the earliest secular women writers to win public fame for their writing rose to prominence a generation later and within the same contexts. Similarly, as chapter 6 shows, the end of the long philogynist season in polite Italian literary culture, at the beginning of the seventeenth century, coincided reasonably closely—given a predictable degree of historical lag—with the marginalization and eventual near disappearance of the figure of the secular woman writer. This may sound entirely obvious and predictable to one approaching the subject from outside. Within a stubbornly patriarchal society, how could the level of women's participation in literary culture *not* be determined fundamentally by elite male social attitudes, positive or negative? How could women gain a hearing within the public literary sphere except through the tolerance of men? The historical correlation just noted has, however, not always been clear in the scholarship, for two principal reasons. One—the more localized, though undoubtedly powerful—has been the influence on the historiography of early modern Italian women's writing of the periodization proposal put forward by Carlo Dionisotti in his classic essay *La letteratura italiana nell'età del Concilio di Trento* (1967), which has remained dominant within studies of this area until very recently.[27] While acknowledging women's longer-term presence as protagonists within Italian literature from the time of Catherine of Siena onward, Dionisotti limited the time in which they can be considered as constituting a true collective presence—"making up a group," in his much-quoted phrase—to a period of around two decades in the mid-sixteenth century: precisely, from 1538, with the first publication of Vittoria Colonna's *Rime,* to around 1560, when, for a variety of economic and sociocultural reasons, the publication of vernacular literature entered a decline.[28] Women's writing was thus framed as the product of a particular, temporally circumscribed phase in the history of Italian literature, when an enterprising publishing industry, based in Venice, was reaching out to the new vernacular reading public created by printing. It is within this short-lived "euphoric" period that Dionisotti locates the emergence of women as published writers, their novelty emblematizing the opening of literature to new practices and readerships.[29]

While Dionisotti's proposal has much power and interest as an analysis of the cultural dynamics of the mid-sixteenth century, taken as a broader sketch for the history of women's writing in Italy, it is notably flawed. To say that women had a "group presence" within Italian literary culture only in the central decades of the century is misleading. On the contrary, as it is one of the purposes of this study to demonstrate, this presence was far more durable than Dionisotti allows for: by at least the last decade of the fifteenth century, women had attained a fairly high-profile place within Italian literature, a place they held, with fluctuations, for over a century, until the early decades of the seventeenth. In many ways, indeed, despite the very striking concentration of published female-authored poetry in the "euphoric" midcentury, it is the later sixteenth century and the early seventeenth that the most impressive advances in women's cultural presence were felt; certainly, it is then that we begin to see women venturing more frequently beyond the bounds of their "core" genre of lyric and occasional poetry and experimenting with genres from the pastoral drama and the dialogue to the religious epic and the polemical treatise. Looking back, as well, from Dionisotti's mid-century period, we can see that although print culture, as he argues, was a major factor in enabling women's writing, it cannot be seen as quite as fundamental and necessary in this regard as he is inclined to suggest; nor, even, can the triumph of the vernacular as the dominant literary language in Italy, causally important in diffusing the phenomenon as it no doubt was. The figure of the secular "learned lady" had already emerged as quite a defined cultural type by the mid-fifteenth century, prior to the introduction of printing, and within contexts in which humanistic Latin was the standard language of exchange. While numbers were few, it would be misleading to represent the humanistically trained women whose writings circulated in this age as exceptional individuals, buoyed into cultural visibility through an irrepressible personal vocation, as Dionisotti suggests we may imagine female writers outside his privileged "group" period of the mid-sixteenth century. Rather, in the same way that we see later, though indisputably on a smaller scale, we already see there a cultural space being crafted for the literary woman into which enterprising individuals of the right background and qualifications might step. Fifteenth-century humanists—or *some* humanists—"needed" literary women in the same way and for some of the same reasons as did their sixteenth-century vernacular descendents. Unless we place them in a historical framework privileging continuity as well as change, we risk jeopardizing our understanding of what those motivating reasons may have been.

In addition to this periodization issue, a further historiographical factor that has tended to impede a full acknowledgment of the importance of Renaissance profeminist discourse as a context for women's writing is the tendency among many feminist critics to assume an oppositional relationship between female writers and the "mainstream" patriarchal culture of the day. While, obviously, individual critics' positions and approaches vary widely, one quite widely shared assumption is that any form of public utterance on women's part in this period was viewed with extreme moral diffidence and that silence was equated with chastity and articulateness with a propensity to sexual "looseness." Emphasis is placed on cultural impulses constraining women's speech and on negative responses to women's cultural agency: paradigmatic in this respect is an incident such as the circulation in late 1430s Verona of a libel against the Nogarola family that connects Isotta Nogarola's famed erudition with her supposed sexual deviance, in an attack sometimes presented as having motivated Nogarola's disheartened withdrawal from the scholarly world.[30] Cumulatively, these emphases have the slightly paradoxical effect of implicitly foregrounding women's agency while, at the same time, portraying the culture of the period as one in which female agency was systematically repressed. If society's interest is seen as lying in the concerted silencing of women, any words that a woman succeeds in articulating become the more "hers" as a result, leading in extreme forms to the romanticized notion of the woman writer as "Philomela" or "defiant muse" or "other voice."[31] Even where a degree of societal facilitation of women's writing is conceded, at least within elite and highly circumscribed circles, emphasis still tends to fall on the skill with which women negotiated their way through the prickly path of conflicting cultural expectations, mimeticizing masculine discourses and manipulating feminine stereotypes to craft a precariously acceptable authorial persona.[32] An agonistic construction of the relationship between female writers and their environment continues to subtend the analysis. There is obviously much historical justification for this interpretive model, and no one would question its basic premise that men and women did not rank as equal citizens within the early modern "republic of letters." It does tend, however, to inhibit serious analysis of the cultural attitudes that enabled women's emergence as writers and to discourage asking *why* particular cultures at particular times should have evolved such enabling stances. The project of this book—to reconnect the narratives of the emergence of women's writing and of the gynephile discourses that laid the basis for this emergence—requires a setting aside of the critical model that sees women writers a priori as interlopers and "thieves of language": successful or doomed would-be gatecrashers of a party to which they have not been invited. Once we begin thinking of women's emergence as literary protagonists as scripted, rather than heroically improvised, it becomes urgent to examine the cultural uses they served and the reasons why the figure of the "new Sappho" gained such durable imaginative purchase within the elite culture of the age. In understanding these reasons, we will also be well placed to understand the causes of women's abrupt near disappearance from Italian literary culture in the early seventeenth century. This is less simply a consequence of Counter-Reformation social conservatism than has often been suggested.

Besides attempting a coherent, contextualized account of the reasons for the emergence and decline of the fifteenth- and sixteenth-century tradition of Italian women's writing, this book also aims to give the first comprehensive—or near comprehensive—historical description and analysis of that tradition. Although there has been much important work in this area in recent years, the majority of studies have centered on single writers and works and have tended, at least until recently, to concentrate on a fairly narrow canon of works.[33] Though it has immeasurably increased recently, and is increasing by the day, the critical coverage of early modern women's writing remains patchy, especially once we venture beyond the relatively well-mapped terrain of single-authored published books into the less negotiable but important hinterlands of "minor" and local authors, whose names often survive attached to a handful of sonnets in an anthology. To begin to have a sense of the real extent of the phenomenon, of its social, temporal, and geographical distribution and its contexts, influences, and genre preferences, there is a great deal more basic work of description and analysis that needs to be done. This book is intended to provide an initial, approximate mapping from which future prospecting can proceed.[34]

A few further clarifying remarks may be useful before proceeding to a chapter summary. An accusation to which books of this kind are obviously vulnerable is that of perpetuating a separatist model of literary history, by reifying nebulous historical constructs such as that of a "tradition" of women's writing. This is a point to be taken seriously: in many ways, it is entirely proper and an encouraging sign that recent anthologies of Italian writing in this period are beginning tentatively to incorporate women's writings into general categories organized by region or genre rather than isolating them, as has been common in the past, in the "virtual *matroneum*" of a section of their own.[35] In many ways, however—abstracting from general theoretical discussions of the legitimacy of considering women's writing a tradition apart—it is practically speaking too early to think in terms of abandoning separate studies of women's writing as a phenomenon, even at the cost of a certain artificiality. Simply, there is far too much basic work to be done still in mapping the extent of the phenomenon, in scrutinizing its periodization, and in analyzing its inevitably distinctive sociocultural dynamics, for the prospect of a future hypothetical gender-integrated literary history to be anything other than distant. One thing this book attempts to show, by conjoining the study of women's writing with the parallel history of men's attitudes to women's writing, is that gender plays a more fundamental role in the "deep structure" of Italian literary culture than is often acknowledged, serving in particular, across time, as a key means of effecting and negotiating stylistic and ideological change. The implications of this would clearly point toward a fully integrated diachronic "gendered history" of Italian literature, in which empirical consideration of the part played by women as patrons, consumers, and producers of literature was seamlessly meshed with an analysis of the discursive role played by gender in the constitution of literary identities and the articulation of literary ideals.[36] In the meantime, however, a valuable purpose can be served by works such as this that aim to provide a contextualized account of the development of women's writing, paying attention both to its textual products and the cultural space that it occupied. That it is possible to write women's history in a nonseparatist spirit is well illustrated, I hope, by this book.

The organization of this volume is chronological. The first chapter focuses on the development of a humanistic profeminist discourse within the courts of fifteenth-century Italy and on women's engagement with Latin humanism in this period both inside and outside the courts. The second examines the implications for women of the rise of the vernacular as the dominant literary language of Italy in the late fifteenth and early sixteenth centuries and covers the careers of the founding figures of the vernacular tradition of women's writing, Veronica Gambara and Vittoria Colonna. The focus of chapter 3 is the rapid diffusion of the practice of women's writing apparent in the middle decades of the sixteenth century, following the remarkable publishing success of Colonna's poetry, which first appeared in print in 1538. One subject of scrutiny here will be the dynamics of women's relation with print culture, though the continuing importance of manuscript circulation will also be stressed. Chapter 4 covers the decades of the 1560s and 1570s, which marked a lull in women's published output after the frenetic energies of the 1550s, while chapter 5 examines the remarkable forty-year period that followed, from the early 1580s, when women began to expand beyond what had primarily been their core genre of lyric verse. Finally, chapter 6 looks at the quite sharp reversal in elite cultural attitudes to women and women's learning that began to be apparent in Italian culture from around the 1590s and that would ultimately be instrumental in bringing the tradition of women's writing to an end. As will be apparent from this summary, there is a partial chronological overlap in the period covered by chapters 5 and 6, with the former encompassing the period of 1580–1620, the latter that of 1590–1650. This structural choice is motivated by a desire to maintain narrative clarity during a period that is dramatically transitional where gender attitudes are concerned: the aim is to convey dialectically the complex relation of innovation and continuity at this time. This was the period that saw both women's fullest integration in literary culture and the first manifestations of the cultural changes that would ultimately remarginalize them: both the apex of women's self-assertion as writers and the beginning of their rapid decline.

A clarification will be useful here with regard to the scope of this work, and, more specifically, what is encompassed by the terms "women's writing." I conceive this here narrowly, more or less along the conventional demarcation lines of "literature" (or perhaps, less anachronistically, "letters") and with a strong bias toward works intended for circulation, through the media of manuscript or print.[37] This excludes, for example, much of the rich body of epistolary writing by women of the Italian Renaissance, and includes only letters clearly intended to be read by circles beyond those of their immediate recipients and to be appreciated and judged as literary works on stylistic and rhetorical, as well as informational and social-affective, grounds.[38] Further excluded, or given a subsidiary role, are writings whose intended or actual audience was self-definingly female and that circulated only among women, such as the intriguing tradition of nuns' chronicles recently unearthed by Kate Lowe and the equally compelling body of convent drama earlier studied by Elissa Weaver.[39] Needless to say, this does not imply any kind of negative assessment of the interest or value of this type of more "private" literary material nor of nonliterary writings such as wills—often in this period extraordinarily rich in narrative and autobiographical material—or of assemblages of recipes and cosmetic prescriptions such as the *Experimenti* attributed to Caterina Sforza (1463–1509).[40] That there would be more inclusive ways of writing a history of Italian women's writing in this period is indubitable. Here, however, my selection of material is constrained by the book's thematic focus on the place of women within the public literary sphere (however we choose to define that slippery term in this period): my concern, more than with women's writing, is perhaps more accurately with "the woman writer," understood as defined cultural type.[41] Ultimately, the subject of this book is Italian women's participation in elite literary culture as protagonists and the complex patterns of integration and marginalization that structured this engagement. This entails a narrowing of perspective, but it is one that is essential in the interest of coherence and focus.

A note might be useful at this point for potential readers of this book better acquainted with other traditions of early modern women's writing. It will be surprising to someone coming to this study from the tradition of English writing, in particular—the area, of course, that has seen the greatest concentration of critical work on women's writing to date—that so little energy has been devoted to clarifying methodologically implicated historical issues relating to authorship, medium, and text status.[42] This is not because modern notions of authorship and the author function, or of the hierarchical relationship of print to other forms of circulation, may be un-problematically imported into a study of this kind. There are certainly points within this study where it is useful to recall that the assignment of a female signature to a work does necessarily imply female authorship or where notions of collaborative authorship may be usefully invoked.[43] It is similarly important to bear in mind that, throughout the period we are looking at, print circulation did not represent the sole or default means for the dissemination of literary texts and that an overprivileging of printed texts as representative can be misleading.[44] It is nonetheless quite striking, when we survey women's literary production in Italy in this period, how much less these questions loom than they do in equivalent studies centered on England. Women published more in Italy in the sixteenth century than elsewhere in Europe, encouraged by greater publishing opportunities, es-pecially at a local level, and by a literary culture within which the "stigma of print" was perhaps lesser and certainly rather differently configured. Re-latedly, Italian women appear to have been relatively unconcerned about publicly identifying as authors and with claiming full ownership of their works. While anonymous and pseudonymous publication is not unknown, the norm seems to have been for women to publish under their own names: only two of the fifty-three poets in Lodovico Domenichi's famous 1559 anthology of female-authored poetry, for example, are identified by their initials rather than their full names, while an anthology of 1565 has nine named female poets to a single more bashful "Lucrezia N."[45] Wendy Wall has noted of English literature in this period that "constrained by the norms of acceptable feminine behavior, women were specifically discour-aged from tapping into the newly popular channel of print" and that "to do so threatened the cornerstone of their moral and social well-being."[46] This cannot be said of Italy: even where we find women of the higher no-bility keeping themselves aristocratically aloof from the "vulgarizing" in-fluence of print, the force of specifically moral constraints on this score seemed to have been relatively weak. Thus we find Vittoria Colonna, for example—a notorious nonpublisher—urged by a figure of no less august a stature than Pietro Bembo to relax her strictures, while, similarly, at a lower but still highly respectable social level, we find Laura Battiferri degli Ammanati in the late 1550s seeking Benedetto Varchi's advice on details of the publication of her *Primo libro delle opere toscane,* with which she was ev-idently closely involved, without sacrifice to her moral reputation.[47] In cer-tain respects, although the quantitative output is obviously lesser, sixteenth-century Italian women's position with respect to publication and authorship seems to map more happily onto that of women in eighteenth-century

England than onto that of their less integrated grandmothers two centuries earlier.[48]

A few more local issues need to be mentioned in conclusion. The first is terminological. Anyone embarking on a critical or historical work that engages with the *querelle des femmes* will soon find him or herself confronting the issue of how best to describe the "prowoman" side of the debate. There is no word that captures the affirmative stance toward women as neatly and uncontroversially as "misogynist" does its negative counterpart: "feminist" risks anachronism while "prowoman" is clumsy and "gynephile" and "philogynist" unidiomatic. "Protofeminist" has some merits, in acknowledging the problem with "feminist," although it in itself begs the complex question of the historical and conceptual relationship between Renaissance gynephilia and modern feminism. In the text that follows, I have not attempted any kind of purist solution but have rather used the terms "feminist," "pro-" or "protofeminist," "prowoman," "gynephile" and "philogynist" as near synonyms, trusting to the reader to apply the necessary historicizing caution in understanding the sense of "feminist" in this context.[49] The term "feminist" is used to pick out the more politicized strands within the more general gynephilia of the age: those that argued for women's capacity for political leadership and intellectual excellence, for example, rather than those that rapturized on their angelic beauty. Even this more politicized tradition of premodern writing on women, however, differs from modern feminism in its lack of any concrete agenda for social reform; as was noted above, this was an age in which conceptual radicalism on gender issues cohabited comfortably with social conservatism, in a manner initially baffling to modern perceptions.

A further point requiring some glossing also regards terminology—or, more precisely, onomastics. In sixteenth- and seventeenth-century Italy, women with a family name ending in "i" or "o" were generally designated with a feminine-inflected version of the name, so that the writer-daughter of the late Cinquecento Venetian medic Giovanni Marinelli was customarily referred to in her lifetime as "Lucrezia Marinella" and the writer-daughter of the mid-Cinquecento humanist Fulvio Peregrino Morato was known as "Olimpia Morata." In later Italian usage, this inflection of surnames was lost, so that a nineteenth- or twentieth-century Italian would more naturally refer to the figures just named as Lucrezia Marinelli and Olimpia Morato. In the late twentieth-century reprise of scholarship on early modern Italian women, practice has come to vary, with Italian scholars generally preferring the modern usage (Marinelli / Morato) and Anglo-American feminist scholarship tending to restore the early-modern version

(Marinella / Morata), except where a long-standing tradition of use of the masculine form has already been established, as in the case of Veronica Franco, Arcangela Tarabotti, and Chiara Matraini.[50] We thus find ourselves in the curious situation where recent editions of one prominent mid-century female poet bear different author names on different sides of the Atlantic, with the "Laura Battiferri" of Enrico Maria Guidi's Italian editions of 2000 and 2005 corresponding to the "Laura Battiferra" of Victoria Kirkham's bilingual one of 2006. I have not attempted in this book to impose any kind of artificial consistency on this differential pattern of naming but have rather broadly followed existing usage, especially that of modern editions, where they exist.[51] This is hardly satisfactory, but it seems preferable to a consistency that would mandate the use of the incongruous-sounding "Veronica Franca," "Chiara Matraina," and "Arcangela Tarabotta" or the equally jarring—at least to Anglo-American ears—"Laura Cereto" or "Giulia Bigolini."

WOMEN'S WRITING IN ITALY, 1400–1650

# CHAPTER ONE

❈ ❈ ❈ ❈

# ORIGINS

## (1400–1500)

❈

The bulk of the present volume is occupied with a "long sixteenth century," comprising the years from around 1490 to 1610: the effective life cycle of the tradition of vernacular women's writing that forms the main subject of the book. This tradition cannot, however, be studied adequately without a consideration of the century or so prior to its inception. It was in the fifteenth century in Italy that secular women writers began to write and circulate their works in numbers and that the figure of the "learned woman" first acquired a focused cultural profile. It was also, connectedly, at this time that humanist discourses celebratory and legitimizing of women's capacity for "virile" achievement attained their mature elaboration, following the experiments of Boccaccio and Petrarch in the previous century. All these developments are essential for understanding later sixteenth-century developments: to study the sixteenth-century tradition of vernacular women's writing without paying attention to its fifteenth-century Latin ancestry would be as misleading as to study twentieth-century women writers without regard to their eighteenth and nineteenth-century predecessors. The relationship of continuity between the two periods is nicely symbolically expressed by the fact that the two great "pioneers" of sixteenth-century vernacular women's writing in the early decades of the sixteenth century, Veronica Gambara (1485–1550) and Vittoria Colonna (?1490–1547), were both genealogically connected to notable fifteenth-century dynasties of "learned women": respectively, the Nogarola of Verona and the Montefeltro of Urbino.[1]

## 1. The "Learned Lady" in Quattrocento Italy: An Emerging Cultural Type

The history of the secular, humanistically educated female *erudite* as a cultural type in Quattrocento Italy has been well documented in its broad lines over the past few decades.[2] A useful initial indicator of the evolution and extent of the phenomenon is the chronological list of fourteenth- and fifteenth-century female Latinists put together by Margaret King and Albert Rabil in their influential 1983 anthology, *Her Immaculate Hand*. The earliest figures included in King and Rabil's list are the Paduan Maddalena Scrovegni (1356–1429) and Battista da Montefeltro Malatesta (1384–1448), the latter best remembered today as the recipient of Leonardo Bruni's *De studiis et litteris* (*On the Study of Literature*).[3] To these might be added Angela Nogarola d'Arco of Verona (d. c. 1436): an interesting figure only now beginning to emerge from the shadows of her more famous nieces.[4] Following these relatively isolated precursors, around the mid-fifteenth century we find a more substantial cluster of young women receiving a sufficiently serious Latin education to attract the praises of contemporary humanists. Most notable among these are Isotta Nogarola (?1418–66), Angela Nogarola's niece, and Costanza Varano (1426–47), Battista da Montefeltro's granddaughter; the others, whose erudition is sometimes testified by mentions in sources rather than any surviving writings, are Isotta Nogarola's sister Ginevra Nogarola (1417–61/68), Cecilia Gonzaga (1425–51), of the ruling family of Mantua, and the two Venetians Costanza Barbaro (b. post 1419) and Caterina Caldiera (d. 1463), the latter two the daughters of noted humanists, respectively Francesco Barbaro (1390–1454) and Giovanni Caldiera (c. 1400–1474).[5] Later female erudites listed by King and Rabil are Ippolita Sforza, Duchess of Calabria (1445–88) and Alessandra Scala (1475–1506), daughter of Bartolomeo Scala (1430–97), chancellor of Florence, as well as the more productive and ambitious Cassandra Fedele of Venice (?1465–1558) and Laura Cereta of Brescia (1469–99).[6] To these should certainly be added the figure of Battista Sforza da Montefeltro (1446–72), Costanza Varano's daughter and Duchess of Urbino, and also Laura Brenzoni Schioppo of Verona (c. 1470–1532), often excluded from accounts of female humanists but one of the highest-profile women writers in Italy at the turn of the sixteenth century.[7] An overview of women's participation in literary culture in this period should also include the rich seam of mainly vernacular convent writing in this period, which may be seen as continuing the great medieval tradition of female mysticism in Italy. Important Quattrocento convent writers include Caterina Vigri (1413–63),

Battista, or Camilla Battista Varano (1458–c. 1524), and Caterina Fieschi Adorno (1447–1510).[8] In addition to these, vernacular writings survive by a handful of secular women writers, most famously the Florentines Lucrezia Tornabuoni (c. 1425–82) and Antonia Pulci (?1452–1501), and the Neapolitan Ceccarella Minutolo (fl. 1470).[9]

Who were these women, and what was their background? As we would expect, almost by definition, all women from this period who received a humanistic education may be categorized very broadly as from the upper strata of society. The same may be said, of course, in very large part, of men who were similarly educated, although, over time, with the diffusion of humanistic learning and its growing importance for careers in chanceries, courts and schools, the "new learning" became an important professional conduit for talented young men from outside the traditional social elites. Where humanistically educated women are concerned, it is useful to distinguish further between women from the very highest ranks of the aristocracy and those lower down the social order. As always, moreover, in Italy, careful attention is also necessary to local geopolitical contexts. Women's precise social position and the cultural traditions of their home cities determined their life outcomes very closely, and a lack of sufficient precision in making the necessary distinctions has led to quite serious misrepresentations within scholarship in this area in the past.[10] Starting from the top of the social spectrum, a distinctive group within the more general category of fifteenth-century learned women—and one especially visible to contemporaries—was constituted by noblewomen from the ruling dynasties of the constellation of large and small states into which Italy was divided in this period. The most influential prototype here was Battista da Montefeltro, who was the daughter of the Count of Urbino, Antonio da Montefeltro (1349–1404), and the wife of the lord of Pesaro, Galeazzo Malatesta (d. 1452). Other examples are Costanza Varano, daughter of the deposed lord of Camerino, Piergentile Varano (1400–1433), and the wife of Alessandro Sforza, lord of Pesaro (1409–73); Battista Sforza, Costanza's and Alessandro's daughter and the wife of Federico da Montefeltro of Urbino (1422–82); and, most exaltedly of all, Ippolita Sforza, daughter of Francesco Sforza of Milan (1401–66) and wife to Alfonso, Duke of Calabria (1448–95), crown prince of the kingdom of Naples. Similar in background to these women but differing in her life choices is the figure of Cecilia Gonzaga, of the ruling house of Mantua, who refused marriage, opting instead to enter a convent. Although unusual in the level of their commitment to learning, these women were not entirely exceptional for their rank; on the contrary, it appears to have been common practice within the ruling dynasties of Italy to educate girls to a high standard, as within the royal households of northern Europe on which they modeled themselves in many respects.[11] Indeed, examining the lives and contexts of the women listed above, one is struck by the extent to which other educated women featured in their family circles. Battista da Montefeltro's sister Anna, in an admiring letter, recognizes Battista's classical studies and "Ciceronian eloquence" as exceptional, but Anna's letter, too, reveals her to be a cultivated woman and a reader of Augustine and Jerome.[12] Battista's sister-in-law and correspondent Paola Malatesta Gonzaga (1393–1449) also had a reputation for learning and was praised by contemporaries for having orchestrated her daughter Cecilia's remarkable humanistic education.[13] Similarly, Ippolita Sforza was clearly encouraged in her learning by her mother, Bianca Maria Visconti (1425–68), to whom a surviving Latin oration by Ippolita, seemingly composed as a school exercise, is addressed.[14] In the course of the fifteenth century, through the agency of such women and their humanist apologists, a composite image progressively emerged of the cultivated dynastic wife or daughter: an image complementary to, and evolving in parallel with, the similarly stereotypical image of the cultivated prince. The ideals are exemplarily illustrated in Piero della Francesca's famous dual portrait of Battista Sforza and Federico da Montefeltro, especially when it is read in conjunction with the remarkable funeral oration for Battista commissioned from the humanist cleric Giannantonio Campano (1429–77) by the grieving Federico, which praises the deceased duchess's eloquence in the highest terms and stresses her descent from an intellectually distinguished female line.[15]

In consequence of their high status and the political importance of their families, women such as Battista da Montefeltro, Ippolita Sforza, and Costanza Varano were without doubt the most visible icons of female erudition of their age. Interesting in this regard is the list of distinguished modern women given in an oration of the 1450s sometimes attributed to a Bolognese woman, Nicolosa Sanuti, which is comprised exclusively of women of this rank.[16] Below this exalted social sphere, but at a relatively bridgeable distance, stand those learned women who derived from the leading families of the great northern Italian cities, such as Angela and Isotta Nogarola in Verona and Maddalena Scrovegni in Padua. While neither clan actually ruled, both the Nogarola and the Scrovegni were among the leading players in their respective cities during the turbulent political season preceding their annexation by the imperial power of Venice in 1405, and the Nogarola, in particular, continued to play a significant role under the new regime. The female scholars of these families corresponded freely with members of at least the more modest of the dynastic families: a poem of Angela Nogarola's shows her on quite intimate terms with Pandolfo

Malatesta (1370–1427), the humanistically inclined lord of Pesaro, while Isotta Nogarola exchanged compliments with Costanza Varano in the 1440s.[17] Among families of the rank of Nogarola and Scrovegni, female learning was less widespread than in the great dynastic families, not least because there was no practical necessity for such learning; unlike Battista da Montefeltro or Costanza Varano, a woman like Isotta Nogarola did not need to be prepared for the eventuality of rule.[18] Whether a particular family of this rank educated its daughters was thus seemingly a matter of choice and intellectual tradition more than custom. While Angela Nogarola was one of the most highly educated women of her day, her sister-in-law, Isotta's mother, Bianca Borromeo, from a comparably noble family, seems to have been illiterate herself, even though she supervised her daughters' education following her husband's premature death.[19] Precisely because of this "gratuitousness," humanistic education in young women of this rank could be seen as socially enobling; in her poem of compliment to Isotta Nogarola, Costanza Varano speaks of the adornment Nogarola has brought to her family, endowing it with it the "elegance equally of manners and sweet wisdom" ("decor[em] pariter morum dulcis pariter que sophiae").[20] Although the compliment seems generic, it is in fact quite precise. While in aristocratic circles generally, the education of women could enhance a family's visibility and cultural standing, the degree of this enhancement obviously depended on the rank of the family concerned. The Nogarola or Scrovegni, though distinguished already, had more to gain on this account than the Montefeltro or Malatesta, still less the Visconti and Sforza, the latter two successive rulers of the northern Italian superpower of the moment, Milan.[21]

The dynamic just noted, of female education as a means of family "ennoblement," is seen far more starkly as we move down the social hierarchy to women like Laura Cereta and Cassandra Fedele. Cereta was the daughter of a Brescian lawyer and was briefly married to Pietro Serina (d. 1486), a merchant from the same city, with business interests also in Venice.[22] Cassandra Fedele came from a family of the rank of *cittadini* in Venice: a peculiarly Venetian status category standing between the ruling patriciate and the *popolo*.[23] She was married in c. 1499 to a physician from Vicenza, Giammaria Mapelli or Mappelli. While the families of both can be fairly described as "'substantial," clearly neither approached the rank of an Isotta Nogarola, still less that of a Costanza Varano or Battista da Montefeltro.[24] Both came from backgrounds in which female learning was the exception, and neither appears to have had female erudite role models within her immediate family circle.[25] Cereta, indeed, speaks feelingly in a letter of the hostility she encountered from women.[26] In the case of both

Fedele and Cereta, it is clear that their education was a distinctive choice on the part of their families, who may be assumed to have encouraged their talented daughters' studies in part for the *decor morum* such learning conferred. A similar case is that of humanist educators, who may have educated their daughters as "walking illustrations of their fathers' pedagogical talents," and perhaps of humanists more generally, whose daughters' literary culture could be seen as flatteringly reflecting their own learning.[27] Such is the case with the Venetians Costanza Barbaro and Caterina Caldiera and the Florentine Alessandra Scala, although, once again here a differentiation should probably be made between the motives of a high-ranking patrician father like Francesco Barbaro and a *cittadino* like Giovanni Caldiera who had more to gain by a gesture of this kind. Bartolomeo Scala, too, though chancellor of Florence under the Medici and a man of considerable wealth and power, came from a modest family background for which the added luster of a brilliant daughter might be useful.[28] Patriotic issues were also by this period beginning to play a part in the diffusion of women's learning: the letter Angelo Poliziano (1454–94) wrote to Cassandra Fedele praising the learning of her less established Florentine "sister erudite" Scala clearly needs to be read on some level as a pitch for the claims of Florentine humanism against those its Venetian "sister republic."[29]

Making such careful social discriminations as these is an important preliminary to any kind of general discussion of the position of the fifteenth-century learned woman, as women's social status and family background had important implications for their scholarly careers. Studies of women intellectuals in Italian Renaissance culture have frequently placed much emphasis on the difficulties of their position, noting that, while male humanists were happy to marvel at these "prodigies of nature" in their writings, female scholars also generated a notable degree of social opprobrium, especially when they came to make the transition from precocious adolescents to adult, sexual women.[30] Social convention, it is claimed, appeared to demand that women set aside their intellectual ambitions on marriage, and a woman who showed a public commitment to the pursuit of learning risked, at best, the wounding hostility—not least from other women—that Laura Cereta records in her letters and, at worst, the public outrage suffered by Isotta Nogarola in the late 1430s, when she became the subject of an anonymous invective accusing her not only of promiscuity but of incest with her brother and drawing an explicit connection between her intellectual pretensions and her supposed sexual deviance.[31] Nogarola's case, in particular, has been given an almost paradigmatic status in modern studies of women's position in Quattrocento culture, with her attacker's vituperative insinuations presented as representative of a widely held hostility to female intellectual pretensions.[32] Isotta's subsequent fate—very unusually for the time, she remained unmarried, while not entering a convent—has been, further, regarded as a "retreat" from a social world in which she could only be regarded as a threatening anomaly.

While there may be some truth in this analysis where the particular case of Isotta Nogarola is concerned, a consideration of the very different situation of contemporary learned women from dynastic families should lead us to doubt its general application.[33] It is not by any means the case that, as has been stated, "there was simply no place for the learned woman in the social environment of Renaissance Italy" nor that learned women were universally perceived as "threats to the natural and social order" or "aroused fear and anger in male contemporaries."[34] In the case of learned women from the ruling dynasties, there is little or no evidence that their intellectual ambitions were met with any form of resistance, either from their families or society in general; on the contrary, as we have seen, the assumption was that women from this background should be educated, and it was regarded not as a deviation but the norm. Nor is there any indication in the sources that the intellectual interests of women in this class were envisaged as limited to the time before their marriage. Battista da Montefeltro's surviving letters and orations mainly date from the period of her marriage to Galeazzo Malatesta, and neither her granddaughter Costanza Varano nor her great-granddaughter Battista Sforza abandoned their studies on marriage.[35] Ippolita Sforza packed a substantial library in her trousseau as she launched on her married life as Duchess of Calabria, and one of her first projects on arriving at her husband's court was to construct herself a *studiolo*.[36] Isabella d'Este (1474–1539), meanwhile, at the end of the century, continued to fret over the inadequacy of her knowledge of Latin well after her marriage to Francesco Gonzaga; far from feeling that her studies should rightly come to an end at her marriage, she appears to have redoubled her efforts.[37] While not as compulsory, certainly, as chastity, piety, and fertility, there is clear evidence that learning was perceived as an attractive quality in a dynastic consort; Anthony D'Elia's recent study of humanistic wedding orations finds erudition and eloquence occurring with a certain frequency as topoi alongside beauty, nobility, and virtue.[38]

It is at lower social levels, where education for women was more exceptional and anomalous, that we tend, predictably, to encounter greater levels of hostility, such as those testified in Laura Cereta's bitter account of the malicious attacks she endured from her female compatriots.[39] Despite the frequent generalizations we find in texts of the period regarding women's "imbecility," fifteenth-century Italian culture in practice worked on an informal two-tier system, in which women of noble rank were conceded to be intellectually "redeemed" by their genetic heritage from the inferiority generally attributed to their sex.[40] The delicate fabric of this socially useful, if largely unarticulated, compromise solution risked disruption by the "paradox" of an intellectually ambitious woman from a non-noble background, and such women, both in the fifteenth century and, to a lesser extent, in the sixteenth, tended to suffer social opprobrium as a result. Even here, however, it would be rash to generalize: while Cereta does appear to have been relatively isolated and underappreciated in her lifetime, this was certainly not the case with contemporaries like Cassandra Fedele, Alessandra Scala, and Laura Brenzoni, whose problem was rather that of fighting their way through the clouds of bland and instrumentalizing laudatory rhetoric that surrounded them at every turn. Whatever her initial novelty and threat value, by the late fifteenth century, the "learned lady" was a familiar and sanctioned enough figure to have been co-opted as a kind of "national treasure," routinely boasted of by compatriots as an honor to her city and her kin. True, these women were adopted more in the role of mascots than fully integrated members of the professional humanistic community; women's existential "otherness" in the period was such that things could have hardly been any other way. Allowing for this, however, the writing woman did have a place by 1500 in Italian literary culture, even if that place was more of the nature of a pedestal or niche than a genuine "seat at the table."

What did these "learned women" write? Here, again, a division on the grounds of the social status of the authors is useful. Most of the Latin works that survive by humanistically educated women from the dynastic families are functional and political in character and composed for particular diplomatic or ceremonial ends. Thus we have an oration of 1433 of Battista da Montefeltro to the Emperor Sigismund (1368–1437), calling for the restoration of her husband, Galeazzo Malatesta, recently deposed from the lordship of Pesaro, and the release of her son-in-law Piergentile Varano of Camerino, languishing in prison during an outbreak of murderous strife with his brothers and coheirs.[41] Similarly, we have an oration by Battista's granddaughter Costanza Varano, delivered nine years later, in 1442, calling on Francesco Sforza of Milan through the medium of his consort Bianca Maria Visconti for the restoration of Camerino to her family: an end attained the following year through the efforts of Costanza's redoubtable mother, Elisabetta Malatesta.[42] These are not literary works in any normal sense of the term but rather carefully scripted diplomatic performances designed to exploit the striking humanistic novelty of female oratory to specific dynastic-political ends. A similar point may be made of the letters and poems we find Maddalena Scrovegni and Angela Nogarola addressing a generation earlier to successive rulers of Padua and Verona; here, again, while the writers' rhetorical and poetic skills are foregrounded, they are clearly writing less as individuals and "creative artists" than as designated spokeswomen for the interests of powerful clans.[43]

A point worth noting is that this political literature by women encompasses two orations, both seemingly delivered in practice by their authors. While the speeches delivered by Battista da Montefeltro in 1443 and by Costanza Varano in 1442 are the only known instances of deliberative oratory on women's part, fifteenth-century instances of demonstrative oratory by women are not rare. Other famous examples include the 14-year-old Ippolita Sforza's 1459 gratulatory oration to the recently elected Pope Pius II and Cassandra Fedele's 1487 speech at the University of Padua commemorating the award of a degree to her kinsman Bertuccio Lamberto.[44] Isotta Nogarola's 1453 oration on St. Jerome, commissioned by the recently elected bishop of Verona, Ermolao Barbaro (1410–71), also gives signs of having been actually delivered.[45] The point is worth stressing, as a widespread critical commonplace, largely based on an overliteral reading of a passage in Leonardo Bruni's *De studiis et litteris*, holds that public speaking was regarded by humanists as lying outside women's proper domain.[46] The evidence is to the contrary. Besides negative examples of the indecorum of women speaking in public, Roman history offered a handful of positive instances, most famously Hortensia, daughter of the orator Quintus Hortensius (114–50 BC), celebrated for a speech delivered during the Second Triumvirate in 42 BC, resisting the imposition of a tax on Roman women.[47] Modern-day female public speakers could thus lay claim to the all-important legitimizing authority of a classical precedent, commended by no less of a rhetorical master than Quintilian and revived in a recent biography by Boccaccio, which lauded Hortensia for her "tireless eloquence" and political courage.[48] It is inconceivable that well-born women like Costanza Varano and Ippolita Sforza would have placed their rhetorical skills on display through public speaking had this been perceived as contrary to feminine decorum or as sexually compromising; both, indeed, delivered orations while marriageable girls, at a time when concerns for propriety were paramount. Nor is it easy to make sense of Bishop Ermolao Barbaro's seeming commission of a publicly delivered oration from Isotta Nogarola if the prospect of a woman speaking in public was perceived as a threat to decorum. While moral concerns certainly existed regarding women and speech, staged and officially sanctioned displays of female eloquence were clearly socially and morally acceptable.[49] Cassandra

Fedele's oration for Lamberto was published four times between 1487 and 1494, while other female speeches, such as Battista and Ippolita Sforza's orations to Pius II, were spoken of by humanists in laudatory terms.[50]

Besides the oration, the most frequent genre of writing practiced by women in fifteenth-century Italy was undoubtedly the letter. Here, again, it is useful to make a distinction between the formal state letter and the informal letter (*epistula familiaris*), the former, naturally, like the political oration, practiced exclusively by women of high estate. Examples of such political letters are Costanza Varano's epistles to Alfonso of Aragon (1443), requesting his help in restoring the Varano to Camerino, and to Pope Eugenius IV (1447), pleading for the commutation of her grandfather Galeazzo Malatesta's excommunication.[51] At the other end of the functionalist spectrum from these circumstantially driven letters are certain of Laura Cereta's moral epistles addressed to fictional or disguised interlocutors ("Lupus Cynicus"; "Europa Solitaria"); these used the format of the letter very transparently as a pretext for what were in effect short moral essays.[52] The most substantial surviving epistolary collections by fifteenth-century women—if we limit ourselves to the "artistic" tradition of the Latin letter intended for public circulation—are Cereta's with 82 and Cassandra Fedele's with 113.[53] Also important and historically groundbreaking, though on a lesser scale, is the letterbook of Isotta Nogarola, amounting to 26 letters, including an expansive consolatory epistle written on commission in 1461 for Jacopo Antonio Marcello for a funerary collection Marcello was putting together to commemorate his dead son. All are impressive attainments, though Cereta's epistolary is generally acknowledged as the most original and distinctive, notable especially for its foregrounding of domestic and family contexts and its broad thematic and tonal range.[54] Fedele's is, by contrast, more "correct" and professional, centering largely on patronage relations and encompassing a glittering international cast list of correspondents, including humanists and statesmen such as Angelo Poliziano and Bartolomeo Scala, two queens—Isabel of Castile (1451–1504) and Beatrice d'Aragona (1457–1508), queen of Hungary—and some of the leading ruler-consorts of northern Italian courts such as Eleonora d'Aragona (1450–93), Duchess of Ferrara, and her daughter Beatrice d'Este (1475–97), Duchess of Milan.[55] Consistently with her rank, and with the earlier date of her writing, Isotta Nogarola's letterbook is more "private" and less patronage-oriented, as well as more exclusively masculine in its interlocutors. Although Nogarola was the recipient of a poem of praise from Costanza Varano, her letters show her interacting principally with males, most characteristically lay and clerical aristocratic humanists such as Lodovico Foscarini (1409–80), Ermolao Barbaro, Niccolò Barbo (?c. 1420–62), and Giuliano Cesarini (1398–?1444).

The genre of the letter collection, which, in a manner characteristic of humanism, blends sententious moral reflection with ethical self-fashioning and enactments of *amicitia,* was not the only one women writers participated took up. Isotta Nogarola and Laura Cereta, for example, also produced longer and more independent prose works.[56] Both are classed in their modern English-language editions as dialogues, but the generic term elides profound differences; in common the two have little more than a basic dialogic structuring and the presence of an authorial figure as protagonist.[57] Nogarola's *Quaestio utrum Adam vel Eva magis peccaverit (Debate on the Equal or Unequal Sin of Adam and Eve)* (1451) is a serious philosophical work, portraying the author discussing the relative guilt of Adam and Eve with the Venetian patrician humanist Lodovico Foscarini in a conversation notable for its dialectical agility and delight in irony and paradox; Nogarola argues throughout for women's inferiority to men—one of the chief grounds of her argument for Eve's lesser sinfulness—yet reveals herself throughout as Foscarini's equal in learning and articulacy, a point reinforced by his admiring comments throughout.[58] Nogarola's dialogue was published over a century after its composition, in 1563, by Count Francesco Nogarola, who gives it a Ciceronian distinctness of setting and occasion, locating it in the Nogarola estate of Castel d'Azzano and adding a third interlocutor, Giovanni Navagero.[59] In its original form, however, the dialogue is presented as a dramatization of an epistolary exchange of views rather than a "live" conversation—so much so that it is legitimate to question whether Foscarini should be credited as coauthor.[60] This unwonted format of a "distanced dialogue" rather poignantly evokes the problems of social decorum constraining women's participation in literary culture at this time; we are here half a century before Bembo's *Gli Asolani* (1505) legitimized the presence of female speakers in philosophical dialogue and three quarters of a century before Castiglione's *Cortegiano* (1528) habituated readers to "mixed' dialogues encompassing clearly identifiable historical speakers.[61] Such considerations of social propriety are entirely remote, by contrast, to Laura Cereta's comic and distinctly "unrealist" *Asinarium funus (On the Death of an Ass)*, her earliest work, dating from around 1485, and placed at the climax of her collection of letters. Taking its cue from Apuleius, the dialogue consists of a series of parodic funeral orations by two variously unreliable rustics, Soldus and Philonacus, followed by a tour de force concluding oration by "Laura" that is used as a pretext in part for introducing recondite details concerning the medicinal use of asses' body parts from Pliny. [62] The work is of its time both in its taste for classical scientific arcana and its exuberant linguistic experimentalism; thematically, as well, it connects with a strain of humanistic satirical writing in its use of the Apuleian-Lucianic motif of the ass.[63] This does not detract, however, from the radical originality of the work, which appears to have disconcerted Cereta's contemporaries; it attracted criticism on its publication, and Cereta did not attempt anything quite as experimental again.

Although the prose production of fifteenth-century female Latinists has long monopolized critical attention in this area, recent articles by Holt Parker have called attention to the existence of a parallel, if more slender, tradition of female-authored Latin verse in this period.[64] In terms of the quantity of their surviving output, the best-represented fifteenth-century Latin female poets are Angela Nogarola and Costanza Varano. Like their prose, these women's poetic output—especially Varano's—interestingly reflects their public diplomatic roles as representatives of powerful families. Thus Varano's poem to her cousin, Gianlucido Gonzaga (1423–48), though cast as a "private" appreciation of Gianlucido's scholarly prowess, may at the same time be seen as reflecting the concern of the Varano-Malatesta to maintain their links with the powerful ruling family of Mantua.[65] A comparable poem in the small oeuvre of Angela Nogarola is her cento addressed to Pandolfo Malatesta of Rimini, teasingly informal in tone—it requests the return of a borrowed manuscript—but clearly functional also in preserving and publicizing an important connection.[66] More urgent and specific diplomatic ends are served by poems like Varano's to Alfonso V of Aragon (1396–1458), accompanying an epistolary plea to help restore the Varano to their lordship of Camerino, and Nogarola's 1387 epigram to Gian Galeazzo Visconti (1351–1402), following his conquest of her home city of Verona.[67] Other poems by women appear to relate more to agendas of personal self-fashioning, such as the poem of admiration addressed in 1441, along with a letter, by the 16-year-old Costanza Varano to Isotta Nogarola and the Greek epigram Alessandra Scala addressed to Poliziano in reply to one from him, the latter a remarkable feat of learning in an age in which such mastery of the language was rare.[68] Poetry independent of correspondence contexts is much rarer in this period, although three such poems are known, all ambitious in scope: Angela Nogarola's awkwardly realized didactic *Liber de virtutibus* (*Book of Virtues*), Isotta Nogarola's far more successful bucolic elegy on the Nogarola family estate at "Cyanum" (Castel d'Azzano), and Laura Brenzoni's miniature Virgilian epic recounting the heroic deeds of the condottiere Roberto Sanseverino (1418–87) during the War of Ferrara from 1482–84, the latter plausibly written when the precocious Brenzoni was no more than 17 years old.[69]

Where vernacular writings are concerned in this period, we find a very different and generally far more localized pattern of composition. The two best-known and most prolific female vernacular writers of the fifteenth century were both Florentine: the patrician Lucrezia Tornabuoni de' Medici, wife of Piero di Cosimo de' Medici (1416–69) and mother of Lorenzo "il Magnifico" (1449–92), and the less socially exalted Antonia Tanini Pulci, wife of the vernacular poet and Medici client Bernardo Pulci (1438–88), the brother of the better-known poets Luca and Luigi. Both Tornabuoni and Pulci wrote exclusively in the vernacular: a considerably less unusual choice in Florence than it would have been elsewhere in the period. The aristocratic practice of humanistically educating young women did not take root in republican Florence as it did in the courts in the fifteenth century; it is not until the 1490s, when the city had drifted some distance toward a quasi-signorial culture under Lorenzo de' Medici, that Florence attained its first nationally famous "learned lady," in the form of Alessandra Scala. At the same time, for patriotic reasons, vernacular literature was more cultivated in the fifteenth century in Florence and Tuscany than elsewhere; where towns like Padua, Verona, and Mantua could lay claim to Livy, Catullus, or Virgil as their literary civic "founding fathers," Florence's chief claim to literary preeminence was modern and vernacular and rested on its status as the real or ideal *patria* of Dante, Petrarch, and Boccaccio.[70] Like his mother, and perhaps influenced by her, Lorenzo de' Medici wrote near exclusively in the vernacular and actively promoted the language in his literary patronage.[71] Similarly, in the case of Pulci, her use of the vernacular does not differentiate her literary production greatly from those of her husband and brothers-in-law.

If literary context, as well as gender, must be seen as a factor in determining Tornabuoni's and Pulci's linguistic practice, gender may probably be seen as a more crucial determinant in their thematic orientation and choices of genre. In a manner that serves to differentiate them from courtly and Veneto female writers almost as clearly as their use of the vernacular, both Tornabuoni and Pulci seem to have limited their literary output to devotional works. Most of Tornabuoni's surviving production consists of writings in two genres, the terza rima or ottava rima religious narrative and the *lauda,* or spiritual canticle.[72] Pulci's output is entirely within the popular genre of the mystery play, or *sacra rappresentazione.* Written for performance, Pulci's plays proved immensely popular, as their sixteenth-century publishing record demonstrates (see appendix A). In

their focus on religious themes and their ostensibly "private" and devotional character, Tornabuoni's and Pulci's ouput conforms far more closely
to traditional circumscriptions of women's proper sphere than does the
overwhelmingly secular production of humanistically educated women
elsewhere. An interesting point of comparison here is Battista da Montefeltro, whose oeuvre encompasses vernacular devotional verse comparable with that of Tornabuoni.[73] In Battista's case, however, this made up
only part of her literary output, which, as we have seen, also included a
public oration before the Emperor Sigismund (1433) as well as a Latin diplomatic epistle (c. 1425) addressed to Pope Martin V.[74] It seems like that it was
only when her public and political life was over—she retired to the Fran-
ciscan convent of Santa Lucia of Foligno following her husband's sale of
his lordship of Pesaro to the Sforza in 1446—that she turned concertedly
to the composition of vernacular religious verse.[75] This points to a significant difference between the position of the women of the ruling elite
within the nominally republican Florence and the seigneurial courts.
While Tornabuoni's position was in some sense comparable with Battista
da Montefeltro's, as the consort of the most powerful man in Florence,
Florentine convention dictated that her fairly substantial influence be exercised essentially behind the scenes.[76] The kind of public diplomatic role
we see assumed with such confidence by da Montefeltro or by Costanza
Varano, or by Bianca Visconti and Ippolita Sforza, would have been perceived in Florence not merely as inappropriate but as politically threatening, precisely because it would have been associated with seigneurial
regimes where power rested with a single dynasty. While there is no reason to doubt the sincerity of her religious inspiration, Tornabuoni's devotional output was thus strategically well judged for a woman in her delicate position, allowing her to stage her literacy and cultural refinement in
a manner that assimilated her to the women of ruling dynasties elsewhere
while keeping her manoeuvers safely within the bounds of gender and political decorum.

The only other secular female vernacular writer of the fifteenth century to leave a substantial body of writing, Ceccarella, or Francesca, Minutolo, offers an interesting counterpoint to Tornabuoni and Pulci. A
Neapolitan noblewoman of high rank and court connections, Minutolo is
known to us for a collection of letters written in around 1470, in a florid
and convoluted style reminiscent of Boccaccio's early writings. Although
unpublished until recently, the *Lettere* were evidently collected for circulation at least to a select manuscript audience, and Minutolo seems to have
enjoyed a certain degree of fame as a writer: allusions to her are found in
other letters of the period, under the classicizing pseudonyms of "sybilla

Minutola" or "sybilla Parthenopea."[77] Minutolo's *Lettere* provide fascinat-
ing, if fragmentary, evidence of noblewomen's participation in literary culture in Naples during the time of Ippolita Sforza's early married life there,
and during the formative years of Eleonora d'Aragona, important as a patron of profeminist culture in her later married life as Duchess of Ferrara.[78] Thematically, Minutolo's letter collection offers a sharp contrast
with both the devout vernacular writings of Tornabuoni and Pulci and the
sober and "virile" epistolary mode cultivated by northern Latinists like
Isotta Nogarola and Costanza Varano. The *Lettere* are eclectic in their subject matter, embracing expressions of homage to princes, critical responses
to literary works, and a letter of self-defense in the face of a verbal attack
as well as one of polite deflection of excessive praise.[79] Minutolo's primary
subject matter in the collection, however, is love, though a love treated in
the stylized and casuistical mode typical of medieval court culture and distanced from autobiographical interpretation by the author, who presents
herself as a discreet scribe of love letters for anonymous "relatives and intimate friends."[80] Despite such precautions, Minutolo shows herself concerned about the possible jeopardy to her reputation such a publication
might bring, and her dedicatory letter, to her fellow nobleman Francesco
Arcella, is defensive even by the standards of the day.[81] Nonetheless, it is
interesting that Minutolo saw fit to publish her letters, and in a collection
that reveals her identity, if discreetly: while the sixteenth century would
see a number of printed volumes of female-voiced love letters, these
tended to appear under conditions of anonymity sufficient for it to be unclear whether the author was a woman.[82] We might be led to reflect that
the conditions of manuscript publication were perhaps more conducive to
such "audacities" than print publication, offering, as they did, the possibility of limiting access to a closely defined audience whose sympathy might
be assumed.[83] The same is perhaps true of another of the very rare secular female writers in the vernacular we know from the fifteenth century,
the Veronese Medea or Amidea degli Aleardi (fl. c. 1405), whose two surviving poems include a striking sonnet of erotic despair, threatening suicide, "Dhè non esser Iasòn, s'io son Medea" ("Pray Do Not Be Jason, Even
if I Am Medea").[84] Together with her Bolognese contemporary Bartolo-
mea Mattugliani, author of a sole surviving poem, and Battista da Montefeltro, whose youthful vernacular lyrics are discussed below, Aleardi represents an intriguing, though ill-documented, early phase in the history of
women's participation in the Italian lyric tradition.[85] Fragmentary though
the evidence for it is, this needs to be taken into account as context when
assessing the careers of early female humanists such as Maddalena Scrovegni and Angela Nogarola. Especially suggestive is the copresence of

Nogarola and Aleardi within Veronese elite culture in the years before the city's fall to Venice in 1405.[86]

Besides this scattering of writings by secular women, we can find a more compact and substantial tradition of female-authored vernacular writing in this period within Italian convents. The outstanding figure here is Caterina Vigri (St. Catherine of Bologna), author among other works of the frequently reprinted *Libro devoto* or *Sette armi spirituali*. Prior to taking vows as an observant Clarissa, Caterina had received a courtly education at Ferrara in the 1420s, where she was invited to be a companion to Margherita d'Este; even if her studies there preceded the foundation of Guarino's famous school, we may assume that they were humanistic in character.[87] Of the same order as Caterina, and also certainly Latin-literate, were the Venetian Illuminata Bembo (c. 1410–93), Caterina's disciple, editor, and biographer, and Battista Varano, daughter of Costanza Varano's cousin Giulio Cesare Varano, who we may assume received the kind of concerted humanistic education common to other girls of her family and age.[88] Besides these highly educated women, all Clarissans, another important female religious writer of the age was the charismatic lay mystic Caterina Fieschi Adorno (St. Catherine of Genoa), whose works, however, reach us through the mediation of male disciples and fall under the complex authorship considerations common to other early female religious writers such as St Catherine of Siena.[89] A point to underline with respect to these religious writings by women is the strong preference shown for the vernacular, even by women whose education would presumably have permitted them to write in Latin, such as Illuminata Bembo or Battista Varano.[90] An informal decorum appears to have pertained in the period, whereby classical Latin was reserved for secular uses and to reach out to masculine audiences, while the vernacular was effectively confined to devotional writings, often intended principally for a female convent audience.[91]

The only female writer of the period we see truly crossing the boundaries between the traditions of humanistic Latin and the religious vernacular is Battista da Montefeltro. Insofar as we can reconstruct it on the basis of her surviving works, Battista's literary trajectory maps this linguistic division quite sharply: we have from her pen, on the one hand, a small corpus of secular Latin writings, written in the course of her public duty as ruler-consort of Pesaro, and, on the other, a body of vernacular poetry near exclusively religious in content.[92] Battista's earliest vernacular poems probably date from the early years of her marriage, which took place in 1405, and attest to her close poetic relationship with her father-in-law, Malatesta Malatesta (d. 1429).[93] Consistently with Malatesta's practice and

with the Petrarchan courtly lyric culture of the time, most of Battista's surviving lyrics from this period are sonnets. The verse that appears to date
from the later years of her life, by contrast, especially during the time of
her religious life in the Clarissan convent of Santa Lucia di Foligno (1446–
48), is principally written in the form of the *lauda,* the most favored vernacular poetic form in monastic contexts of the period, also practiced by
Caterina Vigri. Battista also, however, practiced other metrical forms in
this late poetry: her long prayer to St. Jerome, for example, that serves as
a kind of poetic testament, signaling her Jerome-like renunciation of her
past classical studies, is cast in the form of a terza rima *capitolo.*[94] Producing a critical edition of Battista's quite substantial body of sacred verse
ought to be a priority for the scholarship of fifteenth-century women's
writing: hers is a powerful and refined voice, representing a rather different and less archaizing strain of the *lauda* tradition from that practiced by
Caterina Vigri.[95] Among the benefits of such an edition would be that it
would allow us to gauge better the degree to which Battista's descendent
Vittoria Colonna drew on the tradition of intellectualistic piety to which
she was heir through her maternal Montefeltro heritage in her own, highly
innovative practice of Petrarchizing spiritual lyric, which dominates her
late production of the 1530s and 40s.

## 2. The "Learned Lady" in Theory: Models of Gender Conduct and Their Contexts

As has long been recognized by historians, the figure of the secular female
intellectual of the Renaissance is essentially a construction of humanism.[96] Secular women first emerged as writers, as we have already seen,
precisely in the late fourteenth-century cradle of post-Petrarchan humanism and within the circle of Petrarch's first disciples and imitators: Maddalena Scrovegni was a correspondent of Antonio Loschi (1368–1441) and
Lombardo della Seta (d. 1390), Angela Nogarola of Pandolfo Malatesta.[97]
The first text addressing the problem of women's education was also
one of the first great humanistic educational manifestos more generally,
Leonardo Bruni's *De studiis et litteris,* addressed to Battista da Montefeltro
at some time after her marriage in 1405.[98] A second—as much of a manifesto for the Venetian educational model as Bruni's had been for the Florentine—was written by the Venetian humanist Lauro Quirini (1420–80/
81) for Isotta Nogarola in the late 1440s or early 1450s.[99] Humanists cultivated "literary ladies" and deployed them rhetorically for a variety of
purposes that we see recurring in the vernacular literary culture of the following century: as topics for epideictic invention, as vehicles for homosocial bonding, as ciphers in their social, cultural, and geopolitical self-

positioning, as emblems of their intellectual project. In return for these useful services, they publicized and circulated the names of female scholars and evolved a series of discourses defensive of women's intellectual equality with men. Most specifically, the encomium of a "learned lady" emerged in this period as a recognized epistolary subgenre: by the time Poliziano was composing his tour de force *laudatio* of Cassandra Fedele in the early 1490s, with its string of arcane classical prototypes for the learned woman and its ringing Virgilian incipit "O decus Italiae virgo," implicitly comparing Cassandra to the warrior Camilla, he was conscious of writing in a genre that already included among its distinguished practitioners not only Bruni and Quirini but also Loschi (author of a tribute to Maddalena Scrovegni), Guarino da Verona (1374–1460) (who had preceded Poliziano in comparing the Nogarola sisters to Camilla and Penthesilea), and Lodovico Foscarini (author of a less secularizing tribute to Isotta Nogarola, including the biblical Queen of Sheba among her historical archetypes).[100] Numerous minor Veneto humanists had also already preceded Poliziano in paying tribute to Fedele in Venice, while in nearby Verona, Dante's descendent and homonym Dante Alighieri III (d. 1510) was hailing Laura Brenzoni as an ornament to the city and the world.[101] The tradition of the epistle in praise of a learned *virgo* / virago was sufficiently well established to attract Poliziano as an opportunity for emulative rhetorical display. In turn, his exemplary essay in the genre served further to increase its diffusion.

To contextualize the humanistic stance of supportiveness toward women sufficiently, and to begin to probe its motives, it is necessary to step back from the figure of the "learned lady" and to view this encomiastic discourse within a broader perspective. Humanistic praises of erudite women were a subgenre of a more comprehensive genre of writings laudatory of women's capacities and potential, which cumulatively construct an image of heroic womanhood distinct in many respects from traditional feminine ideals. Again, this broader genre has its roots in the formative period of Italian humanism; indeed, its founding texts were authored by humanism's founding fathers, Petrarch and Boccaccio.[102] The better known of the texts in question is Boccaccio's *De claris mulieribus* (*On Famous Women*), a collection of over a hundred biographies of "famous women," originally drafted in 1361–62 and intended as a counterpart to Petrarch's *De viris illustribus* (*On Illustrious Men*).[103] Preceding this, and a likely source, was a letter of Petrarch's of 1358 (*Familiares*, 21.8) to Anna von Schweidnitz, or Svídnická (1339–62), wife of the Emperor Charles IV (1316–78), congratulating her on the birth of a daughter.[104] As Stephen Kolsky has noted, the letter has a consolatory, as much as a congratulatory, function in context, given the importance for a woman in Anna's position of producing the requisite male heir. Petrarch exploits the delicate rhetorical situation imaginatively, arguing for the dignity of women as manifested by their attainments in classical antiquity and initiating the genre of collections of classical exempla of outstanding women, thematically grouped by learning, military prowess, and family devotion.[105] Together, Petrarch's letter and Boccaccio's treatise established a set of rhetorical norms for the praise of women posited on their capacity to win fame through activities generally considered "masculine," notably intellectual and literary endeavor and political and military leadership. Closely linked in their inception, they embodied two models for humanistic writing on women: the concise theoretical "defense," drawing succinctly on classical exempla as illustrative ballast for the thesis of women's capacity for "masculine" *virtus,* and the more diffuse assemblage of exemplary biographies, privileging narrative interest over analytic coherence.[106] Both models proved productive, and they increasingly came to fuse, producing the mature late fifteenth- and sixteenth-century model of "defense of women," which couples a theoretical defense with an extensive series of coherently marshaled exempla, often organized in accordance with the thematic categories essayed in Petrarch's *Familiares,* 21.8.[107]

The context and framing of Boccaccio's and Petrarch's founding contributions to humanistic writing on women deserve scrutiny, as well as their substance. Petrarch's letter, as we have seen, was addressed to a powerful woman, consort to the emperor and a ruler in her own right, as heiress to a province of Silesia. Boccaccio's treatise, too, is dedicated to a woman in a position of some power, Andrea Acciaiuoli, sister of the Florentine-born grand seneschal of Naples, Niccolò Acciaiuoli (1310–65), and he identifies as his ideal addressee Queen Giovanna I d'Anjou of Naples (1327–82), the only living woman he includes in his list of exempla.[108] Both, then, locate their praise of feminine excellence—or, in Boccaccio's case, exceptional women's ability to "transcend their sex"—within an epideictic discourse addressed to individual women of high estate or actually regnant within regal or imperial courts. This is important to our understanding of the significance of the works, and not simply because a degree of ad hominem flattery must be accounted among their motivating impulses. Court women, and especially women from ruling dynasties, offered a particular problem to conventional constructions of femininity, which in this period depended heavily on biologically deterministic scholastic models of sex difference, stemming ultimately from Aristotle.[109] Within this scholastic view, women were regarded as intrinsically inferior to men and naturally destined to political subordination: men were framed

by nature to command through their superior physical strength and rationality, while women's complementary mental and physical weakness correspondingly fitted them for a subservient role. At the level of behavioral
prescription, this model translated into two distinct, gender-differentiated
codes of conduct, wherein the male virtues of leadership, enterprise, and
articulacy were complemented by the female ones of passivity, silence, and
obedience. This scholastic construction of sex roles meshed relatively
seamlessly with the reality of social practice within the surviving city-
republics of Italy, such as Florence and Venice, where we find humanists
espousing this kind of strictly binary and hierarchical sex-gender system
well into the fifteenth century.[110] Within the princely courts, however—
now the dominant structures in northern and central Italy, as one republican regime after another fell to internal strife and external aggression—a
set of prescriptions mandating female subservience was evidently a more
problematic proposition. While the female succession sometimes found
within northern European monarchic regimes was practically unknown
within the northern and central Italian *signorie,* dynastic consorts did quite
frequently deputize for their husbands during absences and serve as regents if widowed while their sons were still minors; they also often acted
as catalysts for the cultural and social life of the court.[111] That a woman
might need to demonstrate leadership qualities was thus not an unlikely
eventuality, and this was reflected in the education afforded to women in
this position and the works that were dedicated to them. The Neapolitan
statesman Diomede Carafa drafted a weighty *Memoriale* on government
for Eleonora d'Aragona at around the time of her marriage to Ercole
d'Este, while, in her early married life, Eleonora was also the dedicatee of
Antonio Cornazzano's poem *De modo di regere et di regnare* (c. 1478).[112]
Women's profile in the courts was enhanced over the course of the fifteenth century as the Italian dynasties sought to enhance their "monarchic" image by marrying into families of greater antiquity or international
prestige. Consorts such as Barbara of Brandenburg (1423–81) in Mantua
and Eleonora d'Aragona in Ferrara brought to their marriages independent wealth and powerful family contacts: Barbara was the sister-in-law of
King Christian I of Denmark (1426–81), Eleonora the daughter of King Ferrante I of Naples (1423–94). To encompass such "great ladies" within a
scholastic-derived discourse that could logically praise women only for
their expert enactment of subservience was patently incongruous, nor was
it exactly strategic on the part of humanists with an interest in patronage.
Careful as most consorts were to position themselves as devoted and obe-
dient helpmates to their husbands, their relation to the broader courtly
world was of dominance rather than subservience.[113]

It was this quite strident mismatch between scholastic prescription and courtly reality that may be seen as primarily motivating the humanistic re-thinking of feminine virtue. As scholarship since Kristeller has stressed, humanists were primarily rhetoricians and excelled in perceiving rhetori-cal opportunities. Quite an obvious such opportunity was presented by the absence of a Latin praise idiom for highly placed women sufficiently evolved and analytically robust to challenge the discursive dominance of scholasticism in the field of gender. Vernacular culture could fall back on the language of courtly love, which had emerged in medieval Europe partly to address, precisely, the contingency of expressing deference to powerful women. The delicate cadences of vernacular lyric, however, translated with difficulty into the classicizing Latin that was the humanists' trademark, and the spiritualizing bent of Italian courtly lyric sat ill with the secular tasks the courts needed it to perform. What was required, and what humanists supplied with increasing precision, was a discourse capable of refuting essentialist scholastic imputations of female inferiority. In evolv-ing this discourse, they naturally turned initially to the quintessential hu-manistic instrument of the argument from classical history. The scholastic view that located women's political inferiority in their biological "defec-tiveness" was combated by gathering counterevidence of female historical achievement, cumulatively suggesting that sex roles were determined less by biological necessity than by contingent cultural factors. The attractions of this project as an intellectual exercise were manifold, quite indepen-dently of the case being argued: the assemblage of classical exempla of "fa-mous women" offered a showcase for humanists' skills in philology, while the use of rhetorically and historically based argument to counter scholas-tic scientifically based claims lent the debate a metaliterary dimension of methodological critique that could only increase its appeal.[114] Humanists' ingenuity in ferreting out classical exempla of outstanding women is strik-ing: Petrarch's list of learned women in his letter to Anna (Minerva, Isis, Carmenta, Sappho, Proba, the Sybils) includes only two figures—Sappho and Proba—whom modern scholarship would recognize as historical.[115] Countless new names, many culled from obscure texts, some apocryphal, were added to an ever-swelling pantheon over the course of the next two centuries or so.[116] Cumulatively, this patient process of invention and philological archaeology evoked a glittering ancient world of culturally ac-cepted female protagonism modern classicists would struggle to recog-nize, in which respected women poets, philosophers, and inventors com-peted with venerated stateswomen and generals for the admiration of their male peers. While it ranged widely geographically and chronologi-cally, incorporating exempla from ancient Egypt, Assyria, and Persia as well as Greece and Rome, conceptually this ideal gender world of antiquity may be seen as being rooted in the values of the elite of ancient Rome, whose complex view of women as simultaneously "same and other" to men provided a more socially appropriate and rhetorically productive model for the conceptualization of gender difference than Aristotle's relatively monolithic version.[117]

The implications of this discourse regarding the classical attainments of women are explored further later in this chapter. Here it will be useful to continue investigating the motives for its emergence and development. The first and most obvious, already touched on, is dynastic women's growing power within the princely courts of Italy, which made them attractive prospects for literary patronage. Clear-cut examples of this are the dedications of Bartolomeo Goggio's *De laudibus mulierum* (1487), Giovanni Sabadino degli Arienti's *Gynevera, de le clare donne* (1489–90), and Jacopo Filippo Foresti's *De plurimis claris selectisque mulieribus* (1497), to, respectively, Eleonora d'Aragona, Duchess of Ferrara, Ginevra Sforza Bentivoglio (1440–1507), wife of the lord of Bologna, and Beatrice d'Aragona, Eleonora's sister and queen-consort of Hungary.[118] All three were women of influence, prestige, and wealth in their own right, capable of delivering the kind of benefits humanists sought in their patronage efforts. At the same time, however, these women offered a means of mediated access to the still more powerful patronage of their husbands, serving as "threshold patrons," more approachable than their male counterparts precisely because of their more equivocal status.[119] This dynamic of mediation is important to grasp, as it operated both on a literal and a symbolic level and accounts to a great extent for the cultural salience the figure of the dynastic consort attained at this time. While humanists low in the food chain might in some cases limit their aspirations to the service and patronage of consorts alone—an instance here might be Goggio, a Ferrarese notary probably in Eleonora d'Aragona's direct employ—more ambitious and higher-born humanists cultivated court ladies as part of a more articulated strategy of career advancement and self-positioning.[120] A good example of this from the later fifteenth century, is a figure like Niccolò da Correggio (1450–1508), while the early sixteenth century offers still more notable cases such as Pietro Bembo (1470–1547) and Baldassare Castiglione (1478–1529). For men like these, of distinguished aristocratic or patrician families themselves, the attractions of women as "threshold patrons" were numerous. One was that a mediated patronage relation of this kind allowed them to cast their courtship of power in the soft-focus guise of a courtly devotion to "the ladies," thus reworking as a voluntary chivalric homage to female virtue what would look more like servitude if directed to a male. At a less immediate level, a reason why highborn courtiers were drawn to the women of the courts may have been their shared status as "gilded subordinates" to the princes who were, respectively, their husbands and masters. This allowed dynastic women to serve as flattering proxy figures for male courtiers, simultaneously graced by proximity to power and excluded from its direct exercise. The humanist topos of women as naturally equipped for rule, yet suppressed by political custom, may be seen as having something of the function of a consolatory fiction in this regard.[121] The same ambiguity in their relation to power lent value to court women within their own families' diplomatic strategizing in that it left them free to cultivate relationships of kinship and friendship instrumental to dynastic interests in a more informal and "deniable" manner than would have been possible for their husbands.[122] On the basis of these considerations, it seems reasonable to conclude that court women's "actual," autonomous power was not the sole, or perhaps even the dominant, factor in assessing their importance as patrons and cultural interlocutors. Rather, it was the pivotal place they occupied within a complex and negotiated system of power that allowed them to punch culturally considerably above their weight.

Returning from the context and motivations of humanistic profeminist discourse to the narrative of its emergence and diffusion, the first thing to note is the immense fourteenth- and fifteenth-century fortunes of Boccaccio's De claris mulieribus, which is attested by over a hundred surviving manuscripts and two vernacular translations, one of which exists in two versions.[123] Of course, it would be misleading to place the entire fortuna of this polyvalent and ideologically conflicted text under a profeminist rubric. As Margaret Franklin has recently illustrated in a study of the visual arts legacy of De claris mulieribus, the narrative material assembled by Boccaccio in the work lent itself to quite disparate uses, some tending more to reinforce traditional gender values than aid in the construction of new value schemes.[124] The extensive dissemination of Boccaccio's text did have the effect, however, of familiarizing a wide readership with the figure of the virago, and her various associated topoi, positive and negative, as well as placing in circulation a wide range of illustrative material eminently amenable to rhetorical reuse. Limiting ourselves to the field of immediate interest to us, we may note that De claris mulieribus provided admiring biographies of a number of Greek and Roman "learned women," including, most importantly, the poets Sappho, Cornificia, and Proba, the orator Hortensia, and the scholarly queen Nicaula (the biblical Queen of Sheba).[125] Taken together, these biographies constitute a strongly affirmative account of learning as a laudable activity for women (although, with typical ambivalence, Boccaccio also supplies exempla in which erudition in women is associated with sexual deviance).[126] Especially important in this regard is the life of the Roman poet Cornificia, conjured into substance in a late stage of the text's composition on the evidence of a brief mention in Jerome, and used as an opportunity to exhort women to seek fame through virtuous study rather than "lazily" resigning themselves to a life spent purely in marriage and childrearing.[127] Nicaula is also complimented for devoting herself to study rather than indulging in a rich woman's usual outlets of idleness and luxury, while Proba is praised for not wasting her life "like most women" wielding the needle, the distaff, and the loom. Despite the derogatory moral cast of Boccaccio's take on female "idleness," the remarks just cited are important in the history of profeminist discourse in setting forth an ideal of virtuous cultural attainment for women as not simply laudable but laudable precisely as a transgression of the conventional limitations society placed on women's activity.[128] A similar point is made, more cautiously, with respect to women's key virtue of silence, in Boccaccio's biography of the Roman orator Hortensia, when the triumvirs who hear her plea are seen to reflect that "as much as silence in public was a praiseworthy quality in a woman, still, when the occasion required it, an elegant and seemly flow of language deserved to be extolled."[129]

The degree of currency attained by classical exempla of "famous women," and the legitimizing function they performed with respect to modern female erudites, may be measured by the frequency of their occurrence in writings addressed to fifteenth-century "learned ladies."[130] Thus we find Isotta Nogarola compared by Lauro Quirini to the Sybils, Aspasia, Sappho, Proba, Maesia, Hortensia, Cornelia and Hypatia and by Lodovico Foscarini to Sempronia, Cornificia, Sappho, Nicaula, and the Sybils, while Poliziano's encomium to Cassandra Fedele introduces as points of comparison not merely familiar names such as Hortensia, Cornelia, and Sappho but more recondite figures drawn from his Hellenistic studies, such as the poets Telesilla, Anyte, and Praxilla.[131] As this last example suggests, this highly codified citation system allowed much scope for culturally meaningful customization: Poliziano's Hellenizing selection is clearly intended to underline the superiority of his philological reach with regard to his predecessors. In a similar way, we may see Leonardo Bruni's self-consciously selective proposal as role models to Battista da Montefeltro in the opening page of De studiis et litteris of Cornelia, Sappho, and Aspasia, as reflecting the rhetorical-poetic-theological bent of the curriculum outlined in his treatise, while Quirini's foregrounding of Hypatia in his letter to Nogarola polemically points up the greater philosophical content of his own Venetian counterproposal. The complexity of non-gender-related meaning that the discourse of "women's excellence" acquired in context does not detract from its enabling role in the narrative of women's emergence as writers: on the contrary, the multivalence of this discourse, as well as the opportunities it offered for erudite display and intellectual self-positioning, increased its attraction to humanists and hence the degree of its circulation and the breadth of its acceptance. Besides male humanists intent on mutual agonistic emulation, the strategies of argument associated with this theme were equally available to women, as was its rapidly accumulating stock of classical exempla. Thus we find Nogarola, in her letter to Guarino, authorizing her position with due modesty by noting her lack of any aspiration to rival Cornificia, Nicaula, Faunia, Cornelia, or Portia, while Costanza Varano, in her letter of admiration to Nogarola, compares her to Aspasia and Cornelia.[132] Laura Cereta, meanwhile, in a notable display of erudition, lambasts an apocryphal correspondent, "Bibulus Sempronius," who has displayed doubt regarding women's capacities for intellectual endeavor, with a tour de force list of some twenty-four counterexamples, stretching from the remotest antiquity (the Sybils, the Queen of Sheba) to the present day (Nicolosa Sanuti, Nogarola, Fedele).[133]

Cereta's extension of her list of exempla to embrace modern literary women is worthy of notice as representative of a growing trend in her age. Postclassical women are thinly represented in Boccaccio's De claris mulieribus, with the only living woman included being Queen Giovanna of Naples, and that clearly for strategic reasons. Imitations of Boccaccio's work dating to the later fifteenth century, by contrast, begin tentatively to include modern women among their exemplars of female excellence. Noteworthy in this respect is Sabadino degli Arienti's Gynevera, de le clare donne, mentioned above, which replaces the conventional litany of ancient women entirely with a list of modern exempla, including Battista da Montefeltro, Isotta, Ginevra, and Angela Nogarola, Bianca Maria Visconti, Ippolita Sforza, and Battista Sforza da Montefeltro, as well as his Bolognese compatriot Caterina Vigri. Sabadino explicitly makes claims for these women as the equals of their classical predecessors, reinforcing his point locally through classical analogies in individual vitae: Ippolita Sforza, for example, is compared to Nicaula, a fellow "queen," Angela Nogarola to the poet Cornificia, and the mystic Caterina Vigri to the Erythraean Sybil.[134] Besides Sabadino, unusual for the period in his "modernist" emphases, we find a handful of modern female lives in Vespasiano da Bisticci's Libro delle lodi delle donne (early 1490s), though cast in a more socially conservative Florentine-republican idiom, while, back in the courts, Iacopo

Filippo Foresti's *De plurimis claris selectisque mulieribus* includes copious examples of modern women, some plagiarized from Sabadino, and Mario Equicola's *De mulieribus* (1501) contains extensive praises of Isabella d'Este and her lady-in-waiting and close friend Margherita Cantelmo.[135] The inclusion of modern examples in "famous women" treatises had obvious rhetorical advantages for humanists seeking to ingratiate themselves with courtly women in that it allowed scope for flattering dedicatees both directly and through reference to their ancestors.[136] It also had the effect of far more clearly constructing the category of "famous women" as permeable, in a way that encouraged a dynamic of emulation. A letter of Isabella d'Este's thanking Sabadino for a copy of his treatise, assures him that she will "read it with attention and make every effort to imitate the vestiges of those most illustrious matrons."[137] In a congenital overachiever such as Isabella, it would be unwise to dismiss such language as purely conventional.

Isabella's letter to Sabadino was drafted in a context where the "vestiges of illustrious matrons" were a particularly palpable presence. Recent studies of the fifteenth-century humanistic *querelle des femmes* concur that the most productive contexts for encomiastic writings on women were, precisely, the courts of Ferrara and Mantua in the closing decades of the century, in the circles of Isabella's mother, Eleonora d'Aragona, Duchess of Ferrara and of Isabella herself, as Marchioness of Mantua by marriage. We have already seen that Eleonora was the dedicatee of Bartolomeo Goggio's profeminist treatise, *De laudibus mulierum,* while her sister, Beatrice, was the dedicatee of Iacopo Filippo Foresti's *De plurimis claris selectisque mulieribus.* A series of paintings of classical "famous women" by the Ferrarese painter Ercole de' Roberti has also been associated with Eleonora's patronage, while the same courtly context saw the poet Matteo Maria Boiardo (1434–94) injecting an implicit *querelle* element into his classicizing chivalric romance, *Orlando innamorato* (published in 1483 and in 1495), which constructs the dashing female knight Bradamante as ancestress of the Este dynasty with her husband Ruggiero.[138] Following Eleonora's death in 1493, the 19-year-old Isabella appears to have become a similar animating focus of profeminist discourses. Two works associated with her circles are Mario Equicola's *De mulieribus* (c. 1500) and Agostino Strozzi's *Defensio mulierum* (c. 1501), both dedicated to one of Isabella's closest associates, Margherita Cantelmo, and the former, as we have seen, containing extensive praises of Isabella, into whose service Equicola was later assumed.[139] The treatises of Goggio, Strozzi, and Equicola represent an important novelty within the fifteenth-century Italian debate on women as the first treatises to attempt an explicit theoretical consideration of women's role and status rather than relying on what might be inferred

from a historical listing of women's attainments. As such, they are generally seen as a key precedent for the mature sixteenth-century theoretical
debate on women, represented by such authors as Baldassare Castiglione,
himself originally a product of the Mantuan court.

In assessing the reasons for this striking concentration of profeminist
culture in late fifteenth-century Mantua and Ferrara, commentators have
tended to call attention to the intelligence and energy of Eleonora and Isabella as prime motivating forces. There is certainly truth in this: as we
have seen, Eleonora in particular represents an outstanding example of the
type of the "trophy consort," empowered by the distinction and influence
of her natal family, and her skills as a ruler—quite frequently called into
practice by her husband's absences and illnesses—won her much acclaim
in Ferrara and beyond.[140] Isabella, though less politically active than her
mother and less advantaged by natal status with respect to her husband,
was remarkable for the ambitiousness of her cultural patronage and the
astuteness of her self-fashioning.[141] It seems entirely plausible that the
presence of two such self-consciously "exemplary" women in close temporal and geographic proximity would have had the effect of generating
an intense production of profeminist literature and art.[142] We should be
wary, however, of lending too much emphasis to Eleonora's and Isabella's
agency in accounting for the feminist developments of their age, or, more
generally, of giving undue weight to the Ferrarese and Mantuan contexts,
important though they undoubtedly were. The 1480s and 1490s saw a striking confluence of female literary talent and protagonism in Italy more generally, with Cassandra Fedele in Venice, Laura Cereta in Brescia, Laura
Brenzoni in Verona, and Alessandra Scala in Florence. In the latter decade,
we begin to hear the first mentions of a new breed of female vernacular
lyricists, including Girolama Corsi Ramos (fl. 1494–1509) in Venice and Cecilia Gallerani (1473–?1536) and Camilla Scarampa (1476–1520) in Milan.[143]
At the same time, throughout courtly Italy, the language of classicizing
female encomium was thriving as perhaps never before: the writings of the
Neapolitan Giosuè Capasso (b. c. 1466–68), for example, dating from the
closing decades of the fifteenth century, show a similar strongly affirmative and "heroizing" language in their descriptions of the noblewomen of
Naples as the Ferrarese treatises, even if they lack the kind of analytic content that distinguishes the works of an Equicola or a Goggio. Interesting
in particular in this regard is Capasso's terza rima encomiastic poem
*Triumphum novem viduarum (Triumph of the Nine Widows)*, which may be
set alongside the texts of Foresti and Sabadino degli Arienti for its dignified portrayal of a series of modern *donne illustri,* in this case a series of
aristocratic Neapolitan widows including Beatrice d'Aragona and Vittoria

Colonna's mentor Costanza d'Avalos, Duchess of Francavilla (1460–1541).[144] Similarly evocative of the gallant tone of Neapolitan court culture of the time is Capasso's dramatic interlude (*farsa*) for Federico I, datable to 1496–1501, which stages a debate between a misogynist voice and a profeminist one, labeled respectively as the voices of Good and Evil, or Right and Wrong (*Bene* and *Male*).[145] As these texts of Capasso's demonstrate, by the late fifteenth century, profeminist discourse was not the preserve of a hyperrefined intellectual avant-garde or limited to a particular court or courts. That women possessed a capacity for moral excellence equivalent to men's had become an established commonplace of court discourse, as had the fact that gallantry toward women was "right" and misogyny, equally categorically, "wrong."

### 3. The "Learned Lady" as Signifier in Humanistic Culture

The context and motives for these late fifteenth-century developments will be examined in more detail in the opening sections of the following chapter. Before proceeding to this, however, it will be useful to return briefly to an issue raised earlier in this chapter: the question of why humanists—or some humanists, including some of the most distinguished—found the figure of the female scholar so attractive as an object of encomium and advice. What were humanists actually doing when they praised "learned ladies," aside from flexing their rhetorical muscles on a modish subject offering much scope for erudite invention, and perhaps, depending on the lady in question, creating or nurturing valuable social contacts? If we look at fifteenth-century humanistic writings addressed to learned women, a commonplace that immediately strikes the eye for its frequency of recurrence is that of the *renovatio studii*. The modern woman writer is characteristically presented as a miraculous reinstantiation of Sappho or Cornificia, lending credibility to classical accounts of female intellectual "virility" that would otherwise have challenged belief. As the Vicentine intellectual Lodovico da Schio wrote to Cassandra Fedele, before hearing of her, he used to think that "the glory of the Muses, women's eloquence, and the whole feminine art of speaking [muliebre genus dicendi] . . . had all but disappeared," nor did he believe that any modern woman could be capable of the attainments of Hortensia and other legendary Roman orators.[146] Sometimes, more extravagantly, the modern "learned lady" is said to outdo her predecessors in antiquity: hailing Cassandra Fedele's talent in his 1491 encomium, Poliziano declares that "no longer will antiquity taunt us with its Muses . . . nor will the Greek classics show off the names of their female poets."[147] What is clearly being talked of here is the all-important and eminently negotiable question of the relationship between classical and modern humanistic learning, with the *virtus* of women metonymically representing the state of development of an entire culture. Initiating the humanistic discourse of ancient female exemplarity in learning, Boccaccio and Petrarch had presented the female writer as a phenomenon of pure classical "pastness": the Probas, Cornificias, Sybils, and Minervas they dwelled on had no correspondents or descendents today.[148] Their fifteenth-century successors, by contrast, could congratulate themselves on coexisting with modern incarnations of such paragons: rather than a stick with which to beat the lamentable state of contemporary literary culture, the learned lady becomes an index of progress toward the ideal of a "renovation of studies." This could take various and nuanced forms. When Lodovico Foscarini praises Isotta Nogarola for outdoing the famous women of antiquity, in a letter heavily stressing her piety and moral exemplarity, he may be taken as adumbrating the superiority of a modern neoclassical Christian culture to the pagan culture of antiquity on which it builds.[149] Poliziano, meanwhile, in contrasting the multitude of ancient learned women with the sole *rara avis* modern-day incarnation of the type in Cassandra Fedele, manages to combine an elegiac sense of the general superiority of the ancients with the self-flattering suggestion that some few highly select moderns might nonetheless be considered to make the grade. As this last example demonstrates with particular clarity, speaking about learned women was, for humanists, often a more or less veiled manner of speaking about learned men. In fact, implicitly underlying the whole humanistic discourse of women's learning is the rhetorical topic of *quanto magis:* if the *women* of classical antiquity or modern humanistic culture were so intellectually empowered, then what more could be said of its men?

These rhetorical maneuverings are important for the argument of the present study, as they constituted one of humanism's prime discursive legacies to successive vernacular culture in the field of gender. As a palpable novelty who was at the same time claimed to be a classical reincarnation, the fifteenth century "learned lady" could, and did, come to emblematize the innovative energies and the success of the humanistic project as a whole. This gave female writers an importance extending well beyond that merited by their concrete numbers and production; they stood in some sense as figureheads, as one of the purest and most visible effects of the humanistic transformation of culture. As Kristeller has noted, classical Latinity aside, a fifteenth-century male humanist's profile might not differ too extraordinarily from that of a "medieval" dictator or notary.[150] Such continuity could hardly be claimed for an Isotta Nogarola or a Cassandra Fedele. Male humanists might prefer to mirror themselves in a Cicero or a Seneca than a Brunetto Latini, but Hortensia or Cornelia were the *only* archetypes for Nogarola or Fedele. This was part of their prestige and one of the reasons for the rhetoric of the "marvelous" and "unique" that continued to cling around them, seemingly as applicable to Fedele or Alessandra Scala, despite a century of precedents, as it had been to Angela Nogarola and Maddalena Scrovegni.

One interesting aspect of humanists' construction of the "learned lady" as emblem of the revival of studies is the way in which it recalls previous epoch-defining feminine constructions in Italian literary culture. Since its earliest days, Italian vernacular literature had invested its identity very heavily in women as textual icons, using them in particular as a means of elaborating and emblematizing successive literary ideals. Clear-cut cases of this are the *stilnovo* lady, distinguished from her poetic predecessors by her enhanced spiritual dimension, and Petrarch's Laura—or, perhaps better, his succession of revised and revisable Lauras, characterized by their volatile mixture of classical and *stilnovo* ingredients. Humanistic Latin learning may be seen in many ways as marking a break with the feminized and eroticized culture of the vernacular lyric, in a manner embodied by the differences in the ideal male authorial personae of the two traditions: tearful and timorously "feminine" in the one case, briskly stoic and self-consciously "virile" in the other.[151] Despite these differences, however, an underlying continuity may be perceived in the persisting role humanism gave to a feminine cultural emblem: this time no pure poetic figment—a Beatrice or a Laura—but a figure endowed with a properly "humanistic" historicity and responded to characteristically not erotically but with a correctly distanced admiring respect. Unlike her vernacular predecessors, the "learned lady" of humanism did not compromise humanists' masculinity through erotic subjection, even if Poliziano in one letter humorously portrays himself as reduced to wavering impotence through an excess of admiration for Cassandra Fedele.[152] Like them, however, she served as a vessel for meaning and a vehicle for male intellectual self-fashioning. Even before the concrete apparition of the modern "learned lady" on the Italian literary scene, this is apparent already in Boccaccio's prototypical life of Proba in *De claris mulieribus,* which uses a feminine figure to emblematize the ideal of a mobilization of classical pagan culture to modern, Christian-educative ends.[153] Of course, it would be misleading to suggest that the figure of the "learned lady" held as central a role within fifteenth-century humanistic culture as her wispier lyric predecessors had within the vernacular tradition in which Boccaccio had received his own training. The female erudite as icon had to take her place within humanism as part of a more articulated pantheon, all mythologized with equal assiduity, including the Ciceronian ideal of the statesman-orator, revered within republican contexts, or the more courtly ideals of the educated prince or Jerome-like classicizing cleric. It was only with the return of the vernacular, at the end of the fifteenth century, that women could return to their medieval literary centrality—though this time, of course, newly equipped with a humanistic-classical "voice."

Her role as emblem of revived classicism was not the sole aspect of the figure of the female erudite that contributed to her utility as a privileged site for the construction of male humanistic identity. Another, relevant especially to women outside the ruling dynasties, was the patent disinterestedness of her intellectual activity. Since social decorum prevented women from taking up any of the professional activities that might be contemplated by similarly educated men, women's learning was, by definition, particularly "pure," undertaken—to adopt a distinction of Lisa Jardine's—in the spirit of a decorative and socially validating "accomplishment" rather than as a practically oriented "profession."[154] This gave them value to male humanists as embodiments of an aristocratic ideal of learning uncontaminated by "base" motives of economic necessity or professional ambition: the "learned lady" stood at the opposite extreme from the despised type of the penurious schoolmaster or low-rent secretary, touting his classical learning for a living. Women, especially unmarried ones, might be satisfyingly imagined in the situation of unworldly scholarly seclusion that male humanists "officially" recommended as the ideal state for contemplative activity but that, in practice—whether out of necessity or disinclination—few were practically in a position to attain. It may be this, as much as the morbid concern with feminine sexual propriety that has often been attributed to them, that inspired male humanists to stress seclusion and apartness from the world in their figurations of women like Maddalena Scrovegni and Isotta Nogarola. Antonio Loschi's Scrovegni in her "temple of chastity" and Lodovico Foscarini's ascetic Nogarola in her "book-lined cell" ("libraria cella") were perhaps as much wistful images of an elusive male scholarly "chastity" as they were attempts to contain a socially anomalous and potentially threatening female erudition.[155] The social standing of women such as Scrovegni and Nogarola also greatly contributed to their mystique and their attractiveness as cultural models; it is noteworthy that of the significant female scholars of the fifteenth century, it was the less socially distinguished Laura Cereta—widow of a merchant—who failed to attract an encomium from a humanist of status.[156]

A slightly different discourse is needed to describe women at the very top of the social hierarchy, those of the ruling families of Italy: here, more

than a chastely contemplative reclusiveness, the model of learning embodied was one of wise rulership and contribution to the public good. That
classical learning played a key role in training for good government was
one of the most central of humanistic axioms, common to republican cultures like Florence and Venice and princely regimes like those of Ferrara
and Mantua. Within the courts, the notion that competence in classical
Latin and rhetoric was an essential part of a prince's education was argued
by humanist teachers with great insistence and success, especially following its glamorous embodiment in the prestigious schools of Guarino at
Ferrara and Vittorino da Feltre at Mantua. Famous incarnations of the educated prince of the Renaissance include Leonello d'Este of Ferrara (1407–
50) and Federico da Montefeltro of Urbino (1422–82), alumni, respectively,
of Guarino and Vittorino and outstanding patrons of culture. Despite
these individual successes, however, in practice, the amount of energy that
princes could devote to cultural self-improvement was inevitably limited;
nor was humanistic excellence the sole, or even the primary, field in which
they could aspire to "glory."[157] Ruler-consorts, meanwhile, recipients of
the same education yet more limited in their fields of activity, were probably in some cases more receptive to the possibility of pursuing their studies and attaining notice for their erudition than their husbands. The type
of the educated ruler-consort on the model of Battista da Montefeltro was
thus useful to humanists as a complementary, and in some ways more realistic, rhetorical counterpart to the ideal of the educated prince. She could
also serve as a veiled role model for the male humanist himself, in a dynamic we have already touched on in the case of the female contemplative. Leonardo Bruni, for example, uses his discussion of the educational
"formation" of the princely consort in De studiis et litteris to adumbrate
more general considerations on the importance of rulers having access to
wise counsel from those close to him.[158] The obvious point of reference
is the consort herself, but it would be naive to read this too literally, as a
prescription for feminine conduct; rather, the ruler-consort, in Bruni's treatise, becomes an idealized embodiment of the tempering role of humanistic study on the exercise of power, standing as proxy for the author and
the brand of politically inflected, Christian-humanist learning he is forg-
ing under her name. As in the case of the reclusive female contemplative
scholar, a feminine figure is here serving the end of male humanistic self-
fashioning. As in that case, furthermore, the model she represents is one
more of utopian ideal than of concrete aspiration, in that the consort-
counselor's rank lent her a position of privileged intimacy with her husband of which no male humanist advisor could dream.

    A final significance attaching to the "learned lady" in fifteenth-century humanist discourse deserves particular attention, not least because of the importance it will assume in the vernacular humanism of the following century. Among the many roles consigned to learned women, one of the most frequently invoked was that of emblematizing the *virtus* of a particular city or region. Thus Isotta Nogarola is lauded by Foscarini as bringing greater glory to the city of Verona than its famous classical monuments, while Lodovico da Schio implicitly compliments Venice on producing a paragon of learning such as Cassandra Fedele by urging Mantua to cease boasting of itself as birthplace to Virgil, Verona as birthplace to Catullus, or Rome as arena to Cicero.[159] As the example of Fedele illustrates, this topos was not limited to use in connection with female intellectuals: eminent sons, as well as eminent daughters, were often invoked in this role. "Learned ladies," however, seem to have lent themselves especially well to this trope, given their rarity value and the long-established cultural tradition of using the feminine as a vehicle for allegorical and symbolic significance. This kind of geopolitical factor is probably more pervasive within the narrative of the emergence of profeminist discourse than is often acknowledged. It may be, for example, that the energetic attempts of Ferrarese intellectuals to exalt the exemplarity of Eleonora d'Aragona in the 1480s and 1490s should be seen as partly motivated by Ferrara's perceived prior underperformance in this field: owing to a variety of circumstances, the duchy suffered a long mid-century hiatus (1449–74) without a "first lady" and was thus notably ill provided with candidates for "famous womanhood" by comparison with dynasties such as the Gonzaga and Sforza.[160] Also clearly inflected by parochial motives is the listing of famous women in Vespasiano da Bisticci's *Libro delle lodi delle donne,* which seeks a little awkwardly to incorporate a series of Florentine women with more expected figures like Battista da Montefeltro and Cecilia Gonzaga.[161] In the Veneto, meanwhile, a striking example of this kind of patriotic exploitation of the figure of the "famous woman" is the multiauthored volume of vernacular verse in praise of Laura Brenzoni found in a manuscript in the Biblioteca Marciana and recently edited by Massimo Castoldi. While centered on the virtues and beauty of Laura herself, the verse contained in the volume makes persistent flattering reference to the city she "honors," and one of the few poems in the collection whose authorship can be identified is by Panfilo Sasso (1455–1527), Veronese by adoption and an active propagandist for the city.[162] Structurally, the Brenzoni manuscript collection looks forward to sixteenth-century verse collections like those for Irene di Spilimbergo (1561) and for Geronima Colonna d'Aragona (1568), which served as showcases, respectively, for the Venetian and Neapolitan Petrarchan traditions.[163] Similarly anticipatory is the Neapolitan Giosuè

Capasso's *Triumphum novem viduarum,* already mentioned, one of the earliest Renaissance instances of what would become a vastly practiced genre in the following century: the list of women from a particular city outstanding for their learning and other virtues.[164]

### 4. Renaissance Particularism and the "Learned Lady"

A final point deserves to be made before we leave the fifteenth century. As has emerged in the preceding analysis, in this formative period of the tradition of the secular female intellectual in Italy, a crucially important role was played by women of the ruling dynasties. It was within the ruling houses, as we have seen, that education for girls was most habitual, most clearly motivated, and most universally socially accepted; even moralists who might have railed against the education of girls from lesser families as morally dangerous would hardly have been likely to raise their heads in public to deny education to a Battista da Montefeltro or a Bianca Maria Visconti. It was women from this elite stratum of society—or those close to it, such as the Nogarola and Scrovegni—who pioneered the new model of publicly displayed learning. It is only at the end of the century that we find women from more modest backgrounds, such as Cassandra Fedele and Laura Cereta, beginning to feature among the Italian pantheon of learned ladies, and it seems safe to conjecture that such women owed their education to the authorizing example their social "betters" had supplied.

This point needs to be underlined, not least because it can supply a partial answer to one of the central questions with which this study is seeking to engage: why it was that early modern Italy proved such an extraordinarily rich terrain for women's emergence as writers. The practice of educating girls from the ruling dynasties was certainly far from unique to Italy in this period; on the contrary, in schooling the future consorts of rulers, Italy was following customs already well established in the royal courts of northern Europe. What was different in Italy—and what gave the phenomenon there a far greater social purchase than it could have attained elsewhere in Europe—is the sheer number of families and individuals embraced within this most elite of social groupings. Northern and central Italy in this period were divided into a myriad of states, ranging from the large and ambitious imperialist powers such as Milan and Venice to small and vulnerable domains such as many in Umbria and the Marches, which struggled to maintain their independence in the face of factionalism and external aggression. Setting aside the few remaining republics in this period, most of these Italian states were ruled by *signorie* or principalities, of a greater of lesser level of dynastic stability, and each of these regimes had its own ruling dynasty—or, more accurately, very often, its

succession of ruling dynasties—each of which, within the limits of its resources, attempted to style itself as a genuine miniature monarchy, with
its court, its seigneurial palace or palaces, and its battery of trappings of
majesty. Any of these provincial ruling dynasties could potentially produce
a "learned lady" of distinction; indeed, as we have seen, some of the best
known come from relatively minor dynasties such as the Varano and
Malatesta, who may have found the cultivation of female erudition a conveniently economical means to cultural salience. When we consider this,
it becomes apparent that, far from the arcane and statistically irrelevant social group they may at first seem, the female members of the ruling families in Italy made up a substantial, if still highly select, cadre of educated
women, who could then, in turn, serve as inspirations and role models to
women of lesser estate. This is particularly the case if we extend our analysis from the female members of existing reigning dynasties to those of local aristocratic families who might aspire to marry into them, or at least to
place their daughters as ladies-in-waiting to the consorts of their lord.

Besides this multiplication of ruling dynasties, and the consequent diffusion of court practices, there were other respects in which Italy's political disunity served to foster the development of women's writing. The
geopolitical fragmentation of northern Italy at this time contributed considerably to its cultural vitality, fostering as it did the proliferation, at a local level, of institutions such as universities and schools, and, from the sixteenth century, literary academies and publishing houses.[165] Competition
was vital here, too. Even within cities such as those of the mainland Veneto
that had lost their political independence by the beginning of the fifteenth
century, patriotic sentiment ensured a continuing urge to cultural distinctness: indeed, it is plausible that cultural activity acquired a compensatory function for cities such as Padua, Vicenza, and Verona following the
loss of their political sovereignty to Venice. The compact and culturally active cities in which Italy abounded proved largely supportive as environments for female writers, especially as they became more established as a
phenomenon, and as the cultural capital that could derive from them became clearer. As we have seen, even in the fifteenth century, we already
find women like Cassandra Fedele, Alessandra Scala, and Laura Brenzoni
being deployed as civic icons. This became far more widespread in the sixteenth century, following the cultural changes that are examined in the following chapter. By the mid- or late sixteenth century, far from being regarded with hostility by their communities, one has a sense that female
writers were being actively fostered and supported: Laura Cereta's sense
of beleaguerment in the Brescia of the 1480s and 1490s is not typical of the
experience of her successors. This is not, of course, to say that women

were fully integrated in civic intellectual culture or that they could necessarily interact freely with their male peers; with few exceptions, literary
gatherings such as academies remained closed to them, let alone more
formal institutions such as universities. We are far, here, nonetheless from
a situation of comprehensive suppression or silencing. Rather, as we have
seen already in the fifteenth century, women's voices could find a hearing
not simply tolerant but eager—always understood, of course, that they
were the "right" women's voices, saying the "right" things in appropriate
ways.

# CHAPTER TWO

❖ ❖ ❖ ❖

# TRANSLATION

## (1490–1550)

❖

As chapter 1 documents, the fifteenth century was crucial for the emergence of the figure of the secular female intellectual in Italy: barely visible at the beginning of the century, by its end she was an established, if still exotic, cultural type. The diffusion of exemplary discourses on "famous women" in Latin and the vernacular had familiarized at least the literate elites of Italy with the notion that women were capable of "virile" achievement and literature had proved one of the fields in which female attainment most easily translated from classical anecdote into modern reality. Despite this, however, while Latin remained the dominant literary language of Italy, the presence of women on the literary scene was necessarily limited. Although, by the end of the fifteenth century, humanistic education was no longer restricted solely to the upper aristocracy, female *erudite* from outside those social strata, such as Cassandra Fedele and Laura Cereta, still remained extremely rare. It was only with the rise of vernacular literature in the late fifteenth century, and especially with the assertion of the *volgare* as the dominant literary language in Italy in the early sixteenth, that the necessary conditions existed for women to become a more substantial presence on the Italian literary scene.

Besides the rise of the vernacular, another, associated circumstantial factor facilitating the diffusion of the practice of women's writing in this period is the ever-increasing impact of the new technology of printing on Italian literary culture. This was a development apparent especially after 1500, even though printing had been introduced into Italy more than three decades earlier. A consequence of the expansion of the printing industry with very significant implications for women was the increasing availability of books and the progressive lowering of their cost. Although these developments were important in expanding literacy as a whole, they may be assumed to have had a particular effect on literacy in women, since women were so much more dependent than men in their acquisition of literacy skills on the availability of books within the home. For women to attend school in this period was still uncommon, although some received an elementary education in convents; where they were educated at all, this tended to occur within the domestic setting, either at the hands of a tutor, in the grander of households, or under the tutorship of parents or other relatives.[1] The likelihood of women acquiring literacy skills thus depended quite crucially on the presence of books within the household. Even without considering the further, more concerted ways in which print culture contributed to the diffusion of women's writing—most apparent around the middle of the century, when publishers avidly reached out for and encouraged this commercially attractive novelty—this alone would be sufficient to lend an epochal significance within the history of women's writing to the transition from manuscript to print.[2]

That said, however, it must be noted that it is only from around the 1540s that the effects of typographical culture begin to be seen in their full force within the history of women's writing. The transition from manuscript to print, in Italy as in Europe in general, was gradual and cumulative rather than sudden and dramatic, and the first decades of the new century cannot be seen as radically novel in this regard. The first slice of time under investigation in this chapter—around 1490–1510—may be seen as still part of this transitional period. It is largely, thus, linguistic and literary rather than technological change that will initially be the focus of analysis here.

## 1. Women, the Courts, and the Vernacular in the Early Sixteenth Century

The reemergence of the vernacular as a force seriously to be reckoned with in Italian literary culture is conventionally dated to the 1470s in Florence, where we see the young Lorenzo de' Medici presiding over a remarkable flourishing of vernacular poetic production in his dual guise as poet and patron. This is not to say that experimentation with the vernacular was entirely absent during the period of Latin humanistic dominance. Where prose writing is concerned, we find a series of important works being produced by Florentine humanists in the 1430s (Alberti's *Della famiglia,* Matteo Palmieri's *Della vita civile,* Leonardo Bruni's lives of Dante and Petrarch), while in poetry we might cite a work like Giusto de' Conti's Pe-

trarchizing lyric collection, *La bella mano,* produced at the court of Rimini
in the 1440s. These signs of interest in the vernacular remained, however,
relatively sporadic and marginal down to around the 1470s or 1480s, and in
this sense it is certainly true to locate the final quarter of the century as the
true moment of "revival." After the brilliant, though short-lived season of
the 1470s in Florence, we find vernacular literature increasingly cultivated
in the northern courts, especially Ferrara under the Este and Milan under
the Sforza, as well as in the south, in the Aragonese kingdom of Naples.[3]
Among the protagonists of the new vernacular culture were distinguished
humanists such as Angelo Poliziano and Iacopo Sannazaro (1456–1530),
who brought a classically trained sensibility to bear on their production in
the *volgare.* The same is true to a lesser extent of humanistically educated
courtier-poets such as Matteo Maria Boiardo and Antonio Tebaldeo (1463–
1537), whose output embraced work in Latin as well as in the *volgare.* The
range of genres practiced in this period was broad, ranging from chivalric
poems like Boiardo's *Orlando innamorato* and mythological-allegorical narratives such as the extraordinary polyglot *Hypnerotomachia Poliphili* (1499)
to the innovative pastoral romance of Sannazaro's *Arcadia* (1502). My emphasis here will however be primarily on the genre of lyric poetry, as it was
in this field, almost exclusively, that women would make their mark in the
initial phase of their emergence as vernacular writers.

Despite the high quality of some Tuscan lyric poetry in this period, notably that of Poliziano and Lorenzo de' Medici, this genre of writing flourished particularly in the princely courts, where it was closely associated
with contemporary musical and performance traditions. While print
played some part in its diffusion, especially after 1500, the prime and most
prestigious means of circulation remained the manuscript *raccolta.* Varied
and experimental in form, much of the poetry of this era was ephemeral
in character: this was an age of meteoric rises in reputation and similarly
rapid falls, hedonistic, restless, and fashion-led. Characteristic of the period's taste for novelty and of its performance orientation is the extraordinary vogue enjoyed by extemporizers such as Serafino Aquilano (1466–
1500) and Bernardo Accolti ("l'Unico Aretino") (1465–1536), two of the
most celebrated poets of the age. The verse tradition of the late fifteenth
and very early sixteenth century is often designated *poesia cortigiana,* to differentiate it from the more purist neo-Petrarchan school that came gradually to dominate from around the second decade of the sixteenth century
under the influence of the great Venetian poet and theorist Pietro Bembo.
While obviously influenced by Petrarch and his imitator Giusto de' Conti,
the *poesia cortigiana* tradition was notably formally eclectic, featuring a
wide metrical range, from Dantean terza rima to more modern forms such

as the *strambotto* and *frottola*. Linguistically, as well, the poetry of this period was quite diverse; even if we except the extremes of experimentation found in the "comic-realist" tradition, "serious" poetry was written mainly in regional koines, though with strong influences from literary Tuscan and, especially orthographically, from Latin.[4]

A feature of the vernacular poetry of this age that distinguished it quite sharply from the more established Latin humanistic tradition was the very prominent role played by women as patrons of and ideal audiences for poetry. This is recognized in the commemorative biography of Serafino Aquilano composed in 1504 by the poet and courtier Vicenzo Colli, or "Calmeta" (c. 1460–1508), important for its critical reflections on the poetic tradition of the day and its contexts.[5] Uncontroversially enough, Calmeta credits Lorenzo de' Medici and his contemporaries with initiating the vernacular revival. The continuation of this work of restoring the vernacular to its "pristine dignity" is attributed, however, to female patrons: Calmeta's former employer Beatrice d'Este, Duchess of Milan, and "other remarkable women of our age."[6] Although Calmeta does not identify these other "singularissime donne" by name, two likely candidates are Beatrice's sister, Isabella d'Este, Marchioness of Mantua, already encountered in chapter I in her legendary role as cultural patron, and Elisabetta Gonzaga di Montefeltro (1471–1526), Duchess of Urbino, famed now principally for her portrayal in Castiglione's *Cortegiano*. Calmeta's assessment of the importance of these and other female patrons is borne out by much evidence. The leading Milanese lyric poet Gaspare Visconti (1461–99) prepared elegant manuscript collections of his verse in the 1490s for both Beatrice d'Este and Bianca Maria Sforza (1472–1510), and Beatrice seems likely to have been the intended dedicatee of the magnificently illustrated copy of Petrarch now found at the Biblioteca Queriniana in Brescia.[7] The massive multiauthored 1504 tribute volume for Serafino Aquilano in which Calmeta's *Vita* was published was dedicated to the Duchess of Urbino, as were numerous other vernacular works, including an early verse collection by Bembo (1507) and another by Panfilo Sasso.[8] Isabella d'Este was the dedicatee of Antonio Tebaldeo's *Rime* (1505), as well as of an important late manuscript *raccolta* of his verse (c. 1520). She was also the recipient of a number of theoretical and critical writings by Calmeta, including a letter discussing the use of terza rima in *capitoli*, elegies, and epistles and a commentary on Petrarch's "extraordinarily subtle and profound canzone," "Mai non vo' più cantare."[9] In addition to her interest in lyric poetry, Isabella was also, of course, famous for her association with the two greatest vernacular narrative poets of the period, Matteo Maria Boiardo and Lodovico Ariosto (1474–1533), the latter of whom was already reading her

draft episodes from his *Orlando furioso* in 1507. Also important as a patron
of literature, as well as music, was Isabella's sister-in-law and rival Lucrezia
Borgia (1480–1519), Duchess of Ferrara, dedicatee of Pietro Bembo's dialogue *Gli Asolani* (1505) and, like Isabella, seemingly sufficiently interested
in poetry to attempt composition herself.[10] Meanwhile in the south, Ippolita Sforza, the Milanese-born Duchess of Calabria, played an important
part in encouraging the nascent vernacular tradition in the kingdom of
Naples, while a prominent role in the later development of this tradition
was later assumed by Costanza d'Avalos, Duchess of Francavilla and dowager ruler of Ischia from 1501, of great importance to the history of Italian
women's writing as inspiration and role model to her niece by marriage
Vittoria Colonna.[11]

   A fine characterization of a noblewoman as prototypical courtly reader
is found at the beginning of one of the key works of this age, Matteo Bandello's *Novelle* (first published in 1554, though mainly written much earlier),
in a *proemio* addressed to Ippolita Sforza Bentivoglio (1481–c. 1520), whom
he credits with having inspired him to collect his novels together.[12]
Though not part of a ruling family at the time when Bandello portrays
her—her natal family, the Sforza, had been deposed from power in Milan
in 1498, while her husband's, the Bentivoglio, had been ejected from
Bologna in 1506—Ippolita's contacts and family tradition made her a reso-
nant figure within the fifteenth- and early sixteenth-century tradition of
culturally active noblewomen; she was related through her father to
Bianca Maria Visconti and to Ippolita Sforza, while Ginevra Sforza Bentivoglio, dedicatee of Sabadino degli Arienti's *Gynevera*, was both her distant cousin and her mother-in-law.[13] Bandello insists in the *proemio* in question on Ippolita's qualifications as a literary critic, portraying her as well
educated in Latin and the vernacular and possessed of remarkable acumen
and excellent literary taste. Presented with verse in either language, she
penetrates its most recondite meanings at a glance, in a manner that reveals her "profound understanding of literature" ("profonda conoscenza
. . . de le buone lettere"). Such are her technical competences, indeed, that
she is capable of delivering close readings of difficult passages in the "poets and historians" in a manner reminiscent of a humanist philologist:

> Meravigliosa cosa certo è quanto profondamente e con sottigliezza gran-
> dissima talora certi passi degli scrittori cribriate, ventiliate, e a parola per
> parola e senso per senso andiate di maniera interpretando, che ogni persona
> che vi sente ne rendete capace.
>
> [It is a remarkable thing, certainly, how profoundly and with what extraor-
> dinary subtlety you will sometimes scrutinize and open up passages of lit-

erature, explicating them word by word and drawing our their sense so that all those listening come to understand them fully.[14]]

Notable here is the mention of an audience: this is not a court lady meekly listening to the disquisitions of her male peers but an authoritative critic herself, and a highly articulate one, quite capable of assuming a quasi-magisterial role. Bandello notes further that he has often seen Ippolita holding her own in literary disputes with her "most erudite" secretary, the poet Girolamo Cittadini, remarking of one such occasion that anyone listening would have thought himself in the presence not of a woman but "one of the most learned and eloquent men of the day."[15] We should obviously be alert to the element of courtly flattery in these praises of Ippolita, as well as to the element of reflected authorial self-praise (it is this paragon of literary insight, after all, who has counseled Bandello to publish his *novelle*). This does not, however, detract from the value of the passage as an exemplary portrait and a gauge of perceptions; the interest here is precisely that a *female* patron-reader should be given this kind of authorizing role.[16]

The reasons why women came to assume so much importance in this period as patrons and privileged readers of poetry are several. Some have already been touched on in chapter 1, notably the salience women of the ruling dynasty enjoyed within the Italian courts, both as prestigious figures themselves and as conduits to their far more powerful male spouses and relatives. As the secular princely courts came to assume ever-greater importance within Italian culture, women's stock rose with it, and, as courts competed fiercely for cultural status, the value of a literate and culturally astute ruler-consort was correspondingly enhanced. This was reflected in the growing numbers of cultural operatives, such as musicians and poets, within the court establishments of rulers' spouses in the later fifteenth and early sixteenth century. Princely consorts had for some time maintained their own independent households, funded through an annual budget drawn from their husbands' treasuries and through the income from property assigned to them on marriage. These households varied in size, obviously, depending on the wealth of the court in question and on the negotiating power of the individual consort, which derived from her natal status and the value of her contacts. While comparisons are not easy given the variability of accounting practices, it seems fairly clear that the size of these establishments increased across the fifteenth and sixteenth centuries, as princes' wives came to take a more visible role in the cultural patronage of the court.[17] Patronage habits, too, changed over this same period, with the preponderantly religious patronage of earlier fifteenth-century dynastic spouses such as Paola Malatesta Gonzaga and Bianca Maria Visconti

giving way to the more hybrid, religious-secular model of a figure such as
Eleonora d'Aragona and the still more emphatically secularizing practice
of the leading ruler-consorts of the following generation, such as Lucrezia
Borgia and Isabella and Beatrice d'Este.[18] We find Borgia and Isabella
d'Este, for example, maintaining quite substantial independent musical establishments: a phenomenon quite novel in this period, even though music had long figured, with dance, among the privileged forms of cultural
self-expression for women at court.[19] Poets, too, figured on their staff, not
least as suppliers of song lyrics, with Borgia from 1505 expensively retain-
ing Antonio Tebaldeo, one of the most celebrated writers of the age.[20]

Besides the concrete importance of dynastic consorts as patrons of literature in this period, more symbolic factors contributed to the enhancement of women's importance as the ideal audience for vernacular poetry.
Between the late fifteenth century and the early sixteenth, the secular
princely court had come to play an ever more central role in Italian culture, both as a concrete center for artistic production and consumption,
and as a "main reference point for the organization of upper-class consciousness."[21] A monument to this shift is Castiglione's *Il libro del cortegiano,* the origins of whose long and intricate process of composition can
be dated to around 1508; here, the court of Urbino figures as the locus
for a magisterial reflection on elite self-fashioning that would serve as a
prompt book for gentlemanly behavior throughout Europe for decades, if
not centuries, to come.[22] As Castiglione's dialogue acknowledges, women
held a pivotal symbolic role in court culture, where they were recognized
as the supreme custodians and arbiters of courtly values. This centrality is
categorically affirmed by Cesare Gonzaga, in the third book of *Il cortegiano,*
when a fellow courtier attempts to argue that to devote an evening to
speaking of women would be a waste of time. On the contrary, Gonzaga
argues:

> come corte alcuna, per grande che ella sia, non po aver ornamento o splen-
> dore in sé, né allegria senza donne, né cortegiano alcun essere aggraziato,
> piacevole o ardito, né far mai opera leggiadra di cavalleria, se non mosso
> dalla pratica e dall'amore e piacer di donne, così ancor il ragionar del corte-
> giano è sempre imperfettissimo, se le donne, interponendovisi, non danno
> lor parte di quella grazia, con la quale fanno perfetta ed adornano la corte-
> giania.

> [ Just as no court, however great, can have any ornament or splendor or hap-
> piness without women, and just as no courtier may be graceful, charming,
> or bold, nor attain excellence in chivalry, without being inspired by female
> company and the desire to win the approval and love of women, so any dis-

cussion of the courtier is doomed to be sadly lacking without that element of feminine grace that can alone perfect and adorn the art of courtiership.[23]]

Important to note in this passage is that women are conceived of as *defining* of the court and structurally necessary to it, in a manner that curiously inverts the Aristotelian formula whereby the "imperfect" female was completed by and perfected by association with the male.[24] For a male poet to dedicate his poetry to a female patron was thus for him to express his allegiance in this symbolic way to the ideal of courtliness and ultimately to the power system that underlay it, for which, as David Quint has recently argued in an important reading of the *Cortegiano,* women provided, in a sense, the "human face."[25] Gallant deference to women served as an attractively mitigated expression of courtiers' real position of subservience to their princes, allowing their courtship of power to be cast in a satisfyingly euphemistic and mutually flattering guise. As critics have noted, the absence of the duke, retired through infirmity, is a crucial factor in determining the relaxed tones of the evening conversations portrayed in the dialogues of the *Cortegiano,* enabling Castiglione to paint the court in the guise of an ideal family, the members of whom are held together by the voluntary "chain of love" constituted by their shared reverence for the duchess.[26]

All these factors are important in explaining women's importance as ideal audience for literature in this period, so much more marked in Ferrara or Mantua or Milan or Naples than in Florence or Venice or Rome. Further to this, however, as a final factor, less specific to the courts, we need to consider vernacular literature's powerful symbolic association with the feminine, marked in Italy since its medieval origins.[27] Women had long served as the ideal readership for vernacular poetry, with Dante famously tracing the origins of the poetic use of the vernacular to poets' desire to make themselves understood to their ladies.[28] This notion was subsequently extended beyond the realm of love lyric to other genres, such as the romance and the *novella* collection, following the example of Boccaccio's *Fiammetta* and *Decameron,* both addressed to a primary audience of "ladies in love." Women's role in these cases as paradigmatic readers of vernacular literature is not to be taken literally: although it is true that women made up an important segment of the vernacular reading public, as they did not of the Latin, their principal function in these instances is as representatives of a broader projected audience of curious and open-minded readers, unbound by the traditionalism and "clerkly" prejudices that might be stereotypically attributed to a Latin-literate audience. Women were also perceived as more adept than men in negotiating the realms of emotion and sentiment, which was important given the thematic centrality of courtly love in vernacular literature at this time. "Ladies" were attributed a role as intuitive authorities on love and as the ultimate arbiters of its casuistries, possessed of an innate *intelletto d'amore* conceived of as in some ways "nobler" than the book-learning a philosopher might laboriously acquire.[29] This cult of women as the ideal audience for vernacular literature was to a large extent a legacy of medieval Provençal culture and thus ultimately reflects a social situation in which women were concretely important as patrons and even as poets themselves. This was far less the case in medieval Italy, but the feminine address of vernacular literature remained an important convention, to be given new life in the period we are looking at, when an influential female audience was once again a reality in the courts.

## 2. Sappho Surfaces: The First Female Vernacular Poets

Up to this point, we have been concentrating on women's role as consumers rather than producers of literature. It was not solely as an audience, however, that women contributed to the poetry of the time. From around the 1470s onward, but especially from the 1490s, we find women writing themselves in the vernacular, in small but increasing numbers. While this early phase in the history of women's emergence as vernacular poets has engaged little critical attention, it forms an important preamble to the more critically visible period datable to around the 1530s and 1540s, when Vittoria Colonna and Veronica Gambara attained national fame for their verse. It is noteworthy in this regard that, in a work written at around the time of the first print publication of Colonna's *Rime* in 1538, Matteo Bandello could already propose a "canon" of seven modern female poets of various degrees of circulation and fame.[30] The earliest references we find to vernacular poetic activity by women derive, appropriately enough, from Florence and, specifically, from the circles of the Medici. The writings of Lucrezia Tornabuoni and Antonia Pulci have already been discussed in chapter 1. Here, we might add the more tenuously attested case of Ginevra de' Benci (1457–c. 1520), famed as the sitter of a portrait by Leonardo. The subject of a poetic cult in Florence in the 1470s recalling that which we have already seen later surrounding the figure of Laura Brenzoni in Verona, de' Benci is also sometimes claimed to have been a poet herself, though at most a single line from her pen survives.[31] Far better documented is another early female poet of Tuscan, and perhaps Florentine, origin, Girolama Corsi, a collection of whose verse survives in a manuscript in the Biblioteca Marciana, copied by the poet and diarist Marin

Sanudo (1466–1536).[32] The sister of the poet and improviser Iacopo Corsi (d. 1493), Corsi seems to have spent most of her adult life in the Veneto, where she moved in circles overlapping to a degree with those of Laura Brenzoni and Cassandra Fedele. Interesting, in particular, is her connection, through her brother, with the Neapolitan condottiere Roberto Sanseverino, whose deeds, as we saw in chapter 1, were the subject of a celebratory Latin poem by Brenzoni.[33] The other two female poets we know of in the late fifteenth century were based in the Sforza court in Milan, one of the most active centers for vernacular poetry in the last decades of the century. One is Cecilia Gallerani, famous as a mistress of Lodovico Sforza's and thought to be the sitter for Leonardo's *Lady with an Ermine.* No surviving works have been identified by Gallerani, although her poetic activity is reasonably well attested, particularly by Bandello, who praises her punningly as "the sharpest of pens."[34] Better documented is Camilla Scarampa of Asti, certainly the most famous female poet before Veronica Gambara, and the object of tributes by poets of the stature of Iacopo Sannazaro and Giulio Cesare Scaligero (1484–1556). Around a dozen poems by Scarampa survive, including a group of eight found together in three separate manuscripts, although the extent of her fame and Matteo Bandello's description of her as "copious Sappho" ("copiosa Saffo") suggest that these are probably the remnants of a substantial *canzoniere.*[35] Finally, around the turn of the century, we may list Gambara herself, who was certainly active as a poet already by 1504, and, less publicly, Maria Savorgnan, famous for her love affair in around 1500–1501 with Pietro Bembo.[36] As was noted above, moreover, both Isabella d'Este and Lucrezia Borgia are also known to have attempted verse composition, although nothing securely attributable to Borgia survives.[37]

As the preceding suggests, although surviving works by female poets from this period are few, there is sufficient evidence of the practice of verse by women for it to be clear that it was something of a vogue in the period. Further, it is apparent from the male-authored literature testifying to the activity of early female poets that this was a novelty generally regarded with enthusiasm and approbation, particularly within the courts.[38] A genre of writing quickly emerged that recreated in the vernacular the Latin humanist tradition of writing in praise of female learning, the most remarkable example of which is Luca Valenziano's terza rima miniature epic, *Il Camilcleo,* describing the birth and girlhood of Camilla Scarampa, seemingly written in the early years of Camilla's marriage in the early 1500s and published in 1513. Valenziano constructs Scarampa as a dashingly Amazonian figure, comparing her to Atalanta in her skills at running and Diana in the hunt. Her education is described in similarly exuberant mythologizing terms: we see her schooled by the Graces and presented with a globe for the study of geography by Minerva herself.[39] Scarampa is portrayed by Valenziano as having defiantly resisted marriage in her late adolescence in order to devote herself to her studies, before being cajoled into relenting by the persuasions of Venus: a detail perhaps based in fact, given that her marriage seems to have occurred relatively late for the period, probably in 1498–1500, when she was already in her mid-20s. Seemingly locatable in the context of this choice is Scarampa's defiant sonnet, "Biasmi pur chi vuol la mia durezza" ("Blame Me if You Will for My Hardness"), which announces the poet's renunciation of love in favor of the pursuit of glory, interestingly appropriating and reframing the Dantean and Petrarchan topos of the "hard" or "stony" lady who denies the lover response.[40]

Interesting, along with Valenziano's poem, as a document of early responses to the figure of the female poet is a sonnet by Gasparo Visconti, admiringly describing a "lady more divine than human"—perhaps Scarampa herself—who, "being already graced with every other talent, tried her hand also at writing verses, coming so immediately to excel in that art that she showed herself . . . to be a thing divine."[41] Visconti's sonnet deserves to be quoted in full for its particularly eloquent expression of a topos we have already encountered in praises of fifteenth-century "learned ladies": the return of the "classical" figure of the female intellectual as symbol of the renaissance of ancient *virtù* in general.

Benigna grazia novamente piove
In terra a noi dal più superno coro,
Per dare a la virtù degno ristoro
Che era già appresso a l'ultime sue prove.
O forse vole una altra volta Iove.
Come già fece, transmutarse in toro,
  o discender dal cello in pioggia d'oro.
O cose tra noi far più excelse e nove;
O ver che 'l biondo Apol lasciando il celo,
A noi celando la sua propria forma,
Vèstese questo legiadretto velo.
Or sia che voglia, il mondo si transforma
E torna in preggio ancor l'antiquo Delo,
E 'l neglecto Elicona se riforma.

[Benign grace newly rains on us here on earth from the highest choir to give new life and dignity to genius (*virtù*), previously almost drained to the dregs. Or perhaps Jove once again wishes to transform himself into a bull or to descend from the heavens in a shower of gold or to bring about new and excellent things among us; or the blond Apollo, leaving the heavens and concealing his true form from us, chooses to garb himself in this most charming veil. Be the cause what it may, the world is transforming, and ancient Delos returning once more to its former glory, and neglected Helicon is reformed.]

The "wondrous" appearance of a female poet seems here to presage the necromantic marvels of a return to the creative arcadia of antiquity, when poetic inspiration rained from the skies and the gods stalked the earth in mortal guise. This transformative fantasy ("il mondo si transforma" [l. 12]) has an intriguing sexual dimension, presumably suggested to Visconti by the unwonted figure of a female poet: thus, the descent on the poet of Platonic divine furor is here first figured in the second quatrain in terms of Jovian rape before being softened in the following tercet into the ambiguous image of a transgendered Apollo. Both images perhaps convey a sense of threat on the part of the poet, as we see the numinous male creative principle descending into mortal and feminine form. At the same time, however, the challenge presented by the female poet—best figured in her guise as a feminized Apollo—is counteracted by the more conventionally feminine image of the poet as Danæ or Europa, impregnated by a divine masculine force.

The equation we find in Visconti's sonnet between the reappearance of the female poet and the renaissance of classical cultural glory is characteristic of this period. As humanistic, and especially Greek, studies progressed in the fifteenth century, the image of classical female poets came more sharply into focus, and Sappho, in particular, became an object of fascination. A series of commentaries by major humanists of the 1470s and 1480s on Ovid's poetic epistle from Sappho to Phaon (*Heroides* 15), laboriously pieced together all that was known of her life and poetry from classical historical and literary sources.[42] Ovid's epistle itself was translated into the *volgare* in 1496 by Giorgio Sommariva, who seems to have sent a copy to Girolama Corsi with an accompanying sonnet comparing her to Sappho.[43] Raphael included Sappho in his *Parnassus,* painted for Pope Julius II in c. 1510–11, and Stephen Campbell has recently argued that Lorenzo Costa's so-called *Allegory of the Court of Isabella d'Este* (c. 1504–6) should in fact be seen as a representation of the crowning of Sappho by Venus.[44] Although Sappho's bisexuality and supposed suicide for love made her morally ambiguous as a role model, the tendency of humanist commentary was to de-emphasize her sexual vagaries and to stress instead her excellence as a poet and "tenth muse." In Boccaccio's twelfth eclogue, published in 1504 in an important compilation of classical and humanistic pastoral poetry, she is presented as a reticent and pure dweller on Parnassus, unjustly slandered by men.[45] It does not seem to have been considered indecorous to compare modern female poets to Sappho: we find such comparisons applied in this period, for example, to both Camilla Scarampa, and Girolama Corsi, the latter of whom, besides the sonnet by Sommariva mentioned above, was also the recipient of a stanza by Antonio Mezzabarba that pronounces her the equal and superior to Sappho specifically as a love poet.[46] Nor did women themselves seem resistant to such comparisons: it has been suggested that portrait medals of the young Vittoria Colonna incorporated references to Sappho, as she had been portrayed by Raphael in the Vatican.[47] Famously described by Horace as *mascula Sappho,* Sappho was especially well equipped to represent the Amazonian "virility" the Renaissance liked to attribute to classical womanhood. The capacity of a culture to generate such a creature could thus become one of the tests of its vigor: a sign that, in Visconti's phrase, the world was once again ready to bring forth "marvelous and unwonted things" ("cose excelse e nove").[48]

If the literature on Sappho in this period offers the most direct and explicit evidence of its growing fascination with the figure of the female poet, the history of the reception of Ovid's *Heroides* in the late fifteenth century offers interesting supporting evidence in this regard. As recent readings of the *Heroides* have stressed, the epistolary self-expression of Ovid's "heroines" collectively constitutes a kind of virtual tradition of women's writing, which, despite its "ventriloquized" character, nonetheless engages richly with the question of how women might constitute themselves as writers within an overwhelmingly male literary tradition.[49] The *Heroides* had enjoyed a solid medieval *fortuna* and are far from a humanistic "rediscovery"; within Italy, Boccaccio had explored their "feminine poetics of abandonment" with particular inventiveness in his vernacular works.[50] An interesting development of the later fifteenth century, however, was the emergence of a "microgenre" of *Heroides* imitations taking as their nominal authors not fictional creations such as Boccaccio's Madonna Fiammetta nor appropriated mythological heroines such as Ovid's Penelope or Dido but rather identifiable contemporary court ladies, characteristically addressing themselves to their husbands.[51] The best-known example of the genre is Niccolò da Correggio's *capitolo* in the voice of his wife, Cassandra Colleoni (1459–1519), "Como Penelopé scrisse al suo Ulisse" ("As Penelope Wrote to Her Ulysses"), purportedly written at the time of the poet's imprisonment following the War of Ferrara.[52] Other fifteenth-century examples include a sequence of four poems written by Giovanni Cosentino (1432–post 1490) in the persona of Ippolita Sforza, two poems by Tebaldeo addressing da Correggio in the voice of a "Beatrice," and a poem by Iacopo Corsi, Girolama's brother, composed in the voice of Lucrezia Malavolti, wife of the condottiere Roberto Sanseverino.[53] It is suggestive that we find such a close coincidence between the sites of production of these *Heroides* imitations and of early vernacular women's writing: aside from the example of the Corsi siblings—she a poet, he an author of female-voiced poetry—we might cite here the contextual proximity of Giovanni Cosentino's verse in the persona of Ippolita Sforza and the letters of Ceccarella Minutolo, discussed in chapter 1, which include epistles of abandonment on the *Heroides* model.[54] The impulse to reanimate the classical phantom of the female writer, fictional or actual (although the presence of Sappho in the *Heroides* cautions against too clear a distinction) seems in this period to have found expression in both fictional-ventriloquized and "literal" forms. It is worth noting in this regard that the earliest surviving poem of Vittoria Colonna is, precisely, a contribution to the "microgenre" of the terza rima *heroid,* in the form of a *capitolo* lamenting her desolation after her husband's capture at the Battle of Ravenna in 1512.[55]

What kind of verse did the female poets of the *poesia cortigiana* tradition write? Of the four poets verse by whom survives (Corsi, Scarampa, Gambara, and Maria Savorgnan), Savorgnan represents something of a case apart in that there is no evidence of her compositions circulating publicly. The only examples of her work we have—three sonnets, two *strambotti,* and a *barzelletta,* all amorous in theme—derive from her private correspondence with Pietro Bembo, in the doubtless carefully edited form in which he arranged to publish it at the end of his life.[56] Also probably not intended for public circulation are two intimate and circumstantial love poems addressed by Girolama Corsi Ramos to an unfaithful lover.[57] Others of Corsi's love poems, by contrast, as well as the erotic verses of Gambara and Scarampa, have more of an air of literary exercises and were clearly considered works that could circulate without jeopardizing their aristocratic young authors' reputation. The majority of Gambara's early poems explore the classic Petrarchan theme of the torments of love, treated in a stylized and stereotypical manner.[58] Camilla Scarampa's amorous verse is more idiosyncratic than Gambara's and her persona less passive and more spirited; more than Gambara's, her voice is reminiscent of that of a later poet such as Gaspara Stampa (?1525–54).[59] Girolama Corsi's verse is again quite distinctive and is more thematically varied and stylistically experimental than Gambara's or Scarampa's, although this may in part simply be due to the fact that more of her poetry survives. As well as amorous verse and occasional poems, Corsi's *canzoniere* encompasses somber mourning sonnets for her brother, murdered in 1493, a comic *barzelletta* cast as a dialogue between an urban wife and her husband, who is subjecting her to an enforced rural idyll in the Paduan countryside, and a vigorous political *sonnetti caudato* chastening Florence for its pusillanimity in ceding to the French in 1494.[60] Also of interest in Corsi's small but rich poetic ouevre is her sonnet in praise of a portrait of herself by Vittore Carpaccio (c. 1460–1525/26): a rare female essay in a subgenre of praise poem originating with Petrarch and mainly deployed erotically, to evoke a visual representation of the female beloved.[61] Metrically, Corsi is typical of her age in experimenting with contemporary music-led forms such as the *barzelletta,* as well as the more classic sonnet. Gambara's early verse similarly includes *strambotti,* ballads, and a *frottola.* In fact, it is in collections of musical settings issued by the presses of Ottavio Petrucci and Andrea Antico, that Gambara's first texts were published in 1505 and 1510, the first secular lyrics by a woman to find their way into print.[62]

The social backgrounds of the female poets we know of in this period are reasonably varied but with a distinct aristocratic bias. Corsi's origins are fairly obscure, although she refers to her "noble blood" ("sangue gentil") in one poem.[63] Gallerani came from a family of socially ambitious court functionaries of no particular distinction, though her affair with Lodovico Sforza led to a prestigious marriage, to the nobleman Lodovico Bergamini, count of San Giovanni in Croce, near Cremona.[64] Gambara and Scarampa, meanwhile, came from established noble families and married into others. Gambara was the daughter of Gianfrancesco Gambara, lord of Pralboino, and married Giberto da Correggio, lord of Correggio (d. 1518). She was also connected through her mother, Alda Pio, to the prominent and intellectually distinguished northern Italian family of the Pio of Carpi, as well as, as we have seen, through her paternal grandmother, to the Nogarola of Verona.[65] Scarampa's background was similar, although less intellectually distinguished than that of Gambara; she came from a wealthy and noble Piedmontese landowning family, allied with the dukes of Milan, and married Ambrogio Guidobono, lord of Brignano, near Tortona (d. 1517).[66] Together with the higher-placed Isabella d'Este, with whom Scarampa, Gallerani, and Gambara all had contacts, these women may be seen as arch-representatives of the model of assertive and enterprising court lady that was imposing itself as such a powerful cultural presence in this period and that would later be crafted so memorably as a literary persona by writers like Castiglione and Bandello.[67] Not only did they write themselves; they were also all active as literary patrons, a fact that obviously contributed to the enhancement and divulgation of their cultural profile. It is notable that both Gambara and Scarampa had other culturally active women in their family circle. Gambara's sister Isotta—

presumably named for Isotta Nogarola—was lauded by Agnolo Firenzuola for the "Ciceronian" elegance of her letters, while her niece, Camilla
Valenti del Verme, was also much praised as a Latinist.[68] Scarampa's niece,
Margherita Pelletta Tizzoni (d. c. 1533), meanwhile, was praised by Bandello for her vernacular verse, including a series of madrigals for Giulia
Gonzaga (1513–66), which he singles out for particular notice.[69] The same
is true of the grandest *letterata* of the age, Vittoria Colonna, whom we
know to have been active as a poet by around 1512. Besides being descended, as already noted, from a dynasty of female erudites stretching
back through Battista Sforza to Costanza Varano and Battista da Montefeltro, Colonna was also close from her early adulthood to her husband's
aunt, Costanza d'Avalos, Duchess of Francavilla, whom we have already
encountered as a literary patron.

We might conclude our survey of this earliest phase in women's emergence as vernacular poets in Italy with a brief glance at a *capitolo* of
Tebaldeo's celebrating the decision of his patron, Isabella d'Este, to devote
herself to the study of poetic composition under his guidance.[70] Among
the numerous tributes to women's poetic skills we will encounter in the
course of this study, Tebaldeo's for Isabella is unusual in concentrating entirely on promise rather than achievement—perhaps strategically, as there
is little evidence that the marchesa's plans for poetic study bore any more
substantial fruits than her sporadic initiatives for improving her Latin.[71]
Regardless of results, however, Tebaldeo's widely published *capitolo* is of
interest as an indication of the degree to which, at the time of its writing,
poetic composition was beginning to join music and literary and artistic
connoisseurship as a desideratum for the aspiring "universal" woman: a
*virtù conveniente a Madonne,* in a phrase of Isabella's herself.[72] Interestingly,
despite its early date (the *capitolo* was first published in 1498), Tebaldeo does
not place any special emphasis on Isabella's sex other than to flatter her
that her beauty will immeasurably enhance the impact of her talent. Certainly, she is portrayed as destined to bring a new luster to Parnassus, but
it is less her sex than her rank that is seen as distinguishing her among its
existing denizens, who are depicted as thrilled at being joined by a poet of
such impeccably blue blood. A further interesting feature of Tebaldeo's
poem is his emphasis on the pleasure that Isabella's new pursuit will give
to her "fortunate lord," Francesco Gonzaga, whose military prowess is
portrayed as the natural subject matter of his wife's poetry:

> Che gaudio arà quando contexta e messa
> udrà da lei ogni sua palma in verso!
> Lui al far serà pronto, al scriver essa.[73]

[What pleasure it will give him when he hears from her all his victories woven into rhyme! He will be ready to act; she to write.]

While in the case of Isabella and Francesco, this was not to be, it is interesting to see foreshadowed here the model of the complementarily talented noble couple that would be later incarnated with such success in Vittoria Colonna and Francesco Ferrante d'Avalos, he a soldier, she a poet whose primary task is that of immortalizing his fame. This harmonious marital solution to the "arms versus letters" dichotomy neatly updates for a court setting the Aristotelian gender-role model whereby the task of a man is to act in the public sphere, that of a woman to conserve his wealth at home. Man's task here is still to "do" and women's to conserve, but this time not in the self-effacing manner envisaged by Aristotle. On the contrary, in conserving the memory of her husband's great deeds and ensuring him his due immortality, the Renaissance literary wife, on this model, simultaneously immortalizes herself.

### 3. Bembo, Petrarchism, and the Reform of Italian Literature

Despite the confidence and vitality of vernacular literature at the turn of the sixteenth century in Italy, the *volgare* was still far at this time from having established itself as a serious rival to Latin except in terms of popular appeal. True, a handful of modern works had been produced in the vernacular that were sufficiently stylistically distinguished to promise classic status, notably Poliziano's *Stanze per la giostra* (1476–78) and Sannazaro's *Arcadia,* while, within the field of lyric, the quality of the productions of poets such as Boiardo and Lorenzo could hardly be dismissed. Despite all this, however, the vernacular tradition could still not look other than callow when placed beside its principal competitor, the humanistic tradition of Latin literature as it had developed from the days of Petrarch and Boccaccio. The linguistic resource late fifteenth-century humanists could call on—classical Latin, as reconstructed through generations of patient philological labor—was an outstandingly rich and mature one, capable of drawing on an ancient and modern literary tradition of unparalleled sophistication and breadth. The vernacular inevitably suffered by comparison, in spite of an impressive late-medieval heritage that included Dante, Petrarch, and Boccaccio. Compared with a "regular" language like Latin, moreover, that had a relatively standardized grammar and usage, the *volgare* could hardly seem other than anarchic. Even if a degree of convergence among the differing regional variants of Italian was provided at the level of the written language by the dual influences of Latin and medieval Tuscan, regional differences in usage were still sufficiently marked for agreed grammatical and syntactic rules—let alone a standardized vocabulary—to seem utterly remote. Even those sufficiently historicizing in their thought on language to acknowledge the possibility that the vernacular might one day advance to the standard of Latin would have been hard-put to envisage this eventuality taking place any time soon. Still in the late fifteenth century, young men of literary talent and ambition, such as Pietro Bembo, Lodovico Ariosto, and Baldassare Castiglione, all born in the 1470s, were careful to win a name for themselves as Latin poets even while experimenting with the *volgare* on the side.

As the mention of these names suggests, however, by the turn of the century, the situation was poised for change, at least in the north of Italy.[74] As the printing industry developed, and the vernacular reading public expanded, the pressure was inexorable for a widening literary deployment of the vernacular. Moreover, as we have seen, the demand for vernacular literature was by no means limited to the "people": a significant and influential portion of the reading public for vernacular literature was found within the courtly elite. It was logical, in these circumstances, that ambitious writers would be drawn to the *volgare;* and, indeed, the first three decades of the sixteenth century would definitively establish the vernacular as a literary language capable of vying with Latin. Key texts of the period include Ariosto's *Orlando furioso* (1515), Castiglione's *Cortegiano,* Bembo's *Prose della volgar lingua* (1525) and *Rime* (1530), and Sannazaro's *Rime* (1530), the last four already in circulation in manuscript well before their late publication dates. In diverse genres—the chivalric romance, the neo-Ciceronian dialogue, the lyric—these works confirmed the vernacular to be capable of remarkable classicizing refinement. The same may be said to varying extents of the newer classical genres "appropriated" for the vernacular in this period, such as comedy (with Ariosto, Machiavelli, and Bernardo Bibbiena), tragedy (with Giovanni Rucellai, Alessandro de' Pazzi and Giangiorgio Trissino), or the Horatian satire (with Ariosto again, and Luigi Alamanni). While Latin was by no means dead as a literary language and confirmed Latinists like Romolo Amaseo (1489–1552) continued to disparage the vernacular as jejune and presumptuous, such a position was already by this period beginning to become marginal in Italy.[75] As hardly needs to be noted, this development was distinctly precocious with regard to the European norm.

The affirmation of vernacular literature in Italy did not take place without conflict. As was noted above, one of the vernacular's "deficiencies" with regard to Latin was its lack of any universally accepted grammatical and lexical norms, and, inevitably, perhaps, in these circumstances, keen debate arose in this period over the form the literary vernacular should take. The details of the different positions of the discussants in the *questione della lingua,* as the linguistic debate of this period is generally referred to, need not concern us here; they vary from proponents of a single dialect (generally Florentine or Tuscan) to advocates of an eclectic supra-regional language or a *lingua cortigiana* corresponding to the usage of the papal court in Rome.[76] Mainly of interest to us here is the outcome of the debate, which was the adherence on the part of most Italians to a model of the literary vernacular based on the fourteenth-century Tuscan of Boccaccio and Petrarch: a position associated with, and given its most forceful articulation by, the increasingly authoritative figure of Bembo.[77] At first meeting with opposition, Bembo's model came to attain widespread acceptance by around 1530, especially following the publication of his linguistic manifesto, the *Prose della volgar lingua.* A notable testimony to the success of Bembo's views was Castiglione's decision to submit his *Libro del cortegiano* to linguistic revision to bring it more closely into accordance with Tuscan norms before its publication in 1528, a gesture the more noteworthy in that Castiglione's text itself cogently argues for a more eclectic and modernizing solution to the linguistic dilemma.[78] Ariosto also Tuscanized his *Furioso* in advance of its third edition in 1532, where Bembo is hailed for his work in distilling a "pure and sweet language" from the dregs of the "dismal parlance of the vulgar."[79]

To understand the appeal that Bembo's linguistic theories held for his contemporaries, it is necessary to consider their context. Counterintuitive though it may seem, Bembo's archaizing linguistic solution had a distinctly practical dimension in a radically disunified political scenario where no one dialect was likely to assert itself through political "natural selection." By selecting as linguistically authoritative a historically and geographically coherent oeuvre (the fourteenth-century Tuscan writings of Petrarch and Boccaccio), Bembo made it possible to regularize vernacular literary usage in a manner that would otherwise have been impossible to achieve. On a practical level, this meant that tools like reference grammars and dictionaries could be compiled for the *volgare* and that printers were able work to standards that would be acceptable across the peninsula. On a symbolic level, it brought the *volgare* up to the status of Latin as a regulated language. Correctness no longer rested on the shifting whims of popular usage; rather, it resided in the elegant pages of Petrarch and the hardly less elegant pages of Boccaccio (Dante, the third *corona,* as is well known, was sidelined by Bembo as too open to dialect and popular use). Effectively, the *volgare,* in Bembo's hands, became a second language, in the manner of Ciceronian Latin, to be acquired through time-consuming study rather than simply being naturally acquired. This lent the vernacular a social exclusivity that redeemed it from the taint of the "vulgar": as Bembo declares in the *Prose* (1.18) through his brother and spokesman Carlo Bembo, the language of literature must remain remote from that of the *popolo* or else lose all "gravity" and "grandeur."[80]

As this statement well illustrates, Bembo's theories have implications that go well beyond the linguistic, narrowly understood. His was a prescription for a reformed literature, rather than simply a reformed language, based on a through-going imitation of Petrarch, conceived of as the closest historical embodiment in the vernacular of a universal aesthetic ideal. Petrarch's excellence is perceived as lying not merely in his extraordinary technical mastery, although Bembo's studies of his technique were meticulous and highly fruitful; more than this, he is seen as embodying an ideal of decorum with powerful moral and social implications. If Castiglione crafted the perfect gentleman in the *Libro del cortegiano*, Bembo's literary prescriptions supplied a language for that social ideal, informed by the same calculated mixture of dignity and charm, or *gravità* and *piacevolezza* in Bembo's ethically charged stylistic terminology. The more extreme, showy, and ephemeral manifestations of *poeisa cortigiana* were implicitly reproached by these neoclassical standards of decorum, rooted in a self-conscious *mediocrità* and *misura*. Castiglione is, as so often, historically accurate—with the aid of hindsight—when he places the courtly improviser Bernardo Accolti ("l'Unico Aretino") in a disparaging bit part on the fringes of his 1507 aristocratic gathering in the *Cortegiano*, where a visionary Bembo takes center stage, discoursing on Neoplatonic love. Castiglione's characterization points up a further important feature of Bembo's cultural "reform": its displacement of the worldly and sensual version of love that had often characterized the tradition of *poesia cortigiana* by a more ethereal and spiritualized passion, based on Petrarch but philosophically bolstered by a fashionable Neoplatonism deriving from Ficino. This is not to deny the continuities in practice between Bembo's Petrarchism and the poetic school in which he had received his own formation; these continuities exist, clearly, but alongside innovations that gave his proposals a compelling air of modernity.

It would be mistaken, of course, to represent Bembo as single-handedly refashioning the Italian poetic tradition. His ideas were successful in part because they were in accordance with existing trends in literary production, at least among a purist avant-garde. The opening decades of the sixteenth century saw a growing trend, in Italian neo-Latin writing, toward a strict and exclusive imitation of Cicero and Virgil—a trend in which Bembo was, again, influential, especially during his years as secretary to

Pope Leo X (1513–21). This Latin Ciceronianism clearly laid the grounds for the success of Bembo's vernacular Petrarchism, which appropriated much of its theoretical superstructure from the existing Latin phenomenon. Within the vernacular, too, Bembo was not entirely a voice in the wilderness in calling for a close imitation of Petrarch as foundational for lyric practice. Already in the south of Italy in the first decades of the sixteenth century, we find an increasingly strict poetics of Petrarchan imitation being practiced by poets such as Sannazaro, Girolamo Britonio (1490–1550), and Benedetto Gareth ("Cariteo") (c. 1450–c. 1514), who anticipate Bembo, for example, in their exclusion of metrical forms not sanctioned by Petrarchan example.[81] Bembo's crucial contribution was to provide, in the *Prose della volgar lingua*, a historical-theoretical legitimation of this practice, as well as a thorough analytic account of Petrarchan stylistics and a systematic guide to Petrarch's linguistic usage. His categorically stated rules gave an alluring aura of rigor to what had previously been, in the vernacular, a much looser trend of practice, and supplied authoritative standards against which the "correctness" of a work might be judged.

What were the implications of Bembo's linguistic and literary reforms for the nascent tradition of writing by women? The tradition of Renaissance Petrarchism initiated in this period has often been perceived in modern criticism as inimical to women or disabling of women's voices, based as it is on the imitation of a master text in which the feminine only features as object.[82] It is nonetheless true that, in empirical terms, the Petrarchan lyric proved notably accommodating to women writers, to the extent that, at least down to around 1560, it remained by far the dominant form of female literary self-expression.[83] The reasons for this are various. One is that—rather in the manner, again, of Castiglione's codification of court conduct—Bembo's codification of the literary *volgare,* although elitist in intent, was relatively democratizing in practice, at least when made available through the medium of print. The *Prose della volgar lingua,* especially its extensive grammatical section, provided clear linguistic standards that made literary Italian teachable and learnable. Especially when digested into more user-friendly linguistic primers, such as Rinaldo Corso's *Fondamenti del parlar toscano* (1549)—dedicated to a woman, his future wife, Lucrezia Lombardi or "Iparca"—these rules made "correct" writing accessible to any literate person equipped with sufficient time and patience.[84] At the same time, Bembo's advocation of a poetic practice based on the close imitation of a single, and readily available, vernacular author, made "high" literature genuinely accessible to the non-Latin-literate, especially when supplementary instruments such as rhyme books began to be produced,

as they rapidly did.[85] Women were naturally among the prime beneficiaries of these compositional facilitations, remaining as they did far less likely
to receive a classical education than men.

Besides this, there were also, however, other, more gender-specific reasons why the reforms introduced by Bembo proved propitious to women's
involvement with literary culture. As was noted above, besides their linguistic and stylistic dimensions, these reforms had an ethical aspect. Bembo
argued in his theoretical writings and illustrated in practice a polite, decorous, and dignified model of literature, self-consciously elitist and courtly
in its social positioning and remote from any taint of vulgarity. The ethical coloring of Bembo's literary model is especially apparent in the field
of erotic literature, where a reverently desexualized, Neoplatonic model of
erotic discourse progressively displaced the often more licentious codes of
the previous tradition.[86] The palpable "decency" of Bembo's literary formula was a key factor in facilitating women's access to the literary world:
while still a "masculine" code, drawing on masculine models, Petrarchism
was far more safely and decorously appropriable by women than other,
less sublimated, modes. This was all the more so in that, while still privileging love as a theme, the Renaissance Petrarchist tradition that took its
cue from Bembo gave a far greater place to nonerotic genres, especially occasional and correspondence verse; rather than the lonely bucolic haunts
of Petrarch's Vaucluse, the ideal locus of lyric production in sixteenth-
century Italy was the court.[87] This, too, was a development propitious to
female writers in that love, however decorously handled, still held certain
risks as a literary topic for women. By the mid-sixteenth century, it was
possible for a woman writer to make a name for herself as a poet almost
without touching the theme of love: this is the case with Laura Terracina
(1519–c. 1577), the most published poet of the century, and of Laura Battiferra (1523–89), one of the most respected. The importance of "society
verse" within the sixteenth-century lyric tradition also gave great prominence and dignity to women as objects; besides the ethereal poetic *madonne*
that Cinquecento poets inherited from their medieval predecessors, their
*canzonieri* were also increasingly peopled with more substantial feminine
presences in the form of named court ladies constructed as paragons of
beauty, grace, nobility, and wit. These were not necessarily "silent" in the
manner of Laura; indeed, as we will see, they were frequently engaged as
poetic interlocutors. These developments are often forgotten in critical discussions of female poets' relation to the Petrarchan tradition, which often
present the latter as though it was still configured in the mid-sixteenth century in its original fourteenth-century form.

For all the reasons just outlined, then, Bembo's literary reforms have a particularly important place in our narrative here. The new model of vernacular literature that took shape in the early sixteenth century under Bembo's aegis was in many ways more amenable to women writers than the earlier *poesia cortigiana* tradition as well as dramatically more so, of course, than the Latin humanistic tradition. Moreover, not only was the new vernacular literature open to women writers; arguably, it might also be said that they played a necessary part in the process of its self-definition. As was noted at the beginning of this section, the new vernacular culture of the Cinquecento was forged in a spirit of agonistic emulation with the powerful and prestigious tradition of humanistic Latin. This differentiated it in part from the late Quattrocento vernacular literary tradition, which had tended to coexist with reasonable equanimity as a junior partner to humanism. That the vernacular's new relation of rivalry with Latin lent itself to being configured in gendered terms is not surprising if we consider the traditional identification of the "mother tongue" with the feminine, which often took on pejorative tones within the polemics of the Latinist rearguard, where the promiscuous social availability of the vernacular is often epitomized by its accessibility to "foolish women" ("*mulierculae*"). In this context, to insist on women's intellectual acumen and capacity for eloquence was a well-judged rhetorical maneuver in that it converted what had traditionally been regarded as a weakness of the *volgare* into one its strengths. As Alison Cornish has noted of the similarly deft move effected two centuries earlier by Guido Cavalcanti (c. 1255–1300) in his philosophical canzone "Donna me prega" ("A Lady Asks Me"), to address a vernacular poem to a female reader whom the poet "paradoxically" qualifies as intellectually noble "turns vernacularization to rarefaction and refinement: a virtuoso demonstration of the power and beauty of the native language with respect to the old imperial one."[88] Where in late thirteenth-century Florence, however, such a gesture might be considered more or less as a rhetorical expedient, within the early sixteenth-century courts, it was considerably more socially grounded. As we have seen, women played a central role in court culture, both at a concrete and a symbolic level. To be accessible to women—to write in the vernacular, rather than Latin—was to be culturally attuned to the court.

It is within these sociocultural and linguistic contexts that we need to locate the philogynistic attitudes displayed with such consistency by Bembo and by other founding authors of the new literature such as Castiglione. To display an affirmative attitude toward women, particularly in regard to their intellectual and moral capacities, was a powerful signifying gesture, carrying a charge of cultural modernity as well as of gallantry and social cachet. We can follow the process of diffusion of this profeminist culture by tracking the changes that Ariosto introduced into his *Orlando furioso* between the 1516 and 1532 editions: where the first had been relatively typical of its age in its contradictory mingling of gynephile and misogynistic elements, the third edition of 1532, published after the appearance of Castiglione's *Cortegiano,* introduces much new narrative material condemnatory of misogyny and celebratory of women's potential for "masculine" achievements.[89] Prominent as well in the 1532 *Furioso* is a lengthy passage heralding the appearance of female writers on the literary scene, ending with an admiring portrayal of Vittoria Colonna as a new archetype of female perfection, combining the traditional feminine qualities of chastity and marital devotion with the novel one of literary excellence.[90] Three years later, in 1535, in the second edition of his *Rime,* Bembo would include poetic exchanges with Colonna and Veronica Gambara among the highly select group of correspondence poems he added as an appendix to illustrate his literary relations.[91] Bembo's poems to the two women played a central role in defining and glamorizing the figure of the literary woman, especially his three sonnets to Colonna, "Cingi le costei tempie dell'amato" ("Crown Her Temples with the Beloved [Laurel]"), "Alta Colonna, e ferma alle tempeste" ("Lofty Column [*Colonna*], Firm against the Storms") and "Caro e sovran de l'età nostra onore" ("Cherished Sovereign Honor of Our Age"), which among them crafted a memorably dignified portrait of his subject, much imitated by subsequent poets.[92] Nor were his exchanges with Gambara and Colonna Bembo's sole public stagings of his creative relationship with women. In his posthumously published *Lettere* of 1552—meticulously put together before his death—his half-century-old epistolary correspondence with Maria Savorgnan was placed before the public eye, though in a carefully edited form (his letters only are published and all indication of her identity is suppressed).[93] This portrays a relationship at once erotic and literary, in which the poet submits his writings to his lover's "sweet file" ("dolce lima") for polishing and speaks of their composition virtually as a collaborative effort.[94] More strikingly still, the letters ideally locate Bembo's early work on Italian grammar within the context of this relationship: a letter of 2 September 1500 speaks of Bembo's having begun to put together "some notes" ("alcune notationi") on language in response to a request of Savorgnan's that he correct her letters to him linguistically.[95] Nor was this vision of a creative dialogue with women purely a retrospective construct. Bembo's poetic correspondence with Veronica Gambara dates from 1504, when the two exchanged sonnets, and the literary sodality he formed around 1502–3 with a group of Venetian contemporaries, the *Compagnia degli Amici* (Company of Friends), was groundbreaking compared to precedents such as the Accademia

Romana and Accademia Pontaniana in agreeing to admit women to its ranks.[96] Bembo's philosophical dialogue, *Gli Asolani*, published in 1505, though written earlier, was also self-consciously innovative in including women among its interlocutors; it is also set in a court ruled by a woman, Caterina Corner, ex-queen of Cyprus (1454–1510), and is dedicated to a woman, Lucrezia Borgia.[97] Slightly later, during his Urbino period, Bembo dedicated his first collection of *Rime* (c. 1510) to Elisabetta Gonzaga, who is also the addressee of his celebrated canzone on the death of his brother Carlo.[98] Given Bembo's consistent engagement with women as poetic interlocutors, it is intriguing to recall the precedent of his father, Bernardo, who had figured among the prime admirers of Ginevra de' Benci in the 1470s in Florence and is likely to have to commissioned the portrait by Leonardo that implicitly celebrates her as poet.[99] Pietro was also, of course, a contemporary and compatriot of Cassandra Fedele, whose exploits he cannot but have noted, and he would also certainly have known of Alessandra Scala through his own and his father's contacts with Poliziano.[100] These precedents are useful in understanding Bembo's alertness to the possibility of women's participation in literature, and his sensitivity to the symbolic work a feminine presence in literary culture might perform. It was nevertheless he, perhaps more than any single figure, who popularized a stance of intellectual engagement with women, taking what had been a relatively local and avant-garde phenomenon and converting it into an imitable, and widely imitated, formula.[101]

One reason for recalling the fifteenth-century precedents that laid the basis for Bembo's engagement with the figure of the female poet is to caution us against more immediate contextualizing interpretations of his cultural philogyny that might otherwise come to mind. The formative period for Bembo's vernacular poetics was one of severe political trauma for the Italian elite, as the peninsula was consumed by a series of crippling wars, triggered by the French invasions of 1494 and 1498. The Wars of Italy, as they are now known, were experienced by contemporaries as signaling the end of the Italian states' proud late-medieval history of political autonomy, conventionally dated to the Treaty of Constance, sealed between the communes of the Lombard League and the Emperor Frederick I Barbarossa in 1183. Effectively, over the decades following 1494, Italy became a battleground, and a rich looting terrain, for the rising European powers of France and Spain. In the process, the most powerful fifteenth-century Italian states, Milan and Naples, lost their independence, never fully to regain it, while the survival of the remaining states hung for decades on a tissue of precarious and ever-shifting alliances.[102] The literature of the period is replete with allusions to Italy's humiliating reduction to servitude, often cast in gender terms as emasculating or feminizing, as famously in the final chapter of Machiavelli's *Il principe,* which portrays a "battered and torn" feminine Italy calling out for a male savior in the form of his wishfully prospected ideal prince.[103] Nor was the theme remote from the linguistic debates of the period; indeed, a chapter in Bembo's *Prose della volgar lingua* explicitly positions the history of the Italian vernacular against the background of the country's political history since the fall of the Roman Empire, with a long period of "contamination" of Latin by the "barbarian" tongues of the various invading peoples followed by a late-medieval phase of linguistic "purification" and culminating in the insuperable moment represented by Petrarch, which coincides politically with the age of restored Italian liberty following the Treaty of Constance.[104] Seen in this light, Bembo's proposal of a restoration of Petrarchan norms can appear nostalgic and psychologically compensatory: an attempt to cauterize the political wounds inflicted by Italy's renewed reduction to "servitude" by reconstituting its integrity and self-determination on a cultural and symbolic level. In this reading, Bembo's proposal of a bigendered poetic culture might be regarded as similarly compensatory, with the presence of a nominal but much-vaunted cluster of female poets serving to preserve the fragile masculinity of the elite males who made up the vast majority of *letterati* in the period. Petrarchism, at its best, was hardly hypermasculine as an authorship stance, focused as it was on the realms of the erotic and affective and structured as it tended to be around the theme of amorous "servitude" to an imperious *midons.* Female poets could be useful in this scenario in supplying a differential pole against which the male Petrarchist's masculinity would be measured. A similar interpretation has been proposed by for the role of the female courtier or *donna di palazzo* in Castiglione's *Cortegiano,* who may be seen, in her subordination, as guarantor of the masculinity of a male courtier "feminized' by his subordination to the prince.[105]

While there may well be some truth in this construction, there are factors that should induce us to be wary about accepting it entirely. First, it would be misleading to present the emergence of the figure of the female poet in the early 1500s purely as a cultural response to the trauma occasioned by the Wars of Italy. On the contrary, as we have seen, the female vernacular poet stepped into a cultural space already created for her humanistic predecessor, the "learned lady," and the ground was already primed for her appearance by the early 1490s. Indeed, far from the female poet being summoned into being by the crisis of the Italian Wars, two female voices, those of Girolama Corsi and Camilla Scarampa, may already be heard among the shocked chorus of Italian poets lamenting the invasions that triggered those wars in the 1490s.[106] Secondly, turning to the evidence of male responses to female poets of the period, we do not find the kind of gender-based stylistic discrimination one might expect within the compensatory scenario. While it is true that we often find female poets' production praised for its "sweetness" and "purity," this kind of adjectivization is not universal nor exclusive to women; on the contrary, we find Vittoria Colonna, for example, frequently praised for the *gravità* or "weightiness" of her poetry, a quality that unquestionably genders as masculine in Bembo's poetics, forming a dialectic with its opposing feminine quality of *piacevolezza,* or charm. The stylistic ideal Bembo sees epitomized most exquisitely in Petrarch consists precisely of a dynamic balance of *gravità* and *piacevolezza,* by contrast with the excessively "grave" Dante or the excessively "pleasing" Cino da Pistoia. The fact that Petrarch can embody this ideal is already indicative that an admixture of the feminine is not regarded as compromising in a male poet, while, correspondingly, the example of Colonna suggests that an admixture of the masculine did not detract from a female poet's appeal. We are at some distance from the model of Castiglione's *Cortegiano,* with its carefully gender-differentiated stylistic prescriptions, mandating a "firm and robust virility" as the basis for the male courtier's behavioral decorum, while stipulating that the court lady should manifest a "delicate and yielding softness" and show "no semblance whatever of a man."[107]

This does not mean, of course, that we should discount the Wars of Italy as a context for the literary developments that form the subject of this chapter. On the contrary, as the section that follows will suggest, the story of Vittoria Colonna's and Veronica Gambara's rise to fame in the years around 1530 is closely enmeshed with the political history of Italy of this period and especially with the Italian elite's difficult negotiation of its relationship with the new, foreign powers in the land. I discuss these factors thoroughly in section 4, but I would like to note here how large a place within the poetic cult of Colonna that developed from the early 1530s was given to her exemplary stoicism in the face of adverse fortune, emblematized by her device of a rock at sea standing firm against the ferocious battering of the waves.[108] The virtue thus evoked is a complex one in gendered terms: virile, certainly, in its courage and constancy but also feminine-inflected in its passivity: this is a feminine "heroics of endurance" in Mary Beth Rose's formula rather than a masculine "heroics of action."[109] Here, it does certainly seem useful to locate Colonna with regard to the situation of the Italian elite during and following the Wars of Italy and to consider the appeal in this period of a stance flatteringly capable of transmuting defeat into a species of moral victory. With her impressive martial lineage, and her providentially symbolic name, evocative of both triumph (*vittoria*) and sustaining strength (*colonna*/column), Colonna seems to have functioned in this period as much as a consolatory embodiment of Italian virility as a subaltern feminine "other."[110]

### 4. "So Dear to Apollo": Veronica Gambara and Vittoria Colonna after 1530

With this discussion of Colonna, we are now clearly beyond the "prehistory" of vernacular women's writing in Italy and fully on the terrain of canonical literary history. The section that follows is devoted to a detailed consideration of the poetic careers of Colonna and Veronica Gambara: key figures to us here as far the most celebrated female writers of their era and as important and durable models for the tradition of women's writing to come. By the time Colonna and Gambara made their first print appearance in the second edition of Bembo's *Rime* of 1535, both were already well known within elite literary circles through the circulation of their lyrics in manuscript, and both had attained notice as poets in Ariosto's *Orlando furioso*, the most popular narrative work of the day. From this point, their fame continued to expand, particularly following the publication of Colonna's *Rime*, which appeared for the first time in a pirated edition in 1538 and proved one of the publishing sensations of the day. By 1543, Colonna had attained the singular distinction of having had a comprehensive stylistic commentary on her poetry published, by the precocious law student and *letterato* Rinaldo Corso (1525–82). She was the first living poet to receive such an accolade, not yet even accorded to Bembo.[111] While Gambara's cult was less notable than Colonna's, she was published substantially in anthologies from 1545 onward and was widely praised as a poet, often in conjunction with Colonna, with whom her literary fortunes were closely meshed. Following their deaths around midcentury (Colonna's in 1547, Gambara's in 1550), the two continued to form the ineluctable starting point for all listings of "modern Sapphos": ninety years after their deaths, in 1640, Margherita Costa still gave Colonna and Gambara pride of place in a trio of feminine presences in an imagined Parnassus.[112] To an extent of which we need to remind ourselves today, Gambara and Colonna were the unquestioned giants within the panorama of Cinquecento women's writing, utterly dwarfing figures who stand large in the modern female critical canon, such as Gaspara Stampa and Veronica Franco.

Of these two poets, we have already briefly encountered Veronica Gambara as one of a number of female poets active in the Lombard and Venetian cultural sphere in the first decade of the sixteenth century. Colonna, slightly younger, began her poetic activity in a literary context less obviously propitious to women's writing: that of Naples, where she was based after her marriage in 1509, although she was born at the Colonna estate of Marino, near Rome.[113] It is likely that Camilla Scarampa served as a role model to both women: Gambara, born in Brescia, must almost certainly have been familiar with her verse, while the tributes to Scarampa by Iacopo Sannazaro and Enea d'Irpino show that her work was also circulating in the south.[114] Unlike Gambara's, Colonna's early poetic career is mainly attested indirectly, as she appears to have destroyed much of her early work or suppressed its circulation. A *capitolo* that survives of hers from around 1512, however, reveals her already an accomplished poet by this time, even if in an idiom closer to the *poesia cortigiana* tradition than to her mature Petrarchist voice.[115] How widely her writing circulated in this period we cannot be sure, although a *canzoniere* published in 1519 by her poetic admirer Girolamo Britonio served to diffuse her reputation as both muse and poet and the dedication to her of an edition of Dante in 1515 to confirm her status as a woman of unusual intellectual standing.[116] From what we can reconstruct of her verse of the time, it seems probable that Colonna's main theme was her love for her husband, Francesco Ferrante d'Avalos, Marquis of Pescara (1489–1525), a prominent imperial general of Spanish descent.[117] Gambara, too, in as much as we may conjecturally date her poems, appears also to have written amorous verse during the time of her marriage, converting her early, stereotypically tortured poetic voice to a more serene idiom of reciprocated love. This seems to have been the time of composition, for example, of what would become one of her most successful lyrics, the madrigal "Occhi lucenti e belli," which would attract at least five musical settings in the course of the sixteenth century, including, most famously, one by Luca Marenzio in the 1580s.[118]

While it can hardly be said that either woman was unknown during their younger years, the national fame of both Colonna and Gambara dates preponderantly from later, during the long period of their respective widowhoods, Gambara's commencing in 1518, Colonna's in 1525. Neither woman remarried: Gambara remained after her husband's death as regent countess of Correggio during the period of her sons' minority, while Colonna moved back within the sphere of her natal family's power base of Rome, where she led a notably pious existence and became increasingly involved with reform-minded evangelical circles. During the period following her husband's death Colonna continued to cultivate her poetry, concentrating now exclusively on the theme of mourning for her dead love on the model of Petrarch's *in morte* verse for Laura. In the later 1520s, two works composed by writers in her circle served to define her figure further and to disseminate her fame: her cousin Pompeo Colonna's *Apologia mulierum* (1526–29)—one of the most radical *querelle* texts of the century in its advocation of women's equal participation in public life—and Paolo Giovio's *Dialogus de viris et foeminis aetate nostra florentibus,* composed in 1528–29.[119] Although neither of these works were published, both circulated in manuscript, with Giovio's, for example, reaching Isabella d'Este, to whom its author gave a presentation copy in 1529, perhaps with a view to gaining financial subvention for a proposed publication.[120] Giovio was also charged on the same journey north to give a copy of some of Colonna's recent poems, from the period of her widowhood, to Bembo, who was in this period to be found in Bologna for the important political congress marking the reconciliation of the papacy and the empire, which culminated in the papal crowning of the Emperor Charles V in February of 1530.[121] This detail is important, as the congress brought together the major political and cultural players in Italy, turning the city temporarily into a extraordinary fulcrum of literary exchange. That Colonna's verse was circulating in the city, soon with Bembo's enthusiastic stamp of approval, was a vital step in her conversion to a kind of national icon. The same context was also vital for the political consolidation and poetic reputation of Gambara, who was present in Bologna in person and in a highly visible capacity, in that her brother Uberto (1489–1549), a prominent cleric who later reached the rank of cardinal, was the papal governor of the city at the time of the congress and thus effectively the event's immediate host.[122]

The political context supplied by the congress of Bologna is important for understanding the fascination that Colonna, and to a lesser extent, Gambara, began to hold for Italian *letterati* in these years. As was noted above, since 1494, the Italian peninsula had been a battleground for the great emerging powers of Europe, France and Spain, the latter from 1519 effectively united with the empire under the rule of Charles V. In 1529, following the definitive defeat of France and the humiliation of its principal Italian ally in the 1520s, the papacy, a settlement was made at Cambrai dictating the terms of what was to prove an extended period of Spanish hegemony in Italy. It was this new political order that was ceremonially inaugurated at the congress of Bologna in 1529–30. As the widow of one of Charles V's leading generals, and as an Italian woman connected by marriage to the prominent Spanish-Neapolitan clan of the d'Avalos, Vittoria Colonna was well placed to stand as a consolatory icon for an Italy now in large part under direct or indirect Spanish rule. Her marriage to Ferrante d'Avalos represented a harmonized union of "modern" Spanish power and ancient Italian aristocracy, cast here flatteringly as a relationship of equals, he excelling in the field of arms, she in letters. Colonna's verse in memory of d'Avalos was charged, then, with a series of political and ideological meanings far beyond their already attractive literal sense of a devoted widow's tireless memorialization of her husband.[123] Nor was it purely on the fame of her dead husband and her own nobility and talent that Colonna could trade: her cousin by marriage, orphaned in childhood and brought up by Colonna practically as a son, was Alfonso d'Avalos (1502–46), Marquis of Vasto, commander of the imperial forces in Italy and later governor of Milan, from 1535. This relationship added considerably to Vittoria Colonna's prestige, while, at the same time, her growing literary reputation conferred a cultural distinction on Vasto, himself an aspiring poet as well as a notable literary patron. As the research of Tobia Toscano has recently illuminated, Vasto played a significant role in Colonna's promotion, most directly, perhaps, through his award of a generous pension to Ariosto in 1531. It was in gratitude for this that Ariosto inserted his extensive praises of Colonna as poet into his reworking of the *Furioso,* in a passage that perhaps did more than any other single tribute in burnishing and divulgating her fame.[124]

Like Colonna, Veronica Gambara was quite closely connected with the now-dominant proimperial interests, although in her case this was the result less of family and marital circumstance than of strategy. The allegiance of the Gambara family had traditionally been to the French, but, as ruler of Correggio, Gambara positioned herself as a devoted fief of the empire, twice hosting the emperor personally at her court and winning a pledge from him for the security of her lands.[125] Her brother Brunoro and her elder son Ippolito (1510–52) both fought in the imperial armies.[126] Charles V features frequently as a subject in Gambara's encomiastic verse, which includes a sequence of four sonnets celebrating his victories in Tunisia in 1535 and a Latin ode lauding him for his defeat of the Protestant Schmalkaldic League in 1547.[127] Seemingly more "private" in character, but similarly politically strategic, are two poems to the Marquis of Vasto, written in the persona of his wife, Maria d'Aragona (1503–68).[128] It is partly within this context as well that we should probably see Gambara's sedulous cultivation of her relationship with Vittoria Colonna, although a further motive is likely to have been to associate herself with this rapidly rising female poetic star. Two sonnet exchanges exist between Colonna and Gambara, dating from 1532 and both initiated by the latter. Gambara was also responsible for commissioning Rinaldo Corso's commentary on Colonna's poetry, a portion of which was published in 1543, with a dedication to Gambara, followed by the entire gloss in 1558.[129] Gambara's efforts in this regard had the effect of soldering further the popular linkage of her name with Colonna's, to the benefit of her own literary reputation. As will be clear from my earlier discussion of Bembo's relations with the two women, however, this linkage was not purely of Gambara's doing. The model of vernacular culture shaped and codified by Bembo required a female creative presence for its ideal completion, and a presence not reducible to a single exceptional figure was evidently much stronger than one that was. The pairing of Colonna and Gambara, and their twin "canonization," was critical to the literary dynamics of Petrarchism in its formative period. It worked particularly well because the two women, though very different as poets, had sufficient in common as social and ethical models to work as mutually reinforcing exempla. Both were well-born, well-connected, pious, and morally impeccable widows, neither of whom had succumbed to the "temptation" of a second marriage. The social dimension of their poetic personae is well conveyed by the description of them by Lilio Gregorio Giraldi in c. 1548–51 as *"principes et poetriae"* ("princesses and poets").[130] This elevated social profile was underlined by their exceptional standard of education; unusually for sixteenth-century female poets, both were capable of writing Latin verse.[131]

Where their writing was concerned, Colonna and Gambara took interestingly different routes in the poetic careers of their maturity, although an area of thematic overlap exists in their production in their dignified occasional verse. Far the less prolific of the two, Gambara largely confined herself to political and occasional verse in her mature output, formally renouncing her youthful amorous poetry in her sonnet to Colonna, "Mentre da vaghi e giovenil peniseri" ("While by Sweet and Errant Youthful Thoughts") (1532).[132] Her verse shows a high level of formal competence, though it is less original and experimental than Colonna's, and at its best has a warmth and ease that are also apparent in Gambara's attractive epistolary voice.[133] Justly famed within her output are her poems of place, such as the ottava rima poem "Con quel caldo desio che nascer suole," which celebrates her return to her home city of Brescia, from which the Gambara had been exiled from 1512 to 1532.[134] An interesting continuity is apparent here with Isotta Nogarola's Latin poem on the Nogarola estate in Castel d'Azzano, perhaps suggestive of a conscious emulation of her distinguished forebear on Gambara's part.[135] Of special interest from the point of view of this study are Gambara's correspondence sonnets to Bembo and Colonna, two of which, in particular, became much-used models for imitation on the part of future female poets. These are "A l'ardente desio ch'ognor m'accende" ("In the Ardent Desire That Has Always Fired Me") to Bembo, the poem of hers published in his 1535 *Rime*, and "O de la nostra etade unica gloria" ("Oh Unique Glory of Our Age"), to

Colonna, placed by Lodovico Domenichi (1515–64) at the head of his selection from Gambara in his anthology of women's poetry of 1559.[136] The
latter is worth quoting as an influential example of a tribute poem from
one female poet to another, a genre, again, with fifteenth-century humanistic roots in Costanza Varano's poem to Isotta Nogarola of the 1440s:[137]

O de la nostra etade unica gloria
Donna saggia, leggiadra, anzi divina,
A la qual reverente oggi s'inchina
Chiunque è degno di famosa istoria,
Ben fia eterna di voi qua giù memoria,
Nè potrà il tempo con la sua ruina
Far del bel nome vostro empia rapina,
Ma di lui porterete ampia vittoria.
Il sesso nostro un sacro e nobil tempio
Dovria, come già a Palla e a Febo, farvi
Di ricchi marmi e di finissim'oro.
E poichè di virtù siete l'esempio,
Vorrei, Donna, poter tanto lodarvi,
Quanto vi riverisco, amo ed adoro.

[Oh unique glory of our age! Wise and graceful lady—nay, divine—before
whom all those living who are worthy of fame's annals bow in reverence,
certainly your own immortality on earth is now assured. Nor will Time
with his all his ruination be able to snatch away your lovely name; instead,
it will be you who carries off an ample victory (*vittoria*) against him. Our
sex should erect a sacred and noble temple to you, as once they were raised
to Pallas and Phoebus, adorned with rich marbles and the most refined gold.
And since you are the epitome of virtue (and/or talent), I would wish, lady,
to be capable of speaking in your praise in a way that could fully convey the
reverence, love, and worship I feel.]

An interesting feature of this sonnet, when compared to the majority of
tributes to Colonna by male writers at this time, is the lack of any allusion
to Colonna's relationship with her husband. Colonna is saluted here as an
intellectual and a figure of independent moral dignity rather than as a
model of wifely devotion and a "living exemplar" of her husband.[138] Also
interesting is the "hermaphroditic" quality of its representation of its heroine: while Gambara's Colonna remains properly feminine (the adjective
"*leggiadra*" has gendered connotations), the implicit comparison of her to
Athena and Apollo complicates and nuances her gender identity.[139] Not
only do the two represent complementary, male and female embodiments

of philosophical and poetic wisdom, but the helmeted Athena, partheno-genetic offspring of Zeus, offers a peculiarly virile model of female *virtù*. Gambara's classicizing language in this sonnet also serves to recall the classical heritage of female poetry and the status of the female poet as metonymically representative of the Renaissance revival of the glories of antiquity. Colonna's answering sonnet ("Di novo il Cielo de l'antica gloria" ["Heaven Once More with Ancient Glory"]) spells out the historical point implicit in Gambara's sonnet while returning her compliment, adducing Gambara's *virtù* in its opening lines as evidence of the return of ancient glory to the world.[140]

Where Gambara renounced love as a theme in her mature poetry, thus ensuring a clear break between the two phases of her career, Colonna, as we have seen, continued to write of her love for her husband after his death, though with a new elegiac inflection. The decision is announced in her reply to Gambara's renunciatory "Mentre da vaghi e giovenil pensieri," "Lasciar non posso i miei saldi pensieri" ("I Cannot Leave My Constant Thoughts"), which counters Gambara's morally inflected rejection of erotic poetry as the expression of wayward mortal passion with a more mystical and Neoplatonizing model of a poetry of love generated by an "immortal cause" ("cagion immortal") and thus capable of penetrating beyond the grave.[141] As a theme, of course, mourning for a dead love had an established Petrarchan precedent. Colonna, however, took the theme in new directions, partly dictated by the "public" and epic character of the figure mourned; besides recounting her desolation at d'Avalos's death and her aspirations to join him in heaven, a self-conscious memorializing vocation takes center stage in her verse, in a manner recognized by contemporaries, who cast her as a new Artemisia erecting a literary mausoleum to her dead husband.[142] Colonna's postmortem verse for d'Avalos was much imitated by subsequent female poets and may be seen as establishing much of the basic idiom for the subsequent female love lyric, proving adaptable to the description of a dignified and "correct" love *in vita* as well as to elegiac uses. Destined to success, especially, were the Neoplatonic and spiritualizing cast that she gave to her description of the love experience and the abstract and descriptively minimalist codes she evolved for the evocation of the male love object, most successfully encapsulated in the metaphor of the Sun (*Sole*), expressive of his uniqueness, dazzling beauty, spiritually generative properties, and Apollonian or Christ-like numinous power.[143] Stylistically, Colonna's verse impressed contemporaries for its remarkable formal mastery and the weightiness and grandeur of its register; on his first acquaintance with her poetry in 1530, Bembo described one of her sonnets as "finer and more ingenious and graver than one would ex-

pect from a woman."[144] While she has sometimes been presented by critics in the past as a timid, if technically expert, imitator of Petrarch, such
an understanding is based on an inattentive reading: a finer-grained examination reveals Colonna as more formally experimental than many of her
male, as well as her female, contemporaries.[145]

Despite the impressive quality of Colonna's verse for her husband, and
its success as a formula, the narrowness of this vein must soon have become constricting for a poet of Colonna's talent. From around the mid-
1530s, in a manner consistent with her ascetic lifestyle, Colonna appears to
have devoted herself near exclusively to religious verse, experimenting
with a mode that, though still recognizably Petrarchan in its idiom, drew
also extensively on mystical literature, with its more sensual and corporeal
language. The resulting fusion is strikingly original and left a deep impression on contemporaries. Although not technically the first poet to attempt to "convert" Petrarchism to a religious vocation—chronological
primacy in this goes to Girolamo Malipiero, with his *Petrarca spirituale* of
1536—Colonna is generally recognized as the true ideal founder of the
Petrarchist genre of *rime spirituali*.[146] The reformation of Petrarch that
Malipiero had sought to realize mechanically through a literal work of systematic piecemeal rewriting of Petrarch becomes in Colonna a process of
free imaginative transcription, in which the despair and ecstasy characteristic of the Petrarchan erotic experience find their "proper" sphere of reference in evoking the fear and hope of the sinful soul in its trajectory to
salvation.[147] Colonna was facilitated in this task of Petrarchan reinscrip-
tion by the existence of long-established traditions of mystical writing that
cast the soul in a feminine guise—as, for example, desiring bride to Christ's
beloved bridegroom. More specifically, she could draw on a distinguished
authorizing tradition of writings by female mystics in particular, including, most importantly, St. Catherine of Siena, whose *Letters* and *Dialogue*
constituted without doubt the most widely published body of writing
by a woman available to her culture prior to her own.[148] Besides poems
of mystic ecstasy and spiritual self-interrogation, Colonna's *rime spirituali*
also comprehended more "objective," epideictic genres, such as praises
of the Virgin and saints and verses commemorating significant events of
the Christian calendar.[149] The result was a collection at least as varied—
indeed, probably more so—than the conventional erotic *canzoniere*. Colonna's foundational role in the tradition of Petrarchan *rime spirituali*
deserves to be underlined in the present context, especially given the widespread critical tendency to attribute to female writers an inevitable position of discipleship with respect to males. Although it is true that this was
generally the case, Colonna's founding role in this genre of religious verse

reminds us that it is not quite a universal rule. Interesting in this regard is the freedom with which later male "spiritual poets" like Luca Contile (1507–74) and Gabriele Fiamma (1533–85) acknowledged Colonna as initiator of the genre, both describing her, further, as the inspiration of their own poetic and spiritual quest.[150]

Although the mention of Fiamma attests to the continuing currency of Colonna's verse in the age of the Counter-Reformation, consideration is due here to its original religious context within the aristocratic wing of the Italian reform movement.[151] As is well known, in the last decade or so of her life, Colonna was closely associated with reform circles, and particularly, increasingly, with the figures often termed *spirituali:* lay thinkers and clerics drawing inspiration from the teachings of the Spanish reformer Juan de Valdés (?1509–41), who resided in Naples from around 1530 until his death, gaining a substantial following among the elites of the city and beyond. Following Valdés's death, a number of his followers congregated in Viterbo, at this time residence of the powerful English cardinal and sympathizer Reginald Pole (1500–58). Colonna, too, transferred there in 1541, developing a close relationship with Pole, her spiritual "son," and remaining in the city for three years before returning to Rome in 1544. Colonna's contacts in this intense period of her spiritual development spanned both high-ranking prelates such as Pole, Bembo, and Giovanni Morone (1509–80), committed to an internal reform of the Church, and more radical figures such as Marcantonio Flaminio (1498–1550), editor and perhaps coauthor of the *Beneficio di Christo,* first published in c. 1542. Most notoriously, in the late 1530s and very early 1540s, she was close to Bernardino Ochino (1487–1564), the charismatic Sienese preacher whose sermons drew crowds of thousands in Rome, Ferrara, Venice, and Florence and who later scandalized the church with his departure for Geneva in 1542. Colonna's own position on the key theological and ecclesiological issues of this time has been much debated, though without any clear resolution. Certainly, her association with Ochino was sufficient to make her suspect in the eyes of the Inquisition, even though she appears to have broken off all contact with him following his flight from Italy.[152] Cardinal Morone, interrogated on Colonna's views in 1550s by the Inquisition, admitted that he feared or suspected (*dubitava*) she may have shared some of Ochino's views, while Pietro Carnesecchi (1508–67), again under interrogation, speculated that she may have held unorthodox views on predestination and justification by faith.[153]

More interesting, however, for the present discussion than any attempt to determine Colonna's precise theological positions is the question of the degree to which her contacts with the *spirituali* and their writings helped to shape the poetic language of her *rime spirituali* and their religious sub-ject matter. Critics agree that her religious verse shares with the writings of the *spirituali* an overwhelming focus on Christ's redemption of hu-manity through the Passion. Faith is conceived of in this context less in doc-trinal and intellectual terms than as a passionate bond between creature and creator, often figured in a powerfully corporeal guise as a melding of blood, tears, and flesh. Whether or not salvation is formally regarded as deriving from "faith alone," the soul is characteristically portrayed in a state of abjection, utterly dependent for its redemption on grace.[154] Be-sides this general, thematic consonance between Colonna's *Rime* and the devotional culture of the *spirituali,* attempts have been made to trace in her poetry more localized linguistic influences, deriving from sources with which she is known to have been familiar, such as Ochino's sermons.[155] There are dangers in such an exercise, however, given the difficulty of dis-entangling the precise influence of the *spirituali* from the broader tradi-tions of evangelical and mystical writing on which the *spirituali* themselves were drawing and from the traditions of vernacular lyric. It also needs to be recalled that, as Abigail Brundin has recently noted, the traffic between Petrarchism and evangelism in this period was not one-way.[156] If a patina of evangelical-reformist language can be detected in Colonna's *Rime,* this is perhaps best conceived of as less the result of a one-way "influence" than the reflection of a broader contemporary process of interchange between these two discourses, understandable when it is considered that both found their ideal textual community within the geographically dispersed realms of the Italian social and cultural elite. Besides Colonna herself, and Bembo, it is not difficult to list Petrarchist lyric poets of the 1540s with marked reformist sympathies, from Luca Contile and Veronica Gambara to Fortunato Martinengo (d. 1553), Rinaldo Corso, Benedetto Varchi (1503–65), and Lodovico Domenichi.

The presence of both Colonna and Gambara in this list provokes reflec-tion on a theme deserving of notice in the present context: the role of reformist religious circles in this period in promoting women's cultural ac-tivity.[157] As has often been observed, a notable feature of Italian reform cir-cles in the period prior to the Council of Trent was the prominent spiritual and cultural role played by aristocratic women; besides Colonna herself, other notable examples from the same Valdesian circles are Caterina Cibo (1501–57), Duchess of Camerino, and Giulia Gonzaga, Countess of Fondi and related to Colonna through her marriage to Vespasiano Colonna. Colonna's sister-in-law, Giovanna d'Aragona (1500–1577), and Giovanna's sister, Maria, wife of Colonna's cousin by marriage, the Marquis of Vasto, may also be listed among Italian noblewomen of the period noted for their reformist sympathies. Beyond Italy, Colonna was in contact with Marguerite d'Angouleme, or Marguerite de Navarre (1492–1549), with whom she had an important epistolary exchange, published several times from 1542 on, while, closer to home, Marguerite's compatriot, Renée de France, or Renata di Francia (1510–76), Duchess of Ferrara, was another eminent reformist connection.[158] While it would be misleading to represent the Italian reform movement as somehow intrinsically "feminist," it does seem unquestionable that the informal networks of friendship and patronage that meshed together Italians of reformist sympathies offered possibilities of spiritual fellowship and intellectual exchange that appealed keenly to powerful women. Further, in a manner that to some degree parallels the place of "learned ladies" within humanism, female "spirituals" served as figureheads for the developing Italian reform movement, functioning in quite complex ways to articulate and embody its social and intellectual ideals. Constance Furey's recent remarks regarding Vittoria Colonna's symbolic role in the movement could be generalized to other female figures in the list just given: "men of letters extolled Colonna to reassure themselves that their intellectual culture was infused with a nonintellectual (feminized) spirituality even as they used her to articulate an ideal of learned piety to which they themselves aspired'.[159] Again, in a pattern we have already encountered in the case of secular culture, the mutual admiration of the women concerned served further to reinforce their iconic status: thus, we find Colonna proposing Marguerite de Navarre in her letters as an unsurpassed example of the union of spiritual excellence and intellectual power, while Rinaldo Corso's commentary on Colonna's poetry, commissioned by Gambara, serves as tribute both to Colonna's poetic genius and, more discreetly, her reformist piety.[160] Through the writings of these women themselves, and of male admirers such as Benedetto Varchi and Ortensio Lando (c. 1508–c. 1553), a compelling image was constructed of an "alternative" religious culture whose otherness with respect to traditional church hierarchies was signaled not least by its promotion of women.[161] An interesting example of this is Lando's essay on women's superiority in his *Paradossi* of 1543, which concludes with a lengthy roll call of current Italian "women of excellence" that also functions tacitly as a who's who of Italian reform.[162] The list evokes an imagined spiritual community in which the "paradoxical" thesis of women's superiority may be countenanced without absurdity: a community as feminized, or bigendered, as the original ideal community of worshipers evangelical meditative traditions portrayed clustered around the cross.

Before leaving this discussion of Colonna and Gambara as poets, an account of the transmission history of their verse may be useful. As has already been noted, Colonna's verse had a rich publishing history, beginning in 1538, when Filippo Pirogallo first issued a volume of her *Rime* in Venice. Four more editions followed by 1540, and a further eight before her death in 1547.[163] An interesting shift is observable within these editions toward a greater emphasis on the *rime spirituali;* where in the 1538 edition these had followed the *amorose,* they increasingly tended to precede in later editions, while, at around the same time, a new frontispiece began to feature in many editions, portraying the author as a nun-like figure kneeling before a crucifix.[164] In 1543, a selection of Colonna's *rime spirituali* was published apart from the *amorose,* along with Rinaldo Corso's commentary, and in 1546, a separate volume of *rime spirituali* was published by Valgrisi in Venice. All these editions of Colonna's verse were published without the consent of its author, who remained aristocratically throughout her life aloof from the "vulgarity" of print, preferring to circulate her poetry instead in manuscript, whether piecemeal, as in the sonnets conveyed to Bembo by Giovio in 1529–30, or in presentation manuscripts compiled for single individual readers, and presented as gifts.[165] Even the offer of Bembo in 1538 to personally oversee an edition of her verse could not persuade her to relent on this point.[166]

If Colonna's reluctance to engage with the press is combined with a marked interest in the manuscript diffusion of her verse among a select coterie of readers, Veronica Gambara seems, by contrast, to have regarded the fate of her poetry with something like a genuine unconcern. Like Colonna, Gambara explicitly rejected the suggestion that she might consider publishing her verse in a printed edition, airily dismissing her writings as foolish scribblings (*sciocchezze*) unworthy of being brought to public notice.[167] The absence of authorized manuscript editions of Gambara's verse suggests that her dismissiveness may not have been feigned, although a letter to Bembo of 1540 suggests that she was sometimes prepared to condone the manuscript dissemination of individual sonnets.[168] This resulted in a distinctly less compact diffusion pattern than we find in the case of most salient female poets of the Italian Cinquecento, with the exception of the Sienese Virginia Martini Salvi (fl. 1551–71) who remains without a collected edition down to our own day. Although quite substantial selections of Gambara's verse were published in anthologies from 1545 onward, and her youthful love poetry continued to enjoy a significant musical *fortuna,* the first edition of her collected poetry outside an anthological context had to wait until 1759.[169]

## 5. Founding Mothers, First Ladies: Gambara and Colonna as Models and Icons

As we have seen, part of Gambara's and Colonna's importance within the present narrative lies in their efficacy as exemplars for future women writers. There was an ethical dimension to this role, as well as a literary one: here were two universally acclaimed female poets who had successfully combined the pursuit of literary excellence with a flawless moral character, thus establishing the respectability of literature as an appropriate activity for women. The dynamic of emulation set in train by their example is well captured in a sonnet of tribute by the Modenese poet Lucia Dell'Oro Bertani (1521–67), which posits Gambara and Colonna (the latter introduced under her title as marchioness of Pescara) as the modern equivalents of the ancient Sappho and Corinna, whose authorizing role they have inherited along with their poetic laurels:

> Ebbe l'antica e gloriosa etade
> Saffo e Corinna, che con dotte piume
> s'alzaro insino al bel celeste lume
> per molte, degne, e virtuose strade.
> Or due, che allor il crin cinge e bontade
> non pur fan d'Aganippe nascer fiume,
> ma spengono ogni falso e rio costume
> con opre eccelse, eterne, uniche e rade;
> tal che l'alta lor fama i pregi ingombra
> de le due prime; e 'n questa e quella parte
> sonar si sente Gambara e Pescara.
> Quest'alme illustri son cagion che ogni arte
> tento per torre alla mia luce l'ombra
> sol perché al mondo un dì si mostri chiara.[170]

[The glorious age of antiquity had Sappho and Corinna, who with their learned pens (punning on the secondary sense of "feathers" or wings") rose to the lovely light of the heavens by many worthy and virtuous routes. Now two ladies, whose locks are crowned with laurel and goodness not only make Aganippe gush forth once more but extinguish every false and wrongful habit with their splendid, eternal, unique and rare deeds. In this way their lofty fame outshines that of the two who preceded them, and all around the names of Gambara and Pescara sound. These illustrious souls are the cause that makes me try all arts to bring out my light (punning on

her name "Lucia") from the shadows, all so that one day it may shine forth
to the world.]

Notable here is the motif, which we have seen numerous times before, of
the female writer as emblem of the revival of antiquity; by the time we
come to the tercets of the poem, indeed, Gambara and Colonna are presented as not only equaling the glories of Sappho and Corinna but as outdoing them. Similar emphases are found in an important passage of Rinaldo Corso's biography of Veronica Gambara, written after her death and
published in 1556 along with a biography of her husband, which stresses
Gambara's position of discipleship to Bembo and locates her as doyenne
to a new feminine poetic tradition parallel to the masculine tradition
headed by Bembo.[171] Corso concludes by identifying the coincidence of
two such poetic luminaries as Bembo and Gambara as one of the great
claims to glory of the present age, which he defines as "golden" ("aurea")
in many respects but further bejeweled by this crowning fact.[172] Corso's
assessment of the merit of his epoch is not explicitly comparative, but a
comparative ranking is implied by the adjective "golden": this is an age that
exceeds other less glorious ones by virtue of the richness of its poetic tradition and especially by virtue of the remarkable fact that this tradition incorporates women as authors alongside men.

A further, particularly revealing, instance of this type of comparative
rhetoric is found in an anonymous commemorative oration delivered in
the Florentine Academy in 1547, shortly after Colonna's death. The tribute
parallels that accorded a few weeks earlier to Bembo, whose passing had
been mourned in the Academy by his disciple Benedetto Varchi, one of the
leading *letterati* of Florence.[173] The oration for Colonna, unusually, takes
the form of a commentary on a sonnet in praise of its subject ("Pur n'ha
la morte dispietata e rea" ["So Cruel and Pitiless Death Has [Deprived the
World"]).[174] The author of the sonnet, like that of the oration, is unidentified, and it is possible that they are the same man. The Florentine oration
is of great interest for the purposes of the present study in that it combines
an appreciation of Colonna with a more general reflection on the cultural
significance of women's writing and the figure of the woman writer. The
text begins with a general consideration of the present state of culture, cast
in terms reminiscent of the preface to Machiavelli's *Discorsi* and similarly
taking to task those who would condemn the modern age to a congenital
state of inferiority with regard to the glories of antiquity. As examples of
the ability of the moderns to rival the attainments of the ancients in arms,
the author cites Giovanni de' Medici ("Giovanni delle Bande Nere") (1498–
1526), the dashing condottiere father of the Duke of Florence, Cosimo I;

in the field of letters, meanwhile, it is the recently deceased Bembo who is singled out as his primary example, although the speaker's references to Ariosto as Virgilian imitator and to Varchi as "our modern Florentine Cicero" serve to reinforce and generalize the point.[175] The speaker's clinching example of the modern era's claim to excellence is, however, the attainments of its women, culminating in Colonna, who is presented as simultaneously embodying the intellectual and artistic genius of a Sappho or Corinna and the moral exemplarity of a Penelope or Lucretia. The use of both Greek and Roman examples in describing Colonna's excellence is strategic. As the speaker notes, "there was great competition for dominance between these two peoples." Nonetheless, as we learn, these great cultures succeeded only in producing women who excelled in the arts (Greece) *or* women who shone by virtue of their moral qualities (Rome), not a woman like Colonna, "no less excellent in the philosophic disciplines and in poetry than remarkable for the fortitude of her spirit and her chastity."[176] The implication is clear: that just as a Sappho or a Lucretia must bow to a woman who can combine their admirable qualities, so the competing ancient cultures that generated them must yield to the culture that could give birth to a Vittoria Colonna.

Up to this point, aside from its geographically particularized treatment of the topos of ancient female virtue, there is nothing particularly novel in the reasoning of the oration. More distinctive is the comparison the author makes between Colonna and Petrarch's Laura, again to the benefit of Colonna. The greatest praise that Petrarch—"the great weaver of amorous verses"—could say of Laura was that she miraculously combined in her person the apparently inimical qualities of beauty and chastity.[177] "He could not, however," the orator goes on to note, "praise her in all honesty for her knowledge of the most holy sciences of natural philosophy and theology, as one can praise our glorious Marchesa. Nor, above all, could he praise her skill in the most divine art of poetry, as our Venetian Petrarch [Bembo] did so beautifully when he said admiringly of her: 'Cingi le costei tempie dell'amato' . . . "[178] The observation is interesting in several regards. In one respect, it simply continues the previous theme of *translatio studii*, adding the age of Petrarch to the list of eras superseded by the present age (a gesture of some assertiveness in itself, considering that Bembo himself had posited Petrarch as a virtually insuperable ideal). At the same time, however, it serves in several ways quite lucidly to define key differences between these two phases of the vernacular lyric tradition: the change in its thematic center of gravity from the amorous to the epideictic / occasional—"Cingi le costei tempie" and the other two sonnets by Bembo to Colonna cited in the text are poems of respectful tribute, not love—and the transition from an exclusively masculine to a bigendered poetic culture. The muse figure defined here for sixteenth-century lyric poetry is one who combines beauty and chastity with intellectual range and cultural competence, in a manner that reflects flatteringly on the refinement and broad-mindedness of the poet. Modernity is defined, in a manner typical of this era, in terms of an attitude to female *virtù*: Bembo's superseding of Petrarch is certified here through the intellectual superiority of his "muse." The cultural dynamic captured here is one that will be important in the following chapter, as we move on to look at Gambara's and Colonna's successors of the 1540s–60s. If female poets flourished in this period as in almost no other, it was in large part because of their utility as "modern Lauras," sharing with previous poetic love objects their role as generators of verse and emblems of poetic inspiration but asserting their superiority and modernity in their novel capacity to "speak back."[179]

❀ ❀ ❀ ❀

# CHAPTER THREE

# DIFFUSION

## (1540–1560)

❀

### 1. Manuscript and Print in the "Age of the Council of Trent"

Out with the old, in with the new. Only months after the Florentine Academy had assembled to take leave of Colonna, the first secular poetic collection by a woman other than Colonna to be published was brought out by Gabriele Giolito in Venice, under the title of *Rime della Signora Tullia di Aragona et di diversi a lei* (1547). The author, the famed courtesan Tullia d'Aragona (1510–56), was stationed in Florence at the time of publication and counted among her literary acquaintance many of the academicians of that city who had gathered to hear the valedictory oration for Colonna; indeed, in a second work of d'Aragona's, also published in 1547, the *Dialogo dell'infinità d'amore,* we see the author in conversation with the man proudly described in the Colonna oration as "our modern Cicero," the poet and critic Benedetto Varchi.[1] It is hard to believe that the timing of these two publications, so shortly after Colonna's death, was fortuitous. With Colonna's disappearance, the world of Italian publishing was bereft of its figurehead female author, and the search for a successor appears to have been intense: besides d'Aragona, a second new author, the Neapolitan Laura Terracina, appeared the following year, also published by Giolito. Terracina's *Rime* proved a notable publishing success, and subsequent volumes by her followed with remarkable rapidity; by 1550, she had four volumes of verse in print, including an intriguing ottava rima *Discorso* (1549), reworking the *proemi* of Ariosto's *Orlando furioso*.[2] Both Terracina and d'Aragona were identified by their admirers quite explicitly as heirs to

Colonna. A sonnet in Terracina's *Rime seconde* of 1549 by Francesco Ferosi hails her as equal to the "lofty Vittoria" ("alta Vittoria") and rejoices in the renascence of Parnassus, which had been "horrid, neglected, and bleak" ("orrido, inculto, ed ermo") since Vittoria's death.[3] Similar themes are found in Terracina's *Discorso,* in a sonnet by Giovanni Cervoni da Colle (1508–c. 1582), who laments the loss of the "noble column" ("gentil colonna") but goes on present her successor Terracina as a "greater gift" ("maggior don") to the world than Colonna herself.[4] More assertive still, not to say hubristic, is a sonnet in d'Aragona's *Rime* by Benedetto Arrighi, which positions Colonna as pale predecessor "moon" to d'Aragona's glorious "sun."[5]

Despite the eagerness of Terracina's and d'Aragona's poetic admirers to dress them in Colonna's distinguished mantle, we are most likely today to be struck by the distance that separates these poets of the newer generation from Colonna and from her fellow poetic role model Veronica Gambara, who is also respectfully referenced by both.[6] The difference in status and lifestyle is perhaps most immediately obvious. Tullia d'Aragona may have claimed descent from the ex-royal dynasty of Naples as a self-declared natural daughter of Cardinal Luigi d'Aragona (1474–1519), but she was in practice a courtesan of disputed birth, dependent for her living on her wits.[7] Terracina, meanwhile, was an impoverished gentlewoman eking out a living on the margins of Neapolitan aristocratic society, seeking patronage from women of the exalted rank to which Colonna had herself belonged.[8] A further difference, clearly related, between these writers and their aristocratic predecessors was their attitude to print. Where, as we have seen, Colonna fastidiously disdained the public circulation of her work through print, and Veronica Gambara affected a complete lack of interest in the fate of her poetic "trifles," Terracina's and d'Aragona's careers are marked by no such reticence. True, in Terracina's earliest volumes and in d'Aragona's *Dialogo,* the authors' modesty is carefully shielded by having the works introduced by male intermediaries, who present the project of print publication as having originated with them.[9] These modesty frames may be reasonably dismissed as mere gestures, however: all available evidence suggests that both authors collaborated willingly in the publication of their works, and certainly the resulting works are highly calculated exercises in authorial self-fashioning and self-promotion. Especially noteworthy is the inclusion in both d'Aragona's and Terracina's verse collections of substantial sections devoted to poetry in praise of the author: a feature highlighted in d'Aragona's title *Rime della Signora Tullia d'Aragona et di diversi a lei* (*Verses by Signora Tullia d'Aragona and by Others Addressed to Her*).[10] Terracina's editions also include engraved profile portraits of the

poet, in a manner perhaps inspired by the inclusion of images of the author in late editions of Colonna. Where Colonna's "portrait" is generic and
perfunctory, however—a kneeling, nun-like figure, intended as a cipher of
piety—Terracina's has an air of having been taken from life and seems calculated to answer readerly curiosities aroused by the many references in
her admirers' verse to her beauty.[11]

Given the sharpness of these generational differences, it would be
tempting to take the new, print-savvy model of female poet embodied,
in their very different ways, by Terracina and d'Aragona as representative
of the new age. As was noted in the introduction to this study, Carlo
Dionisotti's classic essay on "Italian Literature in the Age of the Council of
Trent" posits a close connection between Italian sixteenth-century wom-
en's writing and print culture, seeing the great age of women's writing as
coinciding with an extraordinary moment in the history of vernacular literature, in the 1540s and 50s, when the Venetian publishing industry, strong
from a period of technological and commercial innovation, began to reach
out aggressively to the new public opened up by the expansion of literacy
and the falling price of books.[12] As Dionisotti notes, this was a period of
remarkable cultural vitality: new products were continually launched and
existing ones "improved," new authors sought out and established classics
repackaged, while the literary middlemen known as *poligrafi*—editors,
agents, translators, as well as writers for the press—who had been a feature of the Venetian publishing scene since the late fifteenth century,
gained an ever-higher public profile as mediators between the presses and
the public.[13] In this volatile, relatively "open," and fiercely commercially
competitive world, a space was created for new voices, including women;
indeed, for Dionisotti, the emergence of women's writing, along with the
rapid expansion of translations from the classics and the explosion in publications in "new" genres such as poetry anthologies and letter collections,
figures as a paradigmatic example of the new, market-led literary culture
enabled by print technology.

There is much that is valuable in Dionisotti's argument, and it is certainly not difficult to trace connections between the worlds of commercial
publishing and women's writing in Italy at this time. It is noteworthy that
both d'Aragona's and Terracina's works of the 1540s were published by the
house of Giolito, the prime mover within the market-led, vernacular-
oriented publishing culture on which Dionisotti's analysis is based.[14] Contacts were close between women writers and *poligrafi* such as Lodovico
Domenichi, Lodovico Dolce (1508–68), and Girolamo Ruscelli (1500–1566).
Along with the Naples-based bookseller and talent scout Marcantonio
Passero, Domenichi seems to have had a hand in the discovery of both Ter-

racina and Chiara Matraini (1515–1604), and he later edited an important anthology of women's poetry, published in Lucca in 1559.[15] Ruscelli, meanwhile, was responsible for the earliest publications of Gaspara Stampa, while Dolce, in association with Passero, was instrumental in publishing both Matraini and Isabella Morra (c. 1515/20–c. 1545).[16] A fourth *poligrafo* closely associated with women's writing in this period was Ortensio Lando, already encountered in chapter 2 as the author of a "paradox" on women's superiority to men. Lando figures as editor of three female-authored works in the 1540s and 1550s: Isabella Sforza's *Della vera tranquillità dell'anima* (1544), the *Lettere* (1552) of Lucrezia Gonzaga da Gazzuolo, and, perhaps most strikingly, the 1548 anthology *Lettere di molte valorose donne,* whose subtitle proclaims itself as proof of women's equality with men in eloquence and learning.[17] With Lando, however, we are on more equivocal territory, where the role of editorial facilitation begins to leach into imposture; in all cases, modern criticism credits Lando with at least partial authorship of these works. The fact is an intriguing one, indicating, among other things, the hunger among publishers for female-authored works in this period, demand for which may very well in the late 1540s have temporarily outstripped supply. Furthermore, if Lando's ventriloquizing of female voices represents something of an extreme case, it is not entirely unrepresentative of the proactive character of editorial "outreach" in this period. Volumes such as d'Aragona's *Rime* and *Dialogo* and Terracina's early volumes were kneaded into being with sufficient energy by these poets' editorial and literary mentors for it to be difficult to account them as fully authorial productions, even by the notably elastic standards of the day.

Given the ample evidence of the close involvement of the *poligrafi* in enabling and soliciting women's literary production, it would clearly be misguided to attempt a history of women's writing in this period without giving due prominence to the impact of print. At the same time, however, it would also be mistaken to dwell too extensively or exclusively on this as a factor. As was noted in the introduction to this volume, the chronological limitations Dionisotti places on the phenomenon of women's writing are misleading to the extent that he represents it as a local feature of the "age of the Council of Trent." In fact, as we have already seen, women's writing was already fairly well established within manuscript culture well before the impact of early publications of Colonna's verse began to be felt in the 1540s. Besides the figures mentioned in chapter 2, poets active in the 1520s and 1530s include the prolific, Milan-based Ippolita Clara (1487–1540), author of a substantial *canzoniere* as well as a partial translation of the *Aeneid,* and the singer Barbara Raffacani Salutati in Florence, known for

her musical collaboration with Machiavelli in the production of his come-
dies in 1525–26.[18] It seems likely also that it was at this time that Siena began to emerge as a significant locus of female literary activity, under the
stimulus of the republic's cultural contacts with Naples, which ensured the
early manuscript circulation there of Colonna's verse.[19] Dionisotti's much-
quoted image of the 1538 publication of Colonna's *Rime* as the spark that
ignited sixteenth-century women's writing is therefore misleading, just as
his underlying metaphor of the phenomenon as a wildfire (*fuoco di paglia*)
underestimates its historical duration.[20] Rather than allocating print the
kind of primary constitutive role that has often been attributed to it within
the history of Italian women's writing, we need to conceive of its role in a
more complex and articulated manner, better figured, perhaps, in terms of
smoldering continuities than as brilliant and sudden flarings-up. In the period we are looking at in this chapter, approximately 1547–60, alongside
fully paid-up denizens of the "Gutenburg galaxy," such as Terracina, it is
quite possible still to find women who acquired fame as poets without publishing or seeking to publish their verse; indeed, this continued to be the
norm, rather than the exception, especially within the aristocratic elites.
Even a figure like Tullia d'Aragona cannot be accounted a creation of print
culture without some distortion. D'Aragona was in her late thirties at the
time when her *Rime* and *Dialogo* were published and already demonstrably
active as a poet by the 1530s, following the precedent of courtesans of her
mother's generation, such as the famous Imperia (d. 1511), recorded by Bandello as capable of "not unskilfully composing the occasional sonnet or
madrigal."[21]

   This point is important, as an overemphasis on print culture as the primary context for the emergence of women's writing can lead to distortions
of perspective. The vast majority of critical work on women's writing
in the mid-sixteenth century has been concentrated on five authors who
published single-authored collections of verse: Terracina, d'Aragona, Matraini, Stampa, and Laura Battiferra (1523–89). While these five writers differ widely in their output and social profile, one negative factor unites
them: none unproblematically reflect the aristocratic model of the female
poet represented in the previous generation by Colonna, Gambara, or Camilla Scarampa. Closest to this model among these figures is undoubtedly
Battiferra, author of a volume of poetry published in Florence in 1560 and
the legitimized "natural" daughter of a high-placed cleric at the papal
court, originally from Urbino.[22] Battiferra's genteel background undoubtedly gave her an entrée to elite circles that a less well-placed writer would
have envied. She cannot, however, be straightforwardly positioned as an
aristocratic poet on the model of a Gambara or a Scarampa, not least be-

cause, probably on account of her illegitimacy, she was not married to a man of her own natal rank, but rather to two "new men"—respectively a musician and an artist—whose status depended on their talents.[23] Laura Terracina, as we have seen, also had claims to gentility but held a fairly marginal place within the category of gentlewomen: tellingly, she remained unmarried until late in life, probably her forties, finally marrying a relative, Polidoro Terracina.[24] The writers under discussion most remote from the aristocratic model were Matraini and Stampa, both from backgrounds without even the trammeled claims to nobility of a figure like Terracina or the debatable ones of a Tullia d'Aragona. Matraini came from a family of wealthy and ambitious *popolani* in Lucca, who had lost their position in the city following an involvement with an aborted uprising in 1531. By the time she published her verse, she was a widow of middle rank, with few, if any, connections with the city's patrician elite.[25] Stampa was the daughter of a Paduan jeweler who died early and was brought up by her mother in Venice. She led an irregular life by the standards of the day, mixing mainly with a cosmopolitan circle of musicians and writers associated with the press and conducting a well-publicized sexual affair outside marriage with an aristocrat from the Venetian mainland, Collaltino da Collalto (1523–69). Whether or not she was actually a courtesan, as has been suggested, Stampa's lifestyle was probably comparable with that of a *cortigiana onesta* such as Tullia d'Aragona, though it is questionable whether she enjoyed quite the aristocratic contacts that d'Aragona or a later courtesan like Veronica Franco could boast.[26]

Such were the lives and backgrounds of the women most familiar to us as writers from this period. As will be apparent, they collectively illustrate very clearly the diffusion of the practice of women's writing through society: we can detect here on a more marked scale the same pattern of downward dissemination that was noted in chapter 1 in the case of humanistic Latin in the 1480s and 1490s, with figures like Laura Cereta and Cassandra Fedele. Other female writers in this period from modest backgrounds include Francesca Baffo, briefly lionized in the early 1540s within the same Venetian circles that later championed Stampa; Ippolita Mirtilla, a poetic acquaintance of Stampa's, sometimes, like Baffo and Stampa, identified as a courtesan; and the Florentine Laura Pieri, active in the mid-1550s, a figure who seems to have escaped all critical scrutiny to date.[27] Interesting as it is to note the emergence of these "new voices," however, we should not deceive ourselves that they represented a prevalent model, even in this period. Writing remained, for women, overwhelmingly an aristocratic pastime, and it was still aristocratic female poets who received the greatest share of critical recognition at this time. If we go beyond the

limited picture of sixteenth-century lyric production offered by single-
authored published books, we find the names of numerous aristocratic female poets emerging, many better known and more celebrated in their
lifetime than figures like Matraini and Stampa.[28] A representative selection
of a dozen such writers, illustrative of the geographic range of women's
writing in this period, are, from Piedmont, Leonora Ravoira Falletti; from
Bergamo, in Venetian Lombardy, Isotta Brembati Grumelli (c. 1530–1586 /
87) and Lucia Albani Avogadro (the latter of whom moved to Brescia on
her marriage); from Mantua (though moving to Piacenza on her marriage), Camilla Valenti del Verme (c. 1523–44); from Cremona, Partenia
Gallerati Mainoldi (c. 1526–71); from Siena, Laodomia Forteguerri (1515–
55), Aurelia Petrucci (1511–42), and Virginia Salvi (the latter resident in
Rome from around the 1540s); from Lazio, Ersilia Cortese del Monte
(1529–after 1587); from Naples, Costanza d'Avalos Piccolomini (1501–?1575)
and Dianora Sanseverino de Mendoza (d. 1581), and from Basilicata, within
the Neapolitan cultural sphere, Isabelle Morra. All these women were
from distinguished backgrounds, and many were titled, either by birth or
by marriage: d'Avalos and Cortese were duchesses, Sanseverino a marchioness, Falletti and Brembati countesses, Albani a *cavaliera,* while Isabella
Morra descended from baronial families on both her father's and mother's
sides.[29] Camilla Valenti, meanwhile, was a niece of Veronica Gambara
through her mother Violante, Veronica's sister, and Aurelia Petrucci a descendent of the family that had ruled Siena from 1487 to 1524. Aside from
Camilla Valenti and Partenia Gallerati, both known mainly as Latinists
rather than vernacular poets, verse by all of these women may be encountered in print, in the poetic anthologies that proliferated at this time.[30]
All, however, maintained a distance from the presses themselves, keeping
to the protocol observed by Vittoria Colonna and Veronica Gambara: at
most, they might discreetly accede to a request from a known *letterato* to
contribute a sonnet to a select, invitation-only commemorative verse collection.[31] It seems implausible to see the writing of women like this as in
any very concrete sense stimulated or solicited by print; rather, in writing
verse, they were adopting an activity already established among culturally
ambitious noblewomen earlier in the century and recently given authoritative sanction by the example of Colonna and Gambara. It is not even
clear that most of the poets listed above would necessarily have needed the
medium of print to become acquainted with Colonna's and Gambara's
verse. Even leaving aside Camilla Valenti, who was Gambara's niece, and
Costanza d'Avalos, Colonna's cousin by marriage, we can conjecture with
some certainty that Laodomia Forteguerri, probably active as a poet by the
late 1530s, became acquainted with Colonna's poetry by manuscript trans-

mission, as did, very probably, Isotta Brembati, given that a member of the Brembati clan is credited by Girolamo Ruscelli with supplying him with an important Colonna manuscript in 1558.[32]

A vivid sense of the "hidden iceberg" represented by aristocratic women's writing in this period may be had by considering the fortuitously well-documented case of Lucia Albani of Brescia. Albani's place in the sixteenth-century published record is distinctly modest: two of her poems were published by Ruscelli in a collection of verse by notable Brescian poets in 1553 and a further two in a tribute volume published in 1561 to commemorate the death of the young Friulian noblewoman and artist Irene di Spilimbergo (1540–59). These are hardly representative, however, of the scope of Albani's oeuvre, which includes a fairly substantial body of youthful love poetry that survives in a manuscript copied posthumously under the direction of a proud relative in around the 1570s or 1580s.[33] Albani also wrote in Latin—a sole poem in that language, addressed to a patrician lady of Venice, survives in a manuscript in the Biblioteca Marciana—and was the author, around 1560, of a vernacular philosophical dialogue, now lost.[34] Details of Albani's literary activities of the late 1550s and early 1560s are recorded in the unpublished letters of her distant relative and literary acquaintance, the Venetian lawyer and poet Pietro Gradenigo (d. 1580), known now mainly as the son-in-law of Pietro Bembo through his marriage to Bembo's daughter Elena.[35] Perhaps mindful of the precedent of his father-in-law's relationship with Colonna and Gambara, Gradenigo shows himself notably supportive of Albani's literary aspirations and active in circulating her work among his literary circles in Venice, which included poets of the distinction of Domenico Venier (1517–82) and Girolamo Molin (1500–56).[36] It is clear from Gradenigo's letters that it was he who solicited Albani to contribute to the Spilimbergo volume, holding out to her as a lure the participation of other "honored and illustrious ladies."[37] We also find him, after the publication of the volume, embarrassedly commiserating with her over the "presumptuous" editorializing to which her poems appear to have been subjected in the process.[38] The sequence offers a rare glimpse of the channels through which aristocratic women's writings parsimoniously filtered out into the public universe of print, as well as, perhaps, some indication of the reasons why many remained reluctant to embrace this distastefully "promiscuous" medium. Family tragedy and premature death put an end to Albani's literary career not long after the appearance of the Spilimbergo volume, so it is uncertain whether, had she continued writing, she would have sought further print exposure or would rather have contented herself with the coterie fame she enjoyed through manuscript dissemination of her works.[39] The latter seems more proba-

ble, and not simply on account of a particular "feminine" modesty or reticence. Of her immediate Venetian readership, neither Venier nor Molin
sought to publish his collected verse in his lifetime; nor, indeed, did Gradenigo himself.[40]

The writings of aristocratic poets like these have received little critical
study by comparison with those of more print-friendly poets such as Tullia d'Aragona and Laura Terracina, partly because of the thinness of their
surviving oeuvre in most cases and partly, perhaps, because of an uncon-
scious prejudice that sees publication as an index of merit.[41] The most notable exception to this critical trend is Isabella Morra, whose miniature *canzoniere* of thirteen poems has sustained a remarkable concentration of
scholarly attention, partly stimulated by her tragically isolated life and violent death (she was murdered at the hands of her brothers).[42] Further
critical work in this area would certainly be desirable, not least because it
would provide a fuller context against which the writings of the better-
known poets of the era might be plotted. The point can be made simply
by considering the theme of love. The most-studied text by a woman of
this period is, by a long measure, Gaspara Stampa's *Rime* of 1554, which is
largely erotic in content, recounting the poet's unhappy affair with her
lover Collalto in an inspired reworking of Petrarch's *Rime sparse*.[43] Less co-
piously studied, but still firmly within the modern canon of women's writing, is Chiara Matraini's similarly narrative *Rime e prose* of 1555, which tracks
the same Petrarchan master text more faithfully—though via the filter of
Colonna's authoritative feminine transcription—telling of the poet's reciprocated love for a man whose death tragically bisects the work.[44] Both
works have been justly celebrated in modern criticism for the distinctness
of their voice and the originality of their reworking of Petrarchan tradition. The intensity of the critical attention that has been focused on
Stampa, in particular, has also had the effect of conferring on her a paradigmatic status; implicitly or explicitly, she is often posited in critical literature as epitomizing the predicament of the Italian Renaissance female
poet in her attempt to appropriate a poetic language elaborated by and for
men.

What critical discussions of the poetry of Stampa and Matraini often
fail to recognize, however, is quite how unusual these two writers were
among the female poets of this era in adopting erotic love as such a salient
theme. If we survey the verse of the aristocratic poets just cited, or leaf
through the pages of Domenichi's aristocratically biased 1559 anthology, it
is immediately striking how little love poetry we find.[45] This is not to say
that erotic writings by aristocratic female poets are completely unknown:
Virginia Salvi writes frequently on amorous themes, as does Leonora Fal-

letti, while Lucia Albani's poetic juvenilia are largely devoted to melancholy love poetry reminiscent of Veronica Gambara's early verse.[46] The vast majority of surviving poems by aristocratic women in this period, however, keep to the formula established by the mature Gambara and, to a lesser extent, by Colonna, with occasional and correspondence verse dominating, flanked by *rime spirituali* and high-minded meditations on political and moral themes.[47] One great advantage of this thematic formula was, of course, that it evaded all potential scruples relating to gender decorum, the poetic persona projected attractively combining the traditional feminine prerequisite of introspective piety with the newer demand of poised social engagement. Interestingly, this model of poetic self-fashioning seems to have been considered sufficiently "decent" to have been embraced by at least one nun, Girolama Castellani (fl. 1551) of Bologna, who figures as a poet alongside her secular counterparts in Domenichi's anthology.[48] It is interesting to note that, of the five authors whose verse was published in this period outside an anthology context, those closest socially to the model of the aristocratic female poet may also be seen as adhering to this formula. This is the case very notably of Laura Battiferra, whose *Rime* exclude love, beyond a few chaste statements of marital devotion. It is also true of Laura Terracina: even though the latter includes examples of erotic verse in her earliest volume of *Rime,* these are distanced from any autobiographical purchase by being grammatically framed as male utterances, thus safely consigning them to the status of formal exercises in poetic ventriloquism.[49] Even Tullia d'Aragona, in her *Rime* of 1547, presents herself overwhelmingly as an occasional poet, although her collection comprehends a small, though structurally important, nucleus of poems of sensual love.[50]

This background is illuminating when we return to consider the poetry of Gaspara Stampa and Chiara Matraini, the unusualness of whose thematic and formal choices in their collections should by now be fully apparent. While Petrarch's *Rerum vulgarium fragmenta* remained a vastly important model for mid-sixteenth-century lyric poetry linguistically and stylistically, in other respects, it had been largely superseded. Male, as well as female, writers had by this point more or less abandoned the Petrarchan model of a love *canzoniere* narrating a sole erotic trajectory for the less solipsistic and more dispersive model of verse collection evolved with such success by Bembo. It is an intriguing fact that the two female writers who used the now faintly archaic form of the Petrarchan erotic *canzoniere* in this period were the two who fitted least comfortably with the customary social profile of a poet of their sex and who were thus least equipped to participate to the full in the literary culture of their day. In Matraini's case, at least, we might conjecture that the choice of an ur-Petrarchan form for her verse was partly the result of her cultural isolation; certainly, stationed as she was in provincial Lucca and in a somewhat marginal social position, she was hardly well placed to essay the worldly and dialogic model of verse *raccolta* fashionable in the midcentury, which effectively constructs the poet's identity through his or her social contacts, laid glitteringly out in sequence as in a virtual salon. Stampa's situation is more complex, and there is evidence that she may, by the end of her life, have been attempting to reposition herself socially as a poet by putting together a collection of occasional verse that would have served as her calling card to the broader polite literary world.[51] If that conjecture is correct, however, she could hardly have done so without the consciousness that she was operating from a position of relative weakness by comparison with more entitled contemporaries who had more impressive address books at their command.

These considerations do not, of course, detract from the artistic interest of Stampa's love poetry or that of Matraini; on the contrary, as with Laura Cereta in the previous century, these poets' social "otherness" may well have contributed to the originality that so attracts readers today. It does mean, however, that we should be wary of seeing them as representative or of generalizing from their case. This is particularly important in regard to the question of women's relationship to literary tradition. Readings of women's poetry in this period that take Stampa as paradigmatic tend very often to present that relationship as embattled and indigent. The female poet is pitted against a masculine literary code that gives space to female figures only as silent, idolized objects, and her task is to attempt to craft a voice for herself, unassisted, from the reworked fragments of an alien language. This model works well enough when we apply it to poets who took the Petrarchan love lyric as their primary model, but it is useful to remember that the majority of female poets would not have experienced their relationship with poetic tradition in quite the same way. Petrarchist occasional and correspondence verse as it developed after Bembo was not as intrinsically "masculine" as a tradition as the love lyric; on the contrary, as we have seen, it was one to which women had stood as godmothers, in the person of Colonna and Gambara. Nor was it a tradition of lyric that saw female poets exclusively in conversation with controlling Pygmalion-like male admirers; rather, the poetic correspondence between Colonna and Gambara we saw in the last chapter had established an authoritative model for poetic exchange between women. The tradition of Petrarchizing *rime spirituali,* meanwhile, offered an arena in which female poets might feel a still greater sense of "belonging," given Colonna's widely acknowledged status as founder of the genre. It is misleading, then, extrapolating from the case of a figure like Stampa, to see female poets as inevitably working from a position of extreme discursive disentitlement. Levels of entitlement, rather, varied, depending not simply on gender but also, crucially, on the factor of status. Chiara Matraini prefaces her 1555 *Rime* with a letter addressed to a putative male critic who has pointed out to her the indecorum of the practice of poetry for a woman "not born of the highest blood, nor raised within the most splendid palaces, among copious and most abundant riches."[52] Matraini's letter offers a spirited defense, but her critic's point reflects a widespread and enduring social prejudice. Print culture may have enabled the practice of women's writing to filter down through society to the unwonted reaches of bourgeois Lucca, but its true locus remained, in the eyes of many contemporaries, the "most splendid palaces" in which it had always belonged.[53]

## 2. *Virtù* Rewarded: The Contexts of Women's Writing

As we have seen, women's writing in the middle years of the sixteenth century displays a great deal more continuity with the earlier sixteenth-century manuscript tradition than has sometimes been acknowledged. Rather than regarding this period as marking an abrupt and absolute departure, we should perhaps regard the years of Dionisotti's "euphoric" expansion of print culture as important for our purposes because they saw the widespread diffusion of cultural attitudes and practices that had already evolved within elite circles in the early part of the century. As we have seen in earlier chapters, a new, humanistically inflected philogynistic culture had grown up in the secular princely courts of Italy from the fifteenth century onward, gaining strength and definition in the sixteenth with the rise of vernacular literature. Within the courts, from early in the century, a gallant attitude to women was a virtual prerequisite for establishing a man's claims to gentility, and women were allocated a crucial symbolic role as the ideal audience for vernacular court culture. By the late 1520s, some of the key works of court culture—Castiglione's *Cortegiano* and the poetry of Bembo and Sannazaro—were finally becoming available in printed versions, and the set of cultural attitudes and literary practices that had matured in court circles was beginning to attain a degree of diffusion. The decades that followed, especially the 1540s and 1550s, saw a further, unstoppable process of expansion. The classics of early sixteenth-century court literature—Ariosto, Castiglione, Bembo—poured from the presses in these years in innumerable editions, and much of the new literature of the time reworked these texts' themes and forms in a less chiseled and more ephemeral manner. Many of the values and attitudes of court culture were carried into the new literature, even when it was being scrabbled together at speed by overworked *poligrafi* in Venice. Even exceptions, such as the famously scurrilous Pietro Aretino (1492–1556), may be seen as in some sense confirming the rule in that his countercultural persona presupposes for its impact the polite authorial ethos it subverts. In any case, Aretino and his followers are far less representative of the dominant tone of their culture than such disciples of Bembo as Lodovico Dolce or Benedetto Varchi. Nor were Aretino's followers always consistent in their rejection of polite modes: we find, for example, the satirist and occasional pornographer Niccolò Franco (1515–70) capable, when required, of turning in a work as impeccably "polite" as his *Dialogo dove si ragiona delle bellezze* (1542), set at the small court of Casale Monferrato and featuring a flattering portrait of the noblewoman Bona Soardi di San Giorgio. Mainstream vernacular literature of the period was to an overwhelming extent self-consciously elegant and courtly in manner: Bembo and Castiglione served in this period as models of authorial ethos as much as of linguistic correctness and literary style. The difference lay in the fact that aristocratic attitudes were now routinely being appropriated by those with no "natural" or ascriptive status entitlement. The figure of the courtesan was here prototypical; hence, perhaps, her centrality in the literature of the age.

This is important for us, of course, because among the principal aristocratic signifiers co-opted by the "new" vernacular culture of this era were an attitude of gallantry toward women, and, more broadly, a perception of femininity as generative and emblematic of polite literature. Continuities are most immediately apparent in the quintessentially courtly genre of the "defense of women," which flourished in this period as in no other in Italy. Notable examples of the genre, among works composed in the period, are Vincenzo Maggi's *Brieve trattato dell'eccellentia delle donne* (1545), Domenico Bruni da Pistoia's *Difesa delle donne* (1552), and Luigi Dardano's *La bella e dotta difesa delle donne* (1554), the last of which is ingeniously cast as a series of quasi-judicial orations by famous "women worthies" of antiquity.[54] Highly influential as well were Francesco Coccio's translation of Henricus Cornelius Agrippa's *De nobilitate et praecellentia foeminei sexus* (1544) and Lodovico Domenichi's reworking of the arguments of the same treatise in his dialogue, *La nobiltà delle donne* (1549).[55] These works served to disseminate the theoretical arguments for women's "nobility and excellence" first pieced together by court writers such as Bartolomeo Goggio, Mario Equicola, and Agostino Strozzi in the fifteenth century and also to popularize the historical exempla of exceptional women Boccaccio had begun to collect in *De claris mulieribus*.[56] The Boccaccian exemplary tradition was also given new currency in the elegant 1545 translation of Boccaccio's treatise by the Sienese *poligrafo* Giuseppe Betussi (c. 1515–c. 1573), which adds fifty new lives of modern "illustrious women" to balance Boccaccio's ancients, culminating in a *vita* of Vittoria Colonna, presented as the ultimate modern exemplar of feminine perfection.[57] Betussi's update pointedly revises its fourteenth-century source by limiting its additions to women celebrated on positive grounds, for "some significant achievement arising from greatness of spirit," rather than interpreting its remit broadly enough to encompass also women notorious for vice.[58] As already in the Quattrocento, the names of historical *donne illustri* circulated in this period not only in literary texts but also through visual material of various kinds, including newer media such as historiated majolica and prints, as well as the traditional panel paintings and *cassoni*.[59] One of the most intriguing pieces of evidence of the imaginative appeal these exempla held for sixteenth-century readers is the increasing incidence over the century of the names of classical "women worthies" as Christian names for girls. Some of the most popular, as we might expect, were exempla of chastity (Virginia, Lucretia), or of wifely devotion (Artemisia, Portia, Laodamia), but we also find surprising numbers of girls named after Amazons, not only the safely "domesticated" Hippolyta, but also a less recuperated figure like Penthesilea.[60] Warrior queens such as Zenobia and Sophonisba also fell within the new onomastic reach, as did the armed Roman goddess of wisdom, Minerva, and, more rarely, the Ariostan female knights Bradamante and Marfisa.[61] We may assume that these names were chosen by parents of humanistic or literary bent, and those fired by modern ideals of the "woman of achievement." For this reason, they quite often appear to have been prophetic. Artists and poets of the period bearing such aspirational names include Irene di Spilimbergo, Sofonisba Anguissola (c. 1532–1625), Minerva Bartoli (b. 1562), and Issicratea Monte (1564–?84), as well as Tullia d'Aragona, celebrated by her poetic admirer Niccolò Martelli (1498–1555) as a reincarnation of Cicero, or Tully.[62]

In addition to formal "defenses of women" on the analytic or exemplificatory model, the philogynist literature of the period also encompassed a substantial production of treatises and dialogues on women's physical and spiritual beauty and the beneficial effects of heterosexual love.[63] While this literature is difficult to assimilate to any modern notion of feminism, the beauty discourse, in particular, seeming terminally complicit in the objectification of women, in context, it is clearly to be reckoned on the philogynist side of the *querelle* divide. Misogynist tradition had long cast women as "defect of nature" and as agents, through their sexuality, of degradation and sin. In the face of this tradition, the sixteenth-century Neoplatonically-inflected conceptions of female beauty as a reflection of the divine and of earthly love as a propulsion to spiritual ascent had an important revisionary role. Like so many of the favored genres of mid-sixteenth century literature, the love dialogue and the treatise on beauty had roots in the vernacular literature of the early sixteenth-century courts. Where the former is concerned, important precedents were Bembo's 1505 *Gli Asolani,* Mario Equicola's 1525 *Libro de natura de amore,* and Castiglione's 1528 *Cortegiano,* the last two of which had been circulating in manuscript well before their dates of publication.[64] The most important courtly treatise on female beauty of this period was Giangiorgio Trissino's *I ritratti* (1524) based on an idealized description of Isabella d'Este. In the period under discussion here, important treatises on beauty include Niccolò Franco's *Dialogo dove si ragiona delle bellezze,* Angelo Firenzuola's *Dialogo delle bellezze delle donne* (c. 1542; published 1552), and Federico Luigini's *Libro della bella donna* (1554), while writings on love—frequently cast in the form of dialogues, following the precedent of Bembo and Leone Ebreo, as well as, ultimately, of Plato—include Giuseppe Betussi's *Il Raverta* (1544) and *La Leonora* (1557), Sperone Speroni's *Dialogo d'amore* (1542), and Tullia d'Aragona's *Dialogo dell'infinità d'amore.*[65] Another popular vehicle for love theory was the academic lecture, reflecting the vogue for Neoplatonic theorizing within the literary academies of the time. Noteworthy examples include Alessandro Piccolomini's 1541 *lettura* for the Paduan Accademia degli Infiammati, discussed below, and the five academic lectures by Benedetto Varchi published collectively as *lezzioni d'amore* in the second part of his *Lezzioni* (1561).[66]

Besides this theoretical literature on beauty and love, another popular genre of the age, important for the circulation of philogynist commonplaces, was the encomiastic tribute volume, whether composed for an individual woman, *in vita* or *in morte,* or for the women of a particular city or region. Collections in praise of individuals most frequently took the form of anthologies that collected tributes from a wide range of assiduously solicited poets. Important examples of such "temples" were Girolamo Ruscelli's *Tempio alla divina signora Giovanna d'Aragona* (1554), prototype for the tribute put together for a woman still living, and Dionigi Atanagi's *Rime di diversi nobilissimi et eccellentissimi autori in morte della Signora Irene delle signore di Spilimbergo* (1561) which established the vogue for the postmortem commemorative collection.[67] Many further such volumes followed, in both modes: one study lists eleven from 1563 to the end of the century, without counting manuscript anthologies such as those assembled for the singer Laura Peverara (1550–1601) in the 1570s.[68] By contrast with the multiauthored individual "temple," volumes in praise of the women of a given city were generally the product of a single author, though there are exceptions, such as Muzio Manfredi's *Per donne romane*

(1575). Notable examples of such writings in the period under discussion include Iacopo Campanile's *Opera nuova nomata vero tempio d'amore* (1536)—written in praise of the ladies of Naples but quickly co-opted for Venetian purposes by Niccolò Franco in his plagiarizing *Tempio d'amore* (1536)—and Girolamo Parabosco's *Tempio della fama in lode d'alcune gentil donne veneziane* (1548).[69] While listed here separately for convenience, the various philogynist genres of the age could fuse without difficulty, following a general tendency in the literature of this period toward hybridity of form. A kind of summa of this literature may be seen, for example, in a work by Girolamo Ruscelli of 1552, whose title translates as *Commentary on a Sonnet by the Most Illustrious Lord, the Marquis of Terza, Addressed to the Divine Lady, the Marchioness of Vasto, in Which the Supreme Perfection of Women Is Proved with New and Compelling Arguments. Also Containing Many Observations on the Platonic Scale by Which Created Beings Ascend to the Contemplation of God, and Many More on True Beauty, Grace, and the Vernacular Tongue; and Wherein There Is also Occasion to Name Certain of the Most Outstanding Gentlewomen of the Principal Towns of Italy.*[70] Of interest in this thematic ragbag of modish concerns is the presence of the "vernacular language" as a topic of discussion, alongside the perfection of women and the mysteries of love: though seemingly discrepant, as we saw in chapter 2, this was bound to the themes of femininity and protofeminism by a profound genetic link.

In addition to their prominence as the subject matter of literature—and, increasingly, of course, also as authors—women's role as consumers of literature and as cultural arbiters was also much celebrated in this period. Most immediately, in this regard, we may cite the frequent appearance of women as the dedicatees of literary works. As we might expect, this was particularly common in the case of works dealing with subjects of perceived "women's interest," such as love, beauty, and feminine virtue, although exceptionally one finds works outside these fields being addressed to women, such as Alessandro Piccolomini's astronomical treatises of 1540, *La sfera del mondo* and *Le stelle fisse*, both dedicated to his compatriot Laodomia Forteguerri, or Rinaldo Corso's vernacular grammatical treatise of 1549, dedicated to his future wife Lucrezia Lombardi.[71] Women were frequently the dedicatees of collections of vernacular poetry as well as of editions of vernacular classics; notable examples here are Francesco Sansovino's edition of Boccaccio's *Ameto* (1545), dedicated to Gaspara Stampa, and Antonio Brucioli's 1548 edition of Petrarch's *Sonetti, canzoni, e triumphi*, dedicated to Lucrezia d'Este.[72] We also find dedications to women of classical works translated into the vernacular: examples here include Piccolomini's 1540 translation of Xenophon's *Economia*, dedicated to the Sienese noblewoman Frasia Venturi, Corso's 1566 translation of Virgil's *Eclogues,* dedicated to Ersilia Cortese, and Benedetto's Varchi's 1554 *volgarizzamento* of Seneca's *De beneficiis,* dedicated to Eleonora of Toledo (1522–62), Duchess of Florence.[73] Especially noteworthy in this period was the tradition of dedications to women of translations of Virgil's *Aeneid.* The first was a translation of the second book by Ippolito de' Medici (1511–35) dedicated to Giulia Gonzaga and published in 1539.[74] This was republished the following year, in a multiauthored translation of the first six books, with each book dedicated to a separate lady and with an overall dedication to the Sienese noblewoman Aurelia Tolomei.[75] Six years later, in 1546, Giuseppe Betussi published a translation of the seventh book, dedicated to Collaltina da Collalto, while in 1555 a translation of the seventh and eighth by the obscure Berardino Berardini of Bari came out in Naples with dedications to Isabella and Delia Sanseverino.[76]

In addition to dedications, a further respect in which acknowledgment was frequently made of women's place in Italian cultural conversation was their inclusion as speakers in literary dialogues, a practice that became increasingly common in this period. As so often, writers of the 1540s and 1550s may be seen in this regard as taking their cue from earlier sixteenth-century precedents, in this case the pioneering choices of Bembo (*Asolani*) and Castiglione (*Cortegiano*). As in the case of dedications, women's appearance in dialogues is often constrained to works felt to be thematically appropriate. Thus, we find female speakers in dialogues on beauty, such as Betussi's *Leonora* (Leonora Falletti) and Franco's *Dialogo dove si ragiona delle bellezze* (Bona Soardi di San Giorgio); on love, such as Betussi's *Raverta* (Francesca Baffo), Sperone Speroni's *Dialogo d'amore* (Tullia d'Aragona), and Lattanzio Benucci's unpublished *Dialogo della lontananza* of 1563 (Onorata Tancredi); and on the dignity and nobility of women, such as Speroni's *Dialogo della dignità delle donne* (1542; Beatrice degli Obizzi), and Lodovico Domenichi's *La nobiltà delle donne* (Violante Bentivoglio).[77] Another category in which women feature with a certain frequency are religious dialogues, generally with a reformist coloring: examples here would be Bernardino Ochino's *Dialogi sette* (1542; Caterina Cibo, Duchess of Camerino), Luca Contile's *Dialogi spirituali* (1543; Camilla de' Rossi; Giulia Trivulzio; Camilla di Ricchetta Pallavicini; Virginia Pallavicini Gambara), Juan de Valdés's *Alphabeto christiano* (1545; Giulia Gonzaga), and Ortensio Lando's *Dialogo nel quale si ragiona della consolatione e utilità che si gusta leggendo la sacra Scrittura* (1552; Lucrezia Gonzaga).[78] Rather outside these thematic categories stand Francisco de Hollanda's dialogues on art (1538), which have Vittoria Colonna as an interlocutor along with Michelangelo, and Stefano Maria Ugoni's interesting reform-inflected *Ragionamento* . . .

*dove si ragiona di tutti gli stati dell'humana vita* (1562) featuring Virginia Pallavicini Gambara as one of the speakers.[79] In most of these cases, women appear in mixed company and tend for the most part to take the kind of reticent, enabling part in the conversation familiar from Castiglione's *Cortegiano*. This is not inevitably the case, however: Leonora Falletti takes an unusually assertive role in Betussi's *Leonora,* as does Tullia d'Aragona in Speroni's *Dialogo d'amore* and her own *Dialogo dell'infinità d'amore.*[80] In a considerable novelty, further, two Sienese dialogues of this period, both unpublished until our day, portray conversations taking place in all-female groups. The first, by Marcantonio Piccolomini, on human perfection (1538), includes the poets Laodomia Forteguerri and Frasia Marsi among its speakers, along with Girolama Carli Piccolomini, wife of a *letterato* whose gynephile tendencies are apparent in his dedications.[81] The second, by the reformist Aonio Paleario (c. 1503–c. 1566), on the management of the household (1555), features a less culturally distinguished cast of speakers, though all still from the patrician elite.[82] Again from Siena and also interesting as a counterexample to the rule of female reticence is a dialogue by Marcello Landucci of 1542 set at a Sienese *veglia* (evening gathering), in which an otherwise unidentified *madonna* Atalanta, perhaps Atalanta Donati, entertains a lively mixed company with a virtuoso performance of semiparodic literary commentary, displaying notable articulateness and literary erudition as well as a mastery of deadpan humor.[83]

It is within this relatively "feminized" literary landscape that we need to locate the phenomenon of the diffusion of women's writing in this period. Taken as a whole, this writing had the cumulative effect of reinforcing the sense, already marked in the courtly production of earlier decades, that literature might be considered a natural habitat for women. Treatises on women's "nobility and excellence" argued the case for their intellectual equality with men, and lists of famous classical and modern "learned ladies" supplied role models for aspiring writers. Dedications to women underlined women's judiciousness as cultural interlocutors, as did the appearance of female interlocutors in dialogues, and marked out learning, articulacy, and intellectual curiosity as commendable feminine qualities. At the same time, and through some of the same means, the notion was spreading that feminine respectability was not incompatible with a quest for fame. An exceptionally interesting document of this is the anonymous biography of the young Friulian noblewoman Irene di Spilimbergo that prefaces the verse anthology published in memory of her in 1561 following her tragically early death two years earlier.[84] Irene is portrayed in the *vita* as a multitalented cultural prodigy, turning from poetry to music to art and excelling in all three. A theme that clearly emerges is the epic quality of her

ambition: from her earliest days, we learn, she was "desirous . . . of de-
parting from the common paths of other women," and eager to pursue
enterprises conducive to honor and glory. Competition with others of her
sex is particularly stressed; we are told that Irene was determined that no
woman should outshine her in the arts and that she listened, in consequence, with a "virtuous envy" ("virtuosa invidia") when other women
were praised in her presence.[85] On taking up drawing, under the tutelage
of Titian, Irene's "noble" emulative urge ("generosa emulatione") is so
stirred by seeing a finely executed portrait by the painter Sofonisba Anguissola—the first woman to attain national fame as an artist—that she
cannot rest until she has mastered painting, which she does with miraculous rapidity.[86] What is interesting here is the almost complete absence of
any shade moral reproach for Irene's ambition, even though it is clearly implied that overapplication to her artistic labors contributed to her early
death.[87] On the contrary, she is presented as exemplary, counterbalancing
her "virile" ambition with a feminine grace and modesty of conduct. The
biography concludes with the point that Irene's "singular qualities" fitted
her to be the wife of a prince.[88]

A final detail in Irene's *vita* that is deserving of our attention here is the
account of her earliest education. On account of her precocity, we learn,
she was set at an unusually early age to learn needlework, sententiously
described by the author as "those labors . . . that gentlewomen and high-
born ladies employ to adorn themselves and to flee idleness, the principal
enemy of their sex."[89] In her first sign of greatness, the child Irene swiftly
comes to consider this art a "trivial attainment" ("picciolo acquisto") and
to consider it unworthy of occupying her whole time; on her own initiative, she teaches herself reading and writing.[90] This rejection of traditional
feminine pursuits—and, implicitly, of their moral function as externally
imposed "guards against idleness"—is also found in the peroration of
Giuseppe Betussi's updating of Boccaccio's *De claris mulieribus* (1545), following his climactic life of Vittoria Colonna. Betussi rails against those
women who "throw away their lives in pleasure" instead of devoting themselves, like Colonna, to study, reserving particular scorn for women of the
ruling elite, those "raised in royal palaces, and bearing the name of
princesses or great ladies." How much greater glory these women would
bring on their names, he notes, if instead of "feminine tasks such as ple-
beian women are condemned to by circumstance," they were to devote
themselves rather to "study, to the arts (*virtù*) and letters."[91] This notion
of study and the pursuit of fame as almost a family duty is also found in
Luca Contile's *Dialogi spirituali* where one of the interlocutors, Camilla de'
Rossi, asserts the right of women—"given that we are deprived of almost

all other freedoms"—to at least have the freedom to study, adding that this pursuit "above all other things brings an honorable and remarkable name to their lineage," as well as "no small credit to the feminine condition."[92] Thus we see women, quite explicitly, drawn into the familiar male humanistic discourse of self-elevation through learning and the pursuit of glory, in a manner that confounds traditionalist, Aristotelian conceptions of sex roles.[93] Iconic in this regard is the composite ideal portrait of elite female identity composed in Giuseppe Betussi's *Imagini del tempio della signora Giovanna d'Aragona* of 1556, a follow-up to Girolamo Ruscelli's 1554 tribute volume to the same lady. Betussi's text, one of the most interesting encomiastic constructs of the age, assembles a cast of twenty-four eminent contemporary women, each representing a particular virtue and flanked by a male poetic celebrant in a manner recalling a similar pairing of "muses" and poets in canto 42 of the *Orlando furioso*.[94] The conceit of the work is that these women represent collectively the assembled virtues of the macrosubject of Betussi's encomium, Giovanna d'Aragona, as if in a moral version of the famous classical anecdote of the painter Zeuxis's composition of an "ideal woman" from the assorted elements of the beauties of Croton. The interest of this construct, in the present context, is the mixture it proposes of traditional feminine virtues, such as Modesty, Chastity, Temperance, or Faith, with less expected and more "contemporary" qualities. Notable among the latter are Fame, Glory, and Talent (*Virtù*), represented respectively by the poets Laudomia Forteguerri, Virginia Salvi, and Leonora Falletti.[95] Although the multifaceted feminine ideal celebrated in works such as this and the Spilimbergo *vita* is not new in this period—with her emulative urge and scattergun artistic ambitions, Irene di Spilimbergo might be seen as a miniature Friulian Isabella d'Este—it is certainly in these years that we see this cultural model beginning to trickle down from the highest circles of the Italian aristocracy. Along with a Gonzaga and a Farnese, Betussi includes among his twenty-four virtuous icons women from the minor urban nobility of Siena, Florence, and Modena, while a supplementary list of notable women organized by city and region reinforces this sense of social and geographical spread.[96]

### 3. Women Writers and Their Uses: Case Studies

As earlier chapters of this study have already illustrated, numerous cultural agendas were served by women writers in this period in Italy, many having relatively little to do with women themselves and their desires and ambitions. Most immediately, as we have seen, relationships with women had a notable importance in the self-fashioning of male *letterati*, especially those who strove to excel in vernacular literature. To show deference to women was to show oneself accustomed to moving in the kind of aristocratic circles where women had power and status. This was as important for *poligrafi* like Girolamo Ruscelli and Lodovico Domenichi as it had been of courtiers like Bembo and Castiglione in the previous generation; indeed, one could argue that it was more important for the former as their ascriptive elite status was less assured. A shrewd observation on the cultural dynamic concerned is found in the somewhat unexpected venue of the *Historia monastica* (1561) of the Benedictine monk Pietro Calzolai (1500–1580), in a theoretical preface preceding a collection of encomia of exemplary nuns. Calzolai identifies the urge to praise women's "noble deeds" as the vocation of all "naturally civilized men" ("ogni huomo naturalmente da bene"), adding that such men "consider themselves in praising women at the same time to gain praise for themselves."[97] As Calzolai's formula makes clear, the act of praising women's deeds could in itself be seen as defining of a "huomo da bene," with all that term's attractive connotations of moral decency and social fit. It is this that gives the act of praise its specular and self-referential character in this instance: by praising women, men show themselves to be themselves by definition worthy objects of praise. The more "lofty" the lady praised, moreover, the more flatteringly Calzolai's specular logic operated: hence the appeal of multi-authored tribute volumes such as Ruscelli's or Betussi's for Giovanna d'Aragona, which had the effect of franchising out to a sizeable cluster of poets the borrowed charisma of a scion of the Aragonese royal line. Of course, this self-reflexive praise dynamic was nothing new where encomia of individual women was concerned: Petrarch speaks in one famous poem of "mirroring and burnishing himself" in Laura.[98] What is more novel in this period is the melding of this lyric motif with the broader, courtly ethos of a general gallantry to "the ladies": the sense that, in the words of Bandello, every man's natural duty is to "love, honor, reverence, and celebrate all woman."[99]

Besides the general utility of women in the crafting of male literary personae, female poets had particular uses, serving, not least, in this period, to allow male *letterati* of the generations that came after Bembo to enact their allegiance to the literary and cultural ideals he represented. As we saw at the end of chapter 2, in the context of Vittoria Colonna's funeral tribute in the Accademia Fiorentina, Bembo's poetic novelty was seen, in part, as lying in the new role that women played in his verse, not simply as beautiful objects, or as spiritual inspirations, but as cultured interlocutors and intellectual peers. The poetic friendships Bembo cultivated with Colonna and Veronica Gambara proved an influential and highly imitable

component of his legacy, serving as models, for example, for the relationships with female poets sustained by disciples such as Benedetto Varchi, literary mentor successively to Tullia d'Aragona and Laura Battiferra in Florence in the 1540s and 1550s, and Alessandro Piccolomini, devoted publicist
of Laudomia Forteguerri in Siena and Padua in the 1540s.[100] It is this that
accounts in part for the currency, in all senses, of poetry by women in this
period: Bembo's poetic choices—and, more broadly, the cultural logic that
informed them—had created a demand for the "interactive muse" that the
female educated elite of Italy was eager to supply. It is by thinking about
factors of this kind that we can best begin to account for the extraordinary
success enjoyed by a figure such as Laura Terracina, despite the manifold
artistic deficiencies critics like Croce have denounced with such zeal.[101] As
we have seen, aristocratic female poets tended on the whole in this period
not to publish their writings or to publish them sparingly; to be seen exchanging sonnets in print with a Leonora Falletti or a Lucia Albani was
not a socially easy feat to achieve. Terracina, by contrast, was sufficiently
noble to make the grade as an instrument of social and cultural self-
positioning and yet sufficiently indigent to make herself poetically accessible to potential "admirers" in a way that more securely stationed noblewomen did not. Critics have noted the high proportion of obscure and
unidentifiable figures among Terracina's poetics interlocutors in successive books of her *Rime,* suggesting that these served as relatively "low-rent"
routes to a social-cultural ratification not easily available elsewhere.

Besides these factors, others need to be considered if we are to attain a
full understanding of the cultural functions performed by the literate
woman in this period. As earlier in the century, an affirmative attitude toward women as readers and writers remained in this period a means of displaying one's commitment to the vernacular. This was less important than
it had been within fields such as lyric poetry and narrative, where the
*volgare*'s battle for position had already been won. It remained vital, however, in those areas of cultural practice where Latin remained dominant,
including, very notably, philosophy and science. Gestures such as Piccolomini's dedication to Laodomia Forteguerri of vernacular scientific treatises such as his *La sfera del mondo* or his moral-educational treatise *Insti-
tutione di tutta la vita dell'uomo nato nobile* (1542) clearly demand to be read
in this sense. In these dedications, Forteguerri functions as the embodiment of a potential vernacular audience for science or moral philosophy,
qualified by natural acumen and intellectual curiosity but excluded from
pursuing its interest by an ignorance of Latin: the same audience that
Dante and Cavalcanti had reached out to in their vernacular philosophical
writings some two centuries earlier.[102] The same might be said of a pub-

lication like Francesco Sansovino's edition of Boccaccio's *Ameto* (1545), equipped with a substantial hermeneutic preface addressed to the young Gaspara Stampa. In this case, the cultural operation for which Stampa serves as a figurehead is that of supplying a non-Latin-literate readership with the necessary philological knowledge to appreciate something of the intertextual dimension of a humanistic vernacular text.[103]

Besides their utility in the construction of male literary identity and their continuing mediatory function as synecdochic proxies for a vernacular audience, educated women were amply exploited in the metaliterary rhetoric of this period as embodiments of civic cultural excellence. This was not new, of course: we have already seen examples in the fifteenth century of literate women serving as cultural figureheads for their cities, following the implicit logic, one suspects, that such superfluous distribution of talent could only result from a miraculous oversupply. As the practice of women's writing became more widespread, this role as geocultural signifier gained in prominence, fostered by phenomena such as the provincial diffusion of the printing industry and the fashion for literary academies, which tended to accentuate the development of that particularistic cultural consciousness that is such a defining feature of the Italian literary landscape of this time. By the mid-sixteenth century, along with the mainly Venetian-published "national" literary anthologies that collected verse from Petrarchan poets from all regions of Italy, we find a growing trend toward local anthologies collecting the poetic production of an individual city, often published by a local typographer and showcasing the activity and contacts of a particular local academy. These anthologies frequently vaunted a local female poet, or preferably an artfully contrasted pair, as a token of civic cultural "virility": thus Girolamo Ruscelli's Brescian collection, *Rime di diversi eccellenti autori bresciani* (1553), features the recently deceased Veronica Gambara and the living Lucia Albani, while a 1556 collection published in Lucca features a selection of verse by Chiara Matraini, proudly displaying her in poetic correspondence with "foreign" *letterati* such as Benedetto Varchi and Tomaso Porcacchi (1530–85).[104] Examples like these make their patriotic point only implicitly, but more explicit and controversialist instances are not unknown. Thus we see the Cremonese humanist Marco Girolamo Vida (1470–1566), in an oration of 1550 "against the Pavians" ("adversus Papienses"), listing as one of his proofs of the superiority of his own native city its production of two such prominent female cultural luminaries as the Latinist Partenia Gallerati and the artist Sofonisba Anguissola.[105] The accusation appears to have hit home, given that by the time of Domenichi's female poetic anthology of 1559, we find a Pavian noblewoman, Alda Torelli Lunati, featuring among the poets gathered in the volume.[106] Besides functioning as figureheads in this way for rival cities, we find female poets on one occasion, more sinisterly, performing the same role for rival factions within the same city. This is the case of the Albani and Brembati in Bergamo, locked in a Montague and Capulet-style struggle for supremacy that burst out bloodily in the 1560s with the murder of a scion of the Brembati by two members of the Albani.[107] It seems more than a coincidence that both families produced female poets who attained some degree of national fame: in the case of the Albani, Lucia Albani, sister of the perpetrators of the Brembati murder, in that of the Brembati, Isotta Brembati Grumelli, Emilia Brembati Solza (c. 1530–86), and Minerva Rota Brembati (c. 1534–1566), the latter two the sister and wife, respectively, of the victim.[108]

Investigation of the often intricate and overlapping personal and geocultural agendas served in this period by the nascent tradition of women's writing is best conducted through the examination of case studies. A good starting point here is the verse-collection for Irene di Spilimbergo whose prefatory biography we looked at above. The volume was seemingly put together on the initiative of the Venetian patrician Giorgio Gradenigo (1522–1600), a friend of Irene's mother, Giulia da Ponte, although the dedicatory letter is signed by the *poligrafo* Dionigi Atanagi (1504–73). The collection is of notable quality and scope, bringing together the work of well over a hundred poets in two sections, Latin and vernacular. The aim was clearly to rival and outdo Girolamo Ruscelli's *Tempio* for Giovanna d'Aragona, which had established the vogue for such literary "monuments." Besides commemorating the talent and virtue of the dead Irene, the volume obviously served to display the *pietas* of Gradenigo as chief mourner as well as the literary tastes and contacts that had allowed him to put together such a collection. Meanwhile, the contributors to the volume enjoyed the gratification of figuring in a select, invited company that included some of the most prestigious *letterati* and intellectuals of the day, figures like Benedetto Varchi, Bernardo Tasso, Bernardo Cappello, Domenico Venier, and Luigi Tansillo as well as Titian, to whom are attributed three Latin poems, and the 16-year-old Torquato Tasso (1544–95).[109] The profeminist content of the collection, already pronounced in the prefatory biography, was reinforced by the inclusion of works by a dozen female poets in the vernacular section, where they make up around 13 percent of the total, an unusually high percentage for the time.[110] More perhaps even than the male contributors, the female participants are distinguished by their social elevation, including noblewomen of the status of Dianora Sanseverino, Costanza d'Avalos, and Ippolita Gonzaga as well as well-known poets such as Laura Battiferra, Laura Terracina, and Virginia Salvi.[111]

Besides the shaping factors already considered, the volume for Irene di Spilimbergo may also be seen as having a fairly complex geocultural agenda. Although calculatedly "pan-Italian" in its selection of poets, from the Neapolitans Tansillo and Bernardino Rota to the Florentine Varchi and the Ferrarese Giambattista Pigna and Giambattista Giraldi Cinzio, it nonetheless remains a distinctly Venetian production, masterminded by Gradenigo and featuring a disproportionate number of contributions by poets from Venice and the Veneto.[112] It may thus be seen as an assertion of the centrality of Venice's position within the national literary conversation, with the presence of Titian further serving as a reminder of the distinction of its artistic tradition. The importance the volume attaches to the fragile figure of Irene di Spilimbergo needs to be seen in this context. One very important role female poets could play in a civic context was to serve as a kind of collective interactive muse, stimulating poetry and articulating bonds between male *letterati;* we see this clearly, for example, in Tullia d'Aragona's activities in Florence in the late 1540s and Laura Battiferra's in the same city in the 1550s.[113] Venice was in difficulty in this regard, especially after the death of Gaspara Stampa, who had briefly fulfilled a similar role there in the 1550s, at least for a particular, nonpatrician circle. One of the last remaining republics in Italy, and a city well known for the seclusion in which it kept its patrician women, Venice was singularly ill equipped to produce "public" women poets, especially on the "respectable" model of a Battiferra or a Laodomia Forteguerri; it would not be until the 1580s that women of the Venetian social elite began to venture as writers into the public domain.[114] Of the fifty-nine female poets published in anthologies between 1545 and 1560, only one, Olimpia Malipiero, appears to have been of Venetian patrician background, and Malipiero spent the majority of her adult life in Florence, and so is less of an exception than she appears.[115]

It was perhaps to meet this lack, as much as anything, that Irene di Spilimbergo needed to be "invented"—to supply (at a safe distance) the unifying Venetian muse that the city could not produce for itself. Living in territory governed by Venice, and born to a Venetian mother, Giulia da Ponte, Irene could plausibly be claimed as at least an honorary daughter of the republic.[116] Although her *virtù* remained largely, at the time of her early death, at the level of potential, the breadth of her talents compensated to some degree for her lack of concrete achievements; although there had been musician-poets before (notably Gaspara Stampa), a poet-musician-artist had considerably more novelty, women artists having only very recently surfaced to public notice as a phenomenon, with the growing fame of Sofonisba Anguissola. Quasi-beatified in death, Irene could stand as evidence of Venice's capacity to generate a homegrown "woman worthy," and one who, unlike previous candidates like Gaspara Stampa or Francesca Baffo, possessed the status and impeccable character to merit a "temple" of this kind. She could also, more specifically, as an artist and pupil of Titian's, serve to defend the honor of Venetian art in its rivalry with Florence, particularly acute in this period following the publication of Vasari's *Lives of the Artists* in 1550.[117] If Sofonisba Anguissola had been a protégée of Michelangelo's, Venice could now respond with an equally brilliant protégée of Titian's, even if one whose career had been cut off by death before it had fully begun.

Further evidence of the kind of geocultural negotiation that could be facilitated by women's writing is afforded by the example of another verse collection, published two years before the Spilimbergo volume in Lucca: Lodovico Domenichi's anthology of female poets of 1559, one of the most striking profeminist initiatives of the age. At an immediate level, Domenichi's anthology offers a good example of the benefits that accrued to male *letterati* through association with literary women. Domenichi himself through his editorship succeeded in reaffirming his standing as one of Italy's most committed devotees and enablers of female literary talent, while at the same time the volume allowed him to display his urbanity as poet in his sonnet exchanges with several of his "exhibits."[118] The same cultural capital accrued, at a greater or lesser level, to the other male stakeholders in the volume, such as Domenichi's collaborator, Giuseppe Betussi, and the dedicatee, Giannotto Castiglione (1532–72), of the noble Milanese family of that name.[119] At the same time, beyond these personal stakes, broader, political agendas are visible. As Marie-Françoise Piéjus has noted in an important study of the collection, the selection of poets Domenichi presents is biased socially in favor of aristocratic writers and geographically in favor of Tuscany, with a special emphasis on Siena, *patria* to around a quarter of the volume's fifty-three poets.[120] This choice reflects in part Siena's actual status as a flourishing center for women's writing, but in part it is clearly ideologically conditioned, in ways that will become obvious if we consider the political context of the volume. Four years before the publication of the volume, in 1555, after a long and bitter campaign, Cosimo I Medici, Duke of Florence, had annexed the republic of Siena. He was formally invested with its government in 1557, an event that decisively consolidated Medici power in Tuscany. These events defined the immediate environment in which the anthology project took shape (Domenichi had been based in Florence since 1547 and was a recipient of Medici patronage), even if it may be true that, as he claims in his dedicatory letter, he had been collecting material for the volume for over a decade.[121] Seen in this light, the anthology's showcasing of Sienese women's writing takes on a particular meaning, both imperialistically triumphalist and conciliatory: it simultaneously celebrates the conquest by Florence of a culturally distinguished rival power, seeks morally to legitimize that conquest on grounds of civic harmony, and offers an olive branch to "opposition" writers like Virginia Salvi, who had lived in exile in Rome since her family had been expelled from the city in the 1540s.[122] Besides these more immediate, political motives, the anthology celebrates Florence's, or Tuscany's, accession to what has been called the "system" of the courts by placing Siena's celebrated patrician women writers within the context of a national feminine cultural and social elite. As Piéjus has noted, even the index is eloquent in this regard, sandwiching Virginia Salvi, for example, between Veronica Gambara and Vittoria Colonna and juxtaposing Costanza (or "Gostanza") d'Avalos with the little-known Sienese poet Onorata (or "Honorata") Pecci.[123] Women's writing, as we have seen, had originated in the courts, and Florence, like Venice, had yet to produce a homegrown female poet of distinction, relying instead on "immigrants" such as the Roman Tullia d'Aragona, the Venetian Olimpia Malipiero, and the Urbino-born Laura Battiferra. The opportunity, with the taking of Siena, to appropriate a ready-made contingent of aristocratic Tuscan female poets was clearly not one to be lost.[124]

The last text we might look at as an example in this section is less familiar to Cinquecento scholars than the previous two mentioned, although Diana Robin has called attention to its interest in a recent book. The text in question is a lecture delivered in February 1541 by Alessandro Piccolomini before the Paduan Accademia degli Infiammati on a sonnet by Laodomia Forteguerri. The *lettura* was published shortly afterward in a pirated edition in Bologna, making Forteguerri, whose sonnet was incorporated in the volume, only the third secular Italian female poet to appear in print, after Colonna and Gambara, as well as, of course, the first to gain the honor of an academic commentary on her work.[125] Piccolomini's commentary is presented by the editor of the published edition as of interest to "all men of refined education and noble ladies of lofty spirit who delight in the sweet pleasure of reading Tuscan writings."[126] It is certainly a work that seems to have caught the imagination of Piccolomini's contemporaries, if we are to judge from the imitations it generated. Within a year, in January 1542, a young academician at the Florentine Accademia degli Umidi presented a *lettura* on a sonnet of Colonna's, citing the Forteguerri lecture explicitly as precedent, while the following year, 1543, saw the publication of Rinaldo Corso's commentary on Colonna's religious poems.[127] More capillary influences can probably also be conjectured:

at any rate, it is interesting to note that Piccolomini's audience at the Infiammati lecture probably included the Tuscan exile Benedetto Varchi, who, after his return to Florence in 1543, would do more than any other individual in that city to encourage the practice of women's writing there.[128]

Piccolomini's motives in the cultural exploit of the Forteguerrri *lettura* deserve close attention in this context, as they serve as a kind of summation of this section's discussion. The practice of lecture commentaries on vernacular verse was well established in the Accademia degli Infiammati, one of the most innovative and influential of the Italian sixteenth-century literary academies.[129] Previous commentary choices in the academy had embraced texts both by "canonical" figures such as Petrarch and Bembo and younger poets such as Lodovico Dolce and Giovanni della Casa (1503–56).[130] A commentary on a female contemporary poet was, however, a strikingly new and audacious move on Piccolomini's part, serving to position him on the avant-garde of vernacular literature while also elegantly nodding to the precedent of Bembo as connoisseur of female literary *virtù* and perhaps also to the Paduan intellectual Sperone Speroni (1500–1588), one of the presiding geniuses of the Infiammati, who had broken with tradition to give a notably articulate role to Tullia d'Aragona in his *Dialogo d'amore* (circulating in manuscript since 1537). Piccolomini's gesture in calling attention to the *virtù* of his Sienese compatriot Forteguerri clearly also had a patriotic dimension, underlining Siena's precocity in the cultivation of female poetic talent—a process in which Siena's own literary academy, the Intronati, had played a decisively proactive role.[131] The promotion of Sienese women's writing as synecdoche for the city's literary prowess was something of a leitmotif of Piccolomini's cultural agency at this time; in May of the same year, we find him sending copies of five sonnets by Sienese women to Pietro Aretino, as "a sample of the wit [ingegno] of our Sienese ladies."[132] Besides these more parochial reasons, Piccolomini's choice of an unknown female poet as a subject for academy commentary further served very strikingly to emblematize the modernity of the Infiammati's cultural project, centered around a militant championing of the vernacular within the fields of science and philosophy as well as literature. Women's role as mascots of literary modernity had already been established within humanism and more emphatically, in the early sixteenth century, by Bembo. In Piccolomini's *lettura*, a woman is once again conscripted to this role to define a new phase in the development of the now triumphant *volgare*. The enticing air of novelty that female authorship inevitably carried with it in this period was compounded in this case by the poem's subject matter and treatment. Forteguerri's "Or ten va superbo, or corre altero" ("Now Flow on Proud and Haughty"), the sonnet chosen by

Piccolomini for commentary, is a tribute to Margaret of Austria (1522–83), Charles V's daughter, couched in the language, unwontedly, of Neoplatonic love: Laodomia casts herself as a pining lover, lamenting the absence of her "lovely distant Sun" ("vago almo Sole") in Rome.[133] If one were looking for an epitome of the "new Petrarchism" ushered in by the generation of Bembo and Colonna, one need look no further than Forteguerri's "Or ten va superbo"; as a witty encomiastic construct, deploying to new and courtly ends the amorous vocabulary of Petrarchan lyric; as the product of the quintessential "new author" of the period, the noblewoman-poet; and, finally, as a tribute to the imperial power now hegemonic in Italy, cast in an attractively mitigated feminized form, it is a consummate poetic product of its day.[134]

## 4. Literary Trajectories: Continuity and Change

Considerations of the kind advanced in the previous section are important to keep in mind as we turn to examine the forms taken by women's writing in the period under scrutiny, as they are essential to an understanding of the genesis of the most important formal innovation of this time, the new structural model of verse collection critics have recently come to refer to as the "choral anthology."[135] This subgenre of verse *raccolta* can first be observed, in a particularly elegant form, in Tullia d'Aragona's *Rime* of 1547; then we see it, though in a less structured and manicured form, in Laura Terracina's various volumes of *Rime,* starting in 1548, and finally, in a model closer to d'Aragona's, in Laura Battiferra's *Primo libro delle opere toscane* of 1560. Where the choral anthology differs most substantially from previous models of lyric collection is in its dialogic character, encapsulated in the title form used by both d'Aragona and Terracina, *Poems by Signora X and by Others to Her.* Characteristically, such anthologies gather both the work of a given poet and correspondence verse addressed to her, concluding—in the case of d'Aragona's *Rime* and Terracina's early collections—with a quasi-appendix of poems composed in her praise. These volumes thus locate the female poet at the center of a social network, composed primarily, if not exclusively, of males, and show her perfectly poised between her roles as poet and as object and generator of poetry. This dual role frequently becomes the object of explicit comment in the collections, particularly in the case of the two Lauras, Battiferra and Terracina, the coincidence of whose name with Petrarch's love object provides a trigger for conceits that position the modern poet as an amalgam of Petrarch and Laura.[136] The structure of the choral anthology is thus perfectly calculated to showcase the new "interactive muse" we saw heralded in the Florentine funeral oration for Colonna discussed at the end of chapter 2, providing the poet herself with an arena for displaying her talent and contacts and her poetic "suitors" with a locus for reciprocal validation and genteel competition with their peers.[137] The result has been aptly described as both a "virtual salon" and a "self-glorifying autograph book."[138] Within the genre as a whole, differentiation can be made between d'Aragona's and Battiferra's more courtly model of choral anthology, opening (and in Battiferra's case also closing) with a carefully orchestrated series of poems to its Medici dedicatees, and Terracina's looser and less hierarchical "typographic" model. Also interesting is the difference in inflection between d'Aragona's and Terracina's anthologies and Battiferra's, the former two, especially d'Aragona's, more erotic in the relationships established between the principal and her "suitors," the latter keyed to a more matronly gravity, and modeling its author more as an object of intellectual admiration than of erotic desire.[139]

In addition to the recognized choral anthologies of d'Aragona, Terracina, and Battiferra, it is possible that we are in possession of at least the nucleus of another, lurking unacknowledged within the curiously inchoate volume of *Rime* by Gaspara Stampa published in 1554. As is well known, Stampa's verse was published after her premature death by her sister, Cassandra Stampa, and we have no evidence that the volume as we know it represents the author's own plans. Besides the famous sequence of love poetry to Collaltino da Collalto that has justly attracted the bulk of critics' attention, the collection also, later, includes a sequence of occasional poetry, beginning with paired sonnets to Henri II of France and his Italian queen, Catherine de' Medici. The page is marked off typographically from the preceding sequence in the 1554 volume in a way that seems to suggest at least a nominal section break, and possibly a transition to another manuscript.[140] The two opening sonnets to the king and queen of France are followed by other encomiastic verses, headed by a sonnet to the Florentine poet Luigi Alamanni (1495–1556). The sequence recalls the opening of Tullia d'Aragona's *Rime* and of Laura Battiferra's *Primo libro,* both of which similarly follow a sequence of poems addressed to princes— in their case Cosimo de Medici and his duchess Eleonora—with a homage to a "trophy" poet, in d'Aragona's case, Bembo, in Battiferra's the Roman-Florentine diptych of Annibale Caro (1507–66) and Benedetto Varchi. After this initial sequence, in the 1554 edition as it stands, few of the addressees of Stampa's encomiastic poems can be securely identified, although internal references pick out verses addressed to Domenico Venier, Sperone Speroni, and Girolamo Molin. We may imagine, however, that in a projected published version, introductory rubrics would have identified others, such as the "lovely phoenix" ("alma fenice") of poem 249, a Vene-

tian lady whose beauty and virtue fills her homeland and Italy with wonderment, and the "famous lord" ("chiaro signor") of sonnet 251, famed for
his erudition (*lingue e scienzie*) and his poetic vein.[141] The collection—if
such we can deem it—also includes a series of sonnets of religious peni-
tence and ends with three poems announcing the poet's intent to pursue
her love poetry for Collalto in a Neoplatonizing and sublimated vein.[142] If
my conjecture is correct, it may be that this largely encomiastic sequence
constitutes the nucleus of a courtly and "honest" volume of poetry that
Stampa was putting together toward the end of her life as part of a process
of poetic "rebranding" also attested by her appearance, with a sonnet, in
Ruscelli's *Tempio alla divina signora donna Giovanna d'Aragona*. Indeed, it is
not inconceivable that, had she lived, Stampa would have taken the option
of presenting herself in a published context in this more "unobjectionable"
guise, keeping her dazzling but highly unconventional love poetry for Collalto for an understanding coterie audience in Venice.[143]

Moving down from the level of the *raccolta* to that of the individual
poem, we find strong continuities between women's literary production
in this period and in the earlier period surveyed in chapter 2. The dominant genre of literary production for women remained overwhelmingly
lyric verse in its three major thematic subveins of the period, the erotic,
occasional-epistolary, and religious. As was noted earlier, the latter two
were preponderant, despite the important exceptions of Matraini and
Stampa. Stylistically, Petrarch, as mediated by Bembo and Colonna, remained by far the dominant influence, although Battiferra, at the end of
the period under scrutiny, shows the influence of a later poet like Della
Casa.[144] We also find her experimenting with newer classicizing metrical
forms such as *endecasillabi sciolti*.[145] Within the general formula of "Petrarchism," quite notable differences can be seen between the formal mastery and gravity of tone of a poet like Battiferra—the truest poetic heir in
many ways to Vittoria Colonna in this period—and the calculated colloquiality of a Stampa or the less calibrated colloquiality of a Terracina.
These last two, in fact are not entirely well served by an analysis that takes
Petrarchism, in its classic form, as its yardstick; both, in different ways, may
be better contextualized within more local and idiosyncratic traditions.
Terracina's great debt, especially in her early years as a poet, is to the Neapolitan tradition of the *glosa* or *trasmutazione*, an originally Hispanic form
that enjoyed a remarkable vogue in Italy from the 1540s.[146] The *trasmutazione* consisted of a short ottava rima poem incorporating lines from a
source text, most usually, in this period, Petrarch's *Rime* or Ariosto's *Orlando furioso*. One of the earliest published Italian showcases for the form
was the collection of *Stanze transmutate de l'Ariosto* (1545), which includes

a *trasmutazione* by the aristocratic Neapolitan female poet Dianora Sanseverino, an acquaintance and probably also a patron of Terracina's.[147] It
is within this context that we need to locate Terracina's debut as a poet: indeed, her first published poem, in an anthology of 1546, is a *trasmutazione,*
while the form also figures large, alongside more conventional Petrarchan
forms, in her *Rime* of 1548 and 1549.[148] *Trasmutazioni* aside, moreover, ottava rima dominates metrically in Terracina's early collections in a manner
that sharply differentiates them from, say, d'Aragona's *Rime:* only seven of
the fifty poems addressed to named individuals in the *Rime* of 1548 are, in
fact, sonnets, while the rest are ottava rime *stanze.*[149]

Terracina's deviation from Petrarchan norms is easy to gauge not least
because of this metrical dimension. Gaspara Stampa's is less clearly mea-
surable in these terms, at least if we set aside the presence in her oeuvre
of a series of lyric *capitoli:* a non-Petrarchan form and one more characteristic of the *poesia cortigiana* of the beginning of the century than of the
mature Bembist Petrarchism of the day.[150] For the most part, in Stampa's
verse, it is at a thematic level, and, to a lesser degree, a stylistic one, that
we can register her distance from Petrarchism in its classic form. As critics
have frequently noted, the narrative content of Stampa's love *canzoniere*
was highly unconventional in Petrarchan terms, recounting as it does a
sexual affair ending in disillusionment, with the prospect of a second love
to come. The register and tone of Stampa's verse also often differs from
classic Petrarchism in its greater colloquiality, apparent particularly at the
level of syntax. Both these features of her verse demand to be contextualized with regard to alternative traditions of writing. One important thematic point of reference, as critics have recently noted, is the tradition of
Ovid's *Heroides,* at this point in time easily available in vernacular translation.[151] Another is Boccaccio in his earlier romances, particularly the ventriloquized female voice of the *Fiammettta,* itself a vernacular reworking
of the *Heroides* mode.[152] The effective fusion of Boccaccian and Petrarchan
elements we find in Stampa's verse, though unique and highly original in
its outcome, has much in common with trends in this period within her
immediate circle in Venice, which was made up largely of *poligrafi* and "ir-
regulars" such as Antonfrancesco Doni (1513–74), Francesco Sansovino
(1521–86), and Girolamo Parabosco (c. 1524–57).[153] The writings of figures
like these represent a kind of middle ground in Venice between the scurrility of Aretino's circle and the rarified Petrarchan experimentation of patrician poets like Domenico Venier: more polite and *onesto* than the former
but racier, more ephemeral, and less chiseled than the latter. It is probably
the world of the politer *poligrafi* that constitutes the most productive context for Stampa's verse rather than the "purebred" Petrarchism against

which her production is often measured.[154] Also important is the context of musical performance, to which Janet Smarr has recently called attention in an important study: Stampa was far more celebrated in her day as a musical virtuosa than as a poet, and, to an extent that has not yet been fully registered by the critical tradition, this is probably verse intended more for the ear than the eye.[155] Compositely, Stampa's is a highly distinctive voice within the female-authored lyric of the period, closer in some respects to the directness and verve of a Camilla Scarampa than to the "graver" modern Petrarchism of a Lucia Albani or a Laura Battiferra. Although her verse met with the approval of a shrewd and unconventional contemporary commentator like Ortensio Lando, who describes her unequivocally as a "great poet" ("*gran poeta*"), this was not indisputably "high" verse nor verse fully calculated to appeal to the more mainstream polite tastes of the period.[156] There may be more than a conventional authorial modesty at work in Stampa's sonnet for the *Tempio* for Giovanna d'Aragona ("Questo felice e glorioso tempio" ["This Happy and Glorious Temple"]), which counterposes her "base rhymes" ("*basse rime*") with the unattainable loftiness of style she anticipates in her fellow contributors to the volume.[157]

While lyric verse remained far the dominant genre of women's writing in this period, it was not the only one. As we saw at the beginning of this chapter, in the same year that she published her *Rime,* 1547, Tullia d'Aragona also published an ambitious philosophical dialogue on love, the *Dialogo dell'infinità d'amore,* portraying her in learned conversation with Benedetto Varchi, who may have assisted in the dialogue's composition.[158] D'Aragona's novelty was striking and prompted imitation by other women; a letter from Pietro Gradenigo of 1560 records his receipt of a dialogue by Lucia Albani, which he praises for its display of philosophical and theological knowledge, while a letter of Chiara Matraini's shows her to have been engaged in the composition of a dialogue modeled on Boethius at around the same time.[159] The 1540s and 1550s also saw the posthumous publication of two prose works by Vittoria Colonna: a select collection of religious letters to her cousin Costanza d'Avalos (1544), and a lyrical prose meditation, the *Pianto sopra la passione di Christo* (1556), the latter of which went through a further four editions before 1563.[160] Far the most-published female-authored work of the period, however, outside the field of lyric poetry (or, indeed, within it), was Laura Terracina's *Discorso* on the *proemi* of Ariosto's *Orlando furioso,* which carried her signature genre of the *trasmutazione* into a more structured and larger-scale work.[161] The *Discorso* is made up of a series of *trasmutazioni* on the forty-six initial *stanze* of successive *canti* of the *Orlando Furioso,* making up a series of miniature seven-

stanza "canti," each with its own one-stanza incipit addressed to a separate
individual or collective dedicatee.[162] Terracina used this ingenious form as
a vehicle for a sort of highly original and sui generis lay ministry, developing moral and political themes mainly, but not always, deriving from the
Ariostan *proemi* on which they draw. The task is well suited to her trenchant and unnuanced voice; this is certainly her most successful work ar-
tistically, as well as in terms of its popular appeal. Another intriguing
female-authored didactic work of the period is the *Orazione dell'arte della
guerra* included in Chiara Matraini's *Rime e prose* of 1555, emphatic in its
foray into "masculine" territory and addressed to an imagined audience
of male academicians.[163] A translation by Matraini of Isocrates's moral-
educational oration *To Demonicus* was also published as an independent
work in Florence in 1556, with a dedication to Giulio de' Medici (c. 1532–
1600): again a rare early case of a woman presenting herself publicly in a
teaching role in relation to a male.[164] Besides these less traditional ventures, women continued as well to be active in epistolography, and their
letters were occasionally anthologized, although no dependably attributable single-authored collection of letters by a woman was published in this
period, other than the slim volume by Colonna noted above.[165]

Besides these essays in discursive, didactic and meditative literature, we
also see in this period the first tentative signs of the narrative vocation that
female writers would develop to such effect in the later decades of the century. The only published narrative work of the period that can be fairly securely attributed to a woman, even though we know nothing of the author, is Laura Pieri's historical poem *Quattro canti della guerra di Siena* of
1555, dedicated to Giovanni Giacomo de' Medici (1495–1555).[166] More substantial, but more problematic in its attribution, is the chivalric romance *Il
Meschino* that came out posthumously under the name of Tullia d'Aragona
in 1560.[167] To these, we might add Veronica Gambara's short ottava rima
moralizing narrative "Quando miro la terra ornata e bella" ("When I Look
at the Beauteous Earth Bedecked"), much anthologized in the period—
though generally under the name of Vittoria Colonna—and probably
influential on a later writer such as Moderata Fonte (1555–92).[168] Far the
most important female narrative writer of the day, however, at least in
terms of the quantity and quality of her output, remained unpublished:
the Paduan Giulia Bigolina (c. 1518–before 1569), author of a romance, *Urania*, recently edited and translated by Valeria Finucci and Christopher Nissen, and a *novella* collection apparently of some substance, of which only
a fragment of the dialogic frame and a single *novella* survive.[169] The example of Bigolina, an obviously ambitious writer whose works are lost or
survive only in a slim manuscript record, may lead us to speculate that hers

may not have been the only narrative experiments by women in the period. Indeed, the same letter of Chiara Matraini's from the early 1560s that records her composition of the philosophical dialogue mentioned above also notes that she has written a *novella* based on a "real-life episode" ("caso veramente stato") that has recently taken place in Genoa.[170] No trace remains of either work, although it is likely that material from the dialogue, which we know to have been influenced by Boethius, was incorporated in Matraini's later works, such as the *Dialoghi spirituali* of 1602.

One great novelty of this period compared to the previous one was that, with the accession of Colonna and Gambara to canonical status, female poets of the midcentury were in a position to draw on authoritative female models in their verse instead of having to rely on male-authored texts, as Colonna and Gambara had themselves been largely constrained to do. The degree to which second-generation female poets imitated Colonna and Gambara has only recently begun to become an object of critical scrutiny, but it is already obvious that this imitation was significant and systematic.[171] As Giovanna Rabitti has noted, this imitation had an ethical, as well as a stylistic, dimension; in the same way that Bembo had done for men, Colonna and, to a lesser extent, Gambara supplied women with an appropriable voice and persona, redolent of social entitlement and moral dignity, and, in the case of Colonna and Gambara, the further attraction of a bankable aura of sexual probity.[172] Interesting evidence of the place that this imitation of models could play in a poet's formation is offered by the early poems by Laura Battiferra recently unearthed by Victoria Kirkham, written in the wake of her loss of her first husband, Vittorio Sereni, who died in 1549 when Battiferra was twenty-five.[173] These mold themselves very closely on Colonna's *in mortem* poetry for her husband, far more closely than anything in Battiferra's published collection of 1560. We have a sense here of an apprentice poet finding her voice, in copybook Petrarchist style, by experimentally inhabiting that of a "master," but with the novelty that the "master" was in this case a woman, and one of sufficient poetic standing to underwrite the authorizing process such formative imitation was intended to effect. The same point might be made of Isabella Morra, Laodomia Forteguerri, and Virginia Salvi; of Lucia Albani, whose *canzoniere* shows her drawing on both Colonna and Gambara as influences; and of Chiara Matraini, who takes her homage to Colonna as far as to directly quote from her in the first quatrain of her sonnet "Occhi miei, oscurato è 'l nostro sole."[174] Matraini's tribute is a particularly complex one in that the quatrain reproduced from Colonna is itself in turn assembled, cento-mode, from a series of Petrarchan fragments.[175] Colonna is thus implicitly constructed here as a poetic authority on a par with her own model Petrarch, and a bigendered genealogy is constructed to sustain Matraini's own poetry of mourning.[176]

One effect of these new imitative possibilities was to help delineate what we might call a feminine space within Italian literary culture: not a hermetic one, of course—literary ratification still largely flowed through male channels—but one of increasing definition and importance. An interesting manifestation of this process is the growing number of poems in this period written by women to women, both poems to intimate friends—we can see a subgenre of poems of female *amicitia* growing up in this period, with contributions from Matraini, Stampa, and Olimpia Malipiero—and to more distant acquaintances, often known only by reputation, following the model of Colonna and Gambara's poetic correspondence of the 1530s.[177] Especially interesting, among this last group are poems addressed to other female poets, reciprocated or otherwise: we have exchanges in this period between Laura Battiferra and Laura Terracina, between Battiferra and Lucia Bertani, and between Leonora Falletti and Livia Tornielli, as well as poems by Battiferra to Ersilia Cortese, by Girolama Castellani to Luisa Sigea, and by Laodomia Forteguerri to Alda Torelli Lunati.[178] Domenichi's anthology of 1559 also records circulations of poetic compliments among obscurer Tuscan figures, such as Giulia Braccali Ricciardi and Cornelia Brunozzi Villani of Pistoia, while Laura Terracina's *Rime seconde* has an interesting small group of poems by Neapolitan noblewomen in praise of her verse.[179] Cumulatively, this traffic of compliment had the effect of reinforcing women's "right of residence" within literary culture and implicitly, as well, that of cutting against the exceptionalist rhetoric with which women's poetic attainments were still often acclaimed. The nebulous classical feminine textual community humanists had evoked for fifteenth-century female writers, peopled by its shadowy Cleobulinas, Cornificias, and Corinnas, was gradually being replaced by a more tangible modern sisterhood, which the Domenichi anthology eventually conjured on the page.

Besides this kind of "horizontal" female-female poetic relationship, we also encounter an increasing number of more "vertical" relationships in this period, with poets of a lesser status addressing themselves to high-placed ladies in expression of homage or expectation of patronage. For a surviving precedent here, we need to look back to Ceccarella Minutolo's and Cassandra Fedele's letters to female patrons in the 1470s and 1480s: as we have seen, for the most part, the female vernacular poets of the early sixteenth century were more of a status to figure as literary patrons themselves than to find themselves in the position of courtship.[180] Examples from the period under discussion here range from Laura Terracina's pro-

miscuous collective courtship of the female Neapolitan elite in her successive volumes of *Rime* to the more select and articulated tributes of
Laura Battiferra's *Primo libro,* embracing women from the great families of
the Della Rovere, Cibo, and Colonna as well as her primary patron and
dedicatee, Eleonora of Toledo. Eleonora was also the recipient of poetic
homage by Tullia d'Aragona and Olimpia Malipiero, while Girolama
Castellani addressed laudatory verses to Renée of France and Leonora
d'Este (1515–75) and Gaspara Stampa and Virginia Salvi to the queen of
France, Catherine de' Medici.[181] Partenia Gallerati, meanwhile, in a direct
echo of the patronage strategies of Cassandra Fedele, addressed Latin
epistles to female luminaries of the rank of Anna d'Este (1531–1609) and
Marguerite de Navarre. The most intriguing work produced in this genre
in this period is a sequence of sonnets by Laodomia Forteguerri to Margaret of Austria, dating from the late 1530s or early 1540s, one of which has
already been mentioned as the object of a public lecture by Alessandro Piccolomini. These are distinctive in that they draw on the language of Neoplatonic love to express the devotion of the poet to her "lady," using a device that would later be exploited by poets like Fiammetta Soderini (d.
c. 1575), Maddalena Campiglia (1553–95), and Maddalena Salvetti Acciaiuoli
(d. 1610).[182] In the period we are looking at here, Forteguerri's poems to
Margaret constitute something of a high point in the evolution of a "feminized" literary language: an effect enhanced by their extensive imitation
of Vittoria Colonna, placed here implicitly as a model on a level with Petrarch.[183] Also interesting in this regard is Laura Battiferra's self-referential
pastoral eclogue, "Europa," published in the *Primo libro* of 1560, which portrays the author as "Dafne" in dialogue with "Europa," or Leonora Cibo
Vitelli (1523–94), wife of the condottiere "Chiappino" Vitelli.[184] Unlike
Forteguerri's portrayal of the distant "solar" Margaret, Battiferra's eclogue
casts the female patron as lofty but approachable and graciously appreciative of the "soothing verses" and "sweet words" proffered up to her by her
devoted female bard.[185] We have a vision here, very explicitly, of a female
poetic creativity enabled and authorized by a woman: a model that later
sixteenth-century female writers, as we shall see, would more fully explore.

Before we leave this question of the evolution of female-female modes
of address in mid-sixteenth century lyric, one context, and one patron, are
deserving of particular scrutiny. The context is Florence in the 1540s and
1550s, the patron, the Eleonora, Duchess of Toledo, whom we find, exceptionally, as the dedicatee of two volumes of female-authored poetry,
Tullia d'Aragona's *Rime* and Laura Battiferra's *Primo libro.* The novelty of
this in this period is worth underlining: while the practice of women writ-

ers dedicating their works to female patrons became common later in the century, down to around 1580, it is far more customary to find female-authored works dedicated to men.[186] The conjunction becomes the more intriguing when we consider Florence's general receptiveness to female poets in this period: besides d'Aragona and Battiferra, and the cluster of unknown Florentine poets attested only in Domenichi's anthology, we find the high-profile Olimpia Malipiero active in the city in this period, along with the narrative poet Laura Pieri.[187] The degree to which this may be attributable to Eleonora of Toledo's encouragement is a question that we should take seriously, despite the fact that the Spanish-born Eleonora has traditionally been regarded as an unlikely connoisseur of the Italian *volgare*. Eleonora was the daughter of a notable literary patron, Don Pedro de Toledo (1484–1553), imperial viceroy of Naples, and would have been aware through family connections of the poetic activity of Vittoria Colonna and Laura Terracina.[188] Despite the famed "Hispanic" religious austerity of her conduct, she appears to have countenanced an education for her daughters that encompassed belles lettres as well as music, to judge from the attainments of the gifted and culturally ambitious Isabella Medici Orsini (1542–76).[189] It does not seem implausible to attribute to a woman of Eleonora's cultural astuteness a perception of the capital that might accrue to a female patron through the cultivation of a female "muse," especially since she had before her the example of her immediate predecessor as Duchess of Florence, Margaret of Austria, whose poetic celebration at the hands of Laodomia Forteguerri had gained such widespread acclaim in the early 1540s.[190] If we accept as a hypothesis that Eleonora may have been an active patron of female poetry, rather than a passive recipient of poetic homage, it becomes interesting to observe the development perceptible over the thirteen years that separate d'Aragona's *Rime* of 1547 from Battiferra's *Primo libro* of 1560. Where d'Aragona's verses to Eleonora celebrate her primarily for her beauty and fertility—two of her four poems to the duchess are addressed to her in her role as mother—Battiferra's later verses craft her in a more heroic and political role, casting her as in a queenly guise as ruler of Florence and Siena.[191] She is also given a greater structural salience within the volume: where d'Aragona's collection opens with a sequence of nine poems to Cosimo de' Medici, followed by a lesser sequence of four to his consort, Battiferra's collection accords pride of place to the duchess, to whom the opening and closing sonnets are addressed.[192] Though we are still far from the kind of sustained, monographic act of courtly homage that Maddalena Salvetti would address to Eleonora's successor, Christine of Lorraine, thirty years later in her *Rime toscane* (1590), Battiferra's *Primo libro* is nonetheless notable for the extent to which it shapes itself around its female dedicatee. In the tercets of its stately opening sonnet, "A voi, Donna real, consacro e dono," Battiferra compares herself aspirationally to Petrarch ("he who, singing on the banks of the Sorgue, exalted Laura to such signal honor"), expressing the hope that the greatness of her subject, Eleonora, will sufficiently "illuminate" her own obscure verse to win her a similar fame.[193] Ritual modesty aside, the poem implicitly recognizes the distinctiveness of the poetic tradition of Battiferra's own age with respect to that of Petrarch, registered in the seismic novelty of a model of praise poetry in which women feature not only as object but as *auctor.*

## 5. Women Writers and the Paradox of the Pedestal

Even if the 1540s and 1550s in Italy did not constitute quite the isolated great age of women's writing we encounter in Dionisotti's historical construction, it cannot be denied that it was in many ways a breakthrough period for the nascent tradition. While they remained a minority presence—and a very small one—by comparison with men, women figured very visibly in Italian culture in this period, aided by their very unusualness, which continued to allow them to figure rhetorically as "phoenixes," despite their increasing numbers at this time. The social and geographic dissemination of the practice of women's writing advanced rapidly, facilitated by print and by patriotic competition between cities and regions. Poetry by women, as we have seen, on occasion became the object of academic commentary, and there are instances from this period as well of women being invited to join academies: Laura Terracina was a briefly member of the Neapolitan Incogniti in the 1540s, while both Laura Battiferra and Virginia Salvi were offered membership in academies in Siena in the early 1560s.[194] The rhetoric we have encountered in previous periods, casting women's cultural "resurgence" as an emblem of the glory of the age was cranked up to a new pitch of triumphalism in these years: a letter appended to the first volume of Terracina's *Rime* places the "fineness of female minds" as climactic in a list of fields in which the modern world might be seen as rivaling the attainments of the classical world, along with letters, arms, sculpture, architecture, and "many other most noble *virtù,* which had been long buried following the barbarian invasions."[195] The topos gained purchase from the parallel emergence in this period of notable female artists and musicians. The artist Sofonisba Anguissola has already been mentioned in connection with Irene di Spilimbergo; in music, the 1550s saw the rise to fame of celebrated singers and musicians such as Francesca Bellamano and Polissena Pecorina in Venice.[196] The sense of wonder aroused by this explosion of female talent is well expressed in a project outlined by Betussi in 1556 for a "Muses' chorus of modern women," designed to celebrate the "rare and singular talents" of women as they were revealing themselves in his day in painting, literary composition, and music.[197] Assembled, Betussi claims, these modern muses would make such a dazzling array that Apollo himself would leave "the nine ancient sisters" and instead eagerly seek the company of these.[198]

Despite this triumphalism, however—and the concrete achievement that lay behind it—women's position within literary culture remained marginal. The very incense that was showered on them by male readers was patently trivializing and indicative of an unwillingness to take their work seriously; amid the floods of ink devoted to women's talent in this period, engaged criticism is notably absent. With very few exceptions, women tended to be exclusively measured against women, in lists of "modern muses" often as vapidly universalizing in their praises as the lists of ancient "women worthies" that had preceded them. A strongly-worded protest against this failure of discrimination is found in an unpublished let-ter of Chiara Matraini's of the 1560s, which deserves to be quoted at length as one of the most insightful comments on the ambient conditions of women's writing in this period. The letter is addressed to a frequent cor-respondent of hers at this time, the judge and minor *letterato* Cesare Coc-capani of Carpi, often misleadingly identified in modern critical literature as her lover. It clearly accompanies a literary work that Matraini is sub-mitting to Coccapani for reading and comment, probably her lost philo-sophical dialogue, and is an attempt to head off the stream of undiffer-entiated praise she anticipates from experience as his likely response:

> Credo bene che V.S. mi lode nel core come nelle parole, per esser donna, le quali alla comune bassamente sogliono parlare ne' loro scritti; ma io che oltre il comune uso delle donne che si dilettono di comporre e degli huo-mini che lodevolmente hanno composto o scritto vorrei comporre e scri-vere, non mi par che sieno le cose mie da esser cosi assolutamente giudi-cate, senza menda o contradizione. Però che V.S. quando le vedrà piacciale di proporsi che li venghino da un suo fratello che abbia a mandare i suoi scritti davanti a una pubblica accademia di gran literati, overo da una per-sona strana, acciò meglio senza alcuno affetto o passione possa giudicare e poscia mi scriva l'opinione sua.

> [I certainly believe that your praises of me are genuine, bearing in mind that I am a woman and that women generally write in an undistinguished man-ner. But I wish to write better than the common run of women and also of men who have composed meritorious works; and it does not seem to me that my writings are of a standard to be judged in that kind of absolute way,

as if they had no need for improvement. So when you see them, I would ask
you to imagine that they have been sent by a brother of yours who is planning to unveil his works before a public academy of great literati—or imagine they come from a complete stranger, so you can judge their merit ab-
solutely dispassionately, and then let me know what you think.][199]

Of course, as has been noted above, Matraini was unusually isolated as a
woman writer for social reasons, and we should not assume that her more
privileged sisters suffered the same dearth of critical input of which she
complains here.[200] Nonetheless, her poignant plea for "fraternal" frankness of treatment does capture something general of the irony of women's
literary predicament: condemned to inequality often not through oppres-
sion and hostility but a relentless blanket covering of praise. This was a literary culture that set a high value on women writers but essentially, still,
as cultural signifiers or marketing novelties: what mattered far more than
what they concretely wrote were the meanings that attached to them as
writers. By 1560, women had attained a remarkable degree of literary
recognition by comparison with earlier eras. They were still poised, however, on a niche, or a pedestal, from which it was all too easy to fall.

# CHAPTER FOUR

❀ ❀ ❀ ❀

# INTERMEZZO

## (1560–1580)

❀

One of the most interesting and original of mid-sixteenth-century Italian women writers, mentioned briefly toward the end of the last chapter, was the Paduan Giulia Bigolina, author of a romance, *Urania,* and a *novella* collection seemingly of quite considerable ambition and scale. Bigolina's work anticipates women's writing in the later Cinquecento in its experimentation with narrative forms and in the profeminist sensibility it manifests (as Valeria Finucci has noted, *Urania* contains an embedded dialogue on the "dignity of women" that anticipates the later feminist writings of Moderata Fonte and Lucrezia Marinella [c. 1571–1653]).[1] Bigolina is also geographically prototypical in that the latter decades of the century would see Venice and the Veneto become increasingly important locations for women's writing in Italy, producing, besides the Venetians Fonte and Marinella, the Vicentine Maddalena Campiglia and the Paduans Isabella Andreini (1562–1604) and Valeria Miani Negri (c. 1560–post 1611) as well as numerous lesser writers such as Issicratea Monte of Rovigo. All these writers, however, emerged to public notice no earlier than the late 1570s (Issicratea Monte) and early 1580s (Moderata Fonte), when they were taken up with enthusiasm and found champions and publishers among their male peers. A different fate met Bigolina, writing prose fiction in the 1550s in Padua, as well as Chiara Matraini, who, as we have seen, seems to have attempted a *novella* in the early 1560s. Neither woman's fiction was published in her lifetime, and both Matraini's *novella* and the vast bulk of Bigolina's have vanished: only a single tale remains of the latter's *novella* collection, while *Urania* itself narrowly escaped oblivion, surviving as it does only in a single manuscript.[2]

While the genre novelty of Bigolina's writings, for a woman at the time, may have been a factor in their unpropitious reception, it must also be noted that, by the late 1550s, times were becoming less conducive to experiments in this regard. The 1560s and 1570s saw quite a striking decline in the number of published works by women compared to the 1540s and 50s. Of the works by women that *were* published in this period, the most important in terms of literary quality and contemporary profile is Laura Battiferra's psalm translation *Sette salmi penitenziali* published by the firm of Giunti in Florence in 1564 and reprinted in 1566 and 1570.[3] Important in terms of quality but negligible in terms of profile (it was published semi-clandestinely in Venice and in a very limited print-run) was the *Terze rime* of the Venetian courtesan Veronica Franco (1546–91), published in 1575.[4] We may add to these, among works by well-known names, Laura Terracina's *Settime rime* (or *Rime sovra tutte le donne vedove di questa città di Napoli*) of 1561, published by Matteo Cancer in Naples and her *Seconda parte de' discorsi,* published by the Venetian firm of Valvassori in 1567. Other publications of this period by women, or published under women's names, were the *Segreti* of Isabella Cortese (1561), a book of medical and cosmetic recipes that went through very numerous editions down to the mid-seventeenth century; the *Lettere amorose* of "Madonna Celia, gentildonna romana" (1562); a volume of prognostications, *Le risposte,* by a "Leonora Bianca" (1565); a slim pamphlet of verse by Virginia Salvi and her daughter Beatrice lauding the Venetian poet Celio Magno (1536–1602) for his verses on the victory at Lepanto (1571); and, toward the end of the period, a series of orations (1577–79) by the "girl prodigy" poet-orator Issicratea Monte.[5] To these may be added two posthumous works: the *Lettere* (1563 and 1576) of the controversial Milanese nun and mystic Paola Antonia de' Negri (1508–55) and a version of Isotta Nogarola's 1451 *Questio utrum Adam vel Eva magis peccaverit* (1563), revised by her descendent Francesco Nogarola.[6] While several of these works are interesting in themselves, it is clear from this list that we cannot talk in this period about anything like the same kind of compact and mutually reinforcing corpus of female writing we find in the 1540–60 period, with the verse collections of Colonna, Gambara, d'Aragona, Terracina, Matraini, Stampa, and Battiferra, or that we will find in the period 1580–1600, with the fictional experiments of Moderata Fonte, Isabella Andreini, Maddalena Campiglia, Maddalena Salvetti, and Lucrezia Marinella. Women do not in these intervening decades "make up a group," to use Dionisotti's phrase; they are not sufficient in numbers, or consistent enough in genres of writing attempted, to constitute a collective presence in literary culture.[7] With the exception of Veronica Franco—a purely local, Venetian phenomenon—no new poet emerged in this period capable of emulating the achievements of the past generation, and the fictional forays of Giulia Bigolina and Chiara Matraini in the 1550s remained an isolated phenomenon down to the early 1580s. Single-authored volumes aside, even the poetic anthologies of the period seem thinner than those of the previous two decades in their representation of women, with the exception of thematic volumes in celebration of female subjects where a feminine presence was still evidently considered appropriate.[8] An example would be Dionigi Atanagi's two-volume *De le rime di diuersi nobili poeti toscani* of 1565, the first of which contains one long-deceased female author out of 63 (Veronica Gambara, with 11 unpublished poems) and the second 3 out of 107 (Olimpia Malipiero, Giulia Premarini, and an unknown correspondent of Orsatto Giustinian's, with a grand total of six sonnets among them).[9] Another anthology of the period, *Il secondo volume delle rime scelte da diversi eccellenti autori, nouamente mandato in luce* (1563), edited by the publisher Gabriele Giolito, contains not a single female poet among the 43 authors featured, while Cristoforo Zabata's *Nuova scelta di rime di diversi begli ingegni* (1573) has only one of 24 (Gaspara Stampa, another poet already long dead).[10]

To what reasons should we attribute this temporary but decided occlusion of the Italian tradition of women's writing in the 1560s and 1570s? Should we see it as signaling an ideological shift with regard to gender, away from those affirmative attitudes to women's *virtù* that had characterized Italian elite culture in the earlier part of the century? Or is it better regarded as an unintended side effect of other, less directly gender-related literary-cultural developments? Where the first hypothesis is concerned, it has been suggested that the period toward the end of the Council of Trent (1545–64) saw the beginnings of a "misogynist turn" in Italian culture that would become more marked as the century developed and lead eventually to the suppression of women's hard-won literary voice. Valeria Finucci has invoked this cultural shift as the context for Giulia Bigolina's exploration of feminist themes in *Urania*, for example, arguing that the ideological self-consciousness Bigolina manifests regarding women's social and cultural position may be seen as reactive in this regard.[11] It is difficult, in practice, however, to find very compelling textual evidence in this period for such a development. Of the texts Finucci cites as examples of the "new misogyny," one, at least, Giovanni Battista Modio's symposially structured dialogue *Il convito, overo del peso della moglie* (1554), cannot be unproblematically labeled as such: although it does give some space to traditional misogynistic arguments against marriage, the dialogue concludes with an authoritative speech on the pleasures of a companionate marriage by Alessandro Piccolomini, the "Socrates" of the piece.[12] Better support for Finucci's thesis might seem to be offered by a work like Lodovico Domenichi's *La donna di corte* (1564), which, rather disconcertingly, given the author's past as a "champion of women," argues that women should keep to cultivating their proper virtues of sexual modesty (*pudicitia*) and simplicity (*simplicità*), leaving more ambitious pursuits—including the more advanced reaches of urbane conversation—to men.[13] The value of Domenichi's work as representative of post-Tridentine values, is, however, diminished by its status as a plagiarism of a Latin work of the 1530s by the Aristotelian philosopher Agostino Nifo.[14] While it is undoubtedly interesting to find the author of *La nobiltà delle donne* (1549) choosing as the object of his plagiarism a work of such traditionalist gender values as Nifo's, it would be difficult to pin the notion of a general ideological shift to such a fragile textual base.

In fact, if we look more closely at the reasons for women's literary marginalization in this period, it becomes apparent that, rather than being the victims of any kind of concerted ideological hostility, they seem rather to have been edged to the sidelines by a series of quite complex, intersecting factors, most not obviously connected with gender ideology. One is simply the decline of vernacular literature in general in these years. The imposition of censorship took a toll on the operations of the Venetian publishing industry generally, as printers and editors sought to conform to new rules mandating the prepublication scrutiny of new works to be published. Some fell victims directly to censorship—Gaspara Stampa's publisher, Pietrasanta, run by Ruscelli, was one of these in 1555—while others simply found themselves having to shoulder the expenses involved in confirming the orthodoxy of new works.[15] These were thin years overall for the industry and thinner still where the publication of vernacular literature was concerned, as publishers turned to producing greater proportions of religious works, partly because they saw it as a safer bet with regard to censorship and partly to meet shifting market demands.[16] The mood of the industry was very different from the expansiveness of the 1540s and 1550s, when Giolito in particular had actively reached out to new authors and audiences; this was a period of caution, and women writers—still "marginal" in many respects—probably suffered as a result. To what extent women stopped writing in this period, discouraged by the changed climate, we have no way of knowing, but the shreds of evidence that have reached us suggest that some at least continued to write without publishing their work. A single manuscript preserves for us Laura Battiferra's writings of the later 1560s and 1570s, for example, another, Laura Terracina's unpublished last volume of *Rime,* written in Rome in around 1577, and as we have seen, Giulia Bigolina's *Urania* and the sole surviving *novella* of her substantial collection are contained in a couple of manuscripts.[17] It is not at all improbable that other works composed by women in this period were simply lost.[18]

Besides the reasons already adduced, a further factor that needs to be considered here is the tonal shift in Italian literary culture highlighted by Dionisotti in his classic essay on Italian literature in the age of the Council of Trent, away from the fictional and poetic vernacular diversions of the midcentury toward a more austere and self-consciously erudite cultural model.[19] Dionisotti portrays this as, in some respects, a return to the spirit of fifteenth-century humanism, noting as a feature of the age the strong revival it witnessed in philology and classical scholarship, especially in Florence, with figures like Piero Vettori (1499–1585) and Vincenzo Borghini (1515–80). At the same time, the study of theoretical poetics flourished, both within the universities and outside them, within the urban academies, stimulating heated debates again reminiscent in some ways of the flamboyant polemics of Quattrocento humanism. The impact of neoclassical theory on literary practice was increasingly felt, at the same time that literature was being reshaped by the spiritual imperatives of the Counter-Reformation; a profound literary transformation was under way, whose first great results were seen in this period with Torquato Tasso's *Discorsi dell'arte poetica* (written c. 1564–70) and *Gerusalemme liberata* (1559–75), perfectly expressive in their pairing of the intimate relation between poetry and theory in this period. While the forms most invested in this change were the classical and neoclassical ones—epic poetry, tragedy, comedy, pastoral—lyric poetry, too, was transformed in a classicizing and erudite direction, most decisively through the influence of Giovanni Della Casa, whose *Rime,* published posthumously in 1558, established a powerful new trend in lyric production, continued and developed by younger poets such as Tasso, who featured prominently in the influential multiauthored volume *Rime degli Accademici Eterei* of 1567.[20] As Dionisotti noted, these changes in the formal emphases of Italian literary culture were accompanied by a process of social "re-aristocratization"; where in early decades, largely through the agency of print, a democratizing trend had opened literature to social "outsiders" like Pietro Aretino, by the period we are looking at here, literary practice had become once more almost exclusively the practice of the social elite.[21] The membership of important literary academies such as the Eterei of Padua (1563–68) or the Innominati of Parma (founded 1574) is telling in this regard, as is the marked vogue in this period for works on nobility, precedence, codes of honor, and the etiquette of dueling.[22] As Venetian publishing circles diminished in importance as a locus for cultural interaction, the position of the courts—especially Florence, Parma, Ferrara, Mantua—was correspondingly enhanced.

The implications for women writers of these shifts in the direction of literary culture were quite marked. The re-aristocratization of literary culture was less of an issue in that, even in previous decades, women writers had been drawn preponderantly from the aristocratic elite. Far graver in its impact on women's place in Italian literary culture was the "neohumanistic," erudite, and academic direction that culture took from around 1560. The vernacular poetic culture of Petrarchism, as codified and authorized by Bembo, had been unusually accommodating to women in that it was accessible to those not in possession of a full humanistic education. The "erudite turn" of the period 1560–80 put a stop to this—or, more precisely, it repositioned the genres of writing accessible to most women so that they were no longer at the forefront of literary fashion. By the 1560s, a philological tour de force such as Fulvio Orsini's edition, with Latin translation, of the surviving fragments of Greek women's writing was likelier to catch the eye of the fastidious literary connoisseur than a volume of vernacular verse by a contemporary female author.[23] Nor were women well placed to participate with any conviction in the literary-theoretical debates that were an increasing focus of energy in this period, excluded as they remained from university education and limited as they were generally to vernacular literacy. Indeed, the sole attempt I know of by a woman to engage publicly in such a literary debate in this period serves only to underline their marginalization with respect to this cultural form. In a 1558 volume of pasquinades by Annibale Caro against the Modenese critic Lodovico Castelvetro (1505–71), who had criticized Caro's use of linguistic forms not sanctioned by the literary tradition, two letters by Castelvetro's compatriot Lucia Bertani feature in an appendix also including polemical letters by Caro to Varchi and others of his literary supporters.[24] Bertani's letters, written in 1556 and 1557, express her distress that such a dispute should have risen between the two and offer as a friend of Castelvetro's to take the role as mediatrix in the dispute.[25] Caro's replies voice an initial acceptance of the proposal, followed by a rapid loss of interest when Bertani stipulates that both disputants will need to acknowledge fault. The episodes illustrates well the limited degree to which a female writer might hope to participate in the literary polemics of the day, even where she was not precluded from them by the limits of her education. Considerations of decorum effectively precluded any role as combatant: even if a well-bred woman were to risk entering the fray, a well-bred man would hardly feel himself free to respond to her arguments with any robustness. Virtually the only role a woman might construct for herself within such a debate was the gender-appropriate "Sabine wife" one that Bertani attempts here; as she reminds her correspondent, "women have, as you know, extinguished the fires of war and made of enemies friends."[26] Within an environment in which agonistically structured debate had an important cultural function, however, this was not a role for which there was any particular need.

As has been mentioned already, women's marginalization from Italian literary culture in the 1560s and 1570s was reversed from around 1580 onward, when they began once again to publish in significant numbers. The experience of these "lost" decades was important, however, for the warning it provided of the shallowness of the roots of the new *letteratura femminile*. Women's achievements as writers over the first six decades of the sixteenth century had been very considerable. From a position of virtual invisibility within literary culture, at least as authors, they had attained a place as a vocal and seemingly established minority group. They had precociously produced two uncontroversially canonical authors in Vittoria Colonna and Veronica Gambara as well as a series of striking, if less authoritative, figures such as Terracina, d'Aragona, Battiferra, Stampa, Matraini, Isabella Morra, Virginia Salvi, and Laodomia Forteguerri. In the mid-century period, women constituted just less than 10 percent of the total of authors included in poetic anthologies—hardly parity, of course, but still a notable proportion considering the norms of premodern Western literary culture.[27] Around the same proportion is found in something like Ortensio Lando's list of contemporary poets in his *Sette libri de' cathaloghi [sic]* (1552), where seven female authors are featured among seventy in total.[28] The fact of women's participation in Italian literary culture had already begun to strike foreign observers: Thomas Hoby, in the dedicatory letter to his translation of Castiglione's *Cortegiano* (1560), notes it as a salutary effect of Italy's embrace of the vernacular along with the opening of literary culture to male writers from outside the social elites, such as Pietro Aretino and Giambattista Gelli.[29] The augury implicit in Raphael's *Parnassus*—that Italy might come to match classical antiquity in evolving a literary culture where modern Sapphos would suavely mix with their male peers—must have seemed by around 1560 already to have been happily achieved. An unpublished oration in praise of the vernacular by Curzio Gonzaga (1536–99) delivered to the influential Accademia delle Notti Vaticane in 1563, which offers an interesting snapshot of contemporary writing, structures its argument in a way that was now becoming almost conventional to give a prominent, if neatly circumscribed, place to the phenomenon of women's writing. By contrast with antiquity, which could

boast a sole Sappho, the present age could vaunt a genuine tradition of female writing, which Gonzaga illustrates with a list of some seventeen
named figures, defining this array of talent "the splendor and wonder of
our age" ("splendore, et stupore del nostro secolo").[30] Some seven years
later, the Sicilian writer Girolamo Camerata, reexamining the question of
the relative dignity of the sexes in his *Questione dove si tratta chi più meriti
honore, ò la donna, ò l'huomo* (1567), was able to conclude that, while men
were superior to woman in their aptitude for the *vita activa,* women's more
temperate complexion fitted them better for the literary and contemplative life.[31]

Despite this fighting talk, however, women's place within literary culture was less consolidated than it may have seemed, as we have already observed in tracing developments in the 1560s and 1570s. Their rise to notice
as authors had occurred within the context of a specific genre and idiom:
namely, Petrarchism, as formulated by Pietro Bembo. By the 1560s, this
powerful literary paradigm was crumbling as many of its major exponents
and popularizers aged and died (Lodovico Domenichi in 1564, Bernardo
Cappello and Benedetto Varchi in 1565, Lodovico Dolce in 1568). Others,
like Alessandro Piccolomini (d. 1579) and Girolamo Muzio (d. 1576), who
had survived into the 1570s, had long ago abandoned Petrarchan verse to
devote themselves to philosophy or literary polemic. The narrowness of
women's literary focus is well illustrated in Curzio Gonzaga's oration,
where a long sequence of lists of male writers organized by genres of writing, from lyric poetry to epic to *trattatistica* and dialogue, is followed by a
far shorter list of women famed exclusively for the "charm of their verses"
("leggiadria delle lor rime").[32] This left them extremely vulnerable to a
stylistic shift such as we observe in the midcentury with the growing influence of Della Casa, whose classicizing and formally experimental model
of verse was less accessible to female poets than the preceding Bembist formula had been. Generally, in fact, by comparison with his literary "father,"
Bembo, Della Casa represents a model of poetic activity notably less receptive to intellectual relationships with women. It is notable that, where
Bembo, as we have seen, partly defined himself through his relationship
with female poets such as Colonna and Gambara, and his disciples such as
Varchi and Piccolomini had perpetuated this pattern, Della Casa's select
*canzoniere* bears no trace of such relationships. Even though he figures as
the dedicatee of Gaspara Stampa's posthumous *Rime,* and Cassandra
Stampa speaks in her dedicatory letter of her sister's deep admiration for
his poetry, there is little evidence otherwise of a connection between the
two.[33] No female poet features, either, as a correspondent or addressee in
the 1567 collected verse of the Accademici Eterei, where, in a manner an-

ticipatory of seventeenth-century practice, female singers become the creative icons of choice.[34] Were these developments purely casual? Or should we rather see these elite poets' seeming disinclination to engage poetically with their female peers as consciously revisionary with respect to the mainstream Petrarchism from which they were taking their distance? Most critical accounts of Della Casa's "reform" see his aristocratic stance as a reaction against what was perceived as the vulgarization of Petrarchan lyric—a lowering of the entry barriers facilitated by large-scale and indiscriminate publishing and the availability of aids such as *rimari*. It is not difficult to see how this "barbarian invasion" might have come to be emblematized for some by women's advent on the literary scene, especially given the popularity of a figure such as Laura Terracina, polar opposite to the fastidious Della Casa in her output, both in quantitiative and qualitative terms.[35]

Reviewing women's position within Italian literary culture in the mid-century, then, the impression is one of a friable niche rather than a consolidated platform or, to shift metaphors, a luxuriant flowering unsupported by particularly deep roots. No one could fairly deny by 1560 that female writers had made a significant contribution at least to the lyric tradition in Italy, but it would be naive to conclude from this that they enjoyed full citizenship within the *respublica literaria*. An iconic episode in this regard, to which Victoria Kirkham has recently called attention, was the memorial service for Benedetto Varchi held in Florence shortly after his death in December 1565, where an eyewitness account by Piero Vettori speaks of Laura Battiferra attending the ceremony in Santa Maria degli Angeli screened away from the other mourners in a *matroneum* out of considerations of decorum. Vettori laments the injustice that Battiferra should be "excluded and isolated" ("esclusa e separata") from this ritual gathering of Florence's literary community, noting that her genius and her writings had earned her the right to be "removed from the number of women and accounted entirely a man."[36] While we should be wary of taking this episode as entirely representative—Battiferra herself had earlier commented with frustration on Florence's relative conservatism with respect to women's social and cultural engagement—it does very poignantly convey women's liminal status in literary culture as warily admitted outsiders.[37] Also indicative of this, as the present chapter has illustrated, is the eclipse suffered by women's writing in the 1560s and 1570s, after their strong showing in the 1540s and 1550s—caused, it has been argued here, not so much by the concerted repressive forces of Counter-Reformation ideology as by the "natural rhythms" of changing literary fashion. Although, from the standpoint of, say, 1590, when women had returned in force as writers, the dip of the 1560s and 1570s must have appeared simply a parenthesis, within a longer perspective, this relatively "dead" interlude comes to seem anticipatory of women's later and more definitive seventeenth-century marginalization. Like the half-present Laura Battiferra at the funeral ceremony of her mentor Varchi, women were admitted to literary society under toleration. However celebrated, however feted, however substantial in their attainments, their summary ejection was always on the cards.

❀ ❀ ❀ ❀

# CHAPTER FIVE

# AFFIRMATION

## (1580–1620)

❀

## 1. Women's Writing in the Age of the Counter-Reformation

The phase in the history of early modern Italian women's writing that we are moving on to consider in the present chapter is in many ways the most remarkable of all those examined in this study. In the twenty-three years between 1538 and 1560, twenty new works authored by women were published in Italy, thirteen of which were collections of lyric and occasional poetry.[1] The equivalent period between 1580 and 1602 saw the publication of thirty-seven such works, including pastoral dramas, religious narratives, a chivalric romance, and two volumes of letters as well as the first two substantial female-authored works of feminist polemic, one in the form of a dialogue, the other a treatise.[2] The following ten years saw a further broadening of women's generic range, to encompass tragedy and epic. We find women in this period being admitted to literary academies with a greater frequency than in the midcentury and in a few instances beginning to become involved in editorial activity; Marina Zancan talks in this period of women's "progressive integration within the dynamics of the literary system."[3] Women's presence on the literary scene as writers was complemented by their newer but striking prominence in other fields of creative activity, as painters, musicians, singers, and actresses: this was the age of Lavinia Fontana (1552–1614), of Isabella Andreini, of Maddalena Casulana (c. 1540–c. 1590), of the Ferrarese *concerto delle donne*.[4] The deference paid to women's artistic talent within Italian culture was arguably never so high as in this period; certainly, it would be difficult to claim that it had in any way fallen off from a putative "Dionisottian" high point in the midcentury. While it is true that the later period produced no female writer of the "canonical" status of a Colonna or a Gambara, it could boast in the actress-poet Andreini a certified bestseller to rival Colonna, and figures like Moderata Fonte, Maddalena Campiglia, Margherita Sarrocchi (c. 1560–1618) and Lucrezia Marinella enjoyed widespread fame and respect in their day.[5] If their names did not survive as well as those of predecessors such as Colonna or Stampa—most of these artists are critical "rediscoveries" of the past few decades—this is indicative as much as anything of the general lack of critical fortune of this period of Italian literature. With a few notable exceptions, the male-authored literature of the final decades of the sixteenth century remains itself equally critically unexplored.

Another reason for the critical "invisibility" of late sixteenth-century women writers, until recently, is that this is not a period to which conventional literary historiography would have led one to look for a flourishing of female creativity. This, more than any, was the period when the dictates of the Counter-Reformation were making themselves felt within Italian literary culture. The practice of ecclesiastical censorship of books, first introduced at a national level in 1559, had progressively reshaped Italian publishing, in a manner already noted in chapter 4. The proportion of religious texts published increased sharply in the final decades of the century, while the proportion of vernacular secular literature declined. The relatively tolerant moral climate of the early sixteenth century gave way to a new moral and religious fundamentalism. Censorship struck not only obviously "shocking" works like Machiavelli's *Principe* and Aretino's salacious dialogues between courtesans, which had been freely published in the 1530s, but even a work as seemingly unobjectionable as Castiglione's *Cortegiano,* a mildly bowdlerized version of which was issued in 1584, shorn of anticlerical banter and passing references to the classical concept of "Fortune."[6] At the same time, more generally, in society, the church took an increasingly interventionist line in matters of public morality, seeking, for example, to regulate marriage and bring it within closer ecclesiastical control and to impose stricter discipline within convents.[7] Within the secular and liberal perspective of traditional Italian literary historiography, these developments have tended to be seen in a negative light, and the period to be bleakly portrayed in general as one of authoritarianism and repression. Where women are concerned, the tendency has been, correspondingly, to regard this period as regressive with respect to the social and cultural "advances" of the era immediately preceding it. A common tendency is to contrast the "Renaissance" protofeminism of the late fifteenth and early sixteenth centuries with the post-Tridentine reimposition of traditional gender attitudes: where the former period was capable of honoring the "virago-like" achievements of a figure like Isabella d'Este, the latter preferred a meeker and more domestic model of womanhood, de-emphasizing intellect and culture in favor of the traditional feminine virtues of chastity, modesty, silence, and obedience. Within this construction of gender history, the emergence of women as writers in the fifteenth and sixteenth centuries is seen as the result of a brief interval of enlightenment, rapidly closed by the forces of reaction.[8] Evidence cited in support of this includes the reemergence of traditions of misogynistic writing in the later sixteenth century; the tendency toward a greater insistence on traditional values within conduct books and treatises on women's education; and the tone of defensiveness that one finds increasingly creeping in to the prefatory letters to writings by women, which often assume that the support of a powerful patron will be needed to defend these works from the opprobrium they might otherwise attract.[9] The greater tendency of women writers in this period to engage in explicit feminist polemic has also been attributed to the newly repressive cultural atmosphere of late sixteenth-century Italy; the argument here would be that women became more ideological, and more angry, as they witnessed the gradual suppression of the relatively liberal gender environment that their peers earlier in the century had enjoyed.

While there may well be some elements of truth in this analysis, there is also much that deserves to be questioned. If the effects of the Counter-Reformation had been as uniformly negative for women—and intellectual women, more specifically—as they are sometimes portrayed, it would be hard to explain why this should have been a period in which women enjoyed such relative success and prominence as writers. One would expect, rather, the kind of trajectory that has often been proposed for women's writing by critics following the historiographical model proposed by Dionisotti: a remarkable but short-lived flourishing in the middle of the century, followed by a definitive, or near-definitive, silence. The fact that this silencing does not occur—indeed, that we find almost the contrary—invites us to revisit our assumptions about the Counter-Reformation and its cultural and gender-ideological implications.[10] Looking at Italian literary culture from the particular viewpoint afforded by the tradition of women's writing brings to the fore continuities between the first and second halves of the century. More than a clear-cut trajectory of progressive ideological "closure," the reality of cultural change in this period is more complex and more contextually differentiated. The secular princely courts were still flourishing in this period, with their gaieties still largely untouched by religious austerity, and the culture of gallantry and Neoplatonic adulation of women retained much of its former currency, even though the Petrarchan idiom of the early and mid-Cinquecento was beginning to give way to more experimental forms. Women remained the symbolic muses of vernacular poetry and continued to constitute an important part of its actual audience, although the ever more ambitious theoretical carapace that was rapidly growing up around vernacular literature was beginning to have the effect of shifting the ideal locus of literary consumption from the court to the more masculine environment of the literary academy. Treatises on women's "nobility and excellence" continued to be written in this period and encomiastic "monuments" assembled for individual ladies. Male writers continued to define themselves to a quite notable extent by their espousal of a "profeminist" stance. Nor does any concerted and widespread attempt seem to have been made in this period to compel women to relinquish their cultural ambitions. Although we do find the authors of occasional conduct books warning of the dangers of allowing women access to literature as readers, there is no particular evidence that this advice was universally followed by parents or that levels of literacy among girls were lower in the 1580s than they had been in the 1540s. Rather, attitudes to female education seem to have varied widely, with social status and geocultural context probably the key determining factors.[11] While moralists of the period sometimes argued against literacy in women as potentially corrupting or advocated limiting girls' reading to religious literature, an aristocratic woman might still freely be praised in 1595 for her ability to recite extended passages from Ariosto from memory.[12] Literacy for women had always been a luxury predominantly reserved for an elite, and, within that elite, there is no very clearly perceptible shift in gender-ideological values, at least down to the turn of the seventeenth century. "Renaissance feminism" had, in any case, always been a relatively superficial phenomenon in that it affected only women's cultural standing and not their social, legal, or economic position. Little changed in this respect, at least immediately, with the Counter-Reformation. To see this movement as oppressive of women is thus misleading if it implies the existence of an earlier, "Renaissance" moment of empowerment or emancipation. The truth is that women remained equally oppressed in practical terms for the entirety of the period in question.

In certain respects, indeed, as I have argued elsewhere, the Counter-Reformation was enabling of women writers, paradoxical as that may seem from the perspective of conventional literary historiography.[13] As was noted above, a feature of women's writing in this period that differentiates it from that of the midcentury was the far broader range of genres we find women engaging with in this period. Down to around 1560, women's writing had been largely limited to neo-Petrarchan lyric, in its amorous, occasional, and spiritual variants. It is only in the later period that we find female authors attempting fiction and drama on any scale. This widening of women writers' generic horizons demands to be seen in the context of broader changes within Italian literary culture, which had the effect of morally "purging" vernacular literature of the licentious and sexually charged elements that had characterized large parts of it earlier in the century. This was especially apparent within the more traditionally lascivious genres such as chivalric romance and comedy, although Vittoria Colonna's spiritual "reformation" of Petrarchan lyric in the 1540s might be seen as prototypical in this respect. This process of moral reinvention is often presented in negative terms, as a response to the introduction of censorship. While there is certainly an element of truth there, it is misleading to portray this development as purely reactive; rather, it was in part prompted by internal imperatives of religious sentiment. The example of Colonna, writing emphatically prior to the introduction of the Index, is instructive in this regard. Her *Rime spirituali* had offered a persuasive and precocious model for the spiritual redeployment of the previously "squandered" seductive resources of vernacular literature. It was one that writers of the second half of the century were quick to seize on and develop.[14] The best-known example of this process is Torquato Tasso's transformation of the chivalric romance as practiced by Ariosto and Boiardo into a grand Christian epic mobilizing the power of classical epic to modern evangelical ends. Other authors utilized the popular romance meter of ottava rima for various forms of religious poetry; this period saw the rise of a whole assortment of subgenres of devotional poetry in ottava rima: saints' lives, biblical narratives, and narrative-meditative-psychological fusions such as Luigi Tansillo's hugely popular *Lagrime di San Pietro*.[15] At the same time, the cynical sex comedy of the age of Machiavelli and Ariosto was displaced by more romantic and morally unexceptionable models of comedy and by the new genre of pastoral drama, which characteristically took as its subject the reward of chaste and faithful love.[16] Though little studied today, with the exception of Tasso's *Gerusalemme liberata* and Giambattista Guarini's *Pastor fido*, the "reformed" vernacular literature of this period is richer and more inventive than it is often given credit for; it is a travesty to present it as a mere compromise between artistic creativity and the dead hand of ecclesiastical censorship. Rather, what we see in the period is a fruitful re-engagement with medieval devotional traditions and discursive practices, enriched by the intervening experiences of classical and vernacular humanism: a "new model literature" for a reevangelized age, transforming past models to contemporary ends.

An unintended consequence of this comprehensive "reform" of vernacular literature was to open up a greater space for women within Italian literary culture and to allow for their more comprehensive integration within that culture. Genres such as the comedy, romance, and *novella*, as they had been practiced in the early Cinquecento, were problematic for "decent" women in their frank celebration of extramarital sexual pleasure. While there is much evidence of women ignoring the carping of moralists and enjoying this literature as readers, it is difficult to imagine a respectable woman writer in this period—at least in an Italian context—putting her name publicly with impunity to a work of such a "lascivious" nature.[17] Such problems did not arise with the reborn literature of the post-Tridentine period, which was far more easily morally consonant with a female authorial persona. Indeed, in its piety, gravity, high-mindedness and decorum, this reformed literature was almost more appropriate to a female elite identity as this was crafted in contemporary culture than it was to the male. It is interesting to note in this regard the use made of the female voice in the prototypical case of the "reform" of Petrarchan lyric in the 1540s. Aside from Colonna's role in this process, we might also mention in this connection the simulated female voice we find in the volume *Sonetti, canzoni, et triomphi di m[adonna] Laura in risposta di m[esser] Francesco Petrarcha*, of anonymous authorship, but sometimes attributed to Stefano Colonna, that appeared in 1552.[18] This work takes the form of a series of replies *per le rime* to each of Petrarch's poems in turn, in which Laura, the purported author, rebukes her admirer for his temerity and advises him to lay aside his vain wooing and to concentrate his mind on his soul's salvation. An "errant" male poet is here thus seen corrected by a pious female one, even if fictional, in a sequence that may be seen as in some sense endorsing female authorship as morally and spiritually corrective.[19] Not dissimilar in its underlying assumptions, although the context is very different, is the encomium of the mid-Cinquecento Paduan *novelliere*, Giulia Bigolina, found in a local historical work by her compatriot Bernardino Scardeone (1478–1574). In praising Bigolina for her collection of *novelle*, now lost, Scardeone stresses in particular the moral decency of her work, contrasting it with the more scurrilous model of *novella* collection offered by Boccaccio's *Decameron*. Even though love and its effects have a place in the collection, they are treated with admirable chastity and modesty, in a manner appropriate to "matronly decorum" and conducive to the moral education of readers.[20] As in the *Sonetti, canzoni, et triomphi di m[adonna] Laura*, a paradigm seems to be adumbrated here of the female author as a morally tempering force within literature, correcting the moral deviancy that formed the "darker side" of Italian culture's great medieval literary inheritance. The same thing is hinted at, though in a more equivocal context, in the preface of readers of the chivalric romance *Il Meschino,* published in 1560 with an attribution to Tullia d'Aragona; here d'Aragona, or whoever authored the letter, writes with stern reprobation of the lasciviousness of much of the vernacular literature currently available and promises in her own romance, instead of the culpable pleasures of Boccaccio or Ariosto, a reformed romance fit to be read by "any decent and devout man" and any "married woman, virgin, widow or nun."[21]

Of course, the fact that Counter-Reformation moralism had the effect of facilitating women's integration in literary culture in this sense cannot be taken as an indication of the gynephile credentials of the movement as a whole. A strain certainly existed within Counter-Reformation culture that associated women with sexual sin and urged men to protect themselves against temptation by limiting their interaction with these "daughters of Eve," in a manner implicitly demonizing of courtly traditions of mixed social interaction. The theologian and future cardinal Silvio Antoniano (1540–1603), in his youth an elegant poet who had corresponded with Laura Battiferra, warned in his *Tre libri dell'educatione christiana dei figliuoli* (1584) that to give a literary education to one's daughters was to risk subjecting them to the moral dangers of "inflammable" conversations with young literati as well as to stoke their "feminine" propensity to vainglory and encourage them to assume indecorous positions of intellectual authority.[22] Despite statements such as this, however, it is misleading to see the Counter-Reformation church as representing a concerted front of ideological opposition to women's cultural engagement. Positions varied accorded to context and circumstance, and a figure like Antoniano is no more representative of the age than someone like the Genoese Benedictine and poet Don Angelo Grillo (1557–1629), whom we find exchanging flattering sonnets with Maddalena Campiglia and encouraging the poetic activity of his relative Livia Spinola. To present the Counter-Reformation without nuance as inimical to the Italian tradition of women's writing is thus misleadingly overtidy and overideological. The cultural microclimate in which that tradition had been nurtured was not the creation of a moment, and its demise would prove correspondingly gradual. Even Antoniano in the *Tre libri,* perhaps mindful of his past acquaintance with the irreproachable Battiferra, ultimately mitigates his strictures against female education by conceding that "every rule has exceptions" ("ogni regola può patire qualche eccezione").[23]

## 2. Chivalry Undimmed: The Contexts of Women's Writing

The majority of critical work to date on female writers of the late Cinque-cento has naturally centered on those writers who wrote and published substantial single-authored works, such as Fonte, Franco, Marinella, Andreini, and Campiglia. As in the period of the midcentury, however, it is important to remember that the "visible" tradition of women's writing, as it appears from library catalogues and other listings of published works, represents only a small portion of what was a far larger and more diffused cultural practice. As had been the case since the beginning of the sixteenth century, well-bred women, like their male peers, cultivated poetry as a graceful accomplishment, perhaps occasionally publishing a sonnet in a select anthology or "temple" but otherwise circulating their work only in manuscript. Good examples of such "gentlewomen poets" in this period are Tarquinia Molza (1542–1617) and Orsola or Orsina Bertolaio Cavalletti (1531–92), both long-term residents of the court of Ferrara. Both were celebrated as poets, although Molza was better known as a singer and musician and a leading member of the famous vocal consort, the *concerto delle donne*.[24] Cavalletti was chosen by Tasso as the titular interlocutor of his dialogue on lyric poetry, *La Cavaletta o vero della poesia toscana* (1584), and Molza as that of his dialogue on love, *La Molza, o vero dell'amore* (1583). The philosopher and literary theorist Francesco Patrizi da Cherso (1529–97) also featured Tarquinia Molza as lead speaker in a dialogue on love.[25] Both Cavalletti and Molza were published in their lifetimes only in anthologies. Cavalletti appears, alongside Isabella Andreini, among the poets collected in Giovanni Battista Licino's *Rime di diversi celebri poeti* of 1587, and in a funerary collection of the same year put together for the poet Isotta Brembati, while Molza has sonnets in Muzio Manfredi's *Per donne romane* of 1575, in a famous 1585 tribute volume put together by Scipione de' Monti for Giovanna Castriota Carafa, Marchioness of Nocera, and in two thematic anthologies edited by Giulio Segni and published in Bologna in 1600 and 1601, one a *tempio* to Cardinal Cinzio Aldobrandini, the other in praise of a sacred image of the Virgin.[26] Both Cavalletti and Molza interestingly illustrate the role of family contexts in supporting and enabling women writers: Molza was a granddaughter of the celebrated early sixteenth-century poet Francesco Maria Molza (1489–1544), a correspondent in his time of Veronica Gambara and Vittoria Colonna, while Cavalletti was the wife of a poet, Ercole Cavalletti (1553–89), and mother of another, Barbara Cavalletti Lotti (d. 1599), whom we find figuring alongside her mother in Giacomo Guaccimanni's *Raccolta di sonetti d'autori diversi* of 1623.[27] Another "dynastic" poet of the time, though known to us only by reputation, is Renata or Renata Pico Salviati (d. 1607), daughter of Fulvia da Correggio Pico (1543–1590), Countess of Mirandola, and thus a great-granddaughter of Veronica Gambara through her maternal line.[28]

The work of the period that offers the richest insight into this "invisible" aristocratic culture of female poetry is Stefano Guazzo's intriguing, though little-known dialogue, *Ghirlanda della contessa Angela Bianca Beccaria*, published posthumously in 1595 and probably written in the early 1590s. Guazzo (1530–93) was Piedmontese in origin and a long-term courtier of the Gonzaga in Mantua. Best known now as the author of the quintessential courtesy book of the era, *La civil conversatione* (1574), he was also the author of a volume of *Dialoghi piacevoli* (1584) and a volume of *rime* in honor of Italian noblewomen (1592). The *Ghirlanda* is set in Pavia in 1590, and recounts a purported three-day conversation among a mixed group of speakers assembled in the home of Count Alfonso Beccaria and his wife Luisa. The discussions are structured around the reading of a series of madrigals commissioned by Guazzo from various contemporary poets, collectively constituting an imagined "garland" of praises for the host's cousin, Countess Angela Bianca Beccaria, who is one of the speakers of the dialogue. A notable feature of the *Ghirlanda* is the number of women included among Guazzo's poets, who amount to seven in total, out of fifty-nine, around 12 percent of the whole. Aside from Tarquinia Molza, the female poets of the *Ghirlanda* are very little known, although poems by one, the Genoese Livia Spinola, also feature in two verse collections published in 1589, Angelo Grillo's *Rime* and the 1589 *Mausoleo* edited by Francesco Melchiori in memory of Giuliano Goselini (1525–87), where she figures in the distinguished company of Isabella Andreini, Maddalena Campiglia, and Margherita Sarrocchi.[29] With the exception of Silvia Bendinelli, noted as of relatively humble estate (she is said to be "inferior to many ladies of Piacenza where the goods of fortune are concerned"), most of the female poets named appear well born.[30] Livia Spinola was the descendent of a distinguished Genoese family that had already produced other poets and Laura Beatrice Cappello from the Venetian patrician Cappello family on one side and the noble Martinengo family of Brescia on the other.[31] The two Sienese, Fulvia Spannocchi and Margherita Marescotti, both from well-known patrician families, are said to vie with one another in beauty, grace, and nobility of birth.[32] All are lavishly praised for their virtue and culture, and for the glory they bring on their home cities and on their country, underlining once more the function of women's talent as a synecdochic expression of the *virtù* of the culture that nurtures it. "If I had to name the part of the world," Count Alfonso at one point boasts, "possess-

ing the greatest number of ladies celebrated and outstanding for the loftiness of their intellect, the nobility of their soul, and the scope of their
learning, I would name Europe as that part, and then Italy within Europe."[33]

A particular interest of the *Ghirlanda* from the point of view of the
present argument is the way in which it locates the female poetic excellence it celebrates within the context of a broader discourse on feminine
conduct and ethos. As noted above, the unifying project of the volume is
that of praise for the figure of Countess Angela Bianca Beccaria, whose
physical beauty and moral excellence is progressively spelled out in the
flower and plant symbolism of the garland of poems describing her. More
directly, as well, we find a prose description of the countess in the introduction to the dialogue; this portrait (*piccolo ritratto*) is explicitly held up by
Guazzo as a model for imitation by his daughter Olimpia, who takes the
role here of ideal reader of the work.[34] Striking in Guazzo's description of
Beccaria is his emphasis on her intellectual and cultural profile: after the
briefest of allusions to her "mortal and exterior charms," he moves rapidly
on to speak in rapturous detail of the beauties of her mind. He notes here
first that her studies have equipped her with a universal knowledge equal
to that of a seasoned world traveler such as "the wise Ulysses or the great
Queen of Sheba." She is then complimented on her eloquence, characterized especially by incisiveness and "laconic" concision. In the realm of cultural accomplishments, the countess is complimented on her broad reading and intimate knowledge of vernacular literature, manifested in her
ability to "recite from memory and with fluency and grace Petrarchan canzoni and entire cantos of Ariosto." She is also portrayed as a skilled musician—both singing and playing are specified—and, though in suspiciously
vague terms, as an accomplished writer (a madrigal later in the collection
by Francesco Pugiella suggests that she wrote poetry, talking of her as
"dearer to Apollo than Sappho").[35] It is only at this point in his description—having concluded that the qualities listed are sufficient to win her a
place among as "the most illustrious women in the world" ("le più illustri
donne del mondo")—that Guazzo condescends to mention his heroine's
more "feminine" virtues. Specifically, he commends Beccaria's spirit of
"charity," manifested in the fact that, not content with the excellence of letters, she devotes herself also to the governance of her home and family
and particularly to the education of her daughters.[36] This is a vision of
female excellence reminiscent of that which we saw embodied in midcentury texts like the life of Irene di Spilimbergo discussed in chapter 3.
Chastity, piety, good governance of the household are seen as insufficient
virtues for a noblewoman ambitious of "honor." To be considered "illus-

trious"—an aspiration presented as entirely appropriate in a woman of status—a capacity for educated conversation is necessary, supplemented ideally by poetic and musical skills.[37] Later in the collection, Silvia Bendinelli
is praised for her excellence in "those gifts that are considered the principal ornament of women."[38] These are clearly regarded as intellectual; it is
only as something of an afterthought that Guazzo specifies that Bendinelli
also attends with diligence to her household and family, citing it as a feature deserving of praise that she does not neglect these domestic tasks for
her writing.[39]

A further point of continuity with earlier sixteenth-century culture
well illustrated by Guazzo's *Ghirlanda* is the persisting importance of gallantry to women in defining elite male identity. If the mid-century model
of the *donna illustre* survived into the late sixteenth century, so too did her
counterpart, the supportive "male feminist," appreciative of female eloquence and talent. While a certain amount of "sex war" banter is found in
the *Ghirlanda*—we find the female speakers occasionally compelled to defend their sex against slanders—this is counterbalanced by the general
tone of respect toward the female intellect.[40] Girolamo Torto hails Tarquinia Molza as "the principal ornament and splendor of the city of Modena"; Count Alfonso boasts of a madrigal by Margherita Marescotti that
it shows its writer skilled in "other than the needle and the spindle"; Giulio
Stefano Lana speaks approvingly of Silvia Bendinelli's parents' encouragement of her "virtuous inclination" to the study of letters.[41] The male
speakers' gallantry offers a mirror image of that of the author, determined
to spend his "last years" ("ultimi anni") and perhaps his "last pages" ("ultime carte") in assembling this weighty monument to female *virtù*.[42] Nor
was Guazzo by any means alone in this period in staging himself as a connoisseur of female creativity. Celebrations of female talent persisted as a
popular theme for poetry—though of course outstripped by celebrations
of female beauty—with new subgenres adding themselves as the categories of *virtuose* expanded. Angelo Grillo's *Rime* of 1589 has poems addressed to the poets Maddalena Campiglia, Livia and Laura Spinola, and
Leonora Bernardi as well as to the singer Laura Peverara, the painter Sofonisba Anguissola, and the lutenist Pentisilea Ferri.[43] Curzio Gonzaga's
*Rime* (1591) contain correspondence sonnets to Campiglia, Virginia Salvi,
and the Florentine poet Fiammetta Soderini; those of Mario Colonna and
Pietro Angeli of Barga (1589) to Soderini, again, and to Laura Battiferra;
those of Orsatto Giustinian (1600) to Campiglia, Olimpia Malipiero, Lucrezia Marinella, and the otherwise unknown Lucia Colao Uderzo.[44]
Campiglia's pastoral *Flori* (1588) attracted a shower of applause from contemporary male *letterati,* while Isabella Andreini, in her dual roles as ac-

tress and poet, might easily have assembled a tribute volume from the verses composed in her honor. Andreini's predecessor as actress-poet, Vincenza Armani (d. 1569), was celebrated following her death in a published funeral oration.[45] Most feted, perhaps, of all, the singer Laura Peverara was the subject of a poetic anthology and two published anthologies of madrigals.[46]

Perhaps the supreme exponent in this period of the role of "celebrant of women" was the poet and courtier Muzio Manfredi of Fermo (1535–1607), a ubiquitous figure in the academic culture of the time, though now best remembered as a dramatist (*Semiramis* [1593]; *La Semiramis boscareccia* [1593]; *Il contrasto amoroso* [1602]). In his long career, Manfredi published numerous volumes of poetry, mainly madrigals, almost all devoted to the praise of women.[47] One of his first works published, the anthology *Per donne romane*, of 1575, is prefaced by an open letter "to the ladies" ("Alle donne") in which Manfredi speaks of himself as having "placed all my efforts and study in that manner of letters I thought most pleasing to you and most fitted to exalt your fame: that is the excellency of Poetry, a truly divine art and one appropriate to your divinity."[48] This devotion is manifested in four further volumes, *Cento donne cantate* (1580), *Cento madrigali* (1587), *Cento sonetti . . . in lode delle donne di Ravenna* (1602), and *Madrigali . . . sopra molti soggetti stravaganti composti* (1606), the first three entirely devoted to women, the last including also a handful of poems to men.[49] Manfredi's *Lettere brevissime* (1606) also contain numerous letters to women. Compositely, these volumes portray Manfredi as engaged in an admiring and flirtatious dialogue not only with the cream of Italian aristocratic womanhood but also with *le donne virtuose,* as he refers to them in *Il contrasto amoroso* (2.4). Among the creative women included among the addressees of his poems and letters are the writers Barbara Torelli Benedetti (1546–post 1602), Maddalena Campiglia, Veronica Franco, Fiammetta Soderini, Laura Guidiccioni Lucchesini (1550–99), Tarquinia Molza, Margherita Sarrocchi, Beatrice Salvi (fl. 1571), Barbara Cavalletti, and Semidea Poggi, the singers Laura Peverara and Leonora Sanvitale (1558/59–1582), the actress and poet Diana Ponti (fl. 1582), and the artists Lavinia Fontana, Barbara Longhi (1552–1638), and Fede Galizia (1578–1630).[50] Manfredi also devoted a volume to the praise of his wife, Ippolita Benigni Manfredi, who was herself celebrated as a poet, though little survives to testify to her talent.[51] Along with Ercole and Orsina Cavalletti, and Tomaso Porcacchi and Bianca Aurora d'Este, Manfredi and Ippolita Benigni constitute a new phenomenon in the literature of the period, of married couples of *letterati,* publishing in collaboration or side-by-side.[52] The ultimate in "interactive muses," one might almost suspect Ippolita Benigni qua poet to be a construction of her indefatigable husband. Certainly, his literal "marriage to the muse" sets the seal on his lifetime self-staging as connoisseur of feminine talent.[53]

Besides the kind of vaporous courtly compliment in which Manfredi was such a specialist, a more solid tradition of theoretical defenses of women's "nobility and excellence" also persisted into this period, even though it cannot be claimed that this genre of writing enjoyed the same cultural centrality as it had had in the first half of the century. A typical product of the age is Hercole Filogenio [Ercole Marescotti]'s *Dell'eccellenza delle donne*, published in Fermo in 1589. The work rehearses the by now familiar philosophical arguments for women's dignity, scrupulously citing philosophical loci in its marginal notes, before concluding with a sequence of sonnets addressed to prominent women of the day. Modern women's achievements in literature and art are celebrated, with Marescotti's Bolognese compatriot, the artist Lavinia Fontana, singled out for particular attention, and Marescotti expresses keen regret that the "superstition" and "uncouth suspicion" ("rustica sospitione") of men, and their reluctance to allow their daughters a proper literary education, hold back other women in his home city from expressing their "brilliant intellect" ("felicissimo ingegno") and "inestimable worth ("inestimabil valore").[54] In the light of my earlier argument regarding the supposed intransigence of the Counter-Reformation church with regard to female learning, it is interesting to note that Marescotti was a priest, while the dedicatee of the text, the young Duchess of Bracciano, Flavia Peretti Orsini (1574–1606), was the grandniece of Pope Sixtus V (Felice Peretti), one of the most zealous reforming pontiffs of the Counter-Reformation, who earlier in his career had aroused hostility in Venice for the severity with which he exercised his task as counselor to the Inquisition. Conjunctions such as this should serve in themselves as a warning against any overly sharp gender-ideological contrasts between "Renaissance" and "Counter-Reformation" culture in Italy. Other male-authored examples of late sixteenth and early seventeenth-century treatises on women's "nobility and excellence" include Cornelio Lanci's *Esempi della virtù delle donne* (1590), dedicated to the poet Maddalena Salvetti; Francesco Serdonati's revised and expanded edition of Betussi's translation of Boccaccio's *Delle donne illustri* (1596); and Pietro Andrea Canoniero's *Della eccellenza delle donne* (1606). Rehearsals of the arguments for women's dignity are also found in other works, not specifically dedicated to the theme, such as Annibale Romei's popular *Discorsi* (1585), a dialogue set in the court of Ferrara.[55] Of particular interest from the point of view of "Tridentine values" is Pietro Paolo Ribera's garguantuan *Le glorie immortali de' trionfi et heroiche imprese d'ottocento quarantacinque donne illustri an-*

*tiche e moderne* (1609), authored by an Augustinian canon and dedicated to an abbess.[56] Though distinctly "Counter-Reformation" in the extent to which it privileges examples from biblical and church history—and in the pride of place given to virgin martyrs in its hierarchy of illustrious women—Ribera's treatise still shows strong continuities with the humanistic tradition of "defenses of women," both in its arguments and its exemplification. Ribera has fulsome praise, moreover, for recent female "defenders of women," such as Moderata Fonte and Lucrezia Marinella, lauding the former particularly as "unique in her learning, exemplary in her intelligence, of incomparable power and remarkable capacity" and praising her *Il merito delle donne* (1600) as one of the most admirable works of the day.[57]

Besides personal courtly self-positioning on the part of male authors, regional pride remained a strong factor in promoting the discourse of "women's excellence." The rhetorical value of talented women as "ornaments to the *patria*" was now sufficiently established for it to have become virtually de rigueur for any aspiring town or city to equip itself with such an adornment. The dynamic is well captured in a line from an encomiastic sonnet preceding a collection of poems published in the small Veneto town of Conegliano, near Treviso, in 1610 by the local poet Lucchesia Sbarra Coderta (?1576–1662): "now, Conegliano, through her your fame rises."[58] Following the vogue for poetry anthologies in the mid-Cinquecento, the latter decades of the century saw increasing numbers of local collections, often put together on particular occasions or to honor particular figures. These parochial minianthologies routinely feature at least one female poet: thus a volume of poems published in Verona in 1596 collecting verse by local poets in praise of Chiara Dolfin Corner, wife of the Venetian prefect of the city, the future doge Giovanni Corner or Cornaro (1551–1629), contains a number of poems and an oration by the Veronese noblewoman Ersilia Spolverini, while an elegant anthology of verse by poets from Udine edited by Giacomo Bratteolo in 1597 has seven sonnets by Catella Marchesi, the 12-year-old daughter of the dedicatee, Lidia Marchesi.[59] Similarly, two female poets are included in a 1590 verse anthology published in Treviso to congratulate the local nobleman Count Antonio Collalto on his appointment to a high-ranking military post. One of these, Innocenza Carrai, presumably enjoyed a degree of local fame given that she is cited with her academic name ("la Piscatrice, Accademica Errante"); the other, however, Marina Dalla Torre, seems to have earned her presence simply as the daughter of the compiler of the anthology, Giovanni Dalla Torre.[60] Still more enterprise was shown by the literary theorist Giovanni Antonio Gilio, whose *Topica poetica* of 1580 gives the texts of a number of poems by apocryphal fourteenth-century female poets from his hometown, Fabriano in the Marche.[61] These shadowy figures—one presented as a correspondent of Petrarch's—had first been mentioned by Gilio in a letter of 1564 attempting to engage the support of Alessandro Farnese for a campaign to have Fabriano elevated to the status of a city. The episode is of interest for a number of reasons, not least as an attempt to "write women back" retrospectively into the generative phase of the Italian lyric tradition.[62] Here, however, the point to note is quite how unequivocally the ability to boast of a "famous" woman poet is perceived as conferring status on a town, to the point of almost being regarded as a qualifying attribute of a distinguished civic culture. These considerations must have acted to an appreciable degree to outweigh remaining scruples about the decorum of women putting their names to poetry; in these circumstances, to write as a woman and have one's work circulated could be deemed almost a patriotic act.

It will be noted that, aside from Gilio, all these examples come from towns on the Venetian mainland: Conegliano, Udine, Verona, Treviso. This is indicative of a marked geographical trend in women's writing of this period: virtually no important town in the Veneto in this period failed to produce a female writer of some public recognition. If Vicenza could glory in Maddalena Campiglia, Padua could boast Isabella Andreini and Giulia Bigolina as well as the dramatist Valeria Miani and the apothecary and natural philosopher Camilla Erculiani Greghetti.[63] Rovigo, meanwhile, had Issicratea Monte, who before her premature death had attained considerable fame as a poet and orator, while Verona, besides Ersilia Spolverini, and the earlier Aquilana Prandina or Prandino (d. pre-1556), also produced the poet Veneranda Bragadin Cavallo (fl. 1613–19), active in the early seventeenth century.[64] We also see in this same region, highly unusually, a brief engagement by female poets with the flourishing Italian tradition of rustic dialect poetry, much cultivated in the Veneto in this period: Monte and Campiglia contributed deftly-turned dialect verses to two commemorative collections of the early 1580s, as did two lesser-known poets, the Vicentine noblewoman Bianca Angaran (d. 1600) and the otherwise unidentified Maria Azzalina.[65] The rise of the Veneto in this period as one of the prime centers for women's writing is intriguing and would be deserving of further study.[66] One motive for it may have been a local consciousness of the region's strong fifteenth-century tradition in this respect, with the Nogarola sisters, Maddalena Scrovegni, and Laura Brenzoni, a tradition kept alive through successive sixteenth-century "famous women" listings and the publication of Isotta Nogarola's Dialogus in 1563.[67] The presence of the renowned Lucrezia Gonzaga da Gazzuolo in Fratta, near

Rovigo, from 1541 until her death in 1576, must also have had an effect in stimulating awareness of women's literary potential.[68] This is especially clear in the case of Issicratea Monte, two of whose principal poetic contacts, the poet and dramatist Luigi Groto or Cieco d'Adria (1541–85) and the *letterato* and agronomist Giovanni Maria Bonardo (d. 1584), were both leading figures within the Accademia dei Pastori Frattegiani, the literary academy sponsored by Gonzaga.[69] Another factor to bear in mind when considering the propitiousness of the mainland Veneto as an environment for women's writing is one already noted in chapter 3: the difficulty of the dominant regional power, Venice, in producing its own female writers—at least, outside the ranks of courtesans and *"irregolari"* like Gaspara Stampa and Veronica Franco—given its distinctive social traditions, which kept patrician women fairly strictly to a domestic "separate sphere." It is noteworthy in this regard that Issicratea Monte, still in her teens, was invited to deliver a gratulatory oration to Doge Sebastiano Venier in 1578, in an event that recalled Cassandra Fedele's adolescent prodigies as Venetian *oratrix* in the 1480s. The gesture effectively co-opted the precocious Monte as an exemplar of Venetian feminine worth, following a dynamic already observed with Irene di Spilimbergo and Lucia Albani.[70]

Even as Issicratea Monte was emerging to notice, however, as the latest in a series of "substitute muses" for Venice, however, the city's long-standing absence from the Italian roll call of "respectable" female literary talent was finally drawing to an end. A semianonymous encomiastic sonnet appended to Monte's 1578 oration for Venier probably constitutes the first appearance in print of the prolific Moderata Fonte, who, three years later, would make her more confident "official" debut with the chivalric romance, *Tredici canti del Floridoro.*[71] Over the following two decades, in a series of innovative writings, Fonte and her younger contemporary Lucrezia Marinella placed Venice at the forefront of the mainstream Italian tradition of women's writing for the first time since Fedele's oratorical prowess in the late Quattrocento had first put the city on this particular map. A shift in the social acceptance of the unwonted figure of the female writer in Venice is probably indicated by the difference in the two women's self-naming as authors: where Fonte, venturing into print in the early 1580s, adopted a pseudonym in deference to social decorum, Marinella, whose first appearances were in the mid-1590s, published happily under her own name.[72] Tellingly enough, like their predecessor Fedele, both writers were *cittadine* rather than of patrician status—perhaps the only social background really viable for a "decent" Venetian female writer in this period, given the strength of the social imperative of keeping the republic's patrician breeding stock free from the taint of unseemly cultural display.[73] Interestingly, both Fonte and Marinella had non-Venetian connections in their family circles that may have facilitated their path to literary emergence. Marinella's father, a prominent physician and writer, who was presumably responsible for his daughter's unusually thorough humanistic education, was originally from Modena, the birthplace of Tarquinia Molza and married home of Lucia Bertani. Fonte's guardian and literary advisor Giovanni Niccolò Doglioni (1548–1629), meanwhile, who promoted her writing during her lifetime and wrote her biography after her death, was from Belluno, on the Venetian terra ferma, not far from the birthplace of Irene di Spilimbergo, the great "Venetian" literary icon of her age.[74]

Besides the interesting example of Venice and the Veneto, where the geographical distribution of women writers is concerned, both continuities and discontinuities may be registered in the closing decades of the sixteenth century with the earlier part of the century. One very notable development was the decline of the South as an important center for women's writing. In the first half of the century, Neapolitans—by birth or adoption—figured very prominently among women writers: besides Vittoria Colonna, appropriable by virtue of her long residence on Ischia, Naples could claim writers of the status and visibility of Laura Terracina, Isabella Morra, Dianora Sanseverino, and Costanza d'Avalos, Duchess of Amalfi. In the later sixteenth century, southern women's presence was much reduced, to the extent that the great tribute volume for Giovanna Castriota edited by Scipione de' Monti in 1585, an important document of the southern male-authored lyric tradition, includes only three female poets, one northern (Tarquinia Molza), one southern (Elisabetta Aiutamicristo (?d. c. 1580) of Palermo, the third unidentifiable ("Virginia N").[75] Elsewhere, Tuscany continued to enjoy a reputation as a center for women's writing, although Siena seems to have lost its absolute supremacy in this regard with the loss of its independence in 1556. Two Sienese poets appear in Guazzo's *Ghirlanda,* as we have seen, and Lucca produced at least three noted poets, Silvia Bendinelli, Leonora Bernardi Bellati (also a musician), and Laura Guidiccioni Lucchesini, in addition to the much older Chiara Matraini, who survived into this period and had an extraordinary late burst of literary creativity in the 1580s and 1590s.[76] Florence, meanwhile, after boasting of the "foreigners" Tullia d'Aragona and Laura Battiferra earlier in the century, produced in this period its first homegrown aristocratic poets: Fiammetta Soderini, Lorenza Strozzi (1514–91), and Maddalena Salvetti.[77] Other cities and regions could lay claim to less of a concentration of women writers, although Ferrara, as noted earlier, had Tarquinia Molza and Orsina Cavalletti, and Bologna could boast an impressive microtradition of literary nuns that included Febronia Pannolini and the later Diodata Malvasia and Semidea Poggi.[78] For many, a single figurehead had to suffice: Parma, with Barbara Torelli; Città di Castello, with Francesca Turina Bufalini (1553–1641); even Rome with the remarkable Margherita Sarrocchi.[79] A last city worthy of mention in this context is Genoa, an interesting case since it had barely figured in the earlier part of the century as a locus for female literary production.[80] In this period, by contrast, the poets Laura and Livia Spinola attained some prominence, especially the latter, who, besides featuring in Guazzo's *Ghirlanda*, also has poems in the *Rime* of her cousin Angelo Grillo and figures in both the *Rime* of Giuliano Goselini and a tribute volume for him put together after his death. Another aristocratic Genoese female poet recorded in this period is Novella Doria, whom we find exchanging verse with Bartolomeo Scaramelli in a work of his published in 1585.[81] This microdevelopment seems interesting, given that this was a period when Genoa was more generally working to establish itself on the national literary map, through the efforts of poets such as Grillo, Ansaldo Cebà (1565–1623), and Gabriele Chiabrera (1552–1638) and publishers such as Girolamo Bartoli and, later, Giuseppe Pavoni. Grillo's energetic promotion of the Spinola poets may be seen as part of this more general campaign of patriotic promotion. For a city truly to be able to stake a claim as a center of lyric production, a female poet—or preferably several—was a near necessity. This remained as true in the 1580s and 1590s as it had been in the 1540s and 1550s.

In conclusion, this survey of the contexts of women's writing in the late sixteenth century has found a perhaps unexpected level of continuity with the earlier part of the century in terms of the degree of supportiveness women writers continued to receive within quite significant segments of elite society. It is easy to reach a contrary conclusion based on a few well-known cases: Veronica Franco's enforced combativeness in the face of male slander or the much-quoted phrase of Moderata Fonte's biographer Giovanni Niccolò Doglioni to the effect that she had confined her writing to spare moments in deference to "false notion, so widespread in this city today, that women should excel in nothing but the running of their household."[82] These cases should not be seen as representative, however. Both, significantly, are Venetian, and reflect social attitudes not necessarily universal in Italy, as Doglioni's impatient tone indicates (as we have seen, he was himself a native of Belluno). The attacks on Franco, moreover, seem motivated more by her status as a courtesan than as a woman who dared to write. It is noteworthy that neither Fonte nor her successor Lucrezia Marinella attracted any such similar personal attacks; indeed, we find Fonte cited with pride among the "glories of Venice" in popular guides for visitors to the city, along with the now legendary Cassandra Fedele.[83]

Meanwhile, in nearby Vicenza, Maddalena Campiglia could publish her pastoral *Flori* with an appendix of no fewer than twenty-seven laudatory poems, many contributed by her fellow citizens—this, despite her "irregular" situation, at the time of publication, as a woman living separately from her husband.[84] With luck—if born into the "right" class and the "right" geocultural context—women writers might confidently hope to be as feted by their communities as their literary forebears had been earlier in the century. Indeed, in many ways, simply as a result of decades of habituation, they were now more accepted than ever before. A sense of the historical depth that the tradition of women's writing had now acquired may be had by considering the orations Valeria Miani and Issicratea Monte delivered in 1581 in Padua to celebrate the passage through the Veneto of the dowager empress Maria (1528–1603), widow of Maximilian II (1527–76) and daughter of Charles V.[85] These were likely inspired by the precedent of the oration delivered some quarter-century earlier, in 1556, by the elderly Cassandra Fedele, brought out of her retirement in Venice to greet the queen of Poland, Bona Sforza (1494–57), while it is possible, in turn, that the Fedele oration was itself intended in part as a tribute to the remembered oratorical accomplishments of Bona's grandmother, Ippolita Maria Sforza, whose public debut as an orator dated to around a century earlier.[86] By the late sixteenth century, Italian women's writing could look back on well over a century and a half of recorded tradition, sedulously kept alive in memory by the lists of "famous women" that formed a staple of the *trattatistica* of the time. The degree to which this contributed to their sense of literary "belonging" may be vividly glimpsed in a passage of Campiglia's pastoral *Flori,* where the eponymous heroine, an aspiring poet, recalls the past example of a "Victorious" and Divine" nymph—clearly Vittoria Colonna, already dead some forty years at the time of writing—who had far outshone in her "sweet singing" the most accomplished shepherds of the age.[87]

### 3. A Literature of Their Own? Writing, Ownership, Assertion

Turning from questions of context to the character of women's literary production in this period, we may note some quite distinctive shifts with respect to the tradition discussed in the previous chapters. One, which has already been pointed out, is the extraordinary expansion that we find in this period in the range of literary genres attempted by women. As we have seen, already in the 1540s and 1550s, we can register a tentative "outreach" on women's part beyond their original vernacular territory of lyric poetry. Prose writings were published in this period by Tullia d'Aragona, Chiara Matraini, and Vittoria Colonna, and we know of experiments in verse and prose narrative by Matraini, Giulia Bigolina, and Laura Pieri as well as, possibly, by d'Aragona.[88] Despite these experiments, however, women's writing remained overwhelmingly limited to lyric verse, as it had been since the 1490s. The later sixteenth century marked a radical departure on this score. Looking first solely at narrative and dramatic forms, we find women's engagement with these genres gathering pace fairly rapidly from the early 1580s onwards, when we find Moderata Fonte—perhaps, as we have seen, inspired by Issicratea Monte's successes as an orator in Venice in the late 1570s—publishing in rapid succession an unfinished chivalric romance, *Tredici canti del Floridoro* (1581), a dramatic *libretto per musica, Le feste* (1582), and an ottava rima biblical narrative, *La passione di Christo* (also 1582).[89] Five years later, we find the first female experiment with the modish form of pastoral drama, with Barbara Torelli's unpublished but much lauded *Partenia,* written in Parma, around 1587, followed swiftly by the first published pastorals by women, Maddalena Campiglia's *Flori* and Isabella Andreini's *Mirtilla* (1588).[90] From this point, over the following two decades, the generic range of female-authored narrative and drama continued to expand and diversify. In 1592, the year of her premature death, Moderata Fonte published a follow-up to her *Passione di Christo, La resurretione di Giesù Christo,* while in 1600, there followed, posthumously, her vividly imagined dialogue *Il merito delle donne,* set among a group of female speakers in Venice.[91] Meanwhile, in 1595, Lucrezia Marinella began her long and immensely prolific publishing career with the four-canto ottava rima hagiographic poem, *La Colomba sacra,* recounting the life of the early Christian martyr St. Columba of Sens.[92] Marinella followed this with two further hagiographic works of similar scale, *La vita del serafico e glorioso San Francesco* (1597) and *La vita di Maria Vergine* (1602), on the life of the Virgin, coupling this last, however, with a more expansive prose life of the Virgin that better prefigures her later hagiographic works.[93] From this point, Marinella alternated secular and sacred, verse and prose, in her narrative works, moving from the mainly prose pastoral romance *Arcadia felice* (1605) to the ottava rima mythological poem *Amore innamorato, et impazzato* (1618), while also adding a series of lives of the apostles to the third edition of her *La vita di Maria Vergine* of 1617.[94] Meanwhile, we find the Paduan Valeria Miani initiating her publishing career with a pastoral drama, *Amorosa speranza* (1604), and extending it, most unusually, with a tragedy, *Celinda* (1611), the only female-authored tragedy of the age.[95] Most impressively of all, perhaps, by the measure of the day, we find in 1606 the first essay by a woman at the grandest and most magisterial narrative form of the period, the historical *poema eroico* on the model of Tasso's *Gerusalemme liberata:* this is Margherita Sarrocchi's *La Scanderbeide* (published in its final version in 1623), which recounts the struggles of the fifteenth-century Albanian hero Gjergj Kastrioti ("Scanderbeg") in his struggles against the Turks.[96] Although Sarrocchi's was the only such poem to be completed in the period—the only other female-authored epic of the age, Lucrezia Marinella's *Enrico, overo Bisanzio acquistato,* was published much later, in 1635—we know of several unfinished attempts at epic, such as Maddalena Salvetti's biblical-chivalric poem *David,* of which three completed *canti* were published posthumously in 1611, and a late, untitled poem by Laura Battiferra, also drawing on Old Testament material, of which a short fragment survives in manuscript.[97] Veronica Franco and Maddalena Campiglia were both also reported to be working on epic poems at the time of their deaths in the early to mid-1590s.[98]

In addition to exploring these new genre trajectories, women continued to be active as secular and spiritual poets; indeed, several of the most notable female-authored prose works of the period incorporate quite substantial verse elements.[99] Short verse forms such as the sonnet and madrigal remained important as forms of social currency, in a manner well attested by the provincial anthologies discussed in the previous section, often serving as "entry-level" literature for young writers keen to see their names in print. At the same time, we find more ambitious, single-authored verse-collections being published, as in the earlier part of the century. The outstanding examples here, from the point of view of impact and distribution, were Isabella Andreini's principal volumes of *Rime,* published in 1601 and—posthumously, by her husband—1605.[100] Other important secular female-authored verse collections of the period are Maddalena Salvetti's *Rime toscane* of 1590, and Chiara Matraini's revised *Rime* of 1595 and 1597, effectively a new work compared to the first edition of 1555.[101] To these may be added, rather later in date, two volumes by provincial Veneto writers: the 1610 *Rime* of Lucchesia Sbarra of Conegliano and the three slim volumes of verse published by Veneranda Bragadin between 1613 and 1619.[102] "Spiritual" collections, meanwhile, include Francesca Turina's *Rime spirituali sopra i misteri del santissimo rosario* of 1595 and Lucrezia Marinella's *Rime sacre* of 1602 as well as the volume of Latin hymns published by the Florentine nun Lorenza Strozzi in 1588.[103] Laura Battiferra also left a very substantial collection of mainly spiritual late verse in manuscript at the time of her death in 1589, while Maddalena Salvetti left an unfinished volume of *poesie liriche spirituali,* published posthumously in 1611.[104] If we add in the individual encomiastic works published as pamphlets in the 1590s by Moderata Fonte, Silvia Bendinelli, and Isabella Cervoni, these publications add up to quite a substantial body of work, even if it must be acknowledged that the majority of the collections mentioned were notably small-scale and provincial.[105] Andreini's *Rime* aside, no verse collection by a female poet at this time achieved anything like the national fame or diffusion enjoyed by those of, say, Tullia d'Aragona—still less, Vittoria Colonna or Laura Terracina. Most of the female-authored poetry was this period was, moreover, conservative metrically and stylistically, keeping stoutly to a Petrarchan or late-Petrarchan formula. Again, the only exception is Andreini, who shows herself open, for example, to the formal innovations of Gabriele Chiabrera, the "Ligurian Amphion," as Andreini apostrophizes him in one poem, mingling metrically "light" Chiabreraesque forms such as the *canzonetta* and scherzo in her 1601 *Rime* alongside the fashionable madrigal form and the more traditional Petrarchan sonnet, sestina and canzone.[106]

Where thematics are concerned, the female poets of this period kept to the formula that had for the most characterized female-authored verse in the midcentury, privileging occasional and religious poetry over the more sensitive subject of love. Once again here, Andreini is exceptional, at least in her 1601 *Rime,* which freely mingles love poetry, some quite sensual, with occasional, moral, and religious verse. Andreini negotiates the issue of feminine decorum with panache, referencing her career as an actress in her famous opening sonnet ("S'alcun fia mai che i versi miei negletti") to distance her verse from the Petrarchan autobiographical mode. Just as in her stage performances, she is used to dealing in the currency of "feigned ardors," "imagined loves," "insincere affect," and "false words," so Andreini directs us to read her poetry not as a lyric confessional but as a form of literary histrionics.[107] Reinforcing this point, and adding to the kaleidoscopic *varietas* of the collection, Andreini frequently adopts a male voice in her love lyrics, an expedient already used earlier by Laura Terracina in her first *Rime* of 1548. Leaving aside Andreini, and her predecessor as actress-poet, Vincenza Armani, few other female poets essayed love as a theme, The only exceptions are those women who wrote of love within a "safe" domestic context, such as Francesca Turina Bufalini in the Colonnaesque sequence in mourning of her husband she includes as an appendix to her *Rime spirituali* of 1595, and Lucchesia Sbarra in her more sui generis adaptation of the Petrarchan postmortem mode to express her love for her dead infant son.[108] If there was a degree of self-censorship at work, however, in women's avoidance of love themes, this applied only to the delicate context of first-person lyric poetry. In fictional works of the period, with the conspicuous exception of Marinella, who shows herself programmatically ascetic in this regard, female writers showed themselves willing to experiment with erotic themes.[109] The resulting explorations are of remarkable interest, ranging from Valeria Miani's dramatization in *Amorosa speranza* of a female protagonist divided between duty toward an errant husband and love for a new admirer, to Andreini's celebration of the sensual pleasures of a reciprocal love within marriage in *Mirtilla* and Margherita Sarrocchi's striking portrayal of the moral ambiguities of an adulterous affair in the first version of her *Scanderbeide*.[110] Perhaps especially noteworthy is the veiled or explicit representation in several works of same-sex love between women, a theme already adumbrated in Giulia Bigolina's *Urania* in the 1550s. In the period under discussion here, we find love between women most explicitly treated in Campiglia's *Flori* and in her pastoral eclogue *Calisa* (1589). It is also present, however in Miani's *Celinda* and, more peripherally, in Marinella's *Arcadia felice*, both drawing, like *Urania*, on the motifs of transvestitism and mistaken identity.[111] The theme of chastity, too, and the rejection of sensual love, are given notably interesting development in the female-authored literature of the period. Where a figure like Barbara Torelli's meek and virginal Partenia, in the play of that name, may seem a direct internalizing transcription of patriarchal ideals, Maddalena Campiglia and Moderata Fonte lend the choice of chastity in women less habitual connotations of intellectual autonomy and self-determination, both portraying female figures who reject marriage to pursue a poetic vocation.[112]

The expansion of women writers' generic range in the period after around 1580 may be seen as indicative of a more general trend toward an enhanced confidence and assertiveness on their part and of what Zancan has termed as their "progressive integration within the literary system."[113] One interesting token of this is that we find women in the late sixteenth and early seventeenth centuries occasionally taking on an editorial or mediatory role in the presentation of literary works to the public rather than simply, as had been the case earlier in the century, being the recipients of such meditation on the part of men. There are some marginal precedents for this in the 1560s, where we find poets like Laura Battiferra and Olimpia Malipiero assisting in the process of soliciting works for collections of commemorative verse.[114] We see more of a leading editorial role taken by Veronica Franco in 1575—though admittedly for a much slighter publication—when she coordinated the assembling of a verse collection commemorating the death of Estore Martinengo, Count of Malpaga, near Bergamo, seemingly at the instigation of Estore's brother, Francesco, to whom she dedicated the work. The volume—printed without a publisher's name or date—contains verse by twelve poets, all male with the exception of Franco herself, and encompassing such luminaries as Domenico Venier, Orsatto Giustinian, and Celio Magno as well as other less prestigious names. Franco herself is quantitatively the most salient contributor to the collection, with nine poems, although she modestly places herself at the end of the sequence of poets, who are seemingly ranked in descending order of social hierarchy, with the "Clarissimo D. V." (Venier) at the head.[115] Although this is the only instance we know of from the period of a woman editing a verse collection of this kind, we find Maddalena Campiglia in the early 1590s contributing material to publications by Curzio Gonzaga, her friend and relative by marriage: first, in 1591, a series of brief verse summaries (*argomenti*) to the second edition of Gonzaga's chivalric romance, *Il Fidamante* (1591); then, the following year, the dedicatory letter (to Marfisa d'Este Cibo-Malaspina) of Gonzaga's comedy, *Gli inganni*.[116] Finally, and most impressively, we find Lucrezia Marinella in 1606 supplying learned annotations and an allegory for the important edition of Luigi Tansillo's *Lagrime di San Pietro* commissioned by the Venetian publisher Barezzo Barezzi in 1606. In all these cases, especially the last, we see female writers filling precisely the kind of paraliterary tasks that had traditionally been the preserve of men. Nor is their sex particularly highlighted: Barezzi notes simply that he commissioned the Tansillo matter from Marinella on the strength of the learning and intellect that made her universally admired.[117] Together with her *Nobiltà et eccellenza delle donne* (1600), Marinella's annotations to Tansillo mark the high point of women's erudite performance in this period: besides the expected Plato and Aristotle, the philosophical authorities Marinella refers to in her commentary include Plotinus, Xenocrates, Dionysius the Areopagite, Ficino, and Sts. Bernard and Augustine. This level of philosophical erudition was not unprecedented in a woman, of course: humanists such as Isotta Nogarola and Olimpia Morata (1526–55) could probably have equaled it. What is new, rather, is the *status* the volume accords to female erudition: in a move that strikingly inverts the long-established didactic convention of using women as proxies for an "unlettered audience," Marinella's role here as allegorizer is to interpret Tansillo's work for the benefit of readers both female and male.

As a further instance of the enlargement of scope and the "professionalization" (in a loose sense) of women's writing in this period, we might look at the increasingly assertive character in this period of female writers' authorial self-presentation. The best token of this is the change in women's dedicatory practices as they may be charted across the periods 1538–60 and 1580–1602 (see appendix B). A very notable tendency in the earlier period is for works by women to be presented to the dedicatee and the reading public by a male intermediary, who, in most cases, presents the decision to publish as having been taken on his initiative, in the face of the author's modest reluctance. In some cases, this commonplace may have had a basis in fact: as we have seen, early editions of Colonna's poetry do seem genuinely to have been published without her consent. In other cases, however, this kind of "screen" paratext is clearly a rhetorical gesture of modesty being staged for the public: this seems likely to have been so with Tullia d'Aragona's *Dialogo,* Laura Terracina's first two volumes of *Rime,* and Chiara Matraini's *Rime* and *Oratione d'Isocrate a Demonico.* In only seven of the seventeen works listed between 1538 and 1560 (inclusive) do we find the dedicatory letter to a work written by the author herself, and four of these are by the prolific and precociously "commercial" Terracina, who rather skews the statistics in this regard.[118] These proportions are dramatically reversed in the later period, 1580–1602, where twenty-three of the twenty-six works listed are presented by the author.[119] One factor in this shift may, of course, be the gradual societal acceptance of the norms of typographical culture in this period and a move away from the aristocratic prejudices against print that still endured in the first half of the sixteenth century. Even if this is a general shift, however, it seems much denser in significance where women are concerned in that the prejudice against "public appearances" by women were stronger and more ideologically charged. Taken in conjunction with other developments in this period, such as the broadening of women's writing from quasi-autobiographical to more "objective" genres, and the occasional appearance of women themselves in mediatory or editorial roles, it confirms the sense that—even if they often continued to present themselves, with conventional modesty, as approaching authorship with trepidation and a sense of inadequacy— women were in practice increasingly comfortable in assuming an authorial role. This may not, of course, have applied equally across all segments of the literate elite from which women writers were drawn: as we saw in the previous section, the retiring aristocratic lady writer was not a vanished species in this period. In some cases, however, what we seem to see in this period is the adumbration of a more "professional" authorial type, engaged with the press and concerned with her diffusion and public image in a way that in some senses prefigures the eighteenth-century "woman of letters."

A further, and intriguing, development that emerges clearly from a comparative scrutiny of women writers' dedicatory practices across the three quarters of a century or so from 1538 to 1602 is the increasing tendency of women writers to address their works to female dedicatees. Of our seventeen earlier works (1538–1560) listed in the appendix, only six are dedicated to women, and one of these, Laura Terracina's *Seste rime* of 1558, published in Lucca with a dedication to Elisabetta della Rovere Cibo, Marchioness of Massa (1529–61), turns out, on closer inspection, to be a red herring.[120] The default route in this period, then, appears to be for works by women authors to be presented by male "mediators" and dedicated to male addressees. The model is perfectly embodied in Lodovico Domenichi's 1559 anthology of women's poetry, which was put together by Domenichi with help from Giuseppe Betussi and is prefaced by two dedicatory letters, from Domenichi to Giannotto Castiglione and from the publisher to Gerardo Spada. Although Domenichi notes that he had considered the possibility of choosing a female dedicatee—going so far as to list possible candidates had he chosen to do so—in practice, the framing of this iconic tribute to women's literary "genius" is emphatically and exclusively male.[121] This model shifts very significantly if we look to the later phase of women's writing, that from 1580 to 1602. By this point, male dedicatees have become a minority: only twelve of the twenty-six works listed for this period have a male figure as a dedicatee, and two of those—Moderata Fonte's *Floridoro,* and Maddalena Campiglia's *Flori*—have dual dedications to a male and a female figure. The remainder of dedications in this period are to women, mainly of the ruling dynasties of Italy, with a scattering to lesser aristocratic figures. The change is noteworthy, especially when we consider it in conjunction with the other tendency noted in this period for women writers to assume authorship of dedicatory letters themselves. In the earlier period, a work dedicated by a female author to a female dedicatee was a rarity: in fact, setting aside the false lead of Terracina's *Seste rime,* the only examples in this period are Tullia d'Aragona's *Rime* of 1547 and Laura Battiferra's of 1560, both dedicated to Eleonora of Toledo, and Terracina's *Quinte rime* of 1552, dedicated to Irene Castriota Sanseverino. In the later period, by contrast, the pattern of works being dedicated by women to women becomes increasingly the norm, to the extent that gender often appears to rank above geography and other factors in determining the choice of dedicatee.[122] This is especially obvious in the case of writers in Venice or the Veneto, where high-profile aristocratic female patrons were not easy to find locally.[123] Thus we find Maddalena Campiglia dedicating her *Flori* to Isabella Pallavicino Lupi, Marchioness of Soragna, near Parma, while Moderata Fonte's dedicatees include Bianca Cappello, Grand Duchess of Tuscany, and Margherita Langosco Parpaglia, Countess of Bastia, wife of the ambassador of Savoy. Fonte's *Merito delle donne,* published, as already noted, posthumously, was similarly dedicated by her daughter to a "foreign" noblewoman of the highest aristocracy, Livia Feltria della Rovere, the young Duchess of Urbino. Fonte's prolific younger contemporary, Lucrezia Marinella, continued this practice, with few exceptions, dedicating her first published work, *La Colomba sacra* to Margherita d'Este, Duchess of Ferrara, and her *Vita del serafico e glorioso San Francesco* to Christine of Lorraine (1565–1637), Grand Duchess of Tuscany, while, later, her *De' gesti heroici e della vita maravigliosa della serafica S[anta] Caterina* (1624) was dedicated to Christine's daughter-in-law and successor as grand duchess Maria Maddalena d'Austria (1589–1631) and her 1605 *Arcadia felice* and 1618 *Amore innamorato* to successive duchesses of Mantua.[124] Even the elderly Chiara Matraini, the dedicatees of whose works tended otherwise to be local to Lucca and of middle-ranking status, falls into this pattern with her 1586 *Considerationi sopra i sette salmi,* dedicated to Lucrezia d'Este della Rovere, Duchess of Urbino, and with her last work, the 1602 *Dialoghi spirituali,* which are dedicated to Marfisa d'Este Cibo-Malaspina. In some cases, a geographical logic can be traced in these dedications. The dedicatee of Fonte's 1581 *Floridoro,* the Venetian-born Duchess of Florence, Bianca Cappello, was a magnet for Venetian writers in search of patronage, while Marinella's dedication of her first work to the Duchess of Ferrara may be explained in part by the fact that her father originated from Modena and was thus, by birth, a subject of the Este.[125] In general, however, it is hard to escape the conclusion that women writers in this period, in dedicating their works, ranked gender very high in their criteria of selection; women were, in this period, clearly selecting their own dedicatees, and their preference was generally for women.[126]

As women's writing oriented itself more decisively toward an ideal audience of elite women, we find discourses developing to accommodate this rhetorical scenario.[127] One of the most notable is a reprise of the language of same-sex erotic homage discussed in chapter 3 in connection with Laudomia Forteguerri's poetry of the 1530s for Margaret of Austria. The most intriguing instance of this is Maddalena Campiglia's pastoral eclogue, *Calisa,* which shows the nymph Flori, representative of the poet, pining with love for her patron, Isabella Pallavicino Lupi, Marchioness of Sorgana, under the guise of the woodland goddess Calisa.[128] Campiglia provocatively underlines the erotic overtones of the discourse by having a male interlocutor, Edreo—a pastoral figure for the poet Muzio Manfredi—initially outraged at this incidence of sapphic passion, before he discovers the "honest" identity of its object.[129] Other instances of this use of erotic language in addressing patrons are found in verse by Fiammetta Soderini for Virginia Fieschi d'Appiano as well as in Maddalena Salvetti's *Rime toscane* in praise of Christine of Lorraine, Grand Duchess of Florence (1565–1637), the latter a remarkably concentrated manneristic exercise in court eulogy.[130] Soderini's *stanze* for Fieschi recall Campiglia's verse for Pallavicino in their use of pastoral-mythological imagery, casting the poet as languishing "Filli" to Fieschi's distant Diana.[131] Salvetti's language, meanwhile, is more classically Petrarchan, recalling, for example, the moment of the poet's Neoplatonic *innamoramento* with the duchess in the breathless tones of an epiphanic vision and lingering blazon-style over the beauties of her "snow-white breast" ("*bianchissimo petto*") and "lovely bare hand" ("*bella ignuda mano*").[132]

　　If these sapphic sorties may be seen partly as explorative mappings on the part of female poets of a potential autonomous, female-authorized literary space, we find the same discursive quest narratively thematized within the female-authored fiction of the age. At the most immediate level here, one might point to the portrayals of all-female creative communities we find in a number of fictional works of the period. The best-known example is the circle of Venetian women we find portrayed in Moderata Fonte's *Il merito delle donne,* acting as a nurturing audience for the didactic discourses and poetic experiments of one of their number, Corinna. Self-consciously utopian though the motif is, the inclusion toward the end of the dialogue of a number of Fonte's encomiastic sonnets to Venetian patrician women hints at an overlap between this ideal female audience and Fonte's real or aspirational readership in Venice.[133] In a more purely fantastic vein, both Lucrezia Marinella's pastoral romance, *Arcadia felice,* and her later epic, *Enrico,* contain visions of exotically imagined "courts" of nymph-like handmaidens under the aegis of benign enchantress-queens.[134] Both are figured as loci of contemplative activity, with the mountain kingdom of *Arcadia felice*'s Erato serving as a virtual astronomical observatory, while the court of *Enrico*'s Erina features a talented female bard, Altea, whom we hear singing learnedly of the marvels of nature.[135] Within the genre of pastoral drama, meanwhile, we find Maddalena Campiglia in her *Flori* adapting the mythological motif of the virgin nymph-votary of Diana to explore the possibility of a female creativity independent of male jurisdiction.[136] The eponymous heroine is quite explicitly presented in the play as a poet, adapting the established pastoral convention of figuring shepherds as practitioners of "song." It is noteworthy that, both here and in Fonte's *Il merito delle donne,* the ideal creative situation for a female writer is posited as one of freedom from any sexual or marital "subjugation" to a man: Fonte's poet-protagonist Corinna is portrayed as determined never to marry, while Campiglia's Flori negotiates herself a relationship of chaste platonic equality with her male soul mate and fellow poet Alessi. The theme is a striking one and one with few precedents, at least within secular female-authored literature.[137] Where traditionally women's sole means of "escape" from their vocation of marriage had been through the convent, in Fonte and Campiglia what is proposed— at least at the level of fantasy—is clearly an uncloistered life free of the constraints of family responsibility, of the kind that male humanists had long counseled as ideally conducive to study. As recent studies have suggested, the emergence of this theme in the female-authored literature of this period needs to be considered in the context of the sharp reduction in marriage rates within the Italian elite in this period and the consequent rise of new tertiary orders such as the *Dimesse* that offered the possibility for women of an uncloistered single life.[138] While this does undoubtedly seem plausible as a context for the questioning of marriage we find in Campiglia and Fonte, another is surely women's growing aspiration to artistic autonomy in this period, expressed both in the fictional exploration of feminized "worlds apart" in works like *Arcadia felice* and *Il merito delle donne* and, in a less fantastic register, in Chiara Matraini's self-portrait at the opening of her *Dialoghi spirituali* in the guise of a scholar happily ensconced in the "little garden" of her study, and "never less alone than when alone."[139]

The mention of Matraini's *Dialoghi spirituali* brings us to a further development in women's writing of this period that deserves to be emphasized here: female authors' increasing willingness to adopt didactic and polemical stances in their writings. Lucrezia Marinella is a prime exhibit here: besides her erudite annotations to Tansillo, she was also the first female author of a fully-fledged academic treatise, *La nobiltà et l'eccellenza delle donne,* seemingly commissioned by the publisher Giambattista Ciotti as a response to Giuseppe Passi's misogynistic *I donneschi difetti* (1599).[140] Other examples of published didactic writings by women in this period are Moderata Fonte's *Il merito delle donne*—though here the didactic portions of the text are specifically targeted to women—and the letter collections of Veronica Franco (1580) and Chiara Matraini (1595 and 1597), both of which contain some pieces that approximate more to short moral essays than conventional "familiar letters."[141] Besides the *Lettere,* which were published with the revised edition of her *Rime,* Matraini also produced four new didactic, or didactic-meditative, prose works on religious subjects in her late career: besides the *Dialoghi spirituali* and *Considerationi sopra i sette salmi,* she also published the *Meditationi spirituali* in 1581 and the *Breve discorso sopra la vita e laude della beatissima Vergine* in 1590.[142] Maddalena Campiglia's first published work was also in this genre, the *Discorso sopra l'annonciatione della beata Vergine, et la incarnatione del s[ignor] n[ostro] Giesù Christo,* published in Vicenza in 1585.[143] Collectively, these works represent an important development within the history of Italian women's writing of the period. Certainly, tentative attempts had been made by female writers earlier in the century to engage with didactic and polemical genres of writing: Matraini herself, notably, had published an oration on the art of war and a translation of Isocrates in the 1550s, and we also have the examples of Tullia d'Aragona's *Dialogo dell'infinità d'amore* and Laura Terracina's

*Discorso.* Where certain of Matraini's late religious works are concerned as well, a precedent like Vittoria Colonna's *Pianto sopra la passione di Christo* must be considered and, more distantly, the writings of fourteenth- and fifteenth-century female mystics like Catherine of Siena and Catherine of Bologna.[144] Even so, the number and ambition of the didactic writings produced by women in the late sixteenth century is striking, and it would be difficult to find a match in earlier female-authored writing for the confidence and sense of intellectual entitlement we see displayed in works such as Marinella's *Nobiltà et eccellenza* or, very differently, Matraini's *Dialoghi spirituali.* Two developments should be noted in particular: first, the willingness of women in this period to base their claims to didactic authority simply on their learning and experience, without recourse to the topos of divine inspiration, and, secondly, their increasing preparedness to take an instructional or polemical role in relation to men.[145] A notable illustration of these developments, where polemical writing is concerned, is Marinella's *Nobiltà et eccellenza delle donne,* especially in its second edition of 1601, which appends a series of essays combatively engaging with past misogynist texts.[146] More straightforwardly didactic are certain of the letters of Veronica Franco and Chiara Matraini, which portray the authors dispensing moral counsel to male correspondents as well as, in the case of Matraini, engaging in philosophical discussion and issuing theological instruction.[147] The latter's *Dialoghi spirituali,* meanwhile, offers a kind of compendium of didactic and polemical forms, including pedagogical dialogue, dream-vision, and moral harangue, showcasing the author—almost ninety at the time of publication—as a combination of scholar-philosopher and Dantean poet-seer.[148] Circulating publicly in print, these works offered a challenge to the Pauline injunctions against women's teaching as well as more secular warnings about the indecorum of their "holding school, or disputing among men."[149] Nor was this task always engaged with in a spirit of properly "feminine" meekness: Marinella's *Nobiltà et eccellenza delle donne,* for example, blithely announces on its title page the author's "demolition" of Aristotle's views.[150]

Up to this point, the present discussion of didactic writings by women has embraced only the fields of the philosophical (broadly understood) and the theological or devotional. It may be interesting, however, by way of detour, to glance briefly at an author of works of a rather more technical stamp, the lace designer and illustrator Elisabetta or Isabetta Catanea Parasole (1575–c. 1625), author of a series of lace pattern books published in Rome between 1595 and 1616.[151] Like the purveyor of "secrets," Isabella Cortese, her only real predecessor as the female author of a published technical manual, Catanea assumes a didactic voice with confidence within a tradition of instruction that had previously been dominated by male authors. The point perhaps needs underlining where Catanea is concerned, given that lace making might appear such a quintessentially feminine concern. In fact, although women were involved in the manufacture of lace, pattern books tended almost invariably come out under male names, including, most famously, in Italy, that of Titian's relative Cesare Vecellio (c. 1521–c. 1601), author of the four-volume *Corona delle nobili e virtuose donne,* first published in Venice in 1591–94.[152] Catanea appropriates this didactic discourse with considerable panache. Her 1616 *Teatro delle nobili e virtuose donne,* the grandest of her productions, proposes her book as a "theater of womanly skill" ("teatro della donnesca virtù"): both her own—though with due modesty she demurs from claims to excellence—and those of the women who will follow her designs. A witty allusion to the myth of Arachne, moreover, turned as a compliment to her dedicatee, Isabella of Bourbon, infanta of Spain, recalls the textile skills of the goddess of wisdom, Minerva, competitor with and nemesis of Arachne in the Ovidian myth.[153] The skills of the needle are here presented in a distinctly dashing light, as a public arena for female creativity rather than as a site for women's socialization to self-effacing domesticity, as so often in the writings of the time.[154] Similarly, in the dedication of her first book, *Studio delle virtuose dame* (1597), to Juana de Aragona, Duchess of Soma, Catanea presents her homage to the noblewoman as the female equivalent of a man's armed service to his liege.[155] While this ostensibly devalues feminine labors by contrast—Catanea describes herself as a "weak woman," capable of serving only with the female "weapon" of a needle—it has the effect, more implicitly, of elevating her art by association with a privileged masculine field of prowess. In the same dedication, Catanea develops a similarly heroicizing implicit analogy between her needlework skills and epic poetry, speaking of her desire, were her powers greater, to figure the great deeds of her dedicatee's glorious ancestors in her work.[156]

At the same time that they were experimenting with new forms of didactic expression, women were also in this period tentatively beginning to venture beyond the confines of their traditional cultural territory, until this point almost exclusively literary and devotional. This is most apparent, perhaps, in the field of natural science, which features more significantly in women's writings of this than any earlier period, despite precedents such as Laura Cereta's use of Pliny's *Natural History* in her *Asinarium funus.*[157] The best-known instance of this is found in the second book of Moderata Fonte's *Il merito delle donne,* where the learned figure of Corinna speaks at length on natural philosophical topics, while her companion Lucrezia justifies women's right to pursue such knowledge irrespective of men's anticipated scorn.[158] Lucrezia Marinella shows a similar interest in natural philosophy, painting in the Erato of her *Arcadia felice* and the Erina of her *Enrico* two female enchantress-scientists in the mold of Tasso's Mago d'Ascalona, both represented—interestingly, in view of Marinella's own relation with her physician father—as heirs to the learning of a distinguished male line.[159] Given their geographic proximity, it is intriguing to speculate whether either Fonte or Marinella was acquainted with the obscure figure of Camilla Erculiani Greghetti of Padua, who in 1584 published a series of letters on questions within the field of natural philosophy, dedicated to the queen of Poland, Anna Jagiellona Bathory (1523–96), and published in Poland, in Krakow.[160] The speculation is particularly tempting in the case of Fonte given the marked interest she shows in herbal medicine in her dialogue, since Camilla describes herself in the title of her work as an apothecary, using the unfamiliar feminine form, *speziala*.[161] Whether or not any direct acquaintance may be proven, the parallels between the two writers are interesting, notably with regard to the self-consciousness with which both call attention to their trespass onto "masculine" terrain. Fonte's self-justification in the voice of Lucrezia has already been noted. Similarly, Erculiani defines the objective of her *Lettere* as that of as "showing that women are as fitted for all realms of learning as men," further describing herself as "a woman who desires to reflect luster on (*illustrare*) the women of her age."[162]

Besides this cluster of women in the Veneto, the other principal female writer in this period known for her philosophical and scientific interests was Margherita Sarrocchi, whom we know, most unusually for the time, to have been formally tutored in science, as well the humanities, in her youth. Sarrocchi's tutor, the distinguished mathematician Luca Valerio (1552–1617), remained a lifelong friend and introduced Sarrocchi to scientific acquaintances, including Galileo, whom we find her energetically defending in the debates that followed the publication of his *Sidereus Nuncius* in 1610. One letter of Sarrocchi's to Galileo of 1611 recounts an epistolary "duel" with an Augustinian friar of Perugia, concluding with an optimistic prospect of her victory ("I have dealt with worse before, and hope I shall have the better of him, even though I am a woman and he a learned friar").[163] Perhaps more than any other Italian woman of the time, in a figure like Sarrocchi, we may see an anticipation of the new engagement with philosophy and science apparent in later seventeenth-century European female erudites such as Margaret Cavendish, Duchess of Newcastle (1623–73), Princess Elizabeth of Bohemia (1618–80), and Queen Christina of Sweden (1626–89) or, at a more developed and systematic level, in a figure like Anne Conway (1631–79). This model was not destined to develop in Italy, where the cultivation of the "new science" was largely discouraged by the constraints of political and religious censorship, and where women —as we will see in chapter 6—were progressively excluded from intellectual and cultural life.[164] It is nonetheless worth registering the truncated impulse in this direction definable in women's writing from around the 1580s as one element among others in the generally expansive and appropriative dynamic of the times.

## 4. The Twilight of Gallantry

In an intriguing aside in his admiring discussion of Moderata Fonte's *Il merito delle donne* in his *Della dignità e nobiltà delle donne* (1622–28), the seventeenth-century "defender of women" Cristoforo Bronzini notes that Fonte, had she lived, was intending to append to her dialogue a series of "Triumphs of Women Past and Present."[165] Although we have no independent evidence to support Bronzini's contention, the project he attributes to Fonte certainly seems consistent with the self-assertive mood of women's writing in this period; it is interesting that we find a mention of a similar project, a *Parnassus* of contemporary famous women, in an eighteenth-century listing of the works of the painter Lavinia Fontana.[166] This is not to say, of course, that the tone of female creative artists in this period was uniformly optimistic or celebratory: many still anticipated a mocking reaction to their efforts from male contemporaries and drew on a preemptive rhetoric of "feminine" weakness in characterizing their work.[167] Speaking relatively, however, this does seem a moment of remarkable confidence among women writers: a moment when a tradition with, by now, a clear century and half behind it could feel itself coming into its own. Two parallel episodes, in Lucrezia Marinella's *Arcadia felice* and Margherita Sarrocchi's *Scanderbeide* will serve well to illustrate this. Both portray an athletic contest: a literary set piece well established within the traditions of both epic and pastoral and traditionally staged as a showcase for aesthetized male physical prowess. In both texts, in a twist to the conventional formula, the outstanding performer in the games proves a woman: in Marinella's *Arcadia felice,* the exiled princess of Epyrus, Ersilia, disguised as a shepherd, in Sarrocchi's *Scanderbeide,* the dashing archeress Silveria, appearing in her own feminine guise.[168] Penned as they are by women consciously pioneering within traditionally male genres, it is difficult to read the episodes as anything other than transparently self-referential, both asserting women's ability in a straight competition to equal or outdo their male peers. The ideological overtones of the episode are underlined, in particular, in Sarrocchi's version, where we see Silveria's male rivals before the event gleefully anticipating their prospective victory as an opportunity to demonstrate men's superiority to women ("mostrar quanto l'huom la donna avanza").[169]

Seen within this perspective, as parables of women's literary assertion, the episodes in Marinella and Sarrocchi are revealing, as much for the differences in their outcome as the similarities in their initial narrative framing. While the defeated rivals of Marinella's Ersilia take the revelation of her sex relatively pragmatically, responding with a "wonderment" that is only fairly modestly shadowed by "rancor" ("invidia"), Silveria is less fortunate, in that her victory stirs a fury that rapidly leads to violence with fatal effects.[170] Read as a depiction of the response to Sarrocchi's own achievements, the episode is fairly accurate, if obviously somewhat self-flattering. As the first female poet to publish an epic within the new formula for the Christian heroic established by Tasso, Sarrocchi met with a quite unprecedented degree of hostility from male critics: Giambattista Marino (1569–1625) portrays her, notoriously, in his *Adone* as a "squawking magpie" ("loquacissima pica"), disturbing the concert of true poet-"swans," while Tommaso Stigliani (1573–1651)—ironically a fellow target of Marino's in the passage of the *Adone* just cited—pours scorn on her *Scanderbeide* in his *Canzoniero [sic]* as worthy of being sold by the pound to wrap fish.[171] The shift in tone is very striking with respect to the blandly approbatory reception to which women had been accustomed in the Cinquecento and to which Sarrocchi herself had been comfortably habituated from the time of her emergence as a precocious adolescent in the 1570s.[172] It would be a mistake to represent the negative turn in Sarrocchi's reception as a poet as absolute. Rather, as is the case with Silveria, whose athletic victories divide her erstwhile companions into competing camps of attackers and supporters, so Sarrocchi continued to attract respect and admiration alongside hostile responses, culminating in the notable honors accorded her at her funeral in 1617, when she was carried to Santa Maria sopra Minerva "crowned with laurel and accompanied by the virtuosi of the city."[173] What is new, however, is precisely the breakdown in this period of critical consensus, set against a past when women could expect near-universal praise or, at worse, indifference.

Consulting contemporary sources, it is not difficult to detect a series of reasons why Sarrocchi should have attracted a hostility from which previous women writers had been immune. One, alluded to already, was genre: as the first woman to attempt a full-scale Tassesque military epic, Sarrocchi was exposing herself competitively and threatening male literary prerogatives to a far greater extent than women working in more established "feminine" genres such as the lyric. Other factors that might also be taken into account are her purportedly "difficult" nature and her possible transgression of the age's sexual mores, although, as ever in such cases, it is hard to establish the degree to which such accusations were the cause of the hostility she attracted or its effects.[174] One thing that is certain, however, is that, independent of such ad hominem factors, the reaction to Sarrocchi appears in historical perspective as indicative of a quite radical and broadly based shift in male attitudes to women's writing at around this time. Her role in this process appears to have been more that of lightning rod than anything else. As the following chapter demonstrates, by the 1590s, the seemingly eternal honeymoon that women writers had enjoyed with their male peers was beginning to come to a rancorous end; literary misogyny was on the rise and long-established conventions of gallantry were beginning to break down. Within this wider perspective, the episode of Silveria's victory at the games in Sarrocchi's *Scanderbeide,* which we have been reading here in its rancorousness as emblematic of its author's reception, will come to be seen to have a broader application within Italian literary culture as a whole.

# CHAPTER SIX

❀ ❀ ❀ ❀

# BACKLASH

# (1590–1650)

❀

## 1. The Rebirth of Misogyny in Seicento Italy

In 1593, in Bergamo, Muzio Manfredi, whom we encountered in the last chapter as a poet, academician, and professional flatterer of "the ladies," published what must probably be considered his most ambitious and serious work, the tragedy *Semiramis*.[1] The play had been written some years earlier and had attained a degree of fame as one of the plays short-listed for consideration as the opening spectacle at the Teatro Olimpico in Vicenza in 1585 (the modern works were eventually rejected and Sophocles's *Oedipus rex* performed instead).[2] An indication of the high profile the *Semiramis* and its author enjoyed is provided by its weighty appended collection of "verses by most excellent and refined Poets in praise of the Tragedy and its Author" ("Versi di alcuni eccellentissimi e cortesissimi Poeti in laude della Tragedia e del suo Autore").[3] This incorporates poems by no fewer than thirty-nine authors, including five women, one anonymous: those named are Barbara Torelli, Maddalena Campiglia, Veronica Franco, and Andriana Trevisani Contarini.[4] An interesting gender division emerges in the responses of these early readers. The male contributors more or less conform to the rhetoric of hyperbolic praise conventional in such sonnets, with Tasso, for example, blandly stressing the morally educative role of the tragedy's "piteous horror."[5] By contrast, among the female writers contributing, only Franco's corresponds to this model, while those of the other four poets all express outrage and bemusement that a poet famed for his courtly praises of women should have chosen as his subject matter the incestuous passion and murderous cruelty of the legendary Assyrian queen. Barbara Torelli urges Manfredi to return to his previous enterprise of "praising the name of honest and fair women."[6] Campiglia marvels that a poet of love, known in particular for his conjugal devotion, could turn his hand to the description of a "monster."[7] Why, the anonymous poet asked, if Manfredi wished to explore the theme of a female *guerriera*, did he make the perverse choice of Semiramis? Why not, instead, the Amazon queen Hippolyta, mythological archetype of the "domesticated Amazon" and homonym of his wife Ippolita Benigni?[8]

If we turn to the play itself, it becomes easy to see why readers like Torelli and Campiglia regarded Manfredi's *Semiramis* as a provocation. Semiramis was an ambiguous figure who had been regarded over the centuries with mingled respect and condemnation: a ruler and military leader of acknowledged greatness, she was also notorious for her purported cruelty and lust, culminating in incest with her son Ninyas.[9] Manfredi plays to the negative image, adding to Semiramis's usual catalogue of sins the murder of Ninyas's secret wife Dirce (an invented figure) and their two children.[10] To compound the horror of Semiramis's act, we later learn that Dirce was not merely her daughter-in-law but her blood daughter, the product of one of her innumerable adulterous liaisons. A central theme of the tragedy is the political one of the horrors of tyranny, embodied by Semiramis's evil empire. As Lucia Denarosi has noted, the queen herself is characterized intellectually by her Machiavellian vision of politics as a naked struggle for power, which stands in sharp contrast with the Christian ideal of merciful government represented by the high priest Beleso.[11] Within this political thematic, the monstrousness of the queen's incestuous lust represents the unnaturalness of tyranny as a transgression of divine law. This lesson is ostensibly gender-neutral—tyrants are condemned regardless of their sex—but the choice of a woman to embody it is not arbitrary, and neither is the play's privileging of Semiramis's sexual transgression against her son as a synecdoche for her abuses of power. As in previous misogynistically tinged versions of the story from Boccaccio onward, Manfredi's demonization of Semiramis draws implicitly on a sense of female rule in itself as a perversion of the natural order and on an association of power in a woman with sexual aggression and unrestraint. The play serves as a warning not only against tyrants but also, implicitly, against women who fail to know their place; if the queen's polluted body serves as a metaphor for the corruption of the body politic through tyranny, it also stands as a reminder of women's base corporeality and moral weakness and hence their essential unsuitability to rule. As queen consort, Semiramis's duty had been to produce an heir; as queen regent, to devolve power to him after his attainment of majority. Instead, her un-bridled lust for power leads her, in a chilling inversion of her dynastic role, to murder her own offspring and put an end to her line.[12]

The example of Manfredi's *Semiramis* is of interest to us here as a straw in the wind, a precocious indicator of a shift within Italian elite literary cul-ture whose effects began to be visible at around this time. As we saw in chapter 5, strong continuities existed within this culture between the mid- and later sixteenth centuries in respect of gender attitudes. Within the courts, in particular, a stance of gallantry toward women was still defining of civility, as was an appreciation of women's capacity for "heroic" or "vir-ile" attainment. Female artists and poets still found, by and large, an ap-preciative audience for their talents. Within this appearance of continuity, however, signs of change may be sporadically detected, sometimes, as we have just seen with Manfredi, manifested in figures who on other occasions staged themselves unequivocally as champions of women. Torquato Tasso is an interesting case here, and an important one, given his literary cha-risma and the influence he exercised on the rising generation of writers. In terms of gender attitudes, as in so many respects, Tasso reveals himself a transitional figure. On the one hand, we find him exercising the role pi-oneered by Bembo as admiring reader and sympathetic mentor to aspiring female writers (Campiglia, Sarrocchi), and he acknowledged women's contribution to court conversation in his writings, giving the title role in his dialogues on lyric poetry and love respectively to Orsina Cavalletti and Tarquinia Molza.[13] At the same time, he practiced with supreme ingenu-ity and elegance another genre in which Bembo had excelled, the quasi-erotic poetry of courtly compliment: no female cohort of the century was the subject of such an exquisitely polished poetic courtship as the aristo-cratic beauties of the Ferrarese court in the 1570s. Despite these credentials as courtly gallant and connoisseur of female *virtù*, however, we find ele-ments in Tasso's literary self-positioning less in keeping with the profemi-nist traditions of the courts. In his epic, most notably, the *Gerusalemme li-berata,* he reshapes the gender conventions of Ariostan romance to give women more ambiguous and less morally positive roles, displacing his lead *guerriera,* Clorinda, for example, from the Christian to the "enemy" camp and exploiting misogynist associations between female sexuality and de-monic temptation in his development of the figure of Armida.[14] A degree of equivocation is similarly apparent in Tasso's two principal explicit con-tributions to the *querelle des femmes:* his 1582 *Discorso della virtù feminile [sic] e donnesca* and his reply to a misogynistic essay by his cousin Ercole Tasso (d. 1613), published with Ercole's *proposta* in 1593.[15] In the second of these pieces, further discussed below, Torquato takes a profeminist position, countering his cousin's opposition to marriage by arguing for women's vital contribution to men's happiness. The *Discorso della virtù feminile [sic] e donnesca,* by contrast, tends to a revisionist, neo-Aristotelian position, arguing essentially for women's inferiority to men, though with an important concessive clause.

This latter work, the *Discorso,* deserves careful consideration in the present context as an ingenious and revealing attempt to remap the borders between Aristotelian-traditionalist and profeminist conceptions of women's virtue.[16] Tasso opens the treatise by defining two positions in the debate on women's virtue, the first best articulated in Thucydides's dictum that "those women deserve the highest praise whose fame does not extend beyond the walls of their home," the second condoning the notion that women may have a role to play within the public sphere. Essentially, he notes, these positions may be defined as Aristotelian and Platonic, given that Plato in the *Republic* allows for women to have a place among the "guardians" of the city and recommends their being educated accordingly.[17] After much close argumentation, Tasso positions himself as a supporter of the Aristotelian view, which he justifies, however, less on biological-essentialist than on broadly political grounds. His conclusion is firm, nonetheless: a woman's virtue is, in political terms, defined by her subordinate role in the city, which is limited to obeying her husband and to running the household and conserving his wealth and status. "Leadership" virtues such as fortitude and justice are thus irrelevant to her, and she needs only the degree of prudence that is necessary to follow directions. The only real moral virtue relevant to women is temperance, with a special emphasis on sexual continence. As for the virtues of the intellect, and especially the speculative intellect, these are those among the whole spectrum most irrelevant to women's capacity and role.[18]

To this point, Tasso's treatise reads as nothing more than an elegantly phrased restatement of the standard Aristotelian teaching on the virtues of women that profeminist writers since the late fifteenth century had invested such energy in attempting to dismantle. Two thirds of the way through, however, the treatise takes an interesting turn, when Tasso introduces a novel distinction between *la virtù feminile*—the default "feminine virtue" he had been discussing up to that point—and what he calls *la virtù donnesca.* This latter is status-specific, applying not to women of the urban elites ("cittadine"), "gentlewomen of private estate" ("gentildonne private"), or "industrious housewives" ("industriose madri di famiglia") but rather to women of the great dynastic families, such as his dedicatee, Eleonora d'Austria Gonzaga (1534–94), Duchess of Mantua, "descended from an imperial and heroic race."[19] Such women are not subject to the "civic" logic that Tasso has been applying in the first half of the treatise: like kings, "heroic women" stand outside civil society, and their role, like that of kings, is to govern rather than to obey. Logically, then, the virtues necessary to them are the "masculine" virtues of power rather than the "feminine" virtues of subservience: the term *donnesca* itself, which Tasso glosses as *signorile* ("lordly," "appropriate to a ruler"), is already indicative in this regard.[20] This "queenly" virtue, as we might perhaps best translate it, is illustrated in a series of modern examples; these include the two Margarets of Austria (1480–1530 and 1522–86), Cathérine de' Medici of France, and Elizabeth I of England as well as, more locally, Renée de France, Duchess of Ferrara, and her daughters Anna, Lucrezia, and Leonora.[21] Such women are praised for their political wisdom but also for their intellectual acuity and learning; Tasso's list concludes, in fact, with the example of Vittoria Colonna, deserving of "heroic" status on account of her high birth and the supreme embodiment of intellectual *virtù donnesca* in her "noble intellect," "happy eloquence," and "divine poetry."[22] It should be noted that, among all his mandatory hyperbole, Tasso does not praise his superwomen as "honorary men" or as sex-transcending marvels: the term "virile" barely figures in his litany of praise. From the "political" perspective of this treatise, women's "virtue profile" is dictated less by their biological limitations than the nature of their role in society. Women placed at the apex of the social and political hierarchy are required by their position to cultivate the "heroic" virtues from which their sex is normally excluded. They are not, in the process, conceived of as overcoming the intrinsic biological limitations of femininity; rather, they are conceived of from the start as a different species, a kind of heroic "third sex."

The acuity of Tasso's Solomonic solution to the sixteenth-century "woman question" should not be underestimated. While the text's modern readers have tended to see the distinction between *virtù feminile* and *virtù donnesca* in the treatise as opportunistic—an expedient introduced to flatter the dedicatee—in fact, within the context of the contemporary *querelle des femmes,* the distinction is not without weight. As I argue in chapter 1, one of the main motivating impulses for the profeminist tradition that emerged in the fifteenth-century Italian courts was the inadequacy of Aristotle's rigorously binary gender scheme in accounting for contemporary courtly reality.[23] The moral identity of great ladies like Eleonora d'Aragona or Battista da Montefeltro could not be well captured within a theoretical grid that limited women's role to the domestic, and a redefinition and broadening of scholastic definitions of "female virtue" was thus felt to be required. The problem with this new definition, however—ever more clearly apparent as profeminist discourse became more widely diffused with the spread of print—was that it failed to correspond to perceived social reality beyond the elite sphere of the upper nobility and the courts. In the urban elites more generally—and in republics such as Venice—sex roles remained better defined in many ways by Aristotle's binary model. Tasso's status-differentiated model of *virtù feminile e donnesca* provided a finer-grained analysis of sex roles in society and in doing so exposed the generally unarticulated class basis of many of the arguments of the *querelle des femmes*. Essentially, Tasso proves both Aristotelian-traditionalist and Platonic-profeminist perspectives on female virtue to be "right"; they merely capture differing social realities. At the same time, pragmatically, from the perspective of the court intellectual, he provides a formula for the definition of sex roles that corrects the more idealizing humanistic positions with a dose of Aristotelian "rigor" and social realism, without jeopardizing the standing of the eulogistic profeminist discourses that had proved so strategically useful at court. Of course he does so at the expense of women below the level of the great dynastic families, who had benefited for a century at this point from the "trickle-down effect" of court intellectuals' redefinition of female virtue. This was something Lucrezia Marinella was quick to note in her critique of Tasso's *Discorso* in her *La nobiltà et l'eccellenza delle donne* of 1601, where she argues fervently against his position, targeting in particular precisely his attempt to drive an ideological wedge between the "heroic lady" and women in general.[24]

A final notable feature of Tasso's *Discorso* deserves to be noted before we pass on. Arguing that "heroic women" are not to be judged by the standards of normal females, Tasso illustrates his point by rather casually noting that modesty and chastity are no more necessary to such women than these "feminine" virtues are to a male of equivalent status. Semiramis and Cleopatra may rank morally beneath sexually "decent" female rulers such as Zenobia or Artemisia but only in the way in which continent male leaders such as Scipio or Camillus might be judged superior to Caesar or Alexander.[25] This protolibertine argument seems at first sight to open the way for a sympathetic consideration of sexually "transgressive" women, in a manner that may seem refreshing after the grinding insistence on chastity found in so many Renaissance "defenses of women." More likely to have struck contemporary readers, however, is the implicit reinforcement this argument of Tasso's offers to the traditional association of power or learning in women with sexual profligacy; it is suggestive, in this regard, that Manfredi's *Semiramis* dates from only three years after the publication of the *Discorso*. The lascivious spin given to Tasso's thesis by the satirist Traiano Boccalini (1556–1613) in his *Ragguagli di Parnaso* (1612) is illustrative of this possible reading. In one *ragguaglio* of the first book, Boccalini retells the notorious Machiavellian anecdote concerning Caterina Sforza's supposed exposure of her genitals on the battlements of Forlì to taunt a besieging army that had taken her children hostage (the political logic of her gesture being that she could breed more children if her present heirs were killed). Boccalini then goes on, tongue in cheek, to justify what could only have registered to his readers as monstrously indecorous behavior on the grounds that "nobly bred princesses" ("le principesse d'alto sangue") were not held to the scruples of modesty that governed the behavior of ladies of private estate ("le donne private").[26] Besides this oblique jibe of Boccalini's, confirmation that Tasso's treatise was regarded as implicitly equating female power with unchastity is offered by Pierre Le Moyne's *La galerie des femmes fortes* (1647), which explicitly sets out to refute the *Discorso* on this point.[27]

Though hardly feminist in its implications, Tasso's *Discorso della virtù feminile e donnesca* cannot accurately be portrayed as overtly misogynistic: women are not abused or denigrated but simply instructed to keep in their place. Such restraint was not universal: in 1586, four years after the publication of the *Discorso,* and the year after Manfredi's *Semiramis* was under consideration at Vicenza, a treatise appeared in Padua slandering women quite explicitly, "Onofrio Filarco"'s *Vera narratione delle operationi delle donne.*[28] Filarco's treatise prompted refutations by two further Paduan-based *letterati:* "Prodicogine Filarete" (*Difesa delle donne* [1588]), and Giacomo Guidoccio (*Vera difesa alla narratione delle operationi delle donne* [1588]).[29] Meanwhile, in Treviso, the academician Cipriano Giambelli published a *Discorso intorno alla maggioranza dell'huomo e della donna* (1589), arguing the case for men's superiority. This probably stimulated in turn Cesare Barbabianca's *L'Assonto amoroso in difesa delle donne* (1593), also published in Treviso, the dedicatory letter of which laments the way in which "women's nobility and respectability is being horribly ripped apart by a few bold and unjust men."[30] Parochial though this Veneto dispute may seem, it may well have filtered out, if the Florentine Cornelio Lanci in his *Esempi della virtù delle donne* of 1590 could refer indignantly to men's ungallantry in "attributing to women innumerable defects" and daring, even, to attempt the slander of arguing the case for men's greater nobility and dignity.[31] Lanci mentions no names, but the treatises of Filogenio and Giambelli would certainly meet his description. To the Veneto texts already mentioned may be added the popular "humorous dispute" ("piacevole contesa") on marriage between Torquato Tasso and his cousin Ercole, first published in Bergamo in 1593. Although geared to the specific question of the desirability of marriage, much of the debate between the two turns on the merits of women, with the enlivening twist that it is the bachelor Torquato who defends marriage and women while the "misogynist" Ercole is portrayed as having capitulated to matrimony not long after composing his antimarriage discourse. Teasing Ercole about his inconsistency, Torquato suggests that he should now devote himself to composing a palinode in the mode of Stesichorus. If he does not, his cousin suggests, the task may be undertaken by some *"donna eloquente,"* capable not only of rebutting his argument rationally but of terminating the question through the "tacit eloquence" (*"tacita eloquenza"*) of her beauty.[32]

It is intriguing that Tasso should have floated this specter in 1593 of a possible female "defender of women," as one was to surface in the next and more virulent round of these polemics on women. This was triggered by the publication in 1599 in Venice and Milan of an admonitory diatribe against women's vices, *I donneschi difetti* by the academician and *letterato* Giuseppe Passi (1569–c. 1620). Passi's treatise was a substantial work of almost three-hundred pages, divided into thirty-five chapters, the first engaged with definitions and most of the remainder with a particularized account of women's vices.[33] Like "Filarco"'s earlier and presumably slighter work, Passi's *Donneschi difetti* attracted a prompt and heated response, but on this occasion, the polemic was less local and more high profile. Most strikingly, for the first time, the chief respondent was not a man but a woman, Lucrezia Marinella, whose *La nobiltà et l'eccellenza delle donne,* as we have seen, was written as a counterattack against Passi.[34] The posthumous publication of Moderata Fonte's *Il merito delle donne* is also generally seen by critics as having been motivated by this polemical context. Two later treatises, Pieto Andrea Canoniero's 1606 *Della eccellenza delle donne* and Pietro Paolo Ribera's massive *Le glorie immortali de' trionfi et heroiche imprese d'ottocento quarantacinque donne illustri antiche e moderne* of 1609, should also probably be seen primarily as responses to *I donneschi difetti,* although neither author names his adversary directly, with Ribera instead referring generally to poison-tongued "satirists" ("*satirici*") and Canoniero still more discreetly to "certain moderns."[35] Besides these formal responses, there is evidence that Passi's treatise was greeted with outrage by women in his hometown of Ravenna; at least, this supposed anger was taken as an opportunity for the academicians of the city to stage elaborate rituals of appeasement. Thus an anonymous member of the Accademia degli Informi, to which Passi also belonged, published in 1601 a Platonizing lecture by a fellow academician, Giacomo Sasso, intended to reestablish the philogynistic credentials of the academy with the infuriated women of the city.[36] Probably intended as similarly expiatory in character was Manfredi's 1602 volume of sonnets in praise of a hundred ladies of Ravenna.[37]

The most impressive and original of the responses to Passi's *Donneschi difetti* was undoubtedly Marinella's *La nobiltà et l'eccellenza delle donne,* rightly recognized by recent critics as a landmark in the history of women's contribution to the *querelle des femmes.*[38] Marinella's text is constructed as a point-by-point rebuttal of Passi and borrows its structure from *I donneschi difetti* as well as something of its vituperative tone.[39] The treatise first counters Passi's listing of women's vices with a specular enumeration of their virtues, similarly exemplified from classical and modern history and literature. This is followed, more originally, by an equally lengthy and erudite disquisition on the defects of men. Rushed out initially in two months, if we are to believe its author's claim—perhaps to meet the exigencies of a publisher eager to capitalize on the controversy—*La nobiltà* was thoroughly revised and expanded in a second edition that came out in 1601.[40] An addition to this later edition of particular importance was a series of appended chapters attacking the arguments of particular misogynist thinkers, ranging from Aristotle and Boccaccio to Sperone Speroni and Torquato Tasso. This is perhaps the point in the treatise where Marinella's incisiveness as a polemicist can be best gauged—far more so than in the exemplificatory chapters, which are dominated by the parade of erudition mandatory within the genre of "defense."[41] The novelty of *La nobiltà et l'eccellenza delle donne* within the Italian tradition of women's writing needs to be noted: while Giulia Bigolina and Moderata Fonte had preceded Marinella in engaging with the theoretical debate on women's status, both had done so in a fairly localized manner and within fictional and dialogic contexts that calculatedly mitigated the force of their argument. There is no real precedent for *La nobiltà* as a sustained, first-person exercise in female-authored feminist polemic nor one that appropriates so accurately male academic disputational modes. To see a woman engaging successfully in this kind of swaggering duel of erudition with a male combatant must have been a spectacle of remarkable novelty for contemporaries, especially given the long-established tradition of male disputants within the *querelle des femmes* staging themselves as women's chivalric defenders.[42] Marinella's influence is patent on subsequent Italian female polemicists: not only her famous younger Venetian compatriot, the dissident nun Arcangela Tarabotti (1604–52), but also obscurer writers such as Veneranda Bragadin, Bianca Naldi (fl. 1613), and Isabella Sori (fl. 1628), all of whom composed defenses of women in response to male-authored attacks.[43] Nor was the impact of her intervention necessarily limited to Italy: the English Swetnam controversy of 1615, where a misogynist text triggered a series of polemical responses from female or purportedly female authors, may well have been influenced as a publishing "event" by this Italian precedent, which had revealed the attractions as spectacle of such staged literary battles of the sexes.[44]

Aside from Marinella's well-documented treatise, a second female-authored response to Passi has come to the attention of scholars in recent years.[45] This is a short treatise of 1614, cast in the form of a letter addressed to the Venetian bookseller Giacomo Violati by an otherwise unknown woman, Bianca Naldi, writing from Palermo. The text is dedicated by Violati to the Paduan noblewoman Laura Obizzi Pepoli, member of an important noble family of Padua. Naldi, who writes on terms of easy familiarity with Violati, thanks him for sending a copy of Passi's *Donneschi difetti* and presents him with her thoughts in reply. The letter is cast as a simple piece of correspondence between friends, which Naldi claims to have dashed off in hours; in reality, however, it is a fairly closely argued treatise, dwelling particularly on the implications of the Genesis narrative of the creation of Adam and Eve and the relative gravity of their sins, though also encompassing the expected classicizing excurses on women's excellence as revealed in their deeds. A striking feature of the text is the degree of technical theological and canon-law erudition displayed in the portions concerned with biblical issues.[46] This might lead us to be skeptical of its claims to female authorship or at least to suspect that we may be looking at an original letter-defense by a woman augmented with male-authored additions, whether these were added under the aegis of the author or, as is perhaps more likely, under that of the publisher.[47] Either way, the text offers interesting evidence of the continuing currency in the Veneto of the debate over Passi's treatise a decade and a half after its publication as well as the very active part played by publishers like Violati in stirring up and maintaining this interest. *I donneschi difetti* was republished in 1618, still by Passi's original publisher Somasco, while Marinella's *La nobiltà et l'eccellenza delle donne* was republished in 1621.

As will be apparent from the degree of reaction excited by Passi's treatise, *bien pensant* profeminist sentiment was still a force in Italy in this period. It was still important to many male *letterati* to position themselves as supportive of women, and women were still credited, as least on a ritual level, with an important "opinion-making" role. Even the poets contributing sonnets to *I donneschi difetti* seem in some cases to be attempting to distance themselves from the work they are endorsing; one, indeed, Tiberio Sbarra, author of a particularly embarrassed tribute, turns up the following year on the side of the "opposition" as a contributor to the expiatory volume put together by the Accademia degli Informi in Ravenna.[48] Passi himself—however disingenuously—gives the impression in later writings of having been taken by surprise by the opposition to his treatise,

and two of his later works may be seen as palinodic in function: his companion volume to *Il donneschi difetti* on the vices of men (*La monstruosa
fucina delle sordidezze de gl'huomini* [1603]) and his treatise on matrimony
(*Dello stato maritale* [1602]), which contains a concessive treatment of the
merits of women, if one of singularly little conviction.[49] Passi's relative
ease in moving from one *querelle* camp to another is a useful reminder of
the rhetorical character of the debate, as is a description of *I donneschi
difetti* by the encyclopedist Giovanni Felice Astolfi as a work in which "the
feminine sex is elegantly [*gentilmente*] lacerated."[50] Astolfi's appreciation of
Passi's style does not seem to bespeak any particular attraction to his
polemical position; in the same passage, he expresses equal appreciation of
Moderata Fonte, whose *Merito delle donne* he praises as having "returned
all honors to her sex" and having "elevated [women] to the stars with her
pen."[51] It is worth noting in this connection that an important context for
the polemic stirred by Passi, as with the previous debates of the 1580s to
the 1590s in Padua and Treviso, was that of the literary academy. Both Passi
and one of his earliest respondents were members of the Accademia degli
Informi of Ravenna, and, in the earlier debate, both Cesare Barbabianca
("il Solingo") and Cipriano Giambelli ("il Bramoso") identity themselves
by their academic names. Debate, controversy, manufactured outrage were
the lifeblood of such gatherings, more important for their role as socializ-
ing rituals than for the intellectual substance of the material discussed. To
a majority of male readers, such literary spats must have been little more
than an entertaining spectator sport in a world that placed great value on
rhetorical dexterity irrespective of the uses to which it was put.

Looking at its immediate context, then, it might be easy to dismiss the
polemic over Passi as a local outburst of inconclusive ludic posturing. Seen
from a longer perspective, however, the polemic over *I donneschi difetti* may
be seen as a cultural turning point: had Passi lived to the age of his antagonist Marinella, who died in 1653, he would have enjoyed the satisfaction
of knowing his scorned treatise to have been in a literary vanguard rather
than out on a limb. Relatively in abeyance in the sixteenth century, misogynistic discourses of all kinds made a decisive return in the seventeenth,
along with, more generally, discourses assuming a strongly polarized conception of the natural capacities and proper roles of the sexes.[52] Of course,
in noting this shift, we should not exaggerate the extent to which misogyny and its cognate discourses had vanished from the cultural landscape
in the "profeminist" sixteenth century. Aristotelian notions of women's inferiority remained deeply rooted in scientific and philosophical culture
throughout this whole period, while, in literature, misogynist classics like
Boccaccio's *Corbaccio* continued to be consumed with alacrity, and a flour-

ishing tradition of satirical and "realist" verse and prose, centered especially in Venice, defined itself in part by its distance from the idealized vision of women that characterized the dominant Petrarchan tradition.[53] This satirical tradition, however, located itself self-consciously outside the mainstream, in an oppositional posture; for those who aspired to the applause of the courts, there was little inducement to experiment with a genre that risked losing them the sympathy of a potential female readership. What changed in the seventeenth century was that, for a complex set of reasons, the expression of misogynistic sentiment began progressively to gain in social acceptability, especially when it cast itself, as it did in Passi, as moralism or moral satire on the corruption of the age. At the level of the broadest generalization, we can characterize the literature of the Italian seventeenth century—at least until its final decades—as being defined as sharply by its negative or belittling attitudes toward women as the previous century's had been by its affirmative attitudes. The mirroring dynamic is important here. Gender remained in the seventeenth century a privileged field of meaning for the self-fashioning of male *letterati*, as it had been in the sixteenth. The terms were, however, reversed, with the previous century's default gallant stance of a "voluntary servitude" to women displaced by postures of antagonism and dominance.

The principal context in which we need to locate this shift in gender attitudes is the radical change in literary sensibilities that took place in Italy at the turn of the seventeenth century, with the emergence of the movement still generally termed for convenience as the baroque.[54] As with Petrarchism a century earlier, it is possible to see the genesis of baroque literature in gradualist terms, as the product of several decades of fermentation, dating at least from the era of Tasso. Again, however, like Petrarchism, though more emphatically, baroque poetry preferred to present itself in terms of rupture and renewal. Both Petrarchism and the baroque gained their spurs in a formative flurry of controversy, and both were spearheaded by a charismatic and exquisitely representative figurehead— in the case of the former movement, Bembo, urbane *arbiter elegantiae* in youth and in old age venerable spiritual authority, in that of the latter, the wayward, twice-imprisoned Giambattista Marino, illuminatingly compared by Elizabeth Cropper to his fellow Neapolitan Caravaggio in both his tempestuous lifestyle and his self-consciously revolutionary artistic stance.[55] Marino famously defined poetry as the pursuit of the "marvelous" and stressed a capacity for "rule-breaking" ("*saper rompere le regole*") as vital to the poet's craft.[56] The baroque aesthetic, at its most extreme, foregrounded artifice and theatricality and a self-conscious pursuit of the extravagant and spectacular. Perhaps its most characteristic stylistic device was the conceit (*concetto, acutezza*), a witty, recondite, and striking image or comparison, gaining its imaginative purchase precisely through its display of bold conceptual acrobatics. Also associated with the movement is a tendency to exuberant rhetorical ornamentation, apparent equally in poetry and prose. Baroque style thus fairly clearly differentiated itself from the soberer, classicizing stylistic model advocated by Bembo, with its stress on balance, rationality, and discretion and its normative reference to "nature," if in a highly idealized form.[57] First manifesting itself in lyric poetry, and in the relatively "moderate" form typified by Marino, by the beginning of the seventeenth century, the baroque stylistic ideal began to assert its ascendancy both in verse and prose. Dominant in the first half of the century—though it was never uncontested—the vitality of the baroque as a literary style progressively ebbed in the second. By the 1680s, a resurgent classicism was gaining power, strongly rejecting of baroque "decadence" and intent on defining the movement's period of dominance as a wayward parenthesis rather than a new stylistic dawn.

The story of the stylistic adventure of the baroque is of extraordinary importance to the narrative of this volume, as the period of the movement's ascendancy was marked by a virtual ejection of women from the domain of Italian literary culture. To understand the causal logic of this development, it is necessary to examine the gender dimension of the baroque stylistic "revolution": an aspect of the movement that has attracted to this point a remarkable paucity of critical attention. As we have seen clearly in this book, a defining feature of Renaissance Petrarchism was its affirmative and idealizing attitude to women. This was manifested both on an internal level (in that the moral and physical beauties of women were thematically central to Petrarchism) and on an external one (in that women constituted a privileged audience for literature and increasingly featured also as writers). The philogynistic profile of Renaissance Petrarchism was sufficiently characterizing as a feature to present itself irresistibly as a target for opponents of the movement: a phenomenon already apparent in the case of sixteenth-century "resisters" such as Aretino and Niccolò Franco. For a self-definingly rule-breaking movement like the baroque, the "rule" of deference to women was particularly tempting as a transgression opportunity: the more so since an attitude of profeminist gallantry had been the default polite gender pose for so long. Once the taboo surrounding it had lifted, misogyny emerged as a literary theme of undoubted attractiveness, offering the same opportunities for rhetorical display as had the now shop-worn theme of women's "nobility and excellence," but with the advantages of freshness and a greater scope for scurrility and the display of satirical wit. Similarly attractive as a theme, and

similar in its "rule-breaking" appeal, was the exploration of the realms of
the sensual and the sexual, long bleached out of the politer realms of literature in deference to Neoplatonic ideals. An enhanced sensuality was
one of the traits that distinguished the lyric poetry of the baroque from
the Petrarchan tradition, first apparent in Tasso—in many ways, godfather
to the baroque—and accentuated in the poetry of Marino and his followers.[58] Although not intrinsically misogynistic, this more sensual poetic mode had the effect of reinforcing traditional associations between
women and the sexual and carnal that had been arduously prized apart in
the Neoplatonically inflected poetry of Petrarchism, with its insistence on
the possibility of a spiritual love. Also contributing to this effect was the
tendency in baroque poetry to construct variously "imperfect" women as
the object of desire in conscious rejection of the Petrarchan ideal of a su-
perhumanly flawless and rigorously unindividualized blonde beauty.[59]
While the Petrarchan muse had, in her very stylization and interchange-
ability, symbolized a transcendence of the flesh and an ascent to the idea
of beauty, the "tainted" ladies of the baroque manifested their carnality
precisely by virtue of their flaws.

Both these developments—the "sensual turn" in baroque literature
and the resurgence of misogyny as a mainstream cultural attitude—may
be clearly seen, as we have noted, as framed dialectically with regard to Renaissance Petrarchism. If the affirmative attitudes to women that emerged
as widespread in the courts of the early sixteenth century served to define
a group identity for a generation of *letterati* in the process of fashioning a
"modern," courtly vernacular literature, the born-again misogyny of the
early Seicento reflects a parallel process of cultural renegotiation, as the
long-enduring Petrarchist formula gave way under the pressure of newer
and more "contemporary" forms. A revisionist attitude to the previous
century's profeminism was the clearest way to redefine oneself poetically
as "beyond Petrarchism"; as so often in cultural history, artistic "progress"
was figured by a militant rupture with previous ideals. Paradoxically, in
fact, in historical retrospect, we can see that seventeenth-century misogyny performed a cultural role in many respects similar to sixteenth-
century male profeminism, enabling processes of homosocial bonding and
cultural self-positioning among men. Antithetical in appearance, the two
developments look more like cognates when viewed from a more sophisticated analytical perspective—at least, until one considers the consequences for the sex that served as the vehicle of this cultural redefinition.

Of course, it would be misleading to present this literary trend as
defining of seventeenth-century literature in general: Marino's new formula for literature was not universally accepted and imitated, any more

than Bembo's had been a century earlier. The hedonistic character of Marino's poetics, and the eroticism of his verse, met much concerted moral criticism, as might be predicted. His literary "irregularity," too, met with resistance from critics, with his epic-scale mythological poem *Adone*, in particular, triggering a full-scale literary polemic when it was first published in 1623, following an extended period of gestation.[60] Where Petrarchism as a poetic language had proved eminently adaptable to spiritual ends, Marino's more sensual and extravagant mode was less easily co-opted. Insistently self-referential in its ostentation of its own stylistic "extraordinariness," and alien to the sobriety to which at least the "graver" tradition of Petrarchism aspired, it was not an idiom that lent itself easily to a literature that sought to "instruct" as well as "delight." Important centers for classicizing resistance to Marinism included Medicean Florence, which staged itself as custodian to the classic tradition of Tuscan poetry, and the Neapolitan circle of the Accademia degli Oziosi (1611–45), headed by Tasso's disciple and biographer Giambattista Manso.[61] Another key nucleus of resistance to Marino's innovations was Rome during the 1623–44 papacy of Urban VIII (Maffeo Barberini), a poet himself in Latin and the vernacular prior to his pontificate and a famously enthusiastic patron of the arts.[62] It is interesting to note that, within these areas of conservative resistance, attitudes to women tended not to take the same negative and reductively sexual inflections that we have seen characterizing the baroque. An example here is Rome during Urban VIII's pontificate, where we see Anna Colonna (1601–58), the wife of the pope's nephew, Taddeo Barberini, becoming the object of a discreet literary cult reminiscent of those enjoyed by sixteenth century aristocratic muses such as her ancestress Giovanna d'Aragona in the 1540s.[63] There are also signs that Barberini circles were sympathetic, or at least perceived as sympathetic, to the figure of the female writer. It is probably not a coincidence that the complete version of Margherita Sarrocchi's *Scanderbeide* first appeared (posthumously) in 1623, in the same year as Urban VIII's election as pope, and contained a prescient or interpolated passage predicting his accession to the papacy.[64] Urban also figures later the dedicatee of Lucrezia Marinella's *Le vittorie di Francesco il serafico* (1643), while the Barberini cardinal nephews also supported Margherita Costa; her *poema sacro, Cecilia Martire*, was dedicated to Francesco Barberini (1597–1679), addressed in the dedicatory letter as a "great ray of the Barberini Vatican Sun."[65]

On a more provincial and small-scale level, further evidence for a linkage between stylistic conservatism and profeminist gender attitudes in Seicento Italy is offered by the example of Paduan cleric and erudite Giacomo Filippo Tomasini (1595–1655), author of the Petrarchist manifesto

*Petrarcha redivivus* (1635), as well as of numerous works of literary biography.[66] As the title of Tomasini's magnum opus suggests, his resistance took the form less of Barberini-style classicism than a militant championing of the virtues of Petrarch, seen as representing a model of decorous literary practice traduced by the deviations of the "moderns." Tomasini accompanied this stylistic stance with a notably supportive and celebratory attitude to women and women's writing. His *Petrarcha redivivus* not only gives Laura a prominent and dignified role, as a cultivated woman herself as well as Petrarch's muse and chaste love, but also goes so far as to supply Petrarch with a female poetic correspondent in the form of the apocryphal Giustina Levi Perotti of Sassoferrato.[67] More strikingly still, among his other scholarly endeavors were editions of the previously unpublished works of Cassandra Fedele (1636) and Laura Cereta (1640), while the second edition of his compilation of Veneto literary biography, *Elogia virorum literis et sapientia illustrium* (1644), is remarkable for the richness of its female component (women make up eight of his seventy-two "famous men").[68] Tomasini's interest in women's writing bespeaks a patriotic consciousness of the Veneto's rich tradition in the field, and this may also have underwritten the openness to women of the Paduan Accademia dei Ricovrati (founded 1599), which admitted a number of—mainly French—women to its ranks in the later seventeenth century, along with the local figurehead Elena Corner Piscopia (1646–84), the first woman in Europe to receive a university degree.[69] Another Veneto profeminist of Tomasini's generation is the Vicentine nobleman Pietro Paolo Bissari (1595–1663), who corresponded with Arcangela Tarabotti and included a passage supportive of women's participation in intellectual life in his *Le scorse olimpiche* (1648).[70] The mention of Bissari, an enthusiast for Marino, is useful as a warning should we be tempted to draw too absolute equation between baroque or antibaroque stylistic self-positioning and gender attitude; in a literary culture as complex and decentralized as Italy's, things are rarely ever quite so neat. With this caveat, however, it seems safe enough to suggest that some such equation may be made, at least at a level of generalization. Were there any doubts on the matter, we would only need to think of the classicizing Arcadian movement that rose as a powerful alternative to the exhausted late baroque in the final decades of the century; there the connection between stylistic purism and a resurgent gynephilia is too patent to be denied.

Returning from the profeminist margins of Seicento culture to the misogynist mainstream, the quite radical gender revisionism that characterized baroque literature is well illustrated by a work like *La galeria delle donne celebri* (1633) by the Veronese medic and writer Francesco Pona

(c. 1594–c. 1654), which recasts and transforms the popular Renaissance genre of the collection of feminine exempla. Pona's treatise, presented as a sample for a more substantial future work, presents twelve exemplary biographies of *donne illustri,* divided into three categories, of "lubricious," "chaste," and "holy" ("lubriche," "caste," and "sante").[71] As the presence of the first category makes clear, Pona interprets the adjective "celebre" in the morally neutral sense in which Boccaccio had used "clarus" in his *De claris mulieribus,* designating women both "famous" for their glorious deeds and "notorious" for their morally reprehensible ones. This represents a conscious reversal with respect to the sixteenth-century tendency to a more restrictive understanding of the term in parallel contexts: as we saw in chapter 3, for example, Giuseppe Betussi's 1545 appendix to Boccaccio limits itself pointedly to women deserving of praise, in a conscious break with Boccaccian practice.[72] Also revisionary in Pona with respect to sixteenth-century tradition is his division of women by the criterion of sexual probity. Where sixteenth-century "famous women" treatises had commonly divided women by the fields of their endeavor (government, warfare, religion, literature), Pona reductively foregrounds chastity and its absence as defining of women's merit or demerit. In his drooling account of figures famed for their "lubriciousness," Pona is representative of his age's fascination with women's supposedly voracious and all-consuming sexuality as well as with the dangers this represents in the political sphere (Semiramis features prominently in his list in the *Galeria,* while Messalina received his attention elsewhere). Even in his encomia of heroines of chastity such as the inevitable Lucretia, and saints such as the predictable Mary Magdalene, Pona's heavily sexualized descriptions have the effect of privileging his protagonists' implicit "lubriciousness" rather than the moral probity for which they are praised. Revealing in particular is his lascivious description of the sexual allure of Lucretia, dwelling especially on a mole or beauty spot at the corner of her mouth that "gave her an air of natural libidinousness that inflamed her admirers' desires."[73] Distastefully, here, Lucrezia's rape by the tyrannical Sextus Tarquinius is implicitly justified by the peremptory sexuality of his victim, revealed, characteristically enough, by a "telltale" physical flaw.

As this analysis of Pona's *Galeria* makes clear, an accurate audit of Seicento misogyny cannot afford to concentrate simply on its most obvious and explicit manifestations, such as the steady trickle of writings on women's vices and failings that we see being published across the course of the century, paralleling and reversing the tradition of "defenses of women" that had formed such a characteristic element in sixteenth-century culture. Besides dedicated works such as Passi's *I donneschi difetti,*

Francesco Buonisegni's *Del lusso donnesco* (1639), Ferrante Pallavicino's *Retorica delle puttane* (1642), Angelico Aprosio's *La maschera scoperta* (c. 1644) (reworked in a mitigated form as *Lo scudo di Rinaldo* [1646]), and Bonaventura Tondi's *La femina origine d'ogni male, overo Frine rimproverata* (1687), a seventeenth-century misogynistic canon would need to spread its net far more widely to include works as diverse in genre and focus as Ansaldo Cebà's biblical epic, *La reina Ester* (1615), Janus Nicius Erythraeus's sprawling Latin roman à clef, *Eudemia* (1637), Pallavicino's libelous political satire, *Il corriero svaligiato* (1641), Antonio Rocco's pornographic dialogue *Alcibiade fanciullo a scola* (1652), and Giovanni Francesco Loredan's "spiritual novel" (*romanzo spirituale*), *Adamo* (1640).[74] As the names of the several of these writers indicate (Pallavicino, Loredan, Rocco), especially important as a locus of misogynist writing was the libertine Accademia degli Incogniti (1630–61), founded by Loredan (1607–61) in Venice, and including as "home" or corresponding members many of the most important literati of the day.[75] The narrative and nonnarrative writings of the Incogniti were frequently characterized by a notably libertine attitude to sexuality, regarded as morally blameless because natural, in contradiction to the censorious attitude of the church. In practice, however, the Incogniti's espousal of the erotic betrays a predictable double standard: male sexuality was celebrated while that of women attracted a more complex response, mingling prurience, repulsion, fascination, and fear.[76] Especially revealing thematically within the Incogniti's narrative output was the motif of the politically ambitious and sexually corrupt woman, explored perhaps most notoriously in Francesco Pona's *La Messalina*, first published in 1628. Other works in this genre, mainly drawing, like Pona's *Messalina*, on Tacitus, include Ferrante Pallavicino's *Le due Agrippine* (1642) and Antonio Lupis's *La Faustina* (1666) as well as Federico Malipiero's *L'imperatrice ambiziosa* (1640) (on the younger Agrippina) and Niccolò Maria Corbelli's *La Semiramide* (1683).[77] The toxic mixture of sexuality and power in these works fuses discourses condemnatory of political decadence and tyranny with anxieties attending on women's sexual power and the "unnatural" ascendancy it gives them over men. A more benign and mitigated variation on the same theme of sex and power is found in works such as Loredan's drama *La forza d'amore* (1662), which portrays a fictional Armenian queen, Ardemia, initially opposed to marriage in the interest of maintaining her autonomy but brought round to it by the power of love. Here, again, women's power and capacity for self-determination is seen as an aberration and as effeminizing of the men who surround them. Resolution can only be reached through a process of recuperation that sees the "natural order" of sex relations restored.[78]

Naturally, the misogynistic reorientation of Italian literary culture we have been describing did not occur in a vacuum. Audience and patronage contexts are as important to an understanding of this cultural shift as they were in the case of the "feminist" turn of the early sixteenth century. If in the earlier case, the key factor was the rise of the secular princely courts as centers of cultural production, and the increasing prominence of dynastic women as literary patrons and privileged readers, here equally significant is the decline of those same courts, which lessened the importance of elite women as an audience. This trend began early. Already by the early Cinquecento, with the coming of Spanish rule, the great cultural centers of Milan and Naples lost their independent courts, forfeiting in consequence the role of cultural leadership they had exercised for much of the previous century. Elsewhere, courts continued to flourish throughout the sixteenth century, both long-established ones, like Ferrara, Mantua, and Urbino, and ones of more recent foundation like Parma and Piacenza under the Farnese (from 1545) and Florence under the Medici (from 1537). By the end of the century, however, the ancient Este regime in Ferrara was facing extinction, as no heir was produced from any of the three marriages of its last duke, Alfonso II (1533–97). In 1598, following Alfonso's death, the city was claimed by the papacy, its legal overlord, and the Este reverted to a much-reduced rule in Modena. Urbino, too, ceased to function as an independent court in the 1620s when the last Della Rovere duke, Francesco Maria II, left without a male heir after the assassination of his only son, ceded his territory to Pope Urban VIII. The fate of the Gonzaga dynasty in Mantua was less dramatic than that of the Este or Della Rovere, but the city is generally seen as having entered a sharp cultural decline after the death of Duke Vincenzo I in 1612, reaching a nadir with the dissolute Vincenzo II (ruled 1626–27), who sold off the great Gonzaga art collection to Charles I of England.[79] Parma under the Farnese also entered a decline from around the 1620s onward, when it was struck by plague and impoverished by the wars of the ambitious Odoardo I. By around the 1630s, of the great families of Italy, only the Medici and, sporadically, the Savoy dynasty in Turin remained active and innovative as cultural patrons.[80] With the decline of the secular courts, cultural leadership in Italy passed elsewhere: to the independent republic of Venice and the Spanish-controlled republic of Genoa, to the Spanish kingdom of Naples, governed in practice by a viceroy, and, overwhelmingly, to the papal court, in this period at a moment of near-unsurpassed cultural splendor. By comparison with the secular princely courts, these were largely not cultural ambiences naturally propitious to female patronage. The republican regimes of Venice and Genoa explicitly excluded women from political power and tended in consequence also to marginalize them culturally; as Traiano Boccalini notes in his *Ragguagli di Parnaso,* "the great advantage of republics over monarchies is that they are free from the impediment of women."[81] The papal court, meanwhile, was of course ruled by a bachelor clerical elite and thus by definition excluded women from the center of power. Although there were certainly powerful women in Rome, notably the wives of papal nephews and the female relatives of prominent cardinals, these women's position was less "official" than that of the consorts of secular princes, and on the whole they did not generate the same force field of flattery and cultural courtship as had the ladies of the Gonzaga and the Este.[82] It may have been in urban centers enjoying a certain cultural autonomy, such as papal-ruled Bologna, that the opportunities for female agency were greatest: certainly, recent studies have stressed the prominent role women played in the cultural life of that city.[83] There are signs, as well, of an adherence to the ideal of female cultural protagonism in the cities of the mainland Veneto, especially Padua, as we have seen.[84] Impressive and interesting as these regional developments may have been, however, we are nonetheless talking about something quite localized by comparison with the age of, say, Isabella d'Este, when a teeming network of ambitious courts had vied for the glory of cultural preeminence in northern Italy, brandishing the *virtù* of their "famous women" as an ever more significant factor in their competition for prestige.

With the demise of the secular courts, then, women's importance as an audience for literature was in decline from the early seventeenth century onward. With it, for the most part, there perished the discourse on women's "nobility and excellence" cultivated with such enthusiasm in the previous century. This general pattern, apparent at a national level, is most strikingly illustrated through its exceptions: in those few situations where powerful individual female figures were active we find the culture of profeminism surviving. The most notable case of this is Florence in the 1620s, during the minority of Ferdinand II (1621–28), when the Grand Duchy of Tuscany was briefly governed by two female regents, Maria Maddalena d'Austria, wife of the previous ruler, Cosimo II, and Cosimo's mother, Christine of Lorraine. The two women were both descended from major European ruling dynasties and brought to their role as consorts to the dukes of Tuscany a powerful sense of entitlement deriving from their natal status. They may thus be seen as falling into the same category of empowered "trophy consorts" we saw playing such a key role in the courts of the fifteenth and sixteenth centuries—women such as Eleonora d'Aragona in Ferrara in the 1480s and Eleonora of Toledo in Florence in the 1540s and 1550s, the latter of particular relevance as a model because she was a direct dynastic "ancestress" of the two Medici regents.[85] As in these earlier cases, the presence of two such prestigious princely consorts in late six- teenth and early seventeenth-century Florence had the effect of encour- aging the production of literature and art celebratory of women. This was apparent even before the period of the regency. Between 1590 and 1611, five treatises in praise of women were published in Florence, including two works dedicated to the successive grand duchesses, Francesco Serdonati's updating of Boccaccio's *De claris mulieribus* (1596), dedicated to Christine, and Niccolò Lorini's *Elogii delle più principali s[ante] donne del sagro calen- dario* (1617), dedicated to Maria Maddalena.[86] During the period of the re- gency itself, moreover, as Kelly Harness has recently emphasized, the cel- ebration of female *virtù* was elevated to an even more central place within Florentine culture. An especially systematic development of the theme is found in the decorative scheme devised for the villa of Poggio Imperiale, acquired by Maria Maddalena in 1622, which features a series of paintings portraying an inspirational pantheon of heroic women from biblical and secular history.[87] Notable particularly here is the emphasis on queens and rulers, including some famed for military leadership as well as govern- mental acumen: examples here are Sofonisba and Semiramis as well as the biblical Esther and Deborah. Powerful women also frequently featured as protagonists in the dramatic spectacles staged for major court events in the 1620s, with examples ranging from mythological goddesses like Athena and Venus to virgin martyrs like Ursula and Agatha.[88] Florence in this pe- riod was also the locus for the composition and partial publication of the most grandly conceived of all early modern "defenses of women": Cristo- foro Bronzini's epic dialogue *Della dignità e nobiltà delle donne,* representing no fewer than twenty-four days' worth of fictional conversation among a group of mixed speakers in Rome.[89] Female creative *virtù* was also culti- vated in Florence in this period, the most notable example being the com- poser Francesca Caccini (1587–c. 1640), best known for her opera *La libe- razione di Ruggiero dall'isola d'Alcina,* commissioned by Maria Maddalena de' Medici for a performance in 1625.[90] Maria Maddalena was also the ded- icatee of a substantial work of Lucrezia Marinella's—her third addressed to a female member of the Medici dynasty—in the form of her *De' gesti heroici e della vita maravigliosa della serafica S[anta] Caterina.*[91]

A less well-known and more localized instance of a similar dynamic of patronage is apparent in the case of Francesco Agostino della Chiesa's *The- atro delle donne letterate* (1620), along with Bronzini's *Della dignità e nobiltà delle donne* one of the most interesting of seventeenth-century "defenses of women." The *Theatro* is of interest as a rare instance of a work devoted specifically to extolling women's literary attainments and also as a document of the *fortuna* of Lucrezia Marinella, whose arguments in *La nobiltà et l'eccellenza delle donne* are closely echoed in its prefatory "Breve discorso della preminenza e perfettione del sesso donnesco" ("Brief Discussion of the Preeminence and Perfection of the Female Sex").[92] Della Chiesa (?1593–1662), a cleric and native of Saluzzo, of which he eventually became bishop, dedicated his work to Margherita of Savoy (1589–1655), daughter of Duke Carlo Emanuele I of Savoy (1562–1630), and of the infanta Catalina Micaela (1567–97), daughter of King Philip II of Spain. Margherita had been married to Francesco IV Gonzaga, Duke of Mantua and Monferrato, who had died young in 1612, preceded by his only son. The deaths triggered a war between Savoy and Mantua for control of the Duchy of Monferrato, claimed by Margherita and her father against the Gonzaga for her daughter Maria, on the grounds that, as a *feudo feminino,* it had been traditionally inheritable through the female line.[93] By the time of the publication of Della Chiesa's *Theatro,* the Savoy claim to the Duchy, which they had held from 1612–17, had been definitively quashed. Margherita, however, retained a certain status at the court, not least by virtue of the prestige of her Spanish royal connections; she was later briefly appointed regent of Monferrato, in 1628, during a second crisis of the Gonzaga succession, while in 1635, she was appointed vicereine of Portugal by her cousin Philip IV. In the light of his dedicatee's situation, Della Chiesa's strong defense of female rule and his attacks on male usurpation of power take on particular resonance, as did, in the Florentine context, slightly later, Bronzini's less radical musings on the same theme.[94] Certainly, there is reason to think that at the time of the composition of the treatise, Margherita had not reconciled herself to the loss of "her" realm; as a recent study suggests, Margherita's exertions to attain sainthood for her namesake and ancestor, the Blessed Margherita of Savoy (1390–1464), a former Marchioness of Monferrato, should perhaps be seen as a wistful expression by proxy of her moral claim to the territory she had lost.[95]

As these cases and particularly that of the Medici regency well demonstrate, there was nothing intrinsic in sixteenth-century encomiastic discourses on women that precluded them from successful reinvention in the new stylistic idioms of the following century. If this did not happen more frequently, it was because few circumstances offered themselves in which women were sufficiently close to the centers of power to stimulate such an initiative. For the most part, the seventeenth century saw women progressively displaced from their sixteenth-century role as privileged audience for polite literature: a status that had provided the concrete and symbolic foundation for the entire Renaissance profeminist edifice. Symbolic of this change, in some sense, is the poetic *Tempio* edited in 1600 by Giulio

Segni in celebration of Cardinal Cinzio Aldobrandini.[96] This seems, in some ways, a typical late-sixteenth century case of a bigendered poetic anthology, with contributions from Isabella Andreini, Francesca Turina, Febronia Pannolini, Tarquinia Molza, and Maddalena Salvetti (the last, with a *corona* of twelve connected sonnets, numerically one of the best-represented poets in the volume).[97] Nonetheless, that we have here a poetic "temple" addressed to a male figure signals a significant shift. As noted in chapters 3 and 4, this was a genre that had evolved specifically as a vehicle for tributes to "great ladies," from Giovanna d'Aragona and Irene di Spilimbergo to Geronima Colonna and Flavia Peretti Orsini. Here, with the new century, we see it converted to celebrate the aristocratic cardinal or cardinal nephew, the new model patron of the age. Similarly suggestive as a mark of transition is Muzio Manfredi's dedication of his tragedy *Semiramis* to Cardinal Odoardo Farnese (1573–1626): a choice reached, as the dedicatory letter tells us, after much careful thought about a suitable dedicatee. Originally, Manfredi informs us, he had thought of Dorothea, Duchess of Brunswick-Lüneburg (1546–1617), a princess of impeccable descent, as he informs us, related to kings, emperors, and eminent churchmen, as a possible candidate.[98] Thinking further, however, he decided that a tragedy, given its loftiness of genre, should be dedicated to a "perfect, indeed most perfect person" ("persona perfetta e perfettissima"); this finally led him to settle on the august figure of the 20-year-old old Cardinal Farnese. Though Manfredi's indiscreet explicitness is unwonted, the selection process he describes cannot have been too remote from that of many of his contemporaries: vernacular literature was indeed increasingly addressing itself in this period to a male, rather than a female or bigendered reading public. One advantage of this, for the writer of fiction, was, of course, that it allowed for a loosening of literary decorum, to embrace disturbing or sexually explicit material that could with difficulty be addressed to a woman. Manfredi underlines this in a number of poems that half-jokingly reprimand female readers for taking pleasure in his *Semiramis,* despite its violent and scurrilous subject matter. One series of madrigals on the subject, addressed to Virginia Narducci Massini, is headed "Cruel Pleasure" ("Piacimento crudele").[99]

Besides the actual diminution in the power and prominence of court women in the seventeenth century by comparison with the sixteenth, less concrete factors also need to be considered in accounting for their decline from cultural salience. As chapters 1 and 2 detail, the place that high-born women were allotted within the rhetorical system of polite vernacular literature was only partly due to their actual importance as patrons, readers, and taste-setters. Important as well were their roles as mediatory channels for the expression of courtly deference toward male patrons and as elegant symbols of the dignity of the *volgare* as it struggled to disassociate itself from the taint of the "vulgar." Neither of these roles was of great continuing relevance in the period under discussion. With a century of "acceptance" behind it, and a modern tradition that could now, with Tasso, authoritatively vaunt its equality with the great literatures of antiquity, the vernacular was no longer in need of the kind of symbolic "godmothering" that had been supplied a century earlier by an Isabella d'Este or Elisabetta Gonzaga. Nor were delicate mediatory maneuvers any longer very necessary in finessing courtiers' relationships of servitude to their patrons. Within the increasingly absolutist princely regimes of the day, the courtly habit of servitude had evolved to a point at which the indirection of a Castiglione or a Bembo would be otiose: already in the 1580s, Tasso had in his *Malpiglio overo de la corte* signaled the modern court's historical distance from Castiglione in this sense.[100] With this development, increasingly marked as the century progressed, the symbolic utility of the "address to the ladies" as a rhetorical expedient was diminished, and women fell back into what may have been in some sense their "actual" position, as figures for the most part on the margins of power, to be courted or cited sporadically as individuals but not generally privileged as an audience for literature.

Besides these essentially "secular" considerations of audience and patronage, to what extent may the shift in gender attitudes described in this chapter be attributed to the influence of the Counter-Reformation church, generally seen as an engine for social conservatism both generally and with regard to gender roles in particular? This question has already been discussed at some length in chapter 5, but it is one that it seems appropriate to revisit in this context, given the causal centrality often attributed to the church in explaining the misogynist turn we are speaking of here.[101] It is certainly true that fear and suspicion of female sexuality was powerfully rooted within Christian tradition, as was a profound mistrust of female claims to spiritual authority. One of the organizing principles of the reforms set in motion in the Counter-Reformation was to bring female religious orders under closer male control; another was to ensure a more hermetic claustration of nuns from the temptations of the world. Within secular society, church teachings certainly reinforced social pressures toward a strict surveillance of female behavior; given women's status as witting or unwitting agents of sexual temptation, with its concomitants of social and spiritual disorder, their movements and interaction must be tightly controlled, along with their contacts with secular culture.[102] Clerical educational theorists of the late sixteenth century, such as Silvio Antoniano and Agostino Valier, proposed models of female education entirely framed by the imperative of strict behavioral discipline and were happy to sacrifice the still tentatively established secular ideal of the cultivated woman for the "safer" traditionalist formula of unremitting chastity, silence, and obedience. In the light of these considerations, it would be easy to accord the Counter-Reformation church the role of villain of the piece in the ideological shift we have been tracing in this chapter; prima facie, it seems obvious that Renaissance profeminist discourse would be anathema to a socially authoritarian movement of this kind, notably for its questioning of the natural justice of women's subordination to male authority and its insistence on women's status as rational moral agents, capable of withstanding temptation through the exercise of will, even in the absence of external constraint. Some evidence that profeminist arguments were beginning to fall under a new suspicion in this period is offered by the fact that two of the principal male "defenders of women" writing in the 1620s, Cristoforo Bronzini and Francesco Agostino della Chiesa, both found themselves in difficulties with the authorities as the result of their feminist advocacy.[103] Bronzini's *Delle dignità e nobiltà delle donne,* originally scheduled for publication in 1622, was withdrawn from circulation after printing and placed on the Index of Prohibited Books pending correction, to be reissued only in 1624.[104] The criticisms the work attracted are indicated in a manuscript list in the Biblioteca Nazionale of Florence, which reveals the main concerns of Bronzini's anonymous accuser to have been with perceived transgressions of religious orthodoxy.[105] Some of these doctrinal points, however, precisely concern the relation of the sexes. Thus Bronzini's classic profeminist claim that men's domination over women was "unjust and tyrannical" was presumably viewed by the accuser as denying the justice of God's mandate to Eve in Genesis 3.16 that "thy desire shall be to thy husband, and he shall rule over thee."[106] Also arousing the suspicions of Bronzini's anonymous censor was a passage arguing that Eve's having been fashioned by God subsequent to Adam signaled her status as the climatic masterpiece of creation: an argument popularized by Henricus Cornelius Agrippa in his *De nobilitate et praecellentia foeminei sexus* (1529) and unproblematically reiterated by late sixteenth-century "defenders of women" such as Moderata Fonte.[107] Della Chiesa's "Discorso della preminenza del sesso donnesco" caused him no such prepublication problems, even though he would certainly be vulnerable to the accusation of presenting women's subordination to men as unjust. The "Discorso" was, however, cited against Della Chiesa during the process of his appointment as bishop of Saluzzo in 1642, presumably on the grounds that social radicalism of this kind accorded ill with episcopal decorum.[108]

Given these facts, and considering the virtual demise of the genre of "defenses of women" after these two works, it would be tempting to conclude that ecclesiastical censorship was an important factor in suppressing profeminist discourse in this period. This would, however, probably be mistaken. Both Bronzini and Della Chiesa escaped their brush with the forces of containment relatively lightly, perhaps because both enjoyed the patronage of powerful women, respectively Maria Maddalena of Austria and Maria Cristina of France, regent of Savoy (1606–63). The 1624 published edition of Bronzini's *Della dignità e nobiltà delle donne* appears substantially identical to that of the withdrawn 1622 edition, suggesting that the author succeeded in persuading the official censors of the innocuousness of his initial readings.[109] Similarly, whatever objections were made to Della Chiesa's feminist past were not sufficient to impede his appointment as bishop and may reflect political objections to his candidacy as much as any genuine ideological opposition.[110] More than a fear of ecclesiastical censorship, what is likely to account for the virtual disappearance of the genre of "defenses of women" after the 1620s was a lack of strong patronage incentives such as those that had inspired the texts of Bronzini and Della Chiesa, accompanied, perhaps, by the kind of social peer pressure we may infer from a text such as Janus Nicius Erythraeus's biography of Bronzini, which sneeringly insinuates that the latter's profeminism derived from his personal weakness for feminine beauty.[111] More generally, if we look at the contexts and protagonists of seventeenth-century misogyny, it would be difficult to speak of the church or of clerics taking an uncontested leading role in the field, in the way that we can, perhaps, more easily in the case of fifteenth-century humanism or certainly moments in medieval culture. As we have seen, one of the fulcrums of Seicento misogyny was the anticlerical and protolibertine Venetian Accademia degli Incogniti, and one of its more tireless proponents the ex-monk and virulent anticurial satirist Ferrante Pallavicino (1618–44). Countervailingly, it is not difficult to think of monks and secular clerics who contributed notably in this period to the discourse on women's "nobility and excellence," ranging from Silvano Razzi (1527–1613) and Pietro Paolo Ribera (d. 1609) to Della Chiesa, Giacomo Filippo Tomasini, and Filippo Maria Bonini (b. 1612).[112] Rather than seventeenth-century misogyny, we should probably speak rather of "misogynies": mistrust and suspicion of women and condemnation of female vice were topoi common to strains of writing otherwise quite radically ideologically disparate, ranging from the clerical-didactic, actively promoted by the church, to the libertine-erotic, frequently banned by it. Attitudes to the erotic became a particular ideological testing ground, with Venice's intellectuals drawing on their city's traditional philosophical alle-

giance to Aristotelian materialism and its equally customary practical culture of high-end prostitution to articulate a sui generis patriotically inflected cult of sexual freedom, viewed as a badge of Venice's independence
from Rome. At the same time, in Rome and its sphere of influence, a militant and evangelizing piety promoted sexual abstinence as a central element in religious culture, positioning female sexuality, correspondingly, as
a grave threat to the spiritual. Both positions were compatible with misogynist attitudes, the libertine, as we have seen, no less than the clerical, even
if it the former could not draw on quite the same venerable patristic and
scholastic traditions of the latter. Seventeenth-century libertine writings
frequently evince a moral disgust for women's supposed sexual rapacity at
the same time as they celebrate the opportunities women's lasciviousness
afforded for male pleasure. "Halt, audacious hand!" Francesco Pona's
voyeuristic *Messalina* warns the reader in its opening phrase, "Do not touch
what is charming your eye. The beauty that attracts you is cadaverous; the
woman who seems living to you . . . is dead, struck by the lightning bolt
of unchastity."[113]

It is a simplification, then, and a misleading one, to invoke the Counter-
Reformation alone in accounting for the seventeenth century's misogynistic turn. As we saw in chapter 5, by the latter decades of the sixteenth
century, a modified form of Renaissance profeminist culture had evolved,
inflected to the age's new religious imperatives but equally affirmative in
its attitudes to women. The culture of the Medici court in the regency
represents the apex of this Counter-Reformation feminism: "Counter-
Reformation" enough to have attracted accusations of obscurantism and
morbid piety in the past in liberal-secular historiography and "feminist"
enough to have become the subject of fascinated enquiry in recent years
by scholars with an interest in women's cultural agency and patronage.[114]
There was nothing intrinsic in post-Tridentine Catholicism that entailed
the adoption of misogynistic positions; indeed, where patronage or readership concerns dictated an admiring stance with regard to women, material, especially in the form of inspirational exempla, was not difficult to ex-
cavate within the tradition. If humanism had its Zenobia and Lucretia and
Hortensia, the Christian tradition had its Esther and its Catherine of Alex-
andria—even, in Mary Magdalene, a striking case of a sexually profligate
woman redeemed to become a paragon of grace. It is not difficult to imagine that, in an alternative political scenario, the gender profile of Italian
Counter-Reformation culture might look rather different. Examples from
outside Italy are interesting in this regard: the regencies of both Marie de'
Medici (1610–17) and Anne of Austria (1643–51) in France offer compara-

tive instances of a post-Tridentine Catholic culture inflecting to accommodate to the presence of a powerful female figure.[115]

A last matter deserves attention before we leave the question of Seicento misogyny generally to focus on the figure of the female writer in particular: how seriously should we take the often disturbingly virulent misogynist diatribes we find so often in the literature of the day? An untutored response would tend to take Seicento misogynist writings as representing a genuine and widespread animus against the female sex and to imagine the shift from affirmative to negative and belittling views of women as reflecting a societal change for the worse in women's position. This was also the tendency within historical studies until relatively recently, when a protofeminist and relatively open Renaissance was seen as followed by an oppressive, Jesuitical and Spanish-dominated Seicento that forced women into a position of religiously tinged infantilization.[116] While social changes can certainly be traced in this period that had an impact on women's lives, notably the tendency to a reduced marriage rate among the elite, it would be mistaken to represent women's life chances as radically transformed in concrete terms between the sixteenth and seventeenth centuries.[117] Studies on women's patronage of religious architecture in the seventeenth century, for example, show that some elite women of this period enjoyed a notable degree of financial empowerment and cultural visibility, even if the tendency of women to channel their patronage energies in this direction may in some ways be seen as a reversion to fifteenth-century practice.[118] Beyond such empirical details, moreover, it is useful to question the fundamental assumption underpinning the view that Seicento misogynistic writings bespoke a real and widespread anti-woman sentiment, which is that literary discourses of gender may be read as faithful reflections of "actual" gender perceptions of gender relations. Such transparency cannot be simply assumed. Both Cinquecento profeminist discourses and Seicento misogynistic ones need to be seen in the context of the humanistic tradition of epideictic rhetoric, which saw the twin exercises of blame and praise as privileged sites for the display of verbal ingenuity and wit. Read from the perspective of this tradition, the baroque genre of misogynistic invective becomes the mirror image of the Renaissance genre of "praise of women" rather than its antithesis, with both best considered a kind of "society game," usefully facilitating relations among men.[119] A recent essay by Franco Croce sensitively analyzes the exuberant laudatory hyperbole of baroque dedicatory letters, concluding that they should not be seen as "sincere"—or intended to be read as such—nor as the quasi-satirical exaggerations they can easily appear to be to modern readers; rather, they instigate a complicity between writer and dedicatee as coparticipants in a sophisticated rhetorical scenario that subtly flatters the latter's intelligence by implying his ability correctly to "handle" such praise.[120] The same might be said of the misogynistic discourse of the age, and its controversialist discourse in general; not entirely "serious" in its hyperbole—women as monsters, harpies, devils, "toxins of nature"—nor aiming satirically to undermine the position it parodies through hyperbole, it worked rather by constructing a mutually flattering bond between writer and reader, both scripted as practiced connoisseurs of the rhetorical "marvelous."[121] Consideration of this can help us understand otherwise baffling phenomena such as the relationship of touchy mutual affirmation that united the century's prime feminist polemicist, the Venetian nun Arcangela Tarabotti, and one of its most active and authoritative "misogynists," Gianfrancesco Loredan. Loredan facilitated and perhaps financed at least two of Tarabotti's publications, her *Paradiso monacale* (1643) and her *Lettere* (1650), also playing an important role in supplying her with secular (and sometimes scandalous) literary works she could not otherwise easily have come by.[122] She returned the compliment by dedicating her *Lettere* to him, addressing him as her "most worshipful patron" ("patron colendissimo"). Despite the radically changed context, the relation of the two—talented "marginal" woman and authoritative literary mentor—is not unlike that we see in the previous century between Tullia d'Aragona and Benedetto Varchi, or Veronica Franco and Domenico Venier. This seems unexpected, to say the least, given Loredan's preparedness to describe womankind, in a letter addressed to Tarabotti, as "nothing but one great defect . . . a monster of our species . . . worse than death" ("tutta un solo difetto . . . un mostro della nostra specie . . . peggiore della morte").[123]

It seems realistic in these circumstances, as well as historically appropriate, to regard Seicento misogynistic rhetorical stances as, precisely, rhetorical stances rather than expressions of committed existential convictions. If hyperbolic polemic was a rhetorical game, moreover, it was one that women, too, could play: when Tarabotti speaks of the wisdom of ancient Amazons who killed male children at birth, we have no particular reason to think this her "actual," considered position.[124] Despite these mitigating considerations however, it would be mistaken to regard Seicento misogynistic discourse as entirely innocuous either or as having no implications for women's lives. In one specific field, the Seicento "misogynistic turn" can be seen very directly to have constrained women's choices with regard to the previous century: in that of elite women's possibilities for participation in intellectual and literary culture. In the new literary climate of the Seicento, secular women were effectively frozen out of the "republic of letters"; even if a few hardy souls like Tarabotti survived until the 1640s, they did so as a species consciously threatened with extinction. This was a change, of course, that affected only a small minority of privileged women, but it is one, nonetheless, that cannot be dismissed as nugatory. Women had briefly had a voice within Italian literature; in the Seicento, that voice was progressively silenced.

## 2. Misogyny and the Woman Writer: The Redomestication of Female *Virtù*

As a means of approaching the question of how this process of silencing was accomplished, it will be useful first to survey seventeenth-century attitudes to intellectual accomplishment on women's part. As noted at the end of chapter 5, in the context of Margherita Sarrocchi, in the final decades of the sixteenth century, even as women entered what was to prove the climactic phase of early modern feminine literary and artistic creativity, voices were beginning to be heard dissenting from the generally supportive attitude to women's writing that had characterized the politer realms of the male literary elite since the era of Bembo. Tasso's *Discorso della virtù feminile e donnesca* is important in this respect for the sly wedge it places between a queenly elite of women from the great dynastic families, confirmed in their traditional right to the cultivation of "masculine" virtues, and the mass of women below this rank in status for whom a domestically oriented *virtù feminile* was sufficient. This has obvious implications for women's writing, although Tasso does not pursue them: it is clear that, logically, his prescriptions would confine literary activity for women to a statistically minuscule elite. The Aristotelian prescriptions that the treatise espouses defined eloquence as a "masculine" virtue, mandating, instead, silence for women. Women outside the queenly elite, were, moreover, precluded from seeking public notice for their talents, in keeping with Thucydides's prescription, approvingly quoted by Tasso, that a woman's fame should not exceed the bounds of her house. Effectively, then, Tasso's *Discorso* proposes a return to the status quo of the fifteenth and early sixteenth centuries, when the public pursuit of literary excellence was largely limited to court ladies, whose education was dictated by their role. His citing of Vittoria Colonna as an exemplum of *virtù donnesca* is telling in this respect. Historically, as we have seen, the example of Colonna functioned as an enabling precedent for women, serving through the medium of print to diffuse the practice of women's writing from the court elites to broader strata of society. Tasso's *Discorso* implicitly represents this process as based on a category mistake: while Colonna was justified in her literary activities as a *donna* of exceptionally high social standing, this did not sanction her imitation by *femine* whose status properly confined them to a *virtù feminile*. The threat Tasso's position represented to the tradition of women's writing was clearly perceived by Lucrezia Marinella, herself an example of someone his theory would silence if carried to its logical conclusion. Marinella's chapter on the *Discorso* in her *La nobiltà et l'eccellenza delle donne* loftily dismisses Tasso's proposed status-based subdivision of feminine virtue, noting that history supplied countless examples of "heroic" attainments by lower-status women. The semantic distinction between *virtù feminile* and *donnesca* is therefore meaningless: a foolishly touted "novelty concept" ("novella invenzione") that brings nothing of value to the debate. Marinella concludes with a ringing defense of women's aspirations to glory, citing Plutarch's *Mulierum virtutes* to the effect that "the fame of women's achievements in the sciences and in virtuous actions should resound not only in their own cities but in diverse and varying provinces."[125] The mention of "sciences" here, alongside "virtuous actions," suggests that intellectual activity stood at the center of her concerns.

In addition to this restriction of the pursuit of "masculine" *virtù* to a minuscule elite constituted by women from the ruling dynasties, Tasso also, as we have seen, more covertly insinuates that even for this elect group, such a pursuit may not be entirely in order. As will be recalled, the *Discorso della virtù feminile e donnesca* concludes by casually noting that proponents of *virtù donnesca* are not necessarily to be held to the standards of sexual propriety considered appropriate in the common run of women. To contemporary readers, as Tasso can hardly have failed to be aware, this was an observation little short of inflammatory in character: while he is careful not to suggest that cultural "virility" in women was in any way inevitably accompanied by a slippage in sexual virtue, given the sensitivity of the topic, it was hardly necessary to do so in order to awaken suspicion. Where education was concerned, a well-established misogynistic tradition associated learning in women with sexual "deviance" and considered the only way of preventing such deviance to be that of keeping girls from the contamination of letters. This was sufficiently widespread as a prejudice for a sixteenth-century theorist like Lodovico Dolce to have felt the need to devote considerable energy in his *Dialogo della institution delle donne* (1545) to combating this view.[126] Moderata Fonte's *Il merito delle donne* also contains a memorable diatribe on the subject.[127] Throughout much of the sixteenth century, however, this misogynistic position had been in abeyance, at least within a reasonably broad swathe of educated liberal opinion. The exemplary force of famously chaste women writers like

Colonna and Gambara had been powerfully functional in this regard, as also the reasoned advocacy of writers such as Dolce. The extent to which learning and poetic talent in women had become uncoupled from any shadow of unchastity in later sixteenth-century Italy is demonstrated, for example, by the relative infrequency with which Italian female writers of this period had recourse to anonymity or the use of pseudonyms and also by the frequency with which, as we have seen, female poets were co-opted by their hometowns as icons of civic pride. Nonetheless, curiously—and revealingly—however much this "liberal" position on women advanced, it was destined to remain somehow intrinsically and perpetually avant-garde, just as female writers remained rhetorically unique "marvels" and "prodigies" long after their presence in Italian literary culture had become commonplace. Impressive though it was in all kinds of respects, the edifice of Renaissance women's writing remained fragile, with the weak point of its foundation being precisely the claim that learning and poetic fame could be pursued without compromise to a woman's moral status. It was this weak point that opponents of women's education would begin with increasing relentlessness to target in the late sixteenth and early seventeenth century, though the supposed hubris and arrogance of the educated woman made a useful occasional secondary target. So much was socially invested in women's chastity in Italy—particularly the chastity of women of the propertied classes—that the least suspicion that study might jeopardize this investment was sufficient to provoke a retrenchment. The nebulous gains to a family's honor that might derive from its being able to boast of the learning of its women was far outweighed by the danger that, precisely on account of this learning, its women might be regarded as unchaste.

A history of the resurgence to cultural prominence in the seventeenth century of the position that regarded education in women as a danger to their chastity should probably take as its starting point Silvio Antoniano's *Tre libri dell'educatione christiana dei figliuoli* of 1584, already discussed briefly in chapter 5. A theologian and future cardinal, writing at the request of Carlo Borromeo, Antoniano accurately represents a certain, rigorist strain within Counter-Reformation social teaching, and his chapter on the education of girls is dominated by moral concerns. Antoniano acknowledges the desirability of literacy, at least, in girls from prominent noble families, but strains to reduce their education to the minimum necessary, denouncing in particular the tendency of parents to allow their daughters to study under the same tutorship as their brothers and to learn languages and rhetoric and become competent in the exercises of oratory and verse.[128] Such accomplishments, Antoniano argues, can only result in an encouragement of women's "natural" vanity and an assumption by them of positions of intellectual authority directly in contravention of the apostle Paul's interdiction of women taking on the role of instructors of men.[129] Further, and more pressingly, he insinuates that education of one's daughters will jeopardize their moral integrity: parents proud of their daughters' accomplishments will find the temptation irresistible to allow them to display their learning in public, thus placing them in contact with young *letterati* with the risk that potentially dangerous flirtations will result.[130] Antoniano concludes that an appropriate education for a girl will supply her with the limited literacy necessary for a little spiritually edifying reading; for the rest, her girlhood training should be focused on preparing her for the practical exercise of running a household.

While there is no particular reason to think that Antoniano's strictures reflected contemporary practice at the time they were written—perhaps the contrary—his treatise is important as prefiguring what would become a more widespread position. Probably more instrumental in associating female literacy with sexual immodesty in the minds of the Italian elites than the sober discussions of educational theorists, however, were the relentless barbs of satirists such as Traiano Boccalini, whose scurrilous take on the dispensability of decorum on the part of "princesses and great ladies" we have already noted in the context of Caterina Sforza. A sketch in Boccalini's most famous work, the *Ragguagli di Parnaso,* satirizing sixteenth-century literary customs portrays the Sienese Accademia degli Intronati admitting to its ranks the *virtuosissime donne* Vittoria Colonna, Veronica Gambara, and Laura Terracina. The experiment is first successful, as "the academicians, warmed [riscaldati] by the beauty of those ladies, not only attended the gatherings with great frequency, but daily published poetry to amaze the muses themselves." An end is put to these academic frolics, however, by Apollo, who rules that mixed literary interaction can only end in sexual confusion, crudely concluding that "literary exercises among ladies and *virtuosi* resemble the fun and games we see among dogs, which always end after a brief space of time with one of them mounting the other."[131] Boccalini's observations on the subject are found frequently echoed by other seventeenth-century male writers, along with their concomitant conclusion that "the true poetics of women is the needle and the spindle."[132] An interesting instance is that of Giambattista de' Luca's conduct treatise *Il cavaliere e la dama* (1675), which discreetly alludes in passing to Boccalini as an authority on the problems involved in integrating women into intellectual life.[133] De Luca acknowledges the theoretical desirability of education for women, but concludes, echoing Antoniano, that the moral dangers involved in exposing women to letters outweighs any potential benefits, adducing the rather curious argument that culture has the effect of making a woman more attractive and therefore more liable to become a target of seduction. More insidiously, meanwhile, literature is said to work on the soul, fostering an attitude of greater "license" and "liberty" that, over time, will inevitably and "almost insensibly" turn a woman's mind to perilous musings on love. What begins, thus, as a creditable quest for knowledge in women will end in "indecency and the prostitution of chastity": this even if the women involved are "Vittoria Colonnas" and the men of their circle "Senecas and other moral philosophers."[134]

One point of interest in De Luca's discussion of women's education is his extension of the "danger zone" for women beyond the practices of writing and literary conversation targeted by Antoniano and Boccalini to the activity of reading, perceived as intrinsically contaminating, regardless of subject matter, on account of its dangerous broadening of the feminine mind. More conventionally and literal-mindedly, satirists tended to highlight as a danger of feminine literacy the possibility of women coming into contact with sexually charged subject matter. Thus, in an aside in his fantasy novel, *La lucerna* (1625), we find Francesco Pona warning against the folly of encouraging women to leave their natural occupations of the "distaff and spindle" and to acquire the literacy skills that give them access to the *lascivie* of poets like Ovid, Catullus, and Martial. Given these temptation, he concludes, it can be accounted a miracle if any woman "wishing to exceed the limits of her sex" through erudition succeeds in escaping without "staining her soul with vices and filthy abominations."[135] Pona's negative use here of the topos of a woman "exceeding her sex" is worthy of notice, as it points up a significant rhetorical point of distinction between sixteenth profeminist and seventeenth-century antifeminist discourses. Humanistic profeminism had relied heavily on exceptionalist language, even as it attempted to "redeem" the female sex in general: a standard compliment to a woman was that she had succeeded in overcoming the deficiencies of her sex. This did not necessarily imply an essentialist concession to "natural" female inferiority, though that was sometimes implicit: often, it praised a woman, rather, for overcoming the cultural inferiority imposed on women by social constraints. Common variants of the commonplace of "exceeding the feminine" were praising women or their virtues as "virile" and speaking of them "abandoning the needle and the spindle" to take up the sword or the pen. Even references to women as "illustrious" or "famous" implicitly referenced this topos in that an emergence to public notice signified a transcendence of women's default condition of self-effacing invisibility. Within the profeminist discourse that evolved over the fifteenth and sixteenth centuries, this transcendence of the feminine condition was viewed as overwhelmingly positive, to the extent that we can see a writer like Giuseppe Betussi in the mid-sixteenth century warning noblewomen whose ambitions did not extend beyond the domestic that they risked appearing lax besides their more intellectual aspiring peers.[136] Seventeenth-century rhetoric differs quite radically on this point and may be seen in many respects as closer to the Boccaccio of De claris mulieribus than his humanist and sixteenth-century successors. Ambitions in women to "exceed their sex" are generally viewed as morally ambiguous: a flouting of the natural order demanding of some form of correction. "Virility" in women, and especially an urge to excel or dominate, is moreover strongly associated with sexual transgression: the nexus is embodied in figures such as Semiramis and Messalina, among the emerging antiheroines of the day, as we have seen. The same connection was routine in the case of intellectual "overreaching," as is apparent in the passage from Pona just quoted, as well as, less outspokenly, in de Luca: a route is directly traced in both texts from a desire to "transcend one's sex," by abandoning its destined domestic activities for the world of letters, to an inevitable sexual corruption, with its accompanying terminal loss of the defining feminine quality of chastity.

An interesting document of the process of sexualization to which the figure of the female writer was progressively subjected in this period is offered by Alessandro Zilioli's Istoria delle vite de' poeti italiani, which, though unprinted, circulated widely in manuscript in the first half of seventeenth century.[137] Zilioli's Istoria is composed of a series of biographies arranged, Vasari-style, in an teleological narrative of progress to literary perfection, beginning with the age of Dante and ascending to the contemporary climax represented by the "insuperable" Tasso and Marino. Women feature mainly, as we would expect, in the "fifth age" described, consisting essentially of the sixteenth century; they constitute 6 of the 122 writers in this era allotted a vita, or approximately 5 percent of the whole. Of the 6 writers selected, the inevitable Colonna and Gambara are accorded a respectful, if somewhat superficial attention, while Moderata Fonte is praised with particular warmth and given the compliment of a more detailed analysis.[138] The lives of the other three writers, meanwhile, Gaspara Stampa, Tullia d'Aragona, and Laura Terracina, are treated very differently and in a notably prurient tone; here, far more than on the literary quality of their work, which is barely mentioned, Zilioli's stress falls on these writers' sexual history, which is presented as irrevocably entwined with the story of their poetic "seductions." Both Stampa and d'Aragona are depicted as manipulative sirens, adroitly stoking their admirers' desire out of an insatiable desire for praise; the former is even seen, in a novelistic vignette, jeering in bed with her lover Collaltino as hapless suitors vainly serenade her beneath her window.[139] Terracina's life offered less obvious scope for scandal, and Zilioli portrays her more as victim than sexual aggressor. His principal narrative focus—unsubstantiated by external evidence—is the tale of Terracina's involvement with the literary academy of the Incogniti of Naples, which he portrays, Boccalini-style, as fated to end in disaster: Terracina is forced to withdraw her membership after a campaign of relentless sexual harassment by her fellow academicians, culminating in an attempted rape.[140] Zilioli's sexual reductionism in these *vite* is reminiscent of that we have already encountered in Boccalini, when he portrays the academicians of the Intronati expressing their excitement at the presence of women in the academy by eager ejaculations of poetic creativity "that would stagger even the Muses." Similarly, Zilioli portrays Tullia d'Aragona's poetic suitors at one point as a pack of "famished hounds" bearing down on their prey.[141] Beneath the brio of the descriptions here, some quite serious and destructive cultural work is taking place: nothing less than the satirical liquidation of the long-standing sixteenth-century practice of poetic exchange between men and women, which had drawn routinely on a language of erotic courtship as sanitized and ritualized as that employed in courtly dance. This Neoplatonic language had served a crucial function in levering women a place within literary culture and providing a socially intelligible vehicle for this novel form of interaction between the sexes. To sexualize this language, and the exchanges it enabled, was to problematize women's literary position in quite a radical way.

A second example of feminine literary biography also worth highlighting for its more general resonances is the life of Margherita Sarrocchi found in the *Pinacotheca* (1642) of Janus Nicius Erythraeus (Gianvittorio de' Rossi) (1577–1647). Erythraeus's life of Sarrocchi opens with a reasonably whole-hearted tribute to her intellect and poetic talent, noting especially her "virile boldness" ("audacia plane virilis") in attempting the genre of epic.[142] As we rapidly learn, however, this impressive *virtù* was coupled with an almost monstrously difficult character; even by Erythraeus's generally malicious standards, this is an exceptionally unflattering portrait. Sarrocchi's chastity is described scathingly as "famed to be such as is generally that of female poets, musicians, singers, and those who have been lured away from their domestic labors to practice the arts of painting and sculpture."[143] She is also portrayed as hideously vain, bullying of all around her, and pathologically oversensitive to criticism, as well as sufficiently irascible to have alienated the whole of literary Rome had it not been for the mitigatory emollience of her friend and possible lover, the mathematician Luca Valerio, whose task of defusing the hostilities aroused

by Sarrocchi's "intolerable contumacy" ("intolerabilis contumacia") is portrayed as a virtual full-time occupation.[144] While presenting itself merely
as an individual portrait, de' Rossi's biography of Sarrocchi hints at
broader lessons regarding the imprudence of attempts to admit women to
literary society; within a very different genre, his message is not different
from that of Boccalini in the *Ragguagli*. The point is reinforced in his
sharply contrasting portrait of the only other female figure to appear in
the first book of the *Pinacotheca*, the Florentine nun Lorenza Strozzi, who
is praised for her piety, celibacy, and retirement from the temptations of
the world.[145] To reinforce Strozzi's exemplarity as a model for female poet,
de' Rossi counterposes her, in an extended comparison, with Sappho, on
the thin grounds that Strozzi had used Sapphic meter extensively in her
*Hymni* of 1588. As might be expected, the contrast drawn up is a stark one:
on the one hand, the promiscuous and "tribadic" pagan love poet, burning
with the "flames of the most impure loves" ("impurissimorum amorum
flamma"); on the other, the virginal nun, cloistered from the world and
singing of Christian devotion. Measured against this scale, Sarrocchi
would clearly incline more to the Sapphic end of the spectrum than to
Strozzi's. It is perhaps not fortuitous in this context that Erythraeus relates
rumors of Sarrocchi's bisexuality, noting that her enemies were inclined to
slander her with the imputation that "she was a man among women and
a woman among men."[146]

Pervading Erythraeus's treatment of both Sappho and Sarrocchi—and
equally present in a text like Boccalini's *Ragguagli*—is the sense that a
woman who ventures into the male territory of literature is radically out
of place. Specifically, for Erythraeus, the problem seems to arise when she
attempts to compete with the men around her. Both Sappho and Sarrocchi are explicitly said in his text to have rivaled and outshone many male
poets of their day.[147] Lorenza Strozzi is portrayed as a lesser poet (even
though she is said to rival her brother, Ciriaco Strozzi, in honor) and hence,
even aside from her moral exemplarity, already as less of a threat.[148] This
raises the possibility that one contributory factor to the "misogynistic
turn" noted in this chapter may have been a sense that women writers
were beginning to encroach too closely on male prerogatives. This is an interesting question, although any answer can inevitably only be speculative.
It is certainly noteworthy that this change in attitude should have occurred
precisely during the period in which women were emerging most strongly
as authors and claiming their place within literary culture most confidently. Nor should it be overlooked that the first "respectable" female
writer to have attracted genuine vitriol from her male peers was also the
first woman in Italy to publish an epic—namely, Sarrocchi.[149] When fe-

male writers had first appeared on the scene in Italy, they had generally figured as decorously subordinate to the male writers around them, who frequently acted as mediators in presenting the work of their "protégées" to the literary world. Later in the Cinquecento, however, as we have seen, women writers were beginning to show an increasing assertiveness and autonomy. In the 1540s and 1550s, it had been unusual for women to pen their own dedicatory letters or even to give any indication that they had given permission to publish their writings. By the 1580s and 1590s, it was entirely standard for women to take full ownership of their work. At the same time, as we have seen, women were increasingly emboldened to undertake ambitious and large-scale literary projects and were, occasionally at least, taking on "male" literary roles as editors of texts or providers of editorial matter. They were also increasingly happy to use their public platform to speak on gender issues, criticizing the limited opportunities available for women and speculating, at least in fictional contexts, about the possibility of a different social order. Figures such as Maddalena Campiglia, Isabella Andreini, and Lucrezia Marinella were, in their very different ways, becoming increasingly hard to frame within conventional notions of the "lady" poet, the decorous amateur. All were shrewd operators, canny in their self-presentation, and alert to patronage opportunities. All made good use, in particular, of the appeal they had, as women, to potential female patrons and of the "novelty value" female writers possessed in a literary world still overwhelmingly male. It is not difficult to imagine that they may have caused resentment, especially among male poets writing in the vernacular and pitching themselves to the same audiences. Female poets had been flattering as novelties fifty years earlier and useful as a means for male *letterati* to display their gallantry and "progressiveness." Fifty years on some of these Pygmalions may have begun to wonder whether they had inadvertently turned into Frankensteins. Some sense of threat does seem to transpire, beneath the affectionately teasing surface tone, in a letter from Luigi Groto to Issicratea Monte of 1583, complimenting her on the excellence of a sonnet exchange he has seen between his correspondent and Campiglia. "I can think of nothing to say," Groto observes, "other than what St. Augustine said at the death of St. Anthony: 'The unlearned are rising up and seizing the kingdom.'" Now, however, "it is women, or rather young girls, who are rising up and forcibly snatching glory from the hands of men."[150] Less benignly than Groto, Giuseppe Passi fulminates against the ignorance and vanity of supposedly erudite women in his *Donneschi difetti,* concluding starkly "Let women be silent, especially in the presence of men."[151]

Whether or not a degree of protectionism may be detected among its motives, the fact seems beyond debate that the Seicento saw the collapse of the mutual-interest compact that had sustained relations between male and female *letterati* throughout the previous century. Intellectual relations with women were no longer a necessary element in male literary self-fashioning as they had been a century earlier: *canzonieri* could be published rich in dialogic exchange without a single woman featuring as other than object. With no particular advantage accruing to men from women's presence as protagonists in literary culture, they could be summarily jettisoned as interlocutors and as objects of praise. This went particularly for women of a social status requiring a reverently Neoplatonizing tone of address as had been the majority of the previous century's highly respectable female Petrarchists. The new muses and idols of the seventeenth century were, for the most part, actresses and singers who lent themselves more easily and attractively to the more sensual registers of the day. It is telling in this connection that in 1644, the year before Lucrezia Marinella effectively tolled the death knell of the Renaissance tradition of women's writing in her *Essortationi alle donne,* discussed below, the *letterati* of her native Venice brought out a lavish poetic tribute volume to the Roman singer Anna Renzi (c. 1620–c. 1660), star of the first performance of Monteverdi's *Incoronazione di Poppea* and one of the greatest divas of her day.[152]

### 3. Women's Writing in Seicento Italy: Decline and Fall

Where did this leave women writers? As will hardly be surprising, given the unpropitiousness of the literary environment, the seventeenth century proved considerably less fertile a period for women's writing than had the sixteenth. This is not solely a question of numbers, although certainly there was a sharp numerical decline at this time, especially if we look beyond the "headline" figures of women publishing single-authored works to the hinterland of anthologized writers who supplied such cultural depth and reach to the sixteenth-century tradition of women's writing.[153] It is not simply that we see fewer new writers emerging in the Seicento than in the previous century; those writers that did emerge tended to be less culturally integrated than their predecessors and their works enjoyed a lesser prestige and diffusion. This is especially clear if we compare the generation of writers born in the 1550s and 1560s and beginning to publish in the 1580s and 1590s, with that born around the 1590s or the early 1600s, and emerging as writers in the 1620s or 1630s. Where the latter are concerned, it is difficult to think of any, with the exception of Arcangela Tarabotti and Margherita Costa (1600–1664), who attained anything like the fame of a Lucrezia Marinella, a Moderata Fonte, a Margherita Sarrocchi, or a Maddalena Campiglia, still less an Isabella Andreini. Of the prior generation, even relatively "minor" writers such as Maddalena Salvetti, and largely un-published ones such as Barbara Torelli and Tarquinia Molza, still achieved a level of recognition of which an Isabetta Coreglia (fl. 1628–50) or a Barbara Tigliamochi (or Tagliomochi) degli Albizzi (d. 1595) could only dream.[154] As long as literary interaction with women remained functional to the construction of male cultural identities, an impressive range of mechanisms existed to facilitate women's access to the literary arena. Treatises on *donne illustri* or of the glories of particular cities circulated the names and sometimes the biographies of female writers; women were sought after as dedicatees, correspondents, and contributors of prefatory sonnets, and their contributions were regularly solicited for poetic anthologies, especially those in praise of women or with a patriotic angle. It was not difficult for a woman in the sixteenth century to gain a certain visibility through these mechanisms, even without any very notable literary talent to back it. In the seventeenth century, by contrast, the means through which women might attain literary fame were more limited: the *donne illustri* genre fell into disuse after the 1620s, and women were no longer perceived as necessary authorizing fixtures in anthologies and *canzonieri*. Occasional instances are still found where a female writer seemed to serve as a literary mascot for a particular ambience or circle: examples here would include Tarabotti in the 1640s with the Accademia degli Incogniti and Costa's with the Medici court in the late 1630s as well as, at a provincial and "archaic" level, Coreglia's in Lucca in the 1620s. These are short-lived and inconclusive relationships, however, and marked by a notable ambivalence, at least in the former two cases. The ritual deference and respect women could rely on in the sixteenth century was in the seventeenth rarely to be found.

When we come to look comparatively at the social profiles of sixteenth- and seventeenth-century women writers, a very interesting discrepancy is apparent. Virtually absent in the Seicento from the meager roll call of female writers is what had been a key type—almost the default type—of the *letterata* from the fifteenth century onward: the "honest" woman of good family, socially integrated and conventional in her mores. Examples from the sixteenth century, too numerous to list, range from aristocratic urban matrons like Lucia Albani, Giulia Bigolina, and Laodomia Forteguerri to court ladies like Veronica Gambara and Leonora Falletti. The type is paradigmatically defined in Giovanni Niccolò Doglioni's biography of Moderata Fonte (1593), with its portrait of the diligent poet-housewife and, with more aristocratic social inflections, in the biography of Irene di Spilimbergo included in her tribute volume of 1561. Within the seventeenth century, it is difficult to think of a new writer of the era (as opposed to sixteenth-century "survivors" like Francesca Turina and Lucrezia Marinella) who unproblematically embodies this type.[155] The only clear-cut exceptions are Barbara Tigliamochi, author of the chivalric romance *Ascanio errante* (1640), whose patrician Florentine background is comparable to that of late sixteenth-century writers like Fiammetta Soderini and Maddalena Salvetti, and Isabella Sori, of the minor nobility of Alessandria in Piedmont, author of a collection of prose works that came out in Pavia in 1628.[156] Of other possible candidates, Coreglia and Tarabotti are "compromised" by their unconventional lifestyles or attitudes; the former appears not to have married, and spent a period of her youth in Naples, perhaps as a singer, while the latter was a self-declaredly dissident nun.[157] Sara Copio Sullam (c. 1590–1640), otherwise well qualified by wealth and matronly status, can be assimilated to this type only with some difficulty because of her religious "otherness" as a Jew.[158] Margherita Costa, meanwhile, was a classic "irregular" as a singer, actress, and possible courtesan.[159] Tigliamochi aside, moreover, it is notable that no salient secular female writers of the Italian Seicento came from an aristocratic or patrician background. Coreglia was from an obscure, if seemingly fairly well-connected, family from Lucca, Copio from a wealthy and cultivated Venetian Jewish background. Tarabotti came from a reasonably moneyed mercantile family in Venice but still qualified technically as a *popolana*, below the *cittadino* status of Moderata Fonte and Lucrezia Marinella, whose fathers were professional men. If we are looking to find female writers from the upper ranks of society, we need to look in this period to nuns. An example here would the mystic Vittoria Colonna (1610–75), homonym and distant grandniece of the great sixteenth-century poet, who left her mark on religious history as the Venerable Chiara Maria della Passione.[160] Also noteworthy by virtue of their descent are Isabella Farnese (1597–1658) and her more famous sister Francesca (1593–1651), granddaughters of Maddalena Campiglia's patron, Isabella Pallavicino Lupi, Marchioness of Soragna.[161] These cases offer examples of the same kind of dynastic transmission of traditions of female learning that we have already seen numerous times in the fifteenth and sixteenth centuries in families, most famously the Montefeltro-Varano-Colonna and the Nogarola-Gambara-Valenti. Here, however, rather than a secular noblewoman-poet or "learned lady," the end product of the process is a nun.

In accounting for this virtual elimination of the "respectable" woman and noblewoman from the literary scene in the Italian Seicento, there are a number of factors we need to consider. One—though this may perhaps rather be seen as a factor affecting women's literary output more generally—was the dearth of potential female patrons available in this period as a result of the decline of the secular courts. By the late sixteenth and seventeenth century, as we have seen, a practice was developing among women writers of addressing their works fairly systematically to women of the great dynastic families of Italy. Thus Lucrezia Marinella dedicated successive works to the duchesses of Ferrara and Mantua, while Moderata Fonte dedicated her *Floridoro* to Bianca Cappello, Isabella Andreini her *Mirtilla* to Lavinia della Rovere, Margherita Sarrocchi her *Scanderbeide* to Giulia d'Este. As the secular courts dwindled as centers of literary production and consumption, it is likely to have become more difficult for women writers to find prominent female dedicatees with a record of cultural patronage that would promise a sympathetic reception. This may, in turn, have made publishers less inclined to take on their works. In a manner that confirms this hypothesis, where female patrons did continue to exert power, we do find small clusters of female-authored works being published. This is most apparent in Tuscany, where Maria Maddalena of Austria was the dedicatee of Marinella's *De' gesti heroici della serafica S[anta] Caterina* and her daughter-in-law Vittoria della Rovere (1622–94) the dedicatee of Suor Maria Clemente Ruoti's *Iacob Patriarca* (1637), Tigliamochi's *Ascanio errante*, Costa's *Flora feconda* (1640) and Tarabotti's *Antisatira* (1644) as well as, later in the century, a patron of the Pisan *letterata* Maria Sevaggia Borghini (1654–1731).[162] Both women were also patrons of female composers: Maria Maddalena commissioned Francesca Caccini's *La liberazione di Ruggiero dall'isola di Alcina,* while Vittoria della Rovere was the dedicatee of Barbara Strozzi's first book of madrigals (1644).[163] Strozzi speaks in the dedicatory letter of the latter work of her hopes that the grand duchess's protection will serve as protection against potential attackers, casting Vittoria as a "Golden Oak" (a pun on her surname, della Rovere) beneath which she might shelter from the slanderers already prepared in the wings. The protection motif was not a new one (we also find it, for example, in Maddalena Campiglia's dedication of her *Flori* to Isabella Pallavicino), but it is quite possible that it reflected a real defensive need, given the antifeminist tenor of contemporary culture.[164] Seventeenth-century writings by women frequently betray a sense of beleagueredness or defiance, and understandably so: the example of Margherita Sarrocchi in the first decade of the century had made it plain that women were no longer off limits for critics, and the lesson was further reinforced by the sexual insinuations and accusations of plagiarism leveled at Sara Copio and the contestations of authorship leveled at Lucrezia Marinella over her *Vita di Maria Vergine* and at Tarabotti over her *Paradiso monacale.*[165] The dedicatory letter to a work of 1628 by Isabella Sori anticipates attacks on the author by "Zoiluses, Momuses, and Aristarchs," and we find Arcangela Tarabotti a few decades later commenting that to publish in this climate required "real nerve" ("metter alla stampa ci vuole una gran testa").[166] It is not difficult to understand, in these circumstances, why women might seek a possible "shield" in a powerful female dedicatee: a second Diana, as Margherita Costa figures Maria Cristina of France, regent of Savoy, in one dedicatory letter of 1647, capable of rendering any potentially hostile male reader a "new Actaeon" for his pains.[167]

Beyond such external reasons, there were also internal, formal and stylistic reasons why seventeenth-century literary idioms proved less hospitable to women than had the Petrarchism of the previous century. While it is easy to deride Benedetto Croce's statement that the language of the baroque required a "virility" of which female poets were incapable, there is a kernel of truth in this assessment that it is useful in this context to explore.[168] It may first be helpful to recap the reasons why sixteenth-century Petrarchism proved so congenial to female poets, besides its decorous subject matter and its vernacular genetic roots. One was its almost militant conventionality. Petrarchism was an imitative genre within which success derived from a conscious and voluntary adherence to tradition. It was also a self-consciously diligent and disciplined literary idiom and an essentially rationalist and socially conformist one, especially in its mature Cinquecento variant, where occasional and spiritual verse had come to challenge or displace the original thematic primacy of the erotic. Within Bembo's analysis, the art of Petrarch came down to an art of balance, measuring the "masculine" and "feminine" qualities of *gravità* and *piacevolezza* in accordance with a moderation and judgment that seem to combine the aesthetic with the moral. It was a poetic idiom ideally suited to "good boys" or good girls, to the socially integrated and the morally upstanding. It was precisely this quality that made it so attractive to those whose innate literary entitlement was unsure. To women poets—always dogged, even at the peak period for their "acceptance," by the specter of sexual indecorum— the polite and sublimated persona Petrarchism offered to the poet was a reasonably secure mode of defense. In fact, it might even be argued that the peculiar balance of "gravity" and "charm" that Bembo defines as the secret of Petrarchist perfection was one to which female poets were particularly culturally well attuned through their social training. The aesthetic tightrope act Bembo sets the Petrarchist poet corresponds quite closely to Castiglione's prescription for his court lady, whose public persona is framed, precisely, as a difficult balance of the seductive and the "grave." The poetic idiom of the baroque was very different on this score and far less comfortably appropriable by women: if Cinquecento Petrarchism had favored the correct and the decent, the baroque sought to capture the imagination by breaking the rules. Baroque poetry was oriented more consistently toward the "singular" and the "marvelous" than the classically harmonious; it privileged the daring, the exuberant, and the irregular, both in its subject matter and style. Even if it in practice resolved itself in time into a style every bit as imitative and conventional as Petrarchism, its characteristic authorial stance was one of charismatic individualism rather than a self-effacing subordination to tradition. Women writers were distinctly at a disadvantage here, or at least those from "respectable" backgrounds, whose required social persona did not lend itself easily to flamboyant or self-promoting effects. It seems more than a coincidence that the female writer of the century who most confidently embraced baroque conventions of writing was the actress-singer Margherita Costa, whose position allowed her to stage herself as extravagant and "eccentric" (*bizzarra*).[169] For a woman of higher social status and less equivocal fame, such as pose would have been entirely unthinkable. It is notable that, with the exception of Costa, the seventeenth century's female writers may all be categorized stylistically as relatively conservative, to the extent that later Arcadian critics such as Giovanni Mario Crescimbeni (1663–1728) tend to present female writers like Margherita Sarrocchi and Maddalena Salvetti as heroic custodians of stylistic purity in the face of Marino's depravations.[170]

An interesting consideration of the problem of authorial decorum as it confronted the aspiring female writer of the seventeenth century is found in a self-referential pastoral eclogue buried unobtrusively in Isabetta Coreglia's *Rime spirituali e morali* (1628). The poem shows "Nerina," a figure for the author, in conversation with an older male figure, "Avvertito," whose name—presumably an academic epithet—translates approximately as "Prudent" or "Astute." The conversation between the two turns precisely on the question the decorum of Nerina's persona in her verse. Avvertito presents her as talented but hotheaded and contrary and of a "capricious and eccentric temperament" ("capriccioso . . . [e] bizzarro umore"), often finding an outlet in inappropriately pungent witticisms ("motti aspretti & appuntati"). None of the characteristics described would, of course, be out of place in the verse or authorial persona of a contemporary male poet; indeed, Nerina's initial line of defense is to claim that her model in learning these traits was none other than Avvertito himself. In a "respectable" female poet, however, such a style is clearly inappropriate, and Avvertito concludes by presenting her best chance at succeeding in the "courts of the great" as being to cast herself in the guise of a "simple nymph, brought up on the banks of the solitary Serchio."[171] This is indeed Nerina's stance in the bulk of the volume, which gives little hint of the capriciousness or wit for which Avvertito reproaches her in the eclogue; pious and decorous in her subject matter, she is praised in notably gendered terms in the publisher's introduction for the "charm," "purity," "facility" and "sweetness" of her verse.[172] The problem highlighted in the volume, and in its author's career generally, is that the dominant literary mode of the day allowed no easy mode of entry for the "respectable" female writer, while the model of literature mandated by a socially "correct" female persona was one for which no obvious market endured. The wry title of Coreglia's eclogue, "La ninfa vinta" ("The Defeated Nymph"), could stand as an epitaph for more than her youthful literary ambitions. The model of respectable female writer prevalent in the previous century and neatly encapsulated by the "simple nymph of the Serchio" formula was no longer culturally relevant or meaningful in the Seicento and would not be until its final decades.[173] The option of "retooling" for the new culture in a less demure mode was, as Coreglia lucidly saw, similarly unrealistic: to attempt to meet the demands of a "capricious" literary culture within the restrictive bounds of female decorum was an enterprise that must end in defeat.

What did women actually write in the Seicento? We need to concentrate here, for sharpness of focus, on those women who were fully the products of the new century, rather than the survivors of the last: the Costas and Coreglias and Tarabottis rather than the Marinellas and Sarrocchis and Turinas. The first thing one notes immediately when turning to the female-authored writings of the seventeenth century, by comparison with the sixteenth, is quite how much of seventeenth-century female writing is polemical in character: a fact, of course, in itself highly revealing of the different and more hostile environment in which women were now writing. Polemic features relatively little in the writing of women in the previous century, at least before Lucrezia Marinella's *La nobiltà et l'eccellenza delle donne* at the very end of the century. The main exceptions earlier are Laura Terracina's riffs on Ariosto's proems in her *Discorso,* where a moral-polemical tone is virtually mandated by the genre, and Veronica Franco's *Terze rime,* which reflect the author's particular situation as a courtesan. Things change quite sharply in the seventeenth century, when we find a series of explicit and concerted polemical writings by women, mostly defensive in character and directed at specified antagonists. Well-known examples of these include Sara Copio's *Manifesto* of 1621, denying the accusation of the cleric and *letterato* Baldassare Bonifacio, or Bonifaccio (1584–1629), that she had disputed the immortality of the soul, Arcangela Tarabotti's *Antisatira,* replying to a satire on female vanity, *Del lusso donnesco,* by the Sienese academician Francesco Buoninsegni (c. 1600–post

1655), and Tarabotti's *Che le donne siano della spetie degli huomini,* written in response to an anonymous satirical treatise disputing the humanity of women that had come out in Venice under a false imprint in 1647 and that Tarabotti published in Venice in 1651, again under a false imprint and with the transparent pseudonym of Galerana Barcitotti.[174] To this list we may add polemical works by two lesser-known authors, the Veronese *letterata* Veneranda Bragadin and the Piedmontese Isabella Sori. Bragadin's *Rime* of 1619, dedicated to Caterina Medici Gonzaga, Duchess of Mantua, contains a sonnet taking to task the author of a recent, seemingly unpublished *Invettiva contro le donne* and a sardonic letter replying at length to a satire her antagonist has written in response.[175] Sori, a decade later, published a set of epistolary *Difese* against attacks that critics had leveled against her earlier, didactic writings on female conduct, the tenor of her defense making patent the misogynistic character of these attacks.[176] Sori encapsulates well in this work the sense of embattledness that marked the experience of most literary women in this period, speaking of the situation of the intellectually ambitious woman as one of perpetual self-defense. The point is elegantly rendered by a mythological aperçu, that where "the ancients deputed two gods to preside over human wisdom," the masculine Apollo and the feminine Minerva, the former is always depicted pacifically, lyre in hand, while Minerva is portrayed as a "valiant warrior-woman (guerriera) poised for combat and armed from head to toe."[177]

Undoubted champion of the "armed Minervas" of Seicento Italy was Arcangela Tarabotti, and a special place needs to be given within the female-authored polemical literature of the period to Tarabotti's remarkable diatribes against the widespread social practice of committing of young girls to convents for socioeconomic reasons without concern for their vocation. Herself a victim of the abuse, Tarabotti wrote two ferocious attacks on it, *La tirannia paterna* and *L'inferno monacale,* the first published posthumously under a false imprint in 1654, revised and with the title *La semplicità ingannata,* the second unpublished until the late twentieth century.[178] These differ from the other female-authored polemical works of the period as they are not ad hominem pieces, composed in response to preceding male-authored writings; rather, in an unprecedented manner— or preceded only faintly and intermittently in Moderata Fonte's *Il merito delle donne*—they engage concretely and critically with the socioeconomic realities determining women's life choices at the time.[179] Tarabotti's two treatises are astonishing works, filled with a raging messianic fury and written in a vivid, if undisciplined, sui generis idiom that mingles biblical language and imagery with elements drawn from vernacular literature, both "classic"—Dante and Ariosto are particular points of reference—and contemporary, including the writings of the Incogniti.[180] These are works it is extremely difficult to imagine a woman writing in the more integrated literary culture of the previous century: Tarabotti is writing from the margins and capitalizes rhetorically on her position, positioning herself as a prophet in the wilderness calling a male-ordered society to account. Tarabotti's works have frequently been studied in conjunction with the feminist writings of her Venetian predecessors Moderata Fonte and Lucrezia Marinella in a manner that posits a continuity between these writers' works. While this is a valid approach—Tarabotti certainly knew both Fonte and Marinella and quotes them reverently as role-models—it is useful, as well, to recall the abyss that separates their works in content, tone, and literary context. Fonte and Marinella were both writing within the protective shield of the *querelle des femmes* and within a culture that still offered women writers a high degree of supportiveness, despite the boorishness of the occasional Passi. Both were arguing, moreover, for no more in effect than a cultural recognition of the dignity of women; certainly in Marinella and in great part in Fonte, there is little by way of a real call for social reform. Tarabotti, by contrast, was denouncing a concrete social abuse and was writing in a literary environment that took far fewer hostages. Little was to be gained by her through a more conciliatory form of argument, while extremity might win her a hearing. The controversial character of Tarabotti's *Semplicità ingannata* is reflected in its postpublication fortunes; never officially approved in the first place, it was placed on the Index in 1661, seven years after its clandestine appearance.[181]

Where more traditional forms of writing are concerned, women continued as a presence within what had been their "core genre" in the previous century: the collection of lyrical or occasional verse. The first two decades of the century saw a flourishing output of verse collections, including Andreini's three collections of 1601, 1603, and 1605, Marinella's *Rime sacre* of 1603, Lucchesia Sbarra's *Rime* of 1610 and Veneranda Bragadin's of 1614 and 1619.[182] The 1620s, too, saw three volumes of verse published by women: Semidea Poggi's *La Calliope religiosa* (1623), Francesca Turina's *Rime varie* (1628)—an exceptionally interesting and original work—and, in the same year as the latter, Isabetta Coreglia's *Rime spirituali e morali*.[183] After this, production slowed. Unusually within the tradition of women's writing but consistently with several of her male Venetian counterparts, Arcangela Tarabotti appears to have operated exclusively in prose.[184] In the 1630s and 1640s, the only published female writer of nonnarrative verse appears to have been Margherita Costa, who brought out a sequence of fancifully entitled works of the late 1630s, notably *La chitarra* and *Il violino* of 1638 and *Lo stipo* of 1639.[185] Costa's verse collections reflect the structural novelties of the Seicento *canzoniere* in terms of thematic titling and the use of internal thematic and metrical subdivisions, as well as in the use of narrative-thematic titles for individual poems.[186] The only other verse collections to be published before the Arcadian movement began to usher women back on to the literary scene in the 1690s were two volumes of sacred verse by religious women of autonomous spiritual authority, both published posthumously by their admirers: Francesca Farnese's *Rime sacre* (1657), and Maria Alberghetti's *Giardino di poesie spirituali* (1674).[187] Several points may be made about this highly disparate series of publications. One is, of course, the number of nuns figuring as authors: three of ten for the period 1600–1680 (Poggi, Farnese, Alberghetti) and two of three for the half-century from 1630. This marks a "reconventualization" of women's writing apparent more generally in this period; as the world of secular literature became less hospitable to "respectable" women, one sees something like a return to the situation of the late-medieval period, when women's writing was largely cloistered in context and was generally published (Farnese, Alberghetti) only following the author's death. Also noteworthy is the provincial setting of most of the publications listed, with the exception of Costa's works and, much earlier, Marinella's and Andreini's. Sbarra's *Rime* was published in her native Conegliano, Bragadin's in Padua and Verona, Poggi's in Vicenza, Coreglia's in Pistoia, Turina's in Città di Castello. This brings out a general, contextual point: where in the mid-sixteenth century, a woman like Chiara Matraini might have been disadvantaged in her writing career by her provincial setting, in the seventeenth, the opposite was probably true. It was in the smaller and less cutting-edge cultural environments that women probably now had the best chance of finding a supportive environment, tapping into residual perceptions of "local Sapphos" as embodiments of civic prestige.[188] Aside from the example of poets like Coreglia and Turina, one might cite in this connection a figure like the Perugian nun poet Gironda Cerrini (1626–1703), verse by whom, in Latin and the vernacular, figures in locally published volumes of the 1640s and 1650s and who may even have enjoyed the honor of membership of her local literary academy, the Virtuosi.[189]

As has already been mentioned, most of the verse collections produced by seventeenth-century Italian women are conservative, stylistically and in structure. Although Lucchesia Sbarra proclaims her admiration of Marino in a lengthy sequence of praise sonnets, it would be difficult to describe her as a disciple, while the works of Bragadin, Turina, and Coreglia could quite easily have been written in the previous century.[190] The most distinctly "seventeenth-century" of seventeenth-century female poets was, without doubt, Margherita Costa, whose numerous and substantial writ-

ings—with Tarabotti and Marinella, she is the most prolific female writer
of the century—are deserving of a far closer critical scrutiny than they
have hitherto received.[191] Typical of her "productions"—a theatrical
metaphor seems justified—is the 1639 volume *Lo stipo* (*The Jewel Box*), a collection of verses in various genres arranged in a series of seven hierarchi-
cally ordered drawers (*cassettini*), containing works varying from the
"high" (verses in praise of the Medici and other notable figures) to the decidedly "low" (the sixth *cassettino* includes comic poems on, among others,
a syphilitic fortune-teller and a go-between (*messaggiera d'Amore*) who has
forfeited her nose in the service of eros.[192] In some respects, Costa may be
seen as a literary "descendent" of Isabella Andreini, her most significant
precedent as a theatrical performer of literary pretensions. Like Andreini's
*Rime*, Costa's *Lo stipo* serves to showcase her versatility and her capacity for
ventriloquization, which extends, as in the case of Andreini, to the frequent adoption of a masculine voice. By comparison with Andreini, however, who never deflects from a refined late-Petrarchan or Chiabreraesque
idiom, Costa is notably more eclectic, willingly stooping to forms of broad
humor we find in no other female voice of the period. Social satire forms
a notable part of her poetic repertoire, mainly centered on the vanity and
folly of lovers, also a theme of her frequently farcical *Lettere amorose* (1639),
which includes exchanges between ugly, scabrous, one-eyed, and hunch-
backed *innamorati,* male and female, in a parodic exploration of the rhetoric of grotesquerie beloved of many poets of the baroque.[193] Interesting
here, of course, is the extent to which male poetic objects are subjected to
the same mercilessly satirical treatment as the more usual female. One of
the most successful poems of *Lo stipo* is in the voice of an aging toy boy
(*zerbino*), ruefully reflecting on the withering of his once irresistible
charms; here, much of the strength of Costa's satire derives the gender inversion of a frequent theme of misogynist satire.[194] It would be misleading, however, to present Costa on the strength of poems like these as programmatically profeminist, in the manner that one can earlier with writers
like Campiglia or Fonte. On the contrary, Costa follows Andreini (and,
among her closer contemporaries, Semidea Poggi, Maria Clemente Ruoti,
and Barbara Tigliamochi) in occasionally adopting misogynistic and ob-
jectifying idioms in speaking of her sex: women are frequently castigated,
for example, for a vanity and worldliness Costa freely admits she shared in
her youth.[195] Particularly striking in this regard is the pastoral rape narrative found among the *idilli* of Costa's *Il violino,* parodying a poem like
Marino's "I trastulli estivi," even down to the name of the female protagonist, Lilla.[196] As in Marino, the raped girl's resistance is presented as affected, and the poet-rapist remains assured of their mutual pleasure in the

act. Costa, however, complicates this exercise in mimetic identification by adding a typically deflating satirical and neo-Boccaccian ending, as the now deflowered Lilla swiftly abandons her lover for a rival.[197]

As the last example illustrates, an interest of Costa's writing is her willingness to take her writing into territories explored by few, if any, other early modern Italian female writers. Similarly unwonted is her crafting of her authorial persona, reminiscent, of anyone, perhaps faintly of Veronica Franco's in its aura of quasi-masculine "frankness":

> Fù varia la mia vita, e in mille modi
> vissi à mia voglia, e il bene, e il mal provai:
> in libertà vivei, vivei fra' nodi
> di tirannico ardor per duo bei rai:
> provai sincer trattar, trattar con frodi,
> hora sperai goder, hor disperai.[198]

> [My life was varied, and in a thousand ways I lived according to my will and experienced the good and bad of it; I lived in freedom and I lived in the bonds of tyrannical passion for two fine eyes. I experienced straight dealing; I experienced deception; now I hoped for satisfaction, and now I despaired.]

Naturally, this was not a voice or an ethos easily appropriable by women of more sheltered social condition: to proclaim one's life to have been "various," or to have been lived on one's terms, was hardly compatible with feminine decorum.[199] An instructive failed exercise in imitation of Costa is apparent in a verse collection by Isabetta Coreglia that remains in manuscript in the Biblioteca Statale di Lucca, probably composed mainly in the 1640s. By comparison with Coreglia's relatively "straight" *Rime spirituali e morali* of 1628, the later collection shows the influence of Costa's more vivacious model: while we still find here a substantial corpus of occasional verse and *rime spirituali,* there are also genres of poetry in it more characteristic of Costa, such as male-voiced erotic lyrics, whimsical narratively based sketches ("Lover Who, Seeing an Old Man next to a Beautiful Woman, Fell in the Water while Staring at Them"), and moral-autobiographical poems reviewing the author's career.[200] Sealing this essay in poetic discipleship, we find two poems in the collection praising Costa directly, both as poet and as stage performer, captured in her role as Isifile in the opera *Giasone.*[201] Despite her obvious admiration of Costa, however, Coreglia is too much the lady to follow her model directly. On occasion, we do find her effectively exploiting Costa's defiant tone of "frankness," as in her interesting autobiographical poem "La musa libera" ("The Free Muse"), which expresses her determination to renounce worldly ambition and henceforth to write purely for herself.[202] As a "decent woman," however, it would clearly have been difficult for Coreglia to follow Costa fully down the path of baroque *bizzarria*. At one point, indeed, we find her explicitly differentiating herself from her model, in a reply to a poem of Costa's satirizing female vanity in the persona of three cosmetically enhanced society femmes fatales on the warpath, which concludes by warning more demure and less provocative beauties to cede to the mores of the day and "beat a retreat."[203] Coreglia replies with indignation, defending the candor and chastity of her compatriots, the ladies of Lucca, concluding with a sharp command to Costa's "shameless Muse ("Musa sfrontata") to be silent if it can do nothing but accuse innocent women.[204] The encounter is an intriguing one, pitting a now somewhat archaic "pure" feminine literary ethos against a newer, brasher, and more sensual one: in this respect, Costa's "painted ladies" and Coreglia's cosmetically undefiled Amazons of chastity take on a decidedly self-referential aspect.[205] Read in this light, we can only concede the truth of Costa's ironic parting shot regarding the present day's favoring only "shameless beauties" ("le belle sfrontate"). After a promising start, Coreglia's career foundered: her late poetry was unpublished and several other late works are known to us only by their titles. Costa, meanwhile, though complaining of the hostile reception of her verse, remains the most published secular female writer of her generation and of several generations after.

Perhaps the most revealing female *canzoniere* of the Seicento is, paradoxically, one that never came into being: that of the best-known female Jewish writer of early modern Italy, Sara Copio.[206] From a wealthy and cultured background, well educated, musical, and socially well connected both inside and outside the Venetian ghetto, Copio made a striking impression on her contemporaries and was temporarily lionized in Venice in the latter part of the second decade of the century and the early years of the third.[207] Although she made a name for herself as a poet, however, and was clearly a woman of some literary ambition, Copio left only a meager corpus of fourteen poems, a mere eight of which were published in her lifetime, and appears to have abandoned literature altogether for around the last fifteen years of her life.[208] Copio's sad and singular story has been told often in recent years, but it merits retelling in this context. In 1618, as a young married woman, she sent a letter and sonnet of praise to the noted Genoese poet Ansaldo Cebà, praising his epic poem *La reina Ester,* which had been published three years earlier in his home city. Although Cebà responded initially as gallantry demanded, replying with a sonnet comparing Copio to the biblical *bella ebrea* ("lovely Jewess") who was the protagonist of his poem, their relationship did not remain at the level of this kind of worldly exchange of compliments. Rather, from the first, Cebà announces his desire to see his beautiful young correspondent converted to Christianity and to have the satisfaction, in the final, ailing years of his life, of having won a worthy soul from damnation. This triggered what must register as one of the more curious epistolary exchanges of the period: the more so because it survives for us only in a published form that contains only Cebà's part of the correspondence.[209] The volume of *Lettere d'Ansaldo Cebà scritte a Sarra [sic] Copia*, published in 1623, dramatizes what is effectively a struggle of wills, though framed in a stylized language of compliment.[210] Especially interesting from the point of view of the present study is the pitilessly clear grandstand view the Cebà-Copio correspondence offers of the final exhaustion of the Neoplatonic conventions that had served so effectively in the previous century as a vehicle for male-female literary interaction. Both in his letters to Copio themselves and in the running commentary he offers on the exchange in his contemporarily published collected *Lettere,* Cebà portrays himself as wearily putting himself through the motions of literary courtship in the interests of his more authentic religious-salvific project, in an ironic inversion of the Neoplatonic convention where a beautiful woman led a male admirer to God.[211] The purity of his motives, as he portrays them, has the effect of exposing the impurity of Copio's: as she "stubbornly" refuses his conversional advances, he progressively lets fall his initial veil of calculated flattery, revealing her as a woman of importunate ambition who has pushed herself on him in the pursuit of literary fame and who would be better, he suggests, attending to her husband and home than pursuing her inappropriate literary ends.[212] The tone of the work is ultimately set by the double-edged compliment of the opening letter, where Cebà expresses amazement that a young woman should have been so impressed by a poem that "speaks of great things" as to have been "unable to resist" procuring the acquaintance of its writer, noting that he has been forced as a result to "a different opinion of [her] than one generally has of [her] sex."[213] Especially prophetic of the correspondence that follows is the phrase "was unable to resist" ("non ha potuto temperarsi"); here, intellectual outreach in women is subtly tainted with the same overtones of sexual "intemperance" to which Boccalini had given such trenchant expression in his *Ragguagli di Parnaso,* published only six years before the letter was dated.[214] It would be inaccurate to present this complex work as an exercise in textbook misogyny or as wholly negative in its portrayal of its female protagonist; there is evidence that Copio condoned its publication, asking only for one letter to be cut.[215] Its value as a document of the deterioration of male-female literary relations in the early seventeenth century rests, however, precisely on its transitional quality: it stands both as a quasi-parodic epitaph on the long sixteenth-century romance between Italian male writers and their female poet-muses and as a warning of the distinctly chillier climate to come.

For Copio, the chill came early: less than two years after the publication of her letters from Cebà, she became the object of a concerted campaign of defamation from an ex-employee and literary consultant, the Roman poet Numidio Paluzzi (?1587–1625) and his friend and compatriot, the poet-painter Alessandro Berardelli. The story is a convoluted one, and its details unclear, but the most likely reconstruction is that Paluzzi and Berardelli conspired to defraud Copio financially, and she denounced them to the authorities, provoking a series of revenge slanders from the pen of Paluzzi, known to us only by their title, the *Sarraidi*. Following Paluzzi's death from syphilis in 1625, Berardelli brought out a volume of the former's *Rime* with the Venetian publisher Giambattista Ciotti, whose preface claims that what he was publishing was all that he had been able to save from the rapacity of Copio, who had raided Paluzzi's home after his death to remove the evidence that would reveal him as the true author of her works.[216] Copio's literary circle was evidently outraged at this attack, and a series of supportive sonnets to her survives, coupled with *risposte* by her detailing her distress and anger at her betrayal at the hands of Paluzzi, defined in one poem as a "domestic monster" ("domestico mostro"), a "new Hydra" ("Idra novella"), and a "base evil siren" ("vile empia sirena").[217] Even the defenses put together by Copio's supporters, however, may have contributed to her sense of beleagueredness in these years. These sonnets, in fact, are known to us through their appearance in an extraordinary *Ragguagli di Parnaso*-style satire, known by the name of its purported author as the *Codice di Giulia Soliga*, which subjects the dead Paluzzi to a literary Parnassan "trial" featuring a lively cast including Aretino, Boccaccio, Castiglione, Colonna, Gambara, and Andreini.[218] While presenting itself as an outraged defense of a "virtuous and honored gentlewoman" ("virtuosa e onorata Gentildonna"), the *Codice di Giulia Soliga* in fact portrays Copio in an undignified light as foolishly credulous and superstitious; in a suspiciously novelistic intrigue plot, she is shown as having exposed herself to a concerted campaign of extortion by Paluzzi and Berardelli in collaboration with a cast of picaresque sidekicks such as a bawdish washerwoman and a black Spanish *conversa* who lays claim to demonic powers. The text also satirizes Copio's literary and social pretensions, portraying a fictional French aristocratic admirer, consumed with a desire to meet her, as the hook through which Paluzzi succeeded in extracting money and gifts from his credulous employer. More than a genuine defense, we should surely see this fanciful concoction as a satirically inflected exercise in character defamation of a woman whose original aspiration had no doubt been to the kind of genteel literary fame enjoyed by her Christian compatriot Lucrezia Marinella.[219] Copio by this time had already been involved in one public polemic when she had been called on to defend herself against a pamphlet by the cleric and *letterato* Baldassare Bonifacio, that had accused her of disbelief in the immortality of the soul.[220] From the mid-1620s, presumably disillusioned with literature, this initially ambitious aspiring poet disappeared from public view, living out the remaining decade and a half of her life in properly "feminine" seclusion.

Obviously, in assessing a case like Copio's, we should be wary of allowing identification or sympathy cloud our critical judgment: it may indeed be that Paluzzi assisted her, to a greater or lesser extent, in the composition of her verse.[221] It needs to be noted, however, by way of contextualization, that the seventeenth century was something of a golden age for denials of female authorship; as Tarabotti pithily summarized "men stubbornly refuse to admit that women are capable of writing without their help."[222] One early instance here is Margherita Sarrocchi, the first version of whose *Scanderbeide* (1606) is said in its dedicatory letter to have been published to shame those male poets who had appropriated "various of her inventions and *concetti*" as the poem circulated in manuscript, thinking themselves safe in their theft, as "it could never possibly be credited by the world that it had genuinely issued from the mind of a woman."[223] Rumors also circulated concerning the authenticity of Lucrezia Marinella's *Vita di Maria Vergine,* as well as that of Arcangela Tarabotti's *Paradiso monacale,* while Margherita Costa's *Selva di Diana* (1647) also contains a poem denying that she received assistance with her works[224] The move was an obvious means of undermining confidence in women's literary potential: if women had been encouraged to write in the sixteenth century by seeing the plaudits accorded to successful women writers, others were presumably discouraged from writing in the seventeenth by the likelihood of being denied the fruits of their labors. Despite some spirited defense from Tarabotti, whose public replies to her accuser, Angelico Aprosio, are among the rhetorical highlights of her *Lettere* (1650), the cumulative effect of such attacks was gradually to demoralize women out of the literary sphere.[225] Such is the message of Marinella's late treatise *Essortationi alle donne,* and of the dedicatory letter to Margherita Costa's *Gli amori della luna* (1654), where the author speaks of her disillusionment with a search for poetic glory in culture in which literary pursuits are considered "monstrous" in women, and talks of how, as a result, she has retreated into silence and "benighted" ("anottata") herself.[226]

Returning to our consideration of seventeenth-century women's literary output, it must be said that, besides polemic and lyric verse, it would be difficult to think of a genre, however broadly defined, worth singling out as especially typical of women's writing in this period. Where narrative and drama are concerned, as noted in chapter 5, the opening decades of the century saw a remarkably flourishing and varied production, including Marinella's *Arcadia felice* and *Amore innamorato,* Valeria Miani's *Amorosa speranza* and *Celinda,* Maddalena Salvetti's truncated *David,* Cherubina Venturelli's *Rappresentazione di Santa Cecilia* (1612), and Margherita Sarrocchi's *Scanderbeide.* Production of secular narrative and dramatic works by women slowed after this, although Marinella continued to produce substantial hagiographic works (*De' gesti heroici e della vita maravigliosa della serafica S[anta] Caterina* in 1624; *Le vittorie di Francesco il serafico* in 1643; *Holocausto d'amore della vergine Santa Giustina* in 1648), as well as an ottava rima historical epic on the model of Tasso's *Gerusalemme liberata, Enrico, overo Bisanzio acquistato* in 1635.[227] A second, more sui generis narrative poem in ottava rima published in this period is Barbara Tigliamochi's curious 1640 *Ascanio errante,* a thirty-one canto retelling of material from the *Aeneid* and *Odyssey,* interpolated with elements from chivalric and Hellenistic romance, and dedicated to Vittoria della Rovere, Grand Duchess of Tuscany.[228] Margherita Costa also published two ottava rima narrative works in the 1640s: a miniature *poema sacro* of four *canti, Cecilia martire,* published in Rome in 1644 with a dedication to Cardinal Francesco Barberini, and the nine-canto *Flora feconda,* dedicated to Grand Duke Ferdinando II de' Medici, and published in 1640 in Florence with a pendant dramatic work of the same title, dedicated to Vittoria della Rovere.[229] Besides this last, Costa also published a number of other dramatic works, notably her comedy, *Li buffoni* of 1641, dedicated to the comic actor Bernardino Ricci ("Il Tedeschino"), with whom she may have been romantically linked, and her late three-act mythological drama *Gli amori della luna* (1654), dedicated to three brother-princes of the Brunswick-Lüneberg dynasty, Georg Wilhelm (1624–1705), Ernst August (1629–95), and Johann Friedrich (1625–79), the latter a convert to Catholicism from 1651.[230] The two other secular female-authored dramas of the period are more conventional in character, Isabetta Coreglia's two "throwback" pastoral dramas *Dori* (1634) and *Erindo il fido* (1650).[231]

Where nonnarrative prose is concerned, aside from the polemical works mentioned earlier, most works of this period are religious in subject matter and composed by nuns: Arcangela Tarabotti's *Paradiso mona-cale*, Angelica Baitelli's *Vita martirio, et morte di Santa Giulia* (1644), Francesca Farnese's *Lettera spirituale ed esortatoria* (1642) and *Lettere* (1686), and Maria Alberghetti's *Discorsi sopra gli evangelii* (1656), *Meditationi divote sopra l'incarnatione* (1658), *Gioiello di divote meditationi* and *Meditationi sopra la sacra passione* (both 1661). The pattern of "reconventualization" we noted earlier in the case of verse collections thus also obtains here, as does the tendency toward posthumous publication, although the first three works cited in the list above, all from the 1640s, were published during the authors' lifetime. Deserving of special mention within the varied array of seventeenth-century convent literature are two examples of historical writings by nuns, the first examples of this rich genre of literature by cloistered women to find their way into print. The second and better known of these is the posthumously published *Annali* (1657) of Angelica Baitelli (1588–1650), recounting the history of her convent, San Salvatore e Santa Giulia in Brescia.[232] The first, again "particular" in its focus, is the Bolognese Diodata Malvasia's history of the sacred image of the Virgin in the Sanctuary of the Monte della Guardia (1617), like Baitelli's *Annali* a campaigning work, written at a moment when the traditional privileges of the nuns who acted as custodians of the Sanctuary were under threat.[233] Still technically in the class of nuns' writings, but anomalously secular in tone, is Arcangela Tarabotti's *Lettere familiari e di complimento* (1650), reminiscent of Veronica Franco's *Lettere familiari* (1580) as an exercise in epistolary self-portraiture, though Tarabotti's collection is more substantial (256 letters) and broader in range.[234] Tarabotti also published together with the *Lettere* a collection of *Lagrime* in mourning for her close friend and fellow nun, Regina Donà, or Donati (d. 1645): an enterprise whose assemblage may be traced in the *Lettere,* as with Franco's funereal collection for Estor Martinengo.[235] Nonnarrative prose works by secular women in this period are rare, though we should include in this category Lucrezia Marinella's *Essortationi alle donne,* discussed below, which, following a polemical opening, is mainly occupied with instruction on "economic" concerns, such the upbringing of children and the running of a household. Similar, though narrower in its focus, is the *Ammaestramenti e ricordi* (1628) of the Piedmontese Isabella Sori, published along with her feminist *Difese delle donne* and a panegyric of her hometown of Alessandria.[236] Paralleling the two convent histories mentioned above, moreover—though at a less ambitious level—we also find two published historical writings by secular women in this period, Maddalena Salvetti's *Breve memoria della nobiltà della casa degli Accaiuoli* (1611), recounting the history of the distinguished Florentine family into which she had married, and Margherita Costa's *Istoria del viaggio d'Alemagna del serenissimo gran duca di Toscana, Ferdinando Secondo* (c. 1630).[237]

Several of the works discussed in the preceding paragraphs are individually interesting and deserving of study (perhaps especially, of post-1620 works, Marinella's *Enrico* and *Essortationi*, Tarabotti's *Lettere*, Francesca Turina's *Rime varie*, and Costa's *Li buffoni*). It would be difficult, however, to discern in this mixed bag of works anything resembling a "tradition": women do not constitute a "group" here, in Dionisotti's phrase, as they did in both the mid-sixteenth century and, again, in the closing decades of the sixteenth century. It is only perhaps briefly in the early 1640s in Florence, when the presence of Vittoria della Rovere reawakened hopes of a stable female patronage, that we find something of a concentration of female writing, with Costa and Barbara Tigliamochi in Florence, and Tarabotti and Barbara Strozzi dedicating works to the Grand Duchess from outside.[238] It is interesting to note that Costa's and Tigliamochi's publications of the period are accompanied by respectable numbers of laudatory male-authored prefatory sonnets, a sign of literary integration that was becoming relatively rare in this period by comparison with the previous century.[239] This was fugitive, however. For the bulk of the seventeenth century, from, say, 1620 to 1690, women were effectively near invisible in Italian literary culture, publishing, if at all, mainly in provincial centers, in editions that disappeared without notice; in fact, aside from a few works from the first decade of the century, such as Marinella's *La vita di Maria Vergine* and Sarrocchi's *Scanderbeide*, it is difficult to think of a single female-authored work that received a second edition in the seventeenth century.[240] Women tended to surface to public attention as writers, locally or more widely, only when controversy or scandal attached to them, as was briefly the case with Sara Copio in the 1620s and later with Arcangela Tarabotti in the 1640s. Otherwise, women who attained notice as writers often came with a preexisting fame deriving from nonliterary sources, Margherita Costa from her career as a singer and actress, Francesca Farnese and Maria Alberghetti from their roles as foundresses of convents and figures of spiritual authority. Those dependent purely on their literary output for their reputation tended—without the aid of the busy promotional industry that had served in the sixteenth century to circulate "famous women"'s names—to remain firmly on the margins. It is noteworthy that the seventeenth-century female writers who fitted most closely with the "sixteenth-century" model of the retiring gentlewoman—Isabetta Coreglia, Barbara Tigliamochi, Isabella Sori—are those who attained the least fame in their lifetimes and who remain the most obscure to our day. Of women in this category, only Lucrezia Marinella retained a reasonably high public profile, and even she, one has the impression, tended to be respected as a "figure" rather than actively read and discussed. It is notable that even a work like her long-prepared *Enrico,* from which she had proudly announced in 1623 that she awaited "a long and supreme honor," aroused nothing of the literary frisson that had accompanied the circulation of the only previous female-authored epic, Margherita Sarrocchi's *Scanderbeide.*[241] Marinella's impeccable life probably told against her in this regard, making her perhaps mercifully unnewsworthy; not the most malicious tongue could think of much to say against a devout and socially reticent widow and grandmother in her sixties.

It was Marinella, however, from her slightly stagnant position of semi-canonized dignity who unexpectedly offered up in her late *Essortationi alle donne e agli altri* what is probably the bitterest, as well as the most cogent and clear-eyed, analysis of the predicament of the seventeenth-century woman writer the century produced. The *Essortationi* was Marinella's first didactic-polemical work since *La nobiltà et l'eccellenza delle donne,* of which it seems in many ways an explicit palinode or retraction.[242] The first of the eight "exhortations" into which the work is divided, devoted to the question of women's status, reaches conclusions in many ways opposite to those of *La nobiltà et l'eccellenza;* while Marinella does not change her position to the extent of conceding women's inferiority to men, she does argue strongly here for the naturalness and properness of their traditional domestic role, retracting her earlier argument in *La nobiltà* that women's forced exclusion from the public sphere was the result of the "tyrannical usurpation" of men.[243] Showing herself to have retained her earlier talent for paradoxical argument, she presents women's domestic seclusion now as a privilege due to their dignity: "retirement" ("retiratezza") is a state reserved for superior beings, such as, besides women, princes and God.[244] Marinella's volte-face on her previous position is the more intriguing given the publication context of the *Essortationi,* which came out with the Venetian publisher Francesco Valvasense, virtual house publisher to the Accademia degli Incogniti, many of whose members must have been delighted to see Marinella subscribing to a position so consonant with their own.[245] Marinella's first *essortatione* supplied nothing less than a reasoned defense of the position that women should refrain from any ambition to "transcend their sex," voiced by a woman who had done more than any other living to argue for the inauthenticity of such constraints. In the feverish atmosphere of mid-1640s Venice, stirred to a new "sex war" controversy by the publication of Tarabotti's *Antisatira,* Marinella's *Essortationi* had a topicality and surprise value that showed the now 74-year-old author not to have lost her controversialist touch.[246]

If Marinella's position in her first *essortatione* seems clear, if surprising, the second takes the work onto a more ambiguous plane. From the general subject of women's role, Marinella moves on here to the more specific question of the legitimacy of literary aspirations in women. As in the first *essortatione,* she takes a conservative position, arguing that women should refrain from such public exhibitions and keep instead to activities more proper to their sex, symbolized by the inevitable "needle and spindle." Here, however, the grounds of Marinella's arguments have shifted. In rhetorical terms, rather than *honestas,* or propriety, she here makes appeal to *utilitas,* or expediency, arguing that to attempt a literary career, as a woman, is a guaranteed path to misery and failure. Much of the second *essortatione* is taken up with a detailed inventory of the means by which society and culture conspire to repress women's literary ambitions, including ridicule, faint praise ("it will do, for a woman" ["per donna può passare"]), and the kind of accusations of plagiarism and ghostwriting that Marinella had herself suffered in the case of her *Vita di Maria Vergine.*[247] While the formal conclusion of this pitiless analysis is defeatist—in the face of such hostility, women should simply retire hurt—the tone is sufficiently impassioned and bitter for the passage to read less as the traditionalist apologia it claims to be than a kind of extended j'accuse. The ambiguity of Marinella's arguments is compounded by the fact that they are voiced by a woman so clearly intent on ignoring her own advice. Following her compelling case for women's retreat into silence in the second *essortatione,* the work continues for a further six such minitreatises, covering the whole field of domestic *economia* as traditionally conceived, including the choice of a marriage partner and the upbringing of children, and extending further into such traditionally "unfeminine" areas as the formation and conduct of the perfect prince.[248] We have here, then, something of a paradox, in that a work that contains the period's most despondent analysis of women's literary possibilities is also probably the most confident and wide-ranging female-authored secular didactic text of the age. The work is the more remarkable in that portions, at least, of its philosophically inflected "economic" pedagogy is clearly addressed primarily to men rather than women; if Marinella on occasion translates a passage from Latin for the benefit of her female readers (addressed with condescending affection as "amiche mie"), she does not do this consistently and the dedicatee of the work is a high-status male, the Spanish ambassador to Venice, Don Gaspar de Teves de Guzmán (1608–78), Marquis of Fuente.[249] Nor were the *Essortationi* Marinella's only work of this period; on the contrary, this fertile late period also saw two ambitious hagiographical works,

*Le vittorie di Francesco il Serafico* and *Holocausto d'amore della vergine Giustina,*
both with ambitious dedications to, respectively, Pope Urban VIII and
Doge Francesco Molin (1575–1655; elected 1546).[250] As seems clear from the
printer's foreword to the former text, moreover, she was also preparing an
expanded edition of the *Enrico,* with a new and topical digression on the
recent episode (1638) of Marin Cappello's defeat of North African pirates
at Avlona (Vlorë).[251]

It would be mistaken, then, to present Marinella's *Essortationi* in simple terms, as a traditionalist retrenchment on the part of a former fire-
brand now retreating into an embittered old age. There are certainly more
agendas at play in the text, including, almost certainly, a sharp self-
distancing from Arcangela Tarabotti, precisely in 1643–44 establishing herself as a published presence on the Venetian literary scene.[252] Immediate
circumstances aside, however, there can be no doubt of the historical value
of the *Essortationi*'s cruelly accurate snapshot of the position of the aspiring *letterata,* whom Marinella portrays in graphic language as effectively
setting herself up "like those targets used by archers, which are run
through and lacerated by everyone and from every angle."[253] Nor is her
formula for escaping such "laceration"—essentially, retreat into silence
and a traditional feminine identity—inaccurate as a representation of the
effective response of women of her class. The same point is repeatedly
made, though in a very different manner, by Margherita Costa, who evolves
a virtual subgenre of poems earnestly recommending women to abandon
all other pursuits—primarily, love, song, and poetry—to cleave only to
their proper arts of needlework and especially spinning ("filare"). One such
poem, in *La chitarra* (1638), ends emphatically with a resolution on Costa's
part to abandon her poetic and musical vocation for her "true" role as a
domestic goddess, following its last octave (quoted below) with a resolute
"IL FINE" ("THE END"), which belies the 166 pages still to come:

> In quanto a me son ferma, e risoluta
> lasciar la penna, abandonar il canto,
> romper'il suono, e con la lingua muta
> ponere ogni virtute ormai da canto:
> poich'ogni cosa in Donne è mal tenuta,
> e biasmo apporta in loro ogni lor vanto;
> ond'io, che d'homo, e Donna hebbi il trattare,
> hor l'arte mia sarà sol di filare.

> [As for me, I am firmly resolved to lay aside the pen and abandon my song,
> to break off all sound and with mute tongue put all arts away from me.

Since all that women do is seen amiss, and all their finest actions bring them blame, I, who once played the part both of man and woman, will now take as my art nothing but spinning.[254]]

This seems a wholly appropriate note on which to end the present chapter's examination of seventeenth-century women's writing. Although the responses of women like Costa and Tarabotti were sufficiently spirited to give an impression of continuing life, the tradition of women's writing that had held such a relatively high-profile place in Italian literary culture even down to twenty years previously was clearly moribund by the 1640s. Marinella's *Essortationi* and Costa's poetic exhortations to a return to the spinning wheel may both be seen, in their different ways, as epitaphs on this tradition; aside from Tarabotti's *Semplicità ingannata,* clandestinely published in 1654—dating in its original composition to the late 1630s and early 1640s—and Margherita Costa's slight 1654 *Amori della luna,* secular women were effectively to be reduced to their needles and spindles for the following four decades. Even the exception here tends to prove the rule: the erudite Elena Corner Piscopia, who attained widespread fame through as the first woman to attain a university degree (1678), diluted the challenge her intellectual protagonism posed to the accepted feminine norm of silent self-effacement by insisting publicly on the justice of that norm.[255] European leadership in women's participation in literary culture had long since passed to France: a fact of which Italian women writers were not unaware—Tarabotti, who sought repeatedly to have her more controversial works published there, wistfully refers to Paris in a letter to Cardinal Mazarin as "the paradise of women," while Costa, free to travel, was briefly drawn there in search of patronage in the late 1540s.[256] In Italy, meanwhile, the ideal of a literary culture in which women participated alongside men was beginning to fade into a historical memory. When, in a 1640 poem lamenting the hostility with which her verse has been greeted, Margherita Costa recounts a voyage to Parnassus to announce to Apollo her intention to relinquish her literary ambitions, she describes Parnassus as peopled by an impeccably gender-mixed crowd, in which Dante, Petrarch, Bembo, Giovanni Guidiccioni (1480–1541), and Della Casa mingle suavely with Colonna, Gambara, and Sarrocchi.[257] The seductiveness of the scene is evidently compounded for Costa by its resolute historical and poetic "otherness"; the last male figure named (Della Casa) died in 1556, the last female (Sarrocchi) in 1617. For a woman of Costa's generation and of her baroque stylistic heritage, a bigendered *stilnovo*-Petrarchist Parnassus of this kind could only remain a fantasy. Reality was by now quite other: as Boccalini had memorably ruled in his *Ragguagli,* the seventeenth-

century Parnassus was to be male. Costa herself draws the necessary conclusion for women in another of her disconcertingly jaunty manifestos for
the "new domesticity" preached with such barely suppressed bitterness in
Marinella's *Essortationi*:

> . . . già che di filar solo ci tocca
> Lasciamo ogn'altro affare, prendiam la rocca.
>
> [Since all that we are good for is to spin,
> There's nothing for it, ladies: let's begin![258]]

❀ ❀ ❀ ❀

# CODA

Looking back over this volume's examination of women's literary contribution during the sixteenth and seventeenth centuries in Italy, it is hard not to be struck by the uncanny likeness between the social profile of the most representative and successful women writers in a given period and the type of the poetic *donna* to whom male writers of the time most characteristically addressed themselves. The poetic lady of Renaissance Petrarchism was both dazzlingly beautiful and morally unimpeachable, like Laura hiding a "grizzled mind" beneath her "blonde locks."[1] Give or take the blonde locks and beauty, the role was one eminently fitted to a Vittoria Colonna or a Veronica Gambara or a Laura Battiferra, with their impeccable moral character, refined intellectualism, and well-attested spiritual bent. Even a courtesan like Tullia d'Aragona, whose lifestyle did not necessarily qualify her for this model, still sought to conform to it in her verse. The Seicento poetic lady, by contrast, is less ineffable, more approachable, and characterized often by some element of exoticism or piquant individualism (the dark lady, the flawed beauty, the woman of "alien" race). Correspondingly, those Seicento female writers who rose to notice often have this same anecdotal and exotic dimension. The *bella ebrea*, Sara Copio Sullam, is a good example, but so also are the singer and courtesan Margherita Costa and the disenchanted nun Arcangela Tarabotti: all sufficiently deviant from the flawless *gentildonna* model of the Cinquecento to create the requisite "baroque" frisson of response.

This prompts some quite serious reflections. As this book has revealed, the myth of Pygmalion and his statue has a certain explanatory purchase with regard to the early modern Italian female writer: she is, in a sense, a figure created and breathed into life by male desires and male cultural needs.[2] Vital and productive herself, and eminently worthy of study as a creative artist, her existence is, nevertheless, at the same time posited on her discursive value as signifier: where that value declines, as in the seventeenth century, she has little choice but to vanish from the scene. Any study of early modern women's writing in Italy needs to be alert to the cultural forces that conjured the female writer into being and that, for a period of around a hundred years, ensured an exceptionally receptive environment for her writing, at least by the standards of the day. We do the writers of this period no service by overestimating their struggles to have their voice heard or assuming universal and unmodulated hostility on the part of a male literary "establishment." This is a misreading of the situation and can serve only to make us less attentive to historical development and change.

The peculiar history narrated in this book has a happier ending than its gloomy concluding chapter might lead us to predict. By the end of the seventeenth century, a literary reform was in the air as radical as that which had taken place a century earlier. Unlike the "revolution" of the baroque, however, this was not a movement that marched under the insignia of novelty and "marvel"; rather, it presented itself as a return to order following a period of deviance and decay. The agents of reform in this case were a group of *letterati* who grouped themselves in Rome under the name of the Accademia degli Arcadi (founded 1690) and became spokesmen for a militant classicism destined to sweep away the now tired vestiges of the baroque.[3] To the founders of the Arcadian movement, the period preceding theirs marked a lamentable deviation from acceptable standards of taste and judgment, while the sixteenth century represented a stylistic ideal to which new literature should properly aspire. This was a recuperative movement, like humanism, based on a return ad radices. The roots in this case, however, were not merely classical but modern. Reform would be effected through the observation of both classical ideals and their tantalizingly recent instantiation in the "good century" ("buon secolo") that led down to the baroque era's wrong turn.

This is important to our narrative here, because one of the sixteenth-century ideals into which the Arcadian movement breathed new life was that of a literary environment in which female writers would coexist in harmonious complementarity with men. From the 1690s, Italian literary culture began to repopulate with secular women, virtually excluded for the previous half-century, at least outside the protected microclimate of Tuscany, where the long-lived Grand Duchess Vittoria della Rovere (d. 1694) continued the local tradition of patronage of female writers initiated in the previous century by Eleonora of Toledo.[4] Specifically, it saw a return of the figure of the "honest" and socially-integrated—and often aristocratic—female writer, on the sixteenth-century model: a development foreshadowed already in the 1670s in the Veneto with the figure of Elena Corner Piscopia. The Accademia degli Arcadi opened its membership to women, who played *pastorelle* to the Academy's male *pastori*, in something resembling a vastly scaled-up and institutionalized version of Bembo's Compagnia degli Amici two centuries earlier.[5] Poetry by women was included in the multivolume *Rime degli Arcadi* (1716–22) and the first individual figures began to rise to salience, beginning with Maria Selvaggia Borghini, a product of the Tuscan tradition just mentioned, whose verse was published alongside that of Lucrezia Marinella, Veronica Gambara, and Isabella Morra by the French-Neapolitan publisher Antonio Bulifon in 1693.[6] Two other celebrated female poets of the age, both Roman-based, were the aristocratic Petronilla Paolini Massimi (1663–1726), unhappily married to the governor of the Castel Sant'Angelo, and Faustina Maratti Zappi (1679–1745), daughter of the painter Carlo Maratti or Maratta (1625–1713).[7] As in the sixteenth century, these famous names represent only the visible tip of what was a far more substantial buried mass, whose dimensions can only begin to be glimpsed if we look to the anthologies of the day. The Arcadian movement's first anthology of female-authored verse appeared in 1716, edited by "Teleste Ciparissiano" (Giovanni Battista Recanati [1687–1734/35]), who conjured up thirty-five living poets, despite complaining in his preface of the reluctance of many others to venture into print. A decade later, in 1726, the Venetian *letterata* Luisa Bergalli (1703–79) assembled fifty-four living poets in her ambitious *Componimenti delle più illustri rimatrici d'ogni secolo*—perhaps significantly, one more than the fifty-three that Lodovico Domenichi had assembled in 1559.[8]

As is hinted at in the 1693 editorial grouping of the verse of Maria Selvaggia Borghini with that of Marinella, Gambara, and Morra, the rise to public notice of new women writers with the Arcadian movement was accompanied by an energetic literary archaeology of the "old." Between 1692 and 1701, Bulifon's press in Naples reissued works by Laura Terracina (1692, 1694, 1698), Vittoria Colonna (1692, 1693), Laura Battiferra (1694), Isabella Andreini (1696), and Margherita Sarrocchi (1701), also republishing Domenichi's 1559 anthology, as *Rime di cinquanta illustri poetesse*, in 1695.[9] The richness of the earlier tradition of women's writing in Italy supplied the *pastorelle* of Arcadia with a dignified cultural ancestry and an eminently appropriable voice, or voices, inspiring a spirit of literary custodianship realized in Bergalli's remarkable project. The *Componimenti delle più illustri rimatrici d'ogni secolo,* as the title suggests, seeks to fuse the traditions of *ri-*

*matrici antiche* and *moderne,* uniting the historically differentiated corpus found in the existing anthologies of Domenichi and Ciparissiano, and expanding them on the basis of new research, conducted collaboratively with the Venetian erudite Apostolo Zeno (1668–1750).[10] While in one sense Bergalli's anthology may be seen as continuing the work of her predecessors, there is an important conceptual novelty in the notion of an anthology of female writers representing not merely the plenitude of a particular historical moment but a *tradition* self-consciously constructed as such. It is to this Arcadian moment of feminist literary rediscovery that we can trace the strong sense of literary women as a "corporation down the ages" (to use a phrase of Croce's) that we find in a later Italian female writer like Diodata Saluzzo Roero (1774–1840), whose verses hymn a feminine literary succession stretching back through Faustina Maratti and Moderata Fonte to "Veronica" and "Vittoria" to the far distant Sappho.[11]

This is not the moment for a detailed examination of the reasons for and context of the late seventeenth-century Arcadian feminist revival, though, given the themes of this volume, it is worth noting the catalytic role in the academy's formation generally attributed to the presence of Queen Christina of Sweden in Rome.[12] What is of importance to us here, introducing the phenomenon at this late stage, is principally the further confirmation it provides for the cultural patterns traced earlier in this study. Once more here we find attitudes to women and women's writing serving to mark and emblematize a process of literary and cultural redefinition, as with humanism, as, more emphatically, with early sixteenth-century Petrarchism, and as, in a negative sense, with the baroque. For fifteenth-century humanists, women writers had come to symbolize the revival of the literary glories of classical antiquity; for Bembo and his followers in the early sixteenth century, a revived and reclassicized medieval vernacular ideal. For the paladins of the baroque, female writers had become the despised symbolic embodiment of the Petrarchan *regole* against which the new generations now chafed, while, finally, for the late seventeenth-century *pastori* of Arcadia, women had come once again to embody a stylistic ideal, though one still more historically textured than in their previous incarnations, expressive of continuities flowing through antiquity to the medieval and more recent Renaissance literary traditions. One very important significance attaching to the return of women writers with Arcadia was that of a revival of Cinquecento standards of "honesty," propriety, and order, after the lapse of the baroque. As noted in chapter 6, Giovanni Mario Crescimbeni, founder-member and long-term secretary of the academy, casts writers such as Maddalena Salvetti and Margherita Sarrocchi as stylistic "resistance heroines" in his great *Istoria della volgar poesia* (1698), presenting their fidelity to Cinquecento idioms as an implicit reproach to their more wayward male peers who had succumbed to the baroque siren call.[13] Sarrocchi, as the target of abuse from Marino, is given particular salience in this role and is praised for her sagacity in recognizing the "false honor that the seventeenth century initially seemed to promise to its followers," and her "courage in opposing and facing up to the founder of the new school himself."[14] Sarrocchi here becomes representative of an ideal of writerly integrity of equal pertinence to both sexes, in the same manner that the Proba of Boccaccio's *De claris mulieribus* had two and a half centuries earlier at the advent of humanism. In both cases, a "feminine" attribute—piety in Proba, conservatism in Sarrocchi—is reproposed as a corrective in the face of male cultural "decay."[15]

As this last point well illustrates, and as this study as a whole has sought to prove, a proper assessment of the role of female writers within Italian literary history must go beyond the simple task of quantitatively and qualitatively gauging their output relative to men's. Female writers were not simply writers who happened to be female; they were a separate cultural category, with distinct cultural functions, including a highly distinctive vocation, during the period under scrutiny here, as a privileged site for the negotiation of literary change. Once women writers had been charged with the significance they came to assume in humanism and Petrarchism, even their absence from the literary scene took on meaning. As the Arcadians recognized, ushering them back, it was not least through its exclusion of women that the "deviant" Parnassus of the baroque was defined. What this means is that the historiographical model this book has set out to dismantle—that of Dionisotti, which limits women's writing to a short-lived phenomenon of the mid-sixteenth century—is detrimental not only to an understanding of the history of Italian women's writing but of Italian literary history in general. It is only within the broader perspective supplied in a study like the present that we can begin to intuit the role women writers played in articulating large-scale literary and cultural developments such as the emergence of humanism, the rise of the vernacular as a literary language and its codification in Petrarchism, the "revolution" of the baroque, and the "counterrevolution" of Arcadia. That this role has to date been the object of little scrutiny is due in part to the habit of bracketing off "women's writing" as a separate and generally secondary tradition: a habit almost as prevalent, ironically, today as it was in sixteenth-century Italy. Also culpable in this regard is the particular blindness to gender as an analytic category that we find within the critical and literary-historiographical tradition of Italy itself (a recent Italian summa of new approaches to the literary baroque contains no study devoted to gender

among its thirty-six contributions: an omission unimaginable in the Anglo-
phone world).[16] As this study has shown, the patterning of women's emergence as writers, their moments of lionization and their periods in the
wilderness, maps with uncanny and illuminating precision on to the con-
tours of literary change. Equally revealing, one suspects, would be a parallel history of the changing inflections of Italian literary masculinity over
the same period: a work I have come to conceive of in the course of composition of the present volume as its devoutly to be wished "missing twin."

## PUBLISHED WRITINGS BY ITALIAN WOMEN, FIFTEENTH TO SEVENTEENTH CENTURIES

The principal printed sources for this list are Erdmann 1999, 207–21; Zancan 1983, appendix 3; Weaver 2002, 123, 179, 217; and Graziosi 2004, 47–51, 68–70 (on early printed works by mystics and convent writers). The principal electronic sources are the online catalogues of the Istituto Centrale per il Catalogo Unico delle Biblioteche Italiane (ICCU); the Research Libraries Information Network (RLIN); and the British Library, though the specialist websites Italian Women Writers (University of Chicago) and *L'Araba Felice* are also useful.[†] I have included only works for which I have found a record in a current library catalogue.[‡] Works of uncertain authorship are marked by a question mark preceding the author's name; posthumous publications (where this can be ascertained) by square brackets; works published outside Italy by an asterisk. The works published between 1692 and 1698 marked with double asterisks are the editions by Antonio Bulifon discussed in the coda.

### c. 1475

[St. Catherine of Bologna (Caterina Vigri), *Le armi necessarie alla battaglia spirituale* (+ 1500, 1504, 1517, 1522, 1536, 1547, 1571, 1579, 1582, 1589, 1614, 1639, 1652; often entitled *Libro devoto* or *Libretto devoto*)]

[St. Catherine of Siena (Caterina Benincasa), *Libro della divina dottrina* (+ 1497)]

### 1488 (×2)

Cassandra Fedele, *Oratio pro Bertucio Lamberto* (+ *1489, 1494)

### c. 1490

[Antonia Pulci, *La rappresentazione di Sancta Domitilla* (+ 1554, 1555, 1561, 1571, 1578, 1584, 1588, 1594, 1597, 1600)]

[Pulci, *La rappresentazione di San Francesco* (+ 1559)]

[Pulci, *La rappresentazione di Santa Guglielma* (+ 1515, 1538, 1554, 1557, 1560, 1568, 1572 ×2, 1575, 1579, 1580, 1585, 1588, 1594, 1597, 1600 ×3, 1604, 1643, 1620, 1667, 1670, 1700)]

[†] www. lib.uchicago.edu/efts/IWW; www.arabafelice.it/dominae.

[‡] For a list of works by nuns recorded as published but of which no surviving copies have been identified, see Graziosi 2005, 158–60. I have not been able to trace library copies of the following two works listed in Erdmann: "Madonna Giulia," *Uno divoto psalmo con oratione* (Savona: Berruerio, 1521) and Anna Savina Carnovale Sarzano, *Avvisi d'una madre ai suoi figli* (Tortona: Bolla, 1585) (Erdmann 1999, 210, 214, 219). Contarina Ubaldini Gabrielli, *Libro de San Francesco* (Venice: Zoppino, 1519) is included in the sixteenth-century offshoot of the ICCU catalogue (edit16) but with no library copies listed.

1492
[St. Catherine of Siena, *Epistole utili e divote*]

1497
[Angela da Foligno, *Rivelatione e amaistramenti*]

1500[†]
[St. Catherine of Siena, *Epistole divotissime* (+ 1548, 1562, 1584)]

1504
[St. Catherine of Siena, *Dialogo* (+ 1517, 1547, 1579, 1582, 1589)]

1511
[St. Catherine of Siena, *Fioreti [sic] utilissimi extracti dal divoto dialogo*]

1517
[?Pulci, *Rappresentazione di Sancto Antonio Abate* (+ 1547, 1555, 1589, 1600, c. 1600)]

1521
[Foligno, *Libellus spiritualis doctrine* (+ another edition, not before 1521)]
[Camilla da Varano, *Devoto libretto*[‡]]

c. 1525
Anon., *Devotissime compositioni rhytmice e parlamenti a Jesù Christo* (×2 + 1536, 1554, 1558, n.d., 1568, 1574, 1588; sometimes published as *Thesauro della sapientia evangelica* or *Cantici spirituali*)[§]

1536
[Foligno, *Libro utile et devoto* (+ 1542)]

1538
Vittoria Colonna, *Rime* (+ 1539 ×4; 1540 ×2; 1542 ×2; 1544; 1546; 1548; 1552; 1559; 1560)

1543
Colonna, *Rime spirituali* (+ 1546; 1548 ×2; 1586)

---

[†]The 1500 edition of Catherine's letters (by Aldo Manuzio) superseded the very partial 1492 Bologna edition (of only thirty-one letters). The subsequent Venetian editions listed here bear different titles (*Epistole et orationi . . . ; Lettere devotissime . . .*) but substantially reproduce the Aldine text (Zancan 1992, 600 and n. 12).

[‡]See Graziosi 2004, 60.

[§]On this text, see Graziosi 2004, 57–67; on its complex *fortuna*, ibid., 68–69.

1544
Colonna, *Litere [sic] . . . alla duchessa d'Amalfi*
?Isabella Sforza, *Della vera tranquillità dell'animo*

1547
Tullia d'Aragona, *Dialogo dell'infinità d'amore* (+ 1552)
d'Aragona, *Rime* (+ 1549, 1560)

1548
?*Lettere di molte valorose donne,* ed. Ortensio Lando
Laura Terracina, *Rime* (+ 1549, 1550, 1553, 1554, 1555, 1560, 1565 ✕2)

1549
Terracina, *Discorso sopra tutti li primi canti d'Orlando furioso* (+1550 ✕2; revised edition, 1551 + 1554, 1557, 1559, 1560 ✕2, 1561, 1564, 1565, 1567, 1573, 1577, 1579, 1581, 1583 ✕2, 1588, 1598, 1608, 1626, 1638)
Terracina, *Seconde rime*

1550
Terracina, *Quarte rime* (+ 1551, 1560)

c. 1550
[Elena da Bologna, *Brieve e signoril modo dil spiritual vivere* (+ 1554)]
[?Pulci, *La rappresentatione del figliuol prodigo* (+ 1572, 1573, 1579 ✕2, 1583, 1584, 1585, c. 1590, 1591, 1610, 1614, 1615)]
Suor Raffaella de' Sernigi, *La rappresentazione di Moisè* (+ 1578)

1552
?Lucrezia Gonzaga, *Lettere*
?"Dafne di Piazza," *Accademia di enigmi in sonetti* (+ 1561, post-1578)
Terracina, *Quinte rime* (+ 1558, 1560)

1554
Laura Pieri, *Quattro canti della guerra di Siena*
[Gaspara Stampa, *Rime*]

1555
Chiara Matraini, *Prose e rime*

1556
[Colonna, *Pianto sopra la passione di Christo* (+ 1557, 1561, 1562, 1563)]
Matraini, *Oratione d'Isocrate a Demonico*

1558
[Colonna, *Tutte le rime*]
[Olimpia Morata,* *Latina et graeca monumenta*]
Terracina, *Seste rime* (+1560)

1559
*Rime . . . di alcune nobilissime . . . donne,* ed. Lodovico Domenichi

1560
[?d'Aragona, *Il Meschino*]
Laura Battiferra, *Il primo libro delle opere toscane*
Terracina, *Settime rime*

1561
Isabella Cortese, *I segreti* (+ 1565, 1574, 1584, 1588, 1595, 1603, 1614, 1625, 1642, 1665,
    1675, 1677)

1562
[Morata,* *Orationes, dialogi, epistolae, carmina*]
?Celia Romana, *Lettere amorose* (+ 1563, 1565, 1572, 1584, 1594, 1600, 1607, 1612, 1624,
    1628)

1563
[Paola Antonio de' Negri, *Lettere spirituali* (+ 1576)]
[Isotta Nogarola, *Dialogus*]

1564
Battiferra, *I sette salmi penitenziali* (+ 1566, 1570)

1565
?Leonora Bianca, *Le risposte*

1567
Terracina, *Seconda parte de' discorsi* (+ 1584)

1569
[?St. Angela Merici, *Regola della nova compagnia di Santa Orsola in Brescia*]

1570
[Morata,* *Opera omnia* (+ 1580)]

1571
Virgina Salvi and Beatrice Salvi, *Due sonetti . . . a M. Celio Magno; Lettera, e sonetti a
    M. Celio Magno* (×2)

1574
[Merici, *Testamento*]

1575
Veronica Franco, *Terze rime*

1576
Eugenia Calcina, *Priego alla vergine beatissima*

1577
Issicratea Monte, *Oratione . . . nella congratulatione del sereniss[imo] principe Sebastiano Veniero*

1578
Monte, *Oratione . . . nella congratulatione del serenissimo principe di Venetia, Niccolò da Ponte*
Monte, *Seconda oratione . . . nella congratulatione di . . . Sebastiano Veniero*

1580
[Colonna, *Quattordici sonetti spirituali* (musical settings)]
Franco, *Lettere familiari*

1581
Moderata Fonte, *Le feste*
Fonte, *Tredici canti del Floridoro*
Matraini, *Meditationi spirituali*
Monte, *Oratione . . . alla sacra maestà di Maria d'Austria*

1582
Fonte, *La passione di Christo*

1584
Camilla Erculiani, *Lettere di philosophia naturale*

1585
Maddalena Campiglia, *Discorso sopra l'annonciatione della beata Vergine*
Fonte, *Canzon nella morte del ser[enissi]mo principe di Venetia Nicolò da Ponte*

1586
Matraini, *Considerationi sopra i sette psalmi penitenziali*

1587
Silvia Bendinelli, *Corona in morte del serenissimo sig[nor] Ottavio Farnese*

1588

Isabella Andreini, *Mirtilla* (+ 1590 ×2,[†] 1594, 1598, 1599, 1602 (×2, one *in French translation), 1605, 1616)

Andreini, *Epitalamio nelle nozze dell'illustrissimi don Michele Peretti e donna Margherita Somaglia*

Campiglia, *Flori, favola boscareccia*

Lorenza Strozzi, *In singulis totius anni solemnia hymni*

[Battista Vernazza, *Opere spirituali*]

1589

Campiglia, *Calisa*

1590

Maddalena Salvetti, *Rime toscane*

Matraini, *Breve discorso sopra la vita et laude della beatiss[ima] Vergine* (+ 1599, 1665, 1675 + four other editions post-1660[‡])

1592

Isabella Cervoni, *Canzone sopra il battesimo del serenissimo gran prencipe di Toscana* (×2)

Fonte, *La resurretione di Giesu Christo*

1594

?"Emilia N.," *Lettere affettuose*

1595

[Isabella Capece, *Consolatione dell'anima*]

Elisabetta Catanea, *Specchio delle virtuose donne* (+ 1596)

Lucrezia Marinella, *La colomba sacra*

Matraini, *Lettere . . . con le rime* (+ 1597)

Francesca Turina, *Rime spirituali*

1596

Flavia Grumelli, *Vita di Santa Grata*

Ersilia Spolverina, *Ad illustrissimam Claram Corneliam poemata duo*

1597

Catanea, *Studio delle virtuose dame*

Cervoni, *Canzone al christianissimo Enrico quarto*

Cervoni, *Canzone al santissimo padre nostro Papa Clemente VIII*

Marinella, *Vita del serafico e glorioso San Francesco*

---

[†]See Bosi 2003, 99–101, on the Mantuan edition of 1590, ignored in most secondary sources.
[‡]All are undated; for details, see Bullock and Palange 1980, 258–59.

1598
Catanea, *Pretiosa gemma delle virtuose donne* (+ 1600 ×2)
Cervoni, *Orazione [a] Papa Clemente ottavo*

1600
Cervoni, *Tre canzoni in laude de' christianiss[imo] re, e regina di Francia e di Nauarra*
[Fonte, *Il merito delle donne*]
Marinella, *La nobiltà et l'eccellenza delle donne* (+ 1601, 1621)

1601
Andreini, *Rime*

1602
Marinella, *Vita di Maria Vergine* (+ 1610, 1617)
Matraini, *Dialoghi spirituali*

1603
*Andreini, *Rime*
Marinella, *Rime sacre*

1604
Valeria Miani, *Amorosa speranza*

1605
[Andreini, *Rime . . . parte seconda*]
Marinella, *Arcadia felice*
Marinella, *Scielta d'alcune rime sacre*

1606
Margherita Sarrocchi, *La Scanderbeide* (+ 1623, in an expanded version)

1607
[Andreini, *Lettere* (+ 1610, 1611, 1612, 1616)]

1610
Catanea, *Fiori d'ogni virtù*
Lucchesia Sbarra, *Rime*

1611
Miani, *Celinda*
[Salvetti, *David perseguitato*]

1612
Suor Cherubina Venturelli, *Rappresentazione di S[anta] Cecilia vergine et martire*
   (+1631, 1640, 1651, 1668, 1685)

1613
Veneranda Bragadin, *Rime diverse*

1614
Bragadin, *Varie rime* (+ 1619)
Bianca Naldi, *Risposta ad una lettera di Giacomo Violati*

1616
Catanea, *Teatro delle nobili et virtuose donne* (+ 1619, 1620, 1636)

1617
[Andreini, *Fragmenti di alcune scritture* (+ 1627)]
[Andreini, *Lettere, aggiunte li ragionamenti piacevoli* (+ 1620 ×2, 162, 1634, 1638, 1647,
    1652, 1663)]
Diodata Malvasia, *La venuta e i progressi miracolosi della santissima Madonna dipinta
    da San Luca*
Marinella, *Le vite de' dodici heroi di Christo, e de' quattro evangelisti* (with *La vita di
    Maria Vergine*)

1618
Marinella, *Amore innamorato, et impazzato*

1621
Sara Copio Sullam, *Manifesto sull'immortalità dell'anima*

1623
Suor Semidea Poggi, *La Calliope religiosa*

1624
Marinella, *De' gesti heroici . . . della serafica S[anta] Caterina da Siena*

1628
Isabella Coreglia, *Rime spirituali e morali*
Isabella Sori, *Ammaestramenti e ricordi* and *Difese delle donne* (published together)
Turina, *Rime varie*

1630
Margherita Costa, *Istoria del viaggio d'Alemagna del . . . gran duca di Toscana, Ferdi-
    nando Secondo* (undated but c. 1630)
Costa, *La Santa Cecilia, poema sacro* (+ 1644, in a revised version)

1634
Coreglia, *Dori, favola pastorale*

1635
Marinella, *L'Enrico, overo Bisanzio acquistato*

1636
[Fedele, *Epistolae et orationes*]

1637
Suor Maria Clemente Ruoti, *Giacob patriarca*

1638
Costa, *La chitarra*
Costa, *Il violino*

1639
Costa, *Lettere amorose*
Costa, *Lo stipo*

1640
[Laura Cereta, *Epistolae*]
Costa, *Flora feconda, drama*
Costa, *Flora feconda, poema*
Costa, *La selva di cipressi*
Barbara Tigliamocchi, *Ascanio errante*

1641
Costa, *Li buffoni*

1642
Suor Francesca di Gesù Maria (Francesca Farnese), *Lettera spirituale, et esortatoria*

1643
Marinella, *Le vittorie di Francesco il Serafico, li passi gloriosi della diva Chiara.*
Suor Arcangela Tarabotti, *Paradiso monacale*

1644
Suor Angelica Baitelli, *Vita martirio, et morte di S[anta[ Giulia cartaginese* (+ 1657)
Tarabotti, *Antisatira* (+ 1645, 1656)

1645
Marinella, *Essortationi alle donne e agli altri*

1647
Costa, *\*Festa reale per balletto*
Costa, *\*La selva di Diana*
Costa, *\*La tromba di Parnaso*

1648
Marinella, *Holocausto d'amore della vergine Santa Giustina*

1650

Coreglia, *Erindo il fido, favola pastorale*

Tarabotti, *Lettere familiari e di complimento* . . . *le lagrime per la illustrissima signora Regina Donati*

1651

Tarabotti, *Che le donne siano della spetie degli uomini*

Maria Porzia Vignola, *L'obelisco di Piazza Navona*

1653

[Tarabotti, *La semplicità ingannata*][†]

Vignola, *Il vaticinio della Sibilla Tiburtina*

1654

Costa, *Gli amori della luna*

1656

[Maria Alberghetti, *Discorsi sopra gli evangelii*]

1657

[Baitelli, *Annali* . . . *del* . . . *Monasterio di S[an] Salvatore, e S[anta] Giulia di Brescia*]

[Farnese, *Poesie sacre* (+ 1659, 1666, 1668, 1679)]

1658

[Alberghetti, *Meditationi divote sopra l'incarnatione del verbo*]

1661

[Alberghetti, *Gioiello di divote meditazioni*]

[Alberghetti, *Meditationi divote sopra la sacra passione*]

1669

Elena Corner (or Cornaro) Piscopia, *Lettera, ouero colloquio di Christo* (translation of a treatise by Johann Landsperger [1489–1539], via the Spanish of Andres Capilla [d. 1610], + 1673, 1681, 1687, 1688, 1706)

1674

[Alberghetti, *Giardino di poesie spirituali*]

1686

[Farnese, *Lettere*]

---

†Tarabotti's treatise was published with a (false) Leiden imprint, but two separate issues of the edition have been identified, one perhaps published clandestinely in Venice; see Panizza 2004, 29–30.

1688
[Corner Piscopia, *Opera*]

1692
[**Colonna, *Rime* (×2)]
[**Terracina, *Rime* (×2 + 1694)]

1693
[**d'Aragona, *Rime*]
[**Colonna, *Rime spirituali*]
**[Marinella, Isabella da Morra, Veronica Gambara,] and Maria Selvaggia Bor-
    ghini, *Rime*

1694
[**Battiferra, *Rime*]

1695
[***Rime di cinquanta illustri poetesse* (×2)]

1696
[**Andreini, *Rime*]

1698
[**Terracina, *Discorso*]

# DEDICATIONS OF PUBLISHED WORKS BY WOMEN

Works published without a dedication, such as Colonna's *Rime* of 1540, Issicratea Monte's *Seconda oratione,* and Chiara Matraini's *Meditationi spirituali* have been omitted from this list (which is, in any case, not intended to be comprehensive). Where not otherwise stated, all dedications are by the author.

### 1538

Vittoria Colonna, *Rime:* Andrea Vercelli (by Filippo Pirogallo)

### 1544

?Isabella Sforza, *Della vera tranquillità dell'animo:* Otto Truchsess von Waldburg, Bishop of Ausburg (1514–73) (by Ortensio Lando)

### 1547

Tullia d'Aragona, *Dialogo dell'infinità d'amore:* (a) d'Aragona (by Girolamo Muzio); (b) Cosimo I de' Medici (1519–74), Duke of Tuscany

d'Aragona, *Rime:* Eleonora of Toledo (1522–62), Duchess of Tuscany

### 1548

Colonna, *Rime spirituali:* Isabella Villamarino Sanseverino (d. 1559), Princess of Salerno (by Apollonio Campano)

Laura Terracina, *Rime:* Giovanni Vicenzo Belprato (b. c. 1500/10), Count of Anversa (by Lodovico Domenichi)

### 1549

Terracina, *Discorso sopra tutti i primi canti d'Orlando furioso:* Giovanni Bernardino Bonifacio (1517–97), Marquis of Oria

### 1550

Terracina, *Quarte rime:* Pietro Antonio Sanseverino (d. 1559), Prince of Bisignano

### 1552

"Dafne di Piazza," *Academia di enigmi in sonetti:* Pietro Fassina (by Stefano di Alessi)

Terracina, *Quinte rime:* Irene Castriota Scanderbeg Sanseverino (d. 1565), Princess of Bisignano

1554

Laura Pieri, *Quattro canti della guerra di Siena:* Giovanni Giacomo de' Medici (1495–1555), Marquis of Marignano

Gaspara Stampa, *Rime:* Giovanni della Casa (1503–56) (by the author's sister, Cassandra Stampa)

1555

Chiara Matraini, *Rime e prose:* (a) Vincenzo Portico (by Vincenzo Pippi); (b) "M. L." (?Lodovico Domenichi)

1556

Matraini, *Oratione d'Isocrate a Demonico:* (a) Matraini (by the publisher Lorenzo Torrentino); (b) Giulio di Alessandro de' Medici (c. 1533–1600)

1558

Colonna, *Tutte le rime:* Isabella Gonzaga d'Avalos (1537–79), Marchioness of Pescara (by Girolamo Ruscelli)

Terracina, *Seste rime:* Isabetta della Rovere Cibo (1529–61), Marchioness of Massa (purportedly by Terracina, but in fact by Vincenzo Arnolfini)

1560

Laura Battiferra, *Primo libro delle opere toscane:* Eleonora of Toledo

Colonna, *Rime:* Giorgio Gradenigo (Venetian poet) (1522–1600) (by Lodovico Dolce)

Terracina, *Seste rime:* Colantonio Caracciolo (c. 1535–77), Marquis of Vico

1561

Isabella Cortese, *Segreti:* Mario Chaboga, archdeacon of Ragusa

1575

Veronica Franco, *Terze rime:* Guglielmo Gonzaga (1538–87), Duke of Mantova

1578

Issicratea Monte, *Oratione . . . nella congratulatione di . . . Niccolò da Ponte: Dogaressa* Marina Gussoni da Ponte

1580

Franco, *Lettere:* Cardinal Luigi d'Este (1538–86)

1581

Moderata Fonte, *Floridoro:* Francesco I de' Medici (1541–87) and Bianca Cappello de' Medici (1548–87), Grand Duke and Duchess of Tuscany

Monte, *Oratione . . . alla sacra maestà di Maria d'Austria:* Federico Corner (or

Cornaro) (1531–90), Bishop of Padua (not present in all copies; see De Vit 1883, 21 n. 23)

**1582**

Fonte, *La passione di Christo:* Doge Niccolò da Ponte (1491–1585)

**1584**

Camilla Erculiani, *Lettere di philosophia naturale:* Anna of Hapsburg (1523–96), Queen of Poland

**1585**

Maddalena Campiglia, *Discorso sopra l'annonciatione della beata Vergine:* Vittoria Trissino della Frattina (d. 1612)

**1586**

Matraini, *Considerationi sopra i sette salmi:* Lucrezia d'Este della Rovere (1535–98), Duchess of Urbino

**1587**

Silvia Bendinelli, *Corona in morte del serenissimo sig[nor] Ottavio Farnese:* Ranuccio Farnese (1569–1622), Duke Regent of Parma and Piacenza

**1588**

Isabella Andreini, *Mirtilla:* Lavinia della Rovere d'Avalos (1558–1632), Marchioness of Vasto

Campiglia, *Flori:* (a) Isabella Pallavicino Lupi (c. 1545–1623), Marchioness of Soragna; (b) Curzio Gonzaga (Mantuan nobleman-poet) (1536–99)

Lorenza Strozzi, *In singulis totius anni solemnia hymni:* Lattanzio Lattanzi (d. 1587), Bishop of Pistoia

**1589**

Campiglia, *Calisa:* Curzio Gonzaga

**1590**

Maddalena Salvetti, *Rime toscane:* Christine of Lorraine (1565–1637), Grand Duchess of Tuscany

Matraini, *Breve discorso sopra la vita della beatiss[ima] Vergine:* Donna Giuditta Matraini (Matraini's cousin and abbess of the convent of San Bernardo, Pisa)

**1592**

Fonte, *La resurretione di Giesù Christo:* Margherita Langosco Parpaglia, Countess of Bastia

1595

Isabetta Catanea, *Specchio delle virtuose donne:* Felice Maria Orsini Caetani (d. 1596), Duchess of Sermoneta

Lucrezia Marinella, *La Colomba sacra:* Margherita Gonzaga d'Este (1564–1618), Duchess of Ferrara

Matraini, *Lettere . . . con le rime:* Chiara Diodati (by Ottaviano Guidoboni)*

Francesca Turina, *Rime spirituali:* Pope Clement VIII (Ippolito Aldobrandini) (1536–1605)

1597

Catanea, *Studio delle virtuose dame:* Juana de Aragona, Duchess of Soma

Marinella, *Vita del serafico e glorioso San Francesco:* Christine of Lorraine

Matraini, *Lettere . . . con le rime:* Giacomo Nani (by Niccolò Moretti)

1600

Fonte, *Il merito delle donne:* Livia Feltria della Rovere (1585–1641), Duchess of Urbino (by Fonte's daughter Cecilia de' Zorzi)

Marinella, *La nobiltà et l'eccellenza delle donne:* Lucio Scarano (Venetian medic and *letterato*)

1602

Marinellla, *Vita di Maria Vergine:* Doge [Marino Grimani] and Senate of Venice

Matraini, *Dialoghi spirituali:* Marfisa d'Este Cibo-Malaspina (?1553–1608), Princess of Massa and Carrara

1603

Marinella, *Rime sacre:* Eugenia Ceruti Scaini (by Ascanio Collosini, who paid for the publication)

1604

Valeria Miani, *Amorosa speranza:* Marietta Descalzi Uberti (by (a) Miani; (b) the publisher Francesco Bolzetta)†

1605

Isabella Andreini, *Rime:* Cardinal Cinzio Passeri Aldobrandini (1551–1610)

Marinella, *Arcadia felice:* Eleonora de' Medici Gonzaga (1566–1611), Duchess of Mantua

Marinella, *Scielta d'alcune rime sacre:* Cornelia Casale (by the publisher Comin Ventura)

---

*The information given here on the dedications of Matraini's 1595 and 1597 *Lettere . . . con le rime* derives from Bullock and Palange 1980, 214–42. The copies of these works that I have consulted contain no dedicatory letter.

†The dedicatee is named in the text as Marietta Uberti Descalzi, but she is identified in Bolzetta's dedicatory letter as the daughter of the lawyer and academician Ottonello Descalzo; Descalzi, or Descalzi, is thus her family name, Uberti presumably the name of her husband.

1606

Margherita Sarrocchi, *La Scanderbeide:* Costanza Colonna Sforza (b. c. 1555), Marchioness of Caravaggio (by the "Arrotato Accademico Raffrontato")

1611

Maddalena Salvetti, *David perseguitato:* Maria Maddalena de' Medici (1589–1631), Grand Duchess of Tuscany by (a) Salvetti's husband, Zanobi Accaiuoli; (b) Salvetti herself

Valeria Miani, *Celinda:* Eleonora de' Medici Gonzaga

1613

Veneranda Bragadin, *Rime diverse:* Doge Marcantonio Memmo (1536–1615)

1614

Bragadin Cavalli, *Varie rime:* Ferdinando Gonzaga (1587–1626), Duke of Mantua

Bianca Naldi, *Risposta ad una lettera di Giacomo Violati:* Laura Obizzi Pepoli (by Giacomo Violati)

1616

Catanea, *Teatro delle nobili e virtuose donne:* Elizabeth of Austria, infanta of Spain (probably Isabella Clara Eugenia [1566–1633])

1617

Diodata Malvasia, *La venuta et i progressi miracolosi della santissima Madonna dipinta da San Luca :* Cardinal Alessandro Lodovisi (1564–1623), Archbishop of Bologna and future pope (Gregory XV)

1618

Marinella, *Amore innamorato, et impazzato:* Caterina de' Medici Gonzaga (1593–1629), Duchess of Mantua

1619

Bragadin, *Rime:* Caterina de' Medici Gonzaga

1623

Suor Semidea Poggi, *La Calliope religiosa:* Count Onorio Capra

Sarrocchi, *La Scanderbeide,* 2nd ed.: Giulia d'Este (1588–1645) (daughter of Duke of Modena)

1624

Marinella, *De' gesti heroici . . . della serafica S[anta] Caterina da Siena:* Maria Maddalena d'Austria

1628

Isabetta Coreglia, *Rime:* Antonio Bendinelli (by the author, and by Filippo Lippi)

Isabella Sori, *Ammaestramenti e ricordi:* Prudenzia Origoni Picenardi (by the publisher Giovanni Maria Magro)

Turina, *Rime varie:* Anna Colonna Barberini (1601–58), *Prefettessa* of Rome

### 1635
Marinella, *Enrico, overo Bisanzio acquistato:* Doge Francesco Erizzo (1566–1646)

### 1638
Margherita Costa, *Il violino:* Ferdinando II (1610–70), Grand Duke of Tuscany

Costa, *La chitarra:* Ferdinando II

### 1639
Costa, *Lettere amorose:* Cardinal Giancarlo de' Medici (1611–63), brother of Duke Ferdinando II de' Medici

Costa, *Lo stipo:* Lorenzo de' Medici (1599–1648), uncle of Duke Ferdinando II de' Medici

### 1640
Barbara Tigliamocchi degli Albizzi, *Ascanio errante:* Vittoria della Rovere (1622–94), Grand Duchess of Tuscany

Costa, *Flora feconda, drama:* Vittoria della Rovere

Costa, *Flora feconda, poema:* Ferdinando II de' Medici

Costa, *La selva di cipressi:* Charles of Lorraine (1571–1640), Duke of Guise

### 1641
Costa, *Li buffoni:* Bernardino Ricci (actor)

### 1643
Marinella, *Le vittorie di Francesco il serafico, li passi gloriosi della diva Chiara:* Pope Urban VIII (Matteo Barberini) (1568–1644)

### 1643
Arcangela Tarabotti, *Paradiso monacale:* Cardinal Federico Corner (or Cornaro) (1579–1653)

### 1644
Costa, *Cecilia martire:* Cardinal Francesco Barberini (1597–1679)

Tarabotti, *Antisatira:* Vittoria della Rovere

### 1647
Costa, *Festa reale per balletto:* Cardinal Giulio Mazzarino (or Mazarin) (1602–61)

Costa, *Selva di Diana:* Maria Cristina of France (1606–63), Regent of Savoy

Costa, *Tromba di Parnaso:* Anne of Austria (1601–66), Queen of France

1648

Marinella, *Holocausto d'amore della vergine Santa Giustina:* Doge Francesco Molin (1575–1655)

1650

Tarabotti, *Lettere familiari e di complimento:* Giovanni Francesco Loredan (Venetian *letterato*) (1607–61)

1650

Tarabotti, *Lagrime per la illustrissima signora Regina Donati:* Andriana Donà Malipiero (sister of the subject)

1650

Coreglia, *Erindo il fido, favola pastorale:* Conservatori of the Accademia degli Incauti of Naples

1654

Costa, *Gli amori della luna:* Georg Wilhelm (1624–1705), Ernst August (1629–95), and Johann Friedrich (1625–79) of Brunswick-Lüneberg

## Acknowledgments

1. The proceedings of these conferences have been published as Panizza, ed., 2000, and Benson and Kirkham, eds. 2005.

## Introduction

1. Kelly 1984. The essay was first published in 1977.

2. Useful recent bibliographies of scholarship on early modern women are found in successive chapters of Weisner 2000; see also Hufton 1998, 565–613.

3. Fundamental in establishing the theoretical basis of such enquiries was J. W. Scott 1986. For an illustrative sample of studies, see, for European literary and cultural history generally, Ferguson, Quilligan, and Vickers 1986; DeJean 1991; Breitenberg 1996; Mikalachki 1998; Matchinske 1998; M. B. Rose 2002; Rublack, ed. 2002; Ferguson 2003. For Italy, see J. Brown and Davis 1998.

4. Where earlier work is concerned, besides the fundamental Kelso 1978 (originally published in 1956), one might point here, in an Italian context, to late nineteenth-century positivistic historical studies such as Morsolin 1882; Biagi 1887; Luzio and Renier 2006 (originally published 1899–1903); also to the Anglo-American female historiographical tradition represented by Cartwright 2002a and b (originally published 1899 and 1903) and Jerrold 1969 (originally published 1906). On the context of the latter tradition, see B. Smith 1984, 722–23, and Ostermark-Johansen 1999, esp. 283 and 294 n. 57.

5. See Travitsky 1990, esp. 6–7, and Herlihy 1995, 33–56, for revisitations of Kelly's argument that broadly confirm her findings while nuancing them. Where Italy is concerned, however, Herlihy pushes the origin of the constricting processes described by Kelly back to a period between the eleventh and the thirteenth centuries, in a manner that obviously compromises Kelly's periodization (see also on this Hughes 1987, 30–31, and Skinner 2001, 146–47, 164–66, both of whom stress the negative implications for Italian elite women of the rise of the Italian communes). For a critique of Kelly's overreliance on literary sources, mentioned in the text, see J. Brown 1986, 206–7.

6. See on this, in an Italian context, Herlihy 1995, 52–54, and J. Brown 1986, 215–16.

7. See, for example, Skinner 2001, 170; also J. Brown 1986, who identifies an increase in paid labor by Tuscan women in the later sixteenth and early seventeenth centuries after their late-medieval marginalization. For a concise bibliography of literature debating the question of whether this period marked a turning point in the situation of working women, see Weisner 2000, 135; for a summary of the issues, Hufton 1998, 25–26.

8. See, where court women specifically are concerned, in an Italian context, Welch 1995 and 2000; Clough 1996; Manca 2003; Shemek 2005b; also the bibliography cited in ch. 1, nn.110–11, below. More generally, as a sample of recent studies in various fields emphasizing women's agency, see Jones 1990; Cohen and Cohen 1993; Chojnacka 2001; Reiss and Wilkins 2001; Lowe 2003; Hacke 2004; McIver 2006.

9. See notably on this Chojnacki 2000, esp. chs. 5–8.

10. Maclean 1980.

11. Erdmann 1999, 201–4 (France) and 206–21 (Italy). Erdmann lists twenty published women writers for Germany (204–6); seventeen for England (199–200); thirteen for Spain and Portugal (224–25); and three for the Netherlands (224). Of course, as scholars such as Margaret Ezell have recently stressed, publication should not be overprivileged as an index of women's literary activity in this period. On the greater publishing opportunities available to Italian women, see ch. 1, n. 165, below.

12. Woods-Marsden 1998, 195–96.

13. Newcomb 1986, 96.

14. For examples of women's election to literary academies, see Fahy 2000 and n. 194 in ch. 3 and n. 3 in ch. 5 below. For women as public speakers, see the text between nn. 41 and 46 in ch. 1 and between nn. 84 and 86 in ch. 5. For women's appearances in poetic anthologies of the period, see Cerrón Puga 2005; Erdmann 1999, 130–34; 221–24; Robin 2007, passim; and chs. 3–5 below, passim.

15. For bibliographies of Italian works on women, see Fahy 1956, 47–55, and Piéjus 1980, 162–65; also, for Europe in general, Kelso 1978, 326–424, and Erdmann 1999, 1–98, 155–98.

16. Benson 1992, 49–50; Jordan 1990 passim; Cox 1995a, 515.

17. On the origins of this humanistic discourse, see ch. 1, sec. 2.

18. The phrase ("cette mini-révolution copernicienne") is from Piéjus 1994b, 80.

19. See ch. 3, sec. 2.

20. For an influential analysis of this tendency, see Jardine 1986 (amalgamating two earlier studies, Jardine 1983 and 1985).

21. For further comment on this, see Cox 1995a, 517–20.

22. As examples of this position with regard to the texts cited, see Schiesari 1989, esp. 73–75, 79–80; Günsberg 1991; Finucci 1992.

23. Burckhardt 1990, 250, and Tomalin 1982.

24. For a recent study that clearly brings out the relation of the scholastic conception of woman and the humanistic reaction to it, see Allen 2002.

25. See ch. 6.

26. The dangers of such "evolutionary" narratives of the emergence of feminism are cogently examined (in an English context) in Ezell 1993; see esp. ch. 1.

27. Dionisotti 1999, 227–54, esp. 237–39.

28. Dionisotti 1999, 238 ("soltanto nella letteratura del medio Cinquecento le donne fanno gruppo").

29. For the term "euphoric" see Dionisotti 1999, 243–44 ("il momento espansivo, euforico della letteratura italiana").

30. On the incident and its prominence in modern scholarship, see the text in ch. 1 between nn. 30 and 32. More generally, for discussions of moral constraints on women's speech in this period, see Jones 1990, 15–28 (though cf. ibid., 30), and Wall 1993, 280. On the corresponding difficulty, for women, of publishing or circulating their written works, see Jones 1990, 27–29, and Wall 1993, 280–81, 283, though cf. Summit 2000, 8, 167–68, for caveats regarding the applicability of speech proscriptions to the situation of writing.

31. Series of female-authored works entitled The Defiant Muse and The Other Voice in Early Modern Europe are published, respectively, by the Feminist Press at CUNY and the University of Chicago Press. The series editors' introduction to the latter offers a good example of the critical stance described here: see especially the sections "The Problem of Speech" and "The Problem of Knowledge." On the myth of Procne and Philomela in women's poetry of this period, see Jones 1991. More generally, on the historiographical notion of the female writer as "outcast" and its romantic origins, see Ezell 1993, 25–26.

32. As an example of this approach, see the justly influential Jones 1990.

33. Exceptions are Zancan 1986 (revised and expanded in Zancan 1998, 5–63) and Panizza and Wood 2000, 11–91 (part 1), both, however, included as part of more general histories of Italian women's writing and operating under corresponding constraints of space.

34. Useful resources for this work are the list of published writings by Italian women in Erdmann 1999, 206–23, and the dedicated websites Italian Women Writers (www.lib.uchicago.edu/efts/IWW) and A Celebration of Women's Writing (http://digital.library.upenn.edu/women) (although the latter currently only covers the better-known writers); also the database of verse in sixteenth-century Italian anthologies (http://rasta.unipv.it). For biographical information on lesser-known writers, Bandini Buti 1946 remains indispensable.

35. For the term "virtual matroneum," see Kirkham 2006, 53. As an example of a recent anthology of Italian poetry that "desegregates" female poets, including them within regional and stylistic groupings with comparable male poets, see Danzi, Gorni, and Longhi, eds. 2001.

36. For the notion of such a gendered history within an Italian context, see Barolini 2005, 169–70. The most sustained attempt at such a history to date is Zancan 1998, 5–109.

37. Oral circulation also needs to be considered in some cases, especially in those of female poets known to have been musical performers (Gaspara Stampa, Barbara Salutati, Tarquinia Molza): see Smarr 1991 for some considerations.

38. The division between "literary" and "nonliterary" or "private" and "public" letters is difficult to make in this period: see Lettere 1990 for an interesting borderline case. For studies of "nonliterary" letters by women in this period, see Zarri, ed. 1999; Swain 1986; Shemek 2005b, as well as the references in n. 53 to ch. 1 below.

39. Lowe 2003 and Weaver 2002. With few exceptions, nuns' writings are included in my discussion here only when they were printed or where there is other evidence of their circulation outside the convent.

40. C. Sforza 1894, and Graziani and Venturelli 1987, 141–49.

41. In its concern with the cultural work done by the figure of the "woman writer," especially in articulating and negotiating literary change, the present volume has much in common with Summit 2000, which illuminatingly examines these issues in an English context. See also Findlen 1995 and 2003 on the similarly complex role played by the figure of the female scientist in Enlightenment Italy.

42. For reviews of these issues, in an English context, see Ferguson 1996, esp. 149–52, 156–63; Summit 2000, 8–9; Clarke 2001, 3–14.

43. Books of questionable authorship published under women's names in Italy in this period include ?I. Sforza 1544; Lando, ed. 1548; ?Gonzaga 1552 (all probably wholly or in part authored by Ortensio Lando); di Piazza 1552; ?d'Aragona 1560; Cortese 1561; "Celia Romana" 1562; "Emilia N." 1594; Naldi 1614. For discussion of the attribution issues raised by these works see the relevant entries in the index. On works by Isotta Nogarola and Tullia d'Aragona probably written in collaboration with male contacts, see ch. 1, n. 60, and ch. 3, n. 158, below. Generally, on issues of authorship in the context of women's writing, see DeJean 1991, 3–5, 98–101; Clarke 2001, 4; North 2003, 211–56.

44. This issue is further discussed in chs. 2 and 3 below. On the continuing importance of scribal publication throughout this period, see, for the English context, Love 1993 and A. Marotti 1995; for the Italian, Richardson 2004. On the implications for women writers, see Love 1993, 54–58; A. Marotti 1995, 48–61; Ezell 1987 and 1993; Summit 2000, 186–88.

45. *Rime* 1565a. Ferro 1581, similarly, has a "Costanza L." alongside five named female poets; see ch. 5, n. 59, below. For Domenichi's anonymous poets ("Narda N. Fiorentina" and "Mad. P. S. M."), see Robin 2007, 242. The most famous case of an Italian woman writer in this period who published under a pseudonym is the Venetian Moderata Fonte (1555–92), born Modesta da Pozzo; see ch. 5, n. 72, below, however, on the exceptionalism of her choice. Female authorship may, of course, be concealed behind some attributions of anthology poems listed as "by an unknown author" (see the listings on the website Antologie della lirica italiana (ALI RASTA [http://rasta.unipv.it]), under the heading "autore incerto"). On the problems raised by such cases, see, in an English context, North 2003, esp. 244–56.

46. Wall 1993, 280.

47. Richardson 2004, 42–43; Kirkham 1996.

48. Interesting with respect to these points is Benson 1999, 257, who notes the exceptionality of the Anglo-Italian poet Aemilia Bassano Lanyer (1569–1645) within the context of English women's writing of the period, particularly in regard to her relatively unabashed attitude to print and her public cultivation of patronage relations, and concludes that Lanyer may be seen in these respects as "culturally Italian."

49. "Profeminist" is proposed in Benson 1992, 2, as a means of addressing the problem highlighted here.

50. Fortuitously, other than Franco, most of the other female writers of this period with a substantial modern critical tradition dating back beyond the last decades of the twentieth century tend to be those with surnames that do not inflect, such as Isotta Nogarola, Vittoria Colonna, Isabella da Morra, Veronica Gambara, and Gaspara Stampa.

51. In the case of Laura Battiferri/a, I have used "Battiferra," in keeping with the recent English-language edition. I am aware that my rule of deference to usage preserves some anomalous namings, such as "Francesca Turina Bufalini"— the form used for Turina Bufalini 1628 and 2005 (Turina Bufalini 1595 uses the fully feminine-inflected "Turina Bufalina" in its title, while modern catalogues such as the on-line ICCU catalogue use the masculine "Turini Bufalini").

## Chapter 1. Origins (1400–1500)

1. Gambara was descended through her father from Ginevra Nogarola, Colonna through her mother from Battista da Montefeltro, Costanza Varano, and Battista Sforza da Montefeltro. See Clough 1996, 34, for a family tree clarifying relations between the latter group of women.

2. I have on the whole preferred the more general terms "learned lady" and "female erudite" to that of "female humanist." While "female humanist" would apply well to a figure such as Isotta Nogarola, on the range and seriousness of whose studies see especially Robathan 1944, it is less appropriate for others, such as Ippolita Sforza and Cecilia Gonzaga, the level of whose erudition and scholarly engagement is less clear.

3. On Scrovegni, see King and Rabil 1983, 16, 33; also, more recently, Stevenson 2005, 157–58. On Battista da Montefeltro, see King and Rabil 1983, 16, 35–38; also, for more detail, G. Franceschini 1959; G. Franceschini 1973, 291–310; Clough 1996, esp. 36–39, 44–46; Patrignani 2005, 2:829–49.

4. On Angela Nogarola, see H. Parker 1997, 250–60 (also H. Parker 2002a, 11–13, 18–21, 23–26), and Stevenson 2005, 158–59, 510–12. The Latin text of Nogarola's works may be found in Nogarola 1886, 2:293–326.

5. On Isotta Nogarola, see King 1994, citing editions and bibliography; Allen 2002, 955–69; King and Robin 2004; and Fenster 2005. On Costanza Varano, see Feliciangeli 1894; King and Rabil 1983, 18, 39–44, 53–56; H. Parker 2002b; Allen 2002, 706–11; Patrignani 2005, 2:886–920. On Ginevra Nogarola, see King and Rabil 1983, 3–4, 18 and n. 41; on Cecilia Gonzaga, King and Rabil 1983, 19–20; on Costanza Barbaro, King and Rabil 1983, 19; also Allen 2002, 724–26; on Caterina Caldiera, King 1975, 537–38 nn. 7 and 9, and King and Rabil 1983, 18–19.

6. Two excellent recent studies of Ippolita Sforza are Welch 1995 and Bryce 2002; see also Cutolo 1955; King and Rabil 1983, 20–21, 44–48; Stevenson 2005, 172–73; Bryce 2007. Most commentators assume her to have been thoroughly humanistically competent, though Alessio 1997, 80, questions the extent of her compe-

tence in the classical languages, noting that most works dedicated to her were in the vernacular. On Scala, see King and Rabil 1983, 25; H. Parker 1997, 267–69. On Fedele, see Pignatti 1995; also Robin 1994 and 2000, both citing editions and secondary sources; also, subsequently, Allen 2002, 936–43. On Cereta, see Rabil 1994a and Robin 1997, both citing editions and criticism; also, subsequently Lorenzini 2001a and b; Allen 2002, 969–1045. Regarding Fedele's date of birth, see Jardine 1986, 45 n. 48, who suggests a date of c. 1470, some years later than that usually stated.

7. On Battista Sforza, see Clough 1996, esp. 32, 40–41, 48, and Stevenson 2005, 154–55, 167. On Brenzoni, see Benzoni 1939; Castoldi 1993 and *Rime* 1994, the latter citing existing bibliography at 75 n. 14; Stevenson 2005, 168–69, 443. Regarding Brenzoni's date of birth, sometimes located in 1474 or 1476, I have followed Benzoni 1939, 188. Other fifteenth-century female erudites recorded in Jane Stevenson's 2005 survey of women writers in Latin include Elena Coppoli of Perugia (173–74, 453–54), Polissena Grimaldi of Verona (168, 473), Clara, or Chiara, Lanzavegia, also possibly from Verona (165, 490–91), and Polissena Messalto of Muggia (156, 501). See also n. 16 below on Nicolosa Sanuti of Bologna, sometimes misleadingly recorded as a Latinist.

8. For references, see nn. 87–89 below.

9. For Tornabuoni, see R. Russell 1994d and the bibliography cited there at 438–40; also, subsequently Tylus 2001a and the bibliography cited there at 21 n. 1 and Tomas 2003, esp. 28–29. For Pulci, see Toscani 1994 and the bibliography cited there at 350–52; also, subsequently, Cook and Cook 1996; Bryce 1999; Weaver 2002, 97–104. For Minutolo, see Minutolo 1999, citing existing bibliography.

10. See on this Clough 1996, 54–55, who rightly notes the imprecision of King and Rabil 1983 in this regard.

11. See on this especially Clough 1996, esp. 37–44; also Stevenson 1998, 103–4; 2005, 152–53. Clough notes (43) that the practice of educating girls alongside their brothers was not uncommon in princely households; this, needless to say, would have been quite exceptional in other social contexts. Interesting for its explicitness regarding the class basis of female education is Francesco da Barberino's *Reggimento e costumi di donna* (1314–16), which condones education for girls of aristocratic background while condemning it for those of lower ranks, from merchants downward. The daughters of knights, judges, and doctors form a further partial exception to the ban; here, education is discretionary and depends on family choice. See Barberino 1957, 10–20; Zarri 2000a, 149.

12. Feliciangeli 1894, 15n. Anna da Montefeltro (d. 1434) married Galeazzo Novello "Belfiore" Malatesta of Rimini, retiring to her home city of Urbino after her widowhood in 1400.

13. Paola Malatesta Gonzaga was the sister-in-law of Battista da Montefeltro and daughter of the poet Malatesta Malatesta. On her reputation as a learned woman, see Stevenson 2005, 171. Sabadino degli Arienti 1888, 140, describes her as "eloquentissima," though he does not otherwise mention her learning. On her life and position, see also Welch 2002.

14. King and Rabil 1983, 44–46. On Bianca Maria Visconti, see Welch 2000, 24–29.

15. On Campano's oration, see McManamon 1989, 113–14; 226 n. 80. The text, which was published in 1495, is reproduced in facsimile in Campano 1969. On Piero's double portrait, see Warnke 1998; Woods-Marsden 2002. Although the gender conventionality of Piero's portraits of Federico and Battista has been stressed in recent scholarship (see, for example, Woods-Marsden 2002, 110–12), the structure of the diptych is undoubtedly suggestive of the equal dignity of the spouses as well as of the differences of their roles. It is interesting to note that two other notable fifteenth-century double portraits of ruler-spouses also feature women noted for their learning or associated with "famous women" discourses: these are the portraits of Francesco Sforza and Bianca Maria Visconti in the Pinacoteca di Brera of Milan sometimes attributed to Bonifacio Bembo (c. 1460) and of Giovanni Bentivoglio and Ginevra Sforza Bentivoglio attributed to Ercole de' Roberti in the National Gallery of Washington (c. 1475). For discussion of the Bentivoglio portrait, see D. Brown 2003, 103–5. Further on the genre of spousal ruler-portraits, see Syson 1996.

16. Killerby 1999, 277. The attribution to Sanuti is somewhat misleading, in that Sanuti herself acknowledges her use of a ghostwriter, in the form of a "man of great excellence and talent" who "dignified" her ideas by translating them into Latin; she was not Latin-literate herself ( Killerby 1999, 261 and n. 30). For a detailed discussion of the authorship question, see Lombardi 1998. Beside the "usual suspects"—Battista da Montefeltro, Costanza Varano, Paola Malatesta Gonzaga, Bianca Maria Visconti—Sanuti's list includes Battista's daughter and Costanza's mother Elisabetta Malatesta (1407–77) and Battista's niece Violante Malatesta (1430–93), as well as Ricciarda da Saluzzo (d. 1474), the widow of Niccolò d'Este, and Niccolò's illegitimate daughter Isotta (1425–56).

17. H. Parker 2002a, 11–12, 18–19, and H. Parker 1997, 266–67. Although the Scrovegni were a less ancient and distinguished family than the Nogarola, we may assume that Maddalena Scrovegni was similarly well connected: her family had risen rapidly on account of their wealth and were allied by marriage to the Este as well as to prominent Venetian families like the Correr. On the family and its place in Padua under the Carrara, see Kohl 1998, 174–77.

18. The practical reasons for the education of women from dynastic families are discussed in the body of the text. Later fifteenth-century women of a rank comparable to Nogarola's with a reputation for learning include Silvia Boiardo (Stevenson 2005, 441), Damigella Trivulzio Torelli (d. 1527; Betussi 1545, 194v–95v), and Camilla Scarampa (discussed in ch. 2, sec. 2).

19. The fact that Bianca Borromeo was illiterate is stated in her will; see Nogarola 1886, cxlix, and cf. King and Robin 2004, 5, 29. It is possible that she was able to read but not write: see Strocchia 1999, 32–33 on the frequency of this form of "split literacy"; also Mazzonis 2004, 401, for a famous sixteenth-century example. Stevenson 2005, 160, 163, notes that Bianca was praised by contemporaries for her role in overseeing her children's education.

20. "felices quippe parentes/quam reo r esse tuos, quibus addis nata decorem/ et pariter morum dulcis pariter que sophiae" (H. Parker 1997, 267; the translation is Parker's with slight adjustment).

21. On the social cachet conferred by female education (even at a relatively low level) in a fifteenth-century Florentine context, see Strocchia 1999, 30–31, 34.

22. Robin 1997, 4–5; see also on Cereta's background King and Rabil 1983, 23; Lorenzini 2001b, 329–32. Cereta's mother, Veronica di Leno, came from a family with greater pretensions to nobility.

23. Another of King and Rabil's examples, Caterina Caldiera, falls into the same status category, as did the later sixteenth-century writers Moderata Fonte and Lucrezia Marinella. On the status of *cittadini* in Venice, see Grubb 2000, citing existing bibliography.

24. The term "substantial" is that of King and Rabil 1983, 25.

25. A possible exception is the nun Deodata di Leno, one of Cereta's female correspondents; see Cereta 1997, 115–22. Rabil 1981, 25, 100, and Lorenzini 2001b, 331, identify her as Cereta's sister, although she bears Cereta's mother's family name.

26. King and Rabil 1983, 85–86; Schiesari 1989, 81–83; cf. Cereta 1997, 80–82.

27. The phrase cited in the text is from Stevenson 2005, 154, who gives the example of Battista Guarino (1434–1513). In training up their daughters, humanist fathers may have been aware of the precedent of the Romans Laelia and Hortensia, daughters respectively of Scipio Aemilianus Africanus's friend Gaius Laelius and of the orator Quintus Hortensius, who were portrayed by Quintilian (1.1.6) as reflections or emanations of their fathers' eloquence. On this topos in Roman literature and its implications, see Hallett 1989, esp. 62–63. The pattern can also be found in the sixteenth century, in the case of women such as Olimpia Morata, Partenia Gallerati, and Lucrezia Marinella. For eighteenth-century instances, see Findlen 1995, 176.

28. On Scala's social background—he was a miller's son—see A. Brown 1979, 3.

29. For the letter, see Poliziano 2006, 188–93; for discussion Jardine 1986, 53–55. On Venetian humanism in this period, enjoying unprecedented prestige in consequence of the innovative philological activity of the younger Ermolao Barbaro (1454–c. 1493), see Branca 1981.

30. See on this especially King 1980a, esp. 68–69; King and Rabil 1983, 17, 18–19, 25–26.

31. The text of the invective is reproduced in Segarizzi 1904, 50–54. For discussion, see King 1980a, 76–77.

32. See, for example, King 1980a and also Jardine 1986, 40, and Schiesari 1989, 73.

33. Even in the case of Nogarola it is unclear how absolute her purported "retreat from the world" was and to what extent it was indeed motivated by the anonymous 1438 libel, which, however unpleasant, remained an isolated episode and unrepresentative of contemporaries' general reaction to her. For a useful recent reexamination of the episode and its implications, see Stevenson 2005, 162. Stevenson also contests Margaret King's classic reading of Antonio Loschi's 1389

tribute to Maddalena Scrovegni as paradigmatic of humanists' unease at the figure of the educated woman (see 156–58, and cf. King 1980b).

34. King and Rabil 1983, 25; King 1980b, 76; N. Rossi 2003, esp. 89, 92–93.

35. Stevenson 2005, 167, notes Costanza Varano's continuing studies and dates Battista Sforza's oration to Pope Pius II to 1461, the year following her marriage to Federico da Montefeltro. See also, on Battista, Clough 1996, 40, 48. Outside the ruling families an example of a woman who continued to circulate her works following marriage is Angela Nogarola (H. Parker 2002a, 13 and 20–21; Stevenson 2005, 163). Counterevidence is seemingly offered by the much-discussed case of Ginevra Nogarola, said to have abandoned her studies on marriage (King and Rabil 1983, 18; Nogarola 2004, 88; Stevenson 2005, 163–64), and by a sonnet of Laura Brenzoni's (Castoldi 1993, 76) seeming to suggest that she considered poetry (or perhaps simply love poetry, the immediate context) an inappropriate activity for a married woman like herself. On the general issue of the impact of marriage on women's studies, see Stevenson 2005, 164–65; also, for dynastic women in particular, Clough 1996, 54–55.

36. Bryce 2002.

37. Stevenson 2005, 152–53.

38. A. D'Elia 2004, 110–14. Stevenson 2005, 169, notes in connection with Veronica Gambara's marriage to Giberto da Correggio the tendency of men of that household to select wives known for their learning; the other examples Stevenson cites are Cassandra Colleoni (446) and Ginevra Rangoni (539). At a lower social level, it is interesting to note that Angelo Poliziano's famous letter of encomium of 1491 to Cassandra Fedele (see n. 100 below) assumes that when Cassandra takes a husband, this will enable her scholarship rather than impede it; he seems to envisage the kind of companionate union with a fellow humanist that would be realized in Alessandra Scala's marriage to the Greek poet Michele Marullo.

39. Besides Cereta and Isotta Nogarola, another female writer of the period to suffer slander as a result of her intellectual ambitions was Maddalena Scrovegni, singled out for satirical opprobrium for her learning in the anonymous misogynist poem, *Il Manganello,* dated by its modern editor to 1430–40; see *Manganello* 1982, xviii, 9–10. For the fifteenth-century literary tradition of misogyny generally, see ibid., xv–xvii.

40. Interesting in this regard is the consideration given by the fourteenth-century Florentine physician Dino del Garbo in his commentary on Guido Cavalcanti's philosophical poem "Donna me prega" to the seeming anomaly of Cavalcanti's addressing such a learned work to a woman. Unpacking the significance of the term *donna,* Dino notes that it implies three qualities in a woman that qualify her for such a compliment: maturity, moral integrity, and nobility of birth, the latter defined explicitly, along with her *honestas,* as "dignifying" her ("unde dignitatem habet ex honestate et ex prole generationis sue"). See Cornish 2000, 172, for discussion and references.

41. Feliciangeli 1894, 6; King and Rabil 1983, 35–38; Clough 1996, 45; Allen 2002, 704–6. Battista appears to have played a particularly prominent role within the

leadership of the Pesaro branch of the Malatesta family due to the inadequacy of her husband, Galeazzo, described aptly in Dalarun and Zinelli 2004, 33, as "un parfait incapable" ("completely inept"); see G. Franceschini 1973, 301–5, who notes that she was effectively left as ruler of the city after the deaths of Galeazzo's brothers Carlo (1438) and Pandolfo (1441).

42. Feliciangeli 1894, 24; Clough 1996, 35; also ibid., 33, for the political context. For a translation, see King and Rabil 1983, 39–41; for the Latin text, Feliciangeli 1894, 50–54. On Costanza Varano as orator, see also Allen 2002, 706–9.

43. See H. Parker 2002a, 13 and 20–21 for Nogarola's two poems of 1387 to Gian Galeazzo Visconti, who had recently taken over Verona in a coup and who would hold it until 1402, and of 1404 to Iacopo da Carrara, of the briefly restored former ruling dynasty of the city. For Maddalena Scrovegni's letter of 1388 to Jacopo del Verme, governor of Padua for the Visconti during their short-lived seizure of the city, see King and Rabil 1983, 33–35; Stevenson 2005, 157–58; also, for the context, Kohl 1998, 261–62.

44. For Sforza's oration, see King and Rabil 1983, 46–48, and Stevenson 2005, 172; for Fedele's, King and Rabil 1983, 69–73, and Fedele 2000, 155–59. King and Rabil cite the Latin editions. Fedele's oration was published four times between 1487 and 1494, the first secular work by a woman to be published. For a stylistic analysis of the speech, see Schlam 1986. Fedele is also credited with two further orations, both performed. On her speech in praise of the study of literature, deliverd to the Venetian doge (Agostino Barbarigo, doge from 1486–1501) and Senate, see Fedele 2000, 159–62; on that to the Queen of Poland, Bona Sforza, in 1556, Fedele 2000, 162–64.

45. See Nogarola 2004, 167–74 and also 161–63, on the context of the speech. A letter of Lodovico Foscarini's mentions a further oration by Nogarola, delivered before the pope (Nicholas V, the humanist Tommaso Parentucelli) and cardinals during a jubilee pilgrimage to Rome in 1450 (Nogarola 2004, 136 and n. 71). If this is a reliable notice, Nogarola's speech may have acted as prototype for the later speeches before popes of Ippolita Sforza (1459) and Battista Sforza (1461), both to Pius II (see Stevenson 2005, 167, on Battista's speech). Other women reputed to have composed orations in this period include Battista Petrucci of Siena (1452, to the Emperor Frederick III and Leonora of Portugal; see Killerby 1999, 258) and Nicolosa Sanuti of Bologna (1453; see Killerby 1999 and n. 16 above).

46. The passage in question is found in L. Bruni 2002, 104–5. For examples of readings of it as denying women the study of rhetoric, see, for example, King 1980a, 77; King and Rabil 1983, 14–15; Schiesari 1989, 73, 74; H. Parker 1997, 248; also, with varying emphases, Jardine 1986, 32–33, 35; Jones 1990, 21; Grantham Turner 2003, 74. For more nuanced recent discussions of the passage, see Allen 2002, 698–700, and Stevenson 2005, 154–55. I plan to discuss Bruni's supposed stricture against women studying rhetoric for public speaking in a forthcoming study.

47. On the figure of Hortensia, see Plant 2004, 104–5. Her speech is summarized (or reconstructed) in Appian's *Civil Wars,* 4:32–34, and is also discussed as in Valerius Maximus, *Memorable Sayings and Deeds,* 8.3.3, who, in the same passage,

gives another positive example of a Roman woman speaking in public (Maesia Sentinas, praised for her "virility") as well as a negative one, Gaia Afrania, whose shamelessness is said to have spurred legislation against women speaking in public (Hallett 1989, 66; though cf. Marshall 1990 for a less positive assessment of the figure of Maesia). The 1453 speech attributed to Nicolosa Sanuti consciously evokes the speech of Hortensia, which had been given in similar circumstances; see Stevenson 2005, 147. Nogarola also cites the figures of Hortensia, Maesia, and Afrania in a letter of c. 1439 defending women against the charge of loquaciousness (Nogarola 2004, 99); interesting here is her conversion of Afrania from a negative into a positive example.

48. Quintilian, 1.1.6 (citing Hortensia in the context of the desirability of women being educated in the interest of the education of their children), and Boccaccio 2001, 348–49.

49. For nuanced discussions of the moral anxieties surrounding women's speech, see Jones 1990, 15–28, who distinguishes between courtly and bourgeois contexts; also Erskin 1999. The issue is often oversimplified in criticism in such a way as to suggest that public speech in women was universally condemned.

50. For humanistic praises of female orations, see Clough 1996, 39, 46, 48, and Stevenson 2005, 154–55. On editions of Fedele's speech, see Pignatti 1995, 567, who also lists the laudatory compositions by fellow humanists attached to the various printed editions. Fedele 2000, 154, and Stevenson 2005, 172 n. 170, omit mention of the 1494 Modena edition.

51. H. Parker 2002b, 32–33, 36–38, 42–43, and Clough 1996, 46–47.

52. Stevenson 2005, 146–47.

53. A famous private and practically oriented female-authored vernacular letter collection of the period is that of Alessandra Macinghi Strozzi (1407–71), seventy-three of whose letters survive. For a description of her life and works, citing bibliography to the early 1990s, see Cocco 1994; also, more recently, A. Strozzi 1997; Doglio 2000, 16–18; and, for biography, Crabb 2000. Forty-nine letters of a similar, nonliterary character survive by Lucrezia Tornabuoni; see Tornabuoni 1993. An important earlier Florentine collection is that of Dora Guidalotti del Bene: see Guidalotti del Bene 2003.

54. Cereta's was also the only letter collection by a woman in this period that we know to have been authorially framed and published as a volume, although there is evidence that collections of Costanza Varano's and Isotta Nogarola's letters also circulated (Stevenson 2005, 146–48; Nogarola 2004, 107).

55. On the contrast between Cereta's and Fedele's letter collections, see Robin 1995, 189–90, and Robin 2000, 8.

56. Two lost Latin treatises, *De vera religione* and *De humanae conditionis fragilitate,* are sometimes attributed to Battista da Montefeltro; see Feliciangeli 1894, 15n. Cassandra Fedele is also recorded as having composed a treatise in her later years, *De scientiarum ordine* (Pignatti 1995, 568).

57. Cereta 1997; Nogarola 2004. Cereta herself describes her *Asinarium funus* as an "oration."

58. For discussion of the dialogue, see Allen 2002, 945–55; Nogarola 2004, 138–45; King and Robin 2004, 12–13; Fenster 2005; Smarr 2005a, 32–38; also Jardine 1986, 42–43 n. 40. For the Latin text, see Nogarola 1886, 2:187–216; for an English translation, Nogarola 2004, 145–58.

59. H. Parker 2002a, 14. Francesco Nogarola's edition of the dialogue was dedicated to the recently appointed bishop of Verona, Cardinal Bernardo Navagero (1507–65); hence the insertion as third interlocutor of Bernardo's ancestor Giovanni. See also on Francesco Nogarola's amendments Allen 2002, 966–68, and Smarr 2005a, 137–38. The text of the 1563 edition is reproduced in Nogarola 1886, 2:219–57.

60. King and Robin 2004 argue for Nogarola's final authorship of the text (Nogarola 2004, 140). Smarr, by contrast, represents it as a record of an actual epistolary exchange (Smarr 2005a, 132–33).

61. On the effects of constraints of social decorum in women's representation as speakers in sixteenth-century dialogue, see Cox 2000a.

62. For the Latin text of the dialogue, see Rabil 1981, 118–34; for an English translation, Cereta 1997, 182–202. For discussion, see ibid., 180–82; Rabil 1981, 52–54; Lorenzini 2001a, 142–43; Allen 2002, 991–92, Lorenzini noting the need for further scholarly and critical work.

63. On this theme in humanistic writings, see Selmi 1998; also, more generally, Ordine 1996a and b. Cereta's version lacks the philosophically dense theme of the ass's metamorphosis and seems more purely comic-satirical. On the stylistic vogue for Apuleius in late-Quattrocento prose and the associated interest in Pliny's *Natural History,* see D'Amico 1984, esp. 360–69, and also Cereta 1997, 87.

64. H. Parker 1997, 2002a and b. See also Stevenson 2005, 159 (on Angela Nogarola).

65. The poem opens, indeed, by noting that Costanza is writing following the frequent urging of her father, Piergentile da Varano, and her maternal grandfather, Galeazzo Malatesta. Gianlucido was the son of Galeazzo's sister Paola Malatesta Gonzaga and thus her second cousin. For the text of the poem, see H. Parker 2002b, 39–40; for its context, H. Parker 2002b, 32 and 35 n. 17.

66. For the text, see H. Parker 2002a, 18–19; for discussion, H. Parker 2002a, 11–12 (also in H. Parker 1997, 251–54).

67. For the texts and comment on their context, see H. Parker 2002a, 13, 20 (cf. H. Parker 1997, 254–55), and H. Parker 2002b, 13, 32. For other similarly "diplomatic" poems by the same authors, see H. Parker 2002a, 13, 25–26 (cf. H. Parker, 1997, 255–57), and H. Parker 2002b, 32–33, 47–48, 50–51. Interesting thematically within Angela Nogarola's oeuvre is her short poem to Niccolò de Facino, defending herself against an accusation of plagiarism, which ends by asserting women's natural intellectual equality with men and predicting the emergence of modern female poets to rival the ancients (H. Parker 2002a, 12–13, 19–20, 25). For evidence of poetic activity on the part of Cassandra Fedele, see Pignatti 1995, 566. A sole epigram by her survives.

68. Varano's letter and poem are printed together in H. Parker 2002b, 35–36,

along with a translation at 43–45. The poem is also in H. Parker 1997, 266–67, and the letter (in translation only) in King and Rabil 1983, 55–56. For discussion, see H. Parker 2002b, 32, and Nogarola 2004, 102–3. Nogarola appears to have initiated the exchange, although her letters to Varano are lost. For Scala's epigram, see H. Parker 1997, 267–69. For evidence of Greek study on the part of Costanza Varano and Battista Sforza, see Clough 1996, 39–41 and Fileteco 1992; also Cutolo 1955, 123, and Welch 1995, 124, on Ippolita Sforza's Greek studies.

69. The lengths of the poems are, respectively, 342 lines, 92 lines, and 966 lines. See H. Parker 1997, 258–60, on Angela Nogarola; 260–66, on Isotta Nogarola (also in H. Parker 2002a, 14–15 and 21–23), and Benzoni 1939 on Brenzoni (Stevenson 2005, 167, mentions Brenzoni's poem but misdescribes the subject). The texts of the poems by Isotta Nogarola and Brenzoni may be found in the studies cited. For the complete text of Angela Nogarola's *Liber de virtutibus,* see Nogarola 1886, 2:312–26.

70. Petrarch was born in Arezzo to Florentine exiles and lived in Avignon and northern Italy but was still conventionally claimed as a Florentine. For an overview of the fortunes of the vernacular in the Quattrocento, see Formentin 1996a, citing further bibliography at 207–10.

71. On the relation between Lorenzo's output and that of Lucrezia Tornabuoni, see Tylus 2001a, 26–27.

72. For an overview of these genres and Tornabuoni's practice of them, see Tylus 2001a, 38–45; also, on the *lauda,* Serventi 2004, 79. Tornabuoni's single surviving sonnet (Tornabuoni 1978, 42) is probably indicative of a more extensive practice of the genre, documented in a letter of Poliziano's of 1479 (R. Russell 1994d, 434; Bryce 1999, 144 n. 26), which mentions *"sonetti,"* as well as *"ternari"* (terza rima poems) and *"laude."*

73. See the text between nn. 93 and 95.

74. As noted in the text, Battista delivered an oration to the Emperor Sigismund in 1433 on behalf of members of her family. For her letter to Martin V concerning her sister-in-law Cleofe Malatesta, married to a Byzantine prince and under pressure to convert from Catholicism, see Clough 1996, 45. Clough also mentions on pp. 44–45 an oration that Battista is sometimes reputed to have delivered to the same pope following his election in late 1417. This tradition is questioned by Feliciangeli 1894, 15n, who notes that it may have arisen from a misunderstanding on the part of early biographers such as Sabadino degli Arienti and Foresti.

75. On the dramatic events leading to Battista's decision to retire to Santa Lucia, see G. Franceschini 1973, 304–5.

76. For a careful consideration of the degree of Tornabuoni's influence in Florence and the means by which it was exerted, see Tylus 2001a, 30–38; also Tomas 2003, passim.

77. Morabito 1999, 11; also B. Croce 1953a, 72–75, who cites evidence suggesting that the name was conferred on her by Alfonso, Duke of Calabria.

78. Two of Minutolo's letters are addressed to Eleonora (nos. 2–3 in the mod-

ern edition [Minutolo 1999, 34–37]), while another addresses Ippolita's husband, Alfonso, Duke of Calabria (no. 19, 57–58); see also B. Croce 1953a, 72–74, for two further letters to Alfonso from a manuscript not available to Minutolo's modern editor. Eleonora's later career in Ferrara is discussed in the body of the text.

79. For letters of homage to princes, see, besides those cited in n. 78, no. 24 (Minutolo 1999, 79–80) to Federico d'Aragona (1451–1504), in the voice of "Theophilo"; also, in a slightly different genre, no. 27 (56–57) to Federico's father, Ferdinando d'Aragona, king of Naples, petitioning him for a second husband (Minutolo was married twice, both times to Neapolitan patricians, Francesco Brancaccio and Camillo Capece Piscicelli). For letters commenting on literary texts, see nos. 8, 20, and 25 (43–44, 58–60, 65–66). For the letter of self-defense, which makes an interesting point of comparison with those of Veronica Franco in the following century, see no. 6 (40–41); for deflections of praise, nos. 7–8, 22 (41–44, 62); also B. Croce 1953a, 72–74.

80. Minutolo 1999, 34 ("parenti et strectissimi amici"). The phrase seems to refer specifically to the male-voiced letters of the collection, which are attributed to the multipurpose persona of "Theophilo," also the addressee of numerous letters; those in a female voice are said to be "ficte" ("feigned"). The closest point of comparison for Minutolo's letter collection is offered by Francesco Galeota's *Colibeto,* assembled around the mid-1480s. Galeota appears to have known Mintuolo, who figures in the *Colibeto* as the addressee of a letter, under her literary name of "Sybilla" (no. 28 [Galeota 1987, 155–56; cf. Galeota 1987, 120, 205–6]).

81. Minutolo 1999, 34 (no. 1).

82. See "Celia Romana" 1562; "Emilia N." 1594.

83. The word "audacity" is taken from Mintuolo's dedicatory letter, in a phrase referring to Francesco Arcella's role in spurring her to publication: "Ma in quello me defende tu cohortatore, lo quale me hai incitata ad tal audace fatto" ("But you can defend me as the person who urged me and incited me to such a daring deed" [Minutolo 1999, 34]). The translation is mine, as are all translations in the text and notes except where attributed.

84. Degli Aleardi's surviving poems, consisting, besides the sonnet mentioned in the text (in fact a *sonetto caudato*), is a reply *capitolo* addressed to Niccolò Malpigli of Bologna. Both are reproduced in Pacchioni 1907, 21–24. For discussion, see, besides Pacchioni's article, Bandini Buti 1946, 1:29; Rabboni 2002, 113, 120, 133.

85. On Mattugliani, see Bandini Buti 1946, 2:18. For the text of her surviving poem, a *capitolo* addressed to the short-lived signor of Cremona, Carlo Cavalabò, datable precisely to 1404–6, see Bergalli 1726, 1, 7–15. Other fourteenth and fifteenth-century female vernacular poets found cited in some sources are in many cases apocryphal (see the text in ch. 5 at n. 61 and ch. 6, n. 67, below); poets affected include Lagia or Livia Chiavelli, Leonora Genga, Ortensia di Guglielmo and Giustina Levi-Perotti.

86. On Veronese humanistic culture in this period, see Viti 1996, 541–44. On vernacular lyric, see Rabboni 2002. Medea degli Aleardi was a friend and poetic correspondent of Giovanni Nogarola (d. 1406), Angela's brother and Isotta Noga-

rola's uncle, who was executed for his participation in a conspiracy against the new Venetian regime.

87. See the recent editions of Vigri's works in Vigri 2000a and 2000b; also Tylus 1995 and the studies in Leonardi, ed. 2004. On the period of her education in Ferrara (1422–24), see Sberlati 2004, 92. A useful brief survey of fifteenth-century religious writing in the convents is Zarri 2000b, 79–85; see also Stevenson 2005, 174–76; Dalarun and Zinelli 2004; Graziosi 2004. On the literary culture of fifteenth-century convents more generally, see Gill 1994.

88. The most famous of Varano's numerous writings, edited in Varano 1958, are her autobiographical *Vita spirituale* (1491) and her dialogue on the passion, *Dolori mentali di Gesù*. Bembo's principal work is the *Specchio di illuminazione*, her spiritual biography of Caterina de' Vigri, whom she succeeded as abbess of Corpus Domini, Bologna; see I. Bembo 2001 for an edition. On her background and education, see I. Bembo 2001, xix–xx, xxxv. On the very active intellectual culture of Corpus Domini, encouraged by Caterina, see Zarri 2000a, 156–78, and I. Bembo 2001, xxxix–xl. Another important female-authored "spiritual biography" of the period is that of Eustochia Calefati of Messina (1434–85) by Iacopa Pollicini of Santa Lucia di Foligno; see I. Bembo 2001, xxxix; Zarri 2000b, 83.

89. Zarri 2000b, 84–85.

90. Stevenson 2005, 174–76. An interesting discussion of the relation of secular classical studies to the religious life is found in a letter from the Venetian humanist and cleric Gregorio Correr (1409–64) to Cecilia Gonzaga; see King and Rabil 1983, 92–105, esp. 102–5; Allen 2002, 680–82; Stevenson 2005, 175.

91. The influence of Catherine of Siena is likely to have been fundamental in this association between female devotion and the vernacular. On the circulation of manuscripts of her letters in fifteenth-century Italy, see Zancan 1992, 598–99; on the conventual provenance of the manuscript used by Aldo Manuzio for his important 1500 printed edition, commissioned by a Venetian abbess, see Zancan 1992, 600, and Tylus 2001b, 117.

92. Two religious poems by Battista da Montefeltro have recently been published, in Bernardi Triggiano 1999 and Dalarun and Zinelli 2004. See also da Montefeltro 1847 for an edition of four further poems. On Santa Lucia di Foligno as a context for literary exchange and production, see Gill 1994, 67–69; Dalarun and Zinelli 2004, 21–31; on its contacts with the Bolognese convent of Corpus Domini, where Caterina Vigri was active in these years, see ibid., 30.

93. Interesting examples of Battista's early poetry, including an exchange with Malatesta, are published in Montefeltro 1859; see also Malatesti 1982, 177–80. On Malatesta Malatesta as poet, see ibid.; Angiolini 2002, 46–52. Battista's brother, Guidantonio da Montefeltro, was also known as a poet; see Santagata 1984, 57. See also ibid., 64–65 for brief remarks on Battista as poet.

94. See Bernardi Triggiani 1999, 88–115, for the text of the 175-line poem (incipit "O glorioso padre, almo doctore"), which survives in thirteen manuscripts of the fifteenth and sixteenth centuries. Important with regard to Battista's cultural self-positioning are lines 61–69 (Bernardi Triggiano 1999, 95–96), which recount

the tale of Jerome's famous dream-induced conversion away from his previous overattachment to pagan literature (here emblematized by Cicero and Plato; 1.62); these seem clearly applicable to the author herself, who had taken her vows under the name of Suor Geronima.

95. For a brief comparison of the two poets, see Dalarun and Zinelli 2004, 35; see also, on Caterina's *laude,* Serventi 2004. Professor Tonia Bernardi Triggiano informs me that she is planning an edition of Battista's verse. For a list of existing partial editions (most quite inaccessible), see Dalarun and Zinelli 2004, 34 n. 51.

96. Although female-voiced poetry was not uncommon in medieval Italy (see Kleinhenz 1995; Steinberg 2007, 67–70, 86–89) and claims have been made for the female authorship of some of it, especially that attributed to the so-called "Compiuta Donzella" (on whom see, most recently, Steinberg 2006), there is nothing in the Italian tradition to approach the rich Provençal tradition of the *trobaritz*. Nor is there much evidence to support the various legends we find concerning women's presence in the medieval universities (on which see Stevenson 2005, 149–50). The most direct postclassical role model for aspirant fifteenth-century Italian women authors was likely to have been Catherine of Siena (1347–80), regarded unproblematically in the period as a writer, though modern scholars debate the extent of her literacy (Tylus 2001b, 143 n. 42). On Catherine's relation to the written word, see also, more broadly, Tylus 2008.

97. Malatesta was a personal friend of Petrarch's (Dotti 1987, 313, 315, 416–17; 420–21), as was Della Seta (on whom see Billanovich 1996, 557–79). Loschi, born later, did not know Petrarch directly, but drew on his scholarship and manuscripts in composing his own best-known work, *Inquisitio artis in orationibus Ciceronis* (see Billanovich 1996, 108, 112, 115–16). Nogarola's correspondence with Malatesta and Loschi's with Scrovegni are discussed in the text. On Della Seta's dedication of a treatise in praise of women to Scrovegni see n. 130 below. It is intriguing to note that the earliest Italian female humanists, Scrovegni and Angela Nogarola, were contemporaries of Christine de Pizan (c.1364–c.1430), who was born to Italian parents in Venice, although she moved to France as a very young girl. On the humanistic contacts of Christine's father, the medic and astrologer Tommaso da Pizzano, who lived in Venice for around a decade (1357–68), see Allen 2002, 541.

98. For the text, see L. Bruni 2002; for discussion Allen 2002, 691–70. The date of the work's composition is debated, with proposals as disparate as 1405 and 1429 being suggested: see Clough 1996, 38 and n. 22, and Allen 2002, 691 n. 96. Important to the debate is whether the treatise is conceived of as having been composed as a guide to Battista's own studies, which would suggest an earlier date, or as a suggested program for the education of her daughter Elisabetta (b. 1407).

99. For a translation of Quirini's letter, see King and Rabil 1983, 112–16; Nogarola 2004, 107–13; for the Latin text, Nogarola 1886, 2:9–22. For discussion, see King and Rabil 1983, 111–12; Jardine 1986, 29–31; Nogarola 2004, 103–4. On the distinctive, philosophically-inflected model of humanism cultivated in fifteenth-century Venice and Padua and reflected in Quirini's proposed curriculum, see King 1986, 182–85, 212–14, 224–25, 234–35, and Branca 1981, 132–33, 144–45, 148–55.

100. For translations of Poliziano's letter to Fedele of 1491, see King and Rabil 1983, 126–27; Fedele 2000, 90–91. The Latin text can be found in Poliziano 2006, 188–93. For an incisive analysis of Poliziano's rhetoric in the letter, see Jardine 1986, 48–50. On Loschi's tribute to Scrovegni, see King 1981 and Stevenson 2005, 157–58. For the text of Guarino's letter to Iacopo Foscari, praising the Nogarola sisters, see Guarini 1915–19, 2:292–94; for discussion, Jardine 1986, 35–36, and Nogarola 2004, 41. For Foscarini's letter to Nogarola, see Nogarola 1886, 2:39–51; King and Rabil 1983, 117–21; Nogarola 2004, 131–37. For further examples, see the letters from Guarino and Guiniforte Barzizza (1406–63) to Costanza Varano (Feliciangeli 1894, 57–59; Barzizza and Barzizza 1723, 134–36) and from Guarino's son Girolamo to Isotta Nogarola (Nogarola 1886, 1:93–102, and Nogarola 2004, 43).

101. See, for example, the letters to Fedele from Lodovico da Schio of Vicenza and Girolamo Broianico of Verona in Fedele 2000, 65 and 82–83 (cf. Fedele 1636, 144–46 and 174–76 for the Latin texts). For Dante Aligheri's letter to Laura Brenzoni, mentioned in Benzoni 1939, 187, see Maffei 1731, 215–16.

102. Anticipations of this development might be detected earlier in Dante's representation of women in the *Commedia,* which presents interesting novelties with regard to his earlier works; see Barolini 2005, esp. 171–73, for comment.

103. For the text, see Boccaccio 2001. For a detailed recent study, citing previous literature, see Kolsky 2003. Particularly useful, among previous readings, are McLeod 1991, 59–80; Benson 1992, 9–31; Collina 1996, 108–12. On the relation of the text to Petrarch's *De viris illustribus,* see Kolsky 2003, 40–42.

104. Petrarch had met the Empress Anna during a stay at the Imperial court in Prague in summer 1356, as an envoy of the Visconti (Bayley 1942, 332–33; Dotti 1987, 314–15). On his relations with the Emperor, who had awarded him the title of Count Palatine in 1357, see Bayley 1942; Borchardt 1975.

105. On Petrarch's letter and its relation to Boccaccio's *De claris mulieribus,* see Kolsky 2003, 40–47; Filosa 2004. For the text of the letter, see Petrarca 1942, 61–68. For discussion of Petrarch's role in evolving a classicizing discourse of female exemplarity in his late vernacular poetry, see Cox 2005b, 587–90.

106. The ambiguities of Boccaccio's text have been the focus of much recent criticism; see, for example, the discussions in Jordan 1990, 35–40; McLeod 1991; Benson 1992. Collina 1996, 108–12, usefully stresses the text's literary character, suggesting that it is best approached as a sui generis novella collection rather than a treatise. See also Kolsky 2003, 17–23, xii–xiv, who notes that the text's ideological tensions are in part a legacy of its protracted and complex process of composition. On the *Decameron*'s similar ambiguity with regard to gender issues, see Migiel 2006. Boccaccio was, of course, also the author of one of the foundational texts of vernacular misogynist literature, *Il Corbaccio,* datable to to the mid-1350s or 1360s.

107. Benson 1992, 45, identifies the origin of this fusion in the late fifteenth- and early sixteenth-century treatises of Bartolomeo Goggio (*De laudibus mulierum*) and Agostino Strozzi (*Defensio mulierum*), both of which are discussed in the text.

108. On the effective double dedication of the *De claris mulieribus* (Boccaccio notes in his dedication that he is addressing it to Andrea Acciaiuoli as he dares not aspire to a dedication to Giovanna) see Benson 1992, 12–13, and Kolsky 2003, 114–

15. On the biography of Giovanna—a late addition to the text, as was the dedication to Acciaiuoli—see Benson 1992, 28–31.

109. For a clear statement of Aristotelian thinking on sex and gender and its influence on early modern culture, see Maclean 1980 and Allen 2002, 65–179.

110. The classic instances of this are the accounts of marriage in the Venetian Francesco Barbaro's *De re uxoria* (1416) and the Florentine Leon Battista Alberti's *Della famiglia* (1434–37). For summaries of their arguments, see Jordan 1990, 40–53; Jones 1990, 20–21; Allen 2002, 718–816; 712–24; see also recently, on Barbaro, Frick 2004. Kolsky 1998 usefully contrasts the treatment of marriage in Florentine writings of the fifteenth century, including Alberti, and those produced in court contexts, noting the "radicalism" of the latter as attempts to "rethink the role of women in society" (247). On women's greater visibility within dynastic and courtly regimes, with respect to republics, see also Swain 1986, 175, 191–94; Hughes 1987, esp. 30–31, 41–42; Herlihy 1995, 41, 289; Manca 2003, esp. 92–93; Hurlburt 2006, esp. 532.

111. On the latter role, see the useful observations of San Juan 1991, 70. An extensive general listing of recent bibliography on the position of women in Italian Renaissance court culture is found in Tomas 2003, 8–9 n. 4. For a recent overview of fifteenth-century women's position in Italian court culture, see Welch 2000.

112. For the text of Carafa's *Memoriale,* see Carafa 1988, 97–209; for its date of composition (pre-1477), ibid., 9. The edition also includes a shorter and more narrowly focused *memoriale* for Eleonora's sister, Beatrice d'Aragona, advising her on her conduct during her journey to meet her husband Mattias Corvinus of Hungary in 1476 (211–43). For discussion of both, see Guerra 2005. On Cornazzano's *De modo di regere,* see Zancani 2000, 64–67, and Manca 2003, who focuses on the impressive introductory miniature by Cosmè Tura showing Eleonora being divinely invested the baton of rule. The poem was published in 1517.

113. For an admiring description of Eleonora d'Aragona's role in the court of Ferrara, stressing the power deriving to her from her natal family, see Gundersheimer 1980b. See also the more nuanced accounts of Ippolita Sforza's married life as Duchess of Calabria in Welch 1995 and Bryce 2002; also Shemek 2005b on Isabella d'Este. An early and ambiguous Italian literary response to the phenomenon of the court lady is Dante's portrayal of the Didoesque Francesca da Polenta or Francesca da Rimini (d. c.1285) in canto 5 of his *Inferno.* See Barolini 2000 for a politically contextualized reading of the episode.

114. On the centrality of history and historical exemplification within the humanists' rhetorical method, see Struever 1970; Hampton 1990; Lyons 1990.

115. Carmenta was the mythical early poet-prophetess mentioned in book 8 of the *Aeneid;* she was credited with the invention of the Latin alphabet. The theory of euhemerism, which interpreted classical deities as mythologized versions of originally historical figures, allowed for the claiming as historical of goddesses such as Minerva and Isis.

116. Insightful studies of this tradition and its rhetorical contexts are McLeod 1991 and Collina 1996; see also Pomata 1993, 12–15; Ajmar 2000; Franklin 2006.

117. On the notion of women as "same and other" in Roman elite culture, see Hallett 1989. For a differentiation between Greek and Roman attitudes in this regard, see ibid., 67. As Joan Kelly noted (1984, 21–22), Renaissance humanistic writings on gender stemming from republican bourgeois contexts tend to reproduce the Greek "separatist" model. The point is sometimes misleadingly extended to humanism in general; see, for example, Schiesari 1989, 67.

118. A modern edition exists of Sabadino degli Arienti's treatise (Sabadino degli Arienti 1888). For discussion, see Zaccaria 1978; Benson 1992, 40–44; Collina 1996, 113–14; Sabadino degli Arienti 2001, 56–57; Kolsky 2005, 63–109. On Goggio, see Fahy 1956, 32–36; Gundersheimer 1980a; Benson 1992, 56–64; Kolsky 2005, 175–90. On Foresti, see Zaccaria 1978; Collina 1996, 112–13; Kolsky 2005, 117–37. An earlier (and slighter) encomiastic work on women addressed to a ruler-consort is Antonio Cornazzano's *De mulieribus admirandis* (c. 1466–68); see Benson 1992, 36–37; Zancani 2000, 62–64. See also the semianonymous defense of women written in polemic with the misogynist *Manganello* (c. 1430–40), published in *Manganello* 1982, xxvii–xxx, 47–63.

119. It is clear from the accompanying letter that Sabadino degli Arienti sent with the gift of his *Gynevera* to the 18-year-old Isabella d'Este in 1492 that he was hoping for an introduction to her husband, Francesco Gonzaga (Sabadino degli Arienti 2001, 125). I take the terms "threshold patron" here from Regan 2005, which is useful in respect of the whole question of humanists' relations with court women. See also Zancani 2000, esp. 61–62.

120. Where the late fifteenth century is concerned, the recent biographies by Carolyn James and Stephen Kolsky of Sabadino and Mario Equicola give an opportunity to gauge the role of women in court intellectuals' patronage strategies; see also James's edition of Sabadino's letters (Kolsky 1991; James 1996; Sabadino degli Arienti 2001).

121. An interesting parallel is offered here by Plutarch, whose *Mulierum virtutes,* in one recent reading (McInerney 2003, 342–43) can be seen as reflecting its author's position as a Greek intellectual under the dominion of Rome: "What concerns him is a power relationship in which weaker impacts favourably upon stronger, in which the weaker partner can inspire the stronger and has within it the potential to match the stronger. That is the position he allows women in relation to men and it is the relationship he desires for Greece with Rome" (342). See also the observations on this same dynamic in Castiglione in Freccero 1992, 271.

122. The notion that noblewomen's utility within aristocratic family strategies depended precisely on their status as "outsiders" to power is discussed in a seventeenth-century context in Ago 1992, esp. 260–61. For the period we are looking at, see Shemek 2005b on Isabella d'Este's epistolary negotiation of family interests and Bryce 2007 on Ippolita Sforza's correspondence with Lorenzo de' Medici; also the brief but suggestive remarks of Stevenson 2005, 157–58, on Angela Nogarola and Maddalena Scrovegni's diplomatic activity on behalf of their families.

123. On the manuscript fortunes of the text, see Branca 1958, 1:92–98 and 2:57–

62; Franklin 2006, 10–13. Branca lists 105 surviving manuscripts (16 from the Trecento), as well as 33 recorded but lost. On the translations of the text, by Donato Albanzani da Casentino (d. 1411), dedicated to Niccolò d'Este, Marquis of Ferrara (1383–1441) and Antonio da Sant'Elpidio, the latter Tuscanized by Niccolò Sassetti and published in 1506, see Kolsky 2003, 172–74, and Franklin 2006, 11, citing existing bibliography. More generally on the fortunes of the text, see Kolsky 2003, 172–79; Kolsky 2005; Franklin 2006.

124. Franklin 2006, esp. 57–113.

125. Boccaccio 2001, 180–85 (Nicaula; ch. 43); 192–95 (Sappho; ch. 46); 348–49 (Hortensia; ch. 84); 352–54 (Cornifica; ch. 86); 410–17 (Proba; ch. 97). On the novelty of Boccaccio's celebration of creative women (his biographies also encompass female painters such as Irene and Marcia), see McLeod 1991, 68. A further important document of Boccaccio's interest in the figure of the female writer is his twelfth eclogue, on Sappho; see S. Campbell 2004, 202–3, for discussion.

126. See Boccaccio 2001, 316–19 (Sempronia; ch. 76); 251–53 (Leontium; ch. 60); 436–41 ("Pope Joan"; ch. 101); also, for their counterposition to the virtuous female creatives just listed, Mcleod 1991, 73.

127. On Boccaccio's source, Jerome's translation-revision of Eusebius's *Chronicon,* see Kolsky 2003, 64 and 197 n. 19. On the life of Cornificia as a late addition to *De claris mulieribus,* see ibid., 18; Franklin 2006, 54. The historical evidence for Cornificia is assessed at Stevenson 2005, 33–34.

128. See especially the remark in his life of Cornificia (Boccaccio 2001, 354): "O femineum decus neglexisse muliebria et studiis maximorum vatum applicuisse ingenium!" ("How glorious it is for a woman to scorn womanish concerns and to turn her mind to the study of the great poets!" [trans. Virginia Brown]) (355).

129. Boccaccio 2001, 349 (trans. Virginia Brown; Latin text on p. 348). The example derives from Valerius Maximus, 8.3.3; for the context, see n. 47 above. A similar reception dynamic to that described here may be perceived for Plutarch's *Mulierum virtutes (On the Courage of Women),* rediscovered in the fifteenth century and first translated into Latin in the 1460s by the Florentine humanist Alamanno Rinuccini. While modern critics see Plutarch's text as sharing some of Boccaccio's ambivalence with regard to women's role and capacities (McInerney 2003), Plutarch's exempla were nonetheless eminently co-optable to profeminist ends; he was used, for example, by Strozzi and Equicola, as well as the more conservative Vespasiano da Bisticci (see Kolsky 2005, 154, 160). On the fifteenth-century fortunes of the text (first published in Rinuccini's translation in Brescia in 1485), see Joost-Gaugier 1982, 279–81. On its sixteenth-century diffusion, see Collina 1996, 115.

130. Besides the surviving works detailed below, mention should be made of the lost treatise dedicated to Maddalena Scrovegni by Petrarch's collaborator Lombardo della Seta, entitled *De laudibus aliquot feminarum gentilium aut litteris aut armis illustrium (On the Praises of Some Women of the Ancient World Celebrated in Letters and Arms),* see Billanovich 1996, 574. The work is the more intriguing in that it focuses specifically on the fields of letters and arms, the former, of course, of direct relevance to Maddalena herself.

131. For the figures named, aside from those already discussed, see Plant 2004, 29–33 (Telesilla); 38–40 (Praxilla); 41–42 (Aspasia); 56–60 (Anyte); 101–3 (Cornelia), 245 (Hypatia). See also A. D'Elia 2004, 112, on a wedding oration for Ippolita Sforza comparing her to Aspasia, Diotima, Proba, Hortensia, Macrina (probably St. Macrina the Younger, sister of St. Basil and St. Gregory of Nyssa), and Aemilia Africana (probably Aemilia Paulla, wife of Scipio Africanus and mother to Cornelia, much cited for her learning). A vernacular example of the same rhetorical motif can be seen in *Rime* 1994, 37 (lines 115–17), referring to Laura Brenzoni. The figures named there are Cleobulina, Hortensia, Sappho, and Corinna; also the Greek philosopher Hipparchia (Plant 2004, 245), the Roman poet Sulpitia (Plant 2004, 248), and Lastenia and Assiotea, supposed pupils of Plato (Equicola 2004, 53 n. 48). See also the vernacular poem in praise of Costanza Varano printed in appendix to Feliciangeli 1894, esp. 73, for a comparison of Varano to Sappho, Proba, and Cornificia.

132. See Nogarola 2004, 52, and H. Parker 2002b, 36. Varano also names another, unidentifiable writer, "Elphe" or "Nelpe." It is possible that this may be a scribal distortion of the name Sappho, given Bruni's citation of Aspasia, Cornelia, and Sappho in the opening page of his *De studiis et litteris,* dedicated to her grandmother Battista da Montefeltro.

133. An interesting, if perhaps rhetorically ill-calculated, aspect of Cereta's list is its moral inclusiveness; it happily encompasses learned women generally framed as sexually deviant (Sempronia, Leontium, Semiramis) alongside virtuous exemplars such as Cornelia and Nicaula. Nogarola is more circumspect in this regard, though in a similar list of famous women in a letter to Damiano del Borgo of 1439–40, she cites, along with other Roman female orators Gaia Afrania, censored for her audacity by Valerius Maximus (8.3.2); see Nogarola 2004, 99, and, for the Latin, Jardine 1986, 39 n. 27.

134. A table of these correspondences is found in Kolsky 2005, 231–32. Prior to Sabadino's treatise, we already find a listing of modern "famous women" in the 1453 oration attributed to Nicolosa Sanuti of Bologna; see n. 16 above.

135. Da Bisticci's short series of lives of modern Italian female worthies ("donne istate in Italia degne") are found in da Bisticci 1999, 103–13. On his social conservatism and its context, see Benson 1992, 34, 36–40; also Kolsky 2005, 37–61, esp. 52. Both Benson and Kolsky contrast da Bisticci's life of Battista da Montefeltro with that of Sabadino degli Arienti, bringing out the latter's far greater emphasis on Battista's intellectual attainments and governmental role (Benson 1992, 42–43; Kolsky 2005, 50–52). For Equicola (1470–1525), see Equicola 2004, 38–40; cf. Kolsky 2005, 154. For Foresti, see Kolsky 2005, 119–20. See also A. D'Elia 2004, 111, 113, 115, on the use of modern examples of "famous women" in humanistic wedding orations.

136. See on this Kolsky 2005, 81–82, with reference to Sabadino degli Arienti.

137. Sabadino degli Arienti 2001, 126 n. 4: "legeremola cum attentione et sforzeremose imitare le vestigie di quelle illustri matrone." The letter is dated 3 July 1492. Sabadino also gave a copy of the text to Isabella's mother, Eleonora d'Aragona, whose own mother, Isabella di Chiaramonte, is among the "famous

women" included; see Sabadino degli Arienti 2001, 58 and Kolsky 2005, 81. The question of the degree to which the circulation of "famous women" literature generated existential emulation in female readers is touched on in Collina 1996, 119.

138. On de Roberti's paintings, see Manca 2003, 86–92; Franklin 2006, 131–48. For discussion of the figure of Bradamante in Boiardo, see Tomalin 1982, 83, 91–94, and Marinelli 1986, 52–79. Although she had figured in earlier epics as the sister of Rinaldo, Boiardo's identification of her as cofounder of the Este dynasty was a significant innovation, positing as it did a symbolic genealogical connection between her *virtù* and that of present-day Este women.

139. On Strozzi's *Defensio,* see Fahy 1956, 40–47; Benson 1992, 47–56; Kolsky 2005, 159–69. On Equicola's *De mulieribus,* see Equicola 2004; also Fahy 1956, 36–40, Kolsky 1991, 67–76; Kolsky 2005, 148–58. Another, less innovative "defense of women" from this period, surviving in a single manuscript, is Bernardino Cacciante's *Libro apologetico delle donne* (1503–4), dedicated to Elisabetta Gonzaga; see M. Martini 1982. As in the case of Eleonora d'Aragona, a cycle of "famous women" images has been associated conjecturally with Isabella d'Este's patronage: Andrea Mantegna's celebrated series of grisailles or *bronzi finti* that may have stood over one of the doors of her *studiolo;* see on these Franklin 2006, 148–74, though, compare, for example, S. Campbell 2004, 68.

140. See Gundersheimer 1980b; Tuohy 1996, 40, 98–99; Edelstein 2000; Manca 2003; A. D'Elia 2004, 111–12; Kolsky 2005, 111–13; Franklin 2006, 118–20.

141. The bibliography on Isabella is immense. Useful recent studies, citing previous bibliography, include San Juan 1991; N. Rossi 2003; S. Campbell 2004; Shemek 2005b; Welch 2005, 245–73. See also Kolsky 2005, 113–15, which compares the position and role of Eleonora d'Aragona in Ferrara and Isabella d'Este in Mantua. Isabella's younger sister, the short-lived Beatrice d'Este, Duchess of Milan, showed qualities and ambitions comparable with those of her mother and sister. For a biography, see Cartwright 2002a.

142. A valuable direct testimony to Eleonora's alertness to contemporary pro-feminist discourse is the letter written in her name in 1488 in response to letters of praise from Cassandra Fedele: see Fedele 2000, 29–30; also Fedele 1636, 161–62, for the Latin text. For Eleonora's earlier association with Ceccarella Mintuolo, see n. 78 above.

143. See ch. 2, sec. 1.

144. For the text of the poem, see Capasso 1990, 59–71. The widows are praised for their "intelligence, valor, wisdom, and fortitude" ("ingegno, valor, senno" and "forteze") as well as their beauty and chastity (p. 70, 2.392); see also p. 67 (2.284–86) where Costanza d'Avalos is singled out further for her "great learning" (*summa doctrina*).

145. Capasso 1990, 49–58.

146. Da Schio was rector of the faculty of medicine and philosophy at Padua University at the time that Fedele delivered her oration *Pro Bertucio Lamberti* there in 1487. For the text of the letter, see Fedele 1636, 144–45; for a translation, Fedele

2000, 65. Diana Robin's translation of *muliebre genus dicendi* as "womanish art of speaking" has a more disparaging tone than the original phrase.

147. See Poliziano 2006, 188 for the Latin text. The translation here is based on that of Shane Butler (Poliziano 2006, 189), with some modification.

148. The only postclassical woman Boccaccio credits with learning is the negative example of Pope Joan, whose learning, however, takes a distinctly "medieval" and scholastic form (she is seen is a quasi-university context, lecturing publicly, disguised as a man, in the Curia). This indecorously "professional," "transvestite" model of female learning is contrasted with an aristocratic-classicizing model compatible with feminine social decorum, most perfectly realized in the Christian Proba.

149. Nogarola 1886, 2, 39–51; King and Rabil 1983, 117–21; Nogarola 2004, 131–37.

150. Kristeller 1979, 85–105, esp. 92–93; cf. Witt 2003, 1–5.

151. On humanism and masculinity, see the observations—from various angles—of Ong 1959; P. Parker 1989; Celenza 2004, 115–33. Interesting in this context are the recent analyses of masculinity within the Roman rhetorical texts Renaissance humanists were drawing on in their self-fashioning: see on this Gleason 1995; Connolly 1999; Gunderson 2000; also, for a comparative analysis between Quintilian and Castiglione in this regard, Rebhorn 1993.

152. Jardine 1986, 51–53.

153. Kolsky 2003, 156.

154. Jardine 1986, 56–57.

155. On such figurations of scholarly seclusion for women, see King 1978, 1980a, 74–75; 1980b, who represents such language as gender-specific. As Jane Stevenson has recently noted in the case of Scrovegni, there are grounds for skepticism regarding the literal truth of these representations of learned women's isolation from the world (Stevenson 2005, 157–58). On humanist descriptions of seclusion and asceticism as ideal enabling conditions for scholarship, see S. Campbell 2004, 36–37. Zarri 2000a, 151, notes that the image of Isotta Nogarola found in the illustrations to Foresti 1497 draws on imagery traditionally associated with the figures of Sts. Jerome and Augustine in their studies. For the image (which is in fact generic and was used in the work to introduce the biographies of other literary women), see Kolsky 2005, 143, fig. 6.

156. This relative neglect during her lifetime translated into a more durable exclusion of Cereta from the "canon" of fifteenth-century female erudites: see, for example, Giuseppe Betussi's sixteenth-century update to Boccaccio's *De claris mulieribus* (Betussi 1545), which omits Cereta from its list of fifteenth-century "famous women" while including Angela, Ginevra, and Isotta Nogarola, Laura Brenzoni, and Cassandra Fedele.

157. This is recognized in Enea Silvio Piccolomini's recommendation to Ladislas of Bohemia (1440–57) in his *De liberorum educatione* (1450) that "a moderate level of eloquence will be sufficient for a king" ("satis erit regi facundia mediocris"); for the text and translation, see E. Piccolomini 2002, 244–45; for discussion Pizzani 1991, 325.

158. L. Bruni 2002, 112–13.

159. Fedele 2000, 65.

160. On the quarter-century hiatus in the presence of ducal consorts in Ferrara prior to Eleonora's arrival, see Gundersheimer 1980b, 44. Of the Este family, Sabadino degli Arienti's *Gynevera* records among its "famous women" only Eleonora's mother-in-law Ricciarda da Saluzzo (d. 1474) (Sabadino degli Arienti 1888, 352–60), although we find Isotta d'Este (1426–56), Ercole's half-sister, listed among "famous women" in an earlier text (see n. 16 above). The Gonzaga, meanwhile, could count such fixtures in "famous women" lists as Paola Malatesta Gonzaga, Barbara of Brandenburg, and Cecilia Gonzaga, while the Sforza had Bianca Maria Visconti Sforza and her daughter Ippolita Sforza, as well as, in Sabadino's Sforza-friendly list, Bianca's sister-in-law Elisa Sforza Sanseverino (1401–76).

161. See da Bisticci 1999, 103–13, especially 103, for his praises of the "universally gifted" Andrea Accaiuoli ("donna universale e ripiena di singulari virtù"). Note also in this geopolitical connection Sabadino degli Arienti's promotion of the Bolognese Caterina Vigri in his *Gynevera* and Poliziano's promotion of Alessandra Scala as a Florentine rival to Cassandra Fedele.

162. For a list of poems in the collection referring to Verona, see *Rime* 1994, xiii n. 9. On Sasso (1455–1527), see Fedele 2000, 82–82. For his involvement in the Brenzoni collection, see *Rime* 1994, xiii; for his writings in praise of Verona, see Castoldi 1993, 79–80.

163. *Rime* 1561; *Tempio* 1568.

164. The genre descends from the earlier poetic mode for lists of the most beautiful women of a city, an example of which is mentioned in the second chapter of Dante's *Vita nova* (Alighieri 1996, 32 and note). On later sixteenth-century examples, see the text in ch. 3 between nn. 68 and 69.

165. The listings of writings by women published in sixteenth-century Italy in Erdmann 1999, 206–23, include works published in around twenty-five different locations, ranging from great cities such as Venice (the unchallenged center of the Italian publishing industry), Florence, and Naples to small towns such as Treviso, Lucca, and Bergamo. The contrast with the situation in England, for example, where provincial literary publishing was ill developed, even down to the late seventeenth century (Ezell 1999, 103–21), is notable.

## Chapter 2. Translation (1490–1550)

1. On the education of girls in Renaissance Italy, see Grendler 1989, 87–102; Richardson 1999, 110; also, on convent education in particular, Strocchia 1999; Strocchia, 2003, esp. 180–81, 186, 192.

2. On the relationship of women to print culture in Italy, see Erdmann 1999; Richardson 1999, 144–50; Robin 2003; Robin 2007, esp. 41–78; also ch. 3, sec. 1, of the present volume.

3. For an overview of the developments discussed in this paragraph, see de Robertis 1966; also, more recently, the relevant chapters in Malato 1996a.

4. On the tradition of *poesia cortigiana,* see Ossola and Segre, eds. 2000,

336–41 and the bibliography they cite on p. 521; also, subsequently, Calitti 2004, ch. 2.

5. Kolsky 1990.

6. Calmeta 1959, 72: "In modo che la vulgare poesia e arte oratoria, dal Petrarca e Boccaccio in qua quasi adulterata, prima da Laurenzo Medice e suoi coetanei, poi mediante la emulazione di questa e altre singularissime donne di nostra etade, su la pristina dignitade essere ritornata se comprende."

7. Finotti 2005, 122–23; Frasso, Canova, and Sandal 1990; Gibellini 1997. The volume is dedicated by its anonymous commentator / illustrator to an "alma Minerva di real sangue nata" ("lovely Minerva of royal line") (Gibellini 1997, 75). On the probable identification of this figure with Beatrice, see Gibellini 1997, 76.

8. On dedications of vernacular texts to Elisabetta Gonzaga, see Calitti 2004, 64, 80 n. 183, 109; also Gorni 1989, 53–54, and ch. 1, n. 139, above.

9. Calmeta 1959, 47–55, 87, 89 ("suttilissima e profonda canzone"). The commentary is lost. For a lost narrative work of Calmeta's addressed to Isabella, see Calmeta 1959, xxxiv–xxxv).

10. For Isabella d'Este's studies of poetry, see Luzio 1887, 52–54; 65–68; Gallico 1962; Tebaldeo 1989, 2, pt. 1:15–16 (note on no. 1, line 11). Where Lucrezia Borgia is concerned, our main evidence is a passage in Bembo's Latin poem "Ad Lucretiam Borgiam"; see Finotti 2004, 399–400, for the text (and Finotti 2004, 414–15, for an Italian translation); also Prizer 1993, 190 and n. 26.

11. On Ippolita Sforza, as patron of vernacular literature, see Pieri 1985, 40 and n. 3, and Alessio 1997, 80. On Costanza d'Avalos and her cultural patronage, see Mutini 1962a; Thérault 1968, 45–59; Parenti 1993, 122–24.

12. Bandello 1992–96, 1:2–5 (1.1).

13. Ippolita was the daughter of Carlo Sforza, natural but legitimized son of Duke Galeazzo Maria Sforza I (1444–76). She was married in 1492 to the condottiere Alessandro Bentivoglio (1474–1532), son of Giovanni Bentivoglio, lord of Bologna. On her cultural and literary interests, see Calitti 2004, 106 n. 244, 119; Marani 2000, 57–58; Trento 2000, 40–41; Danzi 1989, 301, 306, 311.

14. Bandello 1992–96, 1:4.

15. "alcuno dei piú dotti e facondi uomini ed eloquentissimi che oggi vivano" (Bandello 1992–96, 1:4 [1.1]). On Cittadini, see Danzi 1989.

16. A more direct testimonial to women's literary-critical skills is a letter of Ceccarella Mintuolo (Minutolo 1999, 58–60 [no. 20]), minutely and critically dissecting a letter that has been sent to her for comment. See also, from the same Neapolitan *ambiente*, the dedicatory letter of Francesco Galeota's *Colibeto* (c. 1486) to Costanza d'Avalos del Balzo, Countess of Acerra, begging her to help in revising his work stylistically "iongendo e mancando le syllabe, cassando e sopra scrivendo, limando segondo il bisogno et al suo recto iudicio se richiede" ("by adding and removing syllables, erasing and revising words and phrases, polishing it as it needs and as your correct judgment demands"; Galeota 1987, 135). The critical acumen Dionisotti recognizes in Vittoria Colonna in the 1530s (Dionisotti 2002, 121–22) should be seen as reflecting this cultural tradition.

17. Welch 2002, 310–12, calculates Paola Malatesta Gonzaga's establishment in the early decades of the Quattrocento as 20–40 servants, rising to over 60 in the 1430s, when her court incorporated the retinue of her daughter-in-law Barbara of Brandenburg. By comparison, Eleonora d'Aragona had around 60 staff on her payroll (*salariati*) along with other nonsalaried attendants (Tuohy 1996, 40, 98–99; see also, on her establishment, Prizer 1993, 188; Gundersheimer 1980b, 51–52). Isabella d'Este's court, meanwhile, comprised 150 employees in 1502 (Prizer 1993, 198–99) and that of Lucrezia Borgia's 66 in 1506 (Prizer 1993, 196–97). The discrepancy between the size of Isabella's and Lucrezia's courts is presumably due to different accounting practices; Prizer 1993, 199, notes that Isabella seems to have maintained her court on approximately the same annual budget as her sister-in-law.

18. On Paola Malatesta's religious patronage, see Welch 2002, 311, 316–17; on that of Bianca Maria Visconti, Welch 2000, 35–38; cf. also Swain 1986, 186 on Barbara of Brandenburg. On Eleonora d'Aragona's religious patronage, see Edelstein 2000, 297–99; on the more secular cultural production associated with her (though not necessarily commissioned by her), Manca 2003.

19. See Prizer 1985 and 1993, comparing Isabella d'Este and Lucrezia Borgia as music patrons, and stressing particularly their pioneering role in the patronage of secular vocal music; also, specifically on Isabella d'Este, Prizer 1980, 2–14. More generally, on the importance of music in court women's education at this time, see H. Brown 1986, 65–67; Prizer 1993, 187–89; Fenlon 1990, 228. On Isabella d'Este as musician, see Prizer 1999.

20. Prizer 1993, 197. On the close connections between Isabella d'Este's literary interests and her musical patronage, see Rubsamen 1943 and Prizer 1999. Both give instances of her commissioning and solicitation of lyrics for musical setting.

21. Martines 1979, 305. On the expanded cultural role assumed by the Italian courts from the fifteenth century, see also Cattini and Romani 1982.

22. On the impact of the work, see Burke 1995.

23. Castiglione 1960, 207–8 (3.3); see also 263–64 (3.52) on women's role in inspiring music and poetry.

24. Similarly, in another passage of the *Cortegiano* (Castiglione 1960, 20 [1.4]; cf. Greene 1979, 185), we hear of the other denizens of the court, male and female, "tempering themselves" through imitation to the "form and quality" of the duchess, who is presented as an insuperable unisex human ideal. Interesting as a later instance of the same notion is Girolamo Ruscelli's later praise of women for their dual "generative power" (*virtù generativa*): while corporeally, they share with men in the power to generate children, spiritually, they have the capacity to generate in men "the purest of thoughts, deeds, and words, along with every praiseworthy custom and all contentment in this world and the next" ("hanno virtù di criare in noi pensieri, atti, e parole santissime [sic], e ogni lodevol costume, e contentezza per questa vita e per l'altra") (Ruscelli 1552, 21v).

25. Quint 2000; also, coming from a different angle, Kelly 1984, 43–44.

26. See, for example, Greene 1979, 182–83; Benson 1992, 75–77. On the place of

women and the feminine in the *Cortegiano,* see the bibliography cited in Cox 2000a, 397 n. 2; also subsequently Quint 2000; Berger 2000, 63–115.

27. See on what follows the important study of Cannata Salamone 2000; also F. Bruni 1986, 109–12; Plebani 1996; Giunta 2002, 397–402.

28. For discussion and contextualization, see Ahern 1992, 6; Plebani 1996, 29; Cornish 2000, 174; Cannata Salamone 2000, 506.

29. The phrase *intelletto d'amore* derives from Dante's famous *canzone* "Donne ch'avete 'ntelletto d'amore," which plays a pivotal role in the poetic trajectory of his *Vita nova* and is later identified in *Purgatorio,* 24:50–51, as the origin of his "new verse" (*nove rime*). For discussions alert to gender issues, see Cornish 2000, esp. 174, and, most recently, Steinberg 2007, 61–94. See also Steinberg 2007, 175, on Dante's inclusion of women among the prospected audience of his philosophical treatise, *Il convivio* and, more generally, on women's supposed authority in the realm of love, Giunta 2002, 402–4.

30. Bandello 1545, 58v. On the date (1536–38) and circumstances of composition of the poem (*Canti XI de le lodi de la s[ignora] Lucretia Gonzaga*), see Bandello 1992–96; 1:30, and Ridolfi 2001, 796. The poets listed are, in order, Vittoria Colonna, Veronica Gambara, Lavinia Colonna, Cecilia Gallerani, Camilla Scarampa, Margherita Tizzoni, and Lucrezia Gonzaga. All are discussed in the text, with the exception of the two youngest, Lavinia Colonna of Zagarolo (1524–67) and Lucrezia Gonzaga of Gazzuolo (1522–76). The latter was a protégée of Bandello's and the prime encomiastic object of the *canti.* Lavinia Colonna is not otherwise attested as a poet, to my knowledge. Gonzaga was frequently lauded by contemporaries for her poetic talent (Ridolfi 2001, 797), although no poems attributed to her have been identified. The fact that women's poetry in Italy predated Colonna's and Gambara's emergence to national fame is noted in Finotti 2005, 122.

31. On de' Benci's role as collective Florentine poetic muse, see D. Brown 2003, 104. For Laura Brenzoni, see the text between nn. 161 and 163 in ch. 1. On the evidence for de' Benci's own poetic activity see Fletcher 1989, 814, and D. Brown 2003, 104, though note the skepticism of Alessandrini 1966, 193.

32. *Rime di Girolama Corsi fiorentina,* ms. It. IX.270 (6367), Biblioteca Marciana, Venice. Two other manuscripts are known containing texts by Corsi, suggesting that her verse circulated to some extent: see *Composizioni poetiche volgari e latine intorno le cose d'Italia sul finire del sec. XV,* ms. It. IX.363 (7386), Biblioteca Marciana, Venice, 24r, and *Rime di vari poeti,* ms. 91, Biblioteca del Seminario, Padua, 82. On the Marciana ms., see V. Rossi 1890, 185 n. 2. For discussion of Girolama Corsi, see V. Rossi 1890, 183–200, Contarino 1983, and Kaplan 2003.

33. For Girolama Corsi's connections with the Sanseverino family, following her brother's death in the service of the family, see V. Rossi 1890, 198–99. On Iacopo Corsi's employment with Roberto Sanseverino, see Parenti 1983, 574; on his career more generally, V. Rossi 1890, 201–15, Calitti 2004, 78 n. 177. A single poem in the vernacular survives by Laura Brenzoni, possibly indicative of a larger production (Castoldi 1993, 76).

34. Bandello 1545, 58v: "mastra del dire, e d'ogni acuto stile." The phrase puns

on the double meaning of "stile" (pen and style). Compare also Bandello's *Novelle,* 1.3 (cited in Rozzo 1982, 419), where Gallerani and Camilla Scarampa are praised together as "two great lights of the Italian tongue" ("due gran lumi de la lingua italiana"), and see Fiorato 1979, 233–34, for further evidence of her activity as poet. Biographical discussions of Gallerani may be found in Bucci 1998 and Bandini Buti 1946, 1:287; see also the literary portrait in Calmeta 1959, 26–31.

35. On Scarampa, see Monti 1924; Leone 1962, 297–300, Rozzo 1982, 424; Strada 2001, 25–26. Monti 1924 prints most of her surviving poems (though with inaccuracies of transcription); see also Leone 1962, 298–99, and Rozzo 1982, 430–32. For a sonnet attributed both to Scarampa and Veronica Gambara, see Gambara 1995, 81–82 (no. 23).

36. For bibliography on Gambara, see R. Russell 1994c, 150–53; also, subsequently, Chimenti 1994 and Kennedy 1994, 134–46; Gambara 1995; Pignatti 1999; McIver 2000; McIver 2001, 160–64; Pertile 1998; Smarr 2001, 25–27; Cox 2005b, 592–97. On Savorgnan, see P. Bembo and Savorgnan 1950; Quaglio 1986; Zancan 1989; M. Pozzi 1994; Chemello 1999, 23–30.

37. See n. 10 above for references. Another possible female poet of this period is Barbara Torelli Bentivoglio Strozzi (1475–1533), known for a single famous sonnet ("Spenta è d'amor la face, il dardo è rotto") on the murder of her second husband, the poet Ercole Strozzi (1473–1508). Given the absence of contemporary supporting evidence for Torelli's poetic activity, it is possible that the sonnet, unpublished at the time, was written in her voice by a male poet. For extensive discussion of the attribution issue, see Catalano 1951, 41–54. A similar but better documented case from the same period is that of Ippolita Torelli Castiglione (1499–1520), wife of Baldassare Castiglione, the author of *Il cortegiano,* who was in the past frequently included in listings of women writers on the basis of a Latin elegy written in her voice by her husband. On the practice of female-voiced poetry by male authors in this period, see the text between nn. 51 and 53 in this chapter.

38. For an exception, see Calmeta's inclusion of "vain women" (*vane donne*), alongside "vulgar courtiers" and "ignorant overreachers" (*temerari ignoranti*), in a scathing account of the amateur poets of his day who, "because they can string two rhymes together . . . consider themselves the peers of Dante and Petrarch" (Calmeta 1959, 5, cited in Curti 2006, 105).

39. Valenziano 1984, 42 (1.175–89) and 44 (2.31–36).

40. See, for example, Leone 1962, 298, lines 1–2 and 5–6 ("Biasmi pure chi vuol la mia durezza, / che seguir voglio il casto mio pensiero. . . . Fugga pur gioventú, venga vecchiezza, / ché sol nella virtú mi fido, e spero"; "Let he who will blame me for my hardness: I wish to follow my chaste intent. . . . Let youth fly past, let old age come: I trust alone in my virtue [or talent]"). Scarampa's poem makes an interesting point of comparison with the similarly themed sonnet attributed by the late Cinquecento Venetian writer Moderata Fonte to Corinna, the militantly single poet-protagonist of her dialogue *Il merito delle donne:* see Fonte 1988, 18–19, and Fonte 1997, 49, for the text; also Cox 2005b, 190–91, for the Petrarchan subtext probably common to both.

41. "Per una singularissima madonna più presto divina che umana che, essendosi dotata d'ogni altra virtù, ancor se misse a far versi, e in un subito si è facta in questo sì excellente che ben dimostra, come ho decto, esser cosa divina" (G. Visconti 1979, 140 [no. 151.201]). Scarampa seems a more likely candidate than Cecilia Gallerani, given that the poem was included in a *canzoniere* addressed to Beatrice d'Este, the wife of Gallerani's lover Lodovico Sforza, although the possibility that it is addressed to a third female poet of the time obviously cannot be ruled out. Another sonnet of Visconti's ("Dolce Madonna mia, non se convene") is addressed to a female poet who has sent him a "choice poem" ("la tua rima elletta") for correction (G. Visconti 1979, 198 [appendix no. 246]).

42. See Poliziano 1971, xi–xiii, for the context. The major fifteenth-century commentaries on the epistle are those by Giorgio Merula (1471), Domizio Calderini (1476), and Angelo Poliziano (1481). Poliziano's, in particular, is notable for its interest in the historical figure of Sappho (Poliziano 1971, xiii).

43. V. Rossi 1890, 185–86.

44. S. Campbell 2004, 199–204.

45. See Boccaccio 1987, 128–41.

46. For Corsi, see V. Rossi 1890, 192–93; for Scarampa, see the text at n. 35 in the present chapter. Only in much later texts, of the late sixteenth and seventeenth centuries, do such references seem to be problematized by Sappho's perceived "indecency": see ch 5, n. 35, and the text between nn. 145 and 146 in ch. 6.

47. Och 2002, 156.

48. Regarding this, see the suggestive discussion of Boccaccio's eclogue on Sappho in S. Campbell 2004, 202–3, where it is noted that Sappho there stands as "a symbol of the lost plenitude and purity of ancient poetry itself."

49. See especially Fulkerson 2004; also Spentzou 2003; Farrell 1998.

50. The phrase quoted here is from Fulkerson 2004, 3. On the presence of the *Heroides* in Boccaccio's *Fiammetta* and *Amorosa visione,* see Hagedorn 2004, 102–29; also, on the former work, Brownlee 1990, 58–69. On a fourteenth-century translation of the *Heroides* composed on the commission of a female reader, see F. Bruni 1986, 116.

51. For discussion, see Vecce 1993, 29–31; Longhi 1989, 395; Phillippy 1992, 5–6. For the term "microgenre" ("microgenere"), see Scala 1990, 104.

52. Vecce 1993, 30; Longhi 1989, 395.

53. On Cosentino's poems, see B. Croce 1953b; on Tebaldeo's poem, Vecce 1993, 30–31; Longhi 1989, 389–92; on Corsi's, V. Rossi 1890, 203–6.

54. See, for example, Minutolo 1999, 52–55 (no. 15).

55. For the text, see V. Colonna 1982, 53–56; for discussion, Scala 1990, 103–4; Vecce 1993.

56. See P. Bembo and Savognan, 1950, 3–4, 7, 34, 42, 43–44. On Savorgnan as poet, see Quaglio 1986; Gorni 1989, 40–41; Zancan 1998, 55–58. On the reasons that probably inhibited her from publishing or circulating her poetry, see Zancan 1989, who contrasts her with the "public" face of Venetian female creativity in Gaspara Stampa.

57. The two sonnets in question, headed "to a Venetian friend" ("*ad amicum vene-tum*"), are found in V. Rossi 1890, 196–97. That Sanudo had such intimate poems of Corsi's in his possession leads Rossi to conclude that he was probably her lover.

58. For examples, see Gambara 1995, 57–71 (nos. 1–14).

59. See especially the sonnet "Chiaro conosco vostra fiera voglia" ("I Clearly See Your Cruel Desire") (Leone 1962, 299), which ends by warning the lover that his ill treatment of her will damage his reputation and lead him to be branded a "nido d'amorosi inganni" ("hive [literally, 'nest'] of amorous deceptions").

60. For examples of Corsi's occasional verse, which includes verses mourning the death of Isabel of Castile (1451–1504) and celebrating the 1496 marriage of Cateruzza Corner (d. 1554), niece of Caterina Corner, queen of Cyprus, see V. Rossi 1890, 191 n. 1 and 192 n. 1. For Corsi's comic *barzelletta*, see ibid., 190–91; for her political sonnet, ibid., 189, and Contarino 1983, 571, who notes its "remarkable mastery of the aggressive metaphorical language of political invective." For Corsi's sonnets on her brother's death, see V. Rossi 1890, 197–99.

61. V. Rossi 1890, 194. On the genre, see Rogers 1986.

62. Gambara 1995, 36. On Gambara's relations with the musical culture of her time, see Vela 1989; Barezzani 1989.

63. V. Rossi 1890, 197.

64. On the status of rulers' mistresses in this period and the possibilities their relationships offered for family advancement, see Ettlinger 1994.

65. On Gambara's life and background, see Chimenti 1989 and Pignatti 1999. A later female poet also connected with the Nogarola was Alda Torelli Lunati of Pavia (see the text at n. 106 in ch. 3), whose aunt by marriage was an Angela Nogarola, homonym of the fifteenth-century poet. The cross-generational transmission of female learning deserves study as a topic within the history of women's education, alongside the better-known phenomenon of humanist fathers educating their daughters. Besides famous beneficiaries such as Colonna and Gambara, an interesting and little-known case is discussed in Ambrosini 2005, 166–68.

66. On Scarampa's life and background, see Rozzo 1982.

67. Emilia Pio, one of the leading female figures in Castiglione's *Cortegiano*, was Veronica Gambara's maternal aunt. Scarampa and Gallerani both figure in the cornice of Bandello's *novella*, 1.1, which shows their verse being expertly discussed by Ippolita Sforza Bentivoglio, in conversation with the poets Girolamo Cittadini and Niccolò Amanio; see Bandello 1992–96, 3–4 (1.1); Finotti 2005, 126–27; Rozzo 1982, 419–20. Useful recent studies of aristocratic northern Italian women in this period, stressing their cultural agency, are found in McIver 2000 and 2001; see also, on a slightly later period, McIver 2006.

68. On Isotta Gambara, see Firenzuola 1993, 182 (the context is Firenzuola's *Epistola in lode delle donne,* c. 1525). On Camilla Valenti, the daughter of Gambara's sister Violante and Valente Valenti of Mantua, see Stevenson 2005, 171, 281, 313. For a contemporary biography, see Betussi 1545, 229v–230v; for praises Domenichi 2004, 11, and B. Tasso 1560a, 271 (44, 71).

69. Bandello 1545, 58v; cf. Fiorato 1979, 235–36. For Bandello's praises of the madrigals to Gonzaga, see Bandello 1992–96, 83–85 (3.17), where he describes them in terms recalling those of Castiglione in characterizing the behavioral style of the perfect court lady as "lovely, spotless, sweet, elegant and very polished, filled with a winning native and pure eloquence, with no trace of affectation" ("belli, candidi, dolci, eleganti e molto tersi e pieni d'una soave facondia nativa e pura, senza veruna affettazione").

70. Tebaldeo 1989, 2, pt. 1:481–84 (no. 286).

71. Luzio and Renier's exalted account of Isabella's humanistic competences is now considered overoptimistic. Regarding her studies of Latin, see Luzio and Renier 2006, 4–5, and compare Kolsky 1984, 59–60.

72. For the phrase *virtù conveniente a Madonne* (applied to music), see Prizer 1999, 10. For the term "universal" in this sense, see Calmeta's sardonic description of a certain "Bianca Lucia" of Milan, a skilled musician and singer, as having aspirations to become "the most universal lady in the world" (*"la più 'niversal donna del mondo"* [Calmeta 1959, 40]). For a tribute to the "universal" talents of Isabella d'Este, see the 1502 tribute of Bernardo Accolti ("l'Unico Aretino") cited in Prizer 1999, 33 n. 82; also Calmeta 2004, 3, for a similar tribute to Beatrice d'Este and, more fully and elegantly, Bembo's "Ad Lucretiam Borgiam" (cited in n. 10 above) on Lucrezia Borgia.

73. Tebaldeo 1989, 2, pt. 1:483.

74. In the south, by contrast, following a period of vitality in the late Quattrocento, the vernacular tradition lapsed in the early Cinquecento, reviving only from around the 1530s onward; see Toscano 1993. More generally, on Italian literature in the period under discussion here, see Formentin 1996b and Fedi 1996b, both of which extensively cite previous literature.

75. On Amaseo's opposition to the vernacular, see Avesani 1960, 661–62. An acute portrayal of the rearguard Latinist position is found in Speroni 1996a, in the person of Lazzaro Bonamico; see also Giraldi 1999, 212–14.

76. For overviews, see Formentin 1996b, 188–207, and Fedi 1996b, 529–29. For a recent contextualizing study centered on Castiglione's linguistic theory, see J. Marino 2001.

77. On Bembo's linguistic theories, see Formentin 1996b, 189–98, for a recent summary. Good overviews of Bembo's career and cultural influence may be found in Mazzacurati 1980 and Fedi 1996b, 529–53, both citing existing bibliography. For a detailed study of the impact of Bembo's linguistic reform on editing practice in Venice in the first decades of the sixteenth century, see Richardson 1994, 48–78.

78. Ghinassi 1963.

79. "puro e dolce idioma . . . volgar uso tetro" (Ariosto 1976, 1210 [46.15.2–3]). On Ariosto's linguistic revision, see Gilbert 1960, 241–42, 253–54. The same operation was carried out retrospectively on Boiardo's *Orlando Innamorato* by Francesco Berni (1497–1536) in his Tuscanized *rifacimento* of the Quattrocento classic (completed by c. 1531); see Weaver 1977 and Woodhouse 1982.

80. "la lingua delle scritture . . . non dee a quella del popolo accostarsi, se non in quanto, accostandovisi, non perde gravità, non perde grandezza" (P. Bembo 1996, 104).

81. Grippo 1996, esp. 18–19, 46; though see also Parenti 1993, 49, for a differentiation between Cariteo's "tempered Petrarchism" ("petrarchismo temperato") and Sannazaro's stricter observance; cf. Parenti 1993, 125 on Britonio, closer to Sannazaro in this regard. On Cariteo, see also Kennedy 2003, 67–73.

82. The classic statement of this is Vickers 1981. On the influence of this essay, see Braden 1996a, 115–17, and Cox 2005b, 584–85, 601 n. 1.

83. The point is made in Braden 1996a, 115–16, and developed in Cox 2005b; see also Cornish 2000, 176–77.

84. On Corso's grammar, see Sanson 2005, esp. 424, on its didactic accessibility with respect to Bembo's *Prose*. On Lucrezia Lombardi, its dedicatee, see ibid., 410–11, 430–31. For an earlier vernacular grammar addressed to a woman, see ibid., 392.

85. For early examples of such *rimari* see Morato 1532 (first published 1528) and Lanfranco 1531.

86. Such, at least, is the case with Bembo's *Rime* proper. Also published quite widely in the sixteenth century were his *Stanze,* originally composed for carnival at Urbino in 1507, which adhere to a worldlier view of love more characteristic of the *poesia cortigiana* tradition (P. Bembo 2003; Calitti 2004, 120–33; Curti 2006, 151–68). His *Motti,* written for the same context, but considerably more licentious, circulated only in manuscript (Curti 2006, 183–217).

87. Richardson 2004, 45, estimates that around 40 percent of Bembo's lyrics had an addressee. Medieval precedents for such correspondence poetry are discussed in Giunta 2002.

88. Cornish 2000, 177–78; cf. ibid., 176–77, on Dante's similarly table-turning defense of the vernacular on the grounds of its universality in *De vulgari eloquentia*.

89. Benson 1992, 123–48; also Shemek 1998, 95–104.

90. Cox 2005a, 17–19. A further addition to the poem in 1532 was an encomium of Veronica Gambara as "so dear to Apollo and the sacred Aonian choir" ("sì grata a Febo e al santo aonio coro"; Ariosto 1976, 1207 (46.3.7–8) (in earlier versions of the poem she had merely been listed among the ladies of Correggio; see Dionisotti 1989, 14–15, for comment).

91. The other poets included in the appendix are the prominent *letterati* Giangiorgio Trissino (1478–1550) and Francesco Maria Molza and the obscure Benedetto Morosini, presumably a member of the noble Venetian family of that name. On the importance of this edition in the history of the diffusion of Colonna's and Gambara's poetry, see Cox 2005b, 592–93.

92. P. Bembo 1960, 609–11 (nos. 125–27).

93. P. Bembo 1552, 130–268. The letters to Savorgnan makes up the "second part" of the fourth volume of Bembo's *Lettere,* the first half of the volume being composed of "public" letters to women, including Colonna and Gambara. The Savorgnan letters may have inspired the two later volumes of female love letters

attributed to "Celia Romana" ("Celia Romana" 1562) and "Emilia N. Fiorentina" ("Emilia N." 1594). The latter is particularly reminiscent of Savorgnan in its highly literate character and its inclusion of verse ("Emilia N." 1594, 20, 39).

94. The reference to Savorgnan's "dolce lima" is found in Bembo's letter of 12 October 1500 (P. Bembo 1552, 4, 222; cf. P. Bembo and Savorgnan 1950, 115–16 [letter 62]). See also his letter of 1 November 1500 (letter 64), which ends by noting the imperfections of an enclosed poem, concluding that "between us we will patch it up" ("tra voi e io le andrem poi racconciando") (P. Bembo 1552, 4, 226; cf. P. Bembo and Savorgnan 1950, 119) and also that of 15 April 1500 (P. Bembo 1552, 4, 144; cf. P. Bembo and Savorgnan 1950, 58), where Bembo asks for help in revising his compositions, insisting that Savorgnan is to consider them her own ("cose, che vostre sono").

95. P. Bembo 1552, 4, 202; cf. P. Bembo and Savognan 1950, 101; also Sanson 2005, 403–4, for discussion.

96. On the Compagnia degli Amici, see Strada 2001, 6–7, and Gnocchi 1999. The statutes of the association stipulated that membership was open to men who were "dotti e letterati" ("educated and lettered") and to women "di chiaro e valoroso ingegno" ("of elevated and keen intelligence"). It is not known how far membership in practice extended beyond the initial founding group, which included the reformist patricians Tommaso Giustinian and Vincenzo Querini.

97. On Bembo's defense of his choice to include women as speakers in *Gli Asolani*, see Cox 2000a, 397 n. 5.

98. See P. Bembo 1960, 34, 630; also Gorni 1989, 53–54.

99. Fletcher 1989.

100. Bembo met Poliziano as a young man in June 1491, when the latter visited Venice (Fedi 1996b, 529–30), the same visit on which Poliziano made the acquaintance of Cassandra Fedele.

101. For a differing perspective on Bembo's self-positioning with regard to women, see Kolsky 1990, 169–70. For overviews of his literary relations with women see Travi 1984, 76–86, and Braden 1996b. Besides Colonna, Gambara, and Savorgnan, Bembo was also in contact with the Sienese poet Virginia Martini Salvi and the Piedmontese Ippolita Clara; see, for Salvi, Bottrigari, ed. 1551, 190–94, and Eisenbichler 2003, 96; for Clara, Albonico 1989, 326–27.

102. Two recent collections of essays on the invasion of 1494 and its political and cultural impact are Abulafia 1995 and Everson and Zancani, eds. 2000.

103. Machiavelli 1995, 169.

104. P. Bembo 1996, 68–70 (1.7). Precedents for this kind of politicized reading of Italian literary and linguistic history are found in Leonardo Bruni.

105. See, for example, with differing inflections, Kelly 1984, 44–45; Finucci 1992, 43; Freccero 1992, esp. 270–71.

106. See the text at n. 60 in the present chapter on Corsi's sonnet on the 1494 invasion; also Leone 1962, 298, for Scarampa's sonnet "Misera Italia, il ciel pure te minaccia" ("Wretched Italy, the Heavens Persist in Their Threats"), seemingly written around 1498 when the French were threatening a second invasion.

107. Castiglione 1960, 209 (3.4): "una certa virilità soda e ferma . . . una tenerezza molle e delicata . . . senza similitudine alcuna d'omo." For comment on the gender dimension of Castiglione's recommendations regarding male and female behavior, see Kelly 1984, 33–34; Fermor 1993, 131–32.

108. Cox 2005a, 25 n. 6.

109. M. B. Rose 2002.

110. It seems appropriate to recall in this context Colonna's characterization by Michelangelo in a poem as "un uomo in una donna" ("a man in a woman"; Cox 2005a, 15). With regard to her martial lineage, note that Colonna was the daughter of Fabrizio Colonna (1450–1520), the model general of Machiavelli's *Arte della guerra* (1521), and the granddaughter on her mother's side of the legendary fifteenth-century condottiere Federico da Montefeltro.

111. For discussion of Corso's commentary, see Bianco 1998a and 1998b; Cinquini 1999; Brundin 2002, 66–68. See also, more generally, on Corso, Sanson 2005, 405–8, 430–31.

112. Costa 1640c, 249. The third figure is Margherita Sarrocchi.

113. The classic biography of Colonna is Jerrold 1969; see also Thérault 1968; Ferino Pagden 1997; Brundin 2005, 6–13; Robin 2007, 3–8, 14–15, 31–35, 79–101. On Colonna as poet, see the bibliography listed in Bassanese 1994a, 91–94; also, subsequently, Kennedy 1994, 114–34; Adler 2000; R. Russell 2000a; de Vivo 2001; Brundin 2001, 2002, 2005; Och 2001 and 2002; Sapegno 2003 and 2005; Cox 2005a; Cox 2005b, 597–601.

114. See Monti 1924, 255–566, and Rozzo 1982, 420. Irpino's poem is especially interesting given his contacts with Costanza d'Avalos's circle in Ischia; see de Vivo 2001, 41; B. Basile 1978, 87–89. A more local female role model perhaps known to Colonna was the fifteenth-century Neapolitan Ceccarella Minutolo. A Neapolitan contemporary of Colonna's who figures as a poet in one sixteenth-century anthology (Bottrigari, ed. 1551) is Giulia d'Aragona (1492–1542), daughter of the last Aragonese king of Naples, Federico IV and Isabella del Balzo.

115. See V. Colonna 1982, 53–56, and, for discussion, Vecce 1993.

116. On the Dante dedication, rare in a sixteenth-century context, see Ranieri 1985, 250–51, and Scala 1990, 100–101; on Britonio's tributes, Ranieri 1985, 252–53; Scala 1990, 101–4; Grippo 1996. See also Och 2002, 156–57, on allusions to Colonna's poetic activity in her early portrait medals, and de Vivo 2001 on her contacts with Neapolitan humanistic circles during the years of her marriage.

117. For probable examples of Colonna's early love poetry, see Toscano 2000, 18, 20; also, more generally, ibid., 13–24, for reflections on her early literary career. If it is not purely generic, Bembo's reference to Colonna's *rime* in his sonnet "Alta Colonna e ferma alle tempeste" (P. Bembo 1960, 610 [no. 126]) as once "sweet and blithe" ("dolci e liete"), now "piteous and sad" ("pietose e meste"), may offer some supporting evidence of the character of her early verse. See, however, also Forni 2005, 72, for evidence that Colonna's earliest poetic activity also comprehended religious verse.

118. For the text, see Gambara 1995, 79–89 (no. 21). On its musical fortunes, see

Barezzani 1989, 138–42. For other examples of Gambara's poetry of reciprocal love, see Gambara 1995, 45–86 (nos. 18–27). A problem to be borne in mind here is that reconstructions of the chronology of Gambara's oeuvre, such as Bullock's, have generally worked from debatable autobiographical assumptions, attributing expressions of amorous frustration to the period before her marriage and those expressive of mutual love to her married life (cf. Gambara 1995, 4). Except in a clear-cut case such as the elegiac sonnet 28 (86–87), which refers to the heaven-ordained "knot" (*nodo*) of marriage, the criterion of stylistic maturity is more reliable as a basis for dating.

119. For the text of Colonna's *Apologia*, see Zappacosta 1972, 199–246, esp. 209–10, 216–18, on the desirability of women's participation in public life; 225–27, 234–35, for praises of Vittoria Colonna. For discussion of the text, see Zappacosta 1972, 159–97; Ranieri 1985, 253; Scala 1990, 105–8, the latter noting its dependence on book 3 of Castiglione's *Cortegiano,* of which Colonna notoriously possessed a manuscript prior to its publication in 1528 (see Castiglione's dedicatory letter to Miguel da Silva, where he reproaches her for circulating it against his wishes). For the text of Giovio's *Dialogus,* see Giovio 1984, 167–321, esp. 267–321, for the third book, on famous contemporary women, which includes *querelle* elements drawn from Pompeo Colonna; see esp. pp. 313–20 for his climactic encomium of Vittoria Colonna. For discussion of the text, see Vecce 1990, 68–81.

120. Vecce 1990, 71, 81. Colonna's *Apologia* survives in only three manuscripts (Zappacosta 1972, 159–61), but it appears to have been known to later *querelle* writers, not least through a passage in Agostino Nifo's *De re aulica* (see Baldelli 1560, IIIr, and cf. Domenichi 1564, 3r–v). Giovio's *Dialogus* is cited in, for example, Lando 2000, 229.

121. On Giovio's mission, see Vecce 1990, 83–84.

122. On the importance of the Bologna context for the transmission of Colonna's verse in northern Italy, see Dionisotti 2002, 119–22, and Toscano 2000, 108–11. On its importance for Gambara, see Pignatti 1999, 16; Dionisotti 1989, 15; Chimenti 1994, 40–45.

123. For more on the reception context of Colonna's poetry of widowhood, see Cox 2005a, 14–19.

124. Toscano 2000, 105–8. See also more generally ibid., 104–20, on d'Avalos's role in promoting Colonna's poetry in northern Italy, esp. pp. 108–11 for his probable role in introducing Colonna's poetry to Bembo. On d'Avalos as poet, see ibid., 99–103.

125. On Gambara's relationship with Charles V, see Chimenti 1994, 37–40, and McIver 2000, 37–38; on her proimperial policy generally, see Pignatti 1999, 69, and Ghidini 1989, 84.

126. On Ippolito da Correggio, see Ghidini 1983b; on Brunoro Gambara, see Chimenti 1994, 42, 62.

127. The ode, in Sapphic meter, was first published in Gambara 1879, 351–53. See Chimenti 1994, who publishes it with the Italian translation of Luigi Amaduzzi (1889), on pp. 49–53. For the 1535 sonnets, see Gambara 1995, 108–12 (nos. 45–48).

128. Gambara 1995, 91–94 (nos. 32–34). Del Vasto had visited Correggio in 1531,

where he met Ariosto (Ghidini 1989, 92–93). It is possible that he was responsible for introducing Colonna's poetry to Gambara, if she had not already encountered it at Bologna the previous year. Gambara's poetic correspondence with Colonna dates from 1532.

129. Corso 1543 and V. Colonna 1558. For secondary literature, see n. 111 above. On Correggio under Gambara as "an active center for the transmission and, more importantly, the study of Colonna's verse," see Toscano 2000, 80.

130. Giraldi 1999, 220. Giraldi goes on to suggest that the poems of the two are read with the greater eagerness ("cupidius") because they are composed "by illustrious matrons."

131. For Gambara's sole surviving Latin poem, see the text at n. 127 in the present chapter; for Colonna's—a reply poem to the Ferrarese poet Daniele Fini—see Pasquazi 1966, liii, 159.

132. Gambara 1995, 102–3 (no. 41).

133. On Gambara's letters, see Selmi 1989, which cites editions.

134. Gambara 1995, 104–6 (no. 43). On this and Gambara's other poems of place, see Smarr 2001, 25–27.

135. On Nogarola's poem, see the text at ch. 1, n. 69.

136. See Gambara 1995, 95–96 (no. 36); 103–4 (no. 42). For discussion of the former sonnet, see Pertile 1998; Cox 2005b, 592–97. Gambara's presence in the Domenichi anthology is detailed in Gambara 1995, 45.

137. See the text at ch. 1, n. 20.

138. A good example of such "uxorial" depictions of Colonna, dating from around the same time as Gambara's sonnet (1532), is Ariosto's laudatory description in the *Furioso,* on which see Cox 2005a, 18–19. For other examples, see P. Bembo 1960, 609, 611 (nos. 125 and 127) and Beaziano 1551, c8r–v; also Toscano 2000, 30–31 and 32–33, for examples from Francesco Berni (the phrase translated in the text ["vivo exempio"] is cited from Toscano 2000, 30). Comparable to Gambara's sonnet, by contrast, in its privileging of Colonna as poet is P. Bembo 1960, 610 (no. 126); see also B. Tasso 1560b, 91–97, 99–106.

139. On the gender connotations of the term *leggiadro,* see Fermor 1993.

140. "Di novo il Cielo de l'antica gloria/orna la nostra etade" (Heaven once more with ancient glory/adorns the present age") (V. Colonna 1982, 209 [E13]).

141. V. Colonna 1982, 35 (no. A1:65).

142. Following the mandate of authorial modesty and drawing on ineffability topoi characteristic of encomiastic verse, Colonna calls attention to this memorializing function of her verse through expressions of her inadequacy to the task. See, for example, her proemial sonnet "Scrivo sol per sfogar l'eterna doglia" ("I Write Only to Relieve My Eternal Pain") (V. Colonna 1982, 3; A1:1) and her important sonnet to Bembo, "Ahi quanto fu a mio sol contrario il fato" ("Alas, How Cruel Was the Fate of My Sun") (V. Colonna 1982, 38; A1:71). For an analysis of the former, see Cox 2005b, 597–601.

143. The metaphor of the sun for the beloved is not original to Colonna; for its rich Petrarchan heritage, see Petrarca 1996, 24, note to 4.12. In Petrarch, how-

ever, this solar imagery competes with the dominant onomastic *senhal* of the laurel tree for Laura, while Colonna's exclusive and exhaustive use of the sun metaphor effectively rebranded it as hers.

144. "Di vero egli è bello e ingenioso e grave, più che da donna non pare sia richiesto." Letter of 9 April 1530 (P. Bembo 1987–93, 3:126 [no. 1078]), discussed in Dionisotti 2002, 119; Cox 2005a, 15. On the centrality of *gravità* as a stylistic ideal in Petrarchism, see Afribo 2001.

145. See, for example, Afribo 2001, 146, on Colonna's metrical originality, as measured by the frequency of her adoption of rhyme schemes in her sonnets not found in Petrarch.

146. Quondam 1991, 204, describes Colonna's *Rime spirituali* as "the great founding work for the whole process of spiritualization of the Petrarchist code" ("il grande libro che fonda il processo stesso di spiritualizzazione del codice petrarchesco"). On Malipiero, see Roche 1989, 91–94, and Quondam 1991, 203–76. For a chronology of publications of *rime spirituali* to 1600, see Quondam 1991, 283–89. For an overview of the genre, see Quondam 2005a, esp. 166–88.

147. On Colonna's spiritual verse, see, most recently, Bardazzi 2001; Brundin 2002; Brundin 2005, esp. 20–22; Forni 2005; U. D'Elia 2006.

148. For sixteenth-century editions of Catherine of Siena's writings, see appendix A. Another possible inspiration is Colonna's ancestress Battista da Montefeltro, manuscripts of whose religious lyrics (discussed in ch. 1, sec. 1) may well have been available to her.

149. Colonna's poetry to the Virgin has attracted particular critical attention in recent years: see R. Russell 2000a; Brundin 2001; Scarpati 2004, 700–702; Forni 2005; U. D'Elia 2006, 119–23. See also Adler 2000, esp. 317–22, more generally on Colonna's treatment of female religious figures in her verse and letters.

150. For Fiamma, see Ossola 1976, 248 n. 28; for Contile, Quondam 1991, 275–76. See also Plaisance 2004, 285, for a similar acknowledgment on the part of the Florentine poet Niccolò Martelli and A. Piccolomini 1549, A4v–A5r, for critical remarks on Colonna's role in expanding the subject matter of lyric poetry beyond the amorous. A further striking tribute to Colonna's founding role in the tradition of *rime spirituali* is found in two sonnets by Tommaso Costo (c. 1560–c. 1613) that open by quoting in its entirety the first quatrain of one of her spiritual sonnet of hers (S1:47); for the texts, see Tansillo 1606, 30–31; on the author (who worked in the 1590s for the D'Avalos family), Costo 1989, xxxvi–xliii. See also Dickinson 1961; Bettoni 2002; Balsamo 2002, 24–26, on the imitation of spiritual verse by Colonna and Veronica Gambara by the French poets Joachim du Bellay (1522–60) and Philippe Desportes (1546–1606).

151. For a useful recent summary of Colonna's religious trajectory of the 1530s and 1540s, citing further bibliography, see Brundin 2005, 13–18. For more detail, see Firpo 1988; Bianca 1993; Collett 2000, ch. 3; Bardazzi 2001.

152. See Fragnito 1972, 785–86; Bardazzi 2001, 71; Bianca 1993, 429–30. On Colonna's relations with Ochino more generally, see Firpo 1988, 212–13, and Bardazzi 2001.

153. Bardazzi 2001, 73. Carnesecchi's suspicions were based on Colonna's association with known "heretics" such as Flaminio and Ochino, the content of some of her *rime,* and her purported heretical readings (Ranieri 1985, 268; Firpo 1988, 221 n. 46; Collett 2000, 84).

154. On the Lutheran doctrine of salvation *sola fide,* shared by many Italian reformers in the 1530s and 1540s, but eventually condemned as heretical by the Catholic authorities, see Brundin 2005, 14–15.

155. Bardazzi 2001. For readings of Colonna's religious verse in the context of the culture of the *spirituali,* see also Ossola 1985, 82–93, and Scarpati 2004, esp. 714–17.

156. Brundin 2002; Brundin 2005, 21.

157. Gambara's connections with the reform movement are far less well established than Colonna's, and it is probably correct to define her position as one of "prudent conformism" (Chimenti 1994, 96). For the influence of reform thought in her circles in Correggio, however, see Chimenti 1994, 92–93; Ghidini 1989, 95–96; Daenens 1999b, 186–87; Bettoni 2002, 40–41. For a recent work emphasizing the Italian reform movement as a context for women's writing, see Robin 2007.

158. On Colonna's exchanges of letters with Marguerite de Navarre, see Collett 2000. Important in particular for this study, on account on their widespread print distribution, is the exchange of letters of February–March 1540 that was included in two important anthologies of the 1540s and 1550s. For the texts, see Collett 2000, 125–26 and 127–28; for translations, ibid., 111–12, 113–14; for discussion, Adler 2000, 312–13; Brundin 2001, 61–62; Robin 2007, 28–30. On the print fortunes of the exchange, see Chemello 1999, 33–35. Sonnets by Marguerite addressed to Colonna are found in Bottrigari, ed. 1551, 13, and Domenichi 1559, 11.

159. Furey 2004, 3. See also, on women's place in the Italian reform movement, C. Russell 2006, 94–95, citing further literature.

160. Brundin 2002.

161. Evocative in this respect is Varchi's late sonnet "Donna che come chiaro a ciascun mostra" ("Lady Who Clearly Shows to All") (Varchi 1555, 258), whose first tercet portrays the newly deceased Caterina Cibo joining Colonna, Bembo, and Valdés in heaven.

162. Lando 2000, 228–35.

163. V. Colonna 1982, 258–64; also V. Colonna 1982, 264–70, for the nine further sixteenth-century editions of Colonna's verse.

164. See Ragionieri 2005, 132 (no. 44) for the image. On the expansion of the selection of *rime spirituali* in published editions of Colonna after 1538, see Bardazzi 2000, 74–75, drawing on the data in V. Colonna 1982, 463–85. On the ordering of the amorous and spiritual verses in successive editions, see Bianco 1998b, 38–39.

165. Colonna is known to have prepared manuscripts of her verse for Michelangelo (now in the Vatican Library, ms. Latino 11539) and for Marguerite de Navarre (perhaps identifiable with ms. Laurenziano Ashburnhamiano 1153 of the Biblioteca Nazionale Centrale in Florence). A third possible gift manuscript,

known to have been in the possession of Francesco della Torre, secretary to Giovanni Matteo Giberti (1495–1543) in the early 1540s, has not been securely identified (V. Colonna 1998, 23–25). On Colonna's gift manuscripts in general, see Brundin 2002, 61–62; on the manuscript for Michelangelo, see Scarpati 2004 and Brundin 2005, 33–39; on that for Marguerite de Navarre, Brundin 2001. On the practice of sending customized gift manuscripts of this kind, see more generally Richardson 2004, 43–44.

166. Richardson 2004, 42–43; see also, on Colonna's resistance to print, Scarpati 2004, 693 n. 2.

167. Letter to Pietro Aretino of 26 August 1536, cited in Dilemmi 1989, 24 n. 12.

168. Richardson 2004, 61.

169. Gambara 1759. For an earlier edition of her verse alongside that of three other female poets, see Gambara 1690. On her sixteenth-century publishing history, see Gambara 1995, 36–49.

170. On Bertani, see Betussi 1556, 101–4; Tiraboschi 1781–86, 1:254–57; Bertoni 1925. Perhaps Bolognese by birth (though she is also claimed as a native by Modena), she was married to Guron Bertani of Modena, brother to Pietro (1501–58), who became a cardinal in 1551 and was a leading figure at the Council of Trent. Since Bertani refers to Colonna and Gambara as alive in this poem, it is likely to date from before 1547. Bertani also wrote a further "fan sonnet" in praise of Gambara alone ("La santa veramente unica ebrea"; for the text, see Stortoni, ed. 1997, 130). Verse by her was published in Bottrigari, ed. 1551, Domenichi 1559, *Rime* 1561, and *Rime* 1565a.

171. Corso 1556, E4r: "Né è maraviglia, che . . . ella, che col Bembo s'allevò, e da lui prese i primi nutrimenti della sacra poesia, tal guida delle donne sia stato [sic] quale esso fù de gli huomini" ("Nor can there be any wonder that . . . knowing Bembo as she did from childhood and having drawn from him her first lessons in the sacred art of poetry, she served as a model for female writers just as he did for male"). Corso is insistent elsewhere in the passage on Gambara's temporal priority among female poets and her status as "perpetual guide" ("perpetua scorta") to those who will come after her, perhaps betraying a degree of anxiety about her reputation relative to that of Colonna.

172. Corso 1556, E4r–v: "Allegrisi per tanto, allegrisi il nostro secolo d'havere havuto il Bembo e insieme questa Donna . . . di concorde volere alla virtù inanimati per dare alla posterità lume et invitarla a seguire i lor vestigi. Aurea veramente in assai cose è stata l'età nostra, ma in questa io la reputo di gemme pretiosissime" ("It has been a great blessing for the present age to have had two such great writers as Bembo and this lady . . . concerted in their pursuit of poetic excellence and serving as beacons and leaders to those who came after them. Rightly has this been called a golden age in many things, but in this I deem it not only golden but adorned with the most precious of jewels").

173. Plaisance 2004, 291. For the text of the oration, see Plaisance 2004, 294–309. Plaisance notes in his introduction (291) that the oration was most likely com-

missioned by the grammarian and Dante commentator Pier Francesco Giam-bullari (1495–1555), who was consul of the academy from 4 March 1547. For evi-dence of Giambullari's interest in Colonna's poetry, see Rabitti 1992, 138–45.

174. For the text of the poem, see Plaisance 2004, 296–97.

175. On Giovanni de' Medici and Bembo as paradigms of modern *virtù*, see Plaisance 2004, 294–95. For Ariosto as Virgilian imitator, see ibid., 302; for Varchi as "il nostro toscano, anzi più tosto fiorentino Cicerone," see ibid., 294–95.

176. The oration's comparison of Colonna to ancient female paradigms of *virtù* is found at Plaisance 2004, 304–8. For the phrases quoted in the text, see ibid., 305 ("già tra loro furono a gran contese della maggioranza questi due popoli") and 295 ("non meno eccellentissima nelle discipline filosofiche e nella poesia che sin-golarissima nella fortezza d'animo e nella pudicizia"). For other examples of the topoi of Colonna as vanquishing the ancients, or as living proof of the legendary marvels attributed to ancient women, see Varchi 1565, 94v, and V. Colonna 1560, A2r (dedicatory letter from Lodovico Dolce to Giorgio Gradenigo).

177. Plaisance 2004, 301: "il gran testor de gli amorosi detti." The speaker goes on to quote the opening lines of Petrarch's sonnet 297: "Due gran nemiche inseme erano agiunte" (Petrarca 1996, 1158).

178. Plaisance 2004: "Ma non poteva gia nella santissima filosofia naturale e so-pra naturale lodarla veramente come si può lodare la nostra gloriosa marchesa, ma sopra tutto nella divinissima poesia, della quale meravigliato il Petrarca veneziano canto divinamente dicendo: *Cingi . . .* " The speaker goes on (302) to quote in full Bembo's two further sonnets on Colonna (see Bembo 1960, 609–11 [nos. 125–27]).

179. Useful here comparatively are the remarks on the role of women writers as defining of literary "modernity" in other contexts in Summit 2000, 16–17.

## Chapter 3. Diffusion (1540–1560)

1. For d'Aragona's *Rime,* see d'Aragona 1547, d'Aragona 1891 (though bearing in mind the inadequacies of this edition, detailed in Jones 2005, 288–95) and d'Aragona 2005 (more faithful than the 1891 edition, though less complete). For the *Dialogo,* see d'Aragona 1912 and 1997. For discussion of the *Rime,* see R. Rus-sell 1994b and the bibliography cited there; also, subsequently, Bausi 1994 (an abridged translation of Bausi 1993); Bassanese 1996, esp. 74–75; Buranello 2000; D. Basile 2001; Hairston 2003 (with a useful bibliography at n. 3); Zanrè 2004, 146–59; Robin 2007, 175–84; Hairston 2008; Baernstein and Hairston 2008. Secondary lit-erature on the *Dialogo* is cited in n. 158 below.

2. On Terracina, see Dersofi 1994b, citing existing literature; also, subsequently Hernando Sanchez 1994, 489–90; Shemek 1998, 126–57; Casapullo 1998; Montella 2001; Robin 2007, 46–47, 54–55, 60–61. It is interesting to note that both Terracina and d'Aragona were operating in regimes with strong imperial affiliations and in which the cultural model represented by Vittoria Colonna had particular reso-nance; see D. Basile 2001, 139–41, on the role of the Spanish-Neapolitan Duchess

of Florence, Eleonora of Toledo, and other members of her family in establishing d'Aragona in Florence.

3. Terracina 1549, 106–7.

4. Terracina 1550a, 81r. Cervoni is probably a relative, perhaps the father, of the late Cinquecento encomiastic poet Isabella Cervoni, also from Colle.

5. d'Aragona, 1547, 39v (no. 54); cf. d'Aragona 1891, 122; also, for commentary, Bausi 1994, 282.

6. D'Aragona imitates Gambara in a prominently placed sonnet to Bembo (d'Aragona 2005, 48; discussed in Jones 1990, 107, and Bausi 1993, 75–76; cf. Gambara 1995, 95–96 [no. 36]). Terracina pays homage to the older poet in a subdedication in her 1549 *Discorso* (Terracina 1550a, 59r [dedication to canto 37]).

7. D'Aragona's mother was a courtesan, Giulia Campana. For debate on the identity of her father, see d'Aragona 1891, xix; R. Russell 1994b, 26; Hairston 2008.

8. Though Terracina could claim with accuracy to be "of ancient nobility," the Terracina family did not rank high in the complex structure of the Neapolitan nobility; notably, they did not have membership of any of the five *Seggi* (assemblies) among which the aristocratic elite was divided. The most thorough examination of the family's status is found in Maroi 1913 (see esp. 29 on their status as "fuori Seggi"); also B. Croce 1976, 279; Montella 2001, 7; and, for background, Hills 2004. Terracina's poverty is referred to quite often in her verse (see esp. Maroi 1913, 70). For a fairly candid admission that she wrote with an eye to financial reward, see the poems cited in B. Croce 1976, 286.

9. D'Aragona 1547 is introduced by a letter from Girolamo Muzio to the author, noting that he had insisted on her publishing the work. The equivalent role is taken in Terracina 1548 by Lodovico Domenichi, who signs the dedication to Giovanni Vincenzo Belprato, Count of Anversa (1549–89), while in Terracina 1549, it is taken by Leonardo Curz, or Kurz, who appears to have financed the publication.

10. The title is imitated in Terracina's second volume of verse (Terracina 1548).

11. Terracina's author portrait from the 1548 *Rime* is reproduced at B. Croce 1976, 281, and in Montella 2001, facing p. 7. For another portrait of her, from *Le medaglie del Doni* (published in Venice by Giolito in 1550), see Jaffe 2002, 171. The second of these portraits, and probably the first, is the work of the Parmese engraver Enea Vico (1523–67).

12. Dionisotti 1999, 227–54. More recently, on print culture in mid-sixteenth century Italy and its implications for literature, see Quondam 1983; di Filippo Bareggi 1988; Richardson 1994, 90–126; Feldman 1995, 47–50; Coppens and Nuovo 2005.

13. On the *poligrafi* and their activities, see especially di Filippo Bareggi 1988; also Grendler 1969; Richardson 1994; Bragantini 1996, esp. 681–99.

14. On Giolito's alertness to the market appeal of women writers, see Coppens and Nuovo 2005, 118–19, 121. The feminist credentials of the owner of the press, Gabriele Giolito, were advertised by contemporaries: see, for example, Dome-

nichi 1549, *Prefatione* (unnumbered, but a7v), where Giolito is described as "hoggimai conosciuto affettionatissimo, e devoto delle Donne" ("well known today for his great affection for and devotion to women").

15. Terracina's first published poem is addressed to Domenichi and appears in an anthology edited by him (*Rime* 1546, 263–65; *Rime* 2001, 380–81). For his role in the publication of Terracina 1548, see n. 9 above; on his role in promoting her print career generally, Robin 2007, 60. On the probable role of the Naples-based Passero in introducing Domenichi to Terracina's verse, see *Rime* 2001, 441. Where Matraini is concerned, the dedicatory letter of Matraini 1556 makes it clear that Domenichi was instrumental in its publication. See also Matraini 1555, 138–40, for an exchange of sonnets between the two. Domenichi's 1559 anthology of women's poetry is discussed in the text.

16. Stampa first appeared in print in *Rime* 1553, edited by Ruscelli, 68v–69r; cf. also Ruscelli, ed. 1555, 149. Ruscelli also effectively owned the Pietrasanta press, publishers of Stampa 1554: see Trovato 1991, 253–54. On Dolce's role in the publication of Matraini and Morra, see Matraini 1989, liv–lv, and Morra 2000, 12–13, 93–94.

17. ?I. Sforza 1544; ?Gonzaga 1552; Lando, ed. 1548. On the Sforza volume, see Erdmann 1999, 126; Daenens 2000, 36; on the Gonzaga volume, Ridolfi 2001, 797; Erdmann 1999, 111–12; on the *Lettere,* most recently, Bellucci 1981; Jordan 1990, 138–43; Daenens 1999b; Pezzini 2002.

18. On Clara, originally from Alessandria in Piedmont, see Albonico 1989; now also in Albonico 2006, 95–122. Her works survive in a single manuscript at El Escorial. On Salutati, who has been recently identified as the subject of an intriguing portrait by Domenico Puligo, see Slim 1961 and 1972, 1:92–95; Rogers 2000; Cecchi 2001, 274–76; Santarelli 2001, 321–22; Davies 2006, 146–48. Interesting evidence of Salutati's poetic activity survives in the form of a *capitolo* in *Raccolta di poesie,* ms. Fondo Antinori 161, Biblioteca Medicea Laurenziana, Florence, 109r–111v.

19. On relations between Siena and Naples between the 1520s and 1550s, see Toscano 2000, 18–19, who notes that Alfonso d'Avalos, Colonna's cousin by marriage and a key figure in the dissemination of her work, was admitted to the Sienese Accademia degli Intronati in 1525. On the importance of Siena as a center for women's writing in the 1540s and 1550s, see n. 131 below.

20. On the first publication of Colonna's *Rime* as a "scintilla caduta nella paglia," see Dionisotti 1999, 238. Graziosi 2005, 149, has called attention to the earlier appearance in print of an anonymous *raccolta* of verse by a nun of the Clarissan convent of Corpus Domini, first published in 1525 under the title of *Devotissime compositioni rhytmice e parlamenti a Jesù Christo* (see appendix A under 1525; also Serventi 2005, 37–38). Erdmann 1999, 213–14, also lists two further religious works published under women's names in 1519 and 1521, neither of which I have been able to consult (see appendix A, p. 235, fn. ‡). Once we take into account also the publication in this period of works by earlier women writers such as Catherine of Siena, Caterina Vigri, Camilla Varano, and Antonia Pulci, it becomes clear that the novelty of the publication of Colonna's *Rime* lies in the fact that these were *secu-*

*lar* writings by a woman, not that they were writings by a woman per se; here, the only precedent appears to be that of Cassandra Fedele's 1487 *Oratio.*

21. Bandello 1992–96, 194 (3.42) ("non insoavemente componeva qualche sonetto o madrigale"). Although d'Aragona's published poems are not easy to date, her sonnet to the preacher Bernardino Ochino (d'Aragona 2005, 58) is probably datable to her time in Ferrara in 1537. It is quite likely that some of the love poetry included in her 1547 *Rime* also dates to the 1530s; certainly, the impassioned and sensual voice of this poetry is closer to the persona of d'Aragona as portrayed in Sperone Speroni's *Dialogo d'amore* than to the platonically "corrected" version we see in her Florentine-period verse. The literature on the figure of the cultured courtesan (*cortigiana onesta*) is now immense. Studies centered particularly on courtesans' literary activity include Bassanese 1988 and 1996; Rosenthal 1992; Robin 2003; Feldman 2006. Besides Imperia and Barbara Salutati, another intriguing early figure of a courtesan writer is Camilla Pisana, who refers in a letter of around 1515–16 to a book she has written: see *Lettere* 1990, 34, no. 4, for the letter and, for discussion and contextualization, Fedi 1996a, 61–65; Bassanese 1996, esp. 71–74. Flosi 2006, 137–41, unconvincingly attempts to identify possible compositions by Camilla among the madrigals set to music by Costanzo Festa (1485–1550).

22. For Battiferra's life, see Kirkham 2006, 11–32; also Kirkham 2000, 2002a. On her verse and its cultural context see also Kirkham 1996 and 1998; Plazzotta 1998; Battiferra 2000.

23. As Victoria Kirkham's researches have confirmed, Battiferra's first husband (d. 1549) was Vittorio Sereni, a musician at the court of Urbino. Her second was the architect and sculptor Bartolomeo Ammanati (1511–92).

24. B. Croce 1976, 279–80. It is notable, in general, that, of the five authors under consideration in this paragraph, only Battiferra and Matraini had "normal" marital careers by the standards of the time. Matraini was married young, to a fellow *lucchese* of comparable status, Vincenzo Cantarini, and was widowed in her mid-twenties. D'Aragona, meanwhile, contracted a marriage of convenience in her thirties to a Silvestro Guicciardi, while Stampa was still unmarried in her late twenties at the time of her death.

25. On Matraini, see Rabitti 1994 and the bibliography cited there; also, subsequently, Rabitti 1999; R. Russell 2000b; Carlson 2005. Javion 1994 is dated in its approach and takes no account of Rabitti's important work on Matraini of the 1980s.

26. Studies of Stampa often present her as frequenting patrician circles in Venice, but the concrete evidence for this is slim (see n. 154 below). The most thorough modern study on Stampa is Bassanese 1982. For bibliographies of critical writings on Stampa, see Bassanese 1994b, 138, 410–13, and Zancan 1998, 178–80. Recent contributions not listed in these sources include Smarr 1991; Philippy 1995, 92–135; Mussini Sacchi 1998; Moore 2000, 58–93; J. Rose 2000, 29–37; Benfell 2005; Chemello 2005; Jones 2005, 295–303.

27. Little is known of the lives of any of these poets. Poems by Baffo were published in Betussi 1543; Cassola 1544; Domenichi 1544; *Rime* 1545; Doni 1552. For modern editions, see Bianchini 1896, 15–18; also, for the poems published by

Domenichi, Domenichi 2004, 114, and *Rime* 2001, 317. For discussion, see Bianchini 1896; Bassanese 1988, 303–7; *Rime* 2001, 408. Mirtilla's poems appear in *Rime* 1553 and Domenichi 1559. Her works are most easily accessible on the website Italian Women's Writing (www.lib.uchicago.edu / efts / IWW). On her relations with Stampa, see Salza 1913, 61–63, who conjecturally identifies her as the daughter of the courtesan Marietta Mirtilla, famous as the addressee of love letters from Antonio Brocardo (d. 1531). Another female writer based in Venice in this period who was more clearly a courtesan is Lucrezia Ruberta, also known as Lucrezia Squarcia: a figure whose aspirations to learning are ridiculed in the satirical *Tariffa delle puttane* of 1535 (Salza 1913, 78–79) but described sympathetically in Betussi 1543 (Salza 1913, 43); she is also the dedicatee of Bandarini ?1545. For Laura Pieri's works, see the text at n. 166. The only discussions I know of Pieri are Moreni 1819, 235–37, and Moreni 1826, 260–61.

28. For some interesting general observations on the discrepancy between modern and sixteenth-century perspectives in this regard, see Cerrón Puga 2005, 106–8.

29. Other aristocratic female poets who appear in anthologies of the period include Ippolita Gonzaga (1531–63), daughter of Ferrante Gonzaga, governor of Milan in the 1540s and 1550s and Duchess through marriage of, sequentially, Tagliacozzo and Mondragone (*Rime* 1561); Livia Tornielli Borromeo (d. 1553), Countess of Arona in Piedmont (Domenichi, ed. 1559); and Isabella Pepoli Riario, daughter of Count Filippo Pepoli and wife of Count Giulio Riario, both of Bologna (Ruscelli, ed. 1555; Domenichi, ed. 1559).

30. Details of these anthology publications are most conveniently available in the lists in Erdmann 1999, 206–23; see also the websites Italian Women's Writing (www.lib.uchicago.edu / efts / IWW) and ALI RASTA (Antologie della lirica italiana / Raccolte a stampa) (http: // rasta.unipv.it) and Robin 2007, 205–42. The most important single source is Domenichi 1559, which includes substantial selections by Leonora Falletti (twenty-two poems) and Virginia Salvi (fifty), among the women under discussion in this paragraph. The Venetian-born but Florentine-based Olimpia Malipiero, also of patrician background, is also well represented, with thirty-three poems.

31. See, for example, the volume for Irene di Spilimbergo of 1561 (*Rime* 1561), which includes poems by Sanseverino, d'Avalos, Albani, Malipiero, and Salvi, as well as Laura Battiferra and Laura Terracina. On the invitation protocol for this volume, see the text between nn. 36 and 37.

32. Toscano 2000, 77. The manuscript in question was that made by Rinaldo Corso for presentation to Veronica Gambara in the 1540s; for the printed version, see Colonna 1558. The Brembati were connected to the Gambara through the marriage of Maddalena Gambara to Marco Coriolano Brembati.

33. For an edition of Albani's *canzoniere,* including the poems published during her lifetime, see Albani 1903. On the circumstances of the transcription of her early verse, see ibid., 35–37, 39–41. A recent biographical-critical study of Albani is Cominelli 2001.

34. For the dialogue, see *Lettere inedite di Pietro Gradenico,* ms. It. X.23 (6526) (letter to Albani from Pietro Gradenigo of 25 December 1560), Biblioteca Marciana, Venice, 105v–106r. For Albani's Latin poem (to Marietta Contarini, probably the author of the poem listed in Stevenson 2005, 448), see *Ad magnificam et pudicissimam Marrietam Contarenam Lucia Albana,* ms. Lat. XII.225 (4410), Biblioteca Marciana, Venice, 37.

35. The letters are contained in the manuscript cited in n. 34, *Lettere inedite di Pietro Gradenico.* The nature of Gradenigo's family connection with Albani is unclear from the letters, although he refers to her frequently as his "parente." See Albani 1903, 12, who notes that Albani's parents were married in the house of a Luigi Gradenigo, described as a relative by marriage (*affine*).

36. See *Lettere inedite di Pietro Gradenico,* ms. It. X.23 (6526) (letter of 31 October 1555), Biblioteca Marciana, Venice, 74r, where Gradenigo recounts the admiration a letter of Albani's aroused in Venier, Molin, and Lodovico Dolce. Gradenigo's correspondence with Albani, omitted from consideration in Cominelli 2001, would merit further attention; the only brief mention I know of in print is Feldman 1995, 134–35.

37. *Lettere inedite di Pietro Gradenico,* ms. It. X.23 (6526) (letter of 20 August 1560; "honorate, et Illustri Donne, e Signore"), Biblioteca Marciana, Venice, 105r. For a list of the female contributors to the volume, see n. 111 below. As a point of comparison, see the letter of 18 April 1560 from Tommaso Porcacchi to Bianca Aurora d'Este in Giovio 1560, 121r–122v, which similarly uses the lure of the participation of high-placed noblewomen to persuade the recipient to contribute to the Spilimbergo volume, singling out for mention Costanza d'Avalos, Ippolita Gonzaga, and Dianora Sanseverino. Porcacchi's approach bore impressive fruit, as d'Este not only contributed to the volume but later married him (di Filippo Bareggi 1988, 164–65; Porcacchi 1585).

38. *Lettere inedite di Pietro Gradenico,* ms. It. X.23 (6526) (letter of 15 November 1561), Biblioteca Marciana, Venice, 99r. Gradenigo clears himself of any interference with his correspondent's texts, blaming the changes on the printers or the volume's editor, Dionigi Atanagi.

39. The Albani family fell into a morass of scandal in 1563 following Lucia's brothers' murder of the scion of a rival Bergamasque clan (see the text between nn. 106 and 108). Lucia's errant husband, Faustino Avogadro, died the following year, and Albani herself was dead by 1568 at the latest (Albani 1903, 23–25).

40. Molin's *Rime* were published almost two decades after his death in 1573, Gradenigo's three years after his in 1583, Venier's not until 1751.

41. For a caution against this tendency in a seventeenth-century English context, see Ezell 1987, 64.

42. On Morra, see Schiesari 1994 and the bibliography cited there; also, subsequently, Morra 1998 and 2000; Malpezzi Price, 1997; Smarr 2001, 9–11; Robin 2007, 73–77. Besides Morra and Albani, on whom see above, of the other ten writers singled out here for attention, those who have received most critical attention are the Sienese Laodomia Forteguerri (Piéjus 1994b, 85–86; Eisenbichler 2001a; Eisen-

bichler 2003, 100–1); Aurelia Petrucci (Stortoni, ed. 1997, 41–43; Eisenbichler 2003, 98–99); and Virginia Salvi (Cerrón Puga 2005, 107–8; Eisenbichler 2003, 95–98). On Brembati, see Jaffe 2002, 281–310; on Sanseverino, Balsano 1988, xvii; on Falletti (with regard to her portrayal in Giuseppe Betussi's dialogue *Leonora*), Bassani 1992, 74–77. On Costanza d'Avalos, see Mutini 1962b; on Gallerati, Guazzoni 1994, 59–62; Stevenson 2005, 281; on Valenti, ch. 2, n. 68, above.

43. The most accessible edition of Stampa's *Rime* is Stampa 1976, though this follows the ordering of the poems in the 1913 edition by Abdelkader Salza (V. Franco and Stampa 1913) rather than that of the 1554 edition (see Jones 2005, 295–303, for the discrepancies; also Zancan 1998, 94–96, on the context of the 1913 edition). An edition restoring the 1554 order is forthcoming from the University of Chicago Press, edited and translated by Jane Tylus. For criticism, see n. 26 above.

44. A critical edition of the text is available (Matraini 1989). For criticism, see n. 25 above.

45. On the preponderance of occasional and religious verse in Domenichi's anthology, see Piéjus 1982, 202–8. See also, more generally, Smarr 2001 on sixteenth-century women poets' deviations from the erotic model of the Petrarchan lyric.

46. See Piéjus 1982, 208–10, on Virginia Salvi's love poetry, and Cominelli 2001 on Albani. Where Salvi is concerned, note that three poets of this name are recorded in sixteenth-century Siena: Virginia Martini Salvi, the best known of the three and the figure referred to here in the text, Virginia Venturi Salvi (sometimes referred to patronymically as "di Matteo," and Virginia Luti Salvi (sometimes referred to patronymically as "di Achille"); see Piéjus 1994a, 331 n. 23.

47. A good example is the *canzoniere* of Olimpia Malipiero in Domenichi 1559, 130–48. A recent reading of Virginia Salvi emphasizing her political poetry is Eisenbichler 2003, 95–98. For brief comment on political verse by Veronica Gambara and Leonora Falletti, see Sears 1996, 87.

48. Domenichi 1559, 61–68. Castellani's verse also appears in Bottrigari, ed. 1551, 257–61. Castellani's collection in the Domenichi anthology (eleven poems) includes some *rime spirituali* but also poetry in praise of Este women, a poetic exchange with Antonio Gaggi, and a sonnet addressed to the Spanish-Portuguese female erudite Luisa Sigea (1522–60) (61). For discussion, see Graziosi 1996, 310, and Graziosi 2005, 162. Graziosi identifies Castellani as a Dominican in the convent of S. Giovanni Battista.

49. Terracina 1548, 33r–48r; Smarr 2001, 2.

50. See d'Aragona 2005, 62–73; also, for discussion, Jones 1990, 113–17; Jones 1991.

51. This hypothesis is discussed in sec. 4.

52. Matraini 1989, 93 ("donna non de' piu alti sangui nata, né dentro i più superbi palagi, fra le copiose e abbondantissime richezze nodrita"). It is clear from Matraini's reply that her critic had reprehended her particularly for writing of love. The addressee of Matraini's letter is identified only as "M. L." While Lodovico Domenichi ["Messer Lodovico"] has been suggested as a candidate, this seems improbable; apart from anything, it seems clear from the text of the letter that Matraini's antagonist is a fellow *lucchese*.

53. The difficulties Matraini experienced as an intellectually ambitious woman in Lucca are well documented in a chronicle of the time (Baroni, ed., *Memorie e vite d'alcuni uomini illustri,* ms. 926, Biblioteca Statale, Lucca, 210r–213v, discussed in Rabitti 1981, 141–49) that portrays her in a lurid light as a femme fatale who dabbles in magic.

54. On Bruni, see Jordan 1990, 167–71; on Dardano, Jordan 1990, 162–67; on Maggi, Fahy 1961, 254–60.

55. Agrippa 1544; Domenichi 1549; cf. Agrippa 1996. Later editions of Coccio's translation of Agrippa (from 1545) also contain an *Orazione in lode delle donne* by Alessandro Piccolomini, seemingly composed in contrition for his salacious *Dialogo della bella creanza delle donne,* also known as *La Raffaella* (1539). For a list of published literature on women in this period, including treatises on conduct and on love and beauty, as well as *querelle* texts, see Piéjus 1980, 162–65. The best overview of the *querelle* in this period probably remains Jordan 1990, though note also the important observations of Daenens 1983.

56. Fifteenth-century profeminist writings are discussed in ch. 1, secs. 2–3, above. Stephen Kolsky has argued for a direct influence of Equicola on Agrippa; see Kolsky 2005, 207–10. On the circulation of exempla of famous women in this period, see Collina 1996, 114–17. For an interesting contemporary critical review of the history of feminist thought, stressing the gradual superceding of a purely example-based defense by one based on philosophical arguments ("ragioni"), see Ruscelli 1552, 14r–15r.

57. On this work, see the bibliography cited in Kolsky 2003, 223 n.10. On the author, see Bassani 1992 and Robin 2007, 108–10. Ranieri 1985, 264–65, details Betussi's literary relationship with Colonna.

58. Betussi 1545, 183r: "alcuna degna operatione cagionata da grandezza di spirito." Betussi's methodological difference from Boccaccio is implicit in his choice of *illustre* as a translation of Boccaccio's *clarus* in his title; see McLeod 1991, 64–65, for comment.

59. An especially intriguing example of "famous women" imagery in historiated majolica, given the morally equivocal character of the exemplum portrayed, is a plate by Francesco Xanto Avelli of 1533 portraying an image of Semiramis's marriage to Ninus and bearing the arms of the recently married Duke and Duchess of Mantua, Francesco Gonzaga and Margherita Paleologo; see Holcroft 1988, 229, 231–34, and Mallett 2007, 128–29.

60. See, for example, Pantasilea Graziani (Borghesi 1571, 44r ); Penthisilea Ferri (Grillo 1589, 73r); Pantasilea dal Corno Masini (Manfredi 1602b, 89); Pantasilea Gozzadini (Murphy 2003, 121).

61. The most famous instances of the Ariostan names are Bradamante and Marfisa d'Este, nieces of Duke Ercole II d'Este of Ferrara (1508–59), although see also Manfredi 1580, 36–38, for a Bradamante Malvezzi. The age also produced at least one Semiramis (Semiramide d'Appiano [1464–1523]) and an Atalanta (see text at n. 83). For some interesting general considerations on female naming in this period, see Grubb 1996, 45–46.

62. Irene was the name of a Roman painter mentioned in Pliny's *Natural History;* Hypsicratea that of the heroic wife of Mithridates of Pontus, who accompanied him into battle dressed as a man. Issicratea Monte is discussed in ch. 5 below; for Minerva Bartoli, see Erdmann 1999, 208. For d'Aragona as "modern Cicero," see d'Aragona 1891, 132; Zanrè 2004, 156. A famous later example of such "prognostic" naming was, of course, Artemisa Gentileschi (1593–1652 / 53).

63. On sixteenth-century writings on female beauty, see Cropper 1976 and 1986; G. Pozzi 1979; Rogers 1988; Erdmann 1999, 3–5; also Barboni 1998 for a more comprehensive bibliography. For the theoretical love literature of the period, see M. Pozzi 1989; Masi 1996, 595–601; ibid., 674, for further bibliography.

64. The composition of Equicola's *Libro* has been dated to c. 1505–9. Castiglione worked on the *Cortegiano* from around 1508–24, although the concluding section on Neoplatonic love took its final shape only in the last redaction of the dialogue. Another important statement of love theory from this period, of noncourtly provenance, is Leone Ebreo's *Dialoghi d'amore* composed probably around 1501–2, though not published until 1535.

65. Modern editions are available of Luigini and Betussi (Zonta 1912); d'Aragona (d'Aragona 1912, 1997); Firenzuola (Firenzuola 1993); Speroni (Speroni 1996b). For secondary literature, see the works cited in n. 63 above and n. 158 below.

66. A. Piccolomini 1541; Varchi 1561. Varchi's lectures date mainly from the 1550s and were delivered before the Infiammati and the Accademia Fiorentina. Varchi also edited and wrote a preface for an important early sixteenth-century philosophical dialogue on love by Francesco Cattani da Diaceto (1561).

67. See Ruscelli, ed. 1555 and *Rime* 1561. For discussion, see, on the former text, Robin 2007, 102–4, 105–7; on the latter, Schutte 1991 and 1992 and Corsaro 1998. On early sixteenth-century precedents for the genre, see Calitti 2004, 61–63. A fifteenth-century manuscript precedent is the volume for Laura Brenzoni discussed at the end of ch. 1, sec. 3. Where the posthumous volumes are concerned, in particular, note Cristiani, ed. 1555 as a precedent to *Rime* 1561.

68. Schutte 1991, 56; see also, on the later fortunes of the genre, Bianco 2001. On the anthologies for Peverara, see ch. 5, n. 46, below.

69. Campanile's work had been written earlier (c. 1517–22). On Franco's plagiarism, see most recently Capata 1998. The date of publication given is that of the first dated edition; another, copies of which are found in the British Library and the Marciana, may date to 1535. For a list of Neapolitan works in this genre published between 1536 and 1563, see Capata 1998, 229, and also Croce 1942.

70. Ruscelli 1552: the full title in Italian reads *Lettura . . . sopra un sonetto dell'illustriss. signor marchese della Terza alla divina signora marchesa del Vasto, ove con nuove e chiare ragioni si pruova la somma perfettione delle DONNE; e si discorrono molte cose intorno alla scala Platonica dell'ascendimento per le cose create alla contemplatione di Dio, et molte intorno alla vera bellezza, alla gratia, e alla lingua volgare. Ove ancora cade occasione di nominare alcune gentildonne delle piu rare d'ogni terra principal d'Italia.* For the publishing context of the text, see Robin 2007, 46–48.

71. On Corso's dedication, see ch. 2, n. 84, above. Piccolomini's dedicatory letter to *De la sfera* is summarized in Eisenbichler 2001a, 295–96. Examples of works on "women's subjects" dedicated to women include Ebreo 1535 to Aurelia Petrucci (by Mariano Lenzi); N. Franco 1536 to Argentina Rangone (also the dedicatee of Aretino's comedy *Il Marescalco,* 1533); N. Franco 1542 to Maria d'Aragona; Betussi 1545 to Camilla Imperiali; Maggi 1545 to Leonora Gonzaga Martinengo; Sansovino 1545 to Gaspara Stampa; Betussi 1556 to Vittoria Colonna di Toledo; Agrippa 1544, to Bona Soardi di San Giorgio; and Luigini 1554 to Lucrezia Gonzaga da Gazzuolo (by Girolamo Ruscelli).

72. On the latter dedication, see Kennedy 1994, 73–74. As examples of contemporary verse-collections dedicated to women, see Domenichi 1544 to Bona Sforza, queen of Poland; Bandello 1545 to Costanza Rangone; A. Piccolomini 1549 to Vittoria Colonna di Toledo; Ruscelli, ed. 1553 to Virginia Pallavicino Gambara. Some poetic commentaries are also found dedicated to women: see Varchi 1545 (by Francesco Sansovino to Gaspara Stampa) and Gelli 1549 (by the author to the poet Livia Tornielli Borromeo)

73. A. Piccolomini 1540; Corso 1566; Seneca 1554.

74. Borsetto 1989, 23–27,

75. Borsetto 1989, 27–36, 157–58, 182–82. The five poets other than de' Medici and the five subdedicatees other than Gonzaga were all Sienese. The former included Alessandro Piccolomini, the latter Aurelia Petrucci.

76. Borsetto 1989, 184–85, 187–88. Besides these dedications to women, two sixteenth-century women are recorded as themselves having translated portions of the *Aeneid:* Ippolita Clara (Albonico 1989, 323) and Emilia Arrivabene Gonzaga (see ch. 5, n. 50, below).

77. See Zonta 1912; N. Franco 1542; Speroni 1996b; Benucci, *Dialogo della lontananza,* ms. 1369, Biblioteca Angelica, Rome, ff. 1–50; Speroni 1996c; Domenichi 1549. See also Finucci 2002, 33–36 (cf. Finucci 2005, 8–9) for an unpublished love dialogue of the 1540s featuring the Paduan writer Giulia Bigolina as speaker. On thematic constraints on dialogues with female speakers, see further Cox 2000a, 393

78. Ochino 1985; Contile 1543; De Valdés 1938; Lando 1552b. De Valdés's and Ochino's dialogues have recently been discussed in Robin 2007, 18–26, 163–69. The relation of women to reform culture in Italy is discussed above in ch. 2, sec. 4. The most prominent female writer involved with the reform movement in the period under discussion here was Olimpia Morata, who eventually married a German protestant and left Italy in 1550. See on her Morata 2003 and the bibliography cited there; also Daenens 1999a; Smarr 2005a, 72–81; Smarr 2005b.

79. Deswarte-Rosa 1992; Agoston 2001, esp. 1185–86; Ugoni 1562.

80. See Cox 2000a, 390–91; also, on the figure of d'Aragona in Speroni's dialogue, Buranello 2000. On d'Aragona's self-portrayal in her own *Dialogo,* see the bibliography cited in n. 158 below.

81. Belladonna 1992; Robin 2007, 130–36. Girolama's husband, Bartolomeo Carli Piccolomini, dedicated his popular ottava rima poem *Edera* (1543) to the poet Virginia di Achille Salvi, a translation of the fourth book of the *Aeneid* (1540) to

Aurelia Petrucci, and a translation of an oration of Cicero's to Emilia degli Ugurgieri. The latter remains in manuscript in Siena: see Belladonna 1992, 51–52.

82. Paleario 1983. The speakers are Cassandra Spannocchi Bellanti, Aurelia Bellanti Bogini, Francesca Spannocchi, and Porzia degli Agazzari.

83. The text is edited in Glénisson-Delanée 1991 (I am grateful to Alex Coller for calling this article to my attention). The poem glossed by *madonna* Atalanta is a gauche *strambotto* purporting to date from the early Italian tradition (87), with the wit of her commentary depending on the discrepancy between the lowliness of her object and the loftiness of the significance she gives to it. See also Belladonna 1992, 62 n. 2, on a further, unpublished Sienese dialogue, by Girolamo Piccolomini, that includes female interlocutors (Frasia Venturi, Onorata Pecci), along with a male speaker also featuring in Landucci's dialogue, Alfonso Piccolomini-Todeschini, Duke of Amalfi, husband of the poet Costanza d'Avalos.

84. *Rime* 1561, A4v–Aa4v. The biography is often attributed to Giorgio Gradenigo, who appears to have masterminded the commemorative project for Irene; for the issue of authorship, see Corsaro 1998, 46–47.

85. *Rime* 1561, A7v: "desiderosa, nell'imprese d'honore, e di Gloria, di uscir della strada commune delle altre"; ibid., A8v–Aa1r: "Teneva . . . fisso il pensiero ad esser tale che nelle cose che ella prendeva per impresa, non le fosse alcuna donna superiore, laonde con virtuosa invidia sentiva le lodi altrui." See also the passage just preceding (A8r) where it is noted that Irene liked to surround herself with poets, "aspettando da loro quella lode, & Gloria ne' loro poemi, che conveniva alle sue virtù" ("expecting from them that praise and glory in their poems that her many talents deserved").

86. *Rime* 1561, Aa2r–v. On Anguissola's extraordinary career, see Garrard 1994 and Wood-Marsden 1998, 191–213.

87. *Rime* 1561, Aa3r. Irene's mortification of her body in the pursuit of art is portrayed in an admiring manner reminiscent of hagiography, as when, warned to take more care of her health, she replies by querying why one should have such regard for "this poor little body, which is nothing other than vile earth and a scattering of dust?" ("A che haver tanto riguardo a questo corpicciuolo, che altro non è che vil fango, e poca polvere?") A nuance of moral distance is at most conveyed in the allusion to her *"sfrenato . . .* appetito di Gloria" (*"unbridled . . .* appetite for Glory" [Aa2r; my italics]).

88. *Rime* 1561, Aa4v.

89. *Rime* 1561, A5v: "Fu per la vivacità del suo ingegno posta molto prima delle altre fanciulle a quei lavori d'ago e di riccami [sic], che sogliono usarsi tra le Gentildonne, e Signore per loro ornamenti, & per fuggire l'otio nemico principale del sesso loro."

90. *Rime* 1561, A5v: "Nel qual tempo parendo a lei picciolo acquisto l'arte del riccamare, & cosa da non tenervi occupati tutti i suoi pensieri; si diede da sé a leggere, et a scrivere." It seems likely that this version of Irene's education had been narratively "improved" to emphasize Irene's talent and agency; as a noblewoman, and as the daughter of a highly literate mother, Giulia da Ponte (on whom see

Chemello 1999, 36–37), it is unlikely that she would not have been destined for a literary education. For a similar heroizing account of a young female intellectual rejecting the pursuit of needlework forced on her in childhood in favor of reading, see Patrizi 1963, 18–19, on Tarquinia Molza (also the translation in Riley 1986, 284). The motif recalls Ariosto's *Orlando furioso*, 37.14.4–6 (Ariosto 1976, 953), where female writers are lauded for exchanging the "needle and cloth" for the pen: "poi che molte, lasciando l'ago e 'l panno/son con le Muse a spegnersi la sete/al fonte d'Aganippe andate, e vanno."

91. Betussi 1545, 232r. A similar attitude is displayed by Betussi's Sienese compatriot Diomede Borghesi, in a sonnet praising Claudia Rangone (1531–93)—the dedicatee of the Spilimbergo volume—for abandoning feminine labors to pursue immortality through learning (Borghesi 1566, 2v).

92. Quondam 1991, 278. For similar defenses of learning as a commendable pursuit for women, see Bandello 1545, 58r–v; also, in a more politicized key, the letters of feminist exhortation by Partenia Gallerati cited in Guazzoni 1994.

93. On the novelty of the ideal of feminine exemplarity represented in the Spilimbergo vita, see Corsaro 1998, 48.

94. Ariosto 1976, 1092–97 (42.78–96).

95. The twenty-four women and their corresponding virtues are listed in Bassani 1992, 82 n. 31, and in Robin 2007, 120–21.

96. Betussi 1556, 52–56. Similar lists are found in Domenichi 1549 and Ruscelli 1552; see Robin 2007, 52, for comment.

97. Calzolai 1561, day 3, 3: "E da questo [women's excellence] nasce ch'ogni huomo naturalmente da bene volentieri favorisca, con le opere, e con le parole gli egregii fatti delle donne, innalzandogli con infinite lodi insino al cielo, parendo loro in lodar quelle, andarne anche lodati essi."

98. Petrarca 1996, 701 (no. 146): "in ch'io mi specchio e tergo." For comment, see Moore 2000, 41–42.

99. Bandello 1992–96, 84 (3.17, preface): "[sono uomini, il cui debito è] naturalmente e d'amare, onorare, riverire e celebrar tutte le donne."

100. For Varchi's relations with Tullia d'Aragona (who described him in a letter as her "maestro" and her "Dante"), see Bausi 1993, esp. 66. On his relations with Laura Battiferra, attested by their interesting letter exchanges, see Kirkham 2005, 319–20, 323–24, 319–20; also, for the Italian text of the letters, Battiferra 1879. Piccolomini's relations with Forteguerri are discussed in the text.

101. B. Croce 1976, 245.

102. On women's role as proxy for an "unlettered" audience in dialogues of this period, see Cox 1992, 45. For the same dynamic in an earlier period, see also Cornish 2000.

103. Boccaccio 1558, A2r–A8v. Sansovino's introductory essay portrays Stampa, in her early twenties, as a beginning student of Latin, describing Ovid, for example, as an author she will "soon be able to read for herself" (A8r: "[il qual] cred'io che in breve voi medesima potrete intender senza fatica"): a point worth noting given the quite widely diffused notion in modern criticism that Stampa had en-

joyed a full humanistic education in her girlhood (see, for example, the sources cited in Robin 2003, 56 n. 34).

104. Ruscelli ed., 1553 and *Rime* 1556b. Albani, Bergamasque by birth, qualifies as Brescian by virtue of her marriage to a Brescian and residence in the city.

105. Vida 1550, 64v–65r; cf. Guazzoni 1994, 59 and 69 nn. 5 and 16. Vida does not name the two in his oration, identifying them, perhaps out of considerations of decorum, only as "two most celebrated virgins of our city" (*duas praeclarissimas virgenes cives nostras*), but he says enough of their attainments to make their identities clear. On Vida's relationship of mentorship to Gallerati, see Guazzoni 1994, 59.

106. Domenichi 1559, 129 and 136–37. Torelli also features in the volume as the addressee of a sonnet by Laodomia Forteguerri; see Eisenbichler 2001a, 301. Besides her role as poet-figurehead, Torelli also served as one of the principal collective muses to the Pavian Accademia degli Affidati: see, for example, the poems to her in their collected verse of 1565 (*Rime* 1565b, 16 [Ognibene Ferrari]; 17–23, 25, 26–27, 36 [Filippo Binaschi], 114, 121–22 [Guido Casone]; 156–59 [Girolamo Bossi], and 255 [Luca Contile]). On Binaschi's poems to her, see M. Maschietto 1968, 486.

107. On the feud, see Cremaschi 1960 and Jaffe 2002, 293–94.

108. On Isotta, mentioned in the text at n. 29, see Jaffe 2002, 281–310. On Emilia, a sonnet by whom is found in *Tempio* 1568, see Mazzucchelli 1753–63, vol. 2, pt. 4:2044–45. Minerva Rota Brembati is recorded as a poet alongside Isotta in B. Tasso 1560, 271 (canto 44.72), though nothing by her survives.

109. The list of poets contributing to the Spilimbergo volume is reproduced in Schutte 1992. For discussion, see Corsaro 1998

110. Compare Cerrón Puga 2005, 106, for an estimate of women's overall representation in published verse anthologies of the period as 9.61 percent (no doubt a slightly inflated figure, as Domenichi's 1559 anthology of all-female poetry is included in her count). The most immediate precedent for the Spilimbergo volume, as a posthumous tribute anthology for a woman, Cristiani, ed. 1555, includes no women among its thirty-one named poets.

111. Besides the six named in the text, the female poets included in the Spilimbergo volume are Bianca Aurora d'Este, Cassandra Giovio, Diamante Dolfi, Lucia Albani, Lucia Bertani, and Olimpia Malipiero. Of those not discussed elsewhere in this study, Cassandra Giovio was from Como, granddaughter of the *letterato* Benedetto Giovio and married to Girolamo Magnocavallo, lord of Gravellona in the territory of Monferrato (Bandini Buti 1946, 1:303–4), and Diamante Dolfi was Bolognese, the daughter of Lorenzo Dolfi and married to a Giambattista Preti (Fantuzzi 1781–94), 3, 256.

112. Venetian poets with a presence in the volume include Bernardo Cappello, Domenico and Marco Venier, Celio and Alessandro Magno, Orsatto Giustinain, Giacomo Zane, Giacomo Tiepolo, Pietro Gradenigo, and Daniele Priuli.

113. For a contemporary perception of this dynamic, see Betussi's description of the Venetian Giulia Ferretti in his *Il Raverta* (1544) as "scuola ed albergo di dotti e virtuosi" ("school and abode of the learned and talented"; Zonta 1912, 56). On d'Aragona's *Rime* as a venue for homosocial bonding between the male poets as-

sembled there as her admirers, see Jones 1990, 104–5. With due modification—Jones represents D'Aragona's *Rime* as an idealized representation of the relationship of a courtesan's circle of clients—the same analysis may be applied to the choral anthologies of poets such as Terracina and Battiferra, as well as to enterprises such as the volume for Irene di Spilimbergo under discussion here.

114. See ch. 5, sec. 2. On the reasons for Venice's failure to nurture native patrician female writers, see Zancan 1989. One Venetian woman of patrician background mentioned in a number of "famous women" listings of the later sixteenth century (e.g. Marescotti 1589, 171) is Foscarina Foscarini Venier, mother of the poets Domenico and Lorenzo Venier. Another, probably not of patrician origins, is Giulia Ferretti, on whom see Betussi, quoted in n. 113 above; also Lando 1552a, 476. See also n. 34 above on Lucia Albani's correspondent Marietta Contarini, seemingly a Venetian patrician from her surname.

115. Piéjus 1982, 204–5.

116. On Irene's Venetian descent, see Schutte 1991, 43–44. A parallel may be drawn here with Lucia Albani, whose literary 'adoption' by the Venetian *letterato* Pietro Gradenigo is discussed in section 1. Although born in Bergamo, Albani was also of Venetian descent through her maternal line (Foresti 1903, 12–13).

117. Roskill 1968.

118. Domenichi 1559 includes examples of poetic correspondence between Domenichi and Lucia Bertani (111, 118); Olimpia Malipiero (145–46); Laodomia da San Gallo (17); Leonora Falletti (73–74), and Livia Tornielli Borromeo (12, 229). For discussions of the anthology, see Piéjus 1982; Shemek 2005a; Cerrón Puga 2005, 113–29; Robin 2007, 50–51, 59–78, 238–42.

119. Castiglione attained prominence shortly after the publication of the volume as *cameriere segreto* to his Milanese compatriot Pope Pius IV (Giovanni Angelo Medici). Betussi, mentioned in the dedicatory letter (Domenichi 1559, 4) as having convinced Domenichi to publish the volume, figures as correspondent of Livia Tornielli Borromeo (12, 229); see also 228 for a poem to him from Leonora Falletti.

120. Piéjus 1982, 201–2; Piéjus 1994a, 316. Piéjus also notes that a Sienese poet, Aurelia Petrucci, is chosen to open the collection and that another, Virginia Salvi, heads the list of poets in quantitative terms.

121. For the context of the anthology's appearance, see Robin 2007, 59, who, however, in my view misleadingly suggests that the collection was a private project of Domenichi's, pursued outside the aegis, and possibly even against the will, of his principal patron, Cosimo de' Medici. Another text of the same period, this time of Sienese authorship, that demands to be seen in the same political context is the poem in praise of Sienese ladies published in Cerretani 1560, 252–60, with a dedication to Eleonora di Toledo, Duchess of Florence.

122. For Salvi's pro-French (and hence anti-imperial) political position, see Eisenbichler 2003, 95–98. Her consistency is praised in Betussi 1556, 88, cited in Piéjus 1994a, 331 n. 24. Interesting in the political context is Domenichi's choice as opening sonnet of Aurelia Petrucci's "Dove stà il tuo valor, Patria mia cara" ("What Has Become of Your Valor, My Dear Fatherland") (for the text of which

see Stortoni, ed. 1997, 42, and Eisenbichler 2003, 98): a lament on the Sienese "republican" propensity to civil discord, penned by a granddaughter of Pandolfo Petrucci (1452–1512), the great protagonist of Siena's last period of seignorial rule.

123. Piéjus 1994a, 202. Indexes were customarily organized alphabetically by forenames in sixteenth-century Italian books.

124. The collection also showcases a number of poets from elsewhere in Tuscany, mostly unattested elsewhere: from Pistoia, Candida Gattesca (34), Giulia Braccali Ricciardi (37), Cornelia Brunozzi Villani (38), and Selvaggia Bracali [sic] Bracciolini (40) and, from Florence, Clarice Medici Strozzi (31), Maria Martelli Panciatichi (39), "Narda N." (121), and Lisabetta da Cepperello (105–8). For lists of the poets in the volume, see Shemek 2005a, 252–53, and Robin 2007, 240–42; also Cerrón Puga 2005, 108–10, who lists contributors to the volume together with other sixteenth-century anthologized female poets, giving geographical provenance in each case.

125. A. Piccolomini 1541; cf. Robin 2007, 148.

126. A. Piccolomini 1541 (prefatory letter by Marcantonio da Carpi): "à tutti quelli non volgarmente notriti huomini, et a tutte quelle gentili, e d'elevato spirito dotate Donne, che prenden piacere nella soavissima lettione delle cose Thoscane."

127. On the 1542 Florentine lecture (the academic debut of Bernardo Canigiani, later one of the founder-members of the Accademia della Crusca), see Plaisance 2004, 110–11; 286–89. The text of the *lettura* is in *Capitoli, composizioni e leggi dell'Accademia degli Umidi,* ms. II.IV.1, Biblioteca Nazionale Centrale, Florence, 210v–217r. Plaisance 2004, 286, also notes two further lectures on Colonna in the Accademia Fiorentina, one in 1545 by Francesco di Niccolò Bottrigari and the other in 1550 by Tommaso Ginori.

128. Varchi contributed a prefatory sonnet in praise of Forteguerri to the printed edition of Piccolomini's *Lettura* (A. Piccolomini 1541, E2r; Varchi 1565, 95r: "Donna leggiadra, al cui valor divino" ["Fair Lady, Whose Divine Worth"]). On his relations with Tullia d'Aragona and Laura Battiferra, see n. 100 above. Varchi was also acquainted with Gaspara Stampa and wrote a mourning sonnet for her posthumous *Rime* of 1554 (Stampa 1976, 57–58), while a sonnet exchange of his with Chiara Matraini is found in an anthology of 1556 (*Rime* 1556b, C1r–v). He also appears to have been in contact with Laura Pieri, who alludes to him warmly as "'l mio . . . Varchi" (literally, "my Varchi") in Pieri 1554, Aiiiir.

129. On the Infiammati, see Samuels 1976 and Vianello 1998.

130. Vianello 1998, 75–77.

131. On Sienese women's writing at this time, and on the remarkably "feminized" literary culture that nurtured it, see the fundamental study of Piéjus 1994a; also, more recently, Belladonna 1992; Eisenbichler 2003; Coller 2006; Robin 2007, 124–59. Piéjus, Belladonna, and Coller all stress the importance of the Intronati, of which Piccolomini was a leading member, in fostering this profeminist culture.

132. *Lettere* 1968, 3:235 (letter of 31 May 1541). For the texts of the sonnets in question, see Cerreta 1958, 163–65, and Robin 2007, 139–41; for the context of their composition, Cerreta 1960, 32–33; Piéjus 1994a, 317–18; Robin 2007, 137–41.

133. For the text of the sonnet, see Eisenbichler 2001a, 299. The phrase quoted in the text, reminiscent of Colonna in its use of the *senhal* of the sun for the beloved, puns untranslatably on two meanings of *vago* ("beautiful" and "wandering" or "errant"—hence the translation "distant"). Forteguerri's poems for Margaret are discussed further in sec. 4 below.

134. The sonnet portrays Margaret's residence in Rome in explicitly imperial terms, speaking of the city (represented by its river, the Tiber) as now, on account of her presence, "carrying the scepter and ruling over the most famous" ("ora porti lo scettro, or hai l'impero / de' più famosi"). On Piccolomini's imperialist political sympathies, see Celse 1973.

135. For the term, see Kirkham 1996, 353, and Hairston 2003, 257.

136. On this motif, see Cox 2006, 140–42. The choral anthology may probably be accounted as one of the instances in which the female-authored Petrarchan tradition proved influential on the male, along with Colonna's "invention" of the genre of *rime spirituali*. Certainly, male-authored poetic *raccolte* from the 1550s also begin to show an increasingly dialogic character from around this time (see, for example, Varchi 1557, which lays out poetic exchanges dialogically on the page, as does d'Aragona 1547). Earlier volumes had tended rather to consign correspondence verse by other poets to an appendix, following the model of Bembo's *Rime* of 1535.

137. The nature of the exercise, and its agonistic dimension, are brought out in Lodovico Domenich's appreciation of Terracina in Domenichi 1549, 238v–239r: "Questa rara e bella giovane non solo per le rime altrui è famosa et illustre, perciocché i più chiari intelletti dell'età nostra hoggi *la cantano a prova,* ma da sè stessa co' propri inchiostri si va acquistando gloriosa fama" ("This rare and beautiful young woman has not only attained fame and glory through others' verses—for the most celebrated minds of our age *compete to hymn her praises*—but she is also acquiring a glorious reputation through the flow of her own inks"; my italics).

138. Kirkham 1996, 353; Jones 1990, 105.

139. Notable in this regard in Battiferra is the lack of the self-advertising "di diversi a lei" section found in d'Aragona 1547 and Terracina 1548 and 1549.

140. Stampa 1554, 117–18. The poems are 246 and 247 in the conventional modern numbering. The break is reflected in modern editions by the heading *Rime varie* (Stampa 1976, 243).

141. The poems for Venier, Speroni, and Molin are nos. 252, 253, and 260 (Stampa 1976, 247–48, 252). Part of the same encomiastic sequence in the 1554 edition (though not in modern editions) is the series of poems on the death of a Venetian nun (Stampa 1554, 122–26; cf. Stampa 1976, 282–87 [nos. 299–303]). They are followed by a sonnet to a Priuli also placed out of sequence in modern edition (no. 286) and then by a sonnet to a Zanni or Zane (no. 254), after which the modern numbering resumes following 1554. On the discrepancy between the 1554 edition and modern editions, see n. 43 above.

142. Stampa 1554, 147–50, 151–52; cf. Stampa 1976, 210–11 (nos. 204–6); 287–92 (nos. 304–11).

143. A published collection of the kind hypothesized here would almost certainly have comprehended correspondence verse addressed to Stampa and perhaps poetry in praise of her. The oddly marooned *proposta* poem by Leonardo Emo we find at the end of the 1554 edition (Stampa 1554, 177) was plausibly intended for this end; see Stampa 1976, 262–63 (nos. 275–76) for her replies. Other verse addressed to Stampa during her lifetime is reproduced in V. Franco and Stampa 1913, 188–91.

144. See Kirkham 2006, 23–24; also, more generally on Battiferra's poetic influences, ibid., 51.

145. This verse form, which Battiferra uses for her translation of an apocryphal hymn by St Augustine (Battiferra 2000, 148–51), was a Cinquecento innovation, introduced by Giangiorgio Trissino. It was used increasingly for translations from the classical languages from the 1530s, most famously by Annibale Caro in his translation of the *Aeneid* (1565); see Martelli 1984, 543–44 and 545–56; also Borsetto 1989, 25 and n. 10. On Battiferra's metrical eclecticism, especially in her later verse, see Kirkham 2006, 8–9.

146. This characteristic verse-form of Terracina's was first identified in Casapullo 1998; see also now Ravasini 2003, esp. 78–81. On the Spanish origins of the form (which dates to the second half of the fifteenth century), see Ravasini and Scoles 1996. I am grateful to Maria Luisa Cerrón Puga for alerting me to Casapullo's study.

147. A musical setting of Sanseverino's poem, by Giandomenico Martoretta, was published in 1548; see Ravasini 2003, p. 86 for the text and pp. 81–83 for discussion; also Balsano 1988, xvii. Ravasini describes Sanseverino as an imitator of Terracina, but it may well be that the obverse was the case, given that Terracina's first poem in this form only appeared in 1546 (see following note). Terracina pays tribute to Sanseverino in a sonnet of the 1548 *Rime* and makes her the dedicatee of the second canto of her 1549 *Discorso*. Her *Quarte* and *Quinte rime* are dedicated, respectively, to Dianora's father and stepmother. Another female-authored *trasmutazione* of the period (using Petrarch's sonnet 134, "Pace non trovo, e non ho da far guerra" as its source text) is Virginia Salvi's "Da fuoco così bel nasce il mio ardore" (Domenichi 1559, 186–90; cf. Eisenbichler 2003, 195).

148. For the 1546 publication, addressed to Lodovico Domenichi and in an anthology published by him, see *Rime* 2001, 380–81.

149. Interestingly, four of the seven individuals addressed in sonnets are non-Neapolitan (Lodovico Domenichi, Benedetto Varchi, Luca Martini, Marcantonio Passero); the others are Luigi Tansillo, Dianora Sanseverino, and an otherwise unidentified "Reverendo di Fundi." See Terracina 1548, 7r, 8v, 11r–v, 31r–v.

150. Stampa 1976, 230–41 (nos. 241–45), 275–77 (296), 279–82 (no. 298); cf. Stampa 1554, 153–67. For discussion, see Phillippy 1995, 111–14, and Chemello 2005, 71. For precedents, see the *capitoli* by Vittoria Colonna (c. 1512) and Barbara Salutati (1520s) discussed above. After Stampa, within the published tradition, Veronica Franco is the only female author to make substantial use of the form.

151. On Stampa's relation to the *Heroides* tradition, see Philippy 1995, 92–135, and Chemello 2005.

152. On the presence of Boccaccio's *Fiammetta* in Stampa's *Rime* see Mussini Sacchi 1998; also Chemello 2005, 60 n. 37; Braden 1996a, 133. On the dependency of the *Fiammetta* on the *Heroides,* see Brownlee 1990, 11, who designates Boccaccio's text an "expanded heroid."

153. On Stampa's relationship with these figures, see Salza 1913, 5–14 (Sansovino); 14–17 (Parabosco); 36–37 (Doni). See also ibid., 5–52, more generally on Stampa's circle. Although off-putting in its approach (Salza's agenda, pursued with disconcerting zeal, was to prove the thesis that Stampa was a courtesan), this study remains unparalleled as a source for Stampa's life and context.

154. Critics often present Stampa as moving in the circles of Domenico Venier, but it is important to note that there is no evidence of contact between the two other than a sonnet by Stampa addressed to him. The same is true of Sperone Speroni, whose only known reference to Stampa is a slanderous epigram (Salza 1917a, 266, cited in Zancan 1998, 51).

155. Smarr 1991. See also on Stampa's musical career, Feldman 1995, 104–8; Feldman 2006, 114–18; De Rycke 2006.

156. Lando 1552a, 475; for the context, see ch. 4, n. 28, below. Lando also praises Stampa in a letter in the ghostwritten *Lettere di Lucrezia Gonzaga* of 1552; see ?Gonzaga 1552, 325; cf. Salza 1913, 29 n. 2.

157. Stampa 1976, 271–72 (no. 290); cf. Ruscelli, ed. 1555, 149. Among the other female contributors to the volume, besides Stampa, was the Bolognese countess Isabella Pepoli Riario (333); the other two, Anna Golfarina (57) and Fausta Tacita (308–11), are otherwise unknown.

158. See d'Aragona 1912 and 1997; also M. Pozzi 1989, 83–87; Smarr 1998; Buranello 2000; Robin 2003, 41–42; Curtis-Wendlandt 2004; Smarr 2005a, 106–17; Grantham Turner 2003, 37–41; Campbell 2006, 21–49. The skepticism concerning d'Aragona's full authorship of the dialogue expressed by male critics in the past may not simply be an expression of sexism, as is implied in, for example, Allaire 1995, 33–34: the dialogue shows a competence in dialectic that would usually imply a university education in its author, unlike the more "oratorical" and less technical style of philosophical discourse practiced, for example, by Matraini in her late religious dialogues (discussed in ch. 5, sec. 3). On the issues surrounding collaborative authorship in studies of women's writing, see DeJean 1991, 71–72; Clarke 2001, 10–12.

159. For Albani, see *Lettere inedite di Pietro Gradenico,* ms. It. X.23 (6526) (letter of 25 December 1560), Biblioteca Marciana, Venice, 105v–106r, praising, among the work's other merits, "il grande acquisto, ch'ella [= Vostra Signoria] ha fatto delle cose della Filosofia, et Teologia Christiana" ("the great advances you have made in philosophy and theology"). For Matraini, see *Lettere e poesie del sig[nor] Cesare Coccapani auditore di Lucca e di donna incerta lucchese,* ms. 1547, Biblioteca Statale, Lucca, 403, 410. In the first of these letters, Matraini speaks of her difficulties in procuring a vernacular copy of Boethius, noting that she had to rely on a Latin

edition for "a certain dialogue I wrote" ("certo Dialogo che io feci"). In the second, she expresses dissatisfaction with what she perceives as the work's excessive verbosity ("di già parmi nel dialogo essere un poco lunga, non interponendo nelle volte versi come usa il Severino Boezio"; "I fear the dialogue is a little too long, as it is not broken up by poems as Boethius's is").

160. For discussion, see Jung-Iglessis 1997; Brundin 2001 and 2002; U. D'Elia 2006, 120–22. On the letters to Costanza d'Avalos, see also Adler 2000, 313–16.

161. Terracina 1550a (first published 1549); Terracina 1551 (revised edition). For a list of reprints, see appendix A. On the popular fortunes of the work, see Grendler 1989, 299, who records its use as a reading primer in Venetian vernacular schools in the 1580s.

162. The last line of each stanza is taken in succession from Ariosto's opening stanza, except in the case of the seventh stanza, where the last two lines are made up of Ariosto's closing couplet. For discussion of the work, see Cox 1997a, 136–37, and Shemek 1998, 126–57.

163. Matraini 1989, 99 ("nobilissimi e studiosi nostri signori Academici"). The text of the oration is found on pp. 99–109. The same device of an address to a nominal academy is also found in Matraini 1602.

164. Matraini 1556. Matraini's translation, which the title makes clear is translated from the Latin rather than the Greek, is unrelated to the previous published translation by Pietro Carrario (Carrario 1555, 21r–28v), which is more concise and workaday and less consciously elevated. Material from both the Oration and the Isocrates translation were reworked by Matraini for her Lettere of 1595 and 1597; see Rabitti 1999, 215–16.

165. For a useful overview of letter writing by sixteenth-century women, see Chemello 1999. As we have seen, Lando, ed. 1548 and ?Gonzaga 1552, though presented as female-authored, are attributed by most commentators to their purported editor Ortensio Lando.

166. Moreni 1819, 235–37, speculates that Pieri may have been the author of a further ottava rima historical poem published anonymously in Florence probably by Lorenzo Torrentino (see ?Pieri 1555, dated by Moreni to 1553). On the literary context of the poem, see d'Ancona 1906, 85 n. 1.

167. On Il Meschino, see Allaire 1995, who regards the work as genuine, arguing for a date of composition of c. 1543–46; also, on the authorship issue, Celani 1891, lvi–lxiii. Julia Hairston promises a fresh look at the question, drawing on new research that addresses some of Celani's concerns, in her forthcoming edition of the poem for the University of Chicago Press. Doubts regarding the Meschino's attribution to d'Aragona are raised by the work's posthumous publication and its sporadically lascivious character (see ch. 5, nn. 17 and 21, below), as well as by the fluctuation between female and male adjectival and verb endings in first-person interjections by the narrator. The absence of any occasional or encomiastic element also seems surprising in a work by d'Aragona.

168. Gambara 1995, 119–25 (no. 54); also ibid., 125, 128–29, on the text's edito-

rial fortunes. For a sequence of allegorizing *stanze* by Fonte that may reflect the influence of Gambara's poem, see Fonte 1988, 173–81; 1997, 241–58.

169. Bigolina 2002, 2004, and 2005. For discussion, see Nissen 2000; 2003, 205–14; 2004; Finucci 2002, 2005.

170. *Lettere e poesie del sig[nor] Cesare Coccapani auditore di Lucca e di donna incerta lucchese,* ms. 1547, Biblioteca Statale, Lucca, 410; cited in Rabitti, 1981, 150 n. 22. A work by Laura Terracina, *Historia di Isabella et Aurelio,* listed by Gigliola Fragnito as among works considered for inclusion on the 1596 Index of Prohibited Books (Fragnito 1997, 272), is probably a phantom (the title is that of the published Italian translation of Juan de Flores's *Grisel y Mirabella* (1495) by "Lelio Aletifilo," or Lelio Manfredi, published frequently from 1521 onward; see Matulka 1931, 463–66, 469–72, 473–75 on the text's Italian fortunes).

171. See on this Rabitti 1992, 149–55; Rabitti 2000; Cox 2005a, 19–22; Cox 2006, 146–48.

172. See esp. Rabitti 1981, 160; Rabitti 1992, 150.

173. Kirkham 2006, 192–98, 418–19.

174. For Isabella Morra, see Grignani 2000, 26; for Salvi, Rabitti 1992, 152–53; for Albani, Cominelli 2001, 264–69, stressing particularly Gambara's influence. For Forteguerri, see n. 183 below. For Colonna's influence on Matraini, see Rabitti 1981, 159–60; Rabitti 1985, 241; Rabitti 2000, 484–85. For the text of the sonnet cited here, Matraini 1989, 85–86 (A88), 243–44 (C44), and cf. V. Colonna 1982, 15 (A1:15).

175. See Borsetto 1983, 190–92; also Javion 1994, 258.

176. More explicitly, Laura Pieri constructs just such a genealogy to legitimize her writing at the opening of her *Quattro canti* (Pieri 1554, A4r): the female figures cited are Colonna, Gambara, d'Aragona, and Terracina, while the males include Dolce, Varchi, Domenichi, Doni, Luigi Alamanni, and (interestingly, given his reputation) Aretino.

177. For poems of friendship, see Matraini 1989, 63 (A67) ("Donna gentil, ch'e' bei pensieri tenete" ["Gentle Lady of Fine Thoughts"], to an unknown addressee); Malipiero in Domenichi 1559, 138 ("Privo di stelle 'l cielo, e del mar l'onde" ["First the Stars of the Sky and the Waves of the Sea"], to an otherwise unidentified "Minia"); Stampa 1976, 275–77 ("Non aspettò giamai focoso amante" ["Never Did An Ardent Lover"], to Ippolita Mirtilla). Laura Battiferra's sonnets in her *Primo libro* to Ortensia Colonna and Lucrezia Soderini might also be loosely assimilated to these poems in their intimacy of register. Besides the sonnet exchange between Colonna and Gambara, Colonna's published epistolary and exchanges with Marguerite de Navarre offered an authoritative and highly self-conscious model for an exchange of compliments between high-placed women: see ch. 2, n. 158, above for references.

178. For the exchange between Battiferra and Bertani, see *Miscellanea poetica del secolo XVI,* ms. 897, Biblioteca Casanatense, Rome, 187r and 188v; Bertoni 1925, 379–80; Battiferra 2006, 326 n.12. For that between Battiferra and Terracina, see Battiferra 2006, 304–7, 446; also ibid., 116–17, 386–87, for Battiferra's sonnet to

Cortese. For the exchange between Falletti and Tornielli, see Domenichi 1559, 118, 232; also ibid., 61, for Castellani's poem to Sigea. For Forteguerri's poem to Alda Torelli, see Eisenbichler 2001a, 301. See Robin 2007, 151, for further examples.

179. On female-female exchanges in Domenichi, see Piéjus 1982, 203; Curran 2005, 283–84 n. 5; Robin 2007, 62–71. For the Terracina group, see Terracina 1549, 91–93. The female poets contributing to the Terracina volume are mainly from the Colonna family (Geronima, Maria, Vittoria Colonna di Toledo, Giovanna d'Aragona Colonna); see also Terracina 1549, 102, for a sonnet to Terracina by Laodomia di San Gallo, also present in the Domenichi collection. Geronima and Vittoria Colonna and Giovanna d'Aragona Colonna also feature among the canto dedicatees of Terracina's *Discorsi,* along with the poets Dianora Sanseverino, Costanza d'Avalos, and Veronica Gambara.

180. An exception is perhaps Girolama Corsi Ramos (discussed in ch. 2, sec. 2) among whose surviving verses are two sonnets celebrating the marriage of Cateruzza Corner, niece of Caterina Corner, queen of Cyprus (V. Rossi 1890, 192 n. 1).

181. For d'Aragona's poems to Eleonora, see d'Aragona 2005, 40–44. For Malipiero's, see Domenichi 1559, 13; see also ibid., 62 and 64–66, for Castellani's poems to the Este and p. 197 for Salvi's poem to Catherine de' Medici (cf. also, for the latter, Eisenbichler 2003, 98). For Stampa's poem to Catherine, mentioned above, see Stampa 1976, 243–44 (no. 247). An interesting rhetorical discussion of female-female poetry is found in the proem to Bandello's *Novelle,* 3.17, addressed to the aristocratic poet Margherita Pelletti Tizzoni (d. c. 1533) and praising a series of madrigals she has written for Giulia Gonzaga. Bandello suggests there that poetry by a woman may be particularly appreciated by a female recipient because it will be assumed to be more objective than verse by a man; it is made clear, however, that this applies only when the poet is, like Margherita, sufficiently high-placed herself to be considered disinterested.

182. See the discussion of Forteguerri's poems in Eisenbichler 2001a, who, however, in my view, overstresses lesbianism as a context; also Robin 2007, 149–58. Another female poet of the period under discussion here who draws on amorous language in a poem to a patron is Girolama Castellani, in her *canzone* to Renée of France in Domenichi 1559, 64–66. For an example of a "straight" encomiastic poem to Margaret of Austria by a female poet (Giulia d'Aragona), see Bottrigari, ed. 1551, 208.

183. See especially, for the influence of Colonna, Forteguerri's sonnet "A che tuo Febo col mio Sol contende?" ("Why Does Your Phoebus Contend with My Sun?") (Eisenbichler 2001a, 299–300) and compare Colonna's "Questo sol, ch'oggi agli vostri occhi splende" ("This Sun That Today Shines in Your Eyes") (V. Colonna 1982, 13 [A1:21]). For Petrarchan precedents for the motif of the "two suns," see Petrarca 1996, 472 (notes on 100, 1–2). More generally, on the use of this imagery in female poets of the time, see R. Russell 2000b, 419–20.

184. Battiferra 2000, 154–64. The poem, seemingly composed around 1560 and a late addition to the collection (Kirkham 1996, 362–63) is of interest as the first at-

tempt by a woman at the genre of pastoral eclogue, later used by Maddalena Campiglia and Isabella Andreini. Leonora Cibo was a poet herself: a sonnet by her is found in F. Tasso 1573, 51, along with poems by Laura Gabrielli Alciati (40), Ortensia Lomellini Fieschi (44), and Battiferra herself (52). For further biographical detail, see Battiferra 2006, 385. On the conspicuous place given to the Cibo-Vitelli couple in Battiferra's *Primo libro* and the patronage interests informing this, see Kirkham 1996, 362, 365–66, 373.

185. "versi . . . soavi," "dolci detti" (Battiferra 2000, 155 [l. 16], 156 [l. 56]).

186. Changes in dedicatory practices in women's works over the course of the century are discussed in ch. 5, sec. 3.

187. On Domenichi's Florentine poets, see n. 124 above. Another purported female writer active in Florence in this period is the pseudonymous "Madonna Daphne di Piazza," author of a popular book of verse riddles addressed to "her lovers the Florentine Academicians" and first published in Venice in 1552. While the author, or authors, have generally been assumed to be male (de Filippis 1948, 17), it is conceivable that Laura Pieri may have had a hand in its composition, in that the punning identification of the "inventrice" (di Piazza 1552, 2r) with a laurel and a stone (*marmo*) would fit well with her name, reading *marmo* as an etymological allusion to her surname (Piero=Pietro=*petrus*/*petra*). Pieri's connections with the comic poets of the Accademia Fiorentina, such as Giambattista Gelli, Giovanni Maria Cecchi, and Antonfrancesco Grazzini, would merit further investigation; all are cited in a passage in Pieri 1554, Aiiiir, along with Aretino and Antonfrancesco Doni.

188. On de Toledo's literary patronage, see Hernando Sánchez 1994, 484–94. On Eleonora's close relationship with her father, see Gaston 2004, 173. Hernando Sánchez 1994, 489–90, discusses Terracina's attempts to secure Pedro de Toledo's literary patronage; see also pp. 95–96 on connections between the de Toledo and Colonna families (Eleonora's brother García was married in 1552 to Vittoria Colonna, homonymous niece of the poet). Recent studies on Eleonora have dramatically revised previous perceptions of her as rigidly pious and culturally inert, stressing her close collaboration with her husband in the political, economic and artistic spheres (see especially Eisenbichler, ed. 2004; also, subsequently, Gáldy 2006). More remains to be done on her involvement with literature, attested by interesting dedications such as those of Doni 1547, D. Bruni 1552, and Seneca 1554 (the last apparently commissioned by Don Pedro on behalf of his daughter). For first steps in this direction, see Robin 2007, 192; also Hernando Sánchez 1994, 475, 492–93.

189. See Cardamone 2002, esp. 3, on Isabella's humanistic education; also Langdon 2006, 146–70. Isabella continued her mother's tradition of patronage of female creatives; see ibid., 9 on her relations with the composer Maddalena Casulana.

190. The likelihood of Eleonora's knowing these poems is the greater in that Margaret—Eleonora's exact contemporary—spent three years in Naples prior to her marriage to Alessandro de' Medici in 1536 (Gáldy 2006, 293). Given Eleonora's

Neapolitan upbringing, it is possible that she knew also of the madrigals of the early 1530s addressed to Giulia Gonzaga by Margherita Tizzoni which Bandello highlights as notable examples of female-female praise poetry (see the text in ch. 2 at n. 69 and ch. 3, n. 181). Interesting evidence of Eleonora's active support of female poets is offered by her involvement in a 1547 decision to exempt Tullia d'Aragona from the wearing of the yellow veil mandated for courtesans in Florence (see D. Basile 2001, 139–41, who discusses Eleonora's possible motives).

191. This corresponds to a more general shift in Eleonora's self-presentation in the later years of her life, discussed in Benson 2004; cf. Edelstein 2004, 71–72. Both date this development to the period of the conquest of Siena (1559–60), although the evidence of D. Bruni 1552 (discussed in Gáldy 2006, 295–98) might incline us to predate it to the early 1550s.

192. Kirkham 1996, 354 n. 7, remarks that the ordering of the initial sequence reverses the usual gender-hierarchical ordering of poems to noble couples in the *Primo libro,* where sonnets to husbands systematically precede those to wives.

193. Battiferra 2006, 84.

194. On Terracina, see Dersofi 1994b, 424. The story often found in biographies that Terracina was forced out of the academy by the unwanted attentions of an admirer is probably apocryphal (Maroi 1913, 42; see also the text in ch. 6 at n. 140 for the source). On Battiferra's invitation to join the Intronati in 1560, see Kirkham 2005, 180; also ibid., 191 n. 8, for further details. The election of Virginia Salvi to the Sienese academy of the Travagliati in 1560 is implicitly presented by one of its members as motivated by rivalry with the Intronati following their election of "the great Battiferra" ("la gran Battiferra"; Fahy 2000, 444 and n. 21). Another possible case of female academy membership in this period is that of Leonora Fallettti, who, on the testimony of Betussi 1556, 57, was invited to join the Milanese Accademia Fenicia, or dei Fenicii (founded c. 1550); see on this latter academy Maylender 1926–30, 2: 356–61.

195. Terracina 1548, 53r: "tant'altre nobilissime virtù, tanto tempo per le Barbariche ingiurie sepolte." The letter, from "il Caudio," is dated 23 December 1546.

196. See Feldman 1995, 31–35; 104; also, more generally, on the emergence of professional female musicians in the sixteenth century, Newcomb 1986.

197. Betussi 1556, 55–56 (the voice is that of "Fame" addressing "Truth"): "ch'io voglio formare con l'autorità e col giuditio tuo un Choro di Muse di donne moderne . . . voglio . . . elegger Donne tali, e celebrarle secondo le rare e singolari doti che miracolosamente alcuna ha nel Canto, altra nella Voce, altra nel Comporre, altra nel Dipingere, & altra nel Suono"). An allusion to a related project is found in Betussi's *Leonora;* see Bassani 1992, 77 n. 20.

198. Betussi 1556, 56: "Apollo potrebbe lasciare l'antiche nove sorelle, & a queste volontariamente congiungersi."

199. The letter is found in *Lettere e poesie del sig[nor] Cesare Coccapani auditore di Lucca e di donna incerta lucchese,* ms. 1547, Biblioteca Statale, Lucca, 410. For discussion, see Rabitti 1981, 152; also, more generally on the Coccapani letters, see ibid., 149–55; Rabitti 1999, 226–34; Carlson 2005, 108–11.

200. For examples of the focused literary mentorship available to more fortunate women, see Bembo's letter to Veronica Gambara of 11 May 1535, cited in
Dilemmi 1989, 31, suggesting a minor amendment to a sonnet she has sent him;
Pietro Gradenigo's letter to Lucia Albani of 7 October 1560 (*Lettere inedite di Pietro
Gradenico,* ms. It. X.23 [6526], Biblioteca Marciana, Venice, 74v), similarly suggesting revisions, and Benedetto Varchi's very detailed discussion of a linguistic issue
raised by Laura Battiferra in a letter to him of c. 1561 (Battiferra 1879, 60–65; trans.
in Battiferra 2006, 328–32).

## Chapter 4. Intermezzo (1560–1680)

1. Finucci 2002, 55–63 (cf. Finucci 2005, 24–30).

2. The Italian text of Bigolina's surviving novella, with a translation, are found
in Bigolina 2005, 46–72. The manuscript containing *Urania* is found in the Biblioteca Trivulziana of Milan.

3. Some of Battiferra's psalm translations were also reprinted in anthologies of
1568 and 1572 (Battiferra 2005, 30). The *Sette salmi* has received little critical attention
to date; see now, however, the edition by Enrico Maria Guidi (Battiferra 2005); also
Battiferra 2006, 218–27, for an annotated text and translation of portions of the volume, and ibid., 45–47, for discussion.

4. Franco's *Terze rime* have attracted much criticism in recent years. For a survey to the early 1990s, see Migiel 1994, 143–44. Subsequent discussions include
Rosenthal 1992, 178–97; 204–55; Bianchi 1993 and 1995 (the latter a reworking of
the former); Jones and Rosenthal 1998, 13–21; Robin 2003, 46–51; Crivelli 2005; also
Jones 2005, 303–5 (on Franco's modern editorial *fortuna*).

5. See ?Cortese 1561, "Celia Romana" 1562, Bianca 1565, B. Salvi and V. Salvi 1571
and Monte 1577, 1578a, 1578b, and 1581. For Monte, see the text between nn. 63 and
65 and at n. 69 in ch. 5. For the publishing history of "Isabella Cortese"'s manual,
see appendix A below and also Erdmann 1999, 211–12. For discussion, see Eamon
1994, 137, 164–65; Lesage 1993; Erdmann 1999, 106–7. Nothing is known of the supposed author, and her existence cannot be assumed, considering that the adoption
of pseudonyms was common in this genre of writing. On the likelihood of female
authorship in the work attributed to Cortese, see Lesage 1993, 166–70. A precedent, as a female-authored compilation of secrets, is the *Experimenti* of Caterina
Sforza, though this was unpublished in the period; see C. Sforza 1894; Graziani and
Venturelli 1987, 141–49. On the publishing fortunes of "Celia Romana"'s *Lettere,*
see appendix A. The genre, and the pseudonymous publication, would lead us to
suspect that the author was a fictional creation, though the fact that a sonnet by a
Celia Romana appears in a verse collection of the period (*Tempio* 1568, 31v) leaves
open the possibility that she may have existed. Similar authorship issues arise with
a later volume of love letters bearing a female signature, "Emilia N" 1594. Leonora
Bianca, the author of the *Risposte* (which I have been unable to examine) has been
tentatively identified with the Veronese noblewoman Bianca Aurora d'Este, wife
of the *poligrafo* Tommaso Porcacchi, and contributor of a poem to the Spilimbergo anthology of 1561 (see nn. 37 and 111 in ch. 3 above).

6. The 1563 Milan edition of Negri's letters—incomplete and without printer's name—was withdrawn in the course of printing and circulated clandestinely. A full edition was published in Rome in 1576. See Firpo 1991, 35–39, 71–73; Prosperi 1994, 230–33. Authorship of the letters was claimed by a disaffected ex-disciple of Negri's, Gian Pietro Besozzi (Firpo 1991, 39, 73). The recent study of Cagni 1989 concludes that authorship was probably collaborative. On Nogarola, see Nogarola 1563 and ch. 1, n. 59 above. Two further works of this period listed in Erdmann 1999, 209 and 221, are Eugenia Calcina, *Priego* [or *Priega*] *alla Vergine beatissima* (Bologna: Giovanni Rossi, 1576) and a volume of *Cantici spirituali* by an anonymous Clarissan nun (Naples: Salviani, 1574). I have not been able to consult either work, but it seems likely that the latter is a late edition of the much-published collection of *Devotissime compositioni rhytmice* first published in 1525 (see appendix A under that date). Also excluded from this list are the writings published under the name of St. Angela Merici in Brescia in 1569–70 (*Regole* and *Testamento*), which share the problematic authorship status of many medieval mystical works (Mazzonis 2004, 401–2).

7. Dionisotti 1999, 238.

8. The most important example is the 1568 *Tempio* to Geronima Colonna, daughter of the Giovanna d'Aragona who had been celebrated in Ruscelli's original *Tempio* of 1554. This contains seven women among its ninety vernacular contributors, although Erdmann 1999, 223, curiously only lists one. The poets included are Celia Romana, Cornelia Cotta, Emilia Brembati Solza, Isotta Brembati Grumelli, Laura Battiferra, Leonora Maltraversa, and Olimpia Malipiero. An even higher proportion (ten out of seventy-nine authors, including well-known figures such as Laura Terracina and Laura Bertani) is found in *Rime* 1565a, for Lucrezia Gonzaga: see Erdmann 1999, 222, for a list of eight of the ten, to whom should be added Diamante Dolfi and "Lucrezia N." Manfredi 1575, a collective volume in praise of Roman ladies, contains seven female poets among its eighty-six named contributors (Erdmann 1999, 222), including the august Virginia Salvi, as well as rising stars such as Tarquinia Molza (b. 1542) and Margherita Sarrocchi (b. c. 1560). Fiammetta Soderini and Laura Guidiccioni Lucchesini also feature as addressees of poems by Manfredi soliciting contributions. An exception to the norm noted here is *Rime* 1564, in memory of Ippolita Gonzaga, herself a poet, which contains only one female author out of fifty-seven identified vernacular authors (Costanza d'Avalos, Duchess of Amalfi [*Rime* 1564, 25]).

9. One of the poems attributed to Gambara by Atanagi ("Ite pensier fallaci e vana speme") is now identified as an early appearance by Veronica Franco. Of the female-authored poems in the second volume, two are by Malipiero, including an exchange of compliments with Premarini, and three by Giustinian's correspondent.

10. See also Marucini 1576, with no female writer among the nine poets included, and contrast the text between nn. 58 and 62 in ch. 5 on similar local anthologies in the period in the later Cinquecento.

11. Finucci 2002, 59, and Finucci 2005, 27–28.

12. Modio 1913 (see ibid., 347–65 for Piccolomini's speech). I have not been able to trace the other work Finucci cites in this connection (Finucci 2005, 28 n. 74), Niccolò Calusio's *Despoteia* (1557). Another text sometimes cited as representative of misogynist literature in this period is Biondo 1546, although this work's relatively early date of publication makes it difficult to identify it straightforwardly as reflecting Counter-Reformation trends.

13. Domenichi 1564; cf. Jordan 1990, 149–50.

14. The work in question is the second book of Nifo's *De re aulica* (published in Naples in 1534), devoted to the lady of the court (*mulier aulica*). Nifo's treatise had been republished in a vernacular translation three years before the appearance of Domenichi's treatise (Baldelli 1560). The plagiarism (which should not surprise us when we recall that Domenichi's earlier *La nobiltà delle donne* was largely a plagiarism of Henricus Cornelius Agrippa) is noted in Kelso 1978, 211. While Domenichi keeps very closely to his source text on the whole, he does mitigate its generalized reflections on women's deficiencies of "ingegno" by noting the existence of exceptions such as Laura Battiferra, "a woman deserving of being remembered with all manner of reverence and honor" ("donna da esser sempre ricordata con ogni maniera di riverenza & honore") (Domenichi 1564, 4v).

15. On the introduction of censorship in this period and its implications for publishing, see, for an overview, Richardson 1994, 140–42; for more detail, Grendler 1977. On the regulations concerning prepublication censorship, see ibid., 145–61. On Ruscelli's association with the Pietrasanta press and on its fate in the 1550s, see Trovato 1991, 253; di Filippo Bareggi 1988, 220, 239 n. 169.

16. See on this Grendler 1977, 129–34; Quondam 1983, 643–44 (looking specifically at Giolito). Religious works went from around 7 percent of the total of Giolito's output in the 1540s to 39 percent in the 1560s and 69 percent in the 1570s, while secular vernacular works went from 53 percent in the 1540s to 24 percent in the 1560s and 11.5 percent in the 1570s (Grendler 1977, 134, table 3).

17. The manuscript of Terracina's *None rime* is found in *Sonetti al sommo Pontefice Gregorio Decimo terzo . . .*, ms. Palatino 229, Biblioteca Nazionale Centrale, Florence (partially published in Montella 2001); that of Battiferra's unpublished works from the early 1560s to the time of her death in *Rime di Laura Battiferri*, ms. 3229, Biblioteca Casanatense, Rome (partially published in Battiferra 2006). Plans for publication were in both cases probably interrupted by the authors' death. Battiferra's project seems to have been for an ambitious edition of her collected verse including her published works from the early 1560s as well as much late spiritual and occasional verse. Terracina's plan was for a narrower collection mainly composed of encomiastic verse addressed to notable figures at the papal court, though it also includes a sequence of *rime spirituali*. Details of the manuscript survival of Bigolina's works are given in Bigolina 2004 and 2005.

18. An example might be the translation of Terence that eighteenth-century historians such as Crescimbeni attribute to the Florentine Fiammetta Soderini (d. c. 1575), an interesting poet whose slim published oeuvre does not reflect the extent of her reputation in her lifetime. For published poems by Soderini, see M.

Colonna and Angeli 1589, 54; Ferentilli 1571, 309–12. For discussion, see Bandini Buti 1946, 1:363; also Kirkham 2006, 44, who notes her friendship with Laura Battiferra. She appears as speaker in Razzi 1568.

19. Dionisotti 1999, 246–52.

20. *Rime* 1567a; *Rime* 1995.

21. Dionisotti 1999, 253.

22. See Erspamer 1982, 55–72, who places the peak of output of literature of this kind in the decades of the 1550s and 1560s.

23. See Orsini 1568; Neri 2003, 13–14.

24. Caro 1558, 250–52 (letter of 7 December 1556) and 261–64 (letter of 22 January 1557); see also pp. 253–60 and 264–66 for Caro's replies, dated respectively 1 January and 3 February 1557. On Bertani, see ch. 2, n. 170, above.

25. Castelvetro is presented as a poetic admirer of Bertani's in Betussi 1556, 103–4. Two sonnets of hers in praise of him are included in Bottrigari, ed. 1551, 210–11.

26. Caro 1558, 252 (letter of 7 December 1556): "anco le donne, come sapete, hanno spente le guerre accese e fatti i nimici amici."

27. Cerrón Puga 2005, 106.

28. Lando 1552a, 472–76. This list is unusual in considering male and female poets together. The seven poets included are Gaspara Stampa ("gran poeta e musica eccellente"), "Ippolita Roma Poetessa Padovana, di cui si leggono dolcissimi versi"—probably Ippolita Mirtilla—Chiara Matraini ("nobile Poetessa di Lucca"), Laura Terracina ("donna di gentilissimo spirito e alto cuore"), Giulia Ferretta ("non solo . . . donna d'honore ma . . . anche poetessa gentile"), Caterina Pellegrini ("d'alto ingegno dotata"), and, in an odd anachronism, Laura Brenzoni ("donna honorata"). Lando's language here seems quite carefully chosen, with a discrimination being made, for example, between Laura Terracina, praised on the grounds of character rather than poetic skill, and the more unequivocally praised Stampa and Matraini. Of the lesser-known poets here, Caterina Pellegrini of Capua had a sonnet exchange with her compatriot Ottaviano della Ratta published in *Rime* 1556a, in which she figures as a widow and a follower of Colonna. She also features with a single sonnet in Domenichi 1559, while a sonnet is addressed to her in Terracina 1558, 86–87. Giulia Ferretti is ironically praised by Lando in his *Sferza degli scrittori* for her forbearance in not publishing, despite having written "endless works in verse and prose" ("et versi et prose senza fine").

29. Hoby lists as examples Colonna, Gambara, Virginia Salvi, Dianora Sanseverino, and Beatrice Loffredo. I have been unable to identify the last. Elsewhere, in his diary of his travels in Italy, Hoby remarks on the literary fame of Sienese women, singling out Laodomia Forteguerri and Virginia Salvi for praise (Hoby 1902, 19).

30. *Oratione di Curtio Gonzaga in lode della lingua italiana*, ms. 4280, Biblioteca Casantense, Rome, 45r–v. For motives presumably of family pride, Gonzaga gives prominence to the figure of Ippolita Gonzaga, attested as a poet only in *Rime* 1561. The other writers named are Colonna, Gambara, Battiferra, Dionora Sanseverino,

Fiammetta Soderini, Irene di Spilimbergo, Laodomia Forteguerri, Virginia Salvi, Caterina Pellegrini, Lucia Albani, Lucia Bertani, Olimpia Caro, Tarquinia Molza, "la Rangona" (probably Claudia Rangoni, 1537–93), "la Paleotti," and "le Coreali." The aristocratic bias of the list is very notable. All the fully identified figures in the list are discussed in the text, aside from Olimpia Caro, who was the daughter of the poet Annibale. Caro is discussed as a poet by Cristoforo Bronzini in the manuscript of the twenty-third day of his *Dialogo della dignità delle donne* of the 1620s (ms. Magl. VIII.1533, Biblioteca Nazionale Centrale, Florence, insert after p. 30). Bronzini describes Olimpia there as having been educated by her father in the classical languages and quotes a sonnet by her mourning Annibale's death. On a later "canon" of women writers found in Gonzaga's *Fidamante* of 1591, see Chemello 2003, 67–69; here, in addition to Ippolita Gonzaga, Colonna, Gambara, Molza, and Soderini, he gives special praise to Maddalena Campiglia, on his relationship with whom see the text in between nn. 115 and 116 in ch. 5.

31. Camerata 1567, esp. 17r–v. The argument is already adumbrated in Castiglione 1960, 217 (3, 13). Camerata illustrates his point (17v) by reference to an unnamed gentlewoman of Bologna, who, in addition to excelling at poetry, has demonstrated her native intellectual talent by mastering Aristotelian logic and philosophy in a remarkably short time.

32. *Oratione di Curtio Gonzaga in lode della lingua italiana*, ms. 4280, Biblioteca Casantense, Rome, 45v. As Fermor 1993 notes, the term *leggiadria* had gendered connotations, denoting a particularly "feminine" grace.

33. Della Casa in fact draws on explicitly misogynistic rhetoric in his antimarriage dialogue *An uxor sit ducenda* (1537), unpublished in his lifetime; see della Casa 1944 for an edition with a contextualizing introduction; also Panizza 1999, 26 n. 52. Della Casa's "authorized" *canzoniere*, published after his death, contains a poem politely declining an invitation to write in praise of a woman, Livia Colonna, on the grounds of his retirement and indifference to worldly glory (della Casa 2001, 167–69 [no. 55]). While this is disingenuous (five sonnets appear under his name in the published collection for Colonna [Cristiani, ed. 1555, 48v, 63r–64v]), it may indicate a degree of detachment from the ritual gynephilia of the poetic culture of his day.

34. For poems to female singers in the Eterei collection, see *Rime* 1995, 127 (no. 95), 145 (no. 126). On seventeenth-century preference in this regard, see the text at n. 152 in ch. 6.

35. Della Casa's semiauthorized, though posthumously published, *Rime* of 1558 contains only sixty-four poems. Recent Italian critics who have described the context of della Casa's poetic reforms often tend (rather unreflectively) to imply that an equation may be made between the "vulgarization" of poetic culture and its admission of women as authors: see, for example, Giuliano Tanturli's characterization of the literary tradition against which della Casa reacted as "ormai affollata di uomini culturalmente di ogni ceto, *e di donne*" ("now crowded with men of all cultural levels *and women*"; my italics) (della Casa 2001, ix). The term "barbarian invasion" in the text is Dionisotti's; see Dionisotti 1999, 245–46.

36. *Rime di Laura Battiferri,* ms. 3229, Biblioteca Casanatense, Rome, 3v ("io, per dire il vero, stimava, che questa rispetto alla grandezza dell'ingegno suo e per lo dono fattole così bello del comporre, dovesse del numero dell'altre donne esser levata, et essere interamente per huomo tenuta"). For a translation of Vettori's letter, and for further discussion, see Battiferra 2006, 77–80, 365.

37. On Florence's social conservatism (presumably by comparison with Rome, where she had lived until 1555), see Battiferra 1891, 22 (letter to Varchi of 14 November 1556) where she complains that she is unable to respond to a sonnet she had received from a male acquaintance out of a concern for "i respetti che mi bisognano avere in questo paese" ("the social niceties I need to observe in this place"). The letter is discussed in Kirkham 1996, 355–56.

## Chapter 5. Affirmation (1580–1620)

1. See appendix A. The count is inclusive of the years 1538 and 1560. Reprints of works by pre-sixteenth century writers such as Catherine of Siena and Antonia Pulci have been omitted from the count, as have works of debated authorship, such as the entries for ?Sforza 1544, ?Gonzaga 1552, and di Piazza 1552, although Tullia d'Aragona's *Meschino* has been included. The entries for Colonna under 1538, 1543, and 1558 have been treated as a single work.

2. See appendix A. The count is again inclusive and omits one work of dubitable authorship ("Emilia N." 1594). The lace pattern books of Isabetta Catanea have also been omitted, as has the entry for Colonna under 1580. It should be noted that this count for these years includes a number of works that are barely more than pamphlets (see, for example, Bendinelli 1587 and the works by Issicratea Monte listed between 1577 and 1581 as well as those by Isabella Cervoni listed between 1592 and 1600); this does not, however, significantly detract from my arguments here.

3. Zancan 1986, 809 ("una progressiva integrazione nelle dinamiche del sistema letterario ed ideologico"); cf. Zancan 1998, 60, for an abridged version of the same passage. Examples of academy memberships offered to women in this period include those to Issicratea Monte (Concordi, Rovigo; see Pietropoli 1986, 60); Isabella Andreini (Intenti, Pavia); and Margherita Sarrocchi (Ordinati and Umoristi, Rome; also possibly Oziosi, Naples; see de Miranda 2000, 61 n. 42). See also the text between nn. 59 and 60 of the present chapter for the more obscure case of Innocenza Carrai of Treviso. In addition to these formal cases of academy membership, there is interesting evidence from this period of more informal interaction between female writers and literary academies in their home cities: see, for example, Cox and Sampson 2004, 6–7, on Maddalena Campiglia's relationship with the Accademia Olimpica of Vicenza; Sampson 2006, 107–8, on Barbara Torelli's with the Accademia degli Innominati of Parma; and Kolsky 2001, 975–77, on Lucrezia Marinella's with the Accademia Veneziana; see also the text between nn. 68 and 69 of the present chapter.

4. On Fontana, see Murphy 2003; Woods-Marsden 1998, 215–22; De Girolami Cheney 2001. On Casulana, see Pescerelli 1979, 5–20; Higgins 1997, 183–84; LaMay

2002. On the Ferrarese *concerto delle donne,* see Durante and Martellotti 1989a. General studies on female artists and musicians in this period include Newcomb 1986; Bowers 1986; Riley 1986; Garrard 1994; Jacobs 1997; Carter 1999. On the emergence to cultural prominence of actresses in this period, see Andrews 2000 and Henke 2002, 85–105. On Andreini in particular, see n. 5.

5. For bibliography on Andreini to the early 1990s, see Dersofi 1994a; also, subsequently, Andrews 2000; Decroisette 2001; MacNeil 2003; Bosi 2003; MacNeil 2005. Among earlier bibliography, Taviani 1984 remains crucial (for an English summary of his argument, see Kerr 2001, 82–89). For Campiglia, see Cox and Sampson 2004, 2 n. 1; also Chemello 2003; Ultsch 2005a and b. For Sarrocchi, see Belloni 1893, 133–40; Borzelli 1935; Favaro 1983, 1:6–23; Cox 2000b, 60–61; Morandini, ed. 2001, 36–50; Pezzini 2005; R. Russell 2006. For Fonte, see Malpezzi Price 1994a, 134–37, and Cox 1997b, 23; also Jordan 1996, 57–61; Jones 1998, 164–73; Kolsky 1999; Kolsky 2001, esp. 979–81; Carinci 2002; Magnanini 2003; Malpezzi Price 2003a and b; Smarr 2005a, 215–30; Finucci 2006a and b. For Marinella, see Malpezzi Price 1994b; also Allen and Salvatore 1992; Jordan 1996, 61–65; Lavocat 1998; Panizza 1999; Benedetti 1999, 454–56; Santacroce 1999–2000; Chemello 2000a; Benedetti 2005; Haskins 2006, the latter containing important new biographical findings.

6. Richardson 1994, 142–43, and Burke 1995, 101–3.

7. On Tridentine marriage regulation, see Dean and Lowe 1998b, 5–6; Hacke 2004, 31–32, 35–36, 89–90. On Tridentine convent reforms, see Hufton 1998, 370–75; Zarri 2000a, 100–117; Lowe 2003, 140–41, 191–92, 231–32, 298, 393–94; also Schutte 2006, esp. 34 (appendix 1) for a useful list of post-Tridentine papal rulings regarding the integrity of convents. Further bibliography is cited in Ray and Westwater 2005, 26 n. 4.

8. For recent examples of this position, see, for example, Panizza and Wood 2000, 5; Malpezzi Price 2003b, 17–18; Finucci 2005, 27–28. See also, in a Spanish context, and with reference to women's religious writing in particular, Weber 1999, esp. 173–76. Robin 2007 also tends to present Counter-Reformation ideology as systematically repressive of profeminist discourse: see p. 77 for the suggestion that Domenichi's 1559 anthology of women's poetry might have met with Inquisition censorship if he had attempted to publish it in Venice and p. 122 for the suggestion that Betussi's *Imagini del tempio* might have been similarly suspect as a celebration of women's *virtù.*

9. On the shift in the tone of educational treatises and conduct books, see most recently Sberlati 1997.

10. A revisionist consideration of the Counter-Reformation's supposed negative social effects on women has asserted itself in recent decades in the field of social history. See, for example, Cohn 1996, 57–75, and the bibliography cited at p. 186 n. 15; also Hufton 1998, 363–423, for a balanced comparative overview of women's lives in Catholic and Protestant Europe in this period, and Hacke 2004, 16–18, for nuanced considerations on the effects of Counter-Reformation moral policies regarding marriage on women's lives in Venice.

11. Interesting in this regard is the remark in Stefano Guazzo's *La civil conver-*

*sazione* on the diversity of views on feminine education in his day: "hoggidì sono tanto diverse le maniere che si tengono nell'allevarle [le fanciulle] . . . che non vi si può dare una determinata regola. . . . Alcuni le fanno ammaestrare nel leggere, nello scrivere, nella poesia, nella musica e nella pittura. Altri a niente più le avvezzano che alla conocchia e al governo della casa" ("there are so many different practices currently followed in the education of girls that no firm rule can be given. . . . Some teach them reading, writing, poetry, music, and painting; others accustom them to nothing but the spindle and the art of household management" [Guazzo 1575, 413]). The subsequent discussion (413–19) proposes a flexible and context-sensitive attitude to feminine education, with the most ambitious education being accorded to young women destined to a career at court (417).

12. The reference is to a passage in Guazzo 1595, discussed between nn. 34 and 35 in the text.

13. Cox 2000b, esp. 53–54.

14. It is interesting that, after a period of abeyance starting in the 1560s, it was in the period under consideration here that Colonna's *Rime spirituali* were once again republished (V. Colonna 1586). The 1580s also saw musical settings of poems by Colonna published by Pietro Vinci (V. Colonna 1580) and Marcantonio Ingegneri and Filippo di Monte (Philippe de Monte); see Trinchieri Camiz, 2003 (I should like to thank Massimo Ossi for directing my attention to this study). Besides the literary interest of the *Rime,* the continuing power of the Colonna family must be accounted as a factor in Colonna's *fortuna;* the Sicilian Vinci, for example, dedicates his Colonna settings to Colonna's grandniece, Vittoria, daughter of the Lepanto hero Marcantonio Colonna (1535–84), who was viceroy of Sicily from 1576 (Trichieri Camiz 2003, 383–84).

15. Tansillo is evocatively described in a 1588 edition of the poem as a "spiritual Ariosto" ("spirituale Ariosto" [Chiesa 2002, 187]). An authoritative overview of the religious literature of this period is finally available in Quondam 2005a, esp. 192–96, for the *Lagrime* tradition and biblically based narrative poetry; see also Chiesa 2002; Ussia 1993; Fragnito 2005, esp. 148–77; and the comprehensive bibliography in Quondam 2005b. On Tansillo, see Toscano 1987. On Tasso as religious poet, see Ardissino 1996, which includes a chapter on his rarely studied *Rime sacre;* also, specifically on his contribution to the *Lagrime* tradition, see T. Tasso 2001; Mazzotta 2000; Imbriani 2001.

16. On the "decency" of pastoral drama and its implications for women as readers, writers, and actors, see Sampson 2006, 102–6. On the moral tone of late sixteenth-century *commedia erudita* and the roles it offered to women, see Coller 2007.

17. This may be one reason for skepticism regarding the attribution to Tullia d'Aragona of the chivalric poem *Il Meschino* published under her name in 1560, which contains some scurrilous subject matter (see n. 21 below).

18. ?S. Colonna 1552. For discussion, see Arbizzoni 1987 and Roche 1989, 90–96.

19. Interesting as a precedent for Stefano Colonna's project are the medieval

*contrasti* or *tenzoni fittizie* that dramatize a dialogue between a courtly male voice and a skeptical female one, alert to the seductive deceptions of courtly language. See on these Steinberg 2007, 66–70 (with particular reference to the collection in ms. Vaticano 3793).

20. Scardeone 1560, 368: "scripsit . . . quasdam comoedias seu fabulas, ad Boccacii morem (servato tamen ubique matronali decoro). . . . In quibus licet de amore tractetur, & intermisceantur amantium affectus: ita tamen & pudice, & modeste omnia ut quam libet honestam matronam decere possit . . . utpote quae et lectorem ad amplectandam virtutem allicere, et a vitiis deterrere facile possint." For the complete passage (given further circulation by its translation / plagiarism in della Chiesa 1620), see Finucci 2002, 23 n. 29; 25 n. 34.

21. D'Aragona 1560, unnumbered preface "Ai lettori" ("è poi tutto castissimo, tutto puro, tutto Cristiano, oue nè in essempi, nè in parole, nè in alcuna altra guisa, è cosa, la quale da ogni onorato & santo huomo, da ogni donna maritata, vergine, vedoua, & monaca non possa leggersi à tutte l'hore"). This statement of authorial intent is belied by the content of the work, which includes passages as salacious as anything in Ariosto (see, for example, d'Aragona 1560, 37r–v [canto 8]) for a scene of the attempted seduction of the hero by a lascivious innkeeper's daughter, whom he "chivalrously" offers instead to his friend. For discussion of the prefatory letter, see Allaire 1995, 35–37. On the question of authorship, see ch. 3, n. 167, above.

22. Antoniano 1584, 153v–154r. For a more thorough discussion of this text, see ch. 6, sec. 2.

23. Antoniano 1584, 154r.

24. On Molza, see Riley 1986 and Stras 1999, 2003. On Cavalletti, see Durante and Martellotti 1989a and Newcomb 1992, 84.

25. Patrizi 1963. Unlike Tasso's dialogues, published shortly after their composition, Patrizi's was not published at the time.

26. Molza figures in the Castriota anthology and *Per donne romane* for her vernacular verse and in Segni's anthologies for her Latin: see Manfredi 1575, 583; *Rime* 1585, 131; Segni 1600, 21; Segni 1601, 61. A selection of her unpublished writings is found in Molza 1750. See also below for Molza's appearance in Stefano Guazzo's *Ghirlanda*. Cavalletti's most substantial anthology appearance is in *Rime* 1587 (twenty-eight poems), though she also makes briefer appearances in Grillo 1589 and Fiamma 1611. See also *Lieti amanti* 1990, 23–24, 44, 123–27, on a madrigal of hers published with a setting by Lelio Bertani (c. 1550–c. 1620) in an anthology of 1586.

27. Guaccimani, ed. 1623, 18–19, 138–40; see also *Rime* 1713, 234–35 and 567.

28. Renea Pico is referred to as a poet in Manfredi 1580, 215 (misnumbered 115); see also Marescotti 1589, 173, where she is praised for her classical learning, apparently embracing Greek as well as Latin. Her mother Fulvia di Correggio was the daughter of Gambara's son Ippolito (1510–52) and wife of Lodovico II Pico della Mirandola (1527–68). Long-term regent of Mirandola following her husband's death, she was celebrated by contemporaries for her rulership skills and culture

(Ghidini 1983a; Longo and Michelassi 2001, 29–32). Manfredi, in the poem cited above, recommends her to her daughter as a suitable subject for epic verse.

29. *Mausoleo* 1589, 77; cf. ibid., 111 (Sarrocchi), 69–71 (Campiglia), and 16 (Andreini). The poem in the *Ghirlanda* is attributed to Lucia Spinola in the index and heading (349), but the poet is referred to as Livia in the body of the text.

30. Bendinelli was the sister of a schoolmaster and Latin poet, Scipione Bendinelli, originally of Lucca (Coreglia 1628, dedicatory letter). Her married name was Baldini, as appears from the title page of a sonnet sequence she published in 1587, mourning the death of Duke Ottavio Farnese (Bendinelli Baldini 1587). Another sonnet of hers, to the Virgin, is found in a publication of her brother's (Bendinelli 1588, A3r) and two more in a 1589 volume of verses published in Piacenza celebrating the marriage of Giovanni Paolo Lupi and Beatrice Obizzi, in which Maddalena Campiglia also appears (Ducchi 1589, A4r, 80).

31. The other female poets of the Spinola family are Maria (fl. 1550) and Laura; see n. 80 to the present chapter. A brief discussion of Cappello is found in Graziosi 1996, 313.

32. Guazzo 1595, 424. The seventh poet named—included in an appendix of latecomers whose poems are printed but not discussed—is Elena Bianca Stanchi. Poems by Spannocchi and Marescotti both also appear in Marchetti 1596, where their names are given as Margherita Silvestri de' Mariscotti and Fulvia Spannocchi de' Tuti. A third Sienese female poet appears there only as "A. P."

33. Guazzo 1595, 116: "se dato à me fosse il carico di nominare quella parte del mondo, ove si truovi maggior copia di donne illustri e pellegrine per l'altezza dell'intelletto, per la nobiltà dell'animo, & per lo splendore delle varie scienze, nominerei l'Europa, e dell'Europa l'Italia." Beccaria goes on to locate the center of excellence in this regard more particularly in Tuscany and Siena.

34. Guazzo 1595, 3–4.

35. On the countess's musical abilities, see Guazzo 1595, 3; on her poetic talents, Guazzo 1595, 42: "Poi che non men di Safo [sic] à Febo amica / Siete, & di lei più bella, & più pudica" ("since you are no less dear to Phoebus than Sappho, and more lovely and chaste than she"). The phrasing here echoes that of a poem by Giulio Stufa praising Gaspara Stampa as "the new Sappho of our day . . . but chaster than her, as more beautiful" ("Questa de' nostri dì Saffo novella / pari a la greca nel tosco idïoma / ma più casta di lei, quanto più bella" [Stampa 1976, 58]). Interestingly, however, in this context, the comparison here sparks a debate on the degree to which "chaster than Sappho" may be accounted a compliment by a decent woman: as one female speaker notes (Guazzo 1595, 46), "if a poet were to call me more chaste than Sappho, or Lesbia, or a public courtesan, I would certainly take it amiss" ("s'un poeta mi dicesse, ch'io son più honesta che Sappho, ò Lesbia, ò altra publica corteggiana, me lo recherei a sdegno").

36. Guazzo 1595, 3–4: "Erano sufficienti tutte queste parti a darle principal ornamento, & splendore fra le più illustri donne del mondo, ma ella qui non si ferma, e perché tutte l'altre virtù dileguano senza il fondamento della carità, ecco la valorosa donna, che persuadendosi di non haver adempiuta la legge con la sola ec-

cellenza delle lettere, & delle cose appartenenti alla cura di se stessa, ha sempre posto . . . studio nel governo della casa, & della famiglia, & particolarmente nel-l'istitutione di quelle due angiolette la Signora Margherita, & la Signora Camilla sue ben nate figliuole" ("These accomplishments would have been sufficient to lend the countess ornament and splendor among the most illustrious ladies of the world, but she does not stop there; rather, since charity is the foundation of all other virtues, this worthy lady, feeling she has not fulfilled her obligations simply through the excellence of her culture and those things connected with her own self-perfection . . . also devotes attention to the running of her household and family and particularly to the education of those two little angels the ladies Margherita and Camilla, her daughters").

37. Guazzo's emphasis here differs interestingly from that of his earlier *Dialogo dell'onor delle donne*, where he has his interlocutor, Annibale Magnacavallo, maintain that chastity and the care of the home as women's prime source of "honor," allowing only subsequently and in passing that cultural attainments may be necessary to attain the "supreme grade of female dignity" ("supremo grado della donnesca dignità" [Guazzo 1590, 507]). The difference in perspective may be status-related, although Guazzo appears to be holding the countess up as an ideal not simply for titled noblewomen but for other women in that he proposes her explicitly to his own daughter, Olimpia Guazzo Curione, as a "mirror of for her life" ("nobilissimo specchio della vostra vita" [Guazzo 1595, 4]).

38. Guazzo 1595, 285–86: "i beni dell'animo e . . . le doti, che recano alle donne principale adornamento."

39. Guazzo 1595, 286: "il che tanto maggior lode le apporta, quanto ella non tralascia alcun'ufficio, ch'appartenga à valorosa matrona ne i commodi del marito, nell'istitutione de' figliuoli, & nel buon governo della casa" ("all this brings her the greater credit in that she does not neglect any task pertaining to a worthy matron, paying due attention to her husband's comforts, the instruction of her children, and the smooth running of her household").

40. See esp. Guazzo 1595, 394–95, for a dispute between the male and female speakers over women's ability to keep secrets; this concludes, however, with a palinodic statement of appreciation of women from Count Claudio Beccaria.

41. Guazzo 1595, 221, 116, 286.

42. Guazzo 1595, 5.

43. Grillo 1589, 26r, 61r (Bernardi; cf. 113v–114r for two sonnets by her to Grillo); 36r–37r (Laura Spinola; cf. 115r for a sonnet from her to Grillo); 42r and 52r (Campiglia); 73r (Ferri); 78r (Peverara, Molza); 84r (Livia Spinola; cf. 116r for a sonnet by her); 48v (Anguissola). The addressees of the poems are identified in the index. All are mentioned elsewhere in this volume, except for Ferri, whom I have been unable to identify. Campiglia is also among the contributors of prefatory verse to the volume, along with Orsina Cavalletti. For a study of Grillo as poet, see Durante and Martellotti 1989b.

44. Gonzaga 1591, 19–21 and 175–76 (Soderini); 26 (Salvi); 165, 182 (Campiglia); M. Colonna and Angeli 1589, 19, 21, 36, 54 (Soderini, who is also the addressee of

much love poetry by the pair); 46, 49–50, 52 (Battiferra); Giustinian and Magno 1600, 69 (Marinella; Colao); 71 (Campiglia); 97 (Malipiero). The addressees of Giustinian's verses may be identified via the index. Colao is internally identified as a poet in the second quatrain of the sonnet to her, which compares her to Sappho. For Mario Colonna's exchanges with Battiferra, see Battiferra 2006, 302–4 and 445 n. 74.

45. Valerini 1570. For discussion, see B. Croce 1958; Henke 2002, 94–100. Valerini's oration is reproduced in F. Marotti and Romei 1991, 27–41, while the sample of Armani's verse included in Valerini's tribute volume may be found in Bartoli 1782, 1:53–59, along with poetic tributes by various contemporary admirers (ibid., 1:59–63).

46. See Newcomb 1975; also, for a comprehensive listing of poems in praise of Peverara and the other ladies of the Ferrarese *concerto delle donne,* Durante and Martellotti 1989a, 223–52, 289–92. On musical tributes to female singers in this period, see Stras 2003.

47. On Manfredi, discussed further in ch. 6, sec. 1, see Calore 1985; Denarosi 1997; Denarosi 2003 passim.

48. Manfredi 1575, unnumbered prefatory letter: "posta tutta la mia fatica e tutto lo studio mio in quella maniera di lettere le quali più vi potessero piacere, e darvi nome: che è l'eccellentia della Poesia, cosa veramente divina e degna della vostra divinità."

49. For another example of a *raccolta* addressed entirely to ladies, see Guazzo 1592. Stras 2003, 145, notes the existence of similar collections of musical encomia.

50. Other women Manfredi praises for their poetic gifts but for whose poetic activity is otherwise unattested or thinly documented include Vittoria Castelletti da Rhò, Renea Pico (see above n. 28), and Emilia Arrivabene Gonzaga, the last of whom Manfredi praises (on hearsay) for a blank-verse translation of Virgil (Manfredi 1587, 40). On Castelletti, see Erdmann 1999, 210; on Gonzaga, Bandini Buti 1946, 1:46.

51. Manfredi's praise volume to his wife (Manfredi 1604) is dedicated by Ippolita herself to Laura d'Este Pico, princess of Mirandola, and contains a madrigal by her. Sasso ed. 1601, an edition of a lecture in praise of women, is dedicated to Ippolita by a member of the Accademia degli Informi of Ravenna and contains poems in praise of her by other academicians, some mentioning her poetic talents. Numerous poems to Ippolita are also found in the closing pages of Manfredi 1602b.

52. A further possible poetic couple is Livia and Alessandro Spinola of Genoa (Chater 1999, 583). See also the sonnet by the actress Virginia Ramponi Andreini to her husband Giambattista Andreini in preface to his *Florinda* (G. Andreini 1606, 9), "Cigno felice, che spiegando i vanni," which presents the two as mutually supportive in their search for artistic "immortality" (I am grateful to Emily Wilbourne for directing my attention to this sonnet). A precedent for this kind of "creative couple," though active in different fields, is offered by Laura Battiferra and Bartolomeo Ammanati in the 1550s; see Kirkham 2002a. Within the visual arts, ex-

amples include Diana Scultori (d. 1612) and Francesco da Volterra (d. 1594) (see Lincoln 2000, 111–45) and Isabetta Catanea and Leonardo Parasole (discussed in sec. 3 below).

53. For an appreciation of Manfredi's talents in this role, see the sonnet by his fellow academician Giulio Morigi (1538–1610) in Manfredi 1602b, 117: "O de le Donne altero e raro Mostro / Che con pronto veder d'occhio cervero / Scorgete in questo e l'altro Emispero [sic] / Quai degne sian del vostro ornato inchiostro" ("O rare and lofty prodigy of women, who, with the sharp sight of your eagle eye, discern in this and the other hemisphere which are deserving of the adornment of your ink").

54. Marescotti 1589, 176: "le quali [the many naturally talented women of Bologna] hoggi rilucerebbero molto, se dall superstitione e rustica sospitione de gli huomini ritenute non fussero; e se a quelle fusse stato da' padri permesso il virtuoso essercitio delle belle lettere."

55. The discussion of women is found on the fifth day of the dialogue, as part of a more general discussion of nobility (Romei 1586, 170–76 [2nd ed.]). The task of "defending women" is given to Ercole Varano, who begins his talk on p. 173 by noting that he would expand at greater length on the subject if so much had not already been said on it ("se delle lodi delle donne non fossero hoggimai piene tutte le carte").

56. Ribera 1609. The treatise is dedicated by the publisher, Evangelista Deuchino, to Valeria Bonomi, abbess of the "convent of Trieste." Deuchino specifies that his sister is a nun at the convent.

57. Ribera 1609, 300: "Fu Poetessa celeberrima, unica di dottrina, d'intelligenza essemplarissima, incomparabile di potenza, di capacità miranda"; "[Il merito] può stare al bilancio di qualunque compositione che in luce uscita sia a' nostri giorni." For an earlier example of a religiously authored work displaying profeminist sentiment see the introduction to day 3 of Calzolai 1561, discussed in ch. 3, sec. 3.

58. "hor, Coneglian, per lei tua fama sale" (Sbarra Coderta 1610, unnumbered prefatory madrigal). The author is unspecified, but we can probably assume is by the author of the preceding sonnet, Giovanni Prandino, perhaps a relative of the poet Aquiliana Prandina of Verona.

59. See Bratteolo, ed. 1597, 114r–15v, for the poems and dedicatory letter A2v for a description of the precocious Catella, who is also praised by the editor in two sonnets at 134v and by Vincenzo Giusti in a madrigal at 79v. Catella's verse appeared in two further anthologies published in Udine in 1598 and 1599 (Erdmann 1999, 215). For the Corner collection, see Varie compositioni 1596; cf. also, for Spolverini's poetic activity, Spolverini 1596. Other occasional collections published in the Veneto in this period including verse by female poets include Ferro 1581 (Clizia Gabrielli, "Costanza L.," Laura Manfredi, Issicratea Monte, Ginevra Pighini, Grazia Santarella) and Polinnia 1609 (Valeria Miani); see also the earlier Rime 1567b (Biana Maria Angaran; "Artemisia D"). More difficult to read is Fratta, ed. 1575, celebrating the Paduan doctorate of Giuseppe Spinelli and containing verse by the courtesan Veronica Franco (see Rosenthal 1992, 101–2), along with two

seemingly pseudonymous figures, "Andromeda Felice" and "Cinzia dalla Fratta." The latter has been speculatively identified with the suspiciously named Dorotea Cortigiana degli Inganni of Vicenza (see most recently Pietropoli 1986, 53 n. 34, following de Vit 1883, 14–15 n. 13), though another possibility is another Vicentine, Cinzia Garzadora; see the discussion in de Vit 1883 just cited and Mantese and Nardello 1974, 21 and n. 24.

60. dalla Torre 1590.

61. Gilio 1580, 75r–77r. The poets in question are Leonora Genga, Ortensia di Guglielmo, and Livia Chiavello.

62. A possible earlier example of this is found in the famous 1527 Giunta anthology of early Italian verse, which attributes a correspondence poem addressed to the thirteenth-century poet Dante da Maino to the probably apocryphal female poet "Monna Nina," or "Nina Siciliana"; see Giunta 2002, 260–62, for discussion. For a later, seventeenth-century example of an invented fourteenth-century female poet, see the text at n. 67 in ch. 6.

63. Little is known of the lives of either Miani or Erculiani, although the name and profession of the former's father (Achille, a lawyer) are recorded in Ribera 1609, 335. On Miani's works, see the text of the present chapter between nn. 84 and 85 and between nn. 94 and 95. On Erculiani, see text between nn. 159 and 162.

64. On Bragadin, see the text between nn. 101 and 102 in the present chapter and at n. 175 in ch. 6. Nothing survives by Prandina, though she is found listed as a poet in various later sixteenth-century works on "famous women" (e.g. Marescotti 1589, 171). A sonnet lamenting her death by Lodovico Corfino is found in *Rime* 1556a, 288. Issicratea Monte, a protégée of the poet Luigi Groto, gained fame through her orations celebrating the elections of doges Sebastiano Venier (1577) and Nicolò da Ponte (1578) and the visit to Rovigo of the dowager empress Maria of Austria in 1581 (Monte 1577, 1578a and b, 1581). She was also known as a dialect poet. The most complete studies of her remain de Vit 1883 and Cessi 1897; see also Milani 1983; Pietropoli 1986, 60, 73; Cox and Sampson 2004, 10 n. 29.

65. Milani 1983. Angaran, later imprisoned for heresy, had earlier appeared with a Tuscan sonnet in *Rime* 1567b, 27r.

66. For a fuller discussion of this point, see Cox and Sampson 2004, 6–7, 10.

67. Angela, Isotta, and Ginevra Nogarola and Laura Brenzoni are included in the listings of Betussi 1545, which was reprinted a number of times down to 1596. The same "canon" survives in Astolfi 1602, along with a fourth Nogarola, Laura, niece to Angela and sister to Isotta and Ginevra.

68. On Gonzaga's own literary activities and her role as local cultural *animatrice,* see Malavasi 1993; also Pietropoli 1986, 53; Malavasi 1989; Ridolfi 2001. An interesting testimony to her eloquence and expertise in matters of poetry is found in Orazio Toscanella's dedication to her of Giovanni Maria Bonardo's *Madrigali,* dated 1563 (Bonardo 1598, 2v–3r).

69. On Monte's relations with Bonardo, see the sonnets in Bonardo 1598, 33, and Bonardo 1600; also de Vit 1883, 13–14. On her relations with Groto, see Mantese and Nardello 1974, 16 n. 14. On the Pastori Frattegiani, see Malavasi 1989. For

a list of the members of the group, see Bonardo 1598, 58v. Besides Gonzaga, who died when Monte was around 12 years old, Monte had a more immediate female poetic model in Maddalena Campiglia, with whom she exchanged sonnets, now lost (Milani 1983, 396 n. 9; see also, on their acquaintance, Mantese and Nardello 1974, 21). De Vit 1883, 8 n. 3 and 14–15 n. 13, gives evidence of learned women in Rovigo in contact with Groto. See also ibid., 13–14 n. 12, for evidence of Monte's acquaintance with Moderata Fonte.

70. Monte 1578a. For Spilimbergo, see text between nn. 115 and 116 in ch. 3; for Albani see n. 116 in ch. 3.

71. The sonnet is attributed to "Madonna M. P." For the identification with Fonte (whose real name was Modesta Pozzo), see de Vit 1883, 13 n. 12.

72. There are no real grounds for regarding Fonte's adoption of a pseudonym as reflecting a general trend among female writers of this period, as is suggested in Robin 2007, 203. The recently rediscovered presentation letter of the *Floridoro* of 1580 (Carinci 2002, 8–9) provides an interesting gloss on Fonte's adoption of an "invented name" ("imaginato nome"): "ho permesso, che siano stampati, questi xiii canti del Floridoro . . . et ciò sotto imaginato nome di Moderata Fonte, poi che il mio vero, et proprio non hò giudicato esser bene di esponer alla publica censura, essendo giovane da marito, et secondo l'uso della città obligata à molti rispetti" ("I gave permission for these thirteen canti of *Floridoro* to be printed . . . under the invented name of Moderata Fonte, for I judged it unfitting to expose my own proper name to public censure, being an unmarried girl and, according to the customs of this city, obliged to be most circumspect"). Marinella, too, was unmarried on the publication of her first work (Marinella 1595).

73. On the rank of *cittadino,* a social status peculiar to Venice, see the text in ch. 1 at n. 23. A sonnet by an otherwise unknown female poet apparently, to judge by her name, of patrician rank (Adriana Trevisani Contarini) appears in Manfredi 1593. This seems, however, rather an exception that proves the rule of patrician women's silence.

74. On Doglioni, see Doglioni 1997, 31 n. 1 and 36 n. 15; on Giovanni Marinelli, Panizza 1999, 3.

75. On Aiutamicristo, see Bandini Buti 1946, 1:22. On her family, originally Pisan bankers, ennobled in the fifteenth century, see Ligresti 1992, 22 n. 32. Her poem in *Rime* 1585, 107, appears to be her only published work, though Erdmann 1999, 223, records three further female poets (Laura, Marta, and Onofria Bonanno) as featuring in a volume of verse by the Palermitan Accademia degli Accesi, published in 1571. Outside Palermo, Giulio Cesare Capaccio, listing southern female poets in his *Il Forastiero* (1634), names only "Tullia Aragonia, Dorotea Acquaviva, Vittoria Colonna, Laura Terracina" as well as "all those much-praised Corinnas and Cleobulinas of antiquity" ("tante Corinne, e Cleobule dall'antichità lodatissime"). I have not found mention of Dorotea Acquaviva in any other source. Capaccio also lays claim to Margherita Sarrocchi, who was born in Naples, though raised in Rome. A Neapolitan writer not listed by Capaccio is the noble Isabella Capece (1569–90), author of a prose *Consolatione dell'anima oue si contengono pie, e*

*deuote meditationi* published in Naples in 1595 by Giovanni Iacomo Carlino and Antonio Pace. I have been unable to consult this last work.

76. For Laura Lucchesini Guidiccioni, author of a famous series of dramatic texts set to music by Emilio de' Cavalieri (1550–1602) and performed at the wedding of Ferdinand I de' Medici and Christine of Lorraine in 1589, see Kirkendale 2001, 185–212. Although Guidiccioni's most important works are lost, see Treadwell 1997, 65–67, for analysis of a surviving text, written for an intermezzo at the 1589 wedding (the text is given at Treadwell 1997, 66). For Silvia Bendinelli, see n. 30 above. Leonora Bernardi is praised for her poetry and musical skills in Grillo 1589, 26r. Verse of hers was published in *Scelta* 1591; Pocaterra 1607; Franciotti 1616. She is also reputed to have composed a lost pastoral drama; see Ultsch 2005b, 372, and Sampson 2006, 103. Matraini's later published works are mainly religious in character (see Matraini 1581, 1586, 1590, 1602). She also published a radical reworking of her 1555 *Rime,* along with an important new sequence of letters, many of them effectively short prose treatises (Matraini 1595 and 1597). For secondary literature, see nn. 101 and 141–42 below.

77. On Soderini, see ch. 4, n. 18, above. Lorenza Strozzi came from a prominent Florentine patrician family and was sister to the humanist Ciriaco Strozzi (1504–65); she was a nun in the Dominican convent of San Niccolò in Prato. Salvetti came from a Florentine patrician family and was the wife of Commendatore Zanobi Accaiuoli (1548–1613), a Medici official. Also active within the Florentine sphere, though born in Colle di Val d'Elsa, was Isabella Cervoni, author of a number of encomiastic *canzoni* published between 1592 and 1600; see appendix A.

78. On these Bolognese nun writers, see Fantuzzi 1781–94, 5:163–64 (Malvasia), 6:270–72 (Pannolini); 7:73 (Poggi); also, on Pannolini, Ribera 1609, 335; Graziosi 2005, 162–63; Stevenson 2005, 300, 525–26. See the text at n. 48 in ch. 3 on the earlier sixteenth-century Bolognese nun poet (fl. 1559) Girolama Castellani. Another, secular Bolonese female poet, known from a single anthology, is Ottavia Grassi (Segni, ed. 1583, E4v). Useful on the Bolognese context are three recent studies of the strong tradition of female creativity there, especially within the visual arts in this period: Murphy 2003, Bohn 2002, and Bohn 2004. Bohn 2002, 53–54, also discusses the female literary tradition in Bologna.

79. The honorary citizenship offered to Tarquinia Molza in 1600 by the city of Rome (Vandelli 1750, 18–22) may reflect an awareness of its lack of homegrown women writers as a weakness; even Sarrocchi was Neapolitan, rather than Roman, by birth. Barbara Torelli Benedetti came from a branch of the noble family in Parma that produced the tragedian Pomponio Torelli (1539–1608). She was well connected within the courts and highly praised, although her principal work, the pastoral drama *Partenia,* remained unpublished. Turina, from a noble family of Città di Castello, married a condottiere, Giulio Bufalini (d. 1583), living for a period after his death in the household of the Colonna of Paliano as companion to the duchess, Lucrezia Tomacelli (d. 1622), before ending her long life in her hometown. On her life, see Corbucci 1901 (with some inaccuracies); Torrioli 1940; Bà 2005, 147–48.

80. The only exception is Maria Spinola, who features in *Rime* 1553 and Domenichi 1559; she may be the mother of the Livia and Laura Spinola discussed in the text.

81. Scaramelli 1585, 109–10.

82. Doglioni 1988, 9: "l'abuso, che corre oggidì in questa citta, che non si vol veder donna virtuosa in altro, che nel governo della casa"; cf. Fonte 1997, 39. For the satirical attacks on Franco by Maffio Venier (1550–86), see A. Zorzi 1986, 93–111, and Rosenthal 1992, 51–57.

83. See Cox 1997b, 21, for references. Tellingly, the less "reputable" Veronica Franco does not figure on these lists.

84. See Campiglia 2004, 31–32, 306, on the encomiastic appendix to *Flori,* and see n. 90 below for bibliography on the play itself. On Campiglia's marital situation at the time of writing, see Cox and Sampson 2004, 2–4.

85. Monte's oration was published shortly after its delivery (Monte 1581) and was reprinted three years later in an anthology edited by Francesco Sansovino (Erdmann 1999, 118–19; cf. de Vit 1883, 20–21). For Miani's, see Ribera 1609, 335.

86. For Fedele's oration for Bona Sforza, see Fedele 2000, 162–64. Ippolita Sforza's oratorical performances are detailed in ch. 1 above.

87. Campiglia 2004, 65 and 316 n. 32; cf. Cox 2005a, 21–22, for comment. Colonna's *rime spirituali* had been republished two years earlier in Verona (V. Colonna 1586).

88. See ch. 3, sec. 4.

89. *Le feste* and *La passione di Christo* have as yet received no sustained critical attention, though see Malpezzi Price 1994a, 129–130; Malpezzi Price 2003b, 31, 34–35. The *Floridoro* has been edited and translated by Valeria Finucci (Fonte 1995, 2006); its dedicatory letter was archivally unearthed by Eleonora Carinci (Carinci 2002). For criticism, see Finucci 1995, 2006a and b; Weaver 1997; Cox 1997a; Cox 2000b, 59–60; Kolsky 1999, Malpezzi Price 2003b, 31–33, 101–21. On connections between Fonte and Issicratea Monte, see de Vit 1883, 13–14 n. 12.

90. Torelli, *Partenia, favola boschereccia,* ms. a.a.1.33, Biblioteca Statale, Cremona; Campiglia 2004; Andreini 1995 and 2002. For discussion, see, on *Partenia,* Riccò 2004, 326–36; Sampson 2004; Sampson 2006, 106–12; also, for a detailed plot summary, Zonta 1906, 206–9. A transcription of the play, which survives in a single manuscript, may be found in Burgess-Van Aken 2007. On Campiglia's *Flori,* see Chemello 2003, 91–99; Cox and Sampson 2004; Ultsch 2005a, 76–87; Sampson 2006, 112–18. Campiglia also wrote a pastoral eclogue, *Calisa:* see the text at n. 128 in the present chapter. On Andreini's *Mirtilla* (already composed by 1587, though only published in 1588; Bosi 2003, 82), see Vazzoler 1992; J. Campbell 1997 and 2002; Doglio 1995; Decroisette 2001, 211–15; Decroisette 2002, 161–69; MacNeil 2003, 37–46 and 122–25; Sampson 2006, 118–23.

91. Fonte 1592 and Fonte 1600, 1988, 1997. For brief discussions of the former work, see Malpezzi Price, 1994a, 130, and Malpezzi Price 2003b, 34–35. On the latter, one of the most thoroughly studied works of this whole period, see, to the mid-1990s, the bibliography cited in Malpezzi Price 1994a, 134–37, and Fonte 1997,

23; also, subsequently, Jordan 1996; Cox 1997b; Jones 1998, 164–73; Kolsky 1999; Kolsky 2001, esp. 979–81; Magnanini 2003; Malpezzi Price 2003a; Malpezzi Price 2003b, esp. 35–36, 122–49; Smarr 2005a, 215–30.

92. Marinella 1595; for discussion, see Benedetti 2005, 95–101.

93. Marinella 1597; Marinella 1602. Translated extracts from the latter work will appear in an edition of Marian writings by sixteenth-century Italian women edited by Susan Haskins, forthcoming from the University of Chicago Press. A brief discussion of the former work is found in Malpezzi Price 1994b, 236.

94. Marinella 1605a and 1998; Marinella 1617; Marinella 1618. An excellent study of *Arcadia felice* is Lavocat 1998. A translation of the work is forthcoming from the University of Chicago Press, edited by Letizia Panizza. On *Amore innamorato,* see Malpezzzi Price 1994a, 237; Panizza 1999, 8–9; Ussia 2001, 31–37, 155–56. A date of first publication of 1598 is frequently given for this last text, but this seems unlikely: I have found no listed copies of the 1598 edition, and it is omitted from the otherwise compendious list of Marinella's publications given in the publisher's preface to her *Arcadia felice* (Marinella 1998, 2). A later date also seems consonant with the scale and ambition of the work, which is one of Marinella's most interesting.

95. For a critical discussion of Miani's works, see Rees 2008; also, on *Amorosa speranza,* Decroisette 2002, 176–82. Valeria Finucci is currently preparing an edition of *Celinda* for the University of Chicago Press's The Other Voice series.

96. Sarrocchi 1623. The version published in 1606 was an early and incomplete redaction of the poem, published, we are told in the dedicatory letter, to defy critics reluctant to believe that the extracts of the work circulating could have been composed by a woman. For a slightly abridged English translation, with a few extracts in Italian, see Sarrocchi 2006; for discussion, Pezzini 2005 and R. Russell 2006.

97. Salvetti 1611 and Battiferra 2006, 256–65. On Marinella's *Enrico* (Marinella 1635), see Belloni 1893, 285–98; Malpezzi Price 1994b, 237–38; Malpezzi Price 2003b, 110–12; Cox 2000b, 60–61; N. Zorzi 2004–5; Benedetti 2005, 102–9. An abridged English translation of the poem, with extracts from the Italian, is forthcoming from the University of Chicago Press, edited by Maria Galli Stampino.

98. For Franco, see Manfredi 1606a, 249 (cf. Franco 1995, 245); for Campiglia, Cox and Sampson 2004, 11 and n. 32. For a later epic poem by Francesca Turina, *Il Florio* (completed 1640), see Corbucci 1901, 40–41, 53–54. Bà 2005, 148, records the work as surviving in the Bufalini archive at San Giustino. For evidence that Isabella Andreini too may have been working on an epic late in her life, see Belloni 1893, 286 n. 4.

99. This is true, for example, of Marinella's *Arcadia felice* and Fonte's *Il merito delle donne* as well of Chiara Matraini's late religious works (1581, 1586, 1590, 1602).

100. The 1605 collection incorporates the poems from 1601 as a *prima parte,* adding a supplement of mainly occasional and correspondence verse. Some of the latter had already been included in a slimmer volume of Andreini's verse published in Paris in 1603. For discussions of Andreini's lyric poetry, see MacNeil 2005 and Giachino 2001b. For a rapid survey of her published writings, see Andrews

2000, 323–29. These include a number of posthumous works published by her husband, of problematic authorship status: see Andreini 1607 and appendix A at 1617.

101. Salvetti 1590 and Matraini 1595, 1597, 1989. Matraini's recent editor Giovanna Rabitti describes the 1590s version as sufficiently different from that of the 1550s to be considered "another book" ("un altro libro, mutato nelle dimensioni e costruito con diverso materiale lirico" [Matraini 1989,15]). On Matraini's revisions of the *Rime,* see Rabitti 1994, 246–49, and MacLachlan 1992; also, on the successive printed editions, Bullock and Palange 1980, 239–43. For a brief discussion of Salvetti, see Rabitti 2000, 491–92.

102. Sbarra Coderta 1610 and Bragadin Cavalli 1613, 1614, 1619. Nothing appears to be known of Bragadin's life. Sbarra (whose date of birth is sometimes given as 1586) was of a noble and cultured family and twice married, the second time to a Rota; see Martin 1990, 29–30, on her brother, the literary patron Pulzio Sbarra (1560–1626).

103. Turina Bufalini 1595 and 2005; Marinella 1603; L. Strozzi 1588. The most discussed of these works is Strozzi's (see Erdmann 1999 127–28; Stevenson 2002; Stevenson 2005, 297–300, 554–56), though Turina's *Rime* has recently received a new edition (Bà 2005). Both Turina's and Marinella's collections show a distinct narrative slant: Turina's, unusually, narrates the life, passion, and glory of Christ in sonnets, while Marinella's incorporates an ottava rima poem telling the story of the sacred theft that brought an icon of the Virgin to the Sanctuary of the Madonna de la Guardia in Bologna. A further, partial edition of Marinella's *Rime,* probably published without the author's permission and containing only nine poems, each illustrated with a woodcut, is Marinella 1605b.

104. Battiferra's late verse remains in a manuscript of her collected works in the Biblioteca Casanatense in Rome (*Rime di Laura Battiferri,* ms. 3229); see Battiferra 2006, 70 n. 2, for a description, and ibid., 82–265, for selections from the manuscript, including some of the late spiritual poems. For Salvetti's religious verse, intended as a collection for Maria Maddalena of Austria, see Salvetti 1611, 53r–66r.

105. Bendinelli Baldini 1587; Fonte 1585; Cervoni 1592 and 1597; see also appendix A for further works by Cervoni.

106. Chiabrera's influence on Andreini is noted in MacNeil 2005, 4–5. For her description of him as the "Ligustro Anfione," see the last line of "Ecco l'Alba ruggiadosa" (Andreini 1601, 23; Andreini 2005, 46). Like Chiabrera himself, Andreini highlights the metrical variety of her *Rime* by organizing the index according to the metrical forms used: in total, the 1601 *Rime* contains 200 sonnets, 125 madrigals, 6 *canzoni,* 10 *canzonette morali,* 2 *sestine,* 2 epithalamia, 2 *centoni,* 3 *capitoli,* 9 *scherzi,* 4 blank-verse *versi funerali,* and 9 pastoral eclogues. In the 1605 addition, by contrast, made up mainly of occasional and correspondence verse, the sonnet form dominates.

107. "finti ardori . . . imaginati amori . . . non leale affetti . . . finti detti." For the text of the sonnet, which demands to be read comparatively with the proemial sonnet of Tasso's *Rime amorose* ("Vere fur queste gioie e questi ardori" ["True

Were These Joys and Ardors"]), as well as of that of Petrarch, see Andreini 2005, 30–31; for discussion, MacNeil 2003, 116, 121–22, and Andrews 2000, 325–26.

108. Turina Bufalini 1595, 149–72 (*In morte del Sig. Giulio Bufalini*), and Sbarra Coderta 1610 (more accessibly, the selection of Sbarra's poems in Bergalli 1726 has a representative sample of her poems on this theme). For Armani, see n. 45 above.

109. The realm of the sensual in Marinella, following a familiar Counter-Reformation and baroque dynamic, tends to be expressed most characteristically in eroticized representations of bodily self-mortification: a tendency especially marked in Marinella 1597 and Marinella 1624. See briefly on this Malpezzi Price 1994b, 235–36; also Lavocat 1998, xliii, on the notable absence of sensual love as a theme in Marinella's secular *Arcadia felice.*

110. See Miani Negri 1604 for the triangle Allliseo-Venalia-Damone. Decroisette 2002, 178–79, proposes a biographical reading, though note Godard 1984, 175–79, and Sampson 2006, 206, on the presence of such a love triangle in Guidobaldo Bonarelli's near-contemporary *Filli di Sciro* (1607); also, on the incidence of "polygonal" love plots in the baroque novella and romance generally, Getto 1969, 327, 360. For Andreini's celebration of marital love in *Mirtilla,* see Coridone's speeches in 4.2, esp. that at Andreini 1995, 123–24; cf. Andreini 2002, 74–75). On the adulterous Calidora-Serano episode in the 1606 *Scanderbeide*—omitted from the 1623 version of the poem perhaps as a result of moral self-censorship—see Cox 1997a, 143–44, and R. Russell 2006, 25–26. Extracts from the episode are given in Morandini, ed. 2001, 39–47.

111. On the theme of same-sex love between women in Campiglia, see Perrone 1996 and Cox and Sampson 2004, 23–27. For Miani, see especially Miani Negri 1611, 14r–16v (1.3), where Celinda recounts her beginning of her love-relationship with Autilio, disguised as the serving maid "Lucinia." For Marinella, see the episode at the end of Book 2 of *Arcadia felice* (Marinella 1998, 80), where the transvestite Ersilia confesses to courting nymphs, seduced by their beauty, and promising them marriage. Also of interest in this connection is the erotically charged friendship of Rosmonda and Silveria in Margherita Sarrocchi's *Scanderbeide;* see especially the scene of their first encounter in canto 14 of the 1606 edition (where they are called Rosana and Clori) and Canto 8 of the 1623 edition (Sarrocchi 1606, 94–97; Sarrocchi 1623, 130–35; Sarrocchi 2006, 240–51).

112. The figures are the eponymous heroine of Campiglia's *Flori* and Corinna, one of the speakers of Fonte's *Merito delle donne.* On the motif of the single life in Fonte, see Cox 1995; in Campiglia, Cox and Sampson 2004, 20–23, and Ultsch 2005a and b.

113. See n. 3 above.

114. Battiferra's work in soliciting verse for a commemorative volume for Benedetto Varchi published in Florence in 1566 is noted in Kirkham 2006, 26 n. 45. Malipiero's similar involvement with the *Tempio* for Girolama Colonna of 1568 is documented in an exchange with Orsatto Giustinian in Giustinian and Magno 1600, 97. Her role seems to have been to encourage her fellow Venetians ("cigni d'Adria") to contribute.

115. The other poets all feature with their full names, despite the volume's being edited by a courtesan (differently from Franco's own *Rime* and *Lettere,* where the names of her correspondents are largely suppressed). Franco's *Lettere familiari* of 1580 contains interesting examples of letters illustrating her editorial work on the Martinengo volume; see esp. letters 32 and 39 (Franco 1998b, 91–93 and 100–1).

116. Decroisette 2002, 170 n. 71, notes on the basis of a phrase in the dedicatory letter that Campiglia seems to have been responsible for ordering the publication of the play ("ordinai che fosse stampata secondo il disegno e desiderio mio" ["I ordered that it should be published in accordance with my plan and desire"]). Campiglia also seems to have been active in commissioning poetry to celebrate the marriage of the son of her patron Isabella Pallavicino Lupi: see Perrone 1996, 46 and the index to Grillo 1589, where Angelo Grillo's sonnet on the marriage (at 29r of the volume) is said to have been composed "ad instanza della Signora Maddalena Campiglia."

117. Tansillo 1606, A 3r: "mi affaticai di haver questa gratia dalla Signora Lucretia Marinella, gentildonna per le sue rare qualità e per lettere amirata [sic] dal mondo, che ella facesse gli Argomenti e le Allegorie a ciascun Canto, oltre ad una [allegoria] universale di tutto il Poema."

118. The others are d'Aragona's *Rime* and Battiferra's *Rime,* both dedicated to Eleonora of Toledo, and Laura Pieri's *Quattro canti della guerra di Siena,* to Giangiacomo de' Medici. I have omitted from the count d'Aragona's *Dialogo* and Matraini's *Oratione d'Isocrate,* both of which have a dedication by the author relating to the original manuscript "donation" and another (by Girolamo Muzio in the first case and Lorenzo Torrentino in the second) claiming the initiative for publishing the work. Terracina's *Rime seconde* is another such complex case and has also been omitted from the count. The overall count of seventeen works omits two works of contested authorship, Isabella Sforza's *Della vera tranquillità dell'anima* and "Dafne di Piazza"'s *Enigmi.* Three of the Colonna editions included in the count (1548, 1558, 1560) are of course posthumous and so present a special case, in that the author could not have composed her own letter. It should be remembered, however, that Colonna never publicly presented her work in print during her lifetime or associated herself with its publication.

119. One of the three exceptions is Moderata Fonte's *Il merito delle donne* of 1600, a posthumously published work by an author who otherwise dedicated all her works herself.

120. The edition was a pirated one, and, when Terracina reissued the volume in 1560, she rededicated to a male dedicatee (not sparing the marchioness a sideswipe in her new dedicatory letter for having failed to express thanks for the previous volume "even if only in words" ("di parole almeno" [Terracina 1560, A4r]). Many of the individual *canti* of Terracina's *Discorso* are dedicated to women; the overall dedicatee is, however, a man, the reformist Giovanni Bernardino Bonifacio, Marchese d'Oria (1517–97). Only "third-person" dedications have been included in this count, excluding cases where the printed version of a text is dedi-

cated to the author herself by a mediatory figure; this is the case with d'Aragona's *Dialogo* and Matraini's *Oratione.*

121. See Shemek 2005a, 243–44 and 257 n. 18, on the framing of the Domenichi volume.

122. The pattern is still more marked in the subsequent twenty-three year period (1603–25 inclusive), where we find only five male dedicatees among eighteen dedications: less than a third of the total.

123. An exception is Issicratea Monte's 1578 congratulatory oration to Doge Niccolò da Ponte, dedicated to the doge's wife, Marina Gussoni da Ponte. An interesting precedent for the trend described here may be seen in the patronage strategies of Cassandra Fedele, in the late fifteenth century, similarly directed toward non-Venetian noblewomen; see Fedele 2000, 17–34.

124. The main exceptions to this pattern in Marinella are *La nobiltà et l'eccellenza delle donne,* dedicated to Lucio Scarano, *La vita di Maria Vergine,* dedicated to the doge (Marino Grimani) and Senate of Venice, and her late *Enrico* and *Holocausto d'amore della vergine Santa Giustina,* dedicated respectively to Doges Francesco Erizzo and Francesco Molin. Fonte, too, dedicated one work, her early *Passione di Christo* to a doge, Niccolò da Ponte.

125. Lavocat 1998, xv–xvi.

126. Interesting recent studies of female patronage of female artists in the visual arts and music include Murphy 2003 and Cusick 1993a. A comparative study of the subject would be desirable. One interesting feature of Italian women's dedicatory practice in this period is the frequency of "speculative" dedications, of the type exemplified in this paragraph, to prominent women with whom the author had no previous acquaintance or ties. This contrasts with the tendency noted by Anne Larsen of French women to choose dedicatees from "within a well-defined [female] rhetorical community *close to home*" (Larsen 1990, 20).

127. On the rhetorical and strategic uses of such female-female dedications, see, in an English context, the recent discussions of Aemilia Lanyer in Lewalski 1985, 207–12; Lewalski 1993, 219–226; Wall 1993, 322–27; Benson 1999, esp. 244, 250–56 (the latter drawing parallels with Italian practice). In a musical context, see the discussion of Maddalena Casulana's dedication of her *Madrigali* to Isabella de' Medici in Higgins 1997, 183–84. See also, more generally, on the practice of female-female dedications in French texts, Larsen 1990 and Losse 1994.

128. For the text of the poem, see Perrone 1996; also Ducchi 1589, 45–53 for an alternative, probably earlier version. For discussion, aside from Perrone's study, see Cox and Sampson 2004, 27–28; Ultsch 2005a, 87–91; Ultsch 2005b, 359–61. For earlier experiments in the genre of pastoral eclogue, by Laura Battiferra, see Battiferra 2000, 154–64; Kirkham 2001; Battiferra 2006, 206–17, 424–25. Isabella Andreini also wrote prolifically in the genre.

129. For Edreo's accusation, see *Calisa* in Perrone 1996, 79 (lines 99–100); for Flori's "confession" and self-defense, ibid. 80 (lines 104–8).

130. Salvetti 1590, 5–112. The sequence to Cristina is followed by a shorter and

more formal section of verse in tribute to Christine's husband, Ferdinand I de' Medici (Salvetti 1590, 115–55); the couple had been married the previous year.

131. Ferentilli 1571, 309–12.

132. Salvetti describes her *innamoramento* most fully in the *canzone* "Volgea ridendo a torno" (Salvetti 1590, 78–84), which recalls Petrarch's 126 ("Chiare, fresche e dolci acque"); see also p. 105 for the sonnet "Chi su la neve mai candida e bella." The phrases quoted in the text are from the former poem (79). An interesting example of the use of Neoplatonic erotic language between women outside a patronage context is found in Laura Beatrice Cappello's poems for Angela Bianca Beccaria in Guazzo 1595, discussed in the text; see especially Guazzo 1595, 534–35; also Guazzo 1595, 538, for a discussion of the two women's "love."

133. Fonte 1988, 149–52; Fonte 1997, 210–15. The sonnets are attributed within the dialogue to Corinna. On the theme of female *amicitia* in Fonte, see Jordan 1996, 58.

134. See Marinella 1998, 242–68, on the mountain realm of Erato; Marinella 1635, 115–21 (5.62–85), for Erina's enchanted island. For discussion of the figure of Erina, see Cox 1997a, 142–43, and Panizza 1999, 14.

135. See Marinella 1998, 265–67, for Erato's observatory; Marinella 1635, 122–23 (5.87, 89–93), for the description of Altea's song.

136. Cox and Sampson 2004, 20–23.

137. An exception is Camilla Scarampa's youthful sonnet "Biasmi pur chi vuol la mia durezza," declaring her unwillingness to marry and her intent instead to devote herself to poetry; see ch. 2, n. 40, above. For the theme of the attractions of studious solitude in convent theater, see Weaver 2002, 208–10.

138. See on this in relation to Fonte, Cox 1995a; in relation to Campiglia, Chemello 2003 esp. 73–85; Cox and Sampson 2004, 22–23; Ultsch 2005b. It is possible that within Fonte's and Campiglia's Veneto context, memories of the figure of the fifteenth-century secular spinster-scholar Isotta Nogarola may also have been an influence in this regard.

139. Matraini 1602, 10–11; cf. for comment Smarr 2005a, 84 and 264 n. 80. The phrase quoted in the text is an echo of Cicero's *De officiis*, 3.1; for its context within the Renaissance male discourse of scholarly solitude, see S. Campbell 2004, 38.

140. For the context of the treatise, see ch. 6, sec. 1. For the text, see Marinella 1600, 1601, 1621; 1999. For discussion, see Malpezzi Price 1994b; also Allen and Salvatore 1992; Jordan 1996, 61–65; Panizza 1999; Santacroce 1999–2000; Chemello 2000a; Kolsky 2001. Of earlier bibliography, Chemello 1983 and 1993 remain fundamental.

141. Fonte 1600, 1988, 1997; Franco 1580, 1998b; also 1998a (selections); Matraini 1595, 1597, 1989. For discussion, see, for Fonte, the bibliography cited in n. 91 above. For Franco, see Favretti 1992; Rosenthal 1992, 116–52 (abridged in Rosenthal 1993, 110–23); Doglio 1994; Bianchi 1998; Jones and Rosenthal 1998, 8–13; Chemello 1999, 38–42; also Bassanese 1996, which discusses Franco's letters comparatively with letters by other Italian courtesans, and, for literary context, Quondam 1981, 54–

58, esp. 57. The only sustained critical discussion of Matraini's *Lettere* to date is Rabitti 1999, 215–25. On their context, see briefly Quondam 1981, 123.

142. Matraini's late works have been relatively little studied; see, however, Rabitti 1994, 246–49, and Smarr 2005a, 81–97, on the *Dialoghi spirituali*. Translated extracts from Matraini 1590 are included in a forthcoming anthology of sixteenth-century Marian writings by Italian women from the University of Chicago Press, edited by Susan Haskins.

143. See on this work and its context Chemello 2003, 76–86; Cox and Sampson 2004, 7–8; Ultsch 2005a, 74–76.

144. New editions of Catherine of Siena's *Dialogo* appeared in 1579, 1582, and 1589 and of her *Lettere devotissime alla Beata Vergine* in 1562 and 1584. Catherine of Bologna's *Libretto devoto* was reprinted in 1571, 1579, 1582, 1589, and 1614.

145. Matraini makes defensive appeal to divine inspiration in the dedicatory letter of her *Considerationi sopra i sette salmi* (Matraini 1586, A2r) but offers no such claims in her later *Dialoghi spirituali,* which present the learning displayed as fully her own.

146. Marinella 1601, 108–34; Marinella 1999, 119–45.

147. See, for Franco, especially letters 4 and 28 (Franco 1998b, 35–41, 84–87); also, for discussion, Rosenthal 1992, 136–38, and Bianchi 1998, 11–12, 15. For Matraini, see especially her moral-educational letter to her son, Federico Cantarini, an adaptation of her 1556 translation of Isocrates; her letter concerning a point of love theory addressed to Lodovico Domenichi; and her letter to a "Messer Teofilo Caldarini" debating theological issues associated with the notion of divine providence (Matraini 1989, 147–52 [Caldarini]; 156–66 [Cantarini]; 188–90 [Domenichi]).

148. Matraini 1602, 10–72, for the four initial didactic dialogues between "Teofila" and "Filocalio"; 73–96, for the dream vision; and 97–98, 100–102, and 104–6, for the concluding short *sermoni,* or harangues, addressed to a seemingly fictional "Accademia dei Curiosi." Evocative in respect of Matraini's self-fashioning in her late career is her commission of an altarpiece in her native Lucca representing the Cumaean Sybil prophesizing to Augustus; see on this the brief mentions in Rabitti 1981, 148, and Smarr 2005a, 93; cf. Rabitti 1981, 148; also the more extended, though sometimes fanciful, discussion in Jaffe 2002, 112–24. The work is attributed to Alessandro Ardenti (d. 1595).

149. 1 Timothy 2:11–12 ("Let the woman learn in silence. . . . I suffer not a woman to teach, nor to usurp authority over the man"); see also 1 Corinthians 34–35 on the inappropriateness of women speaking in church. The secular source cited in the text is Dolce 1545, 20v ("[la donna] non dee esser Maestra di altri, che di se medesima, & de' suoi figliuoli: et non le appartiene tener schola, o disputar tra gli huomini"). The same point is made, with explicit reference to Paul's injunctions, in Antoniano 1584, 153v.

150. Marinella 1601: "non solo si distrugge l'opinione del Boccaccio, d'amendue i Tassi, dello Sperone, di Monsignor di Namur, e del Passi, ma d'Aristotile il

grande anchora" ("not only demolishes the opinion of Boccaccio, both Tassos, Speroni, Monsignor di Namur and Passi, but that of the great Aristotle as well").

151. For a list of Catanea's publications, see appendix A under 1595, 1597, 1598, 1610, and 1616. The most accessible editions are Catanea Parasole 1879, 1884, and 1891. For discussion, see Jacobs 1997, 105–7; di Castro 2004; Witcombe 2004, 293–95. Catanea's principal work as illustrator was her reported collaboration with her husband, the engraver, Leonardo Parasole of Norcia, *detto* Norsini (1570–1630), on Castor Durante's important herbal, the *Herbario nuovo* (1595), see di Castro 2004, 230–31, and Witcombe 2004, 209. For another female illustrator within her circle, Geronima Cagnaccia Parasole, see Erdmann 1999, 135–36, and di Castro 2004, 240.

152. di Castro 2004, 232–33. Shimizu 1999, 79, notes of English pattern books, exclusively authored by men, that "they trained women to follow male authority by repeatedly recreating male-authored designs" and hence are "figures for the type of productivity open to women—*reproductivity*." Catanea's success as an author of pattern books is probably reflected in the spurious attribution of a later book in this genre, *Ornamento nobile per ogni gentil matrona* . . . (published in Venice in 1620), to a "Lucrezia Romana." The work is in fact a reprint of the fifth volume of Cesare Vecellio's *Corona delle nobili e virtuose donne*.

153. Catanea Parasole 1891, 2.

154. On "stitchery" as moral discipline and instrument of female self-effacement, see Shimizu 1999, esp. 76–80, and Cowen Orlin 1999, esp. 184–92. See also, however, by contrast, Jones and Stallybrass 2000, 140, on needlework as a virtuosistic skill, counseled as a route to public "honor."

155. Catanea Parasole 1884, unnumbered.

156. On needlework and poetry as parallel arts, see Jones and Stallybrass 2000, 145–71. Interesting on the artistic potential of needlework is Arcangela Tarabotti's description of the virtuosity in this field of her friend and fellow nun Regina Donà in Tarabotti 1650, 342–43, which she compares to the artistic excellence of Apelles and Protogenes and the technical ingenuity of Archimedes and Archytas. See also Doglioni 1988, 6, and Doglioni 1997, 36, on Moderata Fonte's virtuoso skill in needlework. Interesting particularly here is Doglioni's stress on Fonte's ability to invent freely in her stitchery "without any design or model before her" ("senza disegno, e essempio davanti").

157. See the text at n. 62 in ch. 1; also ch. 3, n. 71, for the dedication of two astronomical treatises to Laodomia Forteguerri in the 1540s.

158. See Fonte 1988, 125, and Fonte 1997, 181, for Lucrezia's metadialogic interjection; Fonte 1988, 81–107, 111–30, and Fonte 1997, 128–61, 166–88, for her scientific disquisitions generally. For discussion, see Chemello 1983, 143–40; Cox 1997, 9–12; Collina 1989, 155–56; Magnanini 2003, who usefully relates Corinna's teachings to the *selva* tradition.

159. See n. 134 above for references; also Panizza 1999, 14, on Erina's relation with her father, Fileno.

160. Herculiana 1584. I have inferred Camilla Erculiani's surname from the La-

tinized version on her title page, "Herculiana" ("Ercoliani" would be another possibility). Connections between Padua and the Polish court were strong in this period, as Anna's husband, the Polish king Stephen Bathory, had studied at the University of Padua, as had some of his senior courtiers. On Moderata Fonte's contribution to a 1583 verse collection in praise of Bathory, see Cox 2004.

161. Specifically, *speziala alle Tre Stelle,* presumably the name of her shop. Some kind of precedent for this kind of scientific engagement by women is offered by the secrets tradition: see ch. 4, n. 5, above on the secrets literature of Caterina Sforza and Isabella Cortese. Erculiani's letters are, however, far more theoretical-speculative in character, even though she on occasion makes reference to her practical familiarity with natural science, as an apothecary, or *speziala.* Nothing is known of Erculiani outside what may be deduced from her letters, which show her to have been the wife of a *speziale,* Giacomo Greghetti. Her letters make mention of other works on which she is engaged in the area of herbal medicine and natural and moral philosophy, including writings on sin, on the movement of the sun, and on the composition of theriac.

162. Herculiana 1584, A2v: "ho voluto con gli studii far conoscere al mondo, che noi siamo atte a tutte le scientie, come gli huomini"; A2r–v: "di donna che desidera di illustrare quelle de suoi tempi."

163. Galilei 1901, 219 (letter of 12 October 1611): "ma io ho chiarito altra barba delle sue, e così spero di far lui, avegna che io sia donna, et egli frate maestro." See also Valerio's letter to Galileo of 29 May 1610 (Galilei 1900, 362), where he describes Sarrocchi as "no less of a promulgator of your genius than I" ("non men di me del valore di V. S. predicatrice"). On Sarrocchi's relations with Galileo, see Favaro 1983, 1:6–23; on those with Valerio, R. Russell 2006, 5, 8, 15. More generally, on testimonies to her polymathic interests, see R. Russell 2006, 7–8, 11.

164. A rare counterexample is the Venetian Elena Corner Piscopia, famed as the first woman to be awarded a university degree (from the University of Padua, in 1678); on her scientific education, see Pighetti 2005, 29–30, 33–34, 119. On the emergence of women as scientists in eighteenth-century Italy, see Findlen 1995, 1999, and 2003.

165. "Trofei delle Donne passate e presenti " (Bronzini 1625, *Giornata quarta,* 117).

166. Murphy 2003, 77. Later, surviving examples of paintings on this theme include that by Gianfrancesco Romanelli (1610–62), commissioned by Cardinal Mazarin in the 1640s from (DeJean 1991, 33–34), and Richard Samuel's *Nine Living Muses of Great Britain* (1779), discussed in Eger 2001.

167. A good example of this kind of defensive rhetoric is the second dedicatory letter of Campiglia's *Flori,* to Curzio Gonzaga (Campiglia 2004, 46). For a sympathetic examination of the problems facing female writers, cast as a dialogue between Campiglia and Barbara Torelli ("Flori" and "Talia"), see Manfredi 1602a, 39–40.

168. For Ersilia's backstory, see Marinella 1998, 82–89; for the episode of the

games, ibid., 54–70. For the parallel episode in Sarrocchi, see Sarrocchi 1623, 155–57 (15:8–29). The likelihood that Marinella influenced Sarrocchi is high, especially given that an important literary contact of Sarrocchi's, Spinello Benci (c. 1565–post 1648), was secretary to Cardinal Ferdinando Gonzaga, son of Leonora Medici Gonzaga, the dedicatee of *Arcadia felice.*

169. Sarrocchi 1623, 155 (15.9). Specifically, the games are seen by Silveria's rivals as a chance to recoup their lost reputation as men ("racquistar la già perduta fama") following her outstanding performance in battle.

170. Marinella 1998, 91.

171. G. Marino 1975, 1:531 (canto 9, stanzas 187–88; the phrase in the text is in stanza 187, line 5), and Stigliani 1625, 455–56 (the sequence *Scherzo sopra un libro goffo*). On the hostility suffered by Sarrocchi in her lifetime, see, for example, Valerio's letter to Galileo of 23 October 1610 cited in Favaro 1983, 1:7, where he speaks of "the puerile war being waged on her by these now hoarse and despised chatterers" ("[la] guerra puerile, che pur le fanno talhora gli hormai rochi e sprezzati parlatori").

172. On Sarrocchi's early literary career, and the plaudits she received for her learning and poetic talent, see Borzelli 1935, 5–23, and R. Russell 2006, 8–10.

173. Orbaan 1920, 279 (entry for 1 November 1617). For a contemporary account of Sarrocchi's polemic with Marino favorable to Sarrocchi, see Delcorno 1975, 130. She is also warmly defended by Cristoforo Bronzini (Bronzini 1625, 131).

174. R. Russell 2006, 13 and n. 30, rightly reexamines traditional interpretations of Sarrocchi's polemic with Marino as a spat between ex-lovers, based on the thin evidence of an insinuation of her biographer, the unreliable Janus Nicius Erythraeus, on whose gender attitudes see ch. 6, n. 143, below.

## Chapter 6. Backlash (1590–1650)

1. Manfredi and Decio 2002. For discussion, see Questa 1989, 73–78, and Denarosi 2003, 302–12.

2. Denarosi 2003, 258.

3. Manfredi 1593, 69r–92r.

4. Contarini (Manfredi 1593, 69r) is otherwise unknown, although her name would suggest a woman from a Venetian patrician background. The anonymous author (81r) self-identifies as one of the women praised in Manfredi 1580. Possible candidates are Vittoria Castelletti da Rhò (Manfredi 1580, 225), Renea Pica (ibid., 214–15 [misnumbered 114–15]), and Semidea Poggi (ibid., 216). The poems by Barbara Torelli, Maddalena Campiglia, and Veronica Franca [sic] are at, respectively, Manfredi 1593, 71r, 83v, and 91v.

5. Manfredi 1593, 91r: "pietoso horrore."

6. Manfredi 1593, 71r: "Deh torna, o Mutio, à le primiere imprese / Loda d'honeste, e belle Donne il nome."

7. Manfredi 1593, 83v: "Mutio, che già d'Amor l'armi cantasti. . . . / Deh, come, e dove mai, carmi trovasti / Da segnar con la man, che mai non erra / Opra di

mostro, che rabbioso atterra/D'honor le leggi?" ("Muzio, who once sang of the arms of Love. . . . Tell me, however and wherever did you find the verses to trace with your unerring hand the works of a monster, who tramples all the laws of honor in its rage?").

8. Manfredi 1593, 81r, *incerta autrice:* "Poscia che celebrar donna guerriera/Pur volevi, e real, deh perché prima/Semiramis d'Hippolita eleggesti?" On Hippolyta as the archetype of the domesticated Amazon, see Schwarz 2000, 205–35.

9. On the figure of Semiramis in classical and medieval tradition, see Questa 1989, 13–36, and Heller 2003, 225–27. As Heller notes (227), Semiramis was used as an example by writers on both sides of the *querelle des femmes.*

10. Ninyas is in Manfredi's text named Nino (Ninus), more usually the name of Semiramis's second husband.

11. Denarosi 2003, 309–10.

12. The tragedy ends with Nino's murder of his mother (as in tradition), followed by his suicide, motivated in part by his horror at his incest with Dirce. The goriness of the work and its incestuous theme recall Seneca; see Questa 1989, 73.

13. On Cavalletti and Molza, see ch. 5, n. 24, above. For Tasso's poetic relationship with Campiglia, see Cox and Sampson 2004, 22, 32; Ultsch 2005b, 357–58; with Sarrocchi, Borzelli 1935, 10 and n. 3; R. Russell 2006, 9–10. The evidence for his relationship with the more socially equivocal Isabella Andreini is more tenuous; for an authoritative discussion of this much-debated topic, see Taviani 1984 (summarized in Kerr 2001, 82–89).

14. On gender and the role of women in the *Gerusalemme liberata,* see Migiel 1993; Benedetti 1996; Zatti 1998, 163–68.

15. A third, slighter contribution is his elegant six-stanza "Stanze in difesa de le donne," written probably in the early or mid-1580s as a reply to a misogynistic text by the Florentine Antonio de' Pazzi (d. 1598); see Doglio 1999, 520–21. On the exchange with Ercole Tasso, see Doglio 1999, 520.

16. For the text, see T. Tasso 1582 and 1997; for description and analysis, Kelso 1978, 276–78; Collina 1996, 106–8; Benedetti 1999; Doglio 1999, 505–13; Dutschke 1984; also the briefer discussions in Maclean 1977, 19–21; Jordan 1990, 147–49; Heller 2003, 11–13. The composition of the *Discorso* can be dated to 1580 (Doglio 1999, 505).

17. T. Tasso 1997, 53–54.

18. T. Tasso 1997, 61. The essentially Aristotelian position of the *Discorso* is restated in Tasso's dialogue, *Il padre di famiglia* (1580), which attributes the virtues of prudence, fortitude, and justice to men, modesty and chastity to women; see Doglio 1999, 513, and Benedetti 1999, 452.

19. T. Tasso 1997, 62: "nata di sangue imperiale ed eroico." Eleonora was the daughter of the Hapsburg Emperor, Ferdinand I (1503–64) and thus by virtue of her natal family superior in rank to her husband, Guglielmo Gonzaga. The semantic distinction Tasso draws on between the words *femmina* and *donna* is of course traditional (for an early use, see Dante, *Vita nova,* 19.1–2: "non ad ogni

donna, ma solamente a coloro che sono gentili e che non sono pure femmine"
["not to every woman, but only to those who are noble and who are not mere females"]), although the definitional use he makes of it in his treatise is novel.

20. T. Tasso 1997, 62.

21. T. Tasso 1997, 68–69.

22. T. Tasso 1997, 69: "l'altezza dell'ingegno e la felicissima eloquenza e la divina poesia."

23. See ch. 1, sec. 2, esp. the text between nn. 108 and 113.

24. See the text of this chapter at n. 125.

25. T. Tasso 1997, 65.

26. Boccalini 1910–12, 1:121 (1.35): "Ma Apollo, che giudicò che il sempre con-
tenersi entri i termini della modestia fosse obbligo delle donne private, disse che
le principesse nate di alto sangue, negli accidenti gravi che occorrevano loro, erano obbligate mostrar virilità" ("Apollo pronounced that to keep always within the
bounds of modesty was the duty only of women of private estate, while high-
born princesses, when exceptional circumstances demanded it, were obliged to
demonstrate virility"). For an examination of the Sforza anecdote in Machiavelli,
see Hairston 2000.

27. Maclean 1977, 83–84; Newman 1996, 86 n. 29.

28. No copy of the text is extant and the identity of "Filarco" has not been established; the tenor of the treatise is reconstructable only from the responses it
generated. The name may be taken from Leon Battista Alberti's dialogue *Deifira,*
where Filarco is the name given to a character who dissuades from love. The main
study of the debate discussed in this paragraph remains Marchesi 1895; see also
Chemello 1983, 102–3 and n. 12. While 1586 is the date conventionally given for the
beginning of the Paduan debate on women, it should be noted that an allusion to
foreign *cavallieri* coming to Padua and attacking Paduan women is already found
in the preface of Camilla Erculiani's *Lettere di philosophia naturale* of 1584 (Herculiana 1584, a4r).

29. The treatise of "Filarete" ("Lover of Virtue") is lost, like Filarco's, while
Guidoccio's survives (Guidoccio 1588), as do those of Giambelli and Barbabianca
mentioned below.

30. Barbabianca 1593, 4: "tutta la nobiltà, & gentilezza delle Donne è misera-
mente lacerata da alcuni temerari, & ingiusti."

31. Lanci 1590, 2v: "[gli uomini] attribuiscono alle Donne innumerabili difetti . . . né contenti di far professione di mostrar' al mondo i mancamenti di
quelle, ardiscono, e con ogni lor ingegno si sforzano voler provare esser più nobili,
e più degni di loro."

32. E. Tasso and T. Tasso 1595, 34v.

33. The treatise also incorporates asides on the iniquities of female vanity and
adornment (chs. 16–18) and on the dangers of listening to female counsel (chs. 19–
20). For discussion of the text, see Conti Odorisio 1979 (37–38), Biga 1989, Panizza
1999, 16–18; Kolsky 2001, 974–75; Heller 2003, 32–33. On its author, see Mordani

1837, 150–55; Bertolotti 1887; Rebonato 2004, 196–97. A secular *letterato* on the fringes of the courts at the time of his composition of *I donneschi difetti*, Passi later (1614) became a monk.

34. On the reaction to Passi's treatise, see Biga 1989, 35–38; Collina 1989, 143–44, Kolsky 2001; Heller 2003, 30–41; also Bronzini 1624, day 1, 30–32.

35. Canoniero 1606, 21–22, and Ribera 1609, 195, 248, 324. The former text is interesting in showing the currency of the debate in Florence.

36. Sasso 1601. The lecture is a reading of a sonnet by Bernardo Tasso. Especially interesting in the current context is the dedicatory letter (to Muzio Manfredi's wife, Ippolita Benigni Manfredi) by "l'Ombroso Accademico Informe"; this attempts to excuse Passi on the grounds that his treatise was not intended as an attack on women generally, but only on those afflicted by vice, and goes on to lament the misunderstanding of his intent and the consequent opprobrium that has fallen on the academy. The fact that the work was published by the same publisher as Passi's treatise, Giovanni Antonio Somasco, prompts a degree of suspicion concerning the extent to which the debate was medium-manipulated; see, on this, Collina 2006; also, more generally, on the role of printers in stoking the *querelle des femmes*, Gray 2000, 19; Anger et al., 1996, xi–xii; Lesser 2004, 115–39.

37. Manfredi 1602b; see Collina 1989, 144; also Bronzini 1624, day 1, 32.

38. See the bibliography cited in ch. 5, n. 140, above.

39. On the relation between *La nobiltà* and Passi's treatise, see Panizza 1999, 20–22, and Kolsky 2001, 974, 977.

40. Marinella refers to the hastiness of the work's composition in a passage in the 1600 edition of *La nobiltà* (Marinella 1600, 12v), apologizing for the relative thinness of the historical exemplification on the grounds that the work was composed "in due mesi." On the likelihood that the work was commissioned by its publisher, Giambattista Ciotti, perhaps under the urging of the Accademia Veneziana, of which Marinella's brother Curzio was a member, see Kolsky 2001, 975 and n. 11; also Collina 2006, 92.

41. For a summary of Marinella's arguments in this section, see Panizza 1999, 25–29.

42. On this tendency in the *querelle des femmes* generally, see Benson 1992, 48. For an example close in time to Marinella, see the dedicatory letter to Barbabianca 1593, which opens with the declaration that "è di costume all'honorata professione di Cavaliere prender la difesa, hor con la spada, hor con la lancia, in tutte l'occasioni delle innocenti Donne" ("It is the custom of the honored profession of chivalry to take up the defense of innocent ladies on all occasions, with sword or lance").

43. See the text between nn. 45 and 47 and between nn. 174 and 177. The Venetian Sara Copio may also have written a defense of women, probably in the early 1620s: see Paluzzi 1626, A4r (cited in Boccato 2005, 115), where "due libri di Paradossi in lode delle Donne contro gli Huomini" ("two books of Paradoxes in praise of women against men") are listed among works authored by (or purporting to be authored) by Copio (see the text at n. 216 for the context).

44. On the controversy surrounding the publication of Joseph Swetnam's *Arraignement of Lewd, Idle, Froward, and Unconstant Women* (1615), see Woodbridge 1984, 81–110; Lewalski 1993, 153–69; Anger et al., 1996; Jones 1997; Lesser 2004, 115–39. The involvement of publishers in stoking the debate is especially reminiscent of the Passi dispute: see n. 36 above and compare Lewalski 1993, 157, Anger et al., 1996, xi–xii, and, most recently and thoroughly, Lesser 2004.

45. The text has been discussed briefly in Kolsky 2001, 987–88, and Collina 2006, 93–94. I am grateful to Professor Kolsky for directing me to the copy of this rare work in the Biblioteca dell' Archiginnasio of Bologna and to Barbara Burgess-Van Aken for procuring me a reproduction of it.

46. See, for example, Naldi 1614, 7, where the text cites textually in sequence works by Peter Lombard, Hugh of St. Victor, Alexander of Hales, Aquinas, Nicholas of Lyra, and the decretalist Henry of Susa ("l'Hostiense"), as well as St. Ambrose and Plautus.

47. Collina 2006, 94, expresses skepticism about the authorship of the text, without giving reasons. A likely culprit as ghostwriter might be the Camaldolese monk Severo Senesi (c. 1550–1633), named in the letter (Naldi 1614, 3, 30) as transmitting the correspondence between Naldi and Violati. Senesi was a coreligionist of Passi's and resident with him in 1614 in the monastery of San Michele di Murano (Viaro 2005, 10 and n. 39). He was also associated with the press, working for Giunta in an editorial capacity (ibid., 11) and seems to have had a hand in having Passi's treatise *Discorso della magia naturale* published by Violati in 1614, under his religious name Pietro Passi (ibid., 10).

48. Passi 1599 (unnumbered; Sbarra's sonnet is sixth in the sequence); cf. Sasso 1601, 4r, 15v–16r, 42v–43r. Sbarra's sonnet for *I donneschi difetti* concludes with the hopeful speculation that Passi's work may simply have been composed as a rhetorical exercise and may be followed by a palinode. His sonnets in Sasso 1601 reveal him as a poetic admirer of Ippolita Manfredi. Other contributors to *I donneschi difetti* who express dissent from the aims of the book or attempt to attenuate its message include Giulio Morigi and Federico Lunardi, both members of the generally profeminist Accademia degli Innominati of Parma.

49. Passi 1602 and 1603. *Dello stato maritale* states in its dedicatory letter that it is written to confound those who have mistakenly seen *I donneschi difetti* as antimarriage in its implications, while *La monstruosa fucina delle sordidezze degli uomini* explicitly positions itself as a counterpart to the earlier treatise: having previously spoken of women polluted by vice ("donne laide"), he will now speak of male "monsters." Mention is made in the same work (Passi 1603, 59r [cited in Kolsky 2001, 986]) of a further planned treatise, *Il porto delle perfettioni donnesche*, intended presumably as a further step in Passi's literary "rehabilitation." Although *Dello stato maritale* is ostensibly palinodic (see, for example, the attack on misogynists as vile slanderers and the respectful mention of male defenders of women at Passi 1603, 54), it remains resolutely traditionalist-patriarchal in its treatment of marriage; see Jordan 1990, 250–51, and Kolsky 2001, 985.

50. Astolfi 1602, 114: "si dilacera assai gentilmente questo Sesso [femminile]."

Rebonato 2004, 197, positions Passi as an imitator of the exuberant encyclopedic writer and protobaroque prose stylist, Tommaso Garzoni (1549–89) and describes him as "un poligrafo di spirito poliedrico e sperimentatore" ("a *poligrafo* of multifaceted and experimental bent"). In the preface to the readers (or "spectators") of Passi 1603, we find him making reference to the classical tradition of paradoxical encomium, suggesting that his writing is to be taken as a rhetorical exercise (although this is within the context of an attack on the vices of men, rather than women). The rhetorical character of the *querelle des femmes* is stressed, in various language contexts, in Daenens 1983; Woodbridge 1984; Gray 2000, esp. 11–29.

51. Astolfi 1602, 114. Astolfi is quoting here from one of the prefatory sonnets to *Il merito delle donne,* by Fonte's son Pietro Zorzi.

52. On seventeenth-century misogyny, see Conti Odorisio 1979, 35–47; Biga 1989; Bolzoni 1989, esp. 204–8; Heller 2003, passim. The exemplificatory portion of F. Visconti 1905 (47–60) is still useful, although his analysis of the phenomenon is very much of its time.

53. On the persistence of Aristotelian thinking of sex and gender in natural philosophy, law, theology and medicine, see Maclean 1980. For editions of the *Corbaccio,* see Piéjus 1980, 159; also the lists in Richardson 1994, 242–50, though see also Richardson 1994, 183 and 222 n. 7, on the reservations on the work's subject matter expressed (disingenuously or otherwise) by some of the work's editors. The best-known new misogynist treatises are Dolce 1542 and Biondo 1546, the latter with a modern edition in Zonta 1913. For examples of misogynist attitudes in Venetian satirical writings on courtesans, see Rosenthal 1992, passim.

54. A useful recent critical revisitation of the cultural-historiographical notion of baroque in an Italian context is F. Croce et al. 2002; see also, more briefly, Battistini 1997; Battistini 2000. Of older literature, Getto 1969 and Asor Rosa 1975 remain valuable. See also the bibliography in Battistini 2000, 292–308, esp. 293–94.

55. Cropper 1991, 193–94. On Marino's poetry, see Fulco 1997, citing existing bibliography. Giambonini 2000, 107–62, illustrates the extraordinary publishing success of Marino's lyric poetry. The only full study in English remains Mirollo 1963.

56. G. Marino 1966, 396. Marino, however, famously stipulates that this rule-breaking should be tempered by a sense of decorum ("la vera regola . . . è saper rompere le regole a tempo e luogo"). A careful study of Marino's relation to the previous lyric tradition is A. Martini 1985.

57. Useful recent concise descriptions of the baroque literary aesthetic can be found in Battistini 1997, 477–79 (cf. Battistini 2000, 20–24), and F. Croce et al. 2002; cf. also Asor Rosa, 1975, 5–10.

58. On the "revolutionary" character of Marino's poetry in this respect, see F. Croce et al. 2002, 35–36, who usefully distinguishes between Marino and his late Cinquecento predecessors in respect of his combination of sensual subject matter and extreme stylistic elaboration. For illustration of this "voluptuous" tendency within baroque lyric, see B. Croce 1967, 312–30, although Croce treats the phenomenon as a symptom of baroque literary "decadence"; cf. also, specifically

on Marino—and again in tones of disapproval—Jannaco and Capucci 1966, 162–65. On the fundamental influence of Tasso on baroque poetry, see, for example, Getto 1969, 65, and Asor Rosa 1975, 3.

59. On this motif of the unconventional love object in late sixteenth- and seventeenth-century poetry, see Bettella 2005, 128–70; also Jannaco and Capucci 1966, 186–87; Getto 1969, 71–73; Doglio 1999, 516–17.

60. On the debate over the *Adone*, see Guardiani 2002; also F. Croce 1955a.

61. Jori 1997, 702–3; cf. de Miranda 2000, 308–10.

62. On resistance to Marino's model of lyric poetry generally in the first half of the Seicento, see Asor Rosa 1975, 141–63; Battistini 1997, 469–71 (cf. Battistini 2000, 25–35); Jori 1997, passim. On the Barberini circle as a key center for this resistance, see Asor Rosa 1975, 142–44; Jori 1997, 683–87; Bolland 2000, 316–17 and notes. More generally, on the literary culture of Barbarini Rome, see the bibliography cited in Giachino 2002, 192, 13. On Barberini art patronage, see J. B. Scott 1991.

63. On Colonna's position in Rome during Urban VIII's pontificate, see J. B. Scott 1991, 62; also Dunn 1994 and 1997 and Bonadonna Russo 1999 (I am grateful to Amy Brosius for supplying me with a copy of the latter). On the celebratory iconography associated with her in Palazzo Barberini, see J. B. Scott 1991, 62–67, 110. Colonna was the dedicatee of a number of poetic works and libretti between her 1528 marriage and Urban's death in 1644, including Turina Bufalini 1628; *Componimenti* 1629; M. Barberini 1637; M. Rossi 1637; Bracciolini 1639. See also Murata 1981 and Hammond 1994 on the operas commissioned by Anna's husband and brothers-in-law, several featuring female protagonists perhaps intended to compliment her; also Hammond 1994, 214–24, on a staged joust held in Piazza Navona by Cardinal Antonio Barberini in 1634 and dedicated to Anna Colonna and her mother-in-law Costanza Barberini. A similar pattern of literary homage toward a powerful woman may be detected in the case of the Neapolitan Accademia degli Oziosi in 1611–15, during the vice-regency of Pedro Fernandez de Castro, Duke of Lemos (1576–1622); see de Miranda 2000, 143–44, on the dedication to the viceroy's wife, Catalina de la Cerda, of a work by the academician Giambattista Composto celebrating the biblical figure of Judith; also de Miranda 2000, 95, on a further work dedicated to her, a 1612 collection in mourning of Margaret of Austria, queen of Spain.

64. As a well-known literary antagonist of Marino and, like the new pope, a one-time member of the short-lived anti-Marinist Accademia degli Ordinati (founded 1608), Sarrocchi was well placed for a "revival" at this time. For Sarrocchi's Barberini prophecy, see Sarrocchi 1623, 197–98 (18.142–44); cf. Sarrocchi 2006, 311–12. On her relations with Marino, see the text at n. 171 in ch. 5; also R. Russell 2006, 12–14.

65. Costa 1644, unnumbered ("gran raggio del Vaticano Sole Barberino"). Numerous poems in praise of the Barberini, and in mourning for the deaths of Urban VIII and his mother, are included in Costa's later *Tromba di Parnaso* (Costa 1647b, 47–50, 60–85). A further dedication of a female-authored work to a figure

within the Barberini circle is that of Francesca Turina's *Rime varie* to Anna Colonna Barberini. This is rather sui generis, however, in that it reflects a personal connection between the two: Turina had lived in the Colonna household until the death of Anna's mother in 1622, and many of the poems in the volume are addressed to the family.

66. Tomasini 2004; cf. Fumaroli 1992, 36–37.

67. See Tomasini 2004, 114–19, on Laura (cf. 319–32) and 120–24 on Giustina (cf. 333–36). For a precedent in terms of the invention of early female poets, see the text at n. 61 in ch. 5 on Gilio 1580: a text we can assume Tomasini knew, since a sonnet he attributes in his discussion to "Giustina" is also found there (Gilio 1580, 76r), attributed to the equally apocryphal Ortensia da Guglielmo. Interesting as evidence of Tomasini's "throwback" Cinquecento attitude are his remarks on Petrarch's delight at seeing Giustina adding to the nobility of her family through her poetic distinction and her emulation of the attainments of ancient "famous women" (123 [335]). See also pp. 106–7 (320) on Laura's devotion to the liberal arts and her aspirations to immortality and glory.

68. Tomasini 1644. The women included are Angela, Ginevra, Isotta, and Laura Nogarola, Laura Cereta, Cassandra Fedele, Issicratea Monte, and Moderata Fonte. On Tomasini's interest in another Veneto *letterata,* his Paduan compatriot Giulia Bigolina, see Finucci 2002, 26.

69. On female admissions to the Ricovrati, which included Madeleine de Scudéry, see Storer 1948. On Elena Corner (or Cornaro, in the frequently used Tuscan form of her name), see F. Maschietto 1978; Derosas 1983; Pighetti 2005. On the strong tradition of women's writing in the Veneto in the fifteenth to sixteenth centuries see the text between nn. 63 and 70 in ch. 5. On the persistence of traditions of female cultural protagonism in the Veneto in the eighteenth century, see Findlen 1999.

70. Bissari 1648, 3–15. Bissari's mention of his compatriot Maddalena Campiglia in a list of notable women writers (11) is suggestive of the local and patriotic motives that may have contributed to his profeminist stance.

71. Pona 1633. For discussion, see Fabrizio-Costa 1986. For a biography of Pona, see Pona 1973, lvii–lix. For other examples of misogyny in his writings, see the text at n. 113 on his *Messalina;* also Pona 1973, 97–123 (2.2–68) for a lurid portrayal of a "courtesan's progress" in his *Lucerna.*

72. See the text at n. 58 in ch. 3. On the tendency in Seicento "famous women" works to counterpose "good" and "bad" feminine exempla, see Collina 1996, 117–19, who rightly notes as a precedent for Pona's *Galeria* Tommaso Garzoni's *Vite delle donne illustri della Scrittura sacra, con l'agiunta delle vite delle donne oscure e laide dell'uno e dell'altro Testamento* (1586) (see Garzoni 1994).

73. Pona 1633, 73: "havea un neo non molto tinto, nel confine della guancia, e della bocca, che le accresceva venustà, e col darle credito di naturalmente libidinosa, infiammava maggiormente gl'Amanti." On the motif of the *neo,* stemming from Tasso, see Getto 1969, 64- 65, and Doglio 1999, 515. On the sexualization of the figure of Lucretia in seventeenth-century misogynistic literature, see Giachino

2002, 213 and n. 75. On Pona's account in particular, see Fabrizio-Costa 1986, 181–82; cf. also ibid., 183–90, on his similarly lascivious account of the life of Mary Magdalene.

74. For discussion, see, on Buoninsegni, Buoninsegni and Tarabotti 1998; Heller 2003, 63–65; on Pallavicino's *La rettorica*, see Pallavicino 1992 and Grantham Turner 2003, 74–87; on Rocco, Rocco 1988, esp. 71–73; Coci 1988, 23–27; Heller 2003, 74–77; Grantham Turner 2003, 88–103; on Erythraeus, Giachino 2002, 200, 212–13; on Loredan, Muscariello 1979, 70–71; Panizza 2006, 110–13. On Pallavicino's *Il corriero svaligiato*, see Pallavicino 1984, esp. 5–10 (letter 5); also ibid., 133–34, and Tarabotti 2004, 148–49, for Arcangela Tarabotti's response; Heller 2003, 73, 75–76; on Aprosio, Biga 1989; Heller 2003, 64, 66–68; Marini 2000, 171–73, 175–76; on Tondi, Conti Odorisio 1979, 37–42; Heller 2003, 263–64, 265–66; on Cebà, Jannaco and Capucci 1966, 453–55; Cavarocchi Arbib 1999, 148–51. See also Muscariello 1979, 68–72, generally on misogyny in the *romanzo spirituale*. On misogynistic themes in Seicento formal satire, see F. Visconti 1905, 47–56, and Limentani 1961, 312–14, 355–64, 367–86.

75. On the Incogniti, see Spini 1983, 145–99; Miato 1998; Muir 2007, esp. 70–107; also, for an overview of their narrative output, Mancini 1982. On their probaroque literary sympathies—the Venetian circles that coalesced in the Incogniti were fierce defenders of Marino in the debate following the publication of the *Adone* in 1623, and the academy's founder, Loredan, was the author of a laudatory biography of Marino (1633)—see Biga 1989, 25, and Guardiani 2002, 189.

76. On the militant sexual libertinism of the Incogniti and its Aristotelian philosophical roots, see Spini 1983, 155–66; Biga 1989, 28–29; Heller 2003, 50–51. On the misogynistic tendency of their writings, see Biga 1989, 27 and 31 n. 7, and Heller 2003, 48–81. On the political context of their writings in the 1630s and early 1640s, the period of their greatest literary dominance in Venice, see Infelise 2006, esp. 60–65

77. I have been unable to consult the last two of these works and rely on the descriptions in Heller 2003. The presence of this theme in the writings of the Incogniti is discussed in Mancini 1982, 218–19, and Heller 2003, 147–49, 273–75. Even where the possibility of heroic virtue in a woman is acknowledged, as in Pallavicino's portrait of the elder Agrippina, Germanicus's wife, we tend to find this tempered with exceptionalist rhetoric: see, for example, Pallavicino 1654, 12, where Germanicus is congratulated on the good fortune of marriage with a woman "who sustains the merit of virtue against the general lubriciousness of the sex" ("donna, la quale sostenga contro la lubricità del sesso, il merito della virtù").

78. On Loredan's play, see Heller 2003, 78–81, and Heller 2006, 151–57. See also Freeman 1996 on the frequency of this same theme in Seicento opera libretti, and Mikalachki 1998, 115–49, and Schwartz 2000 for English comparative material. As Heller 2006 notes, an interesting feature of *La forza d'amore* is its deployment in its opening scenes of rhetoric reminiscent of the feminist writings of figures such as Moderata Fonte and Arcangela Tarabotti; see esp. for this Loredan 1662, 20–25 (1.3) and contrast the palinodic speech of Ardemia at 40–41 (1.7).

79. See Herlihy 1995, 286, for dramatic statistics regarding Mantua's seventeenth-century decline.

80. On the decline of the courts in the seventeenth century, see Galasso 1997, 396–97, and Archi 1962. On Tuscany and Savoy in the same period, see Galasso 1997, 393–96. For an overview of the literary patronage of the Savoy court, see Masoero 1999, 105–10.

81. Boccalini 1910–12, 2:34 (2.6): "il maggior vantaggio che abbiano le republiche sopra le monarchie [è] l'esser libere dall'impedimento delle donne."

82. On the public visibility of female relatives of popes, and their role as unofficial "first ladies," see Waddy 1990, 26–29, and J. B. Scott 1991, 62, both discussing Anna Colonna Barberini (on whom see n. 63 above), as an example.

83. Murphy 2003 (on the later sixteenth century), and Bohn 2004.

84. See the text between nn. 68 and 70.

85. Pictorial evidence suggestive of a conscious self-modeling of later Medici consorts on Eleonora is offered by Justus Sustermans's portrait of Maria Maddalena with her heir Ferdinand II (c. 1623), which imitates the model of Bronzino's famous dynastic portrait of Eleonora with her son Giovanni (c. 1545). See A. Dixon, ed. 2002, 126–27, for reproductions.

86. Serdonati 1596; Lorini del Monte 1617. See also Lanci 1590; Razzi 1595–1606; Canoniero 1606. Serdonati's and Lorini's dedications continue a tradition of "defenses of women" addressed to successive duchesses of Florence initiated with D. Bruni 1552 (dedicated to Eleonora of Toledo) and continuing with Vasolo 1573 (dedicated to Giovanna d'Austria).

87. Harness 2006, 43–55. The suite of rooms in the Palazzo Vecchio decorated for Eleonora of Toledo in the 1550s and 1560s offered a recent Florentine precedent for such a politically oriented gendered scheme, though with different emphases determined by the two women's respective situations, as, respectively, ruler-consort and regent. On the iconography of Eleonora's rooms, see Benson 2004; Tinagli 2004; Gáldy 2006.

88. Harness 2006, 44–45, 68–99, 180–95. See also Harness 2006, 56–61, for a discussion of smaller-scale dramas featuring Maria Maddalena's namesake Mary Magdalene. Within a different genre, see Quint 2004, 66–77, on the warrior heroine Erinta of Francesco Bracciolini's *La croce racquistata* (1611), presented as ancestress of the Medici dynasty and clearly intended as a compliment to the grand duchess.

89. Only four volumes were published (1624, 1625, 1628, and 1632); the first was originally published in 1622 and then withdrawn. A French adaptation was published in 1622 (Bronzini 1622b; cf. Maclean 1977, 33 and n. 35); this claims to be translated from an abridged version of the original that the author had received from Bronzini prior to the work's publication. I have not been able to consult the rare fourth volume of 1632, entitled *Della virtù e valore delle donne illustri,* published by Zanobi Pignoni and dedicated to Christine of Lorraine (Capucci 1972, 464). The entire work survives in manuscript in the Biblioteca Nazionale Centrale of Florence (Magl. VIII.1513–38; I am grateful to Suzanne Cusick for alerting me to the

existence of this manuscript). Born near Ancona, Bronzini was a court official who had worked in Rome before moving to Florence in the service of Cardinal Carlo de' Medici in 1615. For a biography, see Capucci 1972; for discussion of the text, see Jordan 1990, 266–69, and Harness 2006, 43.

90. Two interesting contextualizing analyses of Caccini's *La liberazione* are Cusick 1993b and Harness 2006, 152–62.

91. The work is unusual among Marinella's hagiographic writings for its incorporation of courtly and dynastic elements more reminiscent of chivalric epic: see, for example, the vision of future Medici rulers of Florence granted by God to Catherine in book 5 (Marinella 1624, 148–60). Marinella was in touch with Florentine literary circles through Cristoforo Bronzini, who appears to have sent his *Dialogo* to her for her opinion (see Bronzini 1625, day 4, 89–90, where he proudly cites her approval; also Marinella 1624, 260, for a laudatory mention of Bronzini's work; cf. Panizza 1999, 23–24; Santacroce 1999–2000, 19–22). Marinella's previous Medici dedications had been of her 1605 *Arcadia felice* (Leonora Medici Gonzaga) and her 1618 *Amore innamorato e impazzato* (Caterina Medici Gonzaga).

92. For discussion, see Conti Odorisio 1979, 74–78; Heller 2003, 41–43; Santacroce 1999–2000, 18–19. For a biography of the author, see Stumpo 1998.

93. On the war and the dynastic issues that motivated it, see Parrott 1997, esp. 32, 33–36.

94. See esp. della Chiesa 1620, 23, where he argues that women's exclusion from rule and from public affairs "non procede dall'imperfettione, o mancamento del sesso . . . ma bene dalla potenza de gl'huomini, che a poco a poco hanno usurpato la lor ragione" ("is not due to any imperfection or failing of the sex, but to the power of men, who have gradually usurped all women's rights"). The passage follows a lengthy account of women's achievements as rulers, stressing the local Piedmontese context and ending with praises of the governing skills of Margherita's mother, Catalina (22).

95. Mostaccio 1999, esp. 467. A third seventeenth-century "defense of women," after Bronzino's and della Chiesa's, that stresses women's capacity for rule and denounces their exclusion from government is Filippo Maria Bonini's *La donna combattuta e difesa* (1652). Again, here, an ad hominem encomiastic agenda may be suspected, as the first edition of the work (which I have not been able to consult) is listed as being dedicated to Pelina Spinola, *principessa* of Molfetta. For Bonini's political arguments, see Bonini 1667, 379–81; also ibid., 383–87, for a list of modern "ruler-heroines" ("heroine di stato"; the term is found at 385). For a brief discussion of Bonini's life and works, see Marrè Brunenghi 1996. Interesting in the light of his profeminist self-positioning are his patronage relations with Cardinals Antonio Barberini and Giulio Mazzarino (Mazarin).

96. See Segni 1600; also, for discussion, Giachino 2001b.

97. Segni 1600, 249–60, for Salvetti; also, in the vernacular section, Febronia Pannolini (145–46), Francesca Turina (291–92), Isabella Andreini (298–99). Pannolini also appears, with Molza, in the separately numbered Latin section (respectively at pp. 98 and 21).

98. Manfredi 1593, 7–8. Dorothea was the daughter of King Christian III of Denmark.

99. Manfredi 1606b, 181–83. See also the poem to Isabella Bonelli Torelli in Manfredi 1587, 58, feigning shock that a woman should have expressed a desire to read of such "tragic horror" (*tragico horrore*).

100. Cox 1995b. On the situation of intellectuals in the "age of absolutism," see the bibliography cited in ibid., 913 n. 39. Rosa 1982, 299–301, 306–8, is especially relevant for the period referred to here.

101. For references, see ch. 5, n. 8, above; also, specifically, where the Seicento is concerned, Conti Odorisio 1979, 36, and Fragnito 2005, 284–86, the latter calling attention to the effects of censorship in particular.

102. See the interesting material relating to this in De Boer 2001, 113–15; also De Boer 2001, 102–5 and 108–11, on Counter-Reformation reforms to confessional practice and the organization of church space predicated on the dangers of male exposure to female sexual attraction.

103. A third "defender of women" of this period is Luciano Bursati da Crema, author of *La vittoria delle donne* (1620), a dialogue set in Venice. For discussion, see Jordan 1990, 261–66, and Heller 2003, 39–41.

104. Capucci 1972, 463. The date of the book's proscription was 2 December 1622 (Santacroce 1999–2000, 19 n. 46).

105. The document, found in ms. Magl. VIII.81, Biblioteca Nazionale Centrale, Florence, 3r–6r, is headed *Dichiaratione della mente del Bronzino Autore del* Dialogo della Dignità, e Nobiltà delle Donne (henceforth cited as *Dichiaratione*) and consists of a list of *censure* and a series of revisions (*accommodamenti*) proposed by the author in response.

106. The quotation is from the King James version. For the *censura* in question (the third in the list), see *Dichiaratione*, 3r. Bronzini's *accommodamento* mitigates the statement, stipulating instead that male rule is unjust when women are treated like slaves ("schiave") rather than comrades ("compagne"). On the tradition within Renaissance defenses of women of presenting male rule as a tyranny, see Cox 1995a, 516–19.

107. *Dichiaratione, censura* 7, misnumbered as 8, 3v–4r; cf. Agrippa 1996, 47–48; Fonte 1988, 26; Fonte 1997, 60.

108. Stumpo 1998, 749.

109. This statement is based on a comparison of sample passages of the texts of Bronzini 1622a and Bronzini 1624, focusing on passages criticized by the anonymous censor of the Biblioteca Nazionale Centrale manuscript where it was possible to identify these. I would like to thank Paul Greene for allowing me access to a rare copy of the former edition (another is in the Folger Library).

110. Stumpo 1998, 749, suggests that della Chiesa may have been perceived in Rome as too much of an instrument of the regent of Savoy, Maria Cristina of France, who had sponsored his candidacy for the post.

111. Erythraeus 1645, 113.

112. See Razzi 1595–1606; Ribera 1609; della Chiesa 1620; Tomasini 2004; Bonini

1667. Bonini offers an interesting instance of a seventeenth-century "male feminist," as the author not only of a formal "defense of women," *La donna combattuta e difesa* (see n. 95) but also a number of encomiastic works addressed to women of the Hapsburg dynasty with Italian maternal ancestry, such as Eleonora of Austria (1653–97) (by whom he was employed as secretary) and Claudia Felice or Felicitas of Austria (1653–76).

113. Pona 1628, 5, cited in Heller, 349 n. 28: "Fermati, o mano audace: non toccare ciò che mira l'occhio invaghito. La bellezza che ti lusinga è cadaverosa. Costei, che ti sembra viva e accenna di parlarti e di muoversi, è donna morta. L'ha tocca [sic] il Fulmine della impudicizia."

114. The same might be said, with due modification, of Eleonora of Toledo, again routinely condemned for "Spanish" obscurantism until recently (see Smyth 1997, 89 n. 27). See also, within literary history, Ultsch 2005b, which cautions against false divisions between piety and profeminist self-assertion in the works of a writer like Maddalena Campiglia.

115. Maclean 1977, esp. 64–87, 209–11, and Johnson 1997. Within Italy, Anne of Austria was the dedicatee of Tomasini 1644, notable among seventeenth-century literary biography for its respectful attention to the female tradition, as well as of Costa 1647b, which opens with a lengthy ottava rima poem in praise of the "Minerva-like" queen (1–13, esp. 12). An example of such a female regent in Italy is Maria Cristina of France, mentioned above in connection with her patronage of Francesco Agostino della Chiesa. The dedicatee of Costa 1647c, Maria Cristina was the daughter of Marie de' Medici and regent of Savoy between 1637 and 1648.

116. For a classicly lurid "period" statement of the position ("Terror reigned; the shadow of the Inquisition hung over all things") see F. Visconti 1905, esp. 68–77; also the opening pages of B. Croce 1968, 186–95.

117. On reduced nubility within the elites in this period, and its causes, see the bibliography cited in Ray and Westwater 2005, 25 n. 2. On the reflections of this development in the writings of Fonte, Marinella, and Arcangela Tarabotti, see Cox 1995a.

118. See the text at n. 18 in ch. 2. On female architectural patronage in Counter-Reformation and baroque Rome, see Valone 1992, 1994; Dunn 1994, 1997; Conelli 2004 (the latter also discussing Naples). On the public prestige accruing to women from their architectural patronage in this period, see in particular Valone 1994, 141–46.

119. The term is taken from Armando Marchi's introduction to Pallavicino 1984, xii, where the misogynistic fifth letter of Ferrante Pallavicino's *Il corriero svaligiato*, which aroused the wrath of Arcangela Tarabotti (Pallavicino 1984, 5–10; Tarabotti 2004, 148–49), is dismissed as a "gioco di società . . . più che diatriba vera e propria" ("a society game rather than a genuine diatribe").

120. F. Croce et al. 2002, 28–29.

121. Compare Astolfi's comment quoted in n. 50 above concerning Passi's "elegant laceration" of the feminine sex, and see Heller 2003, 53, on the rhetorical and "theatrical" element in Gianfrancesco Loredan's antifeminist *Bizzarrie*. The phrase

"toxins of nature" translates a phrase in Antonio Lupis's *La Faustina* (Lupis 1696, 9: "veleno della natura").

122. For Tarabotti's relation to Loredan, see Tarabotti 2005, 66–68 and 168–69; Collina 2006, 95–96; Panizza 2006, 112. Collina 2006, 98, speculates that Loredan may have had a hand in the publication of Tarabotti's *Antisatira* as well as in that of her *Paradiso monacale* and *Lettere*. See also, on Tarabotti's relations with Incogniti intellectuals more generally, Heller 2000, 18–21. On Loredan's power within the Venetian publishing industry of the day, see Infelise 2006, 58–59.

123. Loredan's letter is cited in Heller 2006, 141, and Miato 1998, 116 n. 323. Both critics interpret the letter as essentially good-natured teasing between two "unlikely literary colleagues" (Heller 2006, 142). Another interpretation might be that the letter, like Tarabotti's sarcasms about Loredan in her posthumously published *Semplicità ingannata,* should be seen as marking the deterioration of a previously supportive relationship (Panizza 2006, 112 n. 9). See Ray 2006, 187, for an assessment of this curious literary relationship, stressing its volatility; also Panizza 2004, 183–86.

124. Tarabotti 1654, 137, cited in Cox 1995a, 538 n. 68; cf. Lupis 1696, 9. Tarabotti's zest for polemical writing is clearly conveyed in her letter to Nicolas Bretel de Grémonville (1608–48), French ambassador to Venice, reporting on the various replies to her *Antisatira* against Buoninsegni and detailing her proposed counterattacks (Tarabotti, 2005, 157).

125. Marinella 1999, 141; Marinella 1601, 130 ("et io mossa dal parere di Gorgia Leontino, e di Plutarco dico che il grido delle operationi donnesche, parlo in materia di scientie, e d'attioni virtuose, deve risonare non solo nella propria Città, ma in diverse, e varie provincie"). On Marinella's counterargument to Tasso generally, see Benedetti 1999, 453–56, and Panizza 1999, 28.

126. Dolce 1545, 15r–19v. Dolce's arguments regarding women's education are summarized in Grendler 1989, 87–88. On the relation of his text to Juan Luis Vives's *On the Education of a Christian Women* (1523), see Fantazzi 2000, 27–29.

127. Fonte 1988, 168–69, and Fonte 1997, 236–37.

128. Antoniano 1584, 153v: "quanto alle nobili, che devono poi essere madri di famiglia di case maggiori, in ogni modo loderei . . . [che] apprendessero à leggere & scrivere, & numerare mediocremente. Ma che insieme con i figliuoli & sotto la disciplina de i medesimi maestri, imparino le lingue, e sappino orare, & poetare, io per me non lo approvo, ne so vedere che utilità ne possa seguire, ne al ben pubblico, ne al particulare delle medesime zitelle." For discussion of Antoniano's views on female education, see Grendler 1989, 89, and Sanson 2005, 394–95; also, more generally, on his educational theory, Frajese 1987.

129. Antoniano 1584, 153v.

130. Antoniano 1584, 153v–154r.

131. Boccalini 1910–12, 1:66 (1.22): "gli esercizi letterari delle dame co' virtuosi somigliavano gli scherzi e i giuochi che tra loro fanno i cani, i quali dopo brieve tempo tutti forniscono alla fine in montarsi addosso l'uno l'altro." In a later *rag-*

*guaglio,* the courtesan Thaide is controversially admitted to Parnassus (2.36 [Boccalini 1910–12, 2:150–53]).

132. Boccalini 1910–12, 1:66 (1.22): "la vera poetica delle donne era l'aco e il fuso" (the phrase comes from Apollo's reported judgment on the case).

133. De Luca's discussion of female education is found at De Luca 1675, 531–47 (ch. 29). For his reference to Boccalini, see p. 535. A rather summary sketch of his argument can be found in Conti Odorisio 1979, 42–47; cf. 75. For a biography, see Mazzacane 1990. A cleric originally from Venosa, near Naples, De Luca made a successful career in Rome and was elevated to the rank of cardinal in 1681.

134. De Luca 1675, 535. Presumably in deference to his dedicatee, Queen Christina of Sweden, De Luca allows that education should be permitted for "princesses and great ladies," although even these should be careful to moderate their behavior in recognition of "the fragility of their sex" (De Luca 1675, 535, 540). On p. 537 De Luca insists that women of lower status should behave in a status-appropriate manner and not take their cue from women of higher estate, differentiating carefully between "ladies of private estate," "gentlewomen" and "non-nobles" (*popolari*) on this score.

135. Pona 1973, 37 (1.87): "Veramente stimo che si debba a miracolo recare s' alcuna femina, volendo superare il sesso, data alle dottrine e alle lingue, non macchia l'animo di vizii e di sporche abominazioni." On the corrupting influence of Latin poetry, see ibid, 1.86. Pona goes on to make a patriotic concession for his Veronese contemporaries, "the most learned Nogarole" ("le dottissime Nogarole"). For further examples of examples of the theme of the corruption of young women by reading within verse satire in the period, see Limentani 1961, 154–55.

136. See the text at n. 91 in ch. 3.

137. On Zilioli, see Arato 2002, 21–23. References here are to the eighteenth-century manuscript of the text in the Biblioteca Marciana, Venice (*Istoria delle vite de' poeti italiani di Alessandro Zilioli veneziano,* ms. It. X.1 [6394], henceforth cited as Zilio, *Istoria*).

138. The lives of Colonna, Gambara, and Fonte (referred to by her given name, Modesta Pozzo) are in Zilioli, *Istoria,* 104–5, 110, and 144–45, respectively.

139. The Stampa vignette is reminiscent in particular of Boccaccio's misogynistic tale of the scholar and the widow in *Decameron* 8.7. A similarly revealing detail in the life of d'Aragona is Zilioli's comparison of her attractions to those of Cleopatra, frequently cited in misogynistic literature as a type of the emasculating seductress. For Zilioli's life of Stampa, see Zilioli, *Istoria,* 124–25 (reproduced in Salza 1917a, 230–31). For that of d'Aragona, see Zilioli, *Istoria,* 172–73.

140. Zilioli's life of Terracina is found in Zilioli, *Istoria,* 183–84. The anecdote, frequently cited in subsequent accounts of Terracina's life, may be assumed to be apocryphal; aside from anything, there is no evidence in Terracina's case or that of any other sixteenth-century woman admitted to an academy that they attended meetings in person.

141. Zilioli, *Istoria,* 172: "non deve esser maraviglia, se ella abbia avuto tanta

copia d'amanti, e particolarmente fra' poeti, i quali a guisa di veltri affamati, se-guitandola a colpi di sonetti e di canzoni si sforzavano d'atterrarla, e di farla preda delle loro ingorde voglie" ("It should be no wonder that she had a horde of ad-mirers, especially among the poets who pursued her like famished hounds, bran-dishing their sonnets and *canzoni* and trying to bring her to the ground and make her the prey of their greedy desires").

142. Erythraeus stresses the unprecedentedness of this "boldness" on the part of a woman (Erythraeus 1645, 1:259–60): "Nullam ego mulierem, quod quidem meminerim, legi vel audivi, vel ex veteribus vel ex recentibus, quae ausa sit hero-ico carmini manus admovere, illudque perficere" ("I can recall reading or hearing of no other woman, whether among the ancients or the moderns, who has dared to turn her hand to heroic verse and successfully to complete an epic poem"). The Greek Erinna of Telos and the Roman Proba are later cited as partial precedents.

143. Erythraeus 1645, 1:261: "Ea pudicitiae fama, qua solent esse poëtriae, fidicines, cantrices, eaeque quas pingendi fingendique ars à lana et colu abduxit." The phrase is quoted approvingly in Angelico Aprosio's misogynistic *La maschera scoperta*, written in polemic against Arcangela Tarabotti; see Biga 1989, 139. Ery-thraeus was notoriously malicious as a biographer and inclined to misogyny in his writings generally: see, for example, his allusion to Margherita Costa at Ery-thraeus 1645, 3.150, as "non magis canendi artificio, quam turpi quaestu, famosa" ("famous not more for her singing skills than for her shameful profession") and compare the more sympathetic Mandosio 1682–92, 2:26–28 (*centuria* 6.2). The standard study of Erythraeus's life and works remains Gerboni 1899; see also B. Croce 1968, 125–34; Giachino 2002; R. Russell 2006, 13 n. 30. On the treatment of Sarrocchi and Costa in Erythraeus, Aprosio, and Mandosio, see Biga 1989, 105–6 and 139.

144. Erythraeus 1645, 1:260: "Verum ne mortales omnes ab ea odio et iracun-dia inflati discederent, Lucae Valierii contubernalis sui opera fiebat, qui, quoties de re aliqua literaria inter ipsam atque alterum orta lis esset, se interponebat, et intolerabilem mulieris contumaciam sua humanitate lenibat." An interesting re-cent discussion of Sarrocchi's relationship with Valerio is Biagioli 1995, esp. 163–64; see also R. Russell 2006, 5, 15.

145. Erythraeus 1645, 1:249–50.

146. Erythraeus 1645, 1:260: "nec sicut quidam, qui maligne eam laudabant, soliti erant dicere, fuit inter mulieres vir, & inter viros mulier" ("nor is it true, as some malicious gossips liked to say, that she was 'a man among women and a woman among men'" [the quip is from Cicero, *De domo sua*, 139]).

147. Erythraeus 1645, 1:260 (Sarrocchi); 1:249 (Sappho).

148. Erythraeus 1645, 1:249–50. Ciriaco Strozzi (1504–65) was a humanist and philosopher who taught at the universities of Bologna and Pisa.

149. It is interesting to note in this regard that Marino's most famous attack on Sarrocchi, in his *Adone* (9.187.5–8), as a "chattering magpie" croaking of "love and arms" ("d'amori e d'armi") makes specific reference to her pretensions as an epic

poet (the line echoes Ariosto's formula of "arms and love" from the opening line of the *Orlando furioso,* though pointedly reversing the terms).

150. The letter is cited in Milani 1983, 396 n. 9 ("non so che dir altro se non quel che già disse S. Agostino alla morte di S. Antonio: 'si levano gli indotti e ci rapiscono il regno'[;] si levano le donne, anzi le donzelle, e tolgano per forza la gloria del comporre di mano a gli huomini"). The Augustine allusion (comically misapplied, needless to say) is to *Confessions,* 8.8 ("surgunt indocti et coelum rapiunt").

151. "Tacciano dunque le donne, e massimamente dove sono gli huomini." For the passage in question, see Passi 1599, 278–80; also, for discussion, Kolsky 2001, 975 and n. 8.

152. On *Le glorie della signora Anna Renzi romana,* see Heller 2003, 174–75. An earlier Roman counterpart for the volume is the collection *Applausi poetici alle glorie della Signora Leonora Baroni* (Bracciano, 1639). With regard to the role of the female singer as "morally equivocal" cultural icon—in many ways akin to the role played by *cortigiane oneste* in the sixteenth century—see Rosand 1986 on Barbara Strozzi. The sexual connotations of female vocal performance have recently been emphasized (though in an insufficiently nuanced manner) in "new musicological" writings such as Gordon 2004 and Gordon 2006.

153. A rough measure is given by the listings of the Chicago Italian Women Writers website, which at the time of writing lists 194 women writers under its Cinquecento category and 92 for the Seicento. The latter estimate is generous, in that it includes women like Isabella Andreini and Margherita Sarrocchi whose formation was in the sixteenth century, even if they died in the seventeenth (there are far more of these than in the equivalent transition between the fifteenth and sixteenth centuries), as well as a cohort of writers born in the later seventeenth century whose careers were enabled by the profeminist Arcadia movement, discussed in the text. For overviews of Seicento women's writing—relatively little studied as a whole, despite the close attention given to some writers like Arcangela Tarabotti and Sara Copio—see B. Croce 1968, 186–95, and Morandini, ed. 2001.

154. Neither Coreglia nor Tigliamochi has been the subject of serious study, though on the former, see Capucci 1983. Besides her published works—Coreglia 1628, 1634, and 1650—Coreglia left a substantial unpublished collection of mainly poetic writings, now found in the Biblioteca Statale, Lucca (*Raccolta di varie composizioni della sig[no]ra Elisabetta Coreglia di Lucca detta Nerina,* ms. 205, henceforth cited as Coreglia, *Raccolta*). Capucci also mentions two lost works, *Sposalizio spirituale di S[anta] Caterina, con un dialogo de' Santissimi Sacramenti* (1634) and a late work entitled *Absalom,* described as "sacra e tragica": perhaps an epic or a *romanzo spirituale.*

155. Another figure best characterized as a "survivor" is Veneranda Bragadin of Verona, who published volumes of verse in 1614 and 1619. While her life dates are not known, she describes herself in the latter collection as in the autumn of her years, and it is clear from the collection that she is a widow with a grown son.

156. Tigliamochi (d. 1695) was the daughter of Giovanni Battista Tigliamochi and married Tommaso degli Albizzi; the couple had four children. Her husband served the Medici in an administrative capacity, like many Florentine patricians of his background. Almost nothing is known of the life of Sori, who was the daughter of a medic, Giacomo. Her writings comprise three *opuscoli* published together in 1628: a set of twelve letters on female conduct, a further set of twelve "defenses" responding to attacks on the original letters, and a panegyric of the city of Alessandria. For discussion, see Maestri 1993. I am grateful to Bartolomeo Durante and Ruggero Marro of the Biblioteca Aprosiana, Ventimiglia, for their prompt and courteous help in supplying me with a copy of this rare work.

157. On Tarabotti (b. Elena Cassandra Tarabotti), a Benedictine nun at the convent of Sant'Anna di Castello in Venice, see Weaver 1994c, 421–22, and the bibliography cited there; also, subsequently, Tarabotti 1994; Canepa 1996; Buoninsegni and Tarabotti 1998; *"Women Are Not Human"* 1998, 89–159; De Bellis 2000; Heller 2000; Costa-Zalessow 2001, Medioli 2003, Tarabotti 2004; Tarabotti 2005; Weaver 2006a. Tarabotti's "dissidence" is discussed in the text. On Coreglia's life and her period in Naples in the 1630s, see Capucci 1983. Precisely, she appears to have been stationed in Venafro, suggesting a connection with the ruling Peretti family (her 1634 pastoral, *Dori* is dedicated to Francesco Peretti [1595–1653]). Coreglia's *Raccolta* shows her to have later returned to her native Lucca. The conjecture here about her marital status is based on the lack of any mention of a husband or marital name in her works, including the late *Erindo* and on her self-portrait as Nerina in *Dori,* which shows her as impervious to love and enjoying her "dear liberty" ("cara libertade") (Coreglia 1634, 73). Regarding her possible singing career, note that she is praised for her musical talents in a prefatory sonnet to the Lucca manuscript (Francesco Maria Biva, ms. 205, 13v) and that the manuscript contains various *compositioni per musica* (120v ff.).

158. On Copio, see especially the important series of studies by Carla Boccato cited in Boccato 2005, 117 n. 14, and the recent monograph by Umberto Fortis (Fortis 2003); also, among recent studies, Adelman 1999, 146–49; Cavarocchi Arbib 1999, 144–48; da Fonseca Wollheim 1999; Ultsch 2000.

159. For a biography of Costa, see D. Bianchi 1924; also, more recently, Costa-Zalessow 1982, 146–52; Capucci 1984; Morandini, ed. 2001, 114–24; M. Salvi 2004. Born in Rome, Costa made her reputation first in that city as a singer, along with her sister Anna Francesca. She later spent time at the Medici court of Tuscany, at the court of Savoy, and at the royal court of France, before returning to Rome in later life.

160. Dunn 1994, 652, and Dunn 1997, 175. Vittoria was sister to Anna Colonna Barberini (on whom see the text at n. 63). Both sisters benefited in their girlhood from the friendship and perhaps tutorship of the poet Francesca Turina, who seems to have been employed as companion to their mother Lucrezia Tomacelli Colonna (Corbucci 1901, 39).

161. Andretta 1994; Morandini, ed. 2001, 125–31; Graziosi 2005, 163–64. It should be noted that Francesca Farnese's decision to enter a convent is often at-

tributed to a bout of childhood smallpox that may have been considered to disqualify her for marriage. The natal status of two other prominent nun writers of the seventeenth century, Maria Alberghetti (1578–1654) and Maria Porzia Vignola or Vignoli (1632–87), is less clear. The former was Venetian and head of the order of the Dimesse in Padua; the latter, a Dominican, from Viterbo. For the published works of both, see appendix A. An intriguing series of unpublished works by Vignola is listed in Mandosio 1682–92, 2:192–94, including oratorio libretti and a panegyric of Christina of Sweden. Generally, on the post-Tridentine convent as an environment for female learning, see Stevenson 2005, 293–302.

162. On Vittoria della Rovere's relations with Maria Selvaggia Borghini, see Paoli 1999, 508–9; on those with Tarabotti, Weaver 1998, 19–20; Medioli 2003, 73–75, 81–82, 84–89 (the latter revealing Tarabotti to have attempted unsuccessfully in the mid-1640s to interest Vittoria in the publication of her incendiary *La tirannia paterna*). Vittoria was also, late in life, the dedicatee of Corner Piscopia 1688, edited by Benedetto Bachini (Pighetti 2005, 41). Vittoria's literary patronage has received little attention, though see Gigli 1854, 418–19; Graziosi 1992, 329, and Maylender 1926–30, 1:366–67, on her foundation of the all-female Sienese Accademia delle Assicurate (1654). On her activities as art collector, see Barocchi and Gaeta Bertelà, eds. 2005, 1:173–90. In considering her role as a patron of female writers, it is important to note that, beside her Medici marital heritage, Vittoria could draw on the precedent of her grandmother and namesake, Vittoria Farnese della Rovere (1521–1602), duchess of Urbino from 1547 and dedicatee of Laura Battiferra's *Sette salmi penitenziali*.

163. See Cusick 1993b; Harness 2006, 152–62; Rosand 1986, 256 n. 57; 257 n. 64.

164. A particularly close comparison with Strozzi's dedication is offered by Arcangela Tarabotti's dedication of her *Antisatira* to Vittoria della Rovere (Buoninsegni and Tarabotti 1998, 31–33; see esp. 31, where Tarabotti uses the same "shadowing" imagery as Strozzi, and cf. also Costa n.d. (b), 5, for a similar pun on Vittoria della Rovere's name). The hostile reception of the *Antisatira* belies the notion that dedication of a work to a prominent woman offered any actual protection, at least outside her own regional jurisdiction. For earlier examples of this motif in dedications, see Campiglia 2004, 44; also Maddalena Casulana's dedication of her first book of madrigals (1568) to Isabella de' Medici (Pescerelli 1979, 7) and Valeria Miani's dedication of her pastoral *Amorosa speranza* to Marietta Uberti (Miani Negri 1604, A2v).

165. On the attacks on Sarrocchi by Marino and others, see the text at n. 171 in ch. 5. The accusations against Copio are discussed in the text between nn. 215 and 220 of the present chapter.

166. Sori 1628 (and cf. Maestri 1993, 241); Tarabotti 2005, 81.

167. Costa 1647c, a2r ("novello Atteone"). Costa's search for stable female patronage is interestingly illustrated in the work from which this quotation comes, her *Selva di Diana*, published in Paris and reflecting her restless movement in 1647 between Rome, Turin, and the French court. See especially pp. 7–20 for a poem to Maria Cristina and pp. 79–80 for an account of Costa's reception in Paris by

Anne of Austria, who was the dedicatee of her *Tromba di Parnaso* (Costa 1647b); also pp. 21–28 for an interesting earlier sequence of poems to a group of potential female patrons in Alba, near Rome. The *Selva di Diana* is unusual in Costa's oeuvre for its single-minded focus on female patronage, although she had dedicated her *Flora feconda* to Vittoria della Rovere in 1640.

168. B. Croce 1968, 164: "In generale, è notare che le donne letterate furono allora conservatrici, e si astennero quasi affatto dal 'concettizzare' e delle argutezze barocche: stravaganze per le quali par che si richiedesse una sorta di virilità." On Croce's gender attitudes in his critical writings, see Zancan 1998, 87–100; also, more dismissively, Re 2000, 190–91, 193.

169. Costa speaks of her *bizzarria* at Costa 1639a, 292; cf. also Tarabotti 2005, 117, where, in a letter to Loredan, Tarabotti speaks of her "maniera di conversare assai sincera e bizzara" ("very unguarded and eccentric manner of speech").

170. See the text at n. 13 and at n. 14 in the coda. The point regarding women's general stylistic conservatism is less true of the prose of writers like Marinella and Tarabotti than of poetry, though for Marinella see the interesting antibaroque polemic in Marinella 1645, 8, attacking "those who in their writing are always seeking out new coinages and exotic, piquant words, transported and transformed from their natural significance" ("color, li quali nello scrivere le loro compositioni vanno cercando nuovi vocaboli, parole stravaganti, e di salso sapore, trasportate, e transformate dal suo naturale"). The preference expressed there for a simple "historical" style ("un ragionamento schietto, puro, e historico") contrasts with Marinella's earlier stylistic ideals as laid out in the preface to her 1602 *La vita di Maria Vergine* (Marinella 1998, 199–201).

171. Coreglia 1628, 97: "semplice ninfa / nutrita ne le rive / del solitario Serchio" (I have corrected "ninfe," an evident misprint, to "ninfa"). The eclogue as a whole is found on pp. 90–99.

172. Coreglia 1628, iir (letter to the reader by Pier'Antonio Fortunati): "vaghezza," "purità," "facilità," and "dolcezza." The volume is elaborately framed to protect the young author's modesty, in a manner reminiscent of works by women published in the 1540s: a letter from Coreglia to her uncle Antonio Bendinelli, prior of the monastery of S. Bartolomeo in Pistoia, states that she is sending her verse to him entirely privately and with no intention to publish, while another from Filippo Lippi to Bendinelli recounts how the latter sent Coreglia's poems to him for an opinion and that he urged publication.

173. The tension noted here between the demands of literary fashion and the imperative of feminine authorial decorum is implicitly acknowledged in the letter to the reader that prefaces Arcangela Tarabotti's eminently "decorous" *Paradiso monacale* of 1643. Tarabotti's publisher, Guglielmo Oddoni, takes the opportunity to promise there the proximate publication of others of Tarabotti's works "più piccanti, per esser assai più aggiustate al gusto del secolo" ("more piquant [or "daring"], because more attuned to the taste of our day" [Tarabotti 1663 (1643), unnumbered]).

174. On Copio's *Manifesto*, see Boccato 1973 and Fortis 2003, 61–81; 148–56. On

Tarabotti's *Antisatira,* see Buoninsegni and Tarabotti 1998. On her *Che le donne,* see Tarabotti 1994; also *"Women Are Not Human"* 1998, 89–159, for an English translation. The treatise Tarabotti was attacking in her *Che le donne siano della spetie degli huomini* was a vernacular translation of a Latin text generally attributed to the German erudite Acidalius Valens (1567–95), first published in 1595. The original is thought to have been intended as a satire on Socianism rather than a genuine attack on women's claim to human status. The translation, attributed to the pseudonymous "Orazio Plata," was published clandestinely in Venice by Francesco Valvasense, as emerged in the latter's Inquisition trial in 1648 (Infelise 2006, 67). It attracted another response, besides Tarabotti's, in Filippo Maria Bonini's *La donna combattuta e difesa,* on which see n. 95 above.

175. The sonnet is first published in Bragadin's *Rime* of 1614, 72. Her *Rime* of 1619 republished the sonnet (Bragadin Cavalli 1619, 68), adding her antagonist's satire (69–73) and her own long reply letter (74–82). I have been unable to find records of the work under attack, whose title Bragadin gives as *L'Oracolo, over invettiva contro le donne.* The author, cited only by his academic name (l'Accademico Fecondo), may probably be identified with Gabriele Cesana, author of a pastoral drama published by Ciotti in Venice in 1606. Bragadin's *Rime* of 1614 also contains an interesting feminist-themed *Dialogo pastorale* on pp. 84–93.

176. See Sori 1628 and Maestri 1993, 225, 227–28, 235–37. Sori's argument shows familiarity with Marinella's *Nobiltà et eccellenza delle donne,* which she cites at Sori 1628, 16. Both Fonte and Marinella are also cited with admiration in Veneranda Bragadin's dedicatory letter to her 1619 *Rime.*

177. Sori 1628, 5–6; cited in Maestri 1993, 228: "Quelli antichi . . . havendo sopra delle scienze deputato due Dei, un maschio nominato Apollo, e l'altro femina detta Pallade, quello disarmato, e colla lira in mano dipingevano, ma questa qual valorosa guerriera, pronta al combattere, da capo a' piedi armata . . . rappresentavano." Sori's whole preface is of interest as a lucid statement of the position of the seventeenth-century learned woman.

178. The *Inferno monacale* seems to have been intended as part of a neo-Dantean trilogy, with the *Paradiso monacale* and the *Purgatorio delle malmaritate* (either lost or never written); see Tarabotti 2005, 45; also Ray and Westwater 2005, 27 n. 9, on other lost works of Tarabotti's known by their titles.

179. On the distinctiveness of Tarabotti's feminist writings with regard to the tradition, see Medioli 1990, 148; Heller 2006, 146. On the element of social critique present in the writings of Fonte and Marinella, see Cox 1995a.

180. On Tarabotti's literary culture, and on her literary acquaintances, especially among the Incogniti, see Medioli 1990, 137–47, and Panizza 2006. On her use and manipulation of citations in her writings, see also Canepa 1996, 10–11.

181. For an account of the condemnation and the prior examination of the book, see Costa-Zalessow 2001, 319–23.

182. For discussion, see ch. 5, sec. 3.

183. Poggi 1623; Turina Bufalini 1628; Coreglia 1628. None has been the object of criticism.

184. A single poem is attributed to her in a nineteenth-century source (Ray and Westwater 2005, 27 n. 9).

185. Costa 1638a, 1638b, 1639a. Other verse collections by Costa are Costa 1640c—a themed funeral collection, dedicated to Charles of Lorraine, fourth Duke of Guise (who ironically died himself within months of the dedication)—and 1647b and 1647c, dedicated respectively to Maria Christina of Savoy and Anne of Austria. The volumes mentioned in the text are dedicated to Ferdinand II de' Medici, Grand Duke of Tuscany (*Il violino, La chitarra*), and to Lorenzo de' Medici (1599–1648), Ferdinando's uncle. Besides these poetic collections, Costa also published brief occasional pieces see Costa n.d. (a)–(c).

186. For a summary of these developments, see A. Martini 2006.

187. For Farnese, see the bibliography cited at n. 161 above. For brief comments on Alberghetti as poet, see Graziosi 1996, 325–26.

188. Coreglia's position in Lucca, which is well attested by the occasional and correspondence verse in her late manuscript *Raccolta*), may reflect the city's pride in its tradition of women's writing in the sixteenth century, with Chiara Matraini, Laura Guidiccioni, Leonora Bellati Bernardi, and Silvia Bendinelli. An allusion to the last is found in one of the prefatory letters to Corgelia's early *Rime* (Coreglia 1628, iiv).

189. Stevenson 2005, 301. Poems by Cerrini are found in Stefano Tofi's *Trattato dell'indulgenza plenaria* (published in Urbino in 1644) and Giovanni Bonifacio Diaspro's *Sacra lilia poetica . . . in triumphum divi Antonii de Padua* (published in Perugia in 1644); see also Coppetta 1720, 432–38, for a *canzone* published in another local production of 1643. Cerrini's youth at the time of these publications falls into the "child prodigy" pattern not uncommon with such civic figureheads: Issicratea Monte offers another example. Cerrini is later said to have composed a *dramma per musica, Il trionfo di San Filippo Neri*. Another provincial nun poet of the period is Suor Benedetta Gamberini of Ferrara (born Marta Maria [1590–1658]); see *Rime* 1713, 335–36 and 568.

190. Sbarra's sequence in praise of Marino is found in Sbarra Coderta 1610, C7r–D3r.

191. Costa has tended to be dismissed by critics for the carelessness and lack of polish of her verse; see, for example, B. Croce 1968, 162, who dismisses her as "shining only by her ignorance" ("risplende sopratutto per la sua incultura"); also Capucci 1983 and Costa-Zalessow 1982, the latter of whom nonetheless commends her for her humor (148). Morandini, ed. 2001, 115, judges Costa's verse "not always correct, but imbued by a sincere inspiration" ("è una poesia non sempre corretta, eppure pervasa da un'ispirazione sincera"). Costa herself deals with accusations of poetic slackness in her verse with typical aplomb, frankly acknowledging her weaknesses and laughing them off: see, for example, the comic opening poem of *La chitarra* (Costa 1638a, 1–5), reproduced in Morandini, ed. 2001, 117–20.

192. Costa 1639a, 208–17 ("Messsaggiera d'Amore si duole d'haver perduto il naso ne' servigi Amorosi") and 218–21 ("Astrologo offeso da Morbo gallico").

193. Costa 1639b. A selection of Costa's letters was included in a much-pub-

lished anthology of *lettere amorose* along with other classics of the genre from Parabosco to Ferrante Pallavicino and Luca Assarino (*Scielta* 1662): a rare case of a seventeenth-century female writers being anthologized. Interesting as context for Costa's exploration of the rhetoric of the grotesque is a work like Alessandro Adimari's *La Tersicore* (1637), written by one of Costa's closest associates in Florence and a contributor of encomiastic prefatory verse to several of her volumes; this contains fifty poems to variously imperfect women, concluding with a *bella sepolta* ("beautiful corpse"). On the popularity of this kind of verse in the period, see the bibliography cited in n. 59 above.

194. Costa 1639a, 194–207 ("Il [*sic*] Zerbino ravveduto"). See also, for female-authored critiques of male vanity, Buoninsegni and Tarabotti 1998, 68–71, and Marinella 1999, 166–75. On the theme of male vanity in male writers of the time, see Biga 1989, 76.

195. As examples of Costa's confessions of her own past vanity, see, for example, the autobiographical poem at 1638a, 387–97, esp. 391; also 1639a, 178–96, esp. 185. Semidea Poggi's strictures against female vanity, like those of Maddalena Campiglia in her *Discorso sopra l'annonciatione,* are composed in a more purely didactic, "third-person" manner (Poggi 1623, 31–47). For Suor Maria Clemente Ruoti's negative portrayal of women in her *Iacob Patriarca,* see Weaver 1994b, 285–87 (though cf. Weaver 1994b, 289–90, on her later *Natal di Christo*). For Barbara Tigliamochi, see n. 228 below.

196. For the text of the Marino poem, see Ferrero, ed. 1954, 388–91; for Costa's, entitled *Violamento di Lilla narrato dall'istesso Amante,* see Costa 1638b, 17–26.

197. Interesting as a point of comparison, though more transparently satirical, is Costa 1638b, 9–16, a vigorously realized exercise in misogynist diatribe, undermined by its own narrative title ("Amante ingelosito per haver visto una lettera della sua Donna ad altro Amante"; "Lover Provoked to Jealousy By Seeing a Letter from His Lady Addressed to Another Admirer").

198. Costa 1638a, 392. The octave is from one of Costa's most interesting autobiographical poems, "Bella Donna si duole della sua vita passata, e si gode della sua vita presente" ("A Beautiful Woman Laments Her Past Life and Enjoys Her Present"). Also reminiscent of Franco's voice is a poem like 1638a, 280–84, where the poet indignantly rejects the advances of an admirer who has sought to buy her favors, although another poem in the same volume (316–21) implicitly acknowledges her to have been misled in the past by a "cieco desir d'argento e d'oro" ("blind desire for silver and gold") (319).

199. Interesting in regard to this is Costa's self-defense against possible accusations of sexual loucheness in a *capitolo* in *La chitarra* (Costa 1638a, 567–73); her argument here is akin to Andreini's in the prefatory sonnet to her *Rime,* namely, that her exercises in love poetry should be seen merely as exercises in poetic feigning.

200. See, for example, Coreglia, *Raccolta,* 38r–40r and 74r–79r for *rime spirituali;* 31v–33r, 40v–45r, and 46r–49r for poems in praise of paintings by Gaspare Mannucci and Pietro Paolini; 53v for a sonnet in praise of a sermon; 15v, 18v, and 19r for

male-voiced poems; 19v for the comic poem mentioned in the text ("Amante, che veduto un Vecchio a canto a Bella Donna, nel rimirarla cadde ne l'acqua"); also 155r–166r for poems relating to carnival games (cf. Costa 1638a, 547–66). A short section of prose writings at the end of Coreglia's manuscript (198–206) has formal analogies with Costa's *Lettere amorose.*

201. The poems to Margherita Costa, both sonnets, are at Coreglia, *Raccolta,* 20v and 24v. I have not been able to ascertain whether the opera referred to in the second poem is Cavalli's famous *Giasone* of 1649 (my thanks are due to Amy Brosius for suggestions regarding the musicological context of these poems). Another sonnet close by (25r), headed *Per la Sig[no]ra Anna rappresentando Medea,* is perhaps a reference to Anna Renzi.

202. The poem is found at Coreglia, *Raccolta,* 128r–29r. For the influence of Costa's persona, see Coreglia's lines at 129r: "schietto il canto, e puro il dir/povertà mi fa gioir" ("with simple song and pure words, I revel in my poverty") and compare to Costa 1638a, 391: "ma schietta in volto, e schietta nel vestire/bramo di viver ben, per ben morire" ("simple in visage and simple in dress, I desire to live well, in order to die well").

203. Coreglia, *Raccolta,* 202v: "Ch'ora sol belle son le belle ardite/E chi non è sfrontata/Batta con sua beltà la ritirata" ("For now the only beauties are bold beauties: she who is not shameless can beat a retreat with her beauty").

204. Coreglia, *Raccolta,* 203r: "Taccia taccia la Musa/Che sfrontata qual'è, l'honeste accusa" ("Let that Muse be silent who, shameless as she is, accuses the innocent").

205. For Coreglia's description of her heroines as "Amazzone guerriere," see Coreglia, *Raccolta,* 202v. Costa's ironic and knowing use of the morally charged rhetoric of feminine adornment in her poetry is a subject that would reward further investigation; this is, after all, a writer who entitled one of her principal poetic works *Lo stipo* ("The Jewel Box").

206. Another earlier, Italian-Jewish female writer is Debora Ascarelli, who was active around the midcentury in Rome. She is known especially for her translations of liturgical texts, notably by Mosè di Rieti (1388–1460), though a handful of independent poems by her are also known. A volume of her works was published posthumously in Venice in c. 1601–2. The dedicatory letter (by the Roman Jewish publisher David della Rocca) is dated 1562, suggesting that this may be a reprint of an earlier edition. The most detailed study on Ascarelli to date is Ascarelli 1925, which includes her surviving writings; see also Quattrucci 1962.

207. For bibliography on Copio, see n. 158 above. On Jewish culture in Venice in this period, and on Jewish authors' participation in Italian-language literature, see Fortis 2003, 36–48; also, more generally, Davis and Ravid 2001. Of particular interest is Copio's family connection with the leading Jewish intellectual of the time, Leone Modena (1574–1608), author of a famous autobiography, an account of Jewish rites, and a tragedy, *Ester* (1619), dedicated to Sara Copio; on this last, see Cavarocchi Arbib 1999, 143–44, 151–57, and Fortis 2003, 44–45.

208. Evidence that Copio wrote considerably more poetry than survives of

hers is provided in Cebà 1623b (discussed in the text), where reference is made of numerous gifts of verse, including at least one *canzone* (Cebà 1623b, 39–40).

209. This is sometimes adduced by critics as an exceptional gesture of suppression and "silencing." Note, however, that Cebà's collected letters (Cebà 1623a) are similarly one-sided in that it contains includes only his own letters and not those of his correspondents. This format was not unusual for love letters; see, for example, "Emilia N." 1594.

210. An excellent literary contextualization of the letters, though differing in perspective from the present analysis, is that of F. Croce 1955b. See also on the exchange Boccato 1974; da Fonseca Wollheim 1999; Fortis 2003, 49–60.

211. See, for example, his summary of the relationship in the dedicatory letter of the volume, to Marcantonio Doria (Cebà 1623b, unnumbered): "io non ricusai di fare l'amore con l'anima sua, per migliorar la condizione della mia" ("I did not refuse to make love to her soul, to improve the condition of my own"). Examples of letters discussing the correspondence with Copio in Cebà's collected letters (Cebà 1623a) include those to Giovanni Battista Spinola on pp. 148, 212–13, and 214 and those to Marcantonio Doria on pp. 321 and 325.

212. This warning is most explicit in Cebà's letter of 10 June 1618 (Cebà 1623b, 9), replying to the news that Copio has taken up the study of astrology: he cautions that excessive study may endanger her health, advising her to proceed with moderation, bearing in mind her duties as a wife and her domestic responsibilities. Disapproval of Copio's "unfeminine" ambitions is also implicit in Cebà's accusation in a late letter that she is ignoring her soul's good for the sake of worldly fame ("Gloria di mondo è quella che voi cercate, mentre per via di lettere procurate di separarvi dal volgo delle femine" [letter of 30 April 1622 (Cebà 1623b, 129)]).

213. "Nuova cosa m'è paruta ch'una giovane donna si sia talmente invaghita d'un poema, che ragiona di cose grandi che non ha potuto temperarsi di procurar la conoscenza di chi l'ha scritto; ond'io mi paio obligato a far di voi altro giudicio che non si suole ordinariamente fare del vostro sesso" (letter 1 of 19 May 1619 [p. 1]).

214. For an analysis of Cebà's first letter in this light, see Ultsch 2000, 77–78.

215. See Copio's letter to Isabella della Tolfa of 8 January 1622 (reproduced in Fortis 2003, 156). Copio remarks in the letter that Cebà's literary executors should have no fear of suppressing the letter in question, since "that blessed soul" ("quella benedetta anima") had ordered the publication "more to honor me, his servant, than out of any ambition of his own" ("più per onorar me, sua serva, che per propria ambizione"). See also Copio's sonnet to Gabriele Zinano (1557–?1635) in Fortis 2003, 127, which proclaims her "heir to the glories of Anselmo" [sic] ("de le virtù d'Anselmo io fatta erede").

216. See Paluzzi 1626, A2v (dedicatory letter to Giovanni Soranzo); cf. ibid., A4r ("Ai cortesi lettori") and Boccato 2005, 115–16.

217. Fortis 2003, 130. The female gendering of the last two epithets is interesting. The sonnets are found in the Giulia Soliga manuscript referenced in n. 218 but may presumably also have circulated separately.

218. The *Codice,* unpublished at the time and surviving in a single manuscript, was first published in Boccato 1987. See also, for discussion, Fortis 2003, 82–90.

219. Fortis 2003, 85, suggests a skeptical reading of this kind.

220. On the Bonifazio episode, see Fortis 2003, 61–81; also Fortis 2003, 150–56, for the text of Copio's *Manifesto* in reply to Bonfazio's accusations.

221. A cryptic comment in a letter of Cebà's (1623b, 55–56 [31 August 1619]) may imply a suspicion that Copio is receiving assistance with her writing: "Voglio ben avvertirvi, che 'l mio gusto intorno al vostro scrivere non è peraventura quello, che v'immaginate; e che, s'io venissi à visitarvi, voi mi piacereste assai più con la chioma ravvolta in capo senza studio dalla vostra mano, che rintrecciata, o disposta dall'artificio della Cameriera" ("I must tell you that my taste regarding your writings may not be that which you imagine. If I were to come to visit you, you would please me more with your hair artlessly tied back by your own hand than braided or disposed by the artifice of your maid").

222. "ostinatamente gli uomini non vogliono che le donne sappiano comporre senza di loro" (Tarabotti 2005, 81). Tarabotti's correspondent here is the Bolognese literary nun Guid'Ascania Orsi (Ray 2006, 179 n. 23; cf. Graziosi 2005, 170–71).

223. Sarrocchi 1606 A2r: "non si potesse mai stimare dal mondo l'ingegno d'una donna essere stato di ciò inventore e facitore." Incredulity as a response to claims of female authorship is also referred to in Guazzo 1595, 13, and in Manfredi 1602a, 40 (2.4).

224. On Marinella, see Marinella 1998, 2–3 (the publisher's foreword to Marinella's *Arcadia felice* [1605]), where he talks of how the *Vita* has been "recognized by a public person as a true offspring of her intellect, to the confusion of malicious slanderers" ("conosciuta . . . vero parto del suo ingegno, da persona publica a confusione de' maligni"). Lavocat 1998, 3 n. 8, speculates that the "public person" may have Lucio Scarano, respected medic-*letterato* and dedicatee of *La nobiltà et l'eccellenza delle donne.* On Tarabotti, see Biga 1989, 62; also Biga 1989, 69, where Biga notes that Aprosio was also responsible for attributing the "true" authorship of Copio's *Manifesto* to Paluzzi. On Costa, see Costa 1647c, 60.

225. See, for example, Tarabotti 2005, 107–8, where Tarabotti ironically requests that Aprosio, as a fellow religious, refrain from continuing to compliment her by esteeming her *Paradiso* to be the product of a male author in order to preserve her from the sin of pride. For other examples of Tarabotti's defenses of her authorship of the *Paradiso,* see Ray 2006, 188 n. 49; also Buoninsegni and Tarabotti 1998, 74–75, where Tarabotti announces that not only did men have no hand in the work's composition but that none would have been involved in its publication had she known at the time of the existence of a female-run print-shop in the city.

226. Costa 1654, dedicatory letter: "l'ignoranza chiama nel nostro sesso monstruoso [sic] le Lettere"; "se non oppressa, disanimata, ho sin qui sotto silenzio annottata me stessa." The letter starts by recounting the author's long literary service to the Medici and lamenting the lack of reward she has received from it.

227. Marinella 1624, 1635, 1643, and 1648. For critical discussions of *Enrico,* see

ch. 5, n. 97, above. Marinella's later hagiographic works have received no critical attention.

228. Tigliamochi's incipit suggests that she earlier wrote pastoral verse ("scherzi vari d'Amor, honesti, e casti/Di Ninfe, e di Pastor leggidari, e belli" [Tigliamochi 1640, 2 (3)]) but I have found no record of this. *Ascanio errante* is unevenly written, veering from epic diction to a more colloquial mode reminiscent of fifteenth-century romance; in this respect, Tigliamochi is closer to Maddalena Salvetti's *David* than the more consistently elevated Marinella and Sarrocchi. The poem also ideologically wavers in its representation of women, juxtaposing heroic female figures designed to compliment the grand duchess with a default misogyny apparent in its numerous asides on women's vanity, timorousness, and cunning.

229. Costa 1644; Costa 1640a; Costa 1640b. Both Costa 1640 a and b are cast in the same mythological idiom, and both recount the same narrative, of Zephyr and Flora's votary journey, advised by Venus and Love, to the Oracle of Jove, where an end to their infertility, their return to their Tuscan homeland, the birth of their child, and its *rapimento* by Jove are all prophesized. The reference is obviously the birth and death of the first-born of the grand ducal couple, the child Cosimo, who was born on 19 December 1639, dying two days later. A precedent for Costa's mythological narrative is offered by Andrea Salvadori's *La Flora* (1628), performed in Florence for the wedding of the grand duke's sister, Margherita de' Medici and Odoardo Farnese; see Harness 2006, 181–88.

230. On *Li buffoni*, the only comedy written by a woman in this period, see M. Salvi 2004. During her short-lived period in France, in 1647, Costa also published a libretto for an equestrian ballet which she had submitted for a competition for a spectacle to be performed at the French court that year (won by Francesco Buti's *L'Orfeo*); see Costa 1647a. The work is dedicated to Cardinal Mazarin.

231. Coreglia 1634 and 1650. Suor Maria Clemente Ruoti's convent drama *Iacob patriarca* should also be mentioned here; see Weaver 1994b, 284–87, and Weaver 2002, 183–87.

232. For discussion, see Evangelisti 1992 and Zarri 2004. More generally, on the practice of history writing in sixteenth and seventeenth-century convents, see Pomata 1993, 19–20, 21–22, and Lowe 2003.

233. For the term "particular" in this context, see Pomata 1993, 16. Malvasia's history has not been studied in any detail to date, though for brief mentions, see Graziosi 1996, 319–20, and Bohn 2004, 268–69. On the polemical context of the work, see Graziosi 1996, 319; also Segni 1601 and Marinella 1603, 9r–12v and 27v–48v; on that of Baitelli's *Annali*, see Evangelisti 1992, 77–79.

234. Tarabotti 2005; for discussion, see Ray and Westwater 2005; Ray 2006; Westwater 2006. Ray 2006, 184 n. 36, notes the similarity between the dedicatory letters of Tarabotti's and Franco's *Lettere* and speculates that Franco's letters may have been known to Tarabotti. The relation between the works deserves further scrutiny.

235. Tarabotti 1650, 323–84. For traces of the *Lagrime* in the *Lettere,* see, for example, Tarabotti 2005, 131–33, where Tarabotti requests mourning poems from her acquaintance Nicolò Crasso (1586–c. 1655) and 169–71, where she solicits a poetic tribute from Giovanni Francesco Busenello (1598–1659), the librettist of *L'incoronazione di Poppea.* The bulk of the *Lagrime* collection is taken up by a lengthy prose tribute by Tarabotti (Tarabotti 1650, 331–76; cf. Tarabotti 2005, 184–85). It is preceded by two poems by Crasso and one anonymous one and followed by a letter to Tarabotti by "l'Eccellentissimo Sig. Dott. Mariotti" (perhaps Benedetto Mariotti, author of a work on the art of encomia published in Pisa in 1637), commending Tarabotti's rhetorical skills in her "oration" and comparing the friendship between the two women to such classic male exempla of friendship as Orestes and Pilades and Lelius and Scipio (Tarabotti 1650, 379). The *Lagrime* are dedicated to Regina's sister, Andriana Donà Malpiero (Tarabotti 1650, 325–26; cf. Tarabotti 2005, 136 n. 1), who is presented as prime mover of its publication (Tarabotti 2005, 170, 185), in a manner again reminiscent of Franco's collection for Martinengo. For discussion of the *Lagrime* project, see Ray 2006, 179–82, who sees it as mainly offering a pretext for the publication of the *Lettere.* For other examples of works by nuns mourning convent friendships, see Graziosi 2005, 168–73.

236. Sori 1628; Maestri 1993, 228–35. Sori's instructions, unlike Marinella's, are concerned specifically with female conduct. As Maestri notes (35), the difference in tone between the meekly conventional teachings of the *Ammaestramenti* and the assertive feminism of Sori's *Difese* is perplexing. At most, a few traces of feminist sentiment may be found in the former work: see for example, Sori 1628, 53–54, which recommends wives' subordination to their husbands but goes on to cite passages lamenting such subordination as "servitude."

237. Salvetti 1611, 67r–72r (misnumbered); Costa c. 1630. Costa's *Istoria,* which she notes is based on information from the ducal secretary Benedetto Guerrini, is presented as a sketch for a possible future biography. The journey narrated took place in 1628.

238. See the text at n. 162. For Costa, see the short poem in Costa n.d. (b), which includes at p. 5 (*stanze 5–6*) an expression of hope in finding poetic patronage from Vittoria, whose "oak" (the Della Rovere family symbol) she identifies as a potential "laurel" for her and Vittoria herself a potential "Apollo and Muse" ("Che la tua Quercia è Lauro; e a' pregi tuoi/In un Musa, ed Apollo esser mi puoi").

239. Costa 1638a has sonnets by the prolific Medicean poet Alessandro Adimari (1579–1649), the librettist Ottavio Tronsarelli, and the aristocratic pastoralist Andrea Barbazza (1581–1656), among others. Adimari also contributed poems to Costa 1638b, along with the librettist Ferdinando Saracinelli, author of the text for Francesca Caccini's *La liberazione di Ruggiero dall'isola d'Alcina.* Costa 1639a has poems by Adimari, Tronsarelli, and the Spanish-Neapolitan poet Miguel de Silveira. Further on Costa's poetic contacts, see Bianchi 1924, 202–3. Tigliamochi's principal literary supporter is the prolific Medici client Girolamo Bartolommei (1584–1662); others of her prefatory sonnets are by clerics, most notably a "Monsignor Salviati" (probably Tommaso Salviati [d. 1571], bishop of Arezzo). Another female-

authored work accompanied by an impressive array of laudatory material is Arcangela Tarabotti's *Paradiso monacale* of 1643; see Collina 2006, 94–95 and n. 8. Among the laudatory voices in this last case are the poet Ciro di Pers, the *Incognito* Gianfrancesco Loredan, and two women, Lucrezia Marinella (with two sonnets) and an "incerta."

240. The principal exception here is Cherubina Venturelli's *Rappresentazione di Santa Cecilia,* which was published a number of times (see appendix A); the consumption dynamic for such *rappresentazioni* is decidedly different, however, from that of other literary works.

241. "del quale [poema] la Compositrice spera un lungo e sommo onore" (Marinella 1624, A3v).

242. Partly, perhaps, because of its extreme rarity, the *Essortationi* has not received the same kind of sustained critical attention as *La nobiltà et l'eccellenza delle donne,* though there are valuable brief discussions in Biga 1989, 38–40; Lavocat 1998, xxii–xxiii, and Kolsky 2001, 982–84. Copies of the *Essortationi* are found in the Biblioteca Aprosiana, Ventimiglia, and the Bibliothèque Mazarine, Paris. I should like to record my gratitude here to Letizia Panizza for procuring a copy of the text for me from the former library.

243. Marinella 1645, 12: "né malvagità per tiraneggiarle, né altra forza esterna [ha] constretta la Donna à star ristretta tra le amiche mura; ma Dio, e la natura, il quale ha constituito l'universo con tanta sapienza, e providenza" ("it is neither a malicious and tyrannical urge [on the part of men] nor any other external force that has constrained women to remain within the friendly walls of home, but rather God and Nature, who have framed the universe with such wisdom and providence"). On Marinella's explicit references to *La nobiltà* in the *Essortationi,* see Kolsky 2001, 982–83. Essentially, she presents her position in the earlier work as an "immature" one (Marinella 1645, 11: "più maturamente considerando").

244. The heading of the first *essortatione* reads, in fact, "Questa Essortatione ci farà accorti, che la retiratezza è propria delle persone in superiorità poste, come di Dio, de' Principi, e delle Donne, à cui la natura, e la prima Causa, l'ha attribuita più, che all'huomo" ("This exhortation serves to make us aware that a retired state is proper to persons of superior rank, such as God, princes, and women, to the last of whom, nature, as prime Cause, has ordained this state more than it has to men").

245. The *Essortationi* are the only work of Marinella's to have been published by Valvasense, who was punished by the authorities for the publication of forbidden books only three years later, in 1648. For his reputation, see Medioli 1990, 161.

246. Tarabotti's *Antisatira* was also published by Valvasense, who appears to have stoked the controversy over the work by passing the pages as they were printed to the polemicist Angelico Aprosio to facilitate his composition of his "counterblast," *La maschera scoperta* (Biga 1989, 63, also cited in Collina 2006, 105). On the controversy excited by the publication of the *Antisatira,* see Biga 1989, 83–92, and Weaver 1998, 26–27; also Tarabotti 2005, 70 n. 2, 157. The 1644–45 controversy is comparable in many ways in its dynamics to that of 1599–1600 triggered

by Passi's *Donneschi difetti,* and it may well be that Marinella's work was commissioned by Valvasense, just as critics have contended her *Nobiltà et eccellenza* was by Giambattista Ciotti. Another possibility is that the *Essortationi* represent a preexisting didactic work to which Marinella was persuaded to add a controversial incipit. On Venetian publishers' roles in stoking controversies of this kind, see Collina 2006.

247. On denials of authorship, see Marinella 1645, 129–30, cited in Biga 1989, 62. More generally, on the means used by men to undermine female authors, see Marinella 1645, 27–31.

248. For the latter discussion, see Marinella 1645, 277–83. Others of the *essortationi* are moral rather than "economic" in nature, urging reticence, modesty in dress and indifference to fugitive physical beauty.

249. For an instance of Marinella translating Latin for her female readership, see Marinella 1645, 170 ("questo voglio volgarizzare, accioché anchora voi, amiche mie, intendiate il senso"). Teves de Guzmán was also the dedicatee of works by a number of Venetian writers, including Bernardo Giustinian's *Historia generale della monarchia di Spagna* (1674) and, closer in time to Marinella, Giacomo Castoreo's *Argelinda* (1650)—also published by Valvasense—and Domenico d'Alessandro's *Il teatro vicentino* (1652). Marinella insists in her dedicatory letter that the *Essortationi* is intellectually worthy of its distinguished recipient, despite its largely "domestic" subject matter, being adorned with "molti fregi filosofici, Aristotelici e Platonici" and "sentenze di Essiodo, e di Homero e d'altri" ("many philosophical ornaments from Aristotle and Plato" and "maxims from Hesiod, Homer, and others" [Marinella 1645, 5]).

250. Marinella's dedication of *Le vittorie* to Urban VIII at the height of the first War of Castro (1641–44) pitting Venice against the Barberini is unexpected; see Infelise 2006, esp. 65, on the political context; also Lavocat 1998, xv–xvi, on Marinella's occasionally ambiguous relationship with her native city. Marinella's late books on St. Francis and St. Justina are remarkable as attempts to fuse hagiographical narrative with philosophical and theological doctrine, the latter incorporated via a dense series of marginal notes. Their tone is well conveyed by the publisher's description in his preface of the former volume as a "theological and philosophical work, in which readers will find a great part of Aristotelian wisdom." As in the case of her earlier *Amore innamorato e impazzato* (see ch. 5, n. 94, above), I have found no evidence of the earlier (1606) version of Marinella's *Holocausto d'amore della vergine Santa Giustina* sometimes listed among her works.

251. Marinella 1643, publisher's foreword (unnumbered); for the historical episode, see Theunissen 1998, 183. The year after the publication of *Le vittorie* saw the beginning of the War of Crete, in which Cappello significantly underperformed, abandoning the defense of Canea; this may account for the nonappearance of Marinella's revised *Enrico.* Another planned but unrealized project of these years may have been a sequel to the *Essortationi;* the published volume ends with the note "Il fine della prima parte" ("End of the first part").

252. The first (and presumably second) *essortationi* are specifically addressed to

"alcune Donne, che bramano, che li loro nomi per via di virtù alte, e nobili, e non sue proprie scorrano per la Città e per la lingua de gli uomini" ("certain women who desire that their names course through the City and circulate on the tongues of men, by virtue of lofty and noble talents not proper to them [as women]"). It is hard to think that anyone other than Tarabotti might be intended here. Marinella had contributed two prefatory sonnets to Tarabotti's *Paradiso monacale* but may well have been alienated from the younger writer when she published the polemical *Antisatira,* especially if au fait with the rumor circulated by Aprosio that Tarabotti had insisted on publishing the work against his advice and that of her brother-in-law, Giacomo Pighetti (Biga 1989, 63, 70–71). Marinella's absence from the roll call of recipients of Tarabotti's published letters lends further credibility to the notion that a degree of hostility existed between the two (see Ray and West-water 2005, 35, on her correspondence with other literary women).

253. Marinella 1645, 2: "come que' segni, che servono a' saggittarii, li quali sono percorsi, e lacerati da ogn'uno, e da ogni parte."

254. The *Grande dizionario della lingua italiana* offers as its fifteenth sense of the verb "filare" an archaic usage (illustrated with a phrase from Michelangelo Buonarroti the Younger (1568–1646), so current in Costa's day) meaning "andare in rovina, ridursi in poverissima condizione" ("to go to rack and ruin"). It is possible that this is intended here as a subsidiary meaning. More generally, on the ideological significance attaching to spinning in early modern culture, see Jones and Stallybrass 2000, 104–33, esp. 111, on associations of spinning with a narrowly defined feminine "simplicity" in contrast to more ambitious and complex textile work such as weaving or needlework.

255. See the preface to her translation of Johann Landsperger's *Letter or Colloquium of Christ,* in Corner 1688, 184; cited in Pighetti 2005, 42 ("L'Ornamento, che rende gratiose le Donne, e famosissime da per tutto, è il silenzio, né son fatte, che per istar in casa, non per andar vagando" ["the Ornament that renders women charming and lends them the highest fame is silence, and they are made to stay at home and not to go wandering abroad"]). Corner's approving citation of this behavioral norm may of course be seen as strategic, prefacing as it does a published work that self-confessedly transgresses it. The need for such strategy is, however, in itself telling.

256. Tarabotti 2005, 197 (and cf. Panizza 2004, 14, for comment); Capucci 1984, 234. For Costa's time in Paris, see also Costa 1647a and 1647b; also Costa 1647c, 79–85, for a rapturous celebration of France as patronage environment. On seventeenth-century French feminism, see Maclean 1977 and DeJean 1991. The genealogical connections between French seventeenth-century feminism and the preceding profeminist culture of sixteenth-century Italy deserve further scrutiny, especially in light of the Italian origins of two women who exercised a formative influences on the French tradition, Marie de' Medici and Catherine de Vivonne, Marquise de Rambouillet (DeJean 1991, 19). The latter's mother was Giulia Savelli, of the Roman baronial family.

257. Costa 1640c, 249. The poem in which the description is found, *Elissa infe-*

*lice* (subtitled "Qui l'Autora sotto nome di Elissa discrive parte della sua sventu-rata vita" [229–56]), is one of Costa's most important autobiographical works, along with the later "Partenza di Roma de l'Autora del anno 1647" in Costa 1647c, 86–95.

258. Costa 1638a, 518. A more literal translation would be: "since all that we are supposed to do is spin, let us leave behind all else, and take up our distaff."

## Coda

1. "sotto biondi capei canuta mente" (Petrarca 1996, 904 [no. 213, line 3]). For other examples of the commonplace, see ibid., 905n.

2. Suggestive in this regard is Castiglione's allusion to the Pygmalion myth in the third book of Castiglione's *Cortegiano,* with reference to Giuliano de' Medici's "formation" of the ideal of the court lady; see Castiglione 1960, 208 (3.4).

3. On the Arcadian movement, see most recently Minor 2006, citing existing literature.

4. On Vittoria della Rovere's patronage of female writers, see the text at nn. 162–63 in ch. 6.

5. See the text at n. 96 in ch. 2. On women in the Arcadia movement, see Graziosi 1992; S. Dixon 1999; Morandini, ed. 2001, 32–35; 202–32; Crivelli 2001, esp. 324–31; also the useful online database Donne in Arcadia (1690–1800) (*www.rose .uzh.ch / crivelli / arcadia*), compiled by Tatiana Crivelli.

6. On Selvaggia Borghini, see Giordano 1994, 66–79, and Paoli 1999.

7. On Maratti and Paolini see Morandini, ed. 2001, 31–32, 167–79, 195–201, 242–43, 244–45, citing existing bibliography in Italian; also Franceschetti 1994 (on Maratti) and Ricaldone 2000, 103–5. Maratti provided the academy with its first love match in her marriage with her fellow Arcadian Giovanni Battista Felice Zappi, with whom she published a joint volume of poetry in 1723.

8. Bergalli 1726. On Bergalli's anthology, see esp. Chemello 2000b; also Curran 2005. The contributors to the volume are listed in Chemello 2000b, 85–88.

9. On Bulifon's publications of female authors, see Graziosi 1992, 338–39. In-teresting as a statement of his feminist intent in these republications is the dedi-catory letter to Bulifon 1695 (to Eleonora Sicilia Spinelli, duchess of Atri).

10. Bergalli explicitly presents her anthology as an heir to the earlier two in her initial note to the reader (unnumbered). For Zeno's contribution to the volume, see Chemello 2000b, 54–56. Bergalli followed the anthology with an edition of Gaspara Stampa (1738), which, while undoubtedly questionable from the point of view of modern editorial practice, had the merit of returning Stampa to poetic circulation by repackaging her in a "morally acceptable" guise. See Zancan 1993, 413–16, and Jones 2005, 299–300.

11. Chemello 2000c, 97–101. See also, more generally, on this sense of cultural "sisterhood" within the Arcadian tradition, Crivelli 2001, esp. 334–40. The phrase of Croce's quoted in the text ("una corporazione lungo i secoli") is cited in Chemello 2000c, 97.

12. After her conversion to Catholicism, Christina lived predominantly in

Rome from 1655 to her death in 1689, and the founder-members of the Accademia degli Arcadi were at least loosely connected with her circles: see Bellina and Caruso 1998, 246–48, and Minor 2006, 115. For socio-political contextualization of Arcadia, see Quondam 1973 (esp. 412–13 for brief comments on the role of women in the academy).

13. On Salvetti, see Crescimbeni 1730–31, 4:53: "con tal buon gusto esercitossi nella Volgar Poesia, che non ostante la corruttela del secolo tutto rilassato a rinvergar nuove forme, e maniere, e a correre alla cieca, e sfrenatamente per l'orme del Marini, acquistò lo stesso onore, e fama, della quale abbondarono i giudiziosi Rimatori del secolo 16" ("she exercised vernacular poetry with such good taste that, despite the corruption of her age, which had lapsed entirely into searching out new forms and manners of poetry and hurtling blindly in the footsteps of Marino, she succeeded in attaining the same honor and fame in which the judicious poets of the sixteenth century so abounded").

14. Crescimbeni 1730–31, 4:146: "Giudiziosa Donna, che seppe conoscere la falsità dell'onore, che a' suoi seguaci promise nel suo ingresso il secolo 17, ed ebbe coraggio d'opporsi, e far testa incontro allo stesso fondatore della novella scuola."

15. As a precedent and perhaps model for this notion of female writers as custodians of stylistic purity, it may be useful to note the Roman notion, voiced, for example, in Cicero's De oratore, 3.45, that women preserved the purity of spoken Latin because the greater seclusion of their lives made them less susceptible to trends of usage ("facilius enim mulieres incorruptam antiquitatem conservant, quod multorum sermonis expertes ea tenent semper, quae prima didicerunt").

16. F. Croce et al. 2002.

# BIBLIOGRAPHY

## Manuscripts

*Ad magnificam et pudicissimam Marrietam Contarenam Lucia Albana.* Ms. Lat. XII.225 (4410), 37. Biblioteca Marciana, Venice.

Baroni, Bernardino, ed. *Memorie e vite d'alcuni uomini illustri.* Ms. 926. Biblioteca Statale, Lucca.

Benucci, Lattanzio. *Dialogo della lontananza.* Ms. 1369.1–50. Biblioteca Angelica, Rome.

Bronzini, Cristoforo. *Dialogo della dignità, e nobiltà delle donne.* Ms. Magl. VIII.1513–38. Biblioteca Nazionale Centrale, Florence.

*Capitoli, composizioni e leggi dell'Accademia degli Umidi.* Ms. II.IV.I. Biblioteca Nazionale Centrale, Florence.

*Composizioni poetiche volgari e latine intorno le cose d'Italia sul finire del sec. XV.* Ms. It. IX.363 (7386). Biblioteca Marciana, Venice.

*Dichiaratione della mente del Bronzino autore del* Dialogo della dignità, e nobiltà delle donne. Magl. VIII.81.3r–6r. Biblioteca Nazionale Centrale, Florence.

*Istoria delle vite de' poeti italiani di Alessandro Zilioli veneziano.* Ms. It. X.1 (6394). Biblioteca Marciana, Venice.

*Lettere inedite di Pietro Gradenico.* Ms. It. X.23 (6526). Biblioteca Marciana, Venice.

*Lettere e poesie del sig[nor] Cesare Coccapani auditore di Lucca e di donna incerta lucchese.* Ms. 1547. Biblioteca Statale, Lucca.

*Miscellanea poetica del secolo XVI.* Ms. 897. Biblioteca del Seminario, Padua.

*Oratione di Curtio Gonzaga in lode della lingua italiana.* Ms. 4280. Biblioteca Casanatense, Rome.

*Raccolta di poesie.* Ms. Fondo Antinori 161. Biblioteca Medicea Laurenziana, Florence.

*Raccolta di varie composizioni della sig[no]ra Elisabetta Coreglia di Lucca detta Nerina.* Ms. 205. Biblioteca Statale, Lucca.

*Rime di Girolama Corsi fiorentina.* Ms. It. IX.270 (6367). Biblioteca Marciana, Venice.

*Rime di Laura Battiferri.* Ms. 3229. Biblioteca Casanatense, Rome.

*Rime di vari poeti.* Ms. 91. Biblioteca del Seminario, Padua.

*Sonetti al sommo Pontefice Gregorio Decimo terzo, et con Sua Santità tutti li cardinali . . . con altri sonetti a particulari gentilhuomini, et donne, conposti [sic] per la signora Laura Terracina.* Libro nono. Ms. Palatino 229. Biblioteca Nazionale Centrale, Florence.

Torelli, Barbara. *Partenia, favola boschereccia.* Ms. a.a.1.33. Biblioteca Statale, Cremona.

## Primary Sources

Only works cited in the notes are listed here. In the interests of space, abbreviated versions of the titles of sixteenth- and seventeenth-century works are generally given. Complete titles (which can often run to several lines) are available from the website of the Istituto Centrale per il Catalogo Unico (ICCU) (http://opac.sbn.it) and (for sixteenth-century works only) its offshoot Edit16 (http://edit16.iccu .sbn.it). Full titles are only given here in the case of titles difficult to abbreviate without losing vital information, such as Betussi 1545, Marinella 1617, and Monte 1578a, and in that of works not listed on the ICCU catalogue, such as Costa n.d. (a)–(c), Marinella 1605b, Naldi 1614, and Sori 1628. Female authors have for the most part here been cited using their family name only (for example, Vittoria Colonna, Lucrezia Marinella), except in the case of some lesser-known figures generally found cited in secondary literature by both their family and married names (for instance, Francesca Turina Bufalini, Lucchesia Sbarra Coderta).

Adimari, Alessandro. 1637. *La Tersicore, o vero scherzi, e paradossi poetici sopra la beltà delle donne.* Florence: Amadore Massi and Lorenzo Landi.

Agnesi, Maria Gaetana, et al. 2005. *The Contest for Knowledge.* Edited and translated by Rebecca Messbager and Paula Findlen. Chicago: University of Chicago Press.

Agrippa, Henricus Cornelius. 1544. *Della nobiltà et eccellenza delle donne.* Translated by Francesco Coccio. Venice: Gabriele Giolito.

———. 1996. *Declamation on the Nobility and Preeminence of the Female Sex.* Edited and translated by Albert Rabil. Chicago: University of Chicago Press.

Albani, Lucia. 1903. *Rime.* Edited by Arnaldo Foresti. Bergamo: Officine dell'Istituto Italiano d'Arti Grafiche.

Alighieri, Dante. 1996. *Vita nova.* Edited by Guglielmo Gorni. Turin: Einaudi.

Andreini, Giambattista. 1606. *La Florinda.* Milan: Girolamo Bordone.

Andreini, Isabella. 1601. *Rime.* Milan: Girolamo Bordone and Pietromartire Locarni.

———. 1605. *Rime.* Milan: Girolamo Bordone and Pietromartire Locarni.

———. 1607. *Lettere.* Venice: Marcantonio Zaltieri.

———. 1995. *Mirtilla.* Edited by Maria Luisa Doglio. Lucca: Maria Pacini Fazzi.

———. 2002. *La Mirtilla: A Pastoral.* Translated with an introduction and notes by Julie D. Campbell. Tempe, AZ: Medieval and Renaissance Texts and Studies.

———. 2005. *Selected Poems of Isabella Andreini.* Edited by Anne MacNeil. Translated by James Wyatt Cook. Lanham, MD: Scarecrow Press.

Anger, Jane, Rachel Speght, Ester Sowernam, and Constantia Munda. 1996. *Defences of Women.* Vol. 4, pt. 1, *The Early Modern Englishwoman: Printed Writings, 1500–1640.* Selected and introduced by Susan Gushee O'Malley. Brookfield, VT: Scolar Press.

Antoniano, Silvio. 1584. *Tre libri dell'educazione christiana dei figliuoli.* Verona: Sebastiano dalle Donne and Girolamo Stringari.

Aprosio, Angelico. 1646. *Lo scudo di Rinaldo overo lo specchio del disinganno, opera di Scipio Glareano*. Venice: Giovanni Giacomo Herz.

Ariosto, Ludovico. 1976. *Orlando furioso*. Edited by Cesare Segre. Milan: Mondadori.

Astolfi, Giovanni Felice. 1602. *Scelta curiosa et ricca officina di varie antiche, e moderne istorie*. Venice: heirs of Melchiorre Sessa.

Baitelli, Angelica. 1644. *Vita martirio, et morte di S[anta] Giulia cartaginese crocifissa*. Brescia: Antonio Rizzardi.

———. 1657. *Annali historici dell'edificatione, erettione, e dotatione del serenissimo Monasterio di S[an] Saluatore, e S[anta] Giulia di Brescia*. Brescia: Antonio Rizzardi.

Baldelli, Francesco. 1560. *Il cortigiano del Sessa*. (Translation of Agostino Nifo, *De re aulica*, 1534.) Genoa: Antonio Belloni.

Bandarini, Marco. ?1545. *Stanze del poeta in lode delle piu famose cortegiane di Venegia*. Venice: n.p.

Bandello, Matteo. 1545. *Canti XI . . . de le lodi de la s[ignora] Lucretia Gonzaga di Gazuolo [sic]*. Agen: Antonio Reboglio.

———. 1992–96. *La prima-quarta parte de le novelle*. 4 vols. Edited by Delmo Maestri. Alessandria: Edizioni dell'Orso.

Barbabianca, Cesare. 1593. *L'assonto amoroso in difesa delle donne*. Treviso: Aurelio Reghettini.

Barberini, Maffeo. 1637. *Poesie toscane*. Edited by Andrea Brogiotti. Rome: Nella Stamperia della Reverenda Camera Apostolica.

Barberino, Francesco da. 1957. *Reggimento e costumi di donna*. Edited by Giuseppe E. Sanson. Torino: Loescher-Chiantore.

Barzizza, Gasparino, and Guinforte Barzizza. 1723. *Opera*. Edited by Giuseppe Alessandro Furietti. Rome: Giovanni Maria Salvioni.

Battiferra, Laura. 1560. *Il primo libro delle opere toscane*. Florence: heirs of Bernardo Giunta.

———. 1564. *I sette salmi penitenziali del santissimo profeta Davit . . . con alcuni . . . sonetti spirituali*. Florence: heirs of Bernardo Giunta.

———. 1879. *Lettere di Laura Battiferri Ammanati a Benedetto Varchi*. Edited by Carlo Gargiolli. Bologna: Gaetano Romagnoli.

———. 2000. *Il primo libro delle opere toscane*. Edited by Enrico Maria Guidi. Urbino: Accademia Raffaello.

———. 2005. *I sette salmi penitenziali del santissimo profeta David con alcuni sonetti spirituali*. Edited by Enrico Maria Guidi. Urbino: Accademia Raffaello.

———. 2006. *Laura Battiferra and Her Circle*. Edited and translated by Victoria Kirkham. Chicago: University of Chicago Press.

Beaziano, Agostino. 1551. *Le rime volgari et latine*. Venice: Gabriele Giolito.

Bembo, Illuminata. 2001. *Specchio di illuminazione*. Edited by Silvia Mostaccio. Florence: Sismel/Edizioni del Galluzzo.

Bembo, Pietro. 1552. *Delle lettere di M. Pietro Bembo*. 4 vols. Venice: Gualtero Scotto.

———. 1960. *Prose e rime*. Edited by Carlo Dionisotti. Turin: UTET.

———. 1987–93. *Lettere*. 4 vols. Edited by Ernesto Travi. Bologna: Commissione per i Testi di Lingua.

————. 1996. *Prose della volgar lingua.* In Pozzi 1996, 1:51–284.

————. 2003. *Stanze.* Edited by Alessandro Gnocchi. Florence: Società Editrice Fiorentina.

Bembo, Pietro, and Maria Savorgnan. 1950. *Carteggio d'amore (1500–1501).* Edited by Carlo Dionisotti. Florence: Le Monnier.

Bendinelli, Scipione. 1588. *Ode . . . alla Madonna de' Miracoli di Lucca.* Translated by Massinissa Bendinelli. Lucca: Vincenzo Busdraghi.

Bendinelli Baldini, Silvia. 1587. *Corona in morte del serenissimo sig[nor] Ottavio Farnese, Duca di Piacenza [e] Parma.* Piacenza: Anteo Conti.

Bergalli, Luisa. 1726. *Componimenti poetici delle più illustri rimatrici d'ogni secolo.* 2 vols. Venice: Antonio Mora.

Betussi, Giuseppe. 1543. *Dialogo amoroso.* Venice: al segno del Pozzo [at the sign of the Well] (Andrea Arrivabene).

————. 1545. *Libro di messer Gio. Boccaccio delle donne illustri, tradotto per m[esser] Giuseppe Betussi, con una additione fatta dal medesimo delle donne famose dal tempo di m[esser] Giovanni fino a i giorni nostri e alcune altre state per inanzi.* Venice: Comin di Trino di Monferrato (at the expense of m[esser] Andrea Arrivabene).

————. 1556. *Le imagini del tempio della signora Giovanna d'Aragona.* Florence: Torrentino.

Bianca, Leonora. 1565. *Le risposte, dove . . . si pronostica e risponde a diverse e molte curiose dimande e richieste circa le cose future.* Venice: Francesco Rampazetto.

Bigolina, Giulia. 2002. *Urania.* Edited by Valeria Finucci. Rome: Bulzoni.

————. 2004. *Urania, the Story of a Young Woman's Love: The Novella of Giulia Camposampiero and Thesibaldo Vitaliani.* Edited and translated by Christopher Nissen. Tempe, AZ: Medieval and Renaissance Texts and Studies.

————. 2005. *Urania: A Romance.* Edited and translated by Valeria Finucci. Chicago: University of Chicago Press.

Biondo, Michelangelo. 1546. *Angoscia doglia e pena, le tre furie del mondo.* Venice: Comin da Trino.

Bissari, Pietro Paolo. 1648. *Le scorse olimpiche.* Venice: Francesco Valvasense.

Boccaccio, Giovanni. 1558. *Ameto comedia delle nimphe fiorentine.* Edited by Francesco Sansovino. Venice: Gabriele Giolito.

————. 1987. *Eclogues.* Translated by Janet Levarie Smarr. New York: Garland.

————. 2001. *Famous Women.* Edited and translated by Virginia Brown. Cambridge, MA: Harvard University Press.

Boccalini, Traiano. 1910–12. *Ragguagli di Parnaso e Pietra del paragone politico.* 2 vols. Edited by Giuseppe Rua. Bari: Laterza.

Bonardo, Giovanni Maria. 1598. *Madrigali.* Venice: Agostino Zoppini and nephews.

————. 1600. *La grandezza, larghezza, e distanza di tutte le sfere, ridotte à nostre miglia.* Venice: Giacomo Zoppini and brothers.

Bonini, Filippo Maria. 1667. *La donna combattuta dall'Empio, e difesa.* Venice: Giovanni Giacomo Hertz.

Borghesi, Diomede. 1566. *Delle rime . . . parti prima-sesta.* Padua: Lorenzo Pasquato.

————. 1571. *Il quinto volume delle rime.* Viterbo: Agostino Colaldo.

Bottrigari, Ercole, ed. 1551. *Libro quarto delle rime di diversi eccellentiss[imi] autori nella lingua volgare.* Bologna: Anselmo Giaccarello.

Bracciolini, Francesco. 1639. *Delle poesie liriche toscane.* Rome: Ludovico Grignani.

Bragadin Cavalli, Veneranda. 1613. *Rime diverse.* Padua: Gasparo Crivellari.

———. 1614. *Varie rime.* Verona: Bortolamio Merlo.

———. 1619. *Rime.* Verona: Angelo Tamo.

Bratteolo, Giacomo, ed. 1597. *Rime di diversi elevati ingegni de la città di Udine.* Udine: Giovanni Battista Natolini.

Bronzini, Cristoforo. 1622a. *Della dignità e nobiltà delle donne . . . settimana prima e giornata prima.* Florence: Zanobi Pignoni.

———. 1622b. *L'advocat des femmes, ou de leur fidelité et constance.* Translated by "S. D. L." Paris: Toussainct du Bray.

———. 1624. *Della dignità, e nobilità delle donne . . . settimana prima, e giornata prima.* Florence: Zanobi Pignoni.

———. 1625. *Della dignità, e nobilità delle donne . . . settimana prima e giornata quarta.* Florence: Zanobi Pignoni.

———. 1628. *Della dignità, e nobilità delle donne . . . settimana seconda, e giornata ottaua.* Florence: Simone Ciotti.

———. 1632. *Della virtù e valore delle donne illustri . . . settimana seconda, giornata settima.* Florence: Zanobi Pignoni.

Bruni, Domenico. 1552. *Difese delle donne.* Florence: heirs of Bernardo Giunti.

Bruni, Leonardo. 2002. *De studiis et litteris liber/The Study of Literature.* In *Humanist Educational Treatises.* Edited and translated by Craig W. Kallendorf, 92–125. Cambridge, MA: Harvard University Press.

Bulifon, Antonio, ed. 1695. *Rime di cinquanta illustri poetesse.* Naples: Antonio Bulifon.

Buoninsegni, Francesco, and Giovanni Battista Torretti. 1638. *Del lusso donnesco, satira menipea [sic] del signor Francesco Buoninsegni . . . con l'Antisatira apologetica di Gio. Battista Torretti.* Venetia: Presso Giacomo Sarzina.

Buoninsegni, Francesco, and Arcangela Tarabotti. 1998. *Satira e Antisatira.* Edited by Elissa Weaver. Rome: Salerno.

Bursati da Crema, Lucrezio. 1622. *La vittoria delle donne.* Venice: Evangelista Deuchino.

Calmeta, Vincenzo. 1959. *Prose e lettere edite e inedite (con due appendici di altri inediti).* Edited by Cecil Grayson. Bologna: Commissione per i Testi di Lingua.

———. 2004. *Triumphi.* Edited by Rossella Guberti. Bologna: Commissione per i Testi di Lingua.

Calzolai, Pietro. 1561. *Historia monastica . . . distinta in cinque giornate.* Florence: Lorenzo Torrentino.

Camerata, Girolamo. 1567. *Questione dove si tratta chi più meriti honore, ò la donna, ò l'huomo.* In *Trattato dell'honor vero, et del vero dishonore.* Bologna: Alessandro Benacci.

Campano, Giannantonio. 1969. *Opera omnia.* Farnborough, UK: Gregg International Publishers.

Campiglia, Maddalena. 1585. *Discorso sopra l'annonciatione della beata Vergine, et la incarnatione del s[ignor] n[ostro] Giesù Christo.* Vicenza: Perin Libraro.

———. 2004. *Flori: A Pastoral Drama.* Edited by Virginia Cox and Lisa Sampson. Chicago: University of Chicago Press.

Canoniero, Pietro Andrea. 1606. *Della eccellenza delle donne.* Florence: Francesco Tosi, alle Scale di Badia (at the request of Simon Grenier, and Iacopo Fabeni, Partners).

Capaccio, Giulio Cesare. 1634. *Il Forastiero.* Naples: Gio. Domenico Roncagliolo.

Capasso, Giosuè. 1990. *Le farse, il trionfo, il lamento.* Edited by Milena Montanile. Naples: Istituto Nazionale di Studi sul Rinascimento Meridionale.

Carafa, Diomede. 1988. *Memoriali.* Edited Franca Petrucci Nardelli. Annoted by Antonio Lupis. Rome: Bonacci.

Carli de' Piccolomini, Bartolomeo. 1543. *Edera.* Venice: Niccolò di Aristotile detto Zopino [sic].

Caro, Annibale. 1558. *Apologia de gli Academici di Banchi di Roma contra m[esser] Lodovico Castelvetro da Modena.* Parma: Seth Viotti.

Carrario, Pietro. 1555. *Tutte le orationi d'Isocrate.* Translated by Pietro Carrario. Venice: Michele Tramezino.

Cassola, Luigi. 1544. *Madrigali.* Venice: Giolito.

Castiglione, Baldassare. 1960. *Il libro del cortegiano.* In *Opere di Baldassare Castiglione, Giovanni della Casa, Benvenuto Cellini,* edited by Carlo Cordié, 5–361. Milan: Ricciardi.

Catanea Parasole, Isabetta. 1879. *Pretiosa gemma delle virtuose donne.* (Reproduction of the Venetian edition of 1600 published by Lucchino Gargano.) Venice: F. Ongania.

———. 1884. *Studio delle virtuose dame.* Rome: Antonio Facchetti, 1597. London: Bernard Quaritch.

———. 1891. *Musterbuch für Stickereien und Spitzen con Elisabetta Parasole, 1616.* (Reproduction of *Teatro delle nobili e virtuose donne* [1616].) Berlin: Ernst Wasmuth.

Cebà, Ansaldo. 1611. *Rime d'Ansaldo Cebà a Leonardo Spinola Francavilla.* Rome: Bartolomeo Zanetti.

———. 1615. *La reina Esther.* Genoa: Giuseppe Pavoni.

———. 1623a. *Lettere d'Ansaldo Cebà ad Agostino Pallavicino di Stefano.* Genoa: Giuseppe Pavoni.

———. 1623b. *Lettere d'Ansaldo Cebà scritte a Sarra [sic] Copia.* Genoa: Giuseppe Pavoni.

"Celia Romana." 1562. *Lettere amorose . . . scritte al suo amante.* Venice: Antonio de gli Antonii.

Cellini, Benvenuto. 2001. *Rime.* Edited by Vittorio Gatto. Rome: Archivio Guido Izzi.

Cereta, Laura. 1640. *Laurae Ceretae brixiensis feminae clarissimae epistolae.* Padua: Sebastiano Sardo.

———. 1997. *Collected Letters of a Renaissance Feminist.* Edited by Diana Robin. Chicago: University of Chicago Press.

Cerretani, Aldobrando. 1560. *L'Eneida in toscano.* Florence: Lorenzo Torrentino.

Cervoni, Isabella. 1592. *Canzone . . . sopra il battesimo del serenissimo gran principe di Toscana.* Florence: Michelangelo Sermartelli.

———. 1597. *Canzone . . . al christianissimo Enrico quarto, re di Francia, e di Navarra sopra la sua conversione.* Florence: Giorgio Marescotti.

Colonna, Mario, and Pietro Angeli. 1589. *Poesie toscane . . . con l'Edipo Tiranno Tragedia di Sofocle* (the latter translated by Angeli). Florence: Bartolomeo Sermartelli.

?Colonna, Stefano. 1552. *Sonetti, canzoni et triumphi di m[adonna] Laura in risposta di m[esser] Francesco Petrarca.* Venice: Comin di Trino.

Colonna, Vittoria. 1558. *Tutte le rime . . . con l'espositione del signor Rinaldo Corso, nuouamente mandate in luce da Girolamo Ruscelli.* Venice: Giovanni Battista and Melchiorre Sessa.

———. 1560. *Rime . . . con l'aggiunta delle rime spirituali, di nuovo ricorrette per m[esser] Lodovico Dolce.* Venice: Giolito.

———. 1580. *Quattordeci [sic] sonetti spirituali della illustrissima et eccellentissima divina Vittoria Colonna . . . messi in canto da Pietro Vinci siciliano.* Venice: heir of Girolamo Scotti.

———. 1586. *Rime spirituali.* Verona: Girolamo Discepoli.

———. 1892. *Carteggio.* 2nd ed. Edited by Ermanno Ferreo and Giuseppe Müller. Annotated supplement by Domenico Tordi. Turin: Loescher.

———. 1982. *Rime.* Edited by Alan Bullock. Bari: Laterza.

———. 1998. *Sonetti in morte di Francesco Ferrante d'Avalos marchese di Pescara: Edizione del ms. XIII G.43 della Biblioteca Nazionale di Napoli.* Edited by Tobia R. Toscano. Milan: Mondadori.

———. 2005. *Sonnets for Michelangelo: A Bilingual Edition.* Edited and translated by Abigail Brundin. Chicago: Chicago: University of Chicago Press.

Componimenti. 1629. *Componimenti poetici di vari autori nelle nozze delli eccellentissimi signori d[on] Taddeo Barberini e d[onna] Anna Colonna.* Rome: Stamperia Camerale.

Contile, Luca. 1543. *Dialogi spirituali divisi in banchetti.* Rome: Baldassare de' Cartolari.

Coppetta, Francesco. 1720. *Rime di Francesco Coppetta, ed altri poeti perugini.* Edited by Giacinto Vincioli. Perugia: heir of Gianni and Francesco Desideri.

Coreglia, Isabetta. 1628. *Rime spirituali, e morali.* Pistoia: Pier'Antonio Fortunati.

———. 1634. *La Dori, favola pastorale.* Naples: Gio[vanni] Domenico Montanaro.

———. 1650. *Erindo il fido, favola pastorale.* Pistoia: Fortunati.

Corner Piscopia, Elena. 1688. *Opera.* Parma: Ippolito Rosati.

Correggio, Niccolò da. 1969. *Opere.* Edited by Antonia Tissoni Benvenuti. Bari: Laterza.

Corso, Rinaldo. 1543. *Dichiaratione fatta sopra la seconda parte delle rime della divina Vittoria Collonna [sic].* Bologna: Giovanni Battista Faelli.

———. 1556. *Vita di Veronica Gambara.* In *Vita di Giberto terzo di Correggio detto il Difensore,* ff. E4r–F3r. Ancona: Astolfo Grandi.

———. 1566. *Le pastorali canzoni di Vergilio tradotte da Rinaldo Corso.* Ancona: Astolfo Grandi.

Cortese, Isabella. 1561. *I secreti.* Venice: Giovanni Bariletto.

Costa, Margherita. c. 1630. *Istoria del viaggio d'Alemagna del serenissimo gran duca di Toscana, Ferdinando Secondo.* Venice: n.p.

———. 1638a. *La chitarra . . . canzoniere amoroso.* Frankfurt: Daniel Wastch.

———. 1638b. *Il violino.* Frankfurt: Daniel Wastch.

———. 1639a. *Lo stipo.* Venice: n.p.

———. 1639b. *Lettere amorose.* Venice: n.p.

———. 1640a. *La Flora feconda, drama.* Florence: Amadore Massi and Lorenzo Landi.

———. 1640b. *Flora feconda, poema.* Florence: Amadore Massi and Lorenzo Landi.

———. 1640c. *La selva di cipressi, opera lugubre.* Florence: Amadore Massi and Lorenzo Landi.

———. 1641. *Li buffoni, commedia ridicola.* Florence: Amadore Massi and Lorenzo Landi.

———. 1644. *Cecilia martire, poema sacro.* Rome: Mascardi.

———. 1647a. *Festa reale per balletto a cavallo.* Paris: Sebastiano Cramoisy.

———. 1647b. *La tromba di Parnaso.* Paris: Sebastiano Cramoisy.

———. 1647c. *La selva di Diana.* Paris: Sebastiano Cramoisy.

———. 1654. *Gli amori della luna.* Venice: Giuliani.

———. n.d. (a). *Al serenissimo Ferdinando II, gran duca di Toscana per la festa di San Gio[vanni] Batista [sic].* Venice: n.p.

———. n.d. (b). *Alla serenissima Vittoria della Rovere, gran duchessa di Toscana per la festa di San Gio[vanni] Batista [sic].* Venice: n.p.

———. n.d. (c). *Alla serenissima Margherita de' Medici duchessa di Parma per l'arrivo in Fiorenza.* Venice: n.p.

Costo, Tommaso. 1989. *Il fuggilozio.* Edited by Corrado Calenda. Rome: Salerno.

Crescimbeni, Giovanni Maria. 1730–31. *Istoria della volgar poesia.* 6 vols. Venice: Lorenzo Basegio.

Cristiani, Francesco, ed. 1555. *Rime di diuersi ecc[ellentissimi] autori, in vita, e in morte dell'ill[ustrissima] s[ignora] Livia Colonna.* Rome: Antonio Barrè.

da Bisticci, Vespasiano. 1999. *Il libro delle lodi delle donne.* Edited by Giuseppe Lombardi. Manziana: Vechiarelli; Rome: Roma nel Rinascimento.

da Montefeltro, Battista. 1847. *Laude ed altre rime spirituali.* Edited by "F. Z. F" (Francesco Zambrini). Imola: Ignazio Galeati.

———. 1859. "Tre sonetti di Batista [sic] da Montefeltro e due di Malatesta Malatesti." Edited by Giuliano Vanzolini. In Francesco Saverio Zambrini, *Raccolta di tutti gli opuscoli d'antichi scrittori inscriti nel giornale L'Eccitamento.* Bologna: Tipografia delle Scienze.

dalla Torre, Giovanni. 1590. *Poesie di diversi eccellenti ingegni trevigiani al conte Antonio Collalto per la sua elezione a collateral generale della Serenissima Repubblica Venetiana.* Edited by Giovanni dalla Torre. Treviso: heirs of Angelo Mazzolini and Domenico Amici.

d'Aragona, Tullia. 1547. *Rime della signora Tullia di Aragona et di diversi a lei.* Venice: Gabriele Giolito.

?————. 1560. *Il Meschino, altramente detto il Guerrino.* Venice: Giovanni Battista and Melchiorre Sessa.

————. 1891. *Le rime.* Edited by Enrico Celani. Bologna: Romagnoli Dall'Acqua.

————. 1912. *Dialogo della infinità di amore.* In *Trattati d'amore del Cinquecento.* Edited by Giuseppe Zonta, 185–248. Bari: Laterza.

————. 1997. *Dialogue on the Infinity of Love.* Edited and translated by Rinaldina Russell and Bruce Merry. Chicago: University of Chicago Press.

————. 2005. *Sweet Fire: Tullia d'Aragona's Poetry of Dialogue and Selected Prose.* Edited and translated by Elizabeth A. Pallitto. New York: George Braziller.

della Casa, Giovanni. 1944. *Se s'abbia da prender moglie.* Edited and translated by Ugo Enrico Paoli. Florence: Le Monnier.

————. 2001. *Rime.* Edited by Giuliano Tanturli. Parma: Ugo Guanda.

della Chiesa, Francesco Agostino. 1620. *Theatro delle donne letterate con un breve discorso della preminenza e perfettione del sesso donnesco.* Mondovì: Giovanni Gislandi and Giovanni Tommaso Rossi.

de Luca, Giovanni Battista. 1675. *Il cavaliere e la dama, overo discorsi familiari nell'ozio tusculano autunnale dell'anno 1674.* Rome: Giacomo Dragondelli.

de Valdés, Juan. 1938. *Alfabeto cristiano: Dialogo con Giulia Gonzaga.* Edited by Benedetto Croce. Bari: Laterza.

di Piazza, Dafne. 1552. *Academia di enigmi in sonetti di madonna Daphne di Piazza a gli academici fiorentini suoi amanti.* Venice: Stefano de Alessi.

Doglioni, Giovanni Niccolò. 1988. "Vita della signora Modesta Pozzo de' Zorzi nominata Moderata Fonte." In Fonte 1988, 3–10.

————. 1997. "Life of Madonna Modesta Pozzo de' Zorzi, Known as Moderata Fonte." In Fonte 1997, 31–40.

Dolce, Lodovico. 1542. *Dialogo piaceuole . . . nel quale messer Pietro Aretino parla in difesa d'i male auenturati mariti.* Venice: Curtio Troiano di Nauò.

————. 1545. *Dialogo . . . della institution delle donne, secondo li tre stati.* Venice: Gabriele Giolito.

————. 1549. *La nobiltà delle donne.* Venice: Gabriele Giolito.

————, ed. 1556. *Stanze di diversi illustri poeti.* 2nd ed. Venice: Gabriele Giolito.

Domenichi, Lodovico. 1544. *Rime.* Venice: Gabriele Giolito.

————, ed. 1559. *Rime diverse d'alcune nobilissime et virtuosissime donne.* Lucca: Vincenzo Busdraghi.

————. 1564. *La donna di corte.* Lucca: Vincenzo Busdraghi.

————. 2004. *Rime.* Edited by Roberto Gigliucci. Turin: RES.

Doni, Anton Francesco. 1547. *Prose antiche di Dante, Petrarcha, et Boccaccio, et di molti alti nobili et virtuosi ingegni.* Florence: Anton Francesco Doni.

————. 1552. *Tre libri di lettere.* Venice: Francesco Marcolini.

Ducchi, Gregorio. 1589. *Rime diversi di molti illustri compositori per le nozze degli illustrissimi signori Gio[vanni] Paolo Lupi marchese di Sorgana e Beatrice Obici [sic].* Piacenza: Giovanni Bazachi.

Ebreo, Leone [Judah Abravanel]. 1535. *Dialogi d'amore*. Rome: Antonio Blado.

"Emilia N." 1594. *Lettere affettuose . . . scritte al cavaliere Bernardino N*. Siena: Ottavio Paiorani.

Equicola, Mario. 2004. *De mulieribus: Delle donne*. Edited by Giuseppe Lucchesini and Pina Tortaro. Pisa: Istituto Editoriali e Poligrafici Internazionali.

Erythraeus, Janus Nicius [Gianvittorio De' Rossi]. 1645. *Pinacotheca imaginum illustrium doctrinae vel ingenii laude virorum, qui, auctore superstite, diem suum obierunt*. 3 vols. Cologne: Jodocus Kalcovius and Partners.

Fedele, Cassandra. 1488. *Oratio pro Bertucio Lamberto*. Venice: Johannes Lucilius Santritter and Hieronymus de Sanctis.

———. 1489. *Oratio pro Bertuccio Lamberto*. Nuremberg: Peter Wagner.

———. 1636. *Clarissimae feminae Cassandrae Fidelis venetae epistolae et orationes*. Edited by Jacopo Filippo Tomasini. Padua: Francesco Bolzetta.

———. 2000. *Cassandra Fedele: Letters and Orations*. Edited and translated by Diana Robin. Chicago: University of Chicago Press.

Ferentilli, Agostino. 1571. *Primo volume della scielta di stanze di diversi autori toscani*. Venice: for the Giunti of Florence.

Ferrero, Giuseppe Guido, ed. 1954. *Marino e i Marinisti*. Milan: Riccardo Ricciardi.

Ferro, Livio. 1581. *Corone et altre rime in tutte le lingue principali del mondo in lode dell'illustre Luigi Ancarano di Spoleto . . . con una oratione dello ecc[ellen]te s[igno]r Antonio Riccobono*. Padua: Lorenzo Pasquati.

Fiamma, Carlo. 1611. *Il gareggiamento poetico*. 10 vols. Venice: Barezzo Barezzi.

Filetico, Martino. 1992. *Iocundissimae disputationes*. Edited and translated by Guido Arbizzoni. Modena: Panini.

Firenzuola, Angelo. 1993. *Opere*. Edited by Adriano Seroni. 3rd ed. Florence: Sansoni.

Fonte, Moderata. 1581. *Tredici canti del Floridoro*. Venice: heirs of Francesco Rampazetto.

———. 1582. *La passione di Christo descritta in ottava rima*. Venice: Domenico and Giovanni Battista Guerra.

———. 1585. *Canzon nella morte del ser[enissi]mo principe di Venetia Nicolò da Ponte*. Venetia: Sigismondo Bordogna.

———. 1592. *La resurretione di Giesù Christo nostro signore, che segue alla Santissima Passione descritta in ottava rima da Moderata Fonte*. Venice: Gio. Domenico Imberti.

———. 1600. *Il merito delle donne*. Venice: Domenico Imberti.

———. 1988. *Il merito delle donne*. Edited by Adriana Chemello. Venice: Eidos.

———. 1995. *Tredici canti del Floridoro*. Edited by Valeria Finucci. Modena: Mucchi.

———. 1997. *The Worth of Women*. Edited and translated by Virginia Cox. Chicago: University of Chicago Press.

———. 2006. *Floridoro: A Chivalric Romance*. Edited by Valeria Finucci and Julia Kisacky. Translated by Julia Kisacky. Chicago: University of Chicago Press.

Foresti, Iacopo Filippo. 1497. *De plurimis claris selectisque mulieribus*. Ferrara: Lorenzo de' Rossi.

Franciotti, Cesare. 1616. *Viaggio alla s[anta] casa di Loreto*. Venice: Giovanni Battista Combi.

Franco, Niccolò. 1536. *Tempio d'amore*. Venice: Francesco Marcolini.

———. 1542. *Dialogo dove si ragiona delle bellezze*. Venice: Antonio Gardane.

Franco, Veronica, ed. 1575. *Rime di diversi eccellentissimi auttori nella morte dell'illustre sign[or] Estore Martinengo conte di Malpaga*. Venice: n.p.

———. 1580. *Lettere familiari a diuersi*. Venice: n.p.

———. 1995. *Rime*. Edited by Stefano Bianchi. Milan: Mursia.

———. 1998a. *Selected Poems and Letters*. Edited by Ann Rosalind Jones and Margaret Rosenthal. Chicago: University of Chicago Press.

———. 1998b. *Lettere*. Edited by Stefano Bianchi. Rome: Salerno.

Franco, Veronica, and Gaspara Stampa. 1913. *Rime*. Edited by Abdelkader Salza. Bari: Laterza.

Fratta, Giovanni, ed. 1575. *Panegirico nel felice dottorato dell'illustre et eccellentissimo signor Giuseppe Spinelli*. Padua: Lorenzo Pasquati.

Galeota, Francesco. 1987. *Le lettere del "Colibeto": Edizione, spoglio linguistico e glossario*. Edited by Vittorio Formentin. Naples: Liguori.

Galilei, Galileo. 1900. *Le opere di Galileo Galilei*. Vol. 10. *Carteggio, 1574–1610*. Florence: G. Barbera.

———. 1901. *Le opere di Galileo Galilei*. Vol. 11. *Carteggio, 1611–13*. Florence: G. Barbera.

Gambara, Veronica. 1690. *Rime delle signore Lucrezia Marinella, Veronica Gambara, ed Isabella Della Morra*. Naples: Antonio Bulifon.

———. 1759. *Rime e lettere*. Edited by Felice Rizzardi. Brescia: Giammaria Rizzardi.

———. 1879. *Rime e lettere*. Edited by Pia Mestica Chiappetti. Florence: G. Barbèra.

———. 1995. *Le rime*. Edited by Alan Bullock. Florence: Olschki; Perth: University of Western Australia.

Garzoni, Tommaso. 1994. *Le vite delle donne illustri della Scrittura sacra: Con l'aggionta delle vite delle donne oscure e laide dell'uno e l'altro Testamento e un discorso in fine sopra la nobiltà delle donne*. Edited by Beatrice Collina. Ravenna: Longo.

Gelli, Giambattista. 1549. *Il Gello sopra un sonetto di m[esser] Francesco Petrarca*. Florence: Lorenzo Torrentino.

Giambelli, Cipriano. 1589. *Discorso intorno alla maggioranza dell'huomo e della donna*. Treviso: Angelo Mazzolini.

Gigli, Girolamo. 1854. *Diario sanese*. Siena: G. Landi and N. Alessandri.

Gilio, Giovanni Andrea. 1580. *Topica poetica*. Venice: Orazio de' Gobbi.

Giovio, Paolo. 1560. *Lettere volgari*. Venice: Giovan Battista and Melchiorre Sessa.

———. 1984. *Dialogus de viris et foeminis aetate nostra florentibus*. In *Dialogi et descriptiones*. Edited by Ernesto Travi and Mariagrazia Penco. Vol. 9 of *Opera*. Rome: Società Storica Comense and Istituto Poligrafico dello Stato.

Giraldi, Lilio Gregorio. 1999. *Due dialoghi sui poeti dei nostri tempi*. Edited by Claudio Pandolfi. Ferrara: Corbo.

Giustinian, Orsatto, and Celio Magno. 1600. *Rime di Celio Magno, et Orsatto Giustiniano*. Venice: Andrea Muschio.

Gonzaga, Curzio. 1591. *Rime*. Venice: heirs of Curzio Troiano Navò (al segno del Leone [at the sign of the Lion]).

?Gonzaga, Lucrezia. 1552. *Lettere . . . con gran diligentia raccolte, e à gloria del sesso feminile nuouamente in luce poste*. Venice: Gualtiero Scotto.

Goselini, Giuliano. 1588. *Rime.* Venice: Francesco Franceschi.

Grillo, Angelo. 1589. *Parte prima-seconda delle rime*. Bergamo: Comin Ventura.

Guaccimani, Giacomo, ed. 1623. *Raccolta di sonetti d'autori diversi, et eccellenti dell'età nostra*. Ravenna: Pietro de' Paoli and Giovanni Battista Giovannelli.

Guarini, Guarino [Guarino da Verona]. 1915–19. *Epistolario*. 3 vols. Edited by Remigio Sabbadini. Venice: Reale Deputazione Veneta di Storia Patria.

Guazzo, Stefano. 1575. *La civil conversatione*. Venice: Altobello Salicato.

———. 1590. *Dialoghi piacevoli*. Venice: Francesco Franceschi Sanese.

———. 1592. *Nuova scielta di rime*. Bergamo: Comin Ventura.

———. 1595. *La ghirlanda della contessa Angela Bianca Beccaria*. Genoa: heirs of Girolamo Bartoli.

Guidalotti del Bene, Dora. 2003. "*Le lettere (1381–1389).*" Edited by Guia Passerini. *Letteratura italiana antica* 4:101–59.

Guidoccio, Giacomo. 1588. *Vera difesa alla narratione delle operationi delle donne . . . insieme con alcune stanze . . . in lode delle gentilissime donne padovane*. Padua: Paolo Meietti.

Herculiana, Camilla. 1584. *Lettere di philosophia naturale*. Krakow: Jan Januszowski.

Hoby, Thomas. 1902. *The Travels and Life of Sir Thomas Hoby, Knight of Bisham Abbey, Written by Himself (1547–64)*. Edited by Edgar Powell. Camden Miscellany 10. London: Royal Historical Society.

Lanci, Cornelio. 1590. *Esempi della virtù delle donne*. Florence: Francesco Tosi.

Lando, Ortensio, ed. 1548. *Lettere di molte valorose donne, nelle quali chiaramente appare non esser né di eloquentia né di dottrina alli huomini inferiori*. Venice: Gabriele Giolito.

———. 1552a. *Sette libri de' cathaloghi*. Venice: Giolito.

———. 1552b. *Dialogo nel quale si ragiona della consolatione e utilità che si gusta leggendo la sacra Scrittura*. Venice: Comin di Trino.

———. 2000. *Paradossi, cioè sentenze fuori del comun parere*. Edited by Antonio Corsaro. Rome: Edizioni di Storia e Letteratura.

Lanfranco, Giovanni Maria. 1531. *Rimario nouo di tutte le concordanze del Petrarcha*. Brescia: Giacomo Filippo Cigoli.

*Lettere*. 1968. *Lettere scritte a Pietro Aretino*. 2 vols. in 4. Bologna: Commissione per i Testi di Lingua. (Orig. pub. 1873.)

*Lettere*. 1990. *Lettere da cortigiane del Rinascimento*. Edited by Angelo Romano. Rome: Salerno.

*Lieti amanti*. 1990. *I lieti amanti: Madrigali di venti musicisti ferraresi e non*. Edited by Marco Giuliani. Florence: Olschki.

Loredan, Giovanni Francesco. 1662. *La forza d'amore, opera scenica*. Venice: Guerigli.

Lorini del Monte, Niccolò. 1617. *Elogii delle più principali s[ante] donne del sagro calendario.* Florence: Zanobi Pignoni.

Luigini, Federico. 1554. *Il libro della bella donna.* Venice: Plinio Pietrasanta.

Lupis, Antonio. 1696. *La Faustina.* Venice: Stefano Curti.

Machiavelli, Niccolò. 1995. *Il principe.* Edited by Giorgio Inglese. Turin: Einaudi.

Malatesti, Malatesta. 1982. *Rime.* Edited by Domizia Trolli. Parma: Studium Parmense.

Malipiero, Girolamo. 1536. *Il Petrarca spirituale.* Venice: Francesco Marcolini.

Malvasia, Diodata. 1617. *La venuta e i progressi miracolosi della s[antissi]ma Madonna dipinta da S[an] Luca posta sul Monte della Guardia dall'anno che ci venne 1160 fin all'anno 1617.* Bologna: heirs of Giovanni Rossi.

Mandosio, Prospero. 1682–92. *Bibliotheca romana.* 2 vols. Rome: Franceso Ignazio Lazzeri.

Manfredi, Muzio. 1575. *Per donne romane.* Bologna: Alessandro Benacci.

———. 1580. *Cento donne cantate.* Parma: Erasmo Viotti.

———. 1587. *Cento madrigali.* Mantua: Francesco Osanna.

———. 1593. *La Semiramis, tragedia.* Bergamo: Comin Ventura.

———. 1598. *La Semiramis, tragedia . . . riveduta e corretta.* 2nd ed. Pavia: Girolamo Bartoli.

———. 1602a. *Il contrasto amoroso, pastorale.* Venice: Giovanni Antonio Somasco.

———. 1602b. *Cento sonetti . . . in lode delle donne di Ravenna.* Ravenna: heirs of Pietro Giovanelli.

———. 1604. *Cento artificiosi madrigali.* Venice: Roberto Meietti.

———. 1606a. *Lettere brevissime.* Venice: Roberto Meietti.

———. 1606b. *Madrigali . . . sopra molti soggetti stravaganti composti.* Venice: Roberto Meietti.

Manfredi, Muzio, and Antonio Decio. 2002. *Semiramis. Acripanda: Due regine del teatro rinascimentale.* Edited by Grazia Distaso. Taranto: Lisi.

Manganello. 1982. *Il Manganello: La reprensione del Cornazzano contra Manganello.* Edited by Diego Zancani. Exeter, UK: University of Exeter.

Marchetti, Silvestro. 1596. *Poesie toscane e latine da diversi autori composte nell'essequie dell'illustre signora Isabella Marescotti de' Ballati, gentildonna sanese.* Siena: Luca Bonetti.

Marescotti, Ercole [Hercole Filogenio]. 1589. *Dell'eccellenza delle donne.* Fermo: Sertorio de' Monti.

Marinella, Lucrezia. 1595. *La Colomba sacra, poema heroico.* Venice: Giovanni Battista Ciotti.

———. 1597. *Vita del serafico et glorioso S[an] Francesco.* Venice: Giovanni Maria Bertano.

———. 1600. *Le [sic] nobiltà et eccellenze delle donne, et i diffetti [sic], e mancamenti de gli huomini.* Venice: Giovanni Battista Ciotti.

———. 1601. *La nobiltà et l'eccellenza delle donne, co' diffetti [sic] et mancamenti de gli huomini.* 2nd ed. Venice: Giovanni Battista Ciotti.

―――. 1602. *La vita di Maria Vergine imperatrice dell'universo, descritta in prosa, et in ottava rima*. Venice: Barezzo Barezzi.

―――. 1603. *Rime sacre . . . fra le quali è un poemetto, in cui si racconta l'historia della Madonna dipinta da San Luca, che è su 'l Monte della Guardia nel territorio di Bologna*. Venice: ad istanza del Collosini [at the expense of Collosini].

―――. 1605a. *Arcadia felice*. Venice: Giovanni Battista Ciotti.

―――. 1605b. *Scielta d'alcune rime sacre della m[olto] illustre sig[nora] Lucretia Marinelli alla illust[re] sig[nora, la signora Cornelia Casale*. Bergamo: Comin Ventura.

―――. 1606. *Vita del serafico e glorioso S[an] Francesco, descritta in ottava rima*. In *Sette canzoni di sette famosi autori in lode del serafico . . . S[an] Francesco e del sacro Monte della Verna*. Edited by Fra Silvestro Poppi. Florence: Giovanni Antonio Caneo and Raffaello Grossi.

―――. 1617. *La vita di Maria Vergine imperatrice dell'universo, descritta in prosa, e in ottava rima, dalla molto illustre sig[nora] Lucretia Marinella, dalla stessa ampliata, et aggiuntevi le vite de' dodici heroi di Christo, e de' quattro evangelisti*. Venice: Barezzo Barezzi.

―――. 1618. *Amore innamorato, et impazzato*. Venice: Giovanni Battista Combi.

―――. 1621. *La nobiltà et l'eccellenza delle donne*. 3rd ed. Venice: Giovanni Battista Combi.

―――. 1624. *De' gesti heroici e della vita maravigliosa della serafica S[anta] Caterina da Siena . . . libri sei*. Venice: Barezzo Barezzi.

―――. 1635. *L'Enrico, overo Bisanzio acquistato*. Venice: Gerardo Imberti.

―――. 1643. *Le vittorie di Francesco il serafico, li passi gloriosi della diva Chiara . . . con ragionamenti, ammaestramenti, e sensi Aristotelici, Platonici, e theologici*. Padua: Giulio Crivellari.

―――. 1645. *Essortationi alle donne et a gli altri se saranno loro a grado . . . parte prima*. Venice: Francesco Valvasense.

―――. 1648. *Holocausto d'amore della vergine Santa Giustina*. Venice: Matteo Leni.

―――. 1998. *Arcadia felice*. Edited by Françoise Lavocat. Florence: Olschki.

―――. 1999. *The Nobility and Excellence of Women and the Defects and Vices of Men*. Edited and translated by Anne Dunhill. Introduction by Letizia Panizza. Chicago: University of Chicago Press.

Marino, Giovanni Battista. 1966. *Lettere*. Edited by Marziano Guglielminetti. Turin: Einaudi.

―――. 1975. *Adone*. 2 vols. Edited by Marzio Pieri. Bari: Laterza.

Marucini, Lorenzo. 1576. *Rime di diversi autori bassanesi*. Venice: Pietro de' Franceschi, e Nepoti.

Matraini, Chiara. 1555. *Rime e prose*. Lucca: Vincenzo Busdraghi.

―――. 1556. *Oratione d'Isocrate a Demonico . . . di latino in volgare, tradotta da madonna Chiara Matraini*. Translated by Chiara Matraini. Florence: Lorenzo Torrentino.

―――. 1581. *Meditationi spirituali*. Lucca: Vincenzo Busdraghi.

―――. 1586. *Considerationi sopra i sette salmi penitentiali del gran re e profeta Davit*. Lucca: Vincenzo Busdraghi.

————. 1590. *Breve discorso sopra la vita e laude della beatissima Vergine e madre del figiuol di Dio . . . con alcune annotationi nel fine del R[everendo] Giuseppe Mozzo-gruaro Napoletano . . . canonico regulare del Salvatore.* Lucca: Vincenzo Busdraghi.

————. 1595. *Lettere . . . con la prima, e seconda parte delle sue rime.* Lucca: Vincenzo Busdraghi.

————. 1597. *Lettere . . . con la prima e seconda parte delle sue rime, con una lettera in difesa delle lettere, e delle armi.* Venice: Nicolò Moretti.

————. 1602. *Dialoghi spirituali . . . con una notabile narratione alla grande Accademia de' Curiosi, e alcune sue rime, e sermoni.* Venetia: Fioravante Prati.

————. 1989. *Rime e lettere.* Edited by Giovanna Rabitti. Bologna: Commissione per i Testi di Lingua.

Mausoleo. 1589. *Mausoleo di poesie volgari et latine in morte del sig[nor] Giuliano Gosellini [sic].* Milan: Paolo Gottardo Pontio.

Miani Negri, Valeria. 1604. *Amorosa speranza, favola pastorale.* Venice: Francecso Bolzetta.

————. 1611. *Celinda, tragedia.* Vicenza: Francesco Bolzetta and Domenico Amadio.

Minutolo, Ceccarella. 1999. *Lettere.* Edited by Raffaelle Morabito. Naples: Edizioni Scientifiche Italiane.

Modio, Giovanni Battista. 1913. *Il convito, overo del peso della moglie.* In *Trattati del Cinquecento sulla donna.* Edited by Giuseppe Zonta, 309–70. Bari: Laterza.

Molino, Girolamo. 1573. *Rime.* Venice: n.p.

Molza, Tarquinia. 1750. *Opuscoli inediti . . . con alcune poesie . . . per l'addietro stampate.* Bergamo: Pietro Lancellotti.

Monte, Issicratea. 1577. *Oratione . . . nella congratulatione del sereniss[imo] principe Sebastiano Veniero.* Venice: Domenico and Giovanni Battista Guerra.

————. 1578a. *Seconda oratione . . . nella congratulatione dell'invitiss[imo] et sereniss[imo] principe di Venetia Sebastiano Veniero, da lei propria recitata nell'illustriss[imo] et eccellentiss[imo] Collegio a sua serenità.* Venice: Domenico and Giovanni Battista Guerra.

————. ?1578b. *Oratione . . . nella congratulatione del serenissimo principe di Venetia, Niccolò da Ponte.* ?Venice: n.p.

————. 1581. *Oratione . . . alla sacra maestà di Maria d'Austria, reina di Boemia, di Ungaria, de' Romani, et grandissima imperatrice, nella venuta di s[ua] maestà a Padova.* Padua: Paolo Meietti.

Morata, Olimpia Fulvia. 2003. *The Complete Writings of an Italian Heretic.* Edited and translated by Holt Parker. Chicago: University of Chicago Press.

Morato, Fulvio Pellegrino. 1532. *Rimario de tutte le cadentie di Dante e Petrarca.* Venice: Antonio Ligname.

Morra, Isabella. 1998. *Canzoniere: A Bilingual Edition.* Edited and translated by Irene Musillo Mitchell. West Lafayette, IN: Bordighera.

————. 2000. *Rime.* Edited by Maria Antonietta Grignani. Rome: Salerno.

Naldi, Bianca. 1614. *Risposta della signora Bianca Naldi da Palermo a una lettera di*

*Giacomo Violati libraro in Venetia, scritta per occasione di ringratiamento, per haverle mandato* I donneschi diffetti [sic] *di Giuseppe Passi Acacdemico Informe di Ravenna nominato l'ardito. All'illustrissima Laura Obizza Pepoli dedicata.* Vicenza: for Giacomo Violati in Venice.

Nogarola, Isotta. 1563. *Dialogus, quo, vtrum Adam vel Eua magis peccauerit quaestio satis nota, sed non adeo explicata, continetur.* Venice: Paolo Manuzio.

———. 1886. *Opera quae supersunt omnia: Accedunt Angelae et Zenevrae Nogarolae epistolae et carmina.* 2 vols. Edited by Eugenius Abel. Vienna: Gerold and Budapest: Kilian.

———. 2004. *Complete Writings: Letterbook, Dialogue on Adam and Eve, Orations.* Edited and translated by Margaret L. King and Diana Robin. Chicago: University of Chicago Press.

Ochino, Bernardino. 1985. *I dialogi sette e altri scritti del tempo della fuga.* Edited by Ugo Rozzo. Torino: Claudiana.

Orsini, Fulvio. 1568. *Carmina nouem illustrium feminarum.* Antwerp: Christophe Plantin.

Paleario, Aonio. 1983. *Dell'economia o vero del governo della casa.* Edited by Salvatore Caponetto. Florence: Olschki.

Pallavicino, Ferrante. 1654. *Le due Agrippine.* Venice: Turrini.

———. 1984. *Il corriero svaligiato, con la lettera dalla prigionia, aggiuntavi la* Semplicità ingannata *di Suor Arcangela Tarabotti.* Edited by Armando Marchi. Parma: Università di Parma.

——— 1992. *La retorica delle puttane.* Edited by Laura Coci. Parma: Fondazione Pietro Bembo and Ugo Guanda.

Paluzzi, Numidio. 1626. *Rime.* Venice: Ciotti.

Passi, Giuseppe. 1599. *I donneschi difetti.* Venice: Giovanni Antonio Somasco.

———. 1602. *Dello stato maritale.* Venice: Giovanni Antonio Somasco.

———. 1603. *La monstruosa fucina delle sordidezze de gl'huomini.* Venice: Giacomo Antonio Somasco.

Patrizi, Francesco. 1963. *L'amorosa filosofia.* Edited by John Charles Nelson. Florence: Le Monnier.

Petrarca, Francesco. 1548. *Sonetti, canzoni, et triomphi di m[esser] Francesco Petrarca.* Edited by Antonio Brucioli. Venice: Antonio Brucioli and brothers.

———. 1942. *Le familiari, libri XX–XXV e indici.* Edited by Umberto Bosco. Vol. 13 of *Edizione nazionale delle opere di Francesco Petrarca.* Edited by Vittorio Rossi and Nicola Festa. Florence: Sansoni, 1926–.

———. 1996. *Canzoniere.* Edited by Marco Santagata. Milan: Mondadori.

———. 2004. *Invectives.* Edited by David Marsh. Cambridge, MA: Harvard University Press.

Piccolomini, Alessandro. 1540. *La economica di Xenofonte.* Venice: al segno del Pozzo [at the sign of the Well] (Andrea Arrivabene).

———. 1541. *Lettura del s[ignor] Alessandro Piccolomini fatta nell'Accademia degli Infiammati.* Bologna: Bartholomeo Bonardo and Marc'Antonio da Carpi.

———. 1549. *Cento sonetti.* Rome: Vincenzo Valgrisi.

Piccolomini, Enea Silvio. 2002. *De liberorum educatione.* In *Humanist Educational Treatises.* Edited and translated by Craig W. Kallendorf, 125–259. Cambridge, MA: Harvard University Press.

Pieri, Laura. 1554. *Quattro canti de la guerra di Siena.* Florence: Bartolomeo Sermartelli.

?———. 1555. *Il felicissimo accordo della magnifica città di Siena con l'illustriss[imo] s[ignor] duca di Fiorenza . . . in ottava rima.* Florence: Lorenzo Torrentino.

Pocaterra, Annibale. 1607. *Due dialoghi della vergogna, con alcune prose e rime.* Reggio: Flavio and Flaminio Bartoli.

Poggi, Semidea. 1623. *La Calliope religiosa.* Vicenza: Francesco Grossi.

*Polinnia.* 1609. *Polinnia per l'illustrissimo [sic] signor Tomaso Contarini, caualiere . . . e podestà di Padoua.* Padua: Francesco Bolzetta.

Poliziano, Angelo. 1971. *Commento inedito all'epistola ovidiana di Saffo a Faone.* Edited by Elisabetta Lazzeri. Florence: Sansoni.

———. 2006. *Letters.* Edited and translated by Shane Butler. Cambridge, MA: Harvard University Press.

Pona, Francesco. 1628. *La Messalina.* In *La lucerna di Eureta Misoscolo Academico Filarmonico . . . con La Messalina et altre composizione [sic] del medesimo.* Venice: n.p. [*La Messalina* has a separate title page, dated 1627.]

———. 1633. *La galeria delle donne celebri.* Bologna: Bartolomeo Cavalieri.

———. 1973. *La lucerna.* Edited by Giorgio Fulco. Rome: Salerno.

Porcacchi, Tomaso. 1585. *Historia dell'origine et successione dell'illustrissima famiglia Malaspina, descritta da Thomaso Porcacchi da Castiglione Arretino [sic], et mandata in luce da Aurora Bianca d'Este sua consorte.* Verona: Girolamo Discepolo.

Pulci, Antonia. 1996. *Florentine Drama for Convent and Festival: Seven Sacred Plays.* Edited by James Wyatt Cook and Barbara Collier Cook. Annotated and translated by James Wyatt Cook. Chicago: University of Chicago Press.

Razzi, Silvano. 1568. *Della economica christiana e civile.* Florence: Bartolomeo Sermartelli.

———. 1595–1606. *Delle vite delle donne illustri per santità.* Florence: heirs of Iacopo Giunti.

Ribera, Pietro Paolo. 1609. *Le glorie immortali de' trionfi et heroiche imprese d'ottocento quarantcinque donne illustri antiche e moderne.* Venice: Evangelista Deuchino.

*Rime.* 1545. *Rime diuerse di molti eccellentiss[imi] auttori [sic] nuouamente raccolte: Libro primo.* Edited by Lodovico Domenichi. Venice: Gabriele Giolito.

*Rime.* 1546. *Rime diuerse di molti eccellentiss[imi] auttori nuouamente raccolte: Libro primo, con nuoua additione ristampato.* Edited by Lodovico Domenichi. Venice: Gabriele Giolito.

*Rime.* 1553. *Il sesto libro delle rime di diuersi eccellenti autori.* Edited by Girolamo Ruscelli. Venice: at the sign of the Well [al segno del Pozzo] (Andrea Arrivabene and Giovanni Maria Bonelli).

*Rime.* 1556a. *Rime di diuersi signori napolitani, e d'altri, nuouamente raccolte et impresse. Libro settimo.* Edited by Lodovico Dolce. Venice: Gabriele Giolito.

*Rime.* 1556b. *De le rime di diversi eccellentissimi autori, nuouamente raccolte. Libro primo.* Lucca: n.p.

Rime. 1561. *Rime di diversi nobilissimi et eccellentissimi autori in morte della signora Irene delle signore [sic] di Spilimbergo.* Edited by Dionigi Atanagi. Venice: Domenico and Giovanni Battista Guerra.

Rime. 1564. *Rime di diversi eccel[lenti] autori in morte della illustrissima sig[nora] d[onna] Hippolita Gonzaga.* Naples: Giovanni Maria Scotto.

Rime. 1565a. *Rime di diversi nobilissimi et eccellentissimi auttori [sic] in lode dell'illustrissima signora . . . donna Lucretia Gonzaga.* Bologna: Giovanni Rossi.

Rime. 1565b [misdated 1545 on title page]. *Rime de gli Academici Affidati di Pavia.* Pavia: Girolamo Bartoli.

Rime. 1567a. *Rime degli Academici Eterei.* Venice: Comin di Trino.

Rime. 1567b. *Rime di diversi illustri autori in lode della s[ignora] Cintia Tiene Bracciadura.* Edited by Diomede Borghesi. Padua: Lorenzo Pasquati.

Rime. 1568. *Rime degli Accademici Occulti con le loro imprese e discorsi.* Brescia: Vincenzo di Sabbio.

Rime. 1585. *Rime et versi in lode della ill[ustrissi]ma et ecc[ellentissi]ma s[igno]ra d[on]na Giovanna Castriota . . . duchessa di Nocera.* Vico Equense: Giuseppe Cacchi.

Rime. 1587. *Rime di diversi celebri poeti dell'età nostra.* Bergamo: Comino Ventura.

Rime. 1713. *Rime scelte de' poeti ferraresi antichi, e moderni.* Ferrara: heirs of Bernardino Pomatelli.

Rime. 1716–22. *Rime degli Arcadi.* 9 vols. Edited by Giovanni Mario Crescimbeni. Rome: Antonio de' Rossi.

Rime. 1994. *Rime per Laura Brenzone Schioppo (dal Codice Marciano it. Cl. IX 163).* Edited by Massimo Castoldi. Bologna: Commissione per i Testi di Lingua.

Rime. 1995. *Rime de gli Academici Eterei.* Edited by Ginetta Auzzas and Manlio Pastore Stocchi. Introduction by Antonio Daniele. Padua: CEDAM.

Rime. 2001. *Rime diverse di molti eccellentissimi autori (1546).* Edited by Franco Tomasi and Paolo Zaja. Turin: RES.

Rocco, Antonio. 1988. *L'Alcibiade fanciullo a scola.* Edited by Laura Coci. Rome: Salerno.

Romei, Annibale. 1586. *Discorsi.* 2nd ed. Ferrara: Vittorio Baldini.

Rossi, Michelangelo. 1637. *Erminia sul Giordano, dramma musicale.* Rome: Paolo Masotti.

Ruscelli, Girolamo. 1552. *Lettura . . . sopra un sonetto dell'illustriss[imo] signor marchese della Terza alla divina signora marchesa del Vasto.* Venice: Giovanni Griffio.

———, ed. 1553. *Rime di diversi eccellenti autori bresciani.* Venice: Plinio Pietrasanta.

———, ed. 1555. *Del tempio alla divina signora donna Giovanna d'Aragona.* Venice: Plinio Pietrasanta.

Sabadino degli Arienti. 1888. *Gynevera, de le clare donne.* Edited by Corrado Ricchi and A. Bacchi della Lega. Bologna: Romagnoli-Dell'Acqua.

———. 2001. *The Letters of Giovanni Sabadino degli Arienti (1481–1510).* Edited by Carolyn James. Florence: Olschki; Perth: University of Western Australia.

Salvetti Accaiuoli, Maddalena. 1590. *Rime toscane.* Florence: Francesco Tosi.

————. 1611. *Il David perseguitato o vero fuggitivo, poema eroico.* Florence: Giovanni Antonio Caneo.

Salvi, Beatrice, and Virginia Salvi. 1571. *Due sonetti di due gentildonne senesi madre e figliuola a m[esser] Celio Magno.* Venice: Domenico and Giovanni Battista Guerra.

Sansovino, Francesco. 1545. *Ragionamento . . . nel quale s'insegna a' giovani uomini la bella arte d'amore.* Venice: Giovanni Farri. Also in Zonta 1912, 151–84.

Sarrocchi, Margherita. 1606. *La Scanderbeide, poema heroico.* Rome: Lepido Facii.

————. 1623. *La Scanderbeide, poema heroico.* Rome: Andrea Fei.

————. 2006. *Scanderbeide: The Heroic Deeds of George Scanderbeg, King of Epirus.* Edited and translated by Rinaldina Russell. Chicago: University of Chicago Press.

Sasso, Giacomo. 1601. *Lettura . . . sopra il sonetto di Bernardo Tasso, "Poi che la parte men perfetta, e bella" . . . con una canzone, e sua sposizione.* Venice: Giacomo Antonio Somasco.

Sbarra Coderta, Lucchesia. 1610. *Rime.* Conegliano: Marco Claseri.

Scaramelli, Baldassare. 1585. *Dui canti del poema heroico di Scanderbec [sic].* Carmagnola: Marc'Antonio Belloni.

Scardeone, Bernardino. 1560. *De antiquitate urbis pataviii, et claris civibus Patavinis, libri tres.* Basle: Nikolaus Episcopius Jr.

*Scelta.* 1591. *Scelta di rime di diuersi moderni autori.* Pavia: heirs of Girolamo Bartoli.

*Scielta.* 1662. *Scielta di lettere amorose . . . con una raccolta di rime amorose, et alquante lettere de Cupido, con la sua risposta.* Venice: Giovanni Battista Cestari.

Segni, Giulio, ed. 1583. *Scelta di varii poemi volgari et latini composti nella partenza dell'eccellentissi[mo] sig[nor] Giovanni] Angelo Papio dalla città di Bologna.* Bologna: Giovanni Rossi.

————, ed. 1600. *Tempio all'illustrissimo et reverendissimo signor Cinthio Aldobrandini, Cardinale S[an] Giorgio, nipote del sommo pontefice Clemente ottavo.* Bologna: heirs of Giovanni Rossi.

————, ed. 1601. *Componimenti poetici volgari, latini, e greci di diversi, sopra la s[anta] imagine della beata Vergine dipinta da San Luca, la quale si serba nel Monte della Guardia presso Bologna, con la sua historia in dette tre lingue scritta da Ascanio Persii.* Bologna: Vittorio Benacci.

Seneca, Lucius Annaeus. 1554. *De' benefizii, tradotto in volgar fiorentino da messer Benedetto Varchi.* Florence: Torrentino.

Serdonati, Francesco. 1596. *Libro di m[esser] Giovanni Boccaccio delle donne illustri, tradotto di latino in volgare per m[esser] Giuseppe Betussi, con una giunta fatta dal medesimo d'altre donne famose, e un'altra giunta fatta per m[esser] Francesco Serdonati, d'altre donne illustri antiche e moderne.* Florence: Filippo Giunti.

Sernigi, Raffaela de.' ?c. 1550. *La rappresentazione di Moisè, quando i Dio [sic] gli dette le leggi in sul Monte Synai, nuovamente ristampata.* Florence: at the expense of Giovanni di Pietro Trevisano.

Sforza, Caterina. 1894. *Experimenti della ex[cellentissi]ma s[igno]ra Caterina Sforza.* Edited by Pier Desiderio Pasolini. Imola: Galeati.

?Sforza, Isabella. 1544. *Della vera tranquillità dell'anima.* Venice: heirs of Aldo Ma-nuzio.

Sori, Isabella. 1628. *Ammaestramenti e ricordi circa a' buoni costumi, che deve insegnare una ben creata madre ad una figlia, divisa in dodeci [sic] lettere, con una particolare aggionta di dodeci difese, fatte contro alcuni sinistri giudicii, fatti sopra de gli medemi [sic] ammaestramenti, e del sesso donnesco: E nel fine un panegirico delle cose più degne dell'illustrissima città d'Alessandria, et di molti pellegrini ingegni usciti da essa.* Pavia: Giovanni Maria Magro.

Speroni, Sperone. 1996a. *Dialogo delle lingue.* In Pozzi 1996, 585–635.

———. 1996b. *Dialogo d'amore.* In Pozzi 1996, 511–63.

———. 1996c. *Dialogo della dignità delle donne.* In Pozzi 1996, 565–84.

Spolverini, Ersilia. 1596. *Ad illustrissimam Claram Corneliam poemata duo.* Verona: Girolamo Discepoli.

Stampa, Gaspara. 1554. *Rime.* Venice: Plinio Pietrasanta.

———. 1976. *Rime.* Introduction by Maria Bellonci. Notes by Rodolfo Ceriello. Mi-lano: Rizzoli.

Stigliani, Tommaso. 1625. *Il canzoniero.* Rome: at the expense of di Giovanni Ma-nelfi; Venice: Evangelista Deuchino.

Strozzi, Alessandra Macinghi. 1997. *Selected Letters.* Edited and translated by Heather Gregory. Berkeley: University of California Press.

Strozzi, Lorenza. 1588. *In singula totius anni solemnia hymni.* Florence: Filippo Giunta.

Tansillo, Luigi. 1606. *Le lagrime di San Pietro . . . poema sacro, et heroico . . . con gli ar-gomenti, ed allegorie di Lucrezia Marinella, et con un discorso nel fine del sig[nor] Tommaso Costo.* Venice: Barezzo Barezzi.

Tarabotti, Arcangela. 1643. See Tarabotti 1663.

———. 1650. *Lettere familiari e di complimento . . . le lagrime . . . per la morte dell'il-lustriss[ima] signora Regina Donati.* Venice: Guerigli.

———. 1654. *La semplicità ingannata.* Leiden: Sambix.

———. 1663 [= 1643]. *Paradiso monacale libri tre, con un soliloquio a Dio.* Venice: Guglielmo Oddoni.

———. 1990. *Inferno monacale.* Edited by Francesca Medioli, 27–107. Turin: Rosen-berg and Sellier.

———. 1994. *Che le donne siano della spetie degli huomini / Women Are No Less Ratio-nal Than Men.* Edited by Letizia Panizza. London: Institute of Romance Stud-ies.

———. 2004. *Paternal Tyranny.* Edited and translated by Letizia Panizza. Chicago: University of Chicago Press.

———. 2005. *Lettere familiari e di complimento.* Edited by Meredith Ray and Lynn Westwater. Introduction by Gabrielle Zarri. Turin: Rosenberg and Sellier.

Tasso, Bernardo. 1560a. *Amadigi.* Venice: Giolito.

———. 1560b. *Rime.* Venice: Giolito.

Tasso, Ercole, and Torquato Tasso. 1595. *Dello ammogliarsi piacevole contesa fra i due moderni Tassi.* 3rd ed. Bergamo: Comin Ventura.

Tasso, Faustino. 1573. *Il secondo libro delle rime toscane.* Turin: Francesco Dolce.

Tasso, Torquato. 1852–55. *Le lettere.* 5 vols. Edited by Cesare Guasti. Florence: Le Monnier.

———. 1582. *Della virtù feminile, e donnesca.* Venice: Bernardo Giunti and brothers.

———. 1997. *Discorso della virtù feminile [sic] e donnesca.* Edited by Maria Luisa Doglio. Palermo: Sellerio.

———. 2001. *Lagrime.* Edited by Maria Pia Mussini Sacchi. Novara: Interlinea.

Tebaldeo, Antonio. 1989. *Rime.* 3 vols. Edited by Tania Basile and Jean-Jacques Marchand. Modena: Panini.

*Tempio.* 1568. *Il tempio della divina signora donna Geronima Colonna d'Aragona.* Padova: Lorenzo Pasquati.

Terminio, Antonio, ed. 1572. *La seconda parte delle stanze di diversi autori.* Venice: Gabriele Giolito.

Terracina, Laura. 1548. *Rime.* Venice: Gabriele Giolito.

———. 1549. *Rime seconde della signora Laura Terracina di Napoli, e di diversi a lei.* Florence: Lorenzo Torrentino.

———. 1550a. *Discorso sopra tutti li primi canti d'Orlando furioso.* Venice: Gabriele Giolito.

———. 1550b. *Quarte rime.* Venice: Giovanni Andrea Valvassori.

———. 1551. *Discorso sopra il principio di tutti i canti d'Orlando furioso.* 2nd ed. Venice: Gabriele Giolito.

———. 1552. *Quinte rime.* Venice: Giovanni Andrea Valvassori.

———. 1558. *Seste rime.* Lucca: Vincenzo Busdraghi.

———. 1560. *Seste rime.* 2nd ed. Naples: Raimondo Amato.

Tigliamochi degli Albizzi, Barbara. 1640. *Ascanio errante.* Florence: Landini.

Tiraboschi, Girolamo. 1781–86. *Biblioteca Modenese.* 6 vols. Modena: Società Tipografica.

Tomasini, Giacomo Filippo. 1644. *Elogia virorum literis et sapientia illustrium.* Padua: Sebastiano Sardi.

———. 2004. *Petrarcha redivivus.* Edited by Massimo Ciavolella and Roberto Fedi. Translated by Edoardo Bianchini and Tommaso Braccini. Pistoia: Libreria dell'Orso.

Tornabuoni, Lucrezia. 1978. *I poemetti sacri di Lucrezia Tornabuoni.* Edited by Fulvio Pezzarossa. Florence: Olschki.

———. 1993. *Lettere.* Edited by Patricia Salvadori. Florence: Olschki.

———. 2001. *Sacred Narratives.* Edited and translated by Jane Tylus. Chicago: University of Chicago Press.

Turina Bufalini, Francesca. 1595. *Rime spirituali sopra i misterii del santissimo rosario.* Rome: Domenico Gigliotti.

———. 1628. *Rime.* Città di Castello: Santi Molinelli.

———. 2005. *Rime spirituali sopra i misteri del santissimo rosario.* Edited by Paolo Bà. *Letteratura italiana antica* 6:147–223.

Ugoni, Stefano Maria. 1562. *Ragionamento . . . nel quale si ragiona di tutti gli stati dell'humana vita.* Venice: Pietro da Fine.

Valenziano, Luca. 1984. *Opere volgari*. Edited by Maria Pia Mussini Sacchi. Introduction by Ugo Rozzo. Tortona: Centro Studi Matteo Bandello e la Cultura Rinascimentale.

Valerini, Adriano. 1570. *Oratione . . . in morte della diuina signora Vincenza Armani, comica eccellentissima . . . con alquante leggiadre e belle compositioni di detta signora Vincenza*. Verona: Sebastiano and Giovanni dalle Donne.

Varano, Camilla Battista (Blessed). 1958. *Le opere spirituali*. Jesi: Scuola Tipografica Francescana.

Varchi, Benedetto. 1545. *Lettura . . . sopra un sonetto della gelosia di mons[ignor] della Casa*. Edited by Francesco Sansovino. Mantua: Venturino Ruffinelli.

———. 1549. *Due lezzioni*. Florence: Torrentino.

———. 1555. *De' sonetti . . . parte prima*. Florence: Lorenzo Torrentino.

———. 1557. *De' sonetti . . . colle risposte, e proposte di diversi, parte seconda*. Florence: Lorenzo Torrentino.

———. 1561. *La seconda parte delle lezzioni di M. Benedetto Varchi nella quale si contengono cinque lezzioni d'Amore*. Florence: Giunti.

———. 1565. *I sonetti . . . novellamente messi in luce*. Venice: Plinio Pietrasanta.

*Varie compositioni*. 1596. *Varie compositioni scritte in lode de l'illustrissimo sig[nor] Giouanni Cornaro, capitanio di Verona; e de l'illustrissima sig[nora] Chiara Delfina sua consorte*. Verona: Girolamo Discepoli.

Vasolo, Scipione. 1573. *La gloriosa eccellenza delle donne e d'amore*. Florence: Giorgio Marescotti.

Vida, Marco Girolamo. 1550. *Cremonensium orationes III adversus papienses in controversia principatus*. Cremona: n.p.

Vigri, Caterina (St.). 2000a. *Laudi, trattati, e lettere*. Edited by Silvia Serventi. Florence: Sismel-Edizioni del Galluzzo.

———. 2000b. *Sette armi spirituali*. Edited by Antonella degli Innocenti. Florence: Sismel-Edizioni del Galluzzo.

Visconti, Gasparo. 1979. *I canzonieri per Beatrice d'Este e per Bianca Maria Sforza*. Edited by Paolo Bongrani. Milan: Fondazione Arnoldo e Alberto Mondadori.

*"Women Are Not Human": An Anonymous Treatise and Responses*. 1998. Edited and translated by Theresa Kenney. New York: Crossroad.

Zabata, Cristoforo, ed. 1573. *Nuova scelta di rime di diversi begli ingegni*. Genova: Cristoforo Bellone.

Zucconello, Ippolito, ed. 1583. *Del giardino de' poeti in lode del serenissimo re di Polonia . . . Libro secondo*. Venice: Fratelli Guerra. In *Viridiarium poetarum . . .* Venice: at the sign of the Hippogryph [ad signum Hyppogriphi] (Domenico and Giovanni Battista Guerra and heirs of Luigi Valvassori).

## Secondary Sources

Abulafia, David. 1995. *The French Descent into Renaissance Italy, 1494–95: Antecedents and Effects*. Aldershot, UK: Variorum.

Adelman, Howard. 1999. "The Literacy of Jewish Women in early Modern Italy." In Whitehead, ed. 1999, 133–58.

Adler, Sara Maria. 1988. "Veronica Franco's Petrarchan *Terze Rime*: Subverting the Master's Plan." *Italica* 65 (3): 213–33.

———. 1989. "The Petrarchan Lament of Isabella di Morra." In *Donna: Women in Italian Culture*. Edited by Ada Testaferri, 201–21. Toronto: Dovehouse.

——— 2000. "Strong Mothers, Strong Daughters: The Representation of Female Identity in Vittoria Colonna's *Rime* and *Carteggio*." *Italica* 77 (3): 311–30.

Affò, Ireneo. 1969–73. *Memorie degli scrittori e letterati parmigiani*. 7 vols. Bologna: Forni. (Orig. pub. 1883.)

Afribo, Andrea. 2001. *Teoria e prassi della "gravitas" nel Cinquecento*. Introduction by Pier Vincenzo Mengaldo. Florence: Franco Cesati.

Ago, Renata. 1992. "Giochi di squadra: Uomini e donne nelle famiglie nobili del 17° secolo." In Visceglia, ed. 1992, 256–64.

Agoston, Laura Camille. 2005. "Male / Female, Italy / Flanders, Michelangelo / Vittoria Colonna." *Renaissance Quarterly* 58 (4): 1175–1219.

Ahern, John. 1992. "The New Life of the Book: The Implied Reader of the *Vita nuova*." *Dante Studies* 110:1–16.

Ajmar, Marta. 2000. "Exemplary Women in Renaissance Italy: Ambivalent Models of Behaviour." In Panizza, ed. 2000, 243–64.

Albonico, Simone. 1989. "Ippolita Clara." In Bozzetti, Gibellini, and Sandal, eds. 1989, 323–83.

———. 2006. *Ordine e numero: studi sul libro di poesia e le raccolte poetiche nel Cinquecento*. Alessandria: Edizioni dell'Orso.

Alessandrini, Ada. 1966. "Benci, Ginevra de'." In *DBI* 1960–, 8:193–94.

Alessio, Gian Carlo. 1997. "Fra Bernardino Renda e Ippolita Sforza." In *Filologia umanistica per Gianvito Resta*. 3 vols. Edited by Vincenzo Fera and Giacomo Ferraú, 1:61–94. Padua: Antenore.

Allaire, Gloria. 1995. "Tullia d'Aragona's *Il Meschino* as Key to a Reappraisal of Her Work." *Quaderni d'Italianistica* 16 (1): 33–50.

Allen, Sister Prudence, R.S.M. 2002. *The Concept of Woman*. Vol. 2. *The Early Humanist Revolution, 1250–1500*. Grand Rapids, MI: W. B. Eerdmans.

Allen, Prudence, and Filippo Salvatore. 1992. "Lucrezia Marinella and Woman's Identity in the Late Italian Renaissance." *Renaissance and Reformation* 28 (4): 5–39.

Ambrosini, Federica. 2005. *L'eresia di Isabella: Vita di Isabella da Passano signora della Frattina (1542–1601)*. Milan: Franco Angeli.

Andretta, Stefano. 1994. *La venerabile superbia: Ortodossia e trasgressione nella vita di Suor Francesca Farnese (1593–1651)*. Turin: Rosenberg and Sellier.

Andrews, Richard. 2000. "Isabella Andreini and Others: Women on Stage in the Late Cinquecento." In Panizza, ed. 2000, 316–33.

Angiolini, Enrico. 2002. "Le vicende familiari, politiche e militari di Malatesta 'dei Sonetti,' signore di Pesaro." In *La signoria di Malatesta "dei Sonetti" Malatesti (1391–1429)*. Edited by Enrico Angiolini and Anna Falcioni, 19–52. Rimini: Bruno Ghigi.

Arato, Franco. 2002. *La storiografia letteraria nel Settecento italiano*. Pisa: ETS.

Arbizzoni, Guido. 1987. "Una riscrittura cinquecentesca del Petrarca: *I sonetti, le canzoni et i trionfi di M[adonna] Laura.*" In *Scritture di scritture: Testi, generi, modelli nel Rinascimento*, 539–47. Rome: Bulzoni.

Archi, Antonio. 1962. *Il tramonto dei principati*. Bologna: Capelli.

Ardissino, Erminia. 1996. *"L'aspra tragedia": Poesia e sacro in Torquato Tasso*. Florence: Olschki.

Ascarelli, Pellegrino. 1925. *Debora Ascarelli, poetessa*. Rome: Sindicato italiano arti grafiche.

Asor Rosa, Alberto. 1975. *La lirica del Seicento*. Bari: Laterza.

Avesani, Rino. 1960. "Amaseo, Romolo." In *DBI* 1960–, 2:660–66.

Bà, Paolo. 2005. "Le *Rime spirituali* di Francesca Turina Bufalini." *Letteratura italiana antica* 6:147–52.

Baernstein, P. Renée, and Julia H. Hairston. 2008. "Tullia d'Aragona: Two New Sonnets." *MLN* 123 (1) (forthcoming).

Balsamo, Jean. 2002. "Les poètes français et les anthologies lyriques italiennes." *Italique* 5:11–32.

Balsano, Maria Antonella. 1988. "Introduction." In Giandomenico Martoretta, *Il secondo libro di madrigali cromatici a quattro voci 1552*. Edited by Maria Antonella Balsano, i–xxii. Florence: Olschki.

Bandera, Sandrina, and Maria Teresa Fiorio, eds. 2000. *Bernardino Luini and Renaissance Painting in Milan: The Frescoes of San Maurizio al Monastero Maggiore*. Milan: Skira; New York: Abbeville; London: Thames and Hudson.

Bandini Buti, Maria. 1946. *Donne d'Italia: Poetesse e scrittrici*. 2 vols. Rome: Tosi.

Barboni, Emma Maria. 1998. "Il canone della bellezza femminile nella cultura italiana del Cinquecento (con particolare riguardo ad Agnolo Firenzuola): Bibliografia." Banca Dati "Nuovo Rinascimento" (www.nuovorinascimento.org). Posted 10 July 1998.

Bardazzi, Giovanni. 2001. "Le rime spirituali di Vittoria Colonna e Bernardino Ochino." *Italique* 4:61–101.

Barezzani, Maria Teresa Rosa. 1989. "Intonazioni musicali su testi di Veronica Gambara." In Bozzetti, Gibellini, and Sandal, eds. 1989, 125–42.

Barocchi, Paola, and Giovanni Gaeta Bertelà, eds. 2005. *Collezionismo mediceo e storia artistica*. Vol. 2. *Il Cardinale Carlo Maria Maddalena, Don Lorenzo, Ferdinando II, Vittoria della Rovere, 1621–1666*. Florence: SPES.

Barolini, Teodolinda. 2000. "Dante and Francesca da Rimini: Realpolitik, Romance, Gender." *Speculum* 75 (1): 1–28.

———. 2005. "Lifting the Veil? Notes toward a Gendered History of Italian Literature." *Medieval Constructions in Gender and Identity: Essays in Honor of Joan M. Ferrante*. Edited by Teodolinda Barolini, 169–91. Tempe: Arizona Center for Medieval and Renaissance Studies.

Bartoli, Francesco. 1782. *Notizie istoriche de' comici italiani che fiorirono intorno all'anno 1550 fino a' giorni presenti*. 2 vols. Padua: Conzatti a San Lorenzo. Repr., Sala Bolognese: Arnaldo Forni, 1984.

Basile, Bruno. 1978. "Petrarchismo e manierismo nei lirici parmensi del Cinquecento." In *Le corti farnesiane di Parma e Piacenza (1545–1622)*. Vol 2. *Forme e istituzioni della produzione culturale*. Edited by Amedeo Quondam, 71–132. Rome: Bulzoni.

Basile, Deanna. 2001. *"Fasseli gratia per poetessa:* Duke Cosimo I de' Medici's Role in the Florentine Literary Circles of Tullia d'Aragona." In Eisenbichler, ed. 2001, 135–47.

Bassanese, Fiora A. 1982. *Gaspara Stampa.* Boston: Twayne.

———. 1984. "Gaspara Stampa's Poetics of Negativity." *Italica* 61 (4): 335–46.

———. 1988. "Private Lives and Public Lies: Texts by Courtesans of the Italian Renaissance." *Texas Studies in Literature and Language* 30 (3): 295–319.

———. 1994a. "Vittoria Colonna (1492–1547)." In Russell, ed. 1994a, 85–94.

———. 1994b. "Gaspara Stampa (1523?–1554)." In Russell, ed. 1994a, 404–13.

———. 1996. "Selling the Self; or, the Epistolary Production of Renaissance Courtesans." In *Italian Women Writers from the Renaissance to the Present. Revising the Canon.* Edited with an introduction by Maria Ornella Marotti, 69–82. University Park: Pennsylvania State University Press.

———. 2004. "Defining Spaces: Venice in the Poetry of Gaspara Stampa and Veronica Franco." In Ferrara, Giusti, and Tylus, eds. 2005, 91–105.

Bassani, Lucia Nadin. 1992. *Il poligrafo veneto Giuseppe Betussi.* Padua: Antenore.

Battistini, Andrea. 1997. "La cultura del Barocco." In Malato, ed. 1997, 463–559.

———. 2000. *Il barocco: Cultura, miti, immagini.* Rome: Salerno.

Bausi, Francesco. 1993. "'Con agra zampogna': Tullia d'Aragona a Firenze (1545–48)." *Schede umanistiche* n. s. 2:61–91

———. 1994. "Le rime di e per Tullia d'Aragona." In Centre Aixois de Recherches Italiennes 1994, 277–92.

Bausi, Francesco, and Mario Martelli. 1993. *La metrica italiana: Teoria e storia.* Florence: Le Lettere.

Bayley, C. C. 1942. "Petrarch, Charles IV, and the 'Renovatio Imperii.'" *Speculum* 17 (3): 323–41.

Beer, Marina. 1990. "Idea del ritratto femminile e retorica del Classicismo: I *Ritratti di Isabella d'Este* di Gian Giorgio Trissino." *Schifanoia* 10:161–73.

Belladonna, Rita. 1992. "Gli Intronati, le donne, Aonio Paleario e Agostino Museo in un dialogo inedito di Marcantonio Piccolomini, 'Il Sodo Intronato' (1538)." *Bulletino senese di storia patria* 99:48–90.

Bellina, Anna Laura, and Carlo Caruso. 1998. "Oltre il Barocco: La fondazione dell'Arcadia; Zeno e Metastasio: La riforma del melodrama." In Malato, ed. 1998, 507–94.

Belloni, Antonio. 1893. *Gli epigoni della* Gerusalemme liberata, *con un'appendice bibliografica.* Padua: Angelo Draghi.

Bellucci, Novella. 1981. *"Lettere di molte valorose donne . . . e di alcune pettegolette,* overo: Di un libro di lettere di Ortensio Lando." In *"Le carte messaggiere": Retorica e modelli di communicazione epistolare.* Edited by Amedeo Quondam, 255–76. Rome: Bulzoni.

Benedetti, Laura. 1996. *La sconfitta di Diana: Un percorso per la* Gerusalemme liberata. Ravenna: Longo.

———. 1999. "Virtù femminile o virtù donnesca? Torquato Tasso, Lucrezia Marinella ed una polemica rinascimentale." In *Torquato Tasso e la cultura estense.* 3 vols. Edited by Gianni Venturi, 2:449–56. Florence: Olschki.

———. 2005. " Saintes et guerrières: L'héroisme féminin dans l'oeuvre de Lucrezia Marinella." In *Les femmes et l'écriture: L'amour profane et l'amour sacré*. Edited by Claude Cazalé Bérard, 93–109. Paris: Presses Universitaires de Paris X.

Benfell, V. Stanley. 2005. "Translating Petrarchan Desire in Vittoria Colonna and Gaspara Stampa." In *Translating Desire in Medieval and Early Modern Literature*. Edited by Craig A. Berry and Heather Richardson Hayton, 109–31. Tempe, AZ: Arizona Center for Medieval and Renaissance Studies.

Benson, Pamela J. 1992. *The Invention of the Renaissance Woman: The Challenge of Female Independence in the Literature and Thought of Italy and England*. University Park: Pennsylvania State University Press.

———. 1999. "To Play the Man: Aemilia Lanyer and the Acquisition of Patronage." In *Opening the Borders: Inclusivity in Early Modern Europe: Essays in Honor of James V. Mirollo*. Edited by Peter C. Herman, 243–64. Newark: University of Delaware Press.

———. 2004. "Eleonora among the Famous Women: Iconographic Innovation after the Conquest of Siena." In Eisenbichler, ed. 2004, 136–56.

Benson, Pamela J., and Victoria Kirkham, eds. 2005. *Strong Voices, Weak History: Women Writers and Canons in Early Modern Europe*. Ann Arbor: University of Michigan Press.

Benzoni, Antonio. 1939. "Un carme inedito di Laura Brenzoni in lode di Roberto Sanseverino." *Archivio Veneto* s. 5, 24 (47/48): 187–229.

Berger, Harry, Jr. 2000. *The Absence of Grace: Sprezzatura and Suspicion in Two Renaissance Courtesy Books*. Stanford: Stanford University Press.

Bernardi Triggiano, Tonia. 1999. "Piety among Women of Central Italy (1300–1600): A Critical Edition and Study of Battista da Montefeltro-Malatesta's Poem in Praise of St. Jerome." PhD diss., University of Wisconsin-Madison.

Bertolotti, Antonio. 1887. "Muzio Manfredi e Passi Giuseppe [sic] letterati in relazione col Duca di Mantova." *Il Buonarroti* s. 3, 3:118–37; 155–69; 181–86.

Bertoni, Giulio. 1925. "Intorno a tre letterati cinquecenteschi modenesi." *Giornale storico della letteratura italiana* 85:376–80.

Bettella, Patrizia. 2005. *The Ugly Woman: Transgressive Aesthetic Models in Italian Poetry from the Middle Ages to the Baroque*. Toronto: University of Toronto Press.

Bettoni, Anna. 2002. "Il sonetto di Veronica Gambara sulla predestinazione in Du Bellay." *Italique* 5:33–52.

Biagi, Guido. 1887. *Un'etèra romana, Tullia d'Aragona (con ritratto)*. Florence: Roberto Paggi.

Biagioli, Mario. 1995. "Knowledge, Freedom, and Brotherly Love: Homosociality and the Accademia dei Lincei." *Configurations* 3 (2): 139–66.

Bianca, Concetta. 1993. "Marcello Cervini and Vittoria Colonna." *Lettere italiane* 45 (3): 427–39.

Bianchi, Dante. 1924. "Una cortigiana rimatrice del Seicento, Margherita Costa." *Rassegna critica della letteratura italiana* 29:1–31, 187–203.

Bianchi, Stefano. 1993. "Petrarchismo liminare: Tradizione letteraria e 'gioco d'amore' nella poesia di Veronica Franco." In *Passare il tempo: La letteratura del gioco e dell'intertenimento dal 12° al 16° secolo; Atti del convegno di Pienza, 10–14 settembre 1991*. 2 vols. 2:721–37. Rome: Salerno.

———. 1995. "Introduzione." In Franco 1995, 5–39.

———. 1998. "Introduzione." In Franco 1998b, 7–24.

Bianchini, Giuseppe. 1896. *Franceschina Baffo, rimatrice veneziana del secolo 16*. Verona: Fratelli Drucker.

Bianco, Monica. 1998a. "Rinaldo Corso e il *Canzoniere* di Vittoria Colonna." *Italique* 1:35–45.

———. 1998b. "Le due redazioni del commento di Rinaldo Corso alle rime di Vittoria Colonna." *Studi di filologia italiana* 56:271–95.

———. 2001. "Il *Tempio* a Geronima Colonna d'Aragona: Ovvero la conferma di un archetipo." In Bianco and Strada, eds. 2001, 147–81.

Bianco, Monica, and Elena Strada, eds. 2001. *"I più vaghi e i più soavi fiori": Studi sulle antologie di lirica del Cinquecento*. Alessandria: Edizioni dell'Orso.

Biga, Emilia. 1989. *Una polemica antifemminista del '600: La* Maschera scoperta *di Angelico Aprosio*. Ventimiglia: Civica Biblioteca Aprosiana.

Billanovich, Giuseppe. 1996. *Petrarca e il primo umanesimo*. Padua: Antenore.

Boccato, Carla. 1973. "Un episodio della vita di Sara Copio Sullam: Il *Manifesto* sull'immortalità dell'anima." *La Rassegna Mensile di Israel* 39:633–46.

———. 1974. "Lettere di Ansaldo Cebà, genovese, a Sara Copio Sullam, poetessa del Ghetto di Venezia." *La Rassegna Mensile di Israel* 40:169–91.

———. 1987. "Sara Copio Sullam: La poetessa del Ghetto di Venzia: Episodi della sua vita in un manoscritto del secolo 17." *Italia* 6 (1–2): 104–218.

———. 2005. "Le *Rime* postume di Numidio Paluzzi: Un contributo alla lirica barocca a Venezia nel primo Seicento." *Lettere italiane* 57: 112–31.

Bohn, Babette. 2002. "The Antique Heroines of Elisabetta Sirani." *Renaissance Studies* 16 (1): 52–79.

———. 2004. "Female Self-Portraiture in Early Modern Bologna." *Renaissance Studies* 18 (2): 239–86.

Bolland, Andrea. 2000. "Desiderio and Diletto: Vision, Touch, and the Poetics of Bernini's *Apollo and Daphne*." *The Art Bulletin* 82 (2): 309–30.

Bolzoni, Lina. 1989. "Tommaso Campanella e le donne: Fascino e negazione della differenza." *Annali d'italianistica* 7:193–216.

Bonadonna Russo, Maria Theresa. 1999. "Donna Anna Colonna Barberini fra mondanità e devozione." *Strenna dei Romanisti*: 475–95.

Borchardt, Frank L. 1975. "Petrarch: The German Connection." *Studies in Romance Languages* 3:418–31.

Borgerding, Todd M., ed. 2002. *Gender, Sexuality, and Early Music*. New York: Routledge.

Borsetto, Luciana. 1983. "Narciso ed Eco: Figura e scrittura nella lirica femminile del Cinquecento; esemplificazioni e appunti." In Zancan, ed. 1983, 171–233. Venice: Marsilio.

———. 1989. *L'Eneida tradotta: Riscritture poetiche del testo di Virgilio nel 16° secolo*. Padua: Unicopli.

Borzelli, Angelo. 1898. *Il cavalier Giovan Battista Marino (1569–1625)*. Naples: Gennaro M. Priore.

———. 1935. *Note intorno a Margherita Sarrocchi ed al suo poema* La Scanderbeide. Naples: Tipografia Pontificia degli Artigianelli.

Bosi, Kathryn. 2003. "Accolades for an Actress: On Some Literary and Musical Tributes for Isabella Andreini." *Recercare* 15:73–117.

Bowers, Jane. 1986. "The Emergence of Women Composers in Italy, 1566–1700." In Bowers and Tick, eds. 1986, 116–67.

Bowers, Jane, and Judith Tick, eds. 1986. *Women Making Music: The Western Art Tradition, 1150–1950*. Urbana: University of Illinois Press.

Bozzetti, Cesare, Pietro Gibellini, and Ennio Sandal, eds. 1989. *Veronica Gambara e la poesia del suo tempo nell'Italia settentrionale; Atti del convegno (Brescia-Correggio, 17–19 ottobre, 1985)*. Florence: Olschki.

Braden, Gordon. 1996a. "Gaspara Stampa and the Gender of Petrarchism." *Texas Studies in Literature and Language* 38 (2): 115–39.

———. 1996b. "Applied Petrarchism: The Loves of Pietro Bembo." *Modern Language Quarterly* 57 (3): 397–423.

Bragantini, Renzo. 1996. "Poligrafi e umanisti volgari." In Malato, ed. 1996b, 681–754.

Branca, Vittore. 1958. *Tradizione delle opere di Giovanni Boccaccio*. Vol. 1. *Un primo elenco di codici e tre studi*. Rome: Edizioni di Storia e Letteratura.

———. 1981. "L'umanesimo veneziano alla fine del Quattrocento: Ermolao Barbaro e il suo circolo." *Storia della cultura veneta*. Vol. 3, pt. 1. *Dal primo Quattrocento al Concilio di Trento*, 123–75. Vicenza: Neri Pozza.

Breitenberg, Mark. 1996. *Anxious Masculinity in Early Modern England*. Cambridge, UK: Cambridge University Press.

Brown, Alison. 1979. *Bartolomeo Scala 1430–1497, Chancellor of Florence: The Humanist as Bureaucrat*. Princeton: Princeton University Press.

Brown, David Alan, ed. 2003. *Virtue and Beauty: Leonardo's* Ginevra de' Benci *and Renaissance Portraits of Women*. Princeton: Princeton University Press.

Brown, Howard Mayer. 1986. "Women Singers and Women's Songs in Fifteenth-Century Italy." In Bowers and Tick, eds. 1986, 62–89.

Brown, Judith C. 1986. "A Woman's Place Was in the Home: Women's Work in Renaissance Tuscany." In Ferguson, Quilligan, and Vickers, eds. 1986, 206–24. Chicago: University of Chicago Press.

Brown, Judith C., and Robert C. Davis. 1998. *Gender and Society in Renaissance Italy*. London and New York: Longman.

Brownlee, Marina Scordilis. 1990. *The Severed Word: Ovid's* Heroides *and the Novela Sentimental*. Princeton: Princeton University Press.

Brundin, Abigail. 2001. "Vittoria Colonna and the Virgin Mary." *Modern Language Review* 96 (1): 61–81.

———. 2002. "Vittoria Colonna and the Poetry of Reform." *Italian Studies* 57:61–74.

———. 2005. "Introduction." In Colonna 2005, 1–43.

Bruni, Francesco. 1986. "Figure della committenza e del rapporto autori-pubblico: Aspetti della comunicazione nel Basso Medioevo." In *Patronage and Public in the Trecento (Proceedings of the St. Lambrecht Symposium, St. Lambrecht, Syria, 16–9 July 1984)*. Edited by Vincenzo Moleta, 105–24. Florence: Olschki.

Bruni, Roberto L. 2004. "Editori e tipografi a Firenze nel Seicento." *Studi secenteschi* 45: 325–419.

Bryce, Judith C. 1995. "The Oral World of the Early Accademia Fiorentina." *Renaissance Studies* 9 (1): 77–103.

———. 1999. "Adjusting the Canon for Later Fifteenth-Century Florence: The Case of Antonia Pulci." In *The Renaissance Theatre: Texts, Performance, Design*. 2 vols. Edited by Christopher Cairns, 1:133–45. Aldershot, UK: Ashgate.

———. 2002. "'Fa finire uno bello studio et dice volere studiare': Ippolita Sforza and Her Books." In *Bibliothèque d'Humanisme et Renaissance* 64 (1): 55–69.

———. 2007. "Between Friends? Two Letters of Ippolita Sforza to Lorenzo de' Medici." *Renaissance Studies* 21 (3): 340–65.

Bucci, Carlo Alberto. 1998. "Gallerani, Cecilia." In *DBI* 1960–, 51:551–53.

Bullock, Alan, and Gabriella Palange. 1980. "Per una edizione critica delle opere di Chiara Matraini." In *Studi in onore di Raffaele Spongano*, 235–62. Bologna: Massimilano Boni.

Buranello, Roberto. 2000. "*Figura meretricis:* Tullia d'Aragona in Sperone Speroni's *Dialogo d'amore*." *Spunti e ricerche* 15:53–68.

Burckhardt, Jacob. 1990. *The Civilization of the Renaissance in Italy*. Translated by S. G. C. Middlemore. Introduction by Peter Burke. Notes by Peter Murray. Harmondsworth, UK: Penguin.

Burgess-Van Aken, Barbara. 2007. "Barbara Torelli's *Partenia:* A Bilingual Critical Edition." PhD diss., Case Western Reserve University.

Burke, Peter. 1995. *The Fortunes of the* Courtier: *The European Reception of Castiglione's* Cortegiano. Cambridge, UK: Polity.

Cagni, Giuseppe. 1989. "Negri o Besozzi? Come nacque la *vexata quaestio* della paternità delle lettere spirituali dell'Angelica Paola Antonia Negri." *Barnabiti studi* 6:177–217.

Calitti, Floriana. 2004. *Fra lirica e narrativa: Storia dell'ottava rima nel Rinascimento*. Florence: Le Càriti.

Calore, Marina. 1985. "Muzio Manfredi tra polemiche teatrali e crisi del mecenatismo." *Studi romagnoli* 36:27–54.

Campbell, Julie D. 1997. "*Love's Victory* and *La Mirtilla* in the Canon of Renaissance Tragicomedy: An Examination of Salon and Social Debates." *Women's Writing* 4 (1): 103–25.

———. 2002. "Introduction." In Andreini 2002, xi–xxvii.

———. 2006. *Literary Circles and Gender in Early Modern Europe: A Cross-Cultural Approach*. Aldershot: Ashgate Publishing Company.

Campbell, Stephen J. 2004. *The Cabinet of Eros: Renaissance Mythological Painting and the Studiolo of Isabella d'Este*. New Haven: Yale University Press.

Canepa, Nancy L. 1996. "The Writing Behind the Wall: Arcangela Tarabotti's *In-*

*ferno Monacale* and Cloistral Autobiography in the Seventeenth Century." *Forum Italicum* 30 (1): 1–23.

Cannata Salamone, Nadia. 2000. "Women and the Making of the Vernacular Literary Canon." In Panizza, ed. 2000, 498–512.

Capata, Alessandro. 1998. "Nicolò Franco e il plagio del *Tempio d'Amore.*" In *Semestrale di Studi (e testi)* 1:219–32.

Capucci, Martino. 1972. "Bronzini, Cristoforo." In *DBI* 1960–, 14:463–64.

———. 1983. "Coreglia, Isabetta." In *DBI* 1960–, 29:41–42.

———. 1984. "Costa, Margherita." In *DBI* 1960–, 30:232–35.

Cardamone, Donna G. 2002. "Isabella Medici-Orsini: A Portrait of Self-Affirmation." In Borgerding, ed. 2002, 1–25.

Carinci, Eleonora. 2002. "Una lettera autografa inedita di Moderata Fonte (al granduca di Toscana Francesco I)." *Critica del testo* 5 (3): 671–81.

Carlson, Veena Kumar. 2005. "*Rime e lettere:* (Self) Representation and Chiara Matraini." In Ferrara, Giusti, and Tylus, eds. 2005, 106–25.

Carter, Tim. 1999. "Finding A Voice: Vittoria Archilei and the Florentine 'New Music.'" In *Feminism and Renaissance Studies.* Edited by Lorna Hutson, 450–67. Oxford, UK: Clarendon Press.

Cartwright, Julia. 2002a. *Beatrice d'Este, Duchess of Milan 1475–1497.* Honolulu, HI: University Press of the Pacific.

———. 2002b. *Isabella d'Este, Marchioness of Mantua, 1474–1539: A Study of the Renaissance.* 2 vols. Honolulu, HI: University Press of the Pacific.

Casale, Olga Silvana. 1985. "L'epistolario quattrocentesco di Ceccarella Minutolo." In *La critica del testo: Problemi di metodo e esperienze di lavoro, atti del convegno di Lecce, 22–26 ottobre 1984,* 505–17. Rome: Salerno.

Casapullo, Rosa. 1998. "Contatti metrici fra Spagna e Italia: Laura Terracina e la tecnica della glosa." In *Atti del 21° Congresso Internazionale di Linguistica e Filologia Romanza, Centro di Studi Filologici e Linguistici Siciliani, Università di Palermo, 18–24 settembre 1995.* 6 vols. Edited by Giovanni Ruffino, 4:361–89. Tübingen: Max Niemeyer Verlag.

Castoldi, Massimo. 1993. "Laura Brenzoni Schioppo nel Codice Marciano it. Cl. IX 163." *Studi e problemi di critica testuale* 46: 69–101.

Catalano, Michele. 1951. *La tragica morte di Ercole Strozzi e un sonetto di Barbara Torelli.* Vol. 2 of *Lezioni di letteratura italiana,* 37–77. Messina: V. Ferrara.

Cattini, Marco, and Marzio Achille Romani. 1982. "Le corti parallele: Per una tipologia delle corti padane dal 13° al 16° secolo." In *La corte e lo spazio: Ferrara estense.* 3 vols. Edited by Giuseppe Papagno and Amedeo Quondam, 1:47–82. Rome: Bulzoni.

Cavarocchi Arbib, Marina. 1999. "Rivisitando la biblioteca Ester: Implicazioni sottese all'immagine femminile ebraica nell'Italia del Seicento." In Honess and Jones, eds. 1999, 143–57.

Cecchi, Alessandro. 2001. "Machiavelli e gli artisti del suo tempo." In Pontremoli, ed. 2001, 265–79. Florence: Olschki.

Celani, Enrico. 1891. "Introduzione." In *Le rime di Tullia d'Aragona, cortigiana del secolo 16*, iii–lxiii. Edited by Enrico Celani. Bologna: Romagnoli Dall'Acqua.

Celenza, Christopher S. 2004. *The Lost Italian Renaissance: Humanists, Historians, and Latin's Legacy*. Baltimore, MD: Johns Hopkins University Press.

Celse, Mireille. 1973. "Alessandro Piccolomini: L'homme du ralliement." In *Les écrivains et le pouvoir en Italie a l'époque de la Renaissance*, 7–76. Paris: Universitè de la Sorbonne Nouvelle.

Centre Aixois de Recherches Italiennes. 1994. *Les femmes écrivains en Italie au moyen age et à la Renaissance*. Aix-en-Provence: Publications de l'Université de Provence.

Cerreta, Florindo. 1958. "La *Tombaide*: Alcune rime inedite su un pellegrinaggio petrarchesco ad Arquà." *Italica* 35 (3): 162–66.

———. 1960. *Alessandro Piccolomini letterato e filosofo senese del Cinquecento*. Siena: Accademia degli Intronati.

Cerrón Puga, María Luisa. 2005. "Le voci delle donne e la voce al femminile: Vie del petrarchismo in Italia e in Spagna." In Crivelli, Nicoli, and Santi, eds. 2005, 103–31.

Cessi, Camillo. 1897. *Quattro sonetti di Issicratea Monte rodigina*. Padua: Tipografia all'Università-Fratelli Gallina.

Chater, James. 1999. "'Such Sweet Sorrow': The *dialogo di partenza* in the Italian Madrigal." *Early Music* 27 (4): 576–88; 590–99.

Chemello, Adriana. 1983. "La donna, il modello, l'immaginario: Moderata Fonte e Lucrezia Marinella." In Zancan, ed. 1983, 95–170.

———. 1988. "Gioco e dissimulazione in Moderata Fonte." In Fonte 1988, ix–lxiii.

———. 1993. "'Il 'genere femminile' tesse la sua 'tela': Moderata Fonte e Lucrezia Marinella." In *Miscellanea di studi*. Edited by Renata Cibin and Angiolina Ponziano, 85–107. Venice: Multigraf.

———. 1999. "Il codice epistolare femminile: Lettere, 'libri di lettere,' e letterate nel Cinquecento." In Zarri, ed. 1999, 3–42.

———. 2000a. "The Rhetoric of Eulogy in Lucrezia Marinella's *La nobiltà et l'eccellenza delle donne*." In Panizza, ed. 2000, 463–77.

———. 2000b. "Le ricerche erudite di Luisa Bergalli." In Chemello and Ricaldone, eds. 2000, 69–88.

———. 2000c. "Omaggio a Clio: Diodata Saluzzo." In Chemello and Ricaldone, eds. 2000, 89–113.

———. 2003. "'Donne a poetar esperte': La 'rimatrice dimessa' Maddalena Campiglia." In *La littérature au féminin*. Special issue, *Versants* n. s. 46:65–101.

———. 2005. "'Tra 'pena' e 'penna': La storia singolare della 'fidelissima Anassilla.'" In Crivelli, Nicoli, and Santi, eds. 2005, 45–77.

Chemello, Adriana, and Luisa Ricaldone. 2000. *Geografie e genealogie letterarie: Erudite, biografe, croniste, narratrici, épistolières, utopiste tra Settecento e Ottocento*. Padua: Il Poligrafo.

Chiesa, Mario. 2002. "Poemi biblici fra Quattrocento e Cinquecento." *Giornale storico della letteratura italiana* 179:161–92.

Chimenti, Antonia. 1994. *Veronica Gambara, gentildonna del Rinascimento: Un intreccio di poesia e di storia*. Reggio Emilia: Magis.

Chojnacka, Monica. 2001. *Working Women of Early Modern Venice*. Baltimore, MD: Johns Hopkins University Press.

Chojnacki, Stanley. 2000. *Women and Men in Renaissance Venice: Twelve Essays on Patrician Society*. Baltimore, MD: Johns Hopkins University Press.

Churchill, Laurie J., Phyllis R. Brown, and Jane E. Jeffrey, eds. 2002. *Women Writing Latin, from Roman Antiquity to Early Modern Europe*. 3 vols. Vol. 3. *Early Modern Women Writing Latin*. New York: Routledge.

Cinquini, Chiara. 1999. "Rinaldo Corso editore e commentatore delle *Rime* di Vittoria Colonna." *Aevum* 73: 669–96.

Clarke, Danielle. 2001. *The Politics of Early Modern Women's Writing*. Harlow, UK: Longman.

Clough, Cecil H. 1996. "Daughters and Wives of the Montefeltro: Outstanding Bluestockings of the Quattrocento." *Renaissance Studies* 10 (1): 31–55.

Cocco, Mia. 1994. "Alessandra Macinghi Strozzi, 1406–71." In Russell, ed. 1994a, 198–206.

Coci, Laura. 1988. "Nota introduttiva." In Rocco 1988, 7–34. Rome: Salerno.

Cohen Elizabeth S., and Thomas V. Cohen. 1993. *Words and Deeds in Renaissance Rome: Trials before the Papal Magistrates*. Toronto: University of Toronto Press.

Cohn, Samuel K., Jr. 1996. *Women in the Streets: Essays on Sex and Power in Renaissance Italy*. Baltimore, MD: Johns Hopkins University Press.

Coldagelli, Ugo. 1972. "Brembati, Giovanni Battista." In *DBI* 1960–, 14:122–24.

Coller, Alexandra. 2006. "The Sienese Accademia degli Intronati and Its Female Interlocutors." *The Italianist* 26 (2): 223–46.

———. 2007. "Ladies and Courtesans in Late Sixteenth-Century *Commedia Grave*: Vernacular Antecedents of Early Opera's *Prime Donne*." *Italian Studies* 62:27–44.

Collett, Barry. 2000. *A Long and Troubled Pilgrimage: The Correspondence of Marguerite D'Angoulême and Vittoria Colonna, 1540–1545*. Princeton: Princeton Theological Seminary (available online).

Collina, Beatrice. 1989. "Moderata Fonte e *Il merito delle donne*." *Annali d'italianistica* 7:142–64.

———. 1996. "L'esemplarità delle donne illustri fra Umanesimo e Controriforma." In Zarri, ed. 1996, 103–19.

———. 2006. "Women in the Gutenberg Galaxy." In Weaver, ed. 2006a, 91–105.

Cominelli, Elena. 2001. "Il canzoniere di Lucia Albani Avogadro." In Selmi, ed. 2001, 1:245–77.

Conelli, Maria Anna. 2004. "A Typical Patron of Extraordinary Means: Isabella Feltria della Rovere and the Society of Jesus." In *Renaissance Studies* 18 (3): 412–36.

Connolly, Joy. 1999. "Mastering Corruption: Constructions of Identity in Roman Oratory." In *Women and Slaves in Greco-Roman Culture*. Edited by Sandra Rae Joshel and Sheila Murnaghan. New York: Routledge.

Contarino, Rosaria. 1983. "Corsi, Girolama." In *DBI* 1960–, 29:570–72.

Conti Odorisio, Ginevra. 1979. *Donna e società nel Seicento: Lucrezia Marinella e Arcangela Tarabotti*. Introdution by Ida Magli. Rome: Bulzoni.

Cook, James Wyatt, and Barbara Collier Cook. 1996. "Florentine Drama for Convent and Festival: Seven Sacred Plays." In Pulci 1996, 38–46.

Coppens, Christien, and Angela Nuovo. 2005. *I Giolito e la stampa nell'Italia del 16° secolo*. Geneva: Droz.

Corbucci, Vittorio. 1901. *Una poetessa umbra: Francesca Turina Bufalini, contessa di Stupinigi [1544–1641]*. Città di Castello: Tipografia dello Stabilimento S. Lapi.

Cornish, Alison. 2000. "A Lady Asks: The Gender of Vulgarization in Late Medieval Italy." *PMLA* 115 (2): 166–80.

Corsaro, Antonio. 1998. "Dionigi Atanagi e la silloge per Irene di Spilimbergo. (Intorno alla formazione del giovane Tasso)." *Italica* 75 (1): 41–61.

Costa-Zalessow, Natalia. 1982. *Scrittrici italiane dal 13° al 20° secolo: Testi e critica*. Ravenna: Longo.

———. 2001. "Tarabotti's *La semplicità ingannata* and Its Twentieth-Century Interpreters, with Unpublished Documents regarding Its Condemnation to the Index." *Italica* 78 (3): 314–25.

Cowen Orlin, Lena. 1999. "Three Ways to Be Invisible in the Renaissance: Sex, Reputation, and Stitchery." In *Renaissance Culture and the Everyday*. Edited by Patricia Fumerton and Simon Hunt, 183–203. Philadelphia: University of Pennsylvania Press.

Cox, Virginia. 1992. *The Renaissance Dialogue: Literary Dialogue in its Social and Political Contexts, Castiglione to Tasso*. Cambridge, UK: Cambridge University Press.

———. 1995a. "The Single Self: Feminist Thought and the Marriage Market in Early Modern Venice." *Renaissance Quarterly* 48 (3): 513–81.

———. 1995b. "Tasso's *Malpiglio overo della corte: The Courtier* Revisited." In *Modern Language Review* 90 (4): 897–918.

———. 1997a. "Women as Readers and Writers of Chivalric Literature." In *Sguardi sull'Italia: Miscellanea dedicata a Francesco Villari*. Edited by Gino Bedani, Zygmunt Baranski, Anna Laura Lepschy, and Brian Richardson, 134–45. Leeds, UK: Society for Italian Studies.

———. 1997b. "Moderata Fonte and *The Worth of Women*." In Fonte 1997, 1–23.

———. 2000a. "Seen but Not Heard: The Role of Women Speakers in Cinquecento Literary Dialogue." In Panizza, ed. 2000, 385–400.

———. 2000b. "Fiction, 1560–1650." In Panizza and Wood, eds. 2000, 52–64.

———. 2004. Biographical entry for Moderata Fonte. Italian Women Writers website, University of Chicago (www.lib.uchicago.edu/efts/IWW).

———. 2005a. "Women Writers and the Canon in Sixteenth-Century Italy: The Case of Vittoria Colonna." In Benson and Kirkham, eds. 2005, 14–31.

———. 2005b. "Sixteenth-Century Women Petrarchists and the Legacy of Laura." *Journal of Medieval and Early Modern Studies* 35 (3): 583–606.

———. 2006. "Attraverso lo specchio: Le petrarchiste del cinquecento e l'eredità di Laura." In *Petrarca: Canoni, esemplarità,* edited by Valeria Finucci, 117–49. Roma: Bulzoni.

Cox, Virginia, and Lisa Sampson. 2004. "Introduction." In Campiglia 2004, 1–35.

Crabb, Ann. 2000. *The Strozzi of Florence: Widowhood and Family Solidarity in the Renaissance.* Ann Arbor: University of Michigan Press.

Cremaschi, Giovanni. 1960. "Albani, Giovanni Giacomo." In *DBI* 1960–, 1:606–7.

Crivelli, Tatiana. 2001. "La sorellanza nella poesia arcadica femminile fra Sette e Ottocento." *Filologia e critica* 26 (3): 321–49.

———. 2005. "'A un luogo stesso per molte vie vassi': Note sul sistema petrarchista di Veronica Franco." In Crivelli, Nicoli, and Santi, eds. 2005, 79–102.

Crivelli, Tatiana, Giovanni Nicoli, and Mara Santi, eds. 2005. *"L'una e l'altra chiave": Figure e momenti del petrarchismo femminile europeo; Atti del Convegno Internazionale di Zurigo, 4–5 giugno 2004.* Rome: Salerno.

Croce, Benedetto. 1942. "Lodi poetiche di dame napoletane del secolo decimosesto." In *Aneddoti di varia letteratura.* 3 vols. 1:257–65. Naples: Riccardo Ricciardi.

———. 1953a. "Ceccarella Minutolo." In *Aneddoti di varia lettura.* 2nd ed. 4 vols. 1:64–76. Bari: Laterza.

———. 1953b. "Giovanni Cosentino." In *Aneddoti di varia lettura.* 2nd ed. 4 vols. 1:95–101. Bari: Laterza.

———. 1958. "Vincenza Armani e Adriano Valerini." In *Poeti e scrittori del pieno e tardo Rinascimento.* 2 vols. 2:171–74. Bari: Laterza.

———. 1967. *Storia dell'età barocca in Italia.* 5th ed. Bari: Laterza.

———. 1968. *Nuovi saggi sulla letteratura italiana del Seicento.* 3rd ed. Bari: Laterza.

———. 1976. "La casa di una poetessa." In *Storie e leggende napoletane,* 235–49. 7th ed. Bari: Laterza.

Croce, Franco. 1955a. "I critici moderato-barocchi, e la discussione sull'*Adone.*" *La Rassegna della letteratura italiana* 59:414–39.

———. 1955b. Review of Eden Sarot, "Ansaldo Cebà and Sara Copio Sullam" (*Italica* 31.3 [1954]: 138–50). In *La Rassegna della letteratura italiana,* s. 7, 59 (1): 148–49.

———. 2002. "Introduzione al Barocco." In Croce et al., eds. 2002, 25–40.

Croce, Franco, et al., eds. 2002. *I capricci di Proteo: Percorsi e linguaggi del Barocco; Atti del convegno di Lecce, 23–26 ottobre 2000.* Rome: Salerno.

Cropper, Elizabeth. 1976. "On Beautiful Women, Parmigianino, Petrarchismo, and the Vernacular Style." *Art Bulletin* 58 (3): 374–94.

———. 1986. "The Beauty of Women: Problems in the Rhetoric of Renaissance Portraiture." In Ferguson, Quilligan, and Vickers, eds. 1986, 175–90.

———. 1991. "The Petrifying Art: Marino's Poetry and Caravaggio." *Metropolitan Museum Journal* 26:193–212.

Curran, Stuart. 2005. "Recollecting the Renaissance: Luisa Bergalli's *Componimenti Poetici* (1726)." In Benson and Kirkham, eds. 2005, 263–86.

Curti, Elisa. 2006. *Tra due secoli: Per il tirocinio letterario di Pietro Bembo.* Bologna: Gedit.

Curtis-Wendlandt, Lisa. 2004. "Conversing on Love: Text and Subtext in Tullia d'Aragona's *Dialogo d'amore.*" *Hypatia* 19 (4): 75–96.

Cusick, Suzanne G. 1993a. "'Thinking from Women's Lives': Francesca Caccini after 1627." In Marshall, ed. 1993, 206–25.

———. 1993b. "Of Women, Music, and Power: A Model from Seicento Florence." In *Musicology and Difference: Gender and Sexuality in Music Scholarship.* Edited by Ruth Solie, 281–304. Berkeley: University of California Press.

Cutolo, Alessandro. 1955. "La giovinezza di Ippolita Sforza, duchessa di Calabria." *Archivio storico per le province napoletane* n.s. 34:119–32.

Daenens, Francine. 1983. "Superiore perché inferiore: Il paradosso della superiorità della donna in alcuni trattati italiani del Cinquecento." In *Trasgessione tragica e norma domestica: Esemplari di tipologie femminili dalla letteratura europea.* Edited by Vanna Gentili, 11–50. Rome: Edizioni di Storia e Letteratura.

———. 1999a. "Olimpia Morata: Storie parallele." In Honess and Jones, eds. 1999, 101–12.

———. 1999b. "Donne valorose, eretiche, finte sante: Note sull'antologia giolitiana del 1548." In Zarri, ed. 1999, 181–207.

———. 2000. "Isabella Sforza: Beyond the Stereotype." In Panizza, ed. 2000, 35–55.

da Fonseca Wollheim, Corinna. 1999. "Acque di Parnaso, acque di Battesimo: Fede e fama nell'opera di Sara Copio Sullam." In Honess and Jones, eds. 1999, 159–70.

Dalarun, Jacques, and Fabio Zinelli. 2004. "Poésie et théologie à Santa Lucia de Foligno: Sur una laude de Battista de Montefeltro." In Leonardi, ed. 2004, 21–45.

D'Amico, John F. 1984. "The Progress of Renaissance Latin Prose: The Case of Apuleianism." *Renaissance Quarterly* 37 (3): 351–92.

d'Ancona, Alessandro. 1906. *La poesia popolare italiana.* 2nd ed. Livorno: Raffaello Giusti.

d'Ancona, Alessandro, and Antonio Medin. 1898. "Rime storiche del sec. 15." *Bullettino dell'Istituto Storico Italiano* 6:17–35.

Danzi, Massimo. 1989. "Girolamo Cittadini, poeta Milanese di primo cinquecento." In Bozzetti, Gibellini, and Sandal, eds. 1989, 296–322.

Danzi, Massimo, Guglielmo Gorni, and Silvia Longhi, eds. 2001. *Poeti del Cinquecento.* Vol 1. *Poeti lirici, burleschi, satirici e didascalici.* Milan: Riccardo Ricciardi.

Davies, Drew Edward. 2006. "On Music Fit for a Courtesan: Representations of the Courtesan and Her Music in Sixteenth-Century Italy." In Feldman and Gordon, eds. 2006, 144–58.

Davis, Robert C. and Benjamin Ravid, eds. 2001. *The Jews of Early Modern Venice.* Baltimore: Johns Hopkins University Press.

Dean, Trevor, and K. J. P. Lowe, eds. 1998a. *Marriage in Italy, 1300–1650.* Cambridge, UK: Cambridge University Press.

———. 1998b. "Introduction: Issues in the History of Marriage." In Dean and Lowe, eds. 1998a, 1–21.

De Bellis, Daniela. 2000. "Attacking Sumptuary Laws in Seicento Venice: Arcangela Tarabotti." In Panizza, ed. 2000, 226–42. Oxford, UK: Legenda.

De Blasi, Nicola, and Alberti Varvaro. 1988. "Napoli e l'Italia meridionale." In *Letteratura italiana: Storia e geografia*. Vol. 2. *L'età moderna*, 235–325. Turin: Einaudi.

De Boer, Wietse. 2001. *The Conquest of the Soul: Confession, Discipline, and Public Order in Counter-Reformation Milan*. Brill: Leiden.

Decroisette, Françoise. 2001. "La première 'divine': Isabella Andreini ou l'invention d'un role." In *Au théâtre, au cinéma, au féminin*. Edited by Mireille Calle-Gruber and Hélène Cixous, 193–215. Paris: L'Harmattan.

———. 2002. "'Satyres au feminine dans la pastorale italienne de la fin du 16e siècle." In *La campagna e la città: Letteratura e ideologia nel Rinascimento; Scritti in onore di Michel Plaisance*. Edited by Giuditta Isotti Rosowsky, 149–82. Florence: Franco Cesati.

De Girolami Cheney, Liana. 2001. "'Lavinia Fontana: A Woman Collector of Antiquity." *Aurora* 2:22–42.

Delcorno, Carlo. 1975. "Un avversario del Marino: Ferrante Carli." *Studi secenteschi* 16:69–155.

Delcorno, Carlo, and Maria Luisa Doglio, eds. 2005. *Rime sacre dal Petrarca al Tasso*. Bologna: Il Mulino.

D'Elia, Anthony F. 2002. "Marriage, Sexual Pleasure, and Learned Brides in the Wedding Orations of Fifteenth-Century Italy." *Renaissance Quarterly* 55 (2): 379–433.

———. 2004. *The Renaissance of Marriage in Fifteenth-Century Italy*. Cambridge, MA: Harvard University Press.

D'Elia, Una Roman. 2006. "Drawing Christ's Blood: Michelangelo, Vittoria Colonna, and the Aesthetics of Reform." *Renaissance Quarterly* 59 (1): 90–129.

De Filippis, Michele. 1948. *The Literary Riddle in Italy to the End of the Sixteeenth Century*. Berkeley: University of California Press.

DeJean, Joan. 1991. *Tender Geographies: Women and the Origins of the Novel in France*. New York: Columbia University Press.

de Miranda, Girolamo. 2000. *Una quiete operosa: Forma e pratiche dell'Accademia napoletana degli Oziosi, 1611–1645*. Naples: Fridericiana Editrice Universitaria.

Denarosi, Laura. 1997. "Il principe e il letterato: Due carteggi inediti di Muzio Manfredi." *Studi italiani* 17:151–76.

———. 2003. *L'Accademia degli Innominati di Parma: Teorie letterarie e progetti di scrittura (1574–1608)*. Florence: Società Editrice Fiorentina.

de Robertis, Domenico. 1966. "L'esperienza poetica del Quattrocento." In *Storia della letteratura italiana*. Vol. 3. *Il Quattrocento e l'Ariosto*. Edited by Emilio Cecchi and Natalino Sapegno, 355–784. Milan: Garzanti.

Derosas, Renzo. 1983. "Corner, Elena Lucrezia." In *DBI* 1960–, 29:174–79.

Dersofi, Nancy. 1994a. "Isabella Andreini (1562–1604)." In Russell, ed. 1994a, 18–25.

———. 1994b. "Laura Terracina (1519–c. 1577)." In Russell, ed. 1994a, 423–30.

De Rycke, Dawn. 2006. "On Hearing the Courtesan in a Gift of Song: The Venetian Case of Gaspara Stampa." In Feldman and Gordon, eds. 2006, 124–32.

Deswarte-Rosa, Sylvie. 1992. *Ideias e imagens em Portugal na época dos descobrimentos: Francisco de Holanda e a teoria da arte*. Lisbon: Difel.

de Vit, Vincenzo. 1883. "Dell'illustre donzella Issicratea Monti." In *Opuscoli letterari editi e inediti*, 7–25. Milan: Bomiardi-Pogliani.

de Vivo, Raffaella. 2001. "Vittoria Colonna e gli umanisti napoletani." In *Napoli viceregno spagnolo: Una capitale della cultura alle origini dell'Europa moderna (secoli 16–17)*. 2 vols. Edited by Monika Bosse and André Stoll, 2:37–55. Naples: Vivarium.

di Castro, Francesca. 2004. "Isabella Catanea Parasole e il teatro delle nobili et virtuose donne." *Strenna dei Romanisti* 65:227–40.

Dickinson, John W. 1961. "Vittoria Colonna, Philippe Desportes, and William Alabaster." *Revue de littérature comparée* 35:112–14.

di Filippo Bareggi, Claudia. 1988. *Il mestiere di scrivere: Lavoro intellettuale e mercato librario a Venezia nel Cinquecento*. Rome: Bulzoni.

Dilemmi, Giorgio. 1989. "'Ne videatur strepere anser inter olores': Le relazioni della Gambara con il Bembo." In Bozzetti, Gibellini, and Sandal, eds. 1989, 23–35.

Dionisotti, Carlo. 1981. "Appunti sul Bembo e su Vittoria Colonna." In *Miscellanea Augusto Campana*. 2 vols. Edited by Rino Avesani, Giuseppe Billanovich, Mirella Ferrari, and Giovanni Pozzi, 1:257–86. Padua: Antenore.

———. 1989. "Elia Capriolo e Veronica Gambara." In Bozzetti, Gibellini, and Sandal, eds. 1989, 13–21.

———. 1999. *Geografia e storia della letteratura italiana*. Turin: Einaudi.

———. 2002. *Scritti sul Bembo*. Edited by Claudio Vela. Turin: Einaudi.

Dixon, Annette, ed. 2002. *Women Who Ruled: Queens, Goddesses, Amazons in Renaissance and Baroque Art*. London: Merrell; Ann Arbor: in association with the University of Michigan Museum of Art.

Dixon, Susan M. 1999. "Women in Arcadia." *Eighteenth-Century Studies* 32 (3): 371–75.

*Dizionario biografico degli italiani (DBI)*. 1960–. 67 vols. to date. Rome: Istituto dell'Enciclopedia Italiana.

Doglio, Maria Luisa. 1994. "Scrittura e 'officio di parole' nelle *Lettere familiari* di Veronica Franco." In Centre Aixois de Recherches Italiennes 1994, 103–17.

———. 1995. "Introduzione." In Andreini 1995, 5–16.

———. 1999. "Il Tasso e le donne: Intorno al *Discorso della virtù feminile e donnesca*." In *Torquato Tasso e la cultura estense*. 3 vols. Edited by Gianni Venturi, 2:505–21. Florence: Olschki.

———. 2000. "Letter-writing, 1350–1650." In Panizza and Wood, eds. 2000, 13–24.

Dotti, Ugo. 1987. *Vita di Petrarca*. Bari: Laterza.

Dunn, Marilyn R. 1994. "Piety and Patronage in Seicento Rome: Two Noblewomen and Their Convents." *Art Bulletin* 76 (4): 644–63.

———. 1997. "Spiritual Philanthropists: Women as Convent Patrons in Seicento Rome." In Lawrence, ed. 1997, 154–88.

Durante, Elio, and Anna Martellotti. 1989a. *Cronistoria del concerto delle dame principalissime di Margherita Gonzaga d'Este*. 2nd ed. Florence: SPES.

———. 1989b. *Don Angelo Grillo, O.S.B., alias Livio Celiano, poeta per musica del secolo decimosesto.* Florence: Studio per Edizioni Scelte.

Dutschke, Dennis. 1984. "Il discorso tassiano *De la virtù feminile e donnesca.*" *Studi tassiani* 32:5–28.

Eamon, William. 1994. *Science and the Secrets of Nature: Books of Secrets in Medieval and Early Modern Culture.* Princeton: Princeton University Press.

Edelstein, Bruce L. 2000. "Nobildonne napoletane e committenza: Eleonora d'Aragona ed Eleonora di Toledo a confronto." *Quaderni storici* 35 (2): 295–329.

———. 2004. "*La fecundissima Signora Duchessa:* The Courtly Persona of Eleonora of Toledo and the Iconography of Abdundance." In Eisenbichler, ed. 2004, 71–97.

Eger, Elizabeth. 2001. "Representing Culture: *The Nine Living Muses of Great Britain* (1779)." In *Women, Writing and the Public Sphere, 1700–1830.* Edited by Elizabeth Eger, Charlotte Grant, Clíona O Gallchoir, and Penny Warburton, 104–32. Cambridge, UK: Cambridge University Press.

Eisenbichler, Konrad. 2001a. "'Laudomia Forteguerri Loves Margaret of Austria.'" In *Same-Sex Love and Desire among Women in the Middle Ages.* Edited by Francesca Canadé Sautman and Pamela Sheingorn, 277–304. New York: Palgrave.

———, ed. 2001. *The Cultural Politics of Duke Cosimo I de' Medici.* Aldershot, UK: Ashgate.

———. 2003. "Poetesse senesi a metà Cinquecento: Tra politica e passione." *Studi rinascimentali* 1:95–102.

———, ed. 2004. *The Cultural World of Eleonora di Toledo, Duchess of Florence and Siena.* Aldershot, UK: Ashgate.

Erdmann, Axel. 1999. *My Gracious Silence: Women in the Mirror of Sixteenth-Century Printing in Western Europe.* Luzern: Gilhofer and Ranschberg.

Erskin, Catherine R. 1999. "The Rei(g)ning of Women's Tongues in English Books of Instruction and Rhetorics." In Whitehead, ed. 1999, 101–32.

Erspamer, Francesco. 1982. *La biblioteca di don Ferrante: Duello e onore nella cultura del Cinquecento.* Rome: Bulzoni.

Ettlinger, Helen S. 1994. "*Visibilis et invisibilis:* The Mistress in Italian Renaissance Court Society." *Renaissance Quarterly* 47 (4): 770–92.

Evangelisti, Silvia. 1992. "Angelica Baitelli, la storica." In *Barocco al femminile.* Edited by Giulia Calvi, 71–95. Rome: Laterza.

Everson, Jane, and Diego Zancani, eds. 2000. *Italy in Crisis: 1494.* Oxford, UK: Legenda.

Ezell, Margaret J. M. 1987. *The Patriarch's Wife: Literary Evidence and the History of the Family.* Chapel Hill: University of North Carolina Press.

———. 1993. *Writing Women's Literary History.* Baltimore, MD: Johns Hopkins University Press.

———. 1999. *Social Authorship and the Advent of Print.* Baltimore, MD: Johns Hopkins University Press.

Fabrizio-Costa, Silvia. 1986. "Édification et érotisme: Le personage de Marie

Madeleine dans la *Galeria* di F. Pona." *Au pays d'Éros: Littérature et érotisme en Italie de la Renaissance à l'âge baroque.* Vol. 1, 173–203. Paris: Université de la Sorbonne Nouvelle.

Fahy, Conor. 1956. "Three Early Renaissance Treatises on Women." *Italian Studies* 11:30–55.

———. 1961. "Un trattato di Vincenzo Maggi sulle donne e un'opera sconosciuta di Ortensio Lando." *Giornale Storico della Letteratura Italiana* 138:254–72.

———. 2000. "Women and Italian Cinquecento Literary Academies." In Panizza, ed. 2000, 438–52.

Fantazzi, Charles. 2000. "Introduction: Prelude to the Other Voice in Vives." In Juan Luis Vives, *The Education of a Christian Women: A Sixteenth-Century Manual.* Edited and translated by Charles Fantazzi, 1–42. Chicago: University of Chicago Press.

Fantuzzi, Giovanni. 1781–94. *Notizie degli scrittori bolognesi.* 9 vols. Bologna: Stamperia di S. Tommaso d'Aquino.

Farrell, Joseph. 1998. "Reading and Writing the *Heroides.*" *Harvard Studies in Classical Philology* 98:307–38.

Favaro, Antonio. 1983. *Amici e correspondenti di Galileo.* 2nd ed. 3 vols. Edited by Paolo Galluzzi. Florence: Libreria Editrice Salimbeni.

Favretti, Elena. 1992. "Veronica Franco: *Rime e Lettere.*" In *Figure e fatti del Cinquecento Veneto,* 73–95. Alessandria: Edizioni dell'Orso.

Fedi, Roberto. 1996a. "From the 'Auctor' to the Authors: Writing Lyrics in the Italian Renaissance." *Quaderni d'Italianistica* 17 (2): 61–74.

———. 1996b. "La fondazione dei modelli: Bembo, Castiglione, Della Casa." In Malato, ed. 1996b, 507–94.

Feldman, Martha. 1995. *City Culture and the Madrigal at Venice.* Berkeley: University of California Press.

———. 2006. "The Courtesan's Voice: Petrarchan Lovers, Pop Philosophy, and Oral Traditions." In Feldman and Gordon, eds. 2006, 105–23.

Feldman, Martha, and Bonnie Gordon, eds. 2006. *The Courtesan's Arts: Cross-Cultural Perspectives.* New York: Oxford University Press.

Feliciangeli, Bernardino. 1894. "Notizie sulla vita e sugli scritti di Costanza Varano-Sforza (1426–1447)." *Giornale Storico della Letteratura Italiana* 23:1–75.

Fenlon, Iain. 1990. "Gender and Generation: Patterns of Music Patronage among the Este, 1471–1539." In *La corte di Ferrara e il suo mecenatismo, 1441–1598: Atti del convegno internazionale, Copenhagen maggio 1987.* Edited by Marianne Pade, Lene Waage Petersen, and Daniela Quarta, 213–32. Copenhagen: Museum Tusculanums Forlag, and Modena: Panini.

Fenster, Thelma S. 2005. "Strong Voices, Weak Minds?: The Defenses of Eve by Isotta Nogarola and Christine de Pizan, Who Found Themselves in Simone de Beauvoir's Situation." In Benson and Kirkham, eds. 2005, 58–77.

Ferguson, Margaret W. 1996. "Renaissance Concepts of the 'Woman Writer.'" In *Women and Literature in Britain, 1500–1700.* Edited by Helen Wilcox, 143–68. Cambridge, UK: Cambridge University Press.

———. 2003. *Dido's Daughters: Literacy, Gender, and Empire in Early Modern England and France*. Chicago: University of Chicago Press.

Ferguson, Margaret W., Maureen Quilligan, and Nancy Vickers, eds. 1986. *Rewriting the Renaissance: The Discourses of Sexual Difference in Early Modern Europe*. Foreword by Catharine R. Stimpson. Chicago: University of Chicago Press.

Ferino Pagden, Silvia. 1997. *Vittoria Colonna: Dichterin und Muse Michelangelos*. Vienna: Kunsthistorisches Museum and Skira.

Fermor, Sharon. 1993. "Movement and Gender in Sixteenth-Century Italian Painting." In *The Body Imaged: The Human Form and Visual Culture since the Renaissance*. Edited by Kathleen Adler and Marcia Pointon, 129–45. Cambridge, UK: Cambridge University Press.

Ferrara, Paul A., Eugenio Giusti, and Jane Tylus, eds. 2005. *Medusa's Gaze: Essays on Gender, Literature, and Aesthetics in the Italian Renaissance, in Honor of Robert J. Rodini*. Boca Raton, FL: Bordighiera Press.

Filosa, Elsa. 2004. "Petrarca, Boccaccio e le *mulieres clarae*: Dalla *Familiare* 21:8 al *De mulieribus claris*." *Annali d'italianistica* 22:381–95.

Findlen, Paula. 1995. "Translating the New Science: Women and the Circulation of Knowledge in Enlightenment Italy." *Configurations* 3 (2): 167–206.

———. 1999. "A Forgotten Newtonian: Women and Science in the Italian Provinces." In *The Sciences in Enlightened Europe*. Edited by William Clark, Jan Golinski, and Simon Schaffer, 313–49. Chicago: University of Chicago Press.

———. 2003. "Becoming a Scientist: Gender and Knowledge in Eighteenth-Century Italy." *Science in Context* 16: 59–87.

Finotti, Fabio. 2004. *Retorica della diffrazione: Bembo, Aretino, Giulio Romano e Tasso. Letteratura e scena cortigiana*. Florence: Olschki.

———. 2005. "Women Writers in Renaissance Italy: Courtly Origins of New Literary Canons." In Benson and Kirkham, eds. 2005, 121–45.

Finucci, Valeria. 1992. *The Lady Vanishes: Subjectivity and Representation in Castiglione and Ariosto*. Stanford: Stanford University Press.

———. 1995. "Moderata Fonte e il romanzo cavalleresco al femminile." In Fonte 1995, ix–xxxix.

———. 2002. "Giulia Bigolina e il romanzo in prosa del Rinascimento." In Bigolina 2002, 13–66.

———. 2003. *The Manly Masquerade: Masculinity, Paternity, and Castration in the Italian Renaissance*. Durham, NC: Duke University Press.

———. 2005. "Giulia Bigolina and Italian Prose Fiction in the Italian Renaissance." In Bigolina 2005, 1–45.

———. 2006a. "When the Mirror Lies: Sisterhood Reconsidered in Moderata Fonte's *Thirteen Cantos of Floridoro*." In *Sibling Relations and Gender in the Early Modern World: Sisters, Brothers, and Others*. Edited by Naomi Miller and Naomi Yavneh, 116–28. Aldershot, UK: Ashgate.

———. 2006b. "Moderata Fonte and the Genre of Women's Chivalric Romance." In Fonte 2006, 1–33.

Finzi, Riccardo. 1959. *Un correggese del Rinascimento: Rinaldo Corso (1525–82)*. Modena: Aedes Muratoriana.

Fiorato, Adelin Charles. 1979. *Bandello entre l'histoire et l'écriture: La vie, l'expérience sociale, l'évolution culturelle d'un conteur de la Renaissance*. Florence: Olschki.

Firpo, Massimo. 1988. "Vittoria Colonna, Giovanni Morone, e gli spirituali." *Rivista di storia e letteratura religiosa* 24:211–61.

———. 1991. "Paola Antonia Negri, monaca angelica (1508–55)." In *Rinascimento al femminile*. Edited by Ottavia Niccoli, 35–82. Bari: Laterza.

Fletcher, Jennifer. 1989. "Bernardo Bembo and Leonardo's Portrait of Ginevra de' Benci." *The Burlington Magazine* 131 (1041): 811–16.

Flosi, Justin. 2006. "On Locating the Courtesan in Italian Lyric: Distance and the Madrigal Texts of Costanzo Festa." In Feldman and Gordon, eds. 2006, 133–43.

Foltran, Daniela. 2004. "Calliope ed Erato: Stile e struttura nella *Babilonia distrutta* di Scipione Errico." *Schifanoia* 26/27:39–99.

Formentin, Vittorio. 1996a. "La 'crisi' linguistica del Quattrocento." In Malato, ed. 1996a, 159–210.

——— 1996b. "Dal volgare toscano all'italiano." In Malato, ed. 1996b, 177–250.

Forni, Giorgio. 2005. "Vittoria Colonna, la 'Canzone alla Vergine,' e la poesia spirituale." In Delcorno and Doglio, eds. 2005, 63–94.

Fortis, Umberto. 2003. *La "bella ebrea": Sara Copio Sullam, poetessa nel ghetto di Venezia del '600*. Turin: Silvio Zamorani.

Fragnito, Gigliola. 1972. "Gli 'spirituali' e la fuga di Bernardino Ochino." *Rivista Storica Italiana* 84:777–813.

———. 1997. *La bibbia al rogo: La censura ecclesiastica e i volgarizzamenti della Scrittura (1471–1605)*. Bologna: Il Mulino.

——— 2005. *Proibito capire: La chiesa e il volgare nella prima età moderna*. Bologna: Il Mulino.

Frajese, Vittorio. 1987. *Il popolo fanciullo: Silvio Antoniano e il sistema disciplinare della Controriforma*. Milan: Franco Angeli.

Franceschetti, Antonio. 1994. "Faustina Maratti Zappi (1679?–1745)." In Russell, ed. 1994a, 226–33.

Franceschini, Chiara. 2004. "*Los scholares son cosa de su excelentia, como lo es toda la Compañia*: Eleonora di Toledo and the Jesuits." In Eisenbichler, ed. 2004, 181–206.

Franceschini, Gino. 1959. "Battista Montefeltro Malatesti, signora di Pesaro." In *Figure del Rinascimento urbinate*, 159–93. Urbino: STEU.

———. 1973. *I Malatesta*. Milan: Dall'Oglio.

Franklin, Margaret. 2006. *Boccaccio's Heroines: Power and Virtue in Renaissance Society*. Aldershot, UK: Ashgate.

Frasso, Giuseppe, Giordana Mariani Canova, and Ennio Sandal, ed. 1990. *Illustrazione libraria, filologia e esegesi petrarchesca tra Quattro e Cinquecento: Antonio Grifo e l'incunabolo queriniano G V 15*. Padua: Antenore.

Freccero, Carla. 1992. "Politics and Aesthetics in Castiglione's *Il Cortegiano*: Book 3 and the Discourse on Women." In *Creative Imitation: New Essays on Renaissance Literature in Honor of Thomas M. Greene*. Edited by David Quint, 251–271. Binghamton, NY: Medieval and Renaissance Texts and Studies.

Freedberg, David. 1989. *The Power of Images: Studies in the History and Theory of Response*. Chicago: University of Chicago Press.

Freeman, Daniel E. 1996. "'La guerriera amante': Representations of Amazons and Warrior Queens in Venetian Baroque Opera." *The Musical Quarterly* 80 (3): 431–60.

Frick, Carole Collier. 2004. "Francesco Barbaro's *De re uxoria*: A Silent Dialogue for a Young Medici Bride." In *Printed Voices: The Renaissance Culture of Dialogue*. Edited by Dorothea Heitsch and Jean-François Vallée, 193–205. Toronto: University of Toronto Press.

Fulco, Giorgio. 1997. "Giovan Battista Marino." In Malato, ed. 1997, 597–652.

Fulkerson, Laurel. 2004. *The Ovidian Heroine as Author: Reading, Writing, and Community in the* Heroides. Cambridge, UK: Cambridge University Press.

Fumaroli, Marc. 1992. "Rhétorique et poétique." *Lettere italiane* 44 (1): 3–40.

Furey, Constance. 2004. "'Intellects Inflamed in Christ': Women and Spiritualized Scholarship in Renaissance Christianity." *Journal of Religion* 84 (1): 1–22.

Galasso, Giuseppe. 1997. "L'egemonia spagnola in Italia." In Malato, ed. 1997, 371–411.

Gáldy, Andrea M. 2006. "Tuscan Concerns and Spanish Heritage in the Decoration of Duchess Eleonora's Apartment in the Palazzo Vecchio." *Renaissance Studies* 20 (3): 293–319.

Gallico, Claudio. 1962. "Poesie musicali d'Isabella d'Este." In *Collectanea historiae musicae* 3:109–19.

Garrard, Mary D. 1994. "Here's Looking at Me: Sofonisba Anguissola and the Problem of the Woman Artist." *Renaissance Quarterly* 47 (3): 556–622.

Gaston, Robert W. 2004. "Eleonora di Toledo's Chapel: Lineage, Salvation, and the War against the Turks." In Eisenbichler, ed. 2004, 157–80.

Gerboni, Luigi. 1899. *Un umanista nel Secento: Giano Nicio Eritreo, studio biografico-critico*. Città di Castello: Lapi.

Getto, Giovanni. 1969. *Barocco in prosa e in poesia*. Milan: Rizzoli.

Ghidini, Alberto. 1983a. "Da Correggio, Fulvia." In *DBI* 1960–, 29:434–36.

———. 1983b. "Da Correggio, Ippolito." In *DBI* 1960–, 29:458–60.

———. 1989. "La contea di Correggio ai tempi di Veronica Gambara." In Bozzetti, Gibellini, and Sandal, eds. 1989, 79–98.

Ghinassi, Ghino. 1963. "L'ultimo revisore del *Cortegiano*." *Studi di filologia italiana* 21:217–64.

Giachino, Luisella. 2001a. "Tra celebrazione e mito: Il *Tempio* di Cinzio Aldobrandini." *Giornale Storico della Letteratura Italiana* 178:404–19.

———. 2001b. "Dall'effimero teatrale alla *quête* dell'immortalità, le *Rime* di Isabella Andreini." *Giornale Storico della Letteratura Italiana* 178:530–53.

―――. 2002. *"Cicero libertinus:* La satira della Roma Barberiniana nell'*Eudemia* dell'Eritreo." *Studi secenteschi* 43:185–215.

Giambonini, Francesco. 2000. *Bibliografia delle opere a stampa di Giambattista Marino.* 2 vols. Florence: Olschki.

Gibellini, Pietro. 1997. "Una nobile lettrice: Il *Canzoniere* del Petrarca commentato e illustrato per Beatrice d'Este." In *La femme lettrée à la Renaissance: Actes du colloque internationale, Bruxelles, 27–29 mars 1996.* Edited by Michel Bastiaensen, 75–93. Herent: Peeters.

Gilbert, Allan. 1960. *"Orlando Furioso* as a Sixteenth-Century Text." *Italica* 37 (4): 239–56.

Gill, Katherine. 1994. "Women and the Production of Religious Literature in the Vernacular, 1300–1500." In Matter and Coakley, eds. 1993, 64–104.

Giordano, Antonella. 1994. *Letterate toscane del Settecento: Un regesto con un saggio su Corilla Olimpica e Teresa Ciamagnini Pelli Fabbroni di Luciana Morelli.* Preface by Riccardo Brusagli and Simonetta Soldani. Florence: All'insegna del Giglio.

Giunta, Claudio. 2002. *Versi a un dedicatario: Saggio sulla poesia italiana del Medioevo.* Bologna: il Molino.

Gleason, Maud. 1995. *Making Men: Sophists and Self-Presentation in Ancient Rome.* Princeton: Princeton University Press.

Glénisson-Delannée, Françoise. 1991. "Une veillée intronata inédite (1542) ou le jeu littéraire à caractère politique d'un diplomate: Marcello Landucci." In *Bollettino sanese di storia patria* 98:63–101.

―――. 1995. "Rozzi e Intronati." In *Storia di Siena.* Vol 1. *Dalle origini alla fine della repubblica.* Edited by Roberto Barzanti, Giuliano Catoni, Mario De Gregorio, 407–22. Siena: Alsaba.

Gnocchi, Alessandro. 1999. "Tommaso Giustiniani, Ludovico Ariosto, e la Compagnia degli Amici." *Studi di filologia italiana* 57:277–93.

Godard, Alain. 1984. "La *Filli di Sciro* de Guidubaldo Bonarelli: Précédents littéraires et nouveaux impératifs idéologiques." In *Réécritures 2: Commentaires, parodies, variations dans la littérature italienne de la Renaissance,* 141–225. Paris: Université de la Sorbonne Nouvelle.

Gordon, Bonnie. 2004. *Monteverdi's Unruly Women: The Power of Song in Early Modern Italy.* Cambridge, UK: Cambridge University Press.

―――. 2006. "The Courtesan's Traffic in Song." In Feldman and Gordon, eds. 2006, 182–99.

Gorni, Guglielmo. 1989. "Veronica e le altre: Emblemi e cifre onomastiche nelle *Rime* del Bembo." In Bozzetti, Gibellini, and Sandal, eds. 1989, 37–57.

Grantham Turner, James, ed. 1993. *Sexuality and Gender in Early Modern Europe: Institutions, Texts, Images.* Cambridge, UK: Cambridge University Press.

―――. 2003. *Schooling Sex: Libertine Literature and Erotic Education in Italy, France, and England, 1534–1685.* Oxford: Oxford University Press.

Gray, Floyd. 2000. *Gender, Rhetoric, and Print Culture in French Renaissance Writing.* Cambridge, UK: Cambridge University Press.

Graziani, Natale, and Gabriella Venturelli. 1987. *Caterina Sforza*. 2nd ed. Milan: Dall'Oglio.

Graziosi, Elisabetta. 1992. "Arcadia femminile: Presenze e modelli." *Filologia e critica* 17:321–58.

———. 1996. "Scrivere in convento: Devozione, encomio, persuasione nelle rime delle monache fra Cinque e Seicento." In Zarri, ed. 1996, 313–31.

———. 2004. "Poesia nei conventi femminili: Qualche repertorio e un testo esemplare." In Leonardi, ed. 2004, 47–72.

———. 2005. "Arcipelago sommerso: Le rime delle monache tra obbedienza e trasgressione." In *I monasteri femminili come centri di cultura fra Rinascimento e Barocco*. Edited by Gianna Pomata and Gabriella Zarri, 145–73. Bologna: Edizioni di Storia e Letteratura.

Greene, Thomas M. 1979. "*Il cortegiano* and the Choice of a Game." *Renaissance Quarterly* 32 (2): 173–86.

Grendler, Paul. F. 1969. *Critics of the Italian World*. Madison: University of Wisconsin Press.

———. 1977. *The Roman Inquisition and the Venetian Press, 1540–1605*. Princeton: Princeton University Press.

———. 1989. *Schooling in Renaissance Italy: Literacy and Learning*. Baltimore, MD: Johns Hopkins University Press.

Grignani, Maria Antonietta. 2000. "Introduzione." In Morra, 2000, 11–38. Rome: Salerno.

Griguolo, Primo. 1984. "Giovanni Maria Bonardo e l'ambiente culturale di Fratta nel '500." In Luciano Alberti et al., *Palladio e il palladianesimo nel Polesine*, 79–85. Padua: F. Muzzio.

Grippo, Marcella. 1996. "La *Gelosia del sole* di Girolamo Britonio." *Critica letteraria* 24: 5–55.

Grubb, James S. 1996. *Provincial Families of the Renaissance: Private and Public Life in the Veneto*. Baltimore, MD: Johns Hopkins University Press.

———. 2000. "Elite Citizens." In *Venice Reconsidered: The History and Civilization of an Italian City-State, 1297–1797*. Edited by John Martin and Dennis Romano, 339–64. Baltimore, MD: Johns Hopkins University Press.

Guardiani, Francesco. 2002. "Le polemiche seicentesche intorno all'*Adone*." In Croce et al., eds. 2002, 177–97.

Guazzoni, Valerio. 1994. "Donna, pittrice, e gentildonna: La nascita di un mito femminile nel Cinquecento." In *Sofonisba Anguissola e le sue sorelle*. Edited by Paolo Buffa, 57–70. Milan: Leonardo Arte.

Guerra, Enrica G. 2005. "Lo spazio del potere: Eleonora e Beatrice d'Aragona nei *Memoriali* di D. Carafa." *Annali dell'Università di Ferrara. Sezione storica* 2:323–61.

Gundersheimer, Werner L. 1980a. "Bartolommeo Goggio: A Feminist in Renaissance Ferrara." *Renaissance Quarterly* 33 (2): 175–200.

———. 1980b. "Women, Learning, and Power: Eleonora of Aragon and the Court of Ferrara." In Labalme, ed. 1980, 43–65.

Gunderson, Eric. 2000. *Staging Masculinity: The Rhetoric of Performance in the Roman World:* Ann Arbor: University of Michigan Press.

Günsberg, Maggie. 1991. "'Donna liberata'? The Portrayal of Women in the Italian Renaissance Epic." In *Women and Italy: Essays on Gender, Culture, and History.* Edited by Shirley Vinal and Zygmunt Baranski, 173–208. London: Macmillan.

Hacke, Daniela. 2004. *Women, Sex and Marriage in Early Modern Venice.* Aldershot, UK: Ashgate.

Hagedorn, Suzanne C. 2004. *Abandoned Woman: Rewriting the Classics in Dante, Boccaccio, and Chaucer.* Ann Arbor: University of Michigan Press.

Hairston, Julia L. 2000. "Skirting the Issue: Machiavelli's Caterina Sforza." *Renaissance Quarterly* 53 (3): 687–712.

———. 2003. "Out of the Archive: Four Newly-Identified Figures in Tullia d'Aragona's *Rime della Signora Tullia d'Aragona e di diversi a lei.*" *MLN* 118 (1): 257–63.

———. 2008. "'Di sangue illustre e pellegrina': Eclipsing the Body in the Lyric of Tullia d'Aragona." In *The Body in Early Modern Italy.* Edited by Julia Hairston and Walter Stephens. Baltimore, MD: Johns Hopkins University Press.

Hallett, Judith. 1989. "Women as Same and Other in Classical Roman Elite." *Helios* 16:59–78.

Hammond, Frederick. 1994. *Music and Spectacle in Baroque Rome: Barberini Patronage under Urban VIII.* New Haven: Yale University Press.

Hampton, Timothy. 1990. *Writing from History: The Rhetoric of Exemplarity in Renaissance Literature.* Ithaca: Cornell University Press.

Hannay, Margaret Patterson, ed. 1985. *Silent but for the Word: Tudor Women as Patrons, Translators, and Writers of Religious Works.* Kent, OH: Kent State University Press.

Harness, Kelley. 2006. *Echoes of Women's Voices: Music, Art, and Female Patronage in Early Modern Florence.* Chicago: University of Chicago Press.

Haskins, Susan. 2006. "Vexatious Litigant, or the Case of Lucrezia Marinella: New Documents concerning Her Life." In *Nouvelles de la république des letters* 1:81–128.

Heller, Wendy. 2000. "'O delle donne miserabil sesso': Tarabotti, Ottavia, and *L'incoronazione di Poppea.*" *Il saggiatore musicale* 7:5–45.

———. 2003. *Emblems of Eloquence: Opera and Women's Voices in Seventeenth-Century Venice.* Berkeley: University of California Press.

———. 2006. *"La forza d'amore* and the *monaca sforzata:* Opera, Tarabotti, and the Pleasures of Debate." In Weaver, ed. 2006a, 141–57.

Henke, Robert. 2002. *Performance and Literature in the Commedia dell'Arte.* Cambridge, UK: Cambridge University Press.

Herlihy, David. 1995. *Women, Family, and Society in Medieval Europe.* Providence, RI: Berghahn Books.

Hernando Sánchez, Carlos José. 1994. *Castilla y Nápoles en el siglo XVI: El virrey Pedro de Toledo, linaje, estado y cultura (1532–53).* [Valladolid]: Junta de Castilla y León, Consejería de Cultura y Turismo.

Higgins, Paula. 1997. "Musical 'Parents' and their 'Progeny': The Discourse of

Creative Patriarchy." In *Music in Renaissance Cities and Courts: Studies in Honor of Lewis Lockwood*. Edited by Jessie Ann Owens and Anthony M. Cummings, 169–86. Warren, MI: Harmonie Park Press.

Hills, Helen. 2004. "'Enamelled with the Blood of a Noble Lineage': Tracing Noble Blood and Female Holiness in Early Modern Neapolitan Convents and Their Architecture." *Church History* 73 (1): 1–40.

Holcroft, Alison. 1988. "Francesco Xanto Avelli and Petrarch." *Journal of the Warburg and Courtauld Institutes* 51:225–34.

Honess, Claire, and Verina R. Jones, eds. 1999. *Le donne delle minoranze: Le ebree e le protestanti d'Italia*. Turin: Claudiana.

Hufton, Olwen. 1998. *The Prospect Before Her: A History of Women in Western Europe, 1500–1800*. 2nd ed. New York: Vintage.

Hughes, Diane Owen. 1983. "Sumptuary Laws and Social Relations in Renaissance Italy." In *Disputes and Settlements: Law and Human Relations in the West*. Edited by John Bossy, 69–99. Cambridge, UK: Cambridge University Press.

———. 1987. "Invisible Madonnas? The Italian Historiographical Tradition and the Women of Medieval Italy." In *Women in Medieval History and Historiography*. Edited by Susan Mosher Stuard, 25–57. Philadelphia: University of Pennsylvania Press.

Hurlburt, Holly S. 2006. "Women, Gender, and Rulership in Medieval Italy." *History Compass* 4 (3): 528–35.

Iannace, Florinda M., ed. 2000. *Maria Vergine nella letteratura italiana*. Stony Brook, NY: Forum Italicum.

Imbriani, Maria Teresa. 2001. "Intertestualità tra le *Lagrime* di Luigi Tansillo e di Torquato Tasso." *Critica letteraria* 29:15–32.

Infelise, Mario. 2006. "Books and Politics in Arcangela Tarabotti's Venice." In Weaver, ed. 2006a, 57–72.

Jacobs, Frederika H. 1997. *Defining the Renaissance* Virtuosa: *Women Artists and the Language of Art History and Criticism*. Cambridge, UK: Cambridge University Press.

Jaffe, Irma B. 2002. *Shining Eyes, Cruel Fortune: The Lives and Loves of Italian Renaissance Women Poets*. New York: Fordham University Press.

James, Carolyn. 1996. *Giovanni Sabadino degli Arienti: A Literary Career*. Florence: Olschki.

Jannaco, Carmine, and Martino Capucci. 1966. *Il Seicento*. 2nd ed. Milan: Vallardi.

Jardine, Lisa. 1983. "Isotto Nogarola: Women Humanists—Education for What?" *History of Education* 12: 231–44.

———. 1985. "'*O Decus Italiae Virgo*,' or The Myth of the Learned Lady in the Renaissance." *The Historical Journal* 28 (4): 799–819.

———. 1986. "Women Humanists: Education for What?" In Anthony Grafton and Lisa Jardine, *From Humanism to the Humanities: Education and the Liberal Arts in Fifteenth and Sixteenth-Century Europe*, 29–57. Cambridge, MA: Harvard University Press.

Javion, Maurice. 1994. "Chiara Matraini: Un 'tombeau' pour Petrarque." In Centre Aixois de Recherches Italiennes 1994, 247–58.

Jerrold, Maud. 1969. *Vittoria Colonna, with Some Account of Her Friends and Her Times.* Freeport, NY: Books for Libraries Press.

Johnson, Géraldine A. 1997. "Imagining Images of Powerful Women: Maria de' Medici's Patronage of Art and Architecture." In Lawrence, ed. 1997, 126–63.

Jones, Ann Rosalind. 1990. *The Currency of Eros: Women's Love Lyric in Europe, 1540–1620.* Bloomington: Indiana University Press.

———. 1991. "New Songs for the Swallow: Ovid's Philomela in Tullia d'Aragona and Gaspara Stampa." In *Refiguring Woman: Perspectives on Gender and the Italian Renaissance.* Edited by Marilyn Migiel and Juliana Schiesari, 263–79. Ithaca, NY: Cornell University Press.

———. 1997. "From Polemical Prose to the Red Bull: The Swetnam Controversy in Women-Voiced Pamphlets and the Public Theater." In *The Project of Prose in Early Modern Europe and the New World.* Edited by Elizabeth Fowler and Roland Greene, 122–37. Cambridge, UK: Cambridge University Press.

———. 1998. "Apostrophes to Cities: Urban Rhetorics in Isabella Whitney and Moderata Fonte." In *Attending to Early Modern Women.* Edited by Susan D. Amussen and Adele Seeff, 155–75. Newark: University of Delaware Press; London: Associated University Presses.

———. 2005. "Bad Press: Modern Editors versus Early Modern Women Poets (Tullia d'Aragona, Gaspara Stampa, Veronica Franco)." In Benson and Kirkham, eds. 2005, 287–313.

Jones, Ann Rosalind, and Margaret Rosenthal. 1998. "Introduction: The Honored Courtesan." In Franco 1998a, 1–22. Chicago: University of Chicago Press.

Jones, Ann Rosalind, and Peter Stallybrass. 2000. *Renaissance Clothing and the Materials of Memory.* Cambridge, UK: Cambridge University Press.

Joost-Gaugier, Christiane. 1982. "Castagno's Humanistic Program at Legnaia and Its Possible Inventor." *Zeitschrift für Kunstgeschichte* 45 (3): 274–82.

Jordan, Constance. 1990. *Renaissance Feminism: Literary Texts and Political Models.* Ithaca: Cornell University Press.

———. 1996. "Renaissance Women Defending Women: Arguments Against Patriarchy." In *Italian Women Writers from the Renaissance to the Present: Revising the Canon.* Edited by Maria Ornella Marotti, 55–67. University Park: Pennsylvania State University Press.

Jori, Giacomo. 1997. "Poesia lirica 'marinista' e 'antimarinista' tra classicismo e barocco." In Malato, ed. 1997, 653–726.

Jung-Iglessis, Eva-Maria. 1997. "*Il Pianto della marchesa di Pescara sopra la passione di Christo.*" *Archivio italiano per la storia della pietà* 10:115–204.

Kaplan, Paul. 2003. "'Io son fatta villanella': An Anti-Pastoral Poem by Girolama Corsi Ramos." *Miscellanea Marciana* 18:81–97.

Kelly, Joan. 1984. "Did Women Have a Renaissance?" In *Women, History, and Theory: The Essays of Joan Kelly,* 19–50. Chicago: University of Chicago Press.

Kelso, Ruth. 1978. *Doctrine for the Lady of the Renaissance.* 2nd ed. Foreword by Katherine M. Rogers. Urbana: University of Illinois Press.

Kennedy, William J. 1994. *Authorizing Petrarch.* Ithaca: Cornell University Press.

———. 2003. *The Site of Petrarchism: Early Modern National Sentiment in Italy, France, and England.* Baltimore, MD: Johns Hopkins University Press.

Kerr, Rosalind. 2001. "The Imprint of Genius: Tasso's Sonnet to Isabella Andreini; A Commentary on Ferdinando Taviani's 'Bella d'Asia: Torquato Tasso, gli attori e l'immortalità.'" *Quaderni d'italianistica* 22 (2): 81–96.

Killerby, Catherine Kovesi. 1999. "'Heralds of a Well-Instructed Mind': Nicolosa Sanuti's Defence of Women and their Clothes." *Renaissance Studies* 13 (3): 255–82.

King, Margaret L. 1975. "Personal, Domestic, and Republican Values in the Moral Philosophy of Giovanni Caldiera." *Renaissance Quarterly* 28 (4): 535–74.

———. 1978. "The Religious Retreat of Isotta Nogarola (1418–1466): Sexism and its Consequences in the Fifteenth Century." *Signs* 3 (4): 807–22.

———. 1980a. "Book-Lined Cells: Women and Humanism in the Early Italian Renaissance." In Labalme, ed. 1980, 66–80.

———. 1980b. "Goddess and Captive: Antonio Loschi's Epistolary Tribute to Maddalena Scrovegni (1389)." *Medievalia et Humanistica* n.s. 10:103–27.

———. 1986. *Venetian Humanism in an Age of Patrician Dominance.* Princeton: Princeton University Press.

———. 1994. "Isotta Nogarola (1418–1466)." In Russell, ed. 1994a, 313–23.

King, Margaret L., and Albert Rabil Jr., ed. 1983. *Her Immaculate Hand: Selected Works by and about the Women Humanists of Quattrocento Italy.* Binghamton, NY: Medieval and Renaissance Texts and Studies.

King, Margaret L., and Diana Robin. 2004. "Introduction." In Nogarola 2004, 1–25.

Kirkendale, Warren. 2001. *Emilio de' Cavalieri "Gentiluomo Romano": His Life and Letters, His Role as Superintendent of all the Arts at the Medici Court, and His Musical Compositions.* Florence: Olschki.

Kirkham, Victoria. 1996. "Laura Battiferra degli Ammanati's *First Book* of Poetry. A Renaissance Holograph Comes out of Hiding." *Rinascimento* 36:351–91.

———. 1998. "Dante's Phantom, Petrarch's Specter: Bronzino's Portrait of the Poet Laura Battferra." *Lectura Dantis* 22–23:63–139.

———. 2000. "Laura Battiferra degli Ammannati benefattrice dei Gesuiti fiorentini." *Quaderni storici* 104 (2): 331–54.

———. 2001. "Cosimo and Eleonora in Shepherdland: A Lost Eclogue by Laura Battiferra degli Ammanati." In Eisenbichler, ed. 2001, 149–75.

———. 2002a. "Creative Partners: The Marriage of Laura Battiferra and Bartolomeo Ammanati." *Renaissance Quarterly* 55 (2): 498–558.

———. 2002b. "La poetessa al presepio: Una meditazione inedita di Laura Battiferra degli Ammanati." *Filologia e critica* 27 (2): 258–76.

———. 2005. "Sappho on the Arno: The Brief Fame of Laura Battiferra." In Benson and Kirkham, eds. 2005, 166–98.

———. 2006. "Introduction." In Battiferra 2006, 1–67. Chicago: University of Chicago Press.

Kleinhenz, Christopher. 1995. "*Pulzelle e maritate*: Coming of Age, Rites of Passage, and the Question of Marriage in Some Early Italian Poems." In *Matrons and Marginal Women in Medieval Society*. Edited by Robert R. Edwards and Vickie Ziegler, 89–110. Woodbridge, UK: Boydell and Brewer.

Kohl, Benjamin G. 1998. *Padua under the Carrara, 1318–1405*. Baltimore, MD: Johns Hopkins University Press.

Kolsky, Stephen. 1984. "Images of Isabella d'Este." *Italian Studies* 39:47–62.

———. 1990. "The Courtier as Critic: Vincenzo Calmeta's *Vita del facondo poeta vulgare Serafino Aquilano*." *Italica* 67 (2): 161–72.

———. 1991. *Mario Equicola: The Real Courtier*. Geneva: Droz.

———. 1998. "Bending the Rules: Marriage in Renaissance Collections of Biographies of Famous Women." In Dean and Lowe, eds. 1998a, 227–48.

———. 1999. "Moderata Fonte's *Tredici Canti del Floridoro*: Women in a Man's Genre." *Rivista di Studi Italiani* 17 (1): 165–84.

———. 2001. "Moderata Fonte, Lucrezia Marinella, Giuseppe Passi: An Early Seventeenth-Century Feminist Controversy." *Modern Language Review* 96 (4): 973–89.

———. 2003. *The Genealogy of Women: Studies in Boccaccio's* De claris mulieribus. New York: Peter Lang.

———. 2005. *The Ghost of Boccaccio: Writings on Famous Women in Renaissance Italy*. Brepols: Turnhout.

Kristeller, Paul O. 1979. *Renaissance Thought and Its Sources*. New York: Columbia University Press.

Labalme, Patricia H., ed. 1980. *Beyond Their Sex: Learned Women of the European Past*. New York: New York University Press.

LaMay, Thomasin. 2002. "Maddalena Casulana: 'My Body Knows Unheard-of Songs.'" In Borgerding, ed. 2002, 41–71.

Langdon, Gabrielle. 2006. *Medici Women: Portraits of Power, Love, and Betrayal*. Toronto: University of Toronto Press.

Larsen, Anne R. 1990. "'Un honneste passetems': Strategies of Legitimation in French Renaissance Women's Prefaces." *L'Esprit Créatur* 30 (4): 11–22.

———. 1997. "Paradox and the Praise of Women: From Ortensio Lando and Charles Estienne to Marie de Romieu." *Sixteenth-Century Journal* 28 (3): 759–74.

Lawrence, Cynthia, ed. 1997. *Women and Art in Early Modern Europe: Patrons, Collectors, and Conoisseurs*. University Park: Pennsylvania State University Press.

Lavocat, Françoise. 1998. "Introduzione." In Marinella 1998, vii–lx.

Leonardi, Claudio, ed. 2004. *Caterina Vigri: La santa e la città; Atti del convegno (Bologna, 13–15 novembre 2002)*. Florence: Sismel-Edizioni del Galluzzo.

Leone, Giuseppe. 1962. "Per lo studio della letteratura femminile del Cinquecento." *Convivium* n.s. 30:293–300.

Lesage, Claire. 1993. "*I Secreti* d'Isabella Cortese." *Chroniques italiennes* 36 (4): 145–78.

Lesser, Zachary. 2004. *Renaissance Drama and the Politics of Publication*. Cambridge, UK: Cambridge University Press.

Lewalski, Barbara Kiefer. 1985. "Of God and Good Women: The Poems of Aemilia Lanyer." In Hannay, ed. 1985, 203–24.

———. 1993. *Writing Women in Jacobean England.* Cambridge, MA: Harvard University Press.

Ligresti, Domenico. 1992. "La feudalità parlamentare siciliana alla fine del Quattrocento." In Visceglia, ed. 1992, 5–30.

Limentani, Uberto. 1961. *La satira nel Seicento.* Milan-Naples: Ricciardi.

Lincoln, Evelyn. 2000. *The Invention of the Italian Renaissance Printmaker.* New Haven: Yale University Press.

Lombardi, Giuseppi. 1998. "Traduzione, imitazione, plagio (Nicolosa Sanuti, Albrecht von Eyb, Niclas von Wyle)." *Semestrale di studi (e testi)* 1:103–38.

Longhi, Silvia. 1989. "Lettere a Ippolito e a Teseo: La voce femminile nell'elegia." In Bozzetti, Gibellini, and Sandal, eds., 1989, 385–98.

Longo, Marina, and Nicola Michelassi. 2001. *Teatro e spettacolo nella Mirandola dei Pico.* Florence: Olschki.

Looney, Dennis, and Deanna Shemek, eds. 2005. *Phaethon's Children: The Este Court and Its Culture in Early Modern Ferrara.* Tempe, AZ: Tempe Center for Medieval and Renaissance Studies.

Lorenzini, Silvia. 2001a. *"Scholastica discipula cum sub favillula humilioris ingenii sopita . . .* per un profilo biografico di Laura Cereta." In Selmi, ed. 2001, 1:119–83.

———. 2001b. "Laura Cereta: Carteggi e corrispondenti." In Selmi, ed. 2001, 1:311–51.

Losse, Deborah N. 1994. "Women Addressing Women: The Differentiated Text." In *Renaissance Women Writers: French Texts / American Contexts.* Edited by Anne R. Larsen and Colette H. Winn, 23–37. Detroit: Wayne State University Press.

Love, Harold. 1993. *Scribal Publication in Seventeenth-Century England.* Oxford, UK: Clarendon Press.

Lowe, K. J. P. 2003. *Nuns' Chronicles and Convent Culture in Renaissance and Counter-Reformation Italy.* Cambridge, UK: Cambridge University Press.

Luzio, Alessandro. 1887. *I precettori d'Isabella d'Este.* Ancona: Morelli.

Luzio, Alessandro, and Rodolfo Renier. 2006. *La coltura e le relazioni letterarie di Isabella d'Este Gonzaga.* Edited by Simone Albonico. Introduction by Giovanni Agosti. 2nd ed. Milan: Silvestre Bonnard.

Lyons, John D. 1990. *Exemplum: The Rhetoric of Example in Early Modern France and Italy.* Princeton: Princeton University Press.

Maclachlan, Elaine, 1992. "The Poetry of Chiara Matraini: Narrative Strategies in the *Rime.*" PhD diss., University of Connecticut.

Maclean, Ian. 1977. *Woman Triumphant: Feminism in French Literature, 1610–52.* Oxford: Clarendon Press.

———. 1980. *The Renaissance Notion of Woman.* Cambridge, UK: Cambridge University Press.

MacNeil, Anne. 2003. *Music and Women of the Commedia dell'Arte in the Late Sixteenth Century.* Oxford: Oxford University Press.

———. 2005. "Introduction." In Andreini 2005, 1–21.

Maestri, Delmo. 1993. "Isabella Sori: Una scrittrice alessandrina del Seicento." *Critica letteraria* 21/22 (79): 225–41.

Maffei, Scipione. 1731. *Verona illustrata, parte seconda*. Verona: Iacopo Vallarsi and Pierantonio Berno.

Magnanini, Suzanne. 2003. "Una selva luminosa: The Second Day of Moderata Fonte's *Il merito delle donne*." *Modern Philology* 101 (2): 278–96.

Malato, Enrico, ed. 1996a. *Storia della letteratura italiana*. Vol. 3. *Il Quattrocento*. Rome: Salerno.

———, ed. 1996b. *Storia della letteratura italiana*. Vol. 4. *Il primo Cinquecento*. Rome: Salerno.

———, ed. 1997. *Storia della letteratura italiana*. Vol. 5. *La fine del Cinquecento e il Seicento*. Rome: Salerno.

———, ed. 1998. *Storia della letteratura italiana*. Vol. 6. *Il Settecento*. Rome: Salerno.

Malavasi, Stefania. 1989. "Cultura religiosa e cultura laica nel Polesine del Cinquecento: Le accademie degli Addormentati e dei Pastori Frattegiani." *Archivio veneto* s. 5, 120 (167): 61–69.

———. 1993. "Lucrezia Gonzaga e la vita culturale a Fratta nella prima metà del Cinquecento." In *Vespasiano Gonzaga e il ducato di Sabbioneta: Atti del convegno Sabbioneta-Mantova, 12–13 ottobre 1991*. Edited by Ugo Bazzotta, Daniela Ferrari, Cesare Mozzarelli, 301–13. Mantua: Accademia Nazionale Virgiliana di Scienze, Lettere ed Arti.

Mallett, J. V. G. 2007. *Xanto: Pottery-Painter, Poet, Man of the Italian Renaissance*. Contributions by Giovanna Hendel, Suzanne Higgott, and Elisa Paola Sani. London: Wallace Collection.

Malpezzi Price, Paola. 1994a. "Moderata Fonte (1555–1592)." In Russell, ed. 1994a, 128–37.

———. 1994b. "Lucrezia Marinella (1571–1653)." In Russell, ed. 1994a, 234–42.

———. 1997. "A Sixteenth-Century Woman Poet's Pursuit of Fame: The Poetry of Isabella di Morra." In *The Flight of Ulysses: Studies in Memory of Emmanuel Hatzantonis*. Edited by Augustus A. Mastri, 146–58. Chapel Hill, NC: Annali d'Italianistica.

———. 2003a. "*Venezia Figurata* and Women in Sixteenth-Century Venice: Moderata Fonte's Writings." In Smarr and Valentini, eds. 2003, 18–34.

———. 2003b. *Moderata Fonte: Women and Life in Sixteenth-Century Venice*. Madison, NJ: Fairleigh Dickinson Press; London: Assocated University Presses.

Manca, Joseph. 2003. "Isabella's Mother: Aspects of the Art Patronage of Eleonora d'Aragona, Duchess of Ferrara." *Aurora* 4:79–94.

Mancini, Albert N. 1982. "La narrativa libertina degli Incogniti." *Forum Italicum* 16 (3): 203–29.

Mantese, Giovanni, and Mariano Nardello. 1974. *Due processi per eresia: La vicenda religiosa di Luigi Groto, il "Cieco d'Adria," e della nobile vicentina Angela Pigafetta-Piovene*. Vicenza: Officine Grafiche.

Marani, Pietro C. 2000. "Bernardino Luini's Frescoes in San Maurizio: Literary Circles, the Lombard Tradition and Central-Italian Classicism." In Bandera and Fiorio, eds. 2000, 53–74.

Marchesi, Giovanni Battista. 1895. "Le polemiche sul sesso femminile ne' secoli 16 e 17." *Giornale Storico della Letteratura Italiana* 74–75:362–69.

Marinelli, Peter V. 1986. *Ariosto and Boiardo: The Origins of* Orlando Furioso. Columbia: University of Missouri Press.

Marini, Quinto. 2000. *Frati barocchi: Studi su A. G. Brignole Sale, G. A. De Marini, A. Aprosio, F. F. Frugoni, P. Segneri.* Modena: Mucchi.

Marino, Joseph. 2001. "A Renaissance in the Vernacular: Baldassare Castiglione's Coining of the Aulic." In Marino and Schlitt, eds. 2001, 3–26.

Marino, Joseph, and Melinda W. Schlitt, eds. 2001. *Perspectives on Early Modern and Modern Intellectual History: Essays in Honor of Nancy S. Struever.* Rochester, NY: University of Rochester Press.

Maroi, Lina. 1913. *Laura Terracina: Poetessa napoletana del secolo 16.* Naples: Francesco Perella.

Marotti, Arthur F. 1995. *Manuscript, Print, and the English Renaissance Lyric.* Ithaca: Cornell University Press.

Marotti, Ferruccio, and Giovanna Romei. 1991. *La commedia dell'arte e la società barocca.* Vol. 2. *La professione del teatro.* Rome: Bulzoni.

Marrè Brunenghi, Franca. 1996. "Un autore dimenticato: Filippo Maria Bonini." In *Studi e documenti di storia ligure in onore di Don Luigi Alfonso per il suo 85° genetliaco,* 305–24. Genoa: Società Ligure di Storia Patria.

Marshall, Anthony J. 1990. "Roman Ladies on Trial: The Case of Maesia of Sentinum." *Phoenix* 44 (1): 46–59.

Marshall, Kimberly. 1993. *Rediscovering the Muses: Women's Musical Traditions.* Boston: Northeastern University Press.

Martelli, Mario. 1984. "Le forme poetiche italiane dal Cinquecento ai nostri giorni." In *Letteratura italiana.* Edited by Alberto Asor Rosa. Vol. 3. *Le forme del testo.* Pt. 1. *Teoria e poesia,* 519–620. Turin: Einaudi.

Martin, Giuliano. 1990. *Casa Sbarra: Un sogno rinascimentale.* Ponzano (Treviso): Viannello.

Martines, Lauro. 1979. *Power and Imagination: City-States in Renaissance Italy.* London: Allen Lane.

Martini, Alessandro. 1985. "Marino postpetrarchista." *Versants* 7:15–36.

———. 2006. "Le nuove forme del canzoniere." In Croce et al., eds. 2002, 199–226.

Martini, Mario. 1982. *Bernardino Cacciante Aletrinate: Contributo allo studio dell'Umanesimo.* Sora: Centro di Studi Soriani.

Maschietto, Francesco Lodovico. 1978. *Elena Lucrezia Cornaro Piscopia (1646–1684), prima donna laureata nel mondo.* Padua: Antenore.

Maschietto, Maria Ludovica. 1968. "Binaschi, Giovanni Filippo." *DBI* 1960–, 10:486–87.

Masi, Giorgio. 1996. "La lirica e i trattati d'amore." In Malato, ed. 1996b, 595–679.

Masoero, Mariarosa. 1999. "Agostino Bucci e l'epica sabauda." In Masoero, Mamino, and Rosso, eds. 1999, 105–22. Florence: Olschki.

Masoero, Mariarosa, Sergio Mamino, and Claudio Rosso, eds. 1999. *Politica e cultura nell' età di Carlo Emanuele I: Torino, Parigi, Madrid; Atti del convegno internazionale di studi (Torino, 21–24 Febbraio 1995).* Florence: Olschki.

Matchinske, Megan. 1998. *Writing, Gender and State in Early Modern England: Identity Formation and the Female Subject*. Cambridge, UK: Cambridge University Press.

Matter, E. Ann, and John Coakley, eds. 1994. *Creative Women in Medieval and Early Modern Italy: A Religious and Artistic Renaissance*. Philadelphia: University of Pennsylvania Press.

Matulka, Barbara. 1931. *The Novels of Juan de Flores and Their European Diffusion: A Study in Comparative Literature*. New York: Institute of French Studies.

Maylender, Michele. 1926–30. *Storia delle Accademie d'Italia*. 5 vols. Bologna: L. Cappelli.

Mazzacane, Aldo. 1990. "De Luca, Giovanni Battista." In *DBI* 1960–, 38:340–47.

Mazzacurati, Giancarlo. 1980. "Pietro Bembo." In *Storia della cultura veneta*. Vol. 3. Pt. 2, 1–59. Vicenza: Neri Pozza.

Mazzonis, Querciolo. 2004. "A Female Idea of Religious Perfection: Angela Merici and the Company of St. Ursula (1535–1540)." *Renaissance Studies* 18 (3): 391–411.

Mazzotta, Giuseppe. 2000. "*Le lagrime della Beata Vergine* di Torquato Tasso." In Iannace, ed. 2000, 39–42. Stony Brook, NY: Forum Italicum.

Mazzuchelli, Giovanni Maria. 1753–63. *Gli scrittori d'Italia cioé notizie storiche, e critiche intorno alle vite, e agli scritti dei letterati italiani*. 2 vols. Brescia: Giambattista Bossini.

McInerney, Jeremy. 2003. "Plutarch's Manly Women." In Andreia: *Studies in Manliness and Courage in Classical Antiquity*. Edited by Ralph M. Rosen and Ineke Sluiter, 319–44. Leiden: Brill.

McIver, Katherine A. 2000. "The 'Ladies of Correggio': Veronica Gambara and Her Matriarchal Heritage." *Explorations in Renaissance Culture* 26 (1): 25–44.

———. 2001. "Two Emilian Noblewomen and Patronage Networks in the Cinquecento." In Reiss and Wilkins, eds. 2001, 159–76.

———, ed. 2003. *Art and Music in the Early Modern Period: Essays in Honor of Franca Trinchieri Camiz*. Aldershot, UK: Ashgate.

———. 2006. *Women, Art, and Architecture in Northern Italy, 1520–1580: Negotiating Power*. Aldershot, UK: Ashgate.

McLeod, Glenda. 1991. *Virtue and Venom: Catalogs of Women from Antiquity to the Renaissance*. Ann Arbor: University of Michigan Press.

McManamon, John. M. *Funeral Oratory and the Cultural Ideals of Italian Humanism*. Chapel Hill: University of North Carolina Press.

Medioli, Francesca. 1990. *L'Inferno monacale di Arcangela Tarabotti*. Turin: Rosenberg and Sellier.

———. 2003. "Arcangela Tarabotti's Reliability about Herself: Publication and Self-Representation (together with a Small Collection of Previously Unpublished Letters)." *The Italianist* 23:54–101.

Miato, Monica. 1998. *L'Accademia degli Incogniti di Giovan Francesco Loredan, Venezia (1630–61)*. Florence: Olschki.

Migiel, Marilyn. 1993. *Gender and Genealogy in Tasso's* Gerusalemme Liberata. Lewiston, NY: Edwin Mellon Press.

———. 1994. "Veronica Franco (1546–91)." In Russell, ed. 1994a, 138–44.

———. 2006. "The Untidy Business of Gender Studies: Or, Why It's Almost Useless to Ask if the *Decameron* Is Feminist." In *Boccaccio and Feminist Criticism*. Edited by Thomas C. Stillinger and F. Regina Psaki, 217–33. Chapel Hill, NC: Annali d'Italianistica.

Mikalachki, Jodi. 1998. *The Legacy of Boadicea: Gender and Nation in Early Modern England*. London: Routledge.

Milani, Marisa 1983. "Quattro donne fra i pavani." *Museum patavinum* 1:387–412.

Minor, Vernon Hyde. 2006. *The Death of the Baroque and the Rhetoric of Good Taste*. Cambridge, UK: Cambridge University Press.

Mirollo, James V. 1963. *The Poet of the Marvelous: Giambattista Marino*. New York: Columbia University Press.

Montella, Luigi. 2001. *Una poetessa del Rinascimento, Laura Terracina: Con le None rime inedite*. 2nd ed. Salerno: Edisud.

Monti, Gennaro. 1924. "Il canzoniere di un'eroina bandelliana." In *Studi letterari*, 250–67. Città di Castello: Il Solco.

Moore, Mary B. 2000. *Desiring Voices: Women Sonneteers and Petrarchism*. Carbondale: Southern Illinois University Press.

Morabito, Raffaele. 1999. "Introduzione." In Minutolo 1999, 3–20.

Morandini, Giuliana, ed. 2001. *Sospiri e palpiti: Scrittrici italiane del Seicento*. Genoa: Marietti.

Mordani, Filippo. 1837. *Vite di ravegnani illustri*. Ravenna: Roveri.

Moreni, Domenico. 1819. *Annali della tipografia fiorentina di Lorenzo Torrentino, impressore ducale*. 2nd ed. Florence: Francesco Daddi.

———. 1826. *Serie d'autori di opere risguardanti la celebre famiglia Medici*. Florence: Magheri.

Morsolin, Bernardo. 1882. *Maddalena Campiglia, poetessa vicentina del secolo 16: Episodio biografico*. Vicenza: Paroni.

Mostaccio, Silvia. 1999. "Le sante di corte: La riscoperta sabauda di Margherita di Savoia-Acaia." In Masoero, Mamino, and Rosso, eds. 1999, 461–73.

Mucci, Silvana. 2001. "Lucrezia Gambara e il cenacolo spirituale di Verola Alghisi." In Selmi, ed. 2001, 1:189–222.

Muir, Edwin. 2007. *The Culture Wars of the Late Renaissance: Skeptics, Libertines, and Opera*. Cambridge, MA: Harvard University Press.

Murata, Margaret. 1981. *Operas for the Papal Court, 1631–68*. Ann Arbor, MI: UMI Research Press.

Murphy, Caroline P. 1999. "'In Praise of the Ladies of Bologna': The Image and Identity of the Sixteenth-Century Bolognese Female Patriciate." *Renaissance Studies* 13 (4): 440–54.

———. 2003. *Lavinia Fontana*. New Haven: Yale University Press.

Muscariello, Mariella. 1979. *La società del romanzo: Il romanzo spirituale barocco*. Palermo: Sellerio.

Mussini Sacchi, Maria Pia. 1998. "L'eredità di Fiammetta: Per una lettura delle *Rime* di Gaspara Stampa." *Studi italiani* 10:35–51.

Mutini, Claudio. 1962a. "D'Avalos, Costanza." In *DBI* 1960–, 4:621–22.

———. 1962b. "D'Avalos, Costanza." In *DBI* 1960–, 4:622–23.

Neri, Camillo. 2003. *Erinna: Testimonianze e frammenti*. Bologna: Patròn.

Newcomb, Anthony. 1975. "The Three Anthologies for Laura Peverara, 1580–83." *Rivista italiana di musicologia* 10:329–45.

———. 1986. "Courtesans, Muses, or Musicians? Professional Women Musicians in Sixteenth-Century Italy." In Bowers and Tick, eds. 1986, 90–115.

———. 1992. Review of Marco Giuliani, *I lieti amanti, madrigali di venti musicisti ferraresi e non* (Florence: Olschki, 1990). *Notes* 49 (1): 83–86.

Newman, Jane O. 1996. "Sons and Mothers: Agrippina, Semiramis, and the Philological Construction of Gender Roles in Early Modern Germany (Lohenstein's *Agrippina*, 1665)." *Renaissance Quarterly* 49 (1): 77–113.

Nissen, Christopher K. 2000. "Subjects, Objects, Authors: The Portraiture of Women in Giulia Bigolina's *Urania*." *Italian Culture* 18 (2): 15–31.

———. 2003. "The Motif of the Woman in Male Disguise from Boccaccio to Bigolina." In *The Italian Novella*. Edited by Gloria Allaire, 201–17. New York: Routledge.

———. 2004. "Introduction." In Bigolina 2004, 1–54.

North, Marcy L. 2003. *The Anonymous Renaissance: Cultures of Discretion in Tudor-Stuart England*. Chicago: University of Chicago Press.

Och, Marjorie. 2001. "Vittoria Colonna and the Commission for a Mary Magdalen by Titian." In Reiss and Wilkins, eds. 2001, 193–223.

———. 2002. "Portrait Medals of Vittoria Colonna: Representing the Learned Woman." In *Women as Sites of Culture: Women's Roles in Cultural Formation from the Renaissance to the Twentieth Century*. Edited by Susan Shifrin, 153–66. Aldershot, UK: Ashgate.

Ong, Walter J. 1959. "Latin Language Study as a Renaissance Puberty Rite." *Studies in Philology* 56:103–24.

Orbaan, J. A. F. 1920. *Documenti sul barocco in Roma*. Rome: Reale Società Romana di Storia Patria.

Ordine, Nuccio. 1996a. *La cabala dell'asino: Asinità e conoscenza in Giordano Bruno*. 2nd ed. Introduction by Eugenio Garin. Naples: Liguori.

———. 1996b. *Giordano Bruno and the Philosophy of the Ass*. Translated by Henryk Baranski in collaboration with Arielle Saiber. New Haven: Yale University Press.

Ossola, Carlo. 1976. "Il 'queto travaglio' di Gabriele Fiamma." In *Letteratura e critica: Studi in onore di Natalino Sapegno*. 5 vols. Edited by Walter Binni et al., 3:239–86. Rome: Bulzoni.

———. 1985. "Introduzione storica." In Juan de Valdés, *Lo Evangelio di San Matteo*. Edited by Carlo Ossola, 11–93. Rome: Bulzoni.

Ossola, Carlo, and Cesare Segre, eds. 2000. *Antologia della poesia italiana: Il Quattrocento*. 2nd ed. Turin: Einaudi.

———, eds. 2001. *Antologia della poesia italiana: Il Cinquecento*. 2nd ed. Turin: Einaudi.

Ostermark-Johansen, Lene. 1999. "The Matchless Beauty of Widowhood: Vittoria Colonna's Reputation in Nineteenth-Century England." *Art History* 22 (2): 270–94.

Pacchioni, Guglielmo. 1907. *Un codice inedito de la Biblioteca Estense: Un poeta ed una poetessa petrarchisti del secolo 15 (complemento ad una notizia data dal Tiraboschi).* Modena: Cooperativa Tipografica.

Panizza, Letizia. 1999. "Introduction to the Translation." In Marinella 1999, 1–34. Chicago: University of Chicago Press.

———, ed. 2000. *Women in Italian Renaissance Culture and Society.* Oxford, UK: Legenda.

———. 2004. "Introduction." In Tarabotti 2004, 1–31. Chicago: University of Chicago Press.

———. 2006. "Reader over Arcangela's Shoulder: Tarabotti at Work with Her Sources." In Weaver, ed. 2006a, 107–28.

Panizza, Letizia, and Sharon Wood, eds. 2000. *A History of Women's Writing in Italy.* Cambridge, UK: Cambridge University Press.

Paoli, Maria Pia. 1999. "'Come se mi fosse sorella': Maria Selvaggia Borghini nella repubblica delle lettere." In Zarri, ed. 1999, 491–534.

Parenti, Giovanni. 1983. "Corsi, Iacopo." In *DBI* 1960–, 29:574–75.

———. 1993. *Benet Garret detto il Cariteo: Profilo di un poeta.* Florence: Olschki.

Parker, Holt. 1997. "Latin and Greek Poetry by Five Renaissance Italian Women Humanists." In *Sex and Gender in Medieval and Renaissance Texts.* Edited by Paul Allen Miller, Barbara K. Gold, and Charles Platter, 247–85. Albany: State University of New York Press.

———. 2002a. "Angela Nogarola (c. 1400) and Isotta Nogarola (1418–66): Thieves of Language." In Churchill, Brown, and Jeffrey, eds. 2002, 11–30.

———. 2002b. "Costanza Varano (1426–47): Latin as an Instrument of State." In Churchill, Brown, and Jeffrey, eds. 2002, 31–53.

Parker, Patricia. 1989. "On the Tongue: Cross Gendering, Effeminacy, and the Art of Words." *Style* 23:445–65.

Parrott, David. 1997. "The Mantuan Succession, 1627–31: A Sovereignty Dispute in Early Modern Europe." *English Historical Review* 112:20–65.

Pasquazi, Silvio. 1966. *Poeti estensi del Rinascimento.* 2nd ed. Florence: Le Monnier.

Patrignani, Giovanna. 2005. "Le donne del ramo di Pesaro." In *Le donne di Casa Malatesti.* Vol. 2. Edited Anna Falcioni, 787–920. Rimini: Bruno Ghigi.

Perrone, Carlachiara. 1996. *"So che donna ama donna": La* Calisa *di Maddalena Campiglia.* Galatina: Congedo.

Pertile, Lino. 1998. "Un 'roco' sonetto per Veronica: Come nasce il 123 delle *Rime* di Pietro Bembo." *Italique* 1:11–24.

Pescerelli, Beatrice. 1979. *I madrigali di Maddalena Casulana.* Florence: Olschki.

Pezzini, Serena. 2002. "Dissimulazione e paradosso nelle *Lettere di molte valorose donne* (1548) a cura di Ortensio Lando." *Italianistica* 31 (1): 67–83.

———. 2005. "Ideologia della conquista, ideologia dell'accoglienza: *La Scanderbeide* di Margherita Sarrocchi (1623)." *MLN* 120 (1): 190–222.

Phillippy, Patricia. 1989. "Gaspara Stampa's *Rime*: Replication and Retraction." *Philological Quarterly* 68 (1): 1–23.

———. 1992. "'Altera Dido': The Model of Ovid's *Heroides* in the Poems of Gaspara Stampa and Veronica Franco." *Italica* 69 (1): 1–18.

———. 1995. *Love's Remedies: Recantation and Renaissance Lyric Poetry*. Lewisburg: Bucknell University Press; London: Associated University Presses.

Piéjus, Marie-Françoise. 1980. "Venus bifrons: Le double idéal féminin dans *La Raffaella* d'Alessandro Piccolomini." In *Images de la femme dans la littérature italienne de la Renaissance: Préjugés misogynes et aspirations nouvelles*. Edited by José Guidi et al., 81–165. Paris: Université de la Sorbonne Nouvelle.

———. 1982. "La première anthologie de poèmes féminins: L'écriture filtrée et orientée." In *Le pouvoir et la plume: Incitation, contrôle, et répression dans l'Italie du 16e siècle*, 193–213. Paris: Université de la Sorbonne Nouvelle.

———. 1994a. "Les poétesses siennoises entre le jeu et l'écriture." In Centre Aixois de Recherches Italiennes 1994, 315–32.

———. 1994b. "La création au féminine dans le discours de quelques poétesses du 16e siècle." In *Dire la Création: La culture italienne entre poétique et poïétique*. Edited by Dominique Budor, 79–90. Lille: Presses Universitaires de Lille.

Pieri, Marzia. 1985. "'Sumptuosissime pompe': Lo spettacolo nella Napoli aragonese." In *Studi di filologia e critica offerti dagli allievi a Lanfranco Caretti*. 2 vols. 1:39–82. Rome: Salerno.

Pietropoli, Giuseppe. 1986. *L'Accademia dei Concordi nella vita rodigiana dalla seconda metà del sedicesimo secolo alla fine della dominazione austriaca*. Padua: Signum.

Pighetti, Clelia. 2005. *Il vuoto e la quiete: Scienza e mistica nel '600; Elena Cornaro e Carlo Rinaldini*. Milan: Franco Angeli.

Pignatti, Franco. 1995. "Fedele, Cassandra." In *DBI* 1960–, 45:566–68.

———. 1999. "Gambara, Veronica." In *DBI* 1960–, 52:68–71.

Pizzani, Ubaldo. 1991. "Discipline letterarie e discipline scientifiche nel *De liberorum educatione* di Enea Silvio Piccolomini." In *Pio II e la cultura del suo tempo (atti del 10 convegno internazionale dell'Istituto di studi Umanistici Francesco Petrarca)*. Edited by Luisa Rotondi, 313–27. Milan: Guerini.

Plaisance, Michel. 2004. *L'Accademia e il suo principe: Cultura e politica a Firenze al tempo di Cosimo I e di Francesco de' Medici*. Rome: Vecchiarelli.

Plant, Ian Michael. 2004. *Women Writers of Ancient Greece and Rome: An Anthology*. Norman: University of Oaklahoma Press.

Plazzotta, Carol. 1998. "Bronzino's Laura." *The Burlington Magazine* 140 (1141): 251–63.

Plebani, Tiziana. 1996. "Nascita e caratteristiche del pubblico di lettrici tra medioevo e prima età moderna." In Zarri, ed. 1996, 23–44.

Pomata, Gianna. 1993. "History, Particular and Universal: On Reading Some Recent Women's History Textbooks." *Feminist Studies* 19 (1): 6–50.

Pontremoli, Alessandro, ed. 2001. *La lingua e le lingue di Machiavelli: Atti del convegno internazionale di studi, Torino, 2–4 dicembre 1999*. Florence: Olschki.

Pozzi, Giovanni. 1979. "Il ritratto della donna nella poesia d'inizio Cinquecento e la pittura di Giorgione." *Lettere italiane* 31 (1): 3–30.

Pozzi, Mario. 1989. "Aspetti della trattatistica d'amore." In *Lingua, cultura, società: Saggi sulla letteratura italiana del Cinquecento,* 57–100. Alessandria: Edizioni dell'Orso.

———. 1994. "'Andrem di pari all'amorosa face': Appunti sulle lettere di Maria Savorgnan." In Centre Aixois de Recherches Italiennes 1994, 87–101.

———, ed. 1996. *Trattatisti del Cinquecento.* 2nd ed. 2 vols. Milan: Ricciardi.

Prizer, William F. 1980. *Courtly Pastimes: The Frottole of Marchetto Cara.* Ann Arbor, Michigan: UMI.

———. 1985. "Isabella d'Este and Lucrezia Borgia as Patrons of Music: The *Frottola* at Mantua and Ferrara." *Journal of the American Musicological Society* 38 (1): 1–33.

———. 1993. "Renaissance Women as Patrons of Music in the North-Italian Courts." In Marshall, ed. 1993, 186–205.

———. 1999. "Una 'Virtù Molto Conveniente a Madonne': Isabella d'Este as a Musician." *Journal of Musicology* 17 (1): 10–49.

Prosperi, Adriano. 1994. "Lettere spirituali." In Scaraffia and Zarri, eds. 1994, 227–51.

Quaglio, Enzo. 1986. "'Intorno a Maria Savorgnan." Pt. 2. "Un 'sidio' d'amore." *Quaderni utinensi* 7–8:77–101.

Quattrucci, Mario. 1962. "Ascarelli (Ascariel), Debora." *DBI* 1960–, 4:370–71.

Questa, Cesare. 1989. *Semiramide redenta: Archetipi, fonti classiche, censure antropologiche nel melodramma.* Urbino: Quattroventi.

Quint, David. 2000. "Courtier, Prince, Lady: The Design of the *Book of the Courtier.*" *Italian Quarterly* 37:185–95.

———. 2004. "Francesco Bracciolini as a Reader of Ariosto and Tasso in *La Croce Racquistata.*" In *L'arme e gli amori: Ariosto, Tasso, and Guarini in Late Renaissance Florence; Acts of an International Conference, Florence, Villa I Tatti, June 27–29, 2001.* 2 vols. Edited by Massimilano Rosa and Fiorella Gioffredi Superbi, 1:59–77. Florence: Olschki.

Quondam, Amedeo. 1973. "L'istituzione arcadica sociologia e ideologia di un'accademia." *Quaderni storici* 23 (2): 389–438.

———, ed. 1981. *"Le carte messaggiere": Retorica e modelli di communicazione epistolare.* Rome: Bulzoni.

———. 1983. "La letteratura in tipografia." In *Letteratura italiana.* Vol 2. *Produzione e consumo.* Edited by Alberto Asor Rosa, 555–686. Turin: Einaudi.

———. 1991. *Il naso di Laura: Lingua e poesia lirica nella tradizione del classicismo.* Modena: Panini.

———. 2005a. "Note sulla tradizione della poesia spirituale e religiosa (prima parte)." In *Semestrale di Studi (e testi)* 16:127–211.

———. 2005b. "Saggio di bibliografia della poesia religiosa." In *Semestrale di Studi (e testi)* 16:213–82.

Rabboni, Renzo. 2002. "Sul canzoniere di Giovanni Nogarola." In *Antichi testi veneti*. Edited by Antonio Daniele, 105–36. Padua: Esedra.

Rabil, Albert Jr. 1981. *Laura Cereta: Quattrocento Humanist*. Binghamton, NY: Medieval and Renaissance Texts and Studies.

———. 1994a. "Laura Cereta (1466–1499)." In Russell, ed. 1994a, 67–75.

———. 1994b. "Olimpia Morata (1503–1555)." In Russell, ed. 1994a, 67–75.

Rabitti, Giovanna. 1981. "Linee per il ritratto di Chiara Matraini." *Studi e problemi di critica testuale* 22:141–65.

———. 1985. "Inediti Vaticani di Chiara Matraini." In *Studi di filologia e critica offerti dagli allievi a Lanfranco Caretti*. 2 vols. 1.225–50. Rome: Salerno.

———. 1992. "Vittoria Colonna, Bembo e Firenze: Un caso di ricezione e qualche postilla." *Studi e problemi di critica testuale* 44:127–55.

———. 1994. "Chiara Matraini (1515–1604)." In Russell, ed. 1994a, 243–52.

———. 1999. "Le lettere di Chiara Matraini tra privato e pubblico." In Zarri, ed. 1999, 209–34.

———. 2000. "Vittoria Colonna as Role Model for Cinquecento Women Poets." In Panizza, ed. 2000, 478–97.

Ragionieri, Pina. 2005. *Vittoria Colonna e Michelangelo*. Edited by Pina Ragionieri. Florence: Mandragora.

Ranieri, Concetta. 1985. "Vittoria Colonna: dediche, libri, e manoscritti." *Critica letteraria* 47:249–70.

Ravasini, Ines. 2003. "Las *Stancias de Ruggiero nuevamente glosadas* de Alonso Nuñez de Reinoso: Una glosa ariostesca de origen italiano." In *Rivista di Filologia e Letteratura Ispaniche* 6:65–86.

Ravasini, Ines, and Emma Scoles. 1996. "Intertestualità e interpretazione nel genere lirico della *glosa*." In *Nunca fue pena mayor (estudios de literatura española en homenaje a Brian Dutton)*. Edited by Ana Menéndez Collera and Victoriano Roncero López, 615–31. Cuenza: Ediciones de la Universidad de Castilla-La Mancha.

Ray, Meredith Kennedy. 2006. "Making the Private Public: Arcangela Tarabotti's *Lettere familiari*." In Weaver, ed. 2006a, 173–89.

Ray, Meredith, and Lynn Westwater. 2005. "Introduzione." In Tarabotti 2005, 25–39.

Re, Lucia. 2000. "Futurism and Fascism, 1914–1945." In Panizza and Wood, eds. 2000, 190–204.

Rebhorn, Wayne A. 1993. "Baldesar Castiglione, Thomas Wilson, and the Courtly Body of Renaissance Rhetoric." *Rhetorica* 11 (3): 241–74.

Rebonato, Alessandro. 2004. "Di alcuni imitatori di Tommaso Garzoni." *Studi secenteschi* 45:195–215.

Rees, Katie. 2008. "Female-Authored Drama in Early Modern Padua: Valeria Miani Negri (c. 1560–post 1611)." *Italian Studies* 63 (1) (forthcoming).

Regan, Lisa K. 2005. "Ariosto's Threshold Patron: Isabella d'Este in the *Orlando Furioso*." *MLN* 120 (1): 50–69.

Reiss, Sheryl E., and David G. Wilkins, eds. 2001. *Beyond Isabella: Secular Women Patrons of Art in Renaissance Italy*. Kirksville, MO: Truman State University Press.

Ricaldone, Luisa. 2000. "Eighteenth-Century Literature." In Panizza and Wood, eds. 2000, 95–106.

Riccò, Laura. 2004. *"Ben mille pastorali": L'itinerario dell'Ingegneri da Tasso a Guarini e oltre.* Rome: Bulzoni.

Richardson, Brian. 1994. *Print Culture in Renaissance Italy: The Editor and the Vernacular Text, 1470–1600.* Cambridge, UK: Cambridge University Press.

———. 1999. *Printing, Writers and Readers in Renaissance Italy.* Cambridge, UK: Cambridge University Press.

———. 2004. "Print or Pen? Modes of Written Publication in Sixteenth-Century Italy." *Italian Studies* 59:39–64.

Ridolfi, Roberta Monica. 2001. "Gonzaga, Lucrezia." In *DBI* 1960–, 57:796–97.

Riley, Joanne Marie. 1986. "Tarquinia Molza (1542–1617): A Case Study of Women, Music, and Society in the Renaissance." In *The Musical Woman: An International Perspective.* Edited by Judith Lang Zaimont, 470–92. Westport, CT: Greenwood Press.

Robathan, Dorothy M. 1944. "A Fifteenth-Century Bluestocking." *Medievalia et humanistica* 2:106–11.

Robin, Diana. 1994. "Cassandra Fedele (1465–1558)." In Russell, ed. 1994a, 119–27.

———. 1995. "Cassandra Fedele's Epistolae (1488–1521): Biography as Ef-facement." In *The Rhetorics of Life-Writing in Early Modern Europe: Forms of Biography from Cassandra Fedele to Louis XIV.* Edited by Thomas F. Mayer and D. R. Woolf, 187–203. Ann Arbor: University of Michigan Press.

———. 1997. "Translator's Introduction." In Cereta 1997, 3–19. Chicago: University of Chicago Press.

———. 2000. "Editor's Introduction." In Fedele 2000, 3–15. Chicago: University of Chicago Press.

———. 2003. "Courtesans, Celebrity, and Print Culture in Renaissance Venice: Tullia d'Aragona, Gaspara Stampa, and Veronica Franco." In Smarr and Valentini, eds. 2003, 35–59.

———. 2007. *Publishing Women: Salons, the Presses, and the Counter-Reformation in Sixteenth-Century Italy.* Chicago: University of Chicago Press.

Roche, Thomas P. 1989. *Petrarch and the English Sonnet Sequences.* New York: AMS Press.

Rogers, Mary. 1986. "Sonnets on Female Portraits from Renaissance North Italy." *Word and Image* 2:291–305.

———. 1988. "The Decorum of Women's Beauty: Trissino, Firenzuola, Luigini and the Representation of Women in Sixteenth Century Painting." *Renaissance Studies* 2 (1): 47–88.

———. 2000. "Fashioning Identities for the Renaissance Courtesan." In *Fashioning Identities in Renaissance Art.* Edited by Mary Rogers, 91–104. Aldershot, UK: Ashgate.

Rosa, Mario. 1982. "La chiesa e gli stati regionali nell'età dell'assolutismo." In *Letteratura italiana.* Vol. 1. *Il letterato e le istituzioni.* Edited by Alberto Asor Rosa, 257–389. Turin: Einaudi.

Rosand, Ellen. 1986. "The Voice of Barbara Strozzi." In Bowers and Tick, eds. 1986, 168–90.

Rose, Judith. 2000. "Mirrors of Language, Mirrors of Self: The Conceptualization of Artistic Identity in Gaspara Stampa and Sofonisba Anguissola." In *Maternal Measures: Figuring Caregiving in the Early Modern Period*. Edited by Naomi J. Miller and Naomi Yavneh, 29–48. Aldershot, UK: Ashgate.

Rose, Mary Beth. 2002. *Gender and Heroism in Early Modern English Literature*. Chicago: University of Chicago Press.

Rosenthal, Margaret F. 1992. *The Honest Courtesan: Veronica Franco, Citizen and Writer in Sixteenth-Century Venice*. Chicago: University of Chicago Press.

———. 1993. "Venetian Women and their Discontents." In Granthan Turner, ed. 1993, 107–32.

Roskill, Mark. W. 1968. *Dolce's* Aretino *and Venetian Art Theory of the Cinquecento*. New York: New York University Press.

Rossi, Nassim E. 2003. "Confronting the *Temple of Chastity:* Isabella d'Este in the Context of the Female Humanists." *Comitatus* 34:88–134.

Rossi, Vittorio. 1890. "Di una rimatrice e di un rimatore del secolo 15: Girolama Corsi Ramos e Jacopo Corsi." *Giornale storico della letteratura italiana* 15:183–219.

Rozzo, Ugo. 1982. "Un personaggio bandelliano: La poetessa Camilla Scarampa." In *Matteo Bandello, novelliere europeo: Atti del convegno internazionale di studi, 7–9 novembre 1980*. Edited by Ugo Rozzo, 419–37. Tortona: Litocoop.

Rublack, Ulinka, ed. 2002. *Gender in Early Modern German History*. Cambridge, UK: Cambridge University Press.

Rubsamen, Walter H. 1943. *Literary Sources of Secular Music in Italy (ca. 1500)*. Berkeley: University of California Press.

Ruggiero, Guido. 1993. "Marriage, Love, Sex, and Renaissance Civic Mentality." In Grantham Turner, ed. 1993, 10–30.

Russell, Camilla. 2006. *Giulia Gonzaga and the Religious Controversies of Sixteenth-Century Italy*. Turnhout, Belgium: Brepols.

Russell, Rinaldina, ed. 1994a. *Italian Women Writers: A Bio-Bibliographical Sourcebook*. Westport, CT: Greenwood Press.

———. 1994b. "Tullia d'Aragona, 1510–1556." In Russell, ed. 1994a, 26–34.

———. 1994c. "Veronica Gambara (1485–1550)." In Russell, ed. 1994a, 145–53.

———. 1994d. "Lucrezia Tornabuoni (1425–82)." In Russell, ed. 1994a, 431–40.

———. 2000a. "Vittoria Colonna's sonnets on the Virgin Mary." In Iannace, ed. 2000, 125–37.

———. 2000b. "Chiara Matraini nella tradizione della lirica femminile." *Forum Italicum* 34 (2): 415–27.

———. 2006. "Margherita Sarrocchi and the Writing of the *Scanderbeide*." In Sarrocchi 2006, 1–57. Chicago: University of Chicago Press.

Salvi, Marcella. 2004. "'Il solito è sempre quello; l'insolito è più nuovo': *Li buffoni* e le prostitute di Margherita Costa fra tradizione e innovazione." *Forum Italicum* 38 (2): 376–99.

Salza, Abdelkader. 1913. "Madonna Gasparina Stampa secondo nuove indagini." *Giornale storico della letteratura italiana* 62:1–101.

———. 1917a. "Madonna Gasparina Stampa e la società veneziana del suo tempo: Nuove discussioni." *Giornale storico della letteratura italiana* 69:217–306.

———. 1917b. "Madonna Gasparina Stampa e la società veneziana del suo tempo: Nuove discussioni" (continuation of 1917a). *Giornale storico della letteratura italiana* 70:1–60, 281–99.

Sampson, Lisa. 2004. "'Drammatica secreta': Barbara Torelli's *Partenia* (c. 1587) and Women in Late Sixteenth-Century Theatre." In *Theatre, Opera, and Performance in Italy from the Fifteenth Century to the Present: Essays in Honour of Richard Andrews*. Edited by Brian Richardson, Simon Gilson and Catherine Keen, 99–115. Leeds: Society of Italian Studies.

———. 2006. *Pastoral Drama in Early Modern Italy: The Making of a New Genre.* Oxford, UK: Legenda.

Samuels, Richard S. 1976. "Benedetto Varchi, the Accademia degli Infiammati, and the Origins of the Italian Academic Movement." *Renaissance Quarterly* 29 (4): 599–634.

San Juan, Rose Marie. 1991. "The Court Lady's Dilemma: Isabella d'Este and Art Collecting in the Renaissance." *Oxford Art Journal* 14 (1): 67–78.

Sanson, Helena. 2003. "*Ornamentum mulieri breviloquentia:* Donne, silenzi, parole nell'Italia del Cinquecento." *The Italianist* 23:194–243.

———. 2005. "Women and Vernacular Grammars in Sixteenth-Century Italy: The Case of Iparca and Rinaldo Corso's *Fondamenti del parlar toscano.*" *Letteratura italiana antica* 6:391–431.

Santacroce, Maria Chiara. 1999–2000. *Aristotele misogino: La difesa delle donne negli scritti di Lucrezia Marinella.* Tesi di laurea: Università degli Studi di Milano, Facoltà di Lettere e Filosofia.

Santagata, Marco. 1984. "La lirica feltresco-romagnola del Quattrocento." In *Rivista di letteratura italiana* 2:53–106.

Santarelli, Cristina. 2001. "Machiavelli e la musica del suo tempo." In Pontremoli, ed. 2001, 315–39.

Sapegno, Maria Serena. 2003. "La costruzione di un *Io* lirico al femminile nella poesia di Vittoria Colonna." In *La littérature au féminin.* Special issue, *Versants* n.s. 46:15–48.

———. 2005. "'Sterili i corpi fur, l'alme feconde' (Vittoria Colonna, *Rime,* A 30)." In Crivelli, Nicoli, and Santi, 31–44.

Sberlati, Francesco. 1997. "Dalla donna di palazzo alla donna di famiglia: Cultura e pedagogia femminile tra Rinascimento e Controriforma." *I Tatti Studies* 7:119–74.

———. 2004. "Tradizione medievale e cultura umanistica in Caterina Vigri." In Leonardi, ed. 2004, 91–114.

Scala, Mirella. 1990. "Encomi e dediche nelle prime relazioni culturali di Vittoria Colonna." *Periodico della Società Storica Comense* 54:95–112.

Scaraffia, Lucietta, and Gabriella Zarri, eds. 1994. *Donna e fede: Santità e vita religiosa in Italia*. Rome: Laterza.

Scarpati, Claudio. 2004. "Le rime spirituali di Vittoria Colonna nel codice vaticano donato a Michelangelo." *Aevum* 78 (3): 693–717.

Schiesari, Juliana. 1989. "In Praise of Virtuous Women? For a Genealogy of Gender Morals in Renaissance Italy." *Annali d'italianistica* 7:66–87.

——. 1994. "Isabella di Morra (c. 1520–1545)." In Russell, ed. 1994a, 279–85.

Schlam, Carl C. 1986. "Cassandra Fidelis as a Latin Orator." In *Acta Conventus Neo-Latini Sanctandreani: Proceedings of the Fifth International Congress of Neo-Latin Studies (St. Andrews, 24 August to 1 September 1982)*. Edited by I. D. McFarlane, 185–91. Binghamton, NY: Medieval and Renaissance Texts and Studies.

Schutte, Anne Jacobsen. 1991. "Irene di Spilimbergo: The Image of a Creative Woman in Late Renaissance Italy." *Renaissance Quarterly* 44 (1): 42–61.

——. 1992. "Commemorators of Irene di Spilimbergo." *Renaissance Quarterly* 45 (3): 524–36.

——. 2006. "The Permeable Cloister?" In Weaver, ed. 2006a, 19–36.

Schwarz, Kathryn. 2000. *Tough Love: Amazon Encounters in the English Renaissance*. Durham, NC: Duke University Press.

Scott, Joan W. 1986. "Gender: A Useful Category of Historical Analysis." *The American Historical Review* 91 (5): 1053–75.

Scott, John Beldon. 1991. *Images of Nepotism: The Painted Ceilings of Palazzo Barberini*. Princeton: Princeton University Press.

Sears, Olivia E. 1996. "Choosing Battles: Women's War Poetry in Renaissance Italy." In *Gendered Contexts: New Perspectives in Italian Cultural Studies*. Edited by Laura Benedetti, Julia Hairston, and Silvia Ross, 79–91. New York: Peter Lang.

Segarizzi, Arnaldo. 1904. "Niccolò Barbo, patrizio veneziano del sec. 15 e le accuse contro Isotta Nogarola." *Giornale Storico della Letteratura Italiana* 43:39–54.

Selmi, Elisabetta. 1989. "Per l'epistolario di Veronica Gambara." In Bozzetti, Gibellini, and Sandal, eds. 1989, 143–81.

——. 1998. "Erasmo, Luciano, Lando: *Funus* e asinità: Storia di un percorso fra 'paradosso' letterario e 'controversia' religiosa." In *Erasmo e il* Funus: *Dialoghi sulla morte e la libertà nel Rinascimento*. Edited by Achille Olivieri, 51–97. Padua: Unicopoli.

Selmi, Elisabetta, ed. (with the assistance of Elisabetta Conti and Maria Moiraghi Sueri). 2001. *La scrittura femminile a Brescia tra il Quattrocento e l'Ottocento*. 2 vols. Brescia: Fondazione Civiltà Bresciana.

Serventi, Silvia. 2004. "Le laudi di Caterina Vigri." In Leonardi, ed. 2004, 79–90.

——. 2005. "Laudi attribuite a Caterina Vigri." In Delcorno and Doglio, eds. 2005, 35–61.

Shemek, Deanna. 1998. *Ladies Errant: Wayward Women and Social Order in Early Modern Italy*. Durham, NC: Duke University Press.

——. 2005a. "The Collector's Cabinet: Lodovico Domenichi's Gallery of Women." In Benson and Kirkham, eds. 2005, 239–62.

——. 2005b. "In Continuous Expectation: Isabella d'Este's Epistolary Desire." In Looney and Shemek, eds. 2005, 269–300.

Shimizu, Stacey. 1999. "The Pattern of Perfect Womanhood: Feminine Virtue, Pattern Books, and the Fiction of the Clothworking Woman." In Whitehead, ed. 1999, 75–100.

Simons, Patricia. 1994. "Lesbian (In)visibility in Italian Renaissance Culture: Diana and Other Cases of *donna con donna.*" *Journal of Homosexuality* 27:81–123.

Skinner, Patricia. 2001. *Women in Medieval Italian Society, c. 500–1200.* London: Longman.

Slim, H. Colin. 1961. "A Motet for Machiavelli's Mistress and a Chanson for a Courtesan." In *Essays Presented to Myron P. Gilmore.* 2 vols. Edited by Sergio Bertelli and Gloria Ramakus, 2:457–72. Florence: La Nuova Italia.

———. 1972. *A Gift of Madrigals and Motets.* 2 vols. Chicago: Published for the Newberry Library by the University of Chicago Press.

Smarr, Janet Levarie. 1991. "Gaspara Stampa's Poetry for Performance." *Journal of the Rocky Mountain Medieval and Renaissance Association* 12:61–84.

———. 1998. "A Dialogue of Dialogues: Tullia d'Aragona and Sperone Speroni." *MLN* 113 (1): 204–12.

———. 2001. "Substituting for Laura: Objects of Desire for Renaissance Women Poets." *Comparative Literature Studies* 38 (1): 1–30.

———. 2005a. *Joining the Conversation: Dialogues by Renaissance Women.* Ann Arbor: University of Michigan Press.

———. 2005b. "Olimpia Morata: From Classicist to Reformer." In Looney and Shemek, eds. 2005, 321–43.

Smarr, Janet Levarie, and Daria Valentini, eds. 2003. *Italian Women and the City.* Madison, NJ: Fairleigh Dickinson University Press; London: Assocated University Presses.

Smith. Alison A. 1994. "Locating Power and Influence within the Provincial Elite of Verona: Aristocratic Wives and Widows." *Renaissance Studies* 8 (4): 439–48.

Smith, Bonnie G. 1984. "The Contribution of Women to Modern Historiography in Great Britain, France, and the United States, 1750–1940." *The American Historical Review* 89 (3): 709–32.

Smyth, Carolyn. 1997. "An Instance of Feminine Patronage in the Medici Court of Sixteenth-Century Florence: The Chapel of Eleonora of Toledo in the Palazzo Vecchio." In Lawrence, ed. 1997, 72–98.

Spentzou, Efrossini. 2003. *Readers and Writer in Ovid's* Heroides: *Transgressions of Genre and Gender.* Oxford: Oxford University Press.

Sperling, Gisela Jutta. 2000. *Convents and the Body Politic in Late Renaissance Venice.* Chicago: University of Chicago Press.

Spini, Giorgio. 1983. *Ricerca dei libertini: La teoria dell'impostura delle religioni nel Seicento italiano.* 2nd ed. Florence: La Nuova Italia.

Steinberg, Justin. 2006. "La Compiuta Donzella e la voce femminile nel manoscritto Vat. Lat. 3793." *Giornale Storico della Letteratura Italiana* 601:1–31.

———. 2007. *Accounting for Dante: Urban Readers and Writers in Late Medieval Italy.* Notre Dame, IN: University of Notre Dame Press.

Stevenson, Jane. 1998. "Women and Classical Education in the Early Modern Period." In *Pedagogy and Power: Rhetorics of Classical Learning*. Edited by Yun Lee Too and Niall Livingstone, 83–109. Cambridge, UK: Cambridge University Press.

———. 2002. "Conventual Life in Renaissance Italy: The Latin Poetry of Suor Laurentia Strozzi (1514–91)." In Churchill, Brown, and Jeffrey, eds. 2002, 109–31.

———. 2005. *Women Latin Poets: Language, Gender, and Authority, from Antiquity to the Eighteenth Century*. Oxford: Oxford University Press.

Stoppelli, Pasquale. 1980. "Chiavelli, Lagia." *DBI* 1960–, 24:641–42.

Storer, Mary Elizabeth. 1948. "French Women Members of the Ricovrati of Padua." *MLN* 63 (3): 161–64.

Stortoni, Laura Anna, ed. 1997. *Women Poets of the Italian Renaissance: Courtly Ladies and Courtesans*. Translated by Laura Anna Stortoni and Mary Prentice Lillie. New York: Italica.

Strada, Elena. 2001. "Carte di passaggio: 'Avanguardie petrarchiste' e tradizione manoscritta nel Veneto di primo Cinquecento." In Bianco and Strada, eds. 2001, 1–41.

Stras, Laurie. 1999. "Recording Tarquinia: Imitation, Parody and Reportage in Ingegneri's 'Hor che 'l ciel e la terra e'l vento tace.'" *Early Music* 27 (3): 358–77.

———. 2003. "Musical Portraits of Female Musicians at the Northern Italian Courts in the 1570s." In McIver, ed. 2003, 145–71.

Strocchia, Sharon T. 1999. "Learning the Virtues: Convent Schools and Female Culture in Renaissance Florence." In Whitehead, ed. 1999, 3–46.

———. 2003. "Taken into Custody: Girls and Convent Guardianship in Renaissance Florence." *Renaissance Studies* 17 (2): 177–200.

Struever, Nancy S. 1970. *The Language of History in the Renaissance: Rhetoric and Historical Consciousness in Florentine Humanism*. Princeton: Princeton University Press.

Stumpo, Enrico. 1998. "Della Chiesa, Francesco Agostino." *DBI* 1960–, 36:748–51.

Summit, Jennifer. 2000. *Lost Property: The Woman Writer and English Literary History, 1380–1589*. Chicago: University of Chicago Press.

Swain, Elizabeth Ward. 1986. "'My Excellent and Most Singular Lord': Marriage in a Noble Family of Fifteenth-Century Italy." *Journal of Medieval and Renaissance Studies* 16 (2): 171–95.

Syson, Luke. 1996. "Zanetto Bugatto, Court Portraitist in Sforza Milan." *The Burlington Magazine* 138 (1118): 300–308.

Taviani, Ferdinando. 1984. "Bella d'Asia: Torquato Tasso, gli attori e l'immortalità." In *Paragone letteratura* 36 (408–10): 3–76.

Thérault, Suzanne. 1968. *Un cénacle humaniste de la Renaissance autour de Vittoria Colonna châtelaine d'Ischia*. Florence: Sansoni; Paris: Didier.

Theunissen, Hans Peter. 1998. "Ottoman-Venetian Diplomatics: The Ahd-names; The Historical Background and the Development of a Category of Political-Commercial Instruments Together with an Annotated Edition of a Corpus of Relevant Documents." *Electronic Journal of Oriental Studies* 1 (2): 1–698.

Tinagli, Paola. 2004. "Eleonora and Her 'Famous Sisters': The Tradition of 'Illustrious Women' in Paintings for the Domestic Interior." In Eisenbichler, ed. 2004, 119–35.

Tomalin, Margaret. 1982. *The Fortunes of the Warrior Heroine in Italian Literature: An Index of Emancipation*. Ravenna: Longo.

Tomas, Natalie R. 2003. *The Medici Women: Gender and Power in Renaissance Florence*. Aldershot, UK: Ashgate.

Torrioli, Igea. 1940. "Francesca Turina Bufalini e la società colta tifernate nel sec. XVI." *L'Alta Valle del Tevere* 8: 1–36.

Toscani, Bernard. 1994. "Antonia Pulci (?1452–?)." In Russell, ed. 1994a, 344–52.

Toscano, Tobia R. 1987. "Note sulla composizione e la pubblicazione de *Le lagrime di San Pietro* di Luigi Tansillo." In *Rinascimento meridionale e altri studi in onore di Mario Santoro*, 437–61. Naples: Società Editrice Napoletana.

———. 1988. "Due 'allievi' di Vittoria Colonna: Luigi Tansillo e Alfonso d'Avalos (con un sonetto inedito della marchesa di Pescara)." *Critica letteraria* 16:739–73.

———. 1993. "Linee di storia letteraria dal regno aragonese alla fine del viceregno spagnolo." In *Storia e civiltà della Campania: Il Rinascimento e l'Età Barocca*. Edited by G. Pugliese Carratelli, 413–39. Naples: Electa.

———. 2000. *Letterati corti accademie: La letteratura a Napoli nella prima metà del Cinquecento*. Naples: Loffredo.

Travi, Ernesto. 1984. "Le donne e il volgare." In *Lingua e vita nel primo Cinquecento*, 76–92. Milan: Edizioni di Storia e letteratura.

Travitsky, Betty S. 1990. "Introduction: Placing Women in the English Renaissance." In *The Renaissance Englishwoman in Print: Counterbalancing the Canon*. Edited by Anne M. Haselkorn and Betty S. Travitsky, 3–41. Amherst: University of Massachusetts Press.

Treadwell, Nina. 1997. "The Performance of Gender in Cavalieri/Guidiccioni's *Ballo* 'O che nuovo miracolo.'" *Women and Music* 1:55–70.

Trento, Dario. 2000. "Alessandro and Ippolita Bentivoglio's Commission for San Maurizio." In Bandera and Fiorio, eds. 2000, 37–44.

Trinchieri Camiz, Franca. 2003. "Music Settings to Poems by Michelangelo and Vittoria Colonna." In McIver, ed. 2003, 377–88.

Trovato, Paolo. 1991. *Con ogni diligenza corretto: La stampa e le revisioni editoriali dei testi letterari italiani (1470–1570)*. Bologna: Il Mulino.

Tuohy, Thomas. 1996. *Herculean Ferrara: Ercole d'Este, 1471–1505, and the Invention of a Ducal Capital*. Cambridge, UK: Cambridge University Press.

Tylus, Jane. 1995. "Mystical Enunciations: Mary, the Devil, and Quattrocento Spirituality." *Annali d'italianistica* 13:219–42.

———. 2001a. "Gender and Religion in Fifteenth-Century Florence." In Tornabuoni 2001, 21–53. Chicago: University of Chicago Press.

———. 2001b. "Caterina da Siena and the Legacy of Humanism." In Marino and Schlitt, eds. 2001, 116–44.

———. 2008. *The Signs of Others: The Writings of Catherine of Siena*. Chicago: University of Chicago Press.

Ultsch, Lori J. 2000. "Sara Copio Sullam: A Jewish Woman of Letters in 17thC Venice." *Italian Culture* 18 (2): 73–86.

———. 2005a. *"Epithalamium interruptum:* Maddalena Campiglia's New Arcadia." *MLN* 120 (1): 70–92.

———. 2005b. "Maddalena Campiglia, 'dimessa nel mondano cospetto'? Secular Celibacy, Devotional Communities, and Social Identity in Early Modern Vicenza." *Forum Italicum* 39 (2): 350–77.

Ussia, Salvatore. 1993. *Il sacro Parnaso: Il lauro e la croce.* Catanzaro: Pullano.

———. 2001. *Amore innamorato: Riscritture poetiche della novella di Amore e Psiche, secoli 15–17.* Vercelli: Mercurio.

Valone, Carolyn. 1992. "Roman Matrons as Patrons: Various Views of the Cloister Wall." In *The Crannied Wall: Women, Religion, and the Arts in Early Modern Europe.* Edited by Craig Monson, 49–72. Ann Arbor: University of Michigan Press.

———. 1994. "Women on the Quirinal Hill: Patronage in Rome, 1560–1630." *Art Bulletin* 76 (1): 129–46.

Vandelli, Domenico. 1750. *Vita di Tarquinia Molza, detta l'Unica.* In Molza 1750, 3–25.

Vazzoler, Franco. 1992. "Le pastorali dei comici dell'arte: La *Mirtilla* di Isabella Andreini." In *Sviluppi della drammaturgia pastorale nell'Europa del Cinque-Seicento, Roma 23–26 maggio 1991.* Edited by Maria Chiabò and Federico Doglio, 281–99. Viterbo: Centro Studi sul Teatro Medioevale e Rinascimentale.

Vecce, Carlo. 1990. "Paolo Giovio e Vittoria Colonna." *Periodico della Società Storica Comense* 54:67–93.

———. 1993. "Vittoria Colonna: Il codice epistolare della poesia femminile." *Critica letteraria,* 21 (78): 3–34.

Vela, Claudio. 1989. "Poesia in musica: Rime della Gambara e di altri poeti settentrionali in tradizione musicale." In Bozzetti, Gibellini, and Sandal, eds. 1989, 399–414.

Vianello, Valerio. 1998. *Il letterato, l'accademia, il libro: Contributi sulla cultura veneta del Cinquecento.* Padua: Antenore.

Viaro, Roberto. 2005. *Il potere della fede: Splendore e tramonto della Vangadizza nelle Fronde sparte del Monaco camaldolese don Severo Senesi.* Treviso: Antilia.

Vickers, Nancy J. 1981. "Diana Described: Scattered Woman and Scattered Rhyme." *Critical Inquiry* 8 (2): 265–79.

Visceglia, Maria Antonietta, ed. 1992. *Signori, patrizi, cavalieri in Italia centro-meridionale nell'età moderna.* Bari: Laterza.

Visconti, Filippo. 1905. *Lo spirito misogino nel secolo 17.* Avellino: Edoardo Pergola.

Viti, Paolo. 1996. "L'umanesimo nell'Italia settentrionale e mediana." In Malato, ed. 1996a, 517–634.

Waddy, Patricia. 1990. *Seventeenth-Century Roman Palaces: Use and the Art of the Plan.* New York: Architectural History Foundation; Cambridge, MA: MIT Press.

Wall, Wendy. 1993. *The Imprint of Gender: Authority and Publication in the English Renaissance.* Ithaca: Cornell University Press.

Waller, Gary F. 1985. "Struggling into Discourse: The Emergence of Renaissance Women's Writing." In Hannay, ed. 1985, 238–56.

Warnke, Martin. 1998. "Individuality as an Argument: Piero della Francesca's Portrait of the Duke and Duchess of Urbino." In *The Image of the Individual. Portraits in the Renaissance.* Edited by Nicholas Mann and Luke Syson, 81–90. London: British Museum.

Weaver, Elissa B. 1977. "The Spurious Text of Francesco Berni's *Rifacimento* of Matteo Maria Boiardo's *Orlando Innamorato.*" *Modern Philology* 75 (2): 111–31.

———. 1994a. "Le muse in convento: La scrittura profana delle monache italiane (1450–1650)." In Scaraffia and Zarri, eds. 1994, 253–76.

———. 1994b. "Suor Maria Clemente Ruoti, Playwright and Academician." In Matter and Coakley, eds. 1994, 281–96.

———. 1994c. "Suor Arcangela Tarabotti (Galerana Baratotti, Galerana Barcitotti) (1604–1652)." In Russell, ed. 1994a, 414–22.

———. 1997. Review of Fonte 1995. *MLN* 112 (1): 114–16.

———. 1998. "Introduzione." In Buoninsegni and Tarabotti 1998, 7–28. Rome: Salerno.

———. 2002. *Convent Theatre in Early Modern Italy: Spiritual Fun and Learning for Women.* Cambridge, UK: Cambridge University Press.

———, ed. 2006a. *Arcangela Tarabotti: A Literary Nun in Baroque Venice* Ravenna: Longo.

———. 2006b. Review of Colonna 2005. *Renaissance Quarterly* 49 (2): 484–85.

Weber, Alison. 1999. "Little Women: Counter-Reformation Misogyny." In *The Counter-Reformation.* Edited by David M. Luebke, 143–62. Oxford: Blackwell.

Weisner, Merry E. 2000. *Women and Gender in Early Modern Europe.* 2nd ed. Cambridge, UK: Cambridge University Press.

Welch, Evelyn S. 1995. "Between Milan and Naples: Ippolita Maria Sforza, Duchess of Calabria." In *The French Descent into Renaissance Italy, 1494–5: Antecedents and Effects.* Edited by David Abulafia, 123–36. Aldershot, UK: Ashgate.

———. 2000. "Women as Patrons and Clients in the Courts of Quattrocento Italy." In Panizza, ed. 2000, 18–34.

———. 2002. "The Art of Expenditure: The Court of Paola Malatesta Gonzaga in Fifteenth-Century Mantua." *Renaissance Studies* 16 (3): 306–17.

———. 2005. *Shopping in the Renaissance.* New Haven: Yale University Press.

Westwater, Lynn Lara. 2006. "The Trenchant Pen: Humor in the *Lettere* of Arcangela Tarabotti." In Weaver, ed. 2006a, 159–72.

Whitehead, Barbara J., ed. 1999. *Women's Education in Early Modern Europe: A History, 1500–1800.* New York: Garland.

Witcombe, Christopher L. C. E. 2004. *Copyright in the Renaissance: Prints and the Privilegio in Sixteenth-Century Venice and Rome.* Leiden: Brill.

Witt, Ronald G. 2003. *"In the Footsteps of the Ancients": The Origins of Humanism from Lovato to Bruni.* 2nd ed. Brill: Leiden.

Woodbridge, Linda. 1984. *Women and the English Renaissance: Literature and the Nature of Womankind, 1540–1620.* Urbana: University of Illinois Press.

Woodhouse, H. F. 1982. *Language and Style in a Renaissance Epic: Berni's Corrections to Boiardo's* Orlando Innamorato. London: MHRA.

Woods-Marsden, Joanna. 1998. *Renaissance Self-Portraiture: The Visual Construction of Identity and the Social Status of the Artist.* New Haven: Yale University Press.

———. 2002. "Piero della Francesca's Ruler Portraits." In *The Cambridge Companion to Piero della Francesca,* 91–114. Cambridge, UK: Cambridge University Press.

Zaccaria, Vittorio. 1978. "La fortuna del *De mulieribus claris* del Boccaccio nel secolo 15: Giovanni Sabbadino degli Arienti, Iacopo Filippo Foresti e le loro biografie femminili (1490–97)." In *Il Boccaccio nelle culture e letterature nazionali.* Edited by Francesco Mazzoni, 519–45. Florence: Olschki.

Zaja, Paolo. 2001. "Intorno alle antologie: Testi e paratesti in alcune raccolte di lirica cinquecentesche." In Bianco and Strada, eds. 2001, 113–45.

Zancan, Marina, ed. 1983. *Nel cerchio della luna: Figure di donna in alcuni testi del 16° secolo.* Venice: Marsilio.

———. 1986. "La donna." In *Letteratura italiana.* Vol. 5. *Le questioni,* 765–827. Turin: Einaudi.

———. 1989. "L'intellettualità femminile nel primo Cinquecento: Maria Savorgnan e Gaspara Stampa." *Annali d'italianistica* 7:42–65.

———. 1992. "Caterina da Siena, *Lettere.'*" In *Letteratura italiana: Le opere.* Vol. 1. *Dalle origini al Cinquecento.* Edited by Alberto Asor Rosa, 593–633. Turin: Einaudi.

———. 1993. "Gaspara Stampa, *Rime.*" In *Letteratura italiana: Le opere.* Vol. 2. *Dal Cinquecento al Settecento.* Edited by Alberto Asor Rosa, 407–32. Turin: Einaudi.

———. 1998. *Il doppio itinerario della scrittura: La donna nella tradizione letteraria italiana.* Turin: Einaudi.

Zancani, Diego. 2000. "Writing for Women Rulers in Quattrocento Italy: Antonio Cornazzano." In Panizza, ed. 2000, 57–74.

Zanrè, Domenico. 2004. *Cultural Non-Conformity in Early Modern Florence.* Aldershot, UK: Ashgate.

Zappacosta, Gugilemo. 1972. "*Apologiae mulierum* libri del Card. Pompeo Colonna." In *Studi e ricerche sull'umanesimo italiano (testi inediti del 15° e 16° secolo),* 157–246. Bergamo: Minerva Italica.

Zarri, Gabriella, ed. 1996. *Donna, disciplina, creanza Cristi dal 15° al 17° secolo: Studi e testi a stampa.* Rome: Edizioni di Storia e Letteratura.

———, ed. 1999. *Per lettera: Scrittura epistolare femminile tra archivio e tipografia, secoli 15–18.* Rome: Viella.

———. 2000a. *Recinti: Donne, clausura, e matrimonio nella prima età moderna.* Bologna: Il Mulino.

———. 2000b. "Religious and Devotional Writing, 1400–1500." Translated by Susan Haskins. In Panizza and Wood, eds. 2000, 79–91.

———. 2004. "La cultura monastica femminile nel Seicento: Angelica Baitelli." In *Arte, cultura e religione in Santa Giulia.* Edited by Giancarlo Andenna, 145–62. Brescia: Grafo.

Zarrilli, Carla. 1997. "Forteguerri, Laudomia." In *DBI* 1960–, 49:153–55.

Zatti, Sergio. 1998. "Dalla parte di Satana: Sull'imperialismo cristiano nella *Gerusalemme liberata.*" In *La rappresentazione dell'altro nei testi del Rinascimento.* Edited by Sergio Zatti, 146–82. Lucca: Maria Pacini Fazzi.

Zonta, Giuseppe. 1906. "La *Partenia* di Barbara Torelli-Benedetti." *Rassegna bibliografica della letteratura italiana* 14:206–10.

———, ed. 1912. *Trattati d'amore del Cinquecento.* Bari: Laterza.

———, ed. 1913. *Trattati del Cinquecento sulla donna.* Bari: Laterza.

Zorzi, Alvise. 1986. *Cortigiana veneziana: Veronica Franco e i suoi poeti (1546–1591).* Milan: Camunia.

Zorzi, Niccolò. 2004–5. "Niceta Coniata fonte dell'*Enrico, ovvero Bisanzio acquistato* (1635) di Lucrezia Marinella." *Incontri triestini di filologia classica* 4:415–28.

# INDEX

Fedele, Cassandra (*cont'd.*)
Poliziano, 18, 24, 29–30, 263n.38, 287n.100;
publication of work of, 10, 181, 243,
265n.50, 297n.20; as Venetian figurehead,
18, 33, 35, 148–49, 181, 350n.68
Felice, Andromeda, 329–30n.59
Feltre, Vittorino da, 32
female voice, in male-authored texts, 49–50,
83, 136, 175, 270n.96, 324–25n.19, 347n.47
Ferrante I, king of Naples, 20
Ferrara, 16, 32, 44, 49, 184; female patronage
in, 26–27, 33, 43, 280nn.17–19; profeminist
discourse in, 26–27, 33, 59–60, 138, 143, 168,
170, 329n.55; women's writing in, 138, 147,
364n.189. *See also* Este women as ad-
dressees/dedicatees of women's writing
Ferretti, Giulia, 307n.114, 320n.28
Fiamma, Gabriele, 71–72
Fieschi, Ortensia. *See* Lomellini Fieschi,
Ortensia
Fieschi Adorno, Caterina (St. Catherine of
Genoa), 2–3, 16
Fieschi d'Appiano, Virginia, 157
Filarco, Onofrio, 172–73, 345n.28–29
Filarete, Prodicogine, 172, 345n.29
Firenzuola, Agnolo, 51–52, 94
Flaminio, Marcantonio, 72, 292n.153
Florence, 38, 125, 180, 186; female power and
patronage in, 116–18, 185–86, 207, 229–30,
361n.162; as locus for women's writing, 2–
3, 6, 13–14, 27, 80, 83–84, 105–6, 117, 129,
147, 207, 222, 229–30, 315n.187, 319–20n.18,
322n.37
Foligno, Angela da, 236
Fontana, Lavinia, 131, 143, 163
Fonte, Moderata (Modesta da Pozzo), 113,
121, 132, 146–47, 150–51, 156, 204, 206,
258n.45, 313n.168, 331nn.71–72, 341n.156; biographies of, 147–48, 200, 205; *Le feste*, 150,
239, 333n.89; *Il merito delle donne*, 144, 150,
156, 158–59, 161–63, 173, 176, 196, 211, 241,
250, 282n.40, 334n.99, 336n.112, 337n.119; *La
passione di Christo*, 150, 239, 249, 333n.89,
338n.124; posthumous fame of, 144, 148,
200, 363n.176; *La resurretione di Giesù
Christo*, 150, 240, 249; *Tredici canti del Floridoro*, 146, 149, 156–57, 207, 239, 248, 331n.72,
333n.89
Foresti, Jacopo Filippo, 22, 25–26
Forteguerri, Laodomia, 86–87, 95, 99, 101,
106–108, 114–17, 309n.133, 314n.183, 320–
21nn.29–30; as author of sonnets to Margaret of Austria, 107–8, 116–17, 157, 315–
16n.190, 309nn.133–34
Foscarini, Lodovico, 10–11, 18, 24, 29, 33,
264n.45

Foscarini Venier, Foscarina, 307n.114
France, women's writing in, xiv, xix, 226,
256n.11, 338n.126, 361–62n.167; profeminist
tradition in, xviii, 192–93, 373n.256. *See also*
Anne of Austria; Christine de Lorraine;
Marguerite de Navarre; Maria Cristina of
France; Medici, Catherine de'; Renée de
France
Franco, Niccolò, 92, 94–96, 178
Franco, Veronica, xxviii, 85, 123, 148, 151, 153–
54, 166, 259n.50, 318n.9, 333n.83, 337n.115,
370n.235; *Lettere*, 221, 239, 248, 337n.115,
369n.234; *Terze rime*, 122, 210, 239, 248,
310n.150, 317n.4, 337n.115
friendship, female, as theme in women's writing, 115, 313n.177, 336n.111, 339n.133, 370n.235
*frottola* (poetic form), 40, 51

Gabrielli Alciati, Laura, 315n.184
Galeota, Francesco, 279n.16
Galilei, Galileo, 162, 342n.163
gallantry to women as courtly attitude, 44,
92, 133–34, 141–43, 163–65, 168
Gallerani, Cecilia, 27, 46, 51, 281n.30, 281–
82n.34, 284n.67
Gallerati, Partenia, 86, 102, 116, 262n.27,
306n.105
Gambara, Brunoro, 67
Gambara, Isotta, 51–52, 284n.68
Gambara, Uberto, 66
Gambara, Veronica, xiv, xxiv, 45–46, 50–52,
64–70, 73, 74–77, 81, 113, 196–97, 218, 259n.1,
263n.38, 284n.62, 289n.127, 292n.157; and
Pietro Bembo, 60, 68, 75, 77, 100–101,
317n.200; biographies of, 77, 200, 293nn.171–
72; fame/poetic cult of, 64–68, 76–77, 79,
114, 127, 230–31, 281n.30, 290n.130, 293nn.170–
72, 320n.29; imitation/influence of, 81, 89,
113–15, 291n.150, 295n.6, 313n.174; as love
poet, 50, 65, 68, 75, 89, 288–89n.118; and
poetic correspondence with Vittoria
Colonna, 67–70, 90, 115, 290n.128,
313n.177
Gambara, Virginia Pallavicini. *See* Pallavicini
Gambara, Virginia
Gamberini, Suor Benedetta, 364n.189
Garbo, Dino del, 263n.40
Gareth, Benedetto ("Cariteo"), 57
Garzadora, Cinzia, 330n.59
Garzoni, Tommaso, 348n.50, 350n.72
Gattesca, Candida, 308n.124
Gelli, Giambattista, 127
gender roles, ix–xi, 19–21, 98–99, 169–71,
272nn.109–10, 273n.117. *See also* Counter-
Reformation: gender attitudes of; "defense
of women" genre